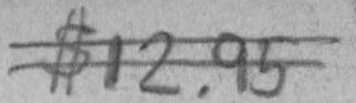

Tools for Homesteaders Gardeners and Small-Scale Farmers

A CATALOG OF HARD-TO-FIND IMPLEMENTS AND EQUIPMENT

BY THE EDITORS OF *ORGANIC GARDENING*®, *THE NEW FARM*®, AND INTERMEDIATE TECHNOLOGY PUBLICATIONS

Edited by
Diana S. Branch

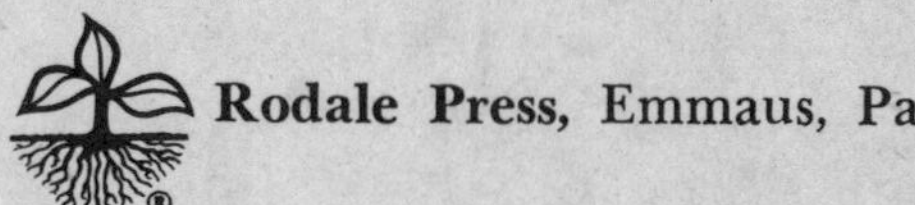

Rodale Press, Emmaus, Pa.

Illustrations by Sally Onopa.
Additional Illustrations by Russell Hoover.

Library of Congress Cataloging in Publication Data
Main entry under title:

Tools for homesteaders, gardeners, and small-scale farmers.

Includes index.
1. Agricultural implements—Catalogs. 2. Garden tools—Catalogs. I. Branch, Diana S. II. Organic gardening and farming. III. Intermediate Technology Publications.
S676.3.T66 631.3 78-18250
ISBN 0-87857-235-X

Printed in the United States of America on recycled paper, containing a high percentage of de-inked fiber.

1 3 5 7 9 10 8 6 4 2

I'd like to dedicate this book to my Grandfather who inspired me to learn the things which made my doing this book possible, and to my Dad who taught them to me.

D.S.B.
2/15/78

Contents

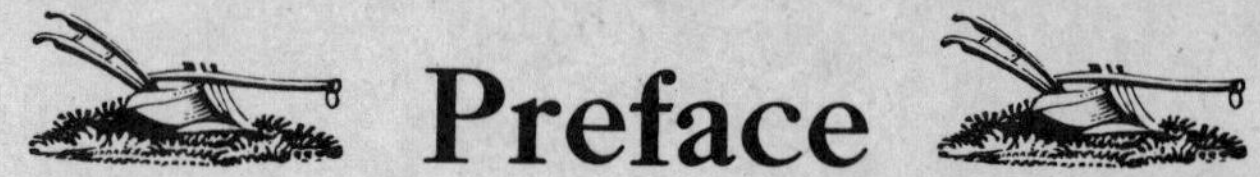

Preface

Tools for Homesteaders, Gardeners, and Small-Scale Farmers is a technology sourcebook, not an exhaustive product listing. We want to show you what tools and implements exist to assist the small farmer and where they can be found. But, to be fair, we have to admit that there are many more sources of tools than we've been able to locate in the past year. If we missed a company you know about and trust, please let us know. If you are interested in distributing any of the products listed, we'd encourage you to write to the manufacturers. Many have expressed an interest in opening new markets.

It must be emphasized that the product descriptions in this book are not evaluations of the products. We are, in most cases, presenting the information provided to us by manufacturers or distributors. If we say more about one product than another, it is because somebody told us more about it. The same is true with photographs. We do not intend photographic coverage to be an endorsement of any product. However, we must confess to discriminating in favor of hard-to-find items both verbally and photographically.

 Acknowledgements 

Guidance in deciding what to include in this book came from three invaluable sources:

The idea for this book grew out of the Intermediate Technology Publications book, *Tools for Agriculture: A Buyer's Guide to Low Cost Agricultural Implements,* by John Boyd. Its object is to provide a source of information on the availability of appropriate tools for the people in developing countries. As the basis of this co-publication, Intermediate Technology Publications have gladly made their written and visual material available to provide the foundation for this book, to which a mass of further information has been added. As a result, the book should prove of inestimable value to farmers and smallholders, not only in North America, but around the world.

Agricultural Engineer, Dr. Biswa Nath Ghosh provided photographs and the technical groundwork for many introductory sections.

Gene Logsdon, a contributing editor for *Organic Gardening and Farming,* revealed many of the needs of the small farmer in North America based upon experiences at his own farmstead in Ohio and those of other small-scale farmers he's met along the way.

Many thanks to all those who contributed photographs and information to this book. Thanks also to the Rodale Press Photo Lab for assisting with the photographs.

My sincere appreciation to Barb Coyle who persevered with research, follow-up, collation, and keeping me organized.

Finally, special thanks to Jerry Goldstein for his guidance and support throughout.

—D.S.B.

Introduction

Finding the right tools can be the most critical need for a small-scale farmer or a large-scale gardener. It can mean the difference between staying on or leaving the land, between a sense of drudgery or a sense of fulfillment, between a successful harvest or a meager crop, between profit or loss.

This catalog will, we hope, help you to find and use the tools you need to produce food. The tools and equipment described in its pages were selected primarily for their value to the homesteader, truck farmer, and the small-scale organic farmer, but backyard gardeners should also find things of interest. This book attempts to fill the gap brought about by what the late E. F. Schumacher of the Intermediate Technology Development Group in London termed "the Law of the Disappearing Middle." As technology steadily moves to higher planes, we are left with primitive, simplistic tools on the one hand, and a very complex, sophisticated technology on the other.

This book intends to show that intermediate-scaled farming is one topic in which people of all lands share common interests and common needs. It is built on five important concepts which we believe to be true:

1. that in many instances the developing nations are ahead of the industrial giants in developing appropriate tools and machines for successful farming on a small scale;
2. that although it may not be readily available everywhere, the technology exists somewhere or has existed at some time in the past to accomplish those tasks which need to be done in an efficient way on the small farm;
3. that it is just a matter of implementing existing knowledge to get these tools to those people who want to put them to work;
4. that to satisfy the need expressed by the small farmer does not mean a technological regression to the primitive techniques practiced on yesterday's small farm, but rather a rediscovery of these techniques, a recognition that they retain relevance to today's small farmer;
5. that what is called for is a modernization of these techniques, applying the technological wisdom of today to the techniques employed in the past.

—Diana Branch, Editor

EXPLORING ALTERNATIVES

Innumerable groups and societies are now concerned with exploring alternatives—alternatives that do not destroy, waste, or pollute our natural resources. More and more individuals are dissatisfied with the mindless repetition of simple tasks imposed by mass production and are seeking greater self-fulfillment and freedom from the tyranny of superficial nine-to-five routines. The movement toward self-sufficiency, homesteading, organic gardening and farming, and natural food is a part of this whole movement.

The problems of agribusiness are also forcing us to explore alternatives. The problems are of both scale and technique: mechanized farming of vast areas with huge machines and widespread use of chemical fertilizers and sprays; the development of food factories; the massive infiltration of artificial ingredients into our foods; the intensive breeding of animals raised in confined conditions for slaughter.

Is more energy being poured into this type of farming than is produced by the harvest? Is the soil's substance being eroded? Do chemical sprays harm the environment more than they benefit the farmer? While surely we need the food, do the means we use to produce it destroy the resources on which we all depend? Are there satisfactory alternatives that could provide as great a volume of production using less-violent means?

These are some of the broad questions that are being asked by more and more people.

There are other related questions, too. As technology moves forward, machines become ever more sophisticated in doing the work of more and more people. In a period of rising unemployment throughout the world, should not this trend be reversed?

Certainly in developing countries, the planners and governments are beginning to have second thoughts. In many cases, the modern high-level technology that was introduced to increase productivity in various fields has proven disastrous for the countries concerned. Western-style technology used scarce supplies of capital and costly fuel, required maintenance beyond the ability of local skills, provided very little employment and even, in some cases, drastically reduced employment. Now, more appropriate alternative methods are being investigated by developing nations. These methods create more employment, use less capital, can be maintained by local skills, increase productivity by successive small increments, and are appropriate to the social and economic requirements of the particular country concerned.

Certainly, the time seems to be ripe for an examination of alternative techniques that could provide some solutions to the mounting concern that is being expressed. There are several lines of investigation that could be followed:

First, existing practices could be modified at the technical level in order to use renewable resources or modify machines so that less pollution is caused and less damage is done to the environment.

The second approach could be to revive and reintroduce an older, tried-and-proven technology using more labor, in which individual skills are needed, providing meaningful work and job satisfaction. These skills may have to be relearned and the technology and tools reworked to suit modern methods and materials.

Third, the scale of modern technology could be changed to meet the needs of a particular area or industry. Centralized production could be changed to small-scale production serving local areas rather than supplying several states. More employment would be provided, with less fuel being wasted on transport. Local preferences could then be catered to, for the establishment of a small industry in a local area has a multiplier effect on the local economy.

In a sense, this book is an amalgam of all three approaches with regard to agriculture and small-scale farming. It contains examples of many different tools and pieces of equipment that can be used in each stage of farming, from plowing to harvesting, from preparing the soil to processing the crop. Some of these tools are based on older, well-tried technologies; some are scaled-down, smaller machines designed for smaller farms; others are designed to use renewable resources to help make organic farming more productive.

This mine of information, carefully gathered and cataloged here, should prove invaluable to farmers, gardeners, and small landholders alike.

—Frank Solomon,
Editor, Intermediate Technology Publications

TOOLS, NOT MACHINES

Throughout the compilation of this book, we have selected the tool over the machine. The difference may be clear-cut in our minds, but not always so distinct in reality, since one and the same product may be a tool *or* machine, depending upon who is using it and how it is being used. A brush in the hand of an artist is a tool. The printing roller that duplicates his painting a billion times into a wallpaper pattern is a machine. There is nothing wrong with a wallpaper machine (though wouldn't it be better if we all decorated our own walls?) just as there is nothing essentially right about an artist's brush. But there is a difference. Peculiar things begin to happen when that difference is extended indefinitely in human activity. The tool remains hand-directed and unhabituated; the machine becomes increasingly more automatic and addictive if its power is not curbed. If you let go of the paint brush, it falls on the floor; the wallpaper machine will go on making wallpaper while you sleep. Because it is so easy to produce with a machine, we inevitably let it produce more than we need. The machine can produce an unlimited supply of wallpaper, but there is never a surplus of art.

Tools humanize; machines dehumanize.

Tools make unique products—each a little different from the other, each speaking eloquently of the tool's user. A machine deals in multiplied sameness no matter who or what operates it. The best machine operators are other machines.

The tool is fragile because it is individual. The machine is powerful because it is collective. In any contest where winning is measured in quantity, it is a mathematical certainty that the machine will win because it can always get there "the fastest with the mostest." As long as economics makes quantity the goal, the machine will devour the tool. And when all the tools are gone, the machine will devour lesser machines. For tyrants, the machine is the ultimate tool.

While our supplies of cheap fossil fuel last, farmers need machines to continue to wrest land away from other farmers for the ultimate aggrandizement of agribusiness. In the new technology, homesteaders, gardeners, and small farmers can live well with tools and have much less need for machines. But they need *lots* of tools.

The magic of any book, we believe, is in the possibilities it raises in the imagination of the reader. There are forgotten tools that could be made again—only better—and future tools not yet dreamed of. The ideas for them could spring from the obsolete tools of the past, so we have included pictures of farm tools from old manuals. Studying the anatomy of a 1930 tractor which is especially suitable to the needs of today's farmstead, a handy person just might be persuaded to build another one—or more.

There is a strong heritage, especially in the United States but elsewhere too, of the farmer as inventor. A large percentage of our inventors came from rural communities, and virtually all the industries which grew up in the United States in the 1800s started on a very small scale, often as one-man operations. Cyrus McCormick, Oliver Evans, Eli Whitney, even Henry Ford—each grew up on a farm. The inventors of tools we still need will most likely come from the ranks of today's small farmers—and their children.

Some tools now marketed for special purposes have uses for growers that the equipment makers didn't foresee. We've tried to include these tools whenever we've been aware of them. For example, a supplier of orchard- and fruit-farming equipment manufactures a mulch spreader for the commercial strawberry grower. The spreader can be placed on a wagon or in the back of a pickup truck. Straw bales are fed into one end and are chopped up and delivered out the back onto the strawberry plants. But the mulcher could be used to lay down straw or spoiled hay between raspberry rows, vegetables, or wherever the farmer needs it.

Common lawn and garden tools have uncommon homestead uses. A grinder-shredder will chop silage for cattle feed out of corn, pumpkins, mangels, or other plants. It will even grind a crude corn and cob meal for cows. A battery-operated hedge trimmer works fine for summer and winter raspberry pruning. A battery- or hand-operated sidewalk edger makes an adequate cutter for strawberry runners. A big ten-tined silage hand fork makes an excellent tool for handling mulching materials like shredded bark. The equally large hand forks we used to call barley forks, with tines closer together than those of a silage fork, are good for shoveling sawdust mulch.

Surely the future looks bright for tool users and toolmakers in the gardening and small farming field. Little imaginative thinking has gone into such tools because technology has been enamored with the concept of Big. All sorts of interesting ideas await development.

We hope this book can help point the way.

—Gene Logsdon,
Organic Gardening

–1– A Picture of the Small Farmer Today

SMALL-SCALE FARMING*

by Jerry Belanger

Pick up almost any issue of *Countryside* and read about the people who are prospering on small farms. Of course it's possible. We prove it every month.

But we're also careful to point out that it isn't easy. Not everyone who dreams of a small farm is going to make it.

Most farmers would be surprised to learn that anyone could be shocked by having their small-farm dreams shattered by an introduction to agribusiness. After all, everyone must certainly know that our farm population has been cut in half since the 1940s, and that the exodus is continuing even now. Everyone (and certainly anyone interested in starting farming) should be aware that only the larger and more-efficient farms are surviving.

If you haven't heard that wheat is selling for less than it brought in 1949, that cattlemen have been selling below the cost of production for more than a year and a half, or that dairymen have been skirting the same situation for several years, you probably haven't done enough homework to be ready to farm. If you don't know that the average U.S. farm encompasses 400 acres and represents an investment of about a quarter of a million dollars, and that the USDA predicts that it will take half a million dollars to break into farming by 1985, you might want to reconsider.

If that's the case, what are magazines like *Countryside* and *Mother Earth News* all about? Is it, as you ask, all a dream?

No, but let's get a few things straight.

To begin with, it's important to understand the distinction between homesteading and farming. If you're talking about producing your own food and preparing for the hard times ahead, that's homesteading. It can be accomplished on a large farm, a small farm, or in town, and since many people in rural homes do not produce their own food or prepare for the future, they are not homesteaders.

Farming, on the other hand, involves producing food for sale or barter.

In *Countryside* magazine as in the countryside itself, there is a lot of overlapping. Some of our topics cover farming, some cover homesteading, and many include both. If you want to be very technical about it (which we never are in the magazine), if you raise rabbits for your own table, you're homesteading; but the minute you sell a fryer, you're farming.

A chicken farmer, then, could be one who has 100,000 birds in cages in climate-controlled, light-regulated buildings . . . or it could be a person who sells a dozen eggs occasionally from the surplus produced by a backyard flock. It shouldn't take much imagination to figure out which one is going to produce eggs at the least cost.

This leads us to the fact that farming is a business. Obviously, you say . . . but it's not obvious to the dreamers. People who don't have enough business acumen to run a popcorn stand envision themselves as farmers, but it won't work. In fact, without knowing and adhering to business principles, even homesteading won't work! The difference, of course, is one of scale. The loss of a couple of dollars on a homestead can be written off as entertainment or exercise or education or any number of other expenses, but a loss on a farm is a loss, period.

This, perhaps, is at the heart of your concern, so let's examine it in closer detail.

* Reprinted with permission, *Countryside*, September 1977.

Any business, in any field, requires capital. You can't even start a lemonade stand without a lemon (or today, perhaps, a synthetic substitute). Farming takes thousands of dollars, depending on the location and type of enterprise. The average Wisconsin dairy farm today represents an investment of $180,000.

In the lemonade business, you'd probably borrow the lemon from your mother. She might not even make you pay her back and almost certainly wouldn't charge interest. But farm debts today stand at more than $1 billion, and those who lend that money expect to be paid back, with interest. Because they expect to be repaid, they examine the borrower's qualifications closely. If all you know about farming is what you've read in *Countryside, Organic Gardening, The New Farm,* and *Mother Earth News,* you probably aren't a very good risk.

So you need training and experience in the business. With the lemonade stand, you must know how to make lemonade, how to make a sign, how to select a location and a nice hot day, how to make change. Certainly no one would start a grocery or hardware store without knowing something about groceries or hardware, without making some type of market survey, and a great deal more. And if anyone thinks farming entails nothing more than buying some land, getting on a tractor, and going to it, well then yes, they're dreaming.

Will you raise cash crops or livestock? Will your crops be corn or soybeans, apples or celery, cabbages or artichokes? Why? Will you raise pigs or sheep or cows? Will your cows be beef animals or dairy animals, your pig enterprise a farrowing operation or a finishing operation or a farrow-to-finish operation? How much experience do you have in whichever you choose? How much capital will it take to get started, how long will it be before you can expect any income, how much money will you need to carry you through that period, what will your cash flow be, what kind of price will you need to make enough money to make a living, what kind of price can you expect in the future?

What kind of machinery will you need, and what do you know about buying, operating, and maintaining it?

And what about marketing? Is there a local market for your pigs or fat lambs, or will you have to ship them a long distance? Is the goat cheese co-op to whom you'll be selling milk established and well managed, or will it fold just about the time you get your herd built up? Or, if you intend to market milk yourself, how thoroughly have you investigated regulations governing such activity, how closely have you figured costs, just how certain are you of your potential market? If you sold a few gallons to the parents of a baby who's allergic to cow's milk, a guy with an ulcer, and a health food nut and assume that counts as valid market research, we can guarantee that you won't be farming very long.

All of this is only the rawest beginning, yet many people who dream of the countryside ignore even these most basic steps.

Now we come to the question of size. Is it really necessary to have hundreds of acres if all you want is a small farm?

Average size varies with location and type of enterprise. An acre of strawberries or asparagus near a major population center might be profitable; an acre of wheat probably would not.

In most cases, a small farm is at a competitive disadvantage if it produces the same products that a large farm in the area produces. The larger farm can make better use of labor and equipment and can more easily acquire operating capital. But we have seen some exceptions.

If a dairy farmer milks 100 cows with an average production of 10,000 pounds and sells that million pounds of milk per year at $9 a hundredweight, he grosses $90,000. The farmer who milks 10 cows of the same caliber grosses $9,000.

If both farmers had the same lineup of equipment, those costs would smother the smaller of the two. If the large farmer had large, fast, new equipment he would accomplish much more than the smaller one with small, slow, old equipment that constantly required repairs. But . . . there could be compensations. If the larger farmer's equipment and other costs were such that his expenses came to $85,000 a year, he'd only have $5,000 left. And if the smaller farmer could hold his costs down to $1,000 a year, he'd have $8,000 left.

A few years ago it would have been tough to find examples of this. New equipment was relatively cheap, there wasn't as much old equipment available, fuel was inexpensive, fertilizers and chemicals constituted a much smaller portion of the farm budget, land costs were lower, taxes were lower, and so forth.

But today, a new combine costs $40,000 or more: an older, smaller one can often be found for $100. Big farmers want—they need—8-, 10-, or 12-bottom plows costing thousands of dollars. They have no use for the old two-bottom out behind the shed, and they sell it for scrap metal prices. An average-size tractor (now about 85 horsepower) will cost more than $10,000; older, smaller models can often be had for under a thousand.

You'll have to be a mechanic if you own the old stuff, and you won't work as many acres in a day. But you'll get the job done. And you won't need nearly as many bushels or gallons or pounds to cover the cost of capital, to repay loans, and pay interest.

Large farmers are extremely shrewd managers. They have to be. They have large equipment because they know exactly what it costs them and what the alternatives are—and because they make money with it.

Small farmers have to do the same. A piece of equipment is not necessarily right just because it's old and small and cheap. Small farmers require the same type of management skills as large farmers; they only apply them differently.

There are several other angles here that can get us off the track. You, the reader, and I have a somewhat different view of the future than most farmers. For the most part, we believe in organic farming, and we're concerned about chemicals in our food and soil. We can see ecological webs that others ignore or are blind to. We are, perhaps, more deeply aware of the real meaning and nature of the energy crisis and its relation to food. We're uneasy about megafarming and disdainful of the middleman with his processing and packaging and advertising and hauling. We think that somehow this is all wrong and that we can make it right.

If you're serious about farming but lack experience, homesteading is certainly one of the best places to begin learning. Or, you might consider formal training and then working as a hired hand. With more experience, you might be able to farm as a renter or on shares. In all of these situations, you'll have to act like an agribusiness farmer, of course, unless you are fortunate enough to find organically inclined people to work with. It's getting easier all the time.

But perhaps the best alternative of all might stem from this encouraging note: fully two-thirds of all American farmers earn more away from their farms than they do from farming.

In organic and other ecological circles, this is generally taken as bad news. More than half the farmers of the 40s have been forced out, and only one-third of those remaining can be said to be full-time farmers. Ninety percent of our food is produced on ten percent of our farms. And yet, if part-time farming is actually twice as common as megafarming, isn't this a golden opportunity? If we can continue to earn a living in town, it doesn't really matter if the farm makes enough money to support us or not. We can learn. We can improve our land, build up our herds and flocks, settle in with machinery that's proper for each individual farm, build up equity, be organic.

It's not the ideal situation, because proper farming requires careful timing and full-time supervision and surveillance, but it's a darn good second choice. For most of us, it's the only logical choice. With study and practice, with good management and sound financial planning, a part-time farm can become a full-time one . . . and if our hopes that agribusiness can't last should prove to be right, such small farms will be in an extremely enviable position.

One thing more. Most organically inclined people know that it takes three to five years to convert a chemical farm to organic methods. But what many do not know is that many farmers believe that it takes five years, even for an experienced farmer, to get to know how to work a particular farm. Every place is different, every situation is different. This is yet another reason for the greenhorn to be cautious.

Yes, it's possible to make a living on a small farm. But it probably takes about as much training and preparation as a career in law or medicine or any other worthwhile profession.

SWEENY AMONG THE DALES

by James C. McCullagh

The Sweeny farm rests across a stream
past a huddle of pubs
and the newsstand in Brecon
which points a hurried finger at the green
and barren hills of Wales.
It is Sunday, when farmers never sleep
but slow down their chores
to take stock of their work
and the week to come.
I see the man Sweeny
moving back and forth
between barn and house
like a windmill.
He motions, like a policeman,
for us to come aboard.

We walk up the snaking hill
like the ones the children draw so well
past the piles of steaming dung
to the courtyard where the ghosts of horses play
among the tools of the fields
graying yet hopeful of return to service.
In the pasture stands a mare
very white against the earth
that knows man Sweeny moves before she does.
"How old," he asks, "do you think she is?"
To be polite and safe I said, "Thirteen."
"Thirty," he said and cradled her
with brown and freckled hands,
feeling her still strong flanks
which have carved the rocky hills for years.
"Horses," Sweeny said, "used to work these hills
before we gave them to the sheep.
But horses are coming back.
I visit auctions up and down the coast
buying equipment for my stable.
Horses are coming back."

On the way to the car Sweeny showed us
a forge "from a local smith who died."
Among the hundredweight of steel,
the hammers and the tongs of silence,
I see a new fist striking the shoe
sending sparks across the dull Welsh earth
igniting fields of harvest wheat
plundered from between the reins.

FARMING IN WALES

by James C. McCullagh

In the absorbing hills of South Wales rests the ten-acre organic farm of Sedley Sweeny and his wife—a picture book farm, complete with Black Welsh Mountain sheep, an array of horse-drawn farm equipment, and compost piles that steam. But this is not Welsh acreage populated by romantics. If you want straight talk about the rigors of organic farming on inhospitable land, Sweeny is the one to go to. He is uncompromising in his advice; he minces no words.

Sweeny and friend.

Let the new farmer (or small-holder, as he would be called in Wales) ponder the following advice from Sweeny: "*hard, long hours* are inescapable, particularly when building up the farm and acquiring the essential skills. The alternative is to accept third-rate results, which, I feel, are the certain paths to failure. One must learn to find recreation in the ever-changing work and the rhythm of the seasons. More leisure should be possible later when the project is running well and one has achieved full co-operation with like-minded neighbors."

Sweeny, an ex-officer in the British Royal Engineers, bemoans the fact that until approximately "a century ago, a peasant child grew up on the land and learned the skills by his father's side. By the age of twelve, the rhythm of the farm life was part of him, and by fifteen, he could tackle practically every job on the holding. He accepted the hardships and joys of subsistence husbandry *because he had no option.* Today, our would-be small-holder jumps in at the deep end with the soft option of the welfare state waiting to rescue him if he fails to swim."

And Sweeny does not underestimate the skill farming demands. "Self-sufficiency farming," he notes, "probably requires more mental and manual skills than most other callings. In olden times, children learned their skills at their parents' knees. But now we have a whole new generation of young people divorced from the land and its traditional crafts. They have to learn from scratch; just like tackling a foreign language, one cannot expect fluency to come quickly to an older person."

While advocating the discipline of self-sufficiency, Sweeny does not romanticize the challenge. "A growing number of people," he remarked, "are opting out of our industrial-economic society in the hope of finding a new and true life of self-sufficiency on the land. The failure rate is high, almost always a result of inexperience and lack of the very considerable skills needed to produce, with certainty, a wide range of products necessary for survival. Our people have become soft and are daunted by the hardship that their grandparents accepted as normal."

Strong words, indeed, but Sweeny practices what he preaches. A center of farm activity is crop production. The three-year crop rotation is a variation of the traditional system used on mixed stock farms in upland Wales. Wheat and rye (one-quarter acre of each) for home milling are autumn-sown by fiddle direct on the inverted sward. Crops are cut by scythe, bound by hand, and placed immediately on tripods to dry and harden. If the crops are carted in time, Sweeny reports that he turns "the hens onto the stubbles for up to a fortnight before cultivating with spring tines. We then sow a crop of grazing oats or rye to provide an early spring bite for house cows."

Sweeny reports that the ground receives a liberal dressing of compost in February or March which is plowed in not more than four inches deep. The ground is then cultivated with spring tines and harrows until a good tilth is obtained. It is then ridged, using a single-furrow horse ridger. Three rows of main-crop potatoes and one-fourth acre of mangolds are sown on the ridge in early May. A single row of peas may also be sown. In late May, a double row of main-crop carrots and in early June, about one-fourth acre of seeds are sown."

According to Sweeny, the dredge corn crop is cut rather green using a scythe of a tractor mower. It is not bound, but put immediately onto a Tyrolean-type three-wire fence so it dries like hay. On the fence, it is quite safe until carted.

Approximately three acres of grass are made into hay. If sufficient material is available, the fields are composted, harrowed, and rolled in mid-April and laid up until cut in early July. The hay is cut with a tractor mower, turned with wooden rakes, put onto tripods, and carted loose when ready.

The individual paddocks are grazed hard by cattle and sheep for five days and rested for up to three weeks, thereby improving the sward and reducing the incidence of intestinal worms in the stock.

Sweeny states that "all grassland is treated with calcinated seaweed, two hundredweight (cwt.) to the acre once every three years; it has also had one dressing of basic slag at ten cwt. in 1975 which has already caused a remarkable growth in white clover."

The Sweenys' one-quarter-acre vegetable garden, in which the crops are rotated on a four-year cycle (potatoes, pulses, cabbage family, roots, and onions), provides practically all-year-round fresh vegetables for the house plus a surplus for sale at the farm gate during the summer. And to extend his season, Sweeny uses an attached greenhouse for early seeding. In fact, he has discovered that he is able to grow tomatoes year-round in his greenhouse, which is quite a feat in Wales where light intensity and sunshine levels are low.

Contrary to how it may seem, Sweeny does not consider his farm a haven of self-sufficiency in a hostile world. He notes that "I am sure that a family could survive on its own in complete isolation, but this would be a rather uncomfortable and insecure subsistence. Three or four neighboring smallholders, working in harmony and pooling their individual skills could live far better. Add a bit of modern technology and life becomes easier, with more leisure time, less drudgery."

And communality is a central feature of the Sweeny experience. For example, his flock of Black Welsh Mountain sheep, consisting of a ram and twelve ewes, graze the acreage on a hillside opposite the farm and are tended unofficially by Sweeny's neighbor. In fact, a spirit of operation seems to pervade this Welsh farming community.

Sweeny acknowledges that when he has hay to cut, he simply has to call his friends. And when he has a sheep to shear, a building to construct, or any formidable task, he does the same thing. And his neighbors do likewise. He is presently equipping a forge, obtained complete from a smithy in the nearby village, which will serve as a communal workshop for him and his neighbors.

Not unlike some farmers in the United States, Sweeny spends some of his time visiting farm auctions, always on the lookout for good, used farm equipment which will serve his needs. This way he is building up an impressive array of horse-drawn equipment for the time when his farm will be plowed, cultivated, and harrowed by horses which, according to Sweeny, "are part of the Welsh hill tradition."

Sweeny senses a genuine back-to-the-land movement in Britain, something he doesn't necessarily greet with open arms. He firmly believes that people, if they are to be successful on the farm, must receive solid training for the job. Accordingly, he hopes to encourage some British agricultural schools to initiate a formal apprenticeship program for would-be farmers. A number of schools have shown considerable interest in this program.

For his part, Sweeny has an apprentice on his farm who is learning the ropes from the ground up. Sweeny emphasizes that "experience comes only with the time, and I would suggest an inexperienced youngster would be unwise to attempt subsistence farming until he spent two years working on a good, mixed farm."

Not everyone would agree with this approach to farm education. However, few, I think, would argue with Sweeny's success. And if you would like to learn more about this fascinating farm in Wales, write for a booklet entitled "Self-Sufficient Small-Holding," which can be obtained from the Soil Association, Walnut Tree Manor, Haugley, Stowmarket, Suffolk, England. Price, $1.

AVI—A VILLAGE CONCEPT

by William R. Lawson

Editor's note: The American Village Institute, teaching the dying skills and concept of self-sufficiency, is a source of hand- and foot-operated tools made from traditional designs and materials.

In many ways the American Village Institute is perhaps the most unusual nonprofit research and educational organization currently active in the field of alternatives. Young, but rapidly growing, the AVI was begun in early 1975 by a small group of dedicated "villagers" who saw the need for a comprehensive institute entirely devoted to teaching people how to become more self-sufficient. Not just to be self-sufficient individuals, but also how to create reasonably self-sufficient communities. It is this emphasis on small-community—or village—development that lies at the heart of the AVI concept.

In order to fully understand the objectives of the AVI, it is first necessary to understand what is meant by the term "village." In brief, a village is defined as a simple composite of family farms, tradespeople, and a marketplace. It is further distinguished by the fact that most of its inhabitants can and do provide most of their own basic necessities, and at least some of their niceties. It is also perhaps the largest form of socioeconomic grouping that can still function entirely on the basis of trade, barter, and the exchange of labor.

With this definition it is easy to see how the village concept can provide a very useful framework for exploring the entire area of self-sufficiency and appropriate technology. By using this village approach, the AVI is developing a broad research and educational program that has many innovative features. One of the most important of these has to do with the study and design of appropriate tools and equipment, and the teaching of the skills necessary to make and use them.

To begin with, the Institute is mostly interested in the development of those tools and methods that are ordinarily associated with traditional crafts, trades, and skills. The reason is simple: no one can be any more self-sufficient than if they can provide their own food, clothing, and shelter, as well as their own tools. [Prior to the industrial revolution that is exactly what most people did—at least within the village structure.] At the same time, the best way to learn these skills is to study them under the guidance of someone who has already mastered them. With this in view, the AVI has begun a comprehensive apprenticeship program that encourages each student to master at least one craft or trade,

An apprentice at the AVI workshop.

and gain at least a working familiarity with all the skills necessary to provide the basics of food, clothing, shelter, *and* tools. Although still in the initial phase of development, it is envisioned that each student who completes the entire course will have the knowledge and ability to create a very comfortable, yet highly self-sufficient way of life.

This focus on tools and related technology is not accidental. In fact, one of the primary reasons the AVI was established was because there were no longer any sources for many of the hand- and foot-operated tools and equipment common to rural America up until the 1940s. The object from the beginning was threefold: first, to make available many of these items that have faded into the past (or are collecting dust in antique shops); second, to reintroduce a new standard of quality in design, craftsmanship, and materials; and third, to provide a reliable method of funding for an apprentice-style craft and trade school. Specific products have not only been selected because of their traditional use, but also because they require a broad range of crafts and skills in the making. They also reflect the type and range of products many students will begin producing once they have established their own shops.

In addition to making traditional tools and equipment, the Institute has also begun to develop many of the older methods and processes that were originally used to make these tools. This begins with the basic methods of extracting and refining raw materials and carries through to the last touches on the final product. For the most part, the emphasis is on the use of hand and foot power—though there is also an attempt to recreate and/or improve upon earlier uses of water, wind, and animal power. This work is aimed at developing a contemporary version of all the tools, hardware, and technology that were typical of an average early American village—as well as the knowledge and skills necessary to use them. The object is not to recreate the past out of curiosity, but rather to regain much of what has been forgotten and integrate that knowledge with what is being learned today.

Three of the implements manufactured by AVI (left to right): a cider press, a corn sheller, and a root cutter.

In addition to the apprenticeship program, the Institute is also developing a more general course of instruction in applied (appropriate) technology. This program was scheduled to begin in early October 1977 and to include a variety of subjects ranging from organic farming to the design and construction of energy-efficient architecture. The emphasis is on teaching the underlying principles upon which all technology is based, and how to apply those principles in the development of contemporary village-scale communities. The Institute is also beginning publication of a series of technical (how-to) manuals that will cover all aspects of self-sufficiency at both the family and village levels. Other publications, like the Institute's bimonthly magazine *The Cider Press,* are intended to provide a more general view of how self-sufficiency can be related to a contemporary village structure.

Perhaps one of the most unique features of the AVI is its growing membership program. Based on the belief that more people will become self-sufficient once it is technically and financially easier to do so, this program offers members the opportunity to contribute their own time, energy, and talents to the overall AVI effort—and in return, receive all the benefits that this combined effort can produce. In many respects this cooperative approach allows individual members to get back considerably more than they put in. It also dramatically increases the effectiveness of the entire organization. For example, the apprenticeship program is open to all members tuition-free (including room & board); in turn, the products made by the apprentices during the course of their training are available to the general membership for the cost of producing them (no profit is added). This serves the dual purpose of providing free training for those who desire it, and highly crafted, exceptionally low-cost tools and equipment for those who need them.

The membership program also provides a much-needed outlet for the many creative people throughout the country who would like to become involved in Alternative research and education, but have been unable to find an organization that can translate their energies into constructive projects. Much of the Institute's research, as well as material for publications, comes from the more than 3,000 members in the United States and many foreign countries. Participating members from many universities, industries, craftshops, and farms across the country provide the Institute with a steady influx of valuable research information, suggestions, and ideas. In fact, many of these people have since become permanent members of the Institute's faculty and staff.

In brief, the village concept has begun to excite the imagination of people everywhere, in every walk of life. It not only provides a framework for the development of appropriate tools and technology, but also promises to become the most direct way for many people to achieve a greater level of control over their basic needs. By working within this concept, the American Village Institute has begun to create a new direction that can get people involved in a very meaningful way. Because of this co-operative approach, the AVI has become a powerful catalyst for change.

MACHINERY ECONOMIZING AND ANTIQUING ON THE SMALL FARM

by Rosalind Cich

Schuyler and Rita Case are self-sufficient farmers from Sharon, Wisconsin. The Cases typify a special breed of small farmer in the United States today. They have farmed all their lives, both having grown up on Illinois farms.

Schuyler Case explained their farming operation: "The two of us work our farm alone. We have 85 head of Holstein cattle, 30 for milking. Our milk has been purchased by a local co-op for more than ten years. Our corn and soybean crops are sold through the local elevators. We grow oats and hay for our own animals and sell what's left." To supplement this internal farm income, Case does a little custom silo filling.

Case feels their farm has several advantages over much larger operations: "Because I have a fairly small place, I can plow using one of the 45 horsepower tractors that I bought 22 years ago. With that and my newer 70 horsepower one, I can cut costs. Sure, I only plant 15 acres a day while my larger

The Case farm: a new home for orphaned machinery.
Gerald Cross

neighbors are plowing 75 to 100 acres with their 150 to 200 horsepower tractors that cost $30,000 to $50,000, but some of those farmers will never be out of debt. They are working for the bank."

"Not only that—with these older tractors, you just add gas to them and four new spark plugs and they'll run. With the new fancy tractors, you need an engineer to overhaul them if something goes wrong. I'm not condemning the farmer who wants a $50,000 tractor with a cab top; I'll just stay out of the fields on those windy days."

"We've learned many different ways to cut costs," said Rita Case. "We cut our grain with a 45-year-old McCormick-Deering eight-foot grain binder we paid $5 for five years ago. We found it in a machine shed on a farm. It was in such good shape that it still wears its original coat of paint. Since we've had it, all we've repaired are the sickle and reel on it, which were both minor jobs."

"Because I've gotten a reputation for collecting old machinery," interjected Case, "I've been able to accumulate some parts through dealers. The ones who've been in business a long time are often excellent sources of old parts for old machines. One, who had no use for the old pieces his company had been storing, gave me a large quantity of them, like sections that go in the sickle of the grain binder. I also buy and keep some machines that are not operable, solely for their parts."

Mrs. Case added, "We realize that no old machine does the job as well as its modern counterpart does. The old equipment took time and labor, and the modern machines take much less time, but they are also much more expensive. Schuyler cuts grain with that old binder. There's a lot of labor involved, because then the grain has to be put through the threshing machine, whereas with the modern combine, one man can do it all with almost no help."

"Although we generally farm modern, we thresh ancient as a hobby," Case noted. "Each year we hold a thresheree on this farm. People come from all over. Many of them have never seen a steam engine before. Our Advance 1910 steam engine weighs 20,000 pounds, and you have to start it at 8 A.M. to get up the steam. We build a fire with wood until we get a full head of steam. Then we start pouring on coal for greater heat, while its black smoke beckons the neighbors. With 125 pounds of steam we can start threshing as long as we stoke the fire and keep the 225-gallon water tank full."

Rita Case smiled, "Our thresheree is a real show. At least 500 people come every year in August. Sometimes we have as many as 1,000. Most of them come primarily to spectate, but many help. Last

Weighing 20,000 pounds, the Advance 1910 steam engine supplies power for threshing.
Gerald Cross

Many volunteers make light work of collecting hand-bound shocks.
Gerald Cross

In action, the belt-driven Belle City 28-inch thresher.
Gerald Cross

year, a lawyer from Milwaukee (more than a 90-minute drive) pitched bundles for three hours. Some work all afternoon, others for 20 minutes. Last year we threshed all afternoon, finishing 12 acres. After we thresh, we have a large dinner to which we invite 100 local people and friends. Everyone brings something. The *Milwaukee Journal* even came to cover last year's event."

The Cases use several machines for threshing. "We have a Belle City 28-inch thresher which is powered by our Advance steam engine. We also use 1932 Case and L. John Deere tractors to pull the wagons. The Case is a C Model, 2-plow, 35 horsepower, and the Deere is 18 horsepower."

"I don't know if you realize that in threshing, the grain is shocked by hand in old twine; you have to use old binder twine because modern baler twine is too heavy. All year 'round, we keep our eyes open for old binder twine at sales. It's still good for use as long as it's been kept inside and dry. Recently, we bought some that was packed in the original bags it came in."

Case continued, "Some of the things we have are too valuable not to take care of. Some of them someday may be more valuable than the enterprise we make our living at. The farmer down the road sold a tractor he bought 35 years ago. He's used it all these years and has taken good care of it. He sold it for $1,100; that's more than he paid for it new. I have two Allis-Chalmers WD 45 tractors that I bought new for $2,200 apiece, 22 years ago. I use them all the time. Even so, right now they're worth $1,200 to $1,400 apiece."

"I have a one-row corn binder in excellent condition. It's a real good one, 35 years old. I would like to use it as a fun thing but it only does one row at a time. It ties the corn into bundles; then they have to be picked up and put into a wagon. Using this machine, it would take ten men to fill a silo in one day, so I just can't spare the time to use it. The one that I use instead is five or six years old, and 110 horsepower. It does two rows at a time; using it, two men can fill a silo in one day. In other words, I don't use old equipment if it's not reasonably efficient. My time is important to me." But, many times older equipment does a perfectly good job.

"I use a hay mower and conditioner that are 15 years old. They're hooked together and pulled with a tractor. My mower is a seven-foot International. My New Idea hay conditioner crimps the hay to dry it sooner. The modern machine that does their work is called a hay bind; it cuts a swath ten feet wide and crimps the hay at the same time. The new machine costs at least $4,000, while my two when new ran about $2,000 together. You could buy used ones for about $500 per pair. Think about it; they're 70 percent as efficient as the new machine. They even have the same operating speed. To me, there's not too much advantage in having a new hay bind."

Rita Case mentioned another machine which could save money for a small farmer: the small tractor-pulled combine. Case elaborated, "From the thresher, the farmers went to a small combine that one man could pull with a tractor with power take-off (a two-plow tractor, 40 horsepower). A man could farm 150 acres, if he wanted to economize, with one of these. As far as I know, they haven't been made for at least ten years, but one of our neighbors bought a nice one at an auction. It's 20 years old, in good condition, can be pulled with his tractor, and cost him around $500. If he'd purchased a modern self-propelled combine, new, they start at around $26,000 and go up to $50,000."

Case talked about another used piece of equipment that the small farm could find valuable. "The Allis-Chalmers G Model tractor is not the kind of machine for a large crop farmer, but I hear they're very useful for the small vegetable farm. The motor's in the back, and they cultivate one row at a time. Most of the ones I see for sale are about 25 years old, but I hear they can be used for so many different jobs that they are handy to have around."

Rita Case offered some tips on collecting antique machinery. "We don't ever go to antique auctions. The prices are too prohibitive. Instead, we attend family farm sales, and a lot of times find pieces in fantastic condition. Of course, all our friends tip us off when they hear about something we would like to have. Also, sometimes we stop at farms when we see interesting pieces out in the yards. We have a 1929 McCormick-Deering 1020 tractor; we are its second owners. This is its first time off the original farm. And we have an old clover hauler in 100 percent working order. There's even a 1929 steel-wheeled tractor Schuyler cuts grain with."

Schuyler Case added some advice on picking out old machinery. First, he pointed out that the machine in perfect working condition should be efficient in its use or it will be a worthless farm addition, as is his one-row corn binder, which is valuable only as an antique.

The second thing he stressed is that the shopper must use his or her mechanical knowledge to check out the machine. Case pointed out, "Remember that the old machinery runs with chains and gears, whereas the modern ones run with pulleys, bearings, and belts. Those parts make modern equipment run smoother. It's an altogether different method of working."

"You can tell if a gear or a chain is worn out; you can tell if it's good. Use your knowledge in dealing with and repairing other machines to pick out and evaluate farm equipment. Then you won't have any problems. Just keep your eyes open and your ears cocked, and you'll hear of all sorts of useful things that are available. Sometimes we drive hours to look at just one piece."

"That's so true," commented Rita Case. "It's become our major form of recreation."

HOW TO BUY AT A FARM AUCTION

by Kennedy P. Maize

You can buy good used homestead tools at very low prices at auctions. Often you can find tools there that you can't find anywhere else.

In the course of a single year, I've purchased the following items at the following fantastic prices:

- A 20-inch Sears chain saw for $9;
- A 7.6-horsepower Gravely tractor with electric starter for $200;
- A perfect scythe, including snath and grass blade, for $8;
- 35 one-pint fruit boxes for $2;
- An assortment of digging irons for $3;
- A five-gallon metal gas can for $2.50;
- A brand new four-drawer full-suspension file cabinet for $30.

I've seen a wide variety of tools and equipment sold at country auctions—cyclone seeders, corn shellers, spokeshaves, nippers, blacksmith tongs, horseshoe nails, grain cradles, and wire strippers—in short, enough good stuff to equip a homestead several times over.

Beyond simple economics, farm auctions are a common form of entertainment and socializing. Going to auctions is a good way to equip yourself, and a fine way to meet nice folks who share some of the same values you do.

A word of warning here—in fact, several words. I'm talking about farm auctions, not antique auctions. It is usually easy to tell the two apart, because auctions are advertised in the local papers and the ad should provide the clue.

For example, an ad appeared in our local daily recently that read like this:

PUBLIC SALE OF FARM EQUIPMENT

Selling for Price Farms, Rodney Dill, and Mr. and Mrs. Jake Scheller on the Robert Mullendore Farm located ten miles south of Hagerstown on the Boonsboro-Williamsport Road four miles west of Boonsboro, and two miles east off Sharpsburg Pike at Lappan's Crossroads on:

FRIDAY, FEBRUARY 13
at 10 a.m.

11 TRACTORS AND FARM EQUIPMENT

John Deere 5010 turbo; JD 4520 diesel w/1400 hrs; JD 4020 diesel w/power shift; JD 4020 gas; MF 165 w/loader; M. Harris 44, two JD A's, Farmall H w/loader; M. Harris 22, cultivators, and two-bottom plow; Ford 8N w/loader; two JD #38 forage harvesters, corn and pickup heads. . . .

And so on for some six inches of small, dark type describing an assortment of farm machinery including some nice horse-drawn equipment and a wide assortment of hand tools.

That is a farm auction. These ads frequently begin with a poignant phrase such as: "Due to quitting farming, I will offer the following at Public Sale located on the premises."

Second- or third-hand tractor attachments can often be picked up at reasonable prices at farm auctions.

Great "finds" can be made at auctions, though some oil and elbow grease may be needed to get parts moving again.

In these parts, the small family farm is a dying institution. Except for a few hardy souls and a sprinkling of crazy homesteaders like us, young folks leave the farm as soon as they can. Surveyor's stakes sprout in the fallow fields, soon to be followed by the early signs of suburban subdivisions. It's a familiar, tragic story. But it puts a lot of equipment on the market for the careful homesteader.

You want to stay away from antique auctions, though. Be wary of auctions that advertise a lot of old guns, coins, or glassware. Prices at those affairs run high and are frequently unpredictable. I've seen a corn sheller worth no more than $10 go for $25 because an antique lover wanted to make a lamp, or a toilet paper holder, or something like that, out of it. So be careful at these kinds of auctions.

Care, of course, is a necessity at all auctions. I'm going to give you six tried and true rules for auction buying which should guarantee getting your money's worth at auctions. But before we get into that, there are some preliminaries you ought to know if you are planning to frequent auctions.

First, almost anything can be, and is, sold at auction. In the case of farm auctions, that means everything including land, houses, livestock, canned and frozen goods, equipment, and clothes. Some time ago I went to an auction where a lovely 15-acre piece of mountain with a fine old stone house was sold. Included in the list of items for sale was a Home Comfort wood stove, a forge in good working order, a shelf full of canned cherries, and a complete World War I Army uniform, right down to the puttees.

If you decide you want to buy something at an auction, keep in mind that most require payment in cash on the day of the sale. This usually permits payment through a local check, but it is a good idea to call the auctioneer beforehand. His number is usually listed in the ad. In the case of big items, such as land, houses, and heavy equipment, the full-payment requirement is usually modified. In these cases, the auctioneer generally wants ten percent on the day of sale and the balance within 30 days. This, too, is frequently specified in the ad.

Sometimes the ad will also specify the bidding system. The most common bidding system at farm auctions around here is the number system. The bidder registers his name and address with a clerk on the site. The clerk will then give the bidder a number on a card. Sales are recorded by the numbers of the successful bidders. It's a good idea to record your purchases on your card as you bid, so that you can compare your record with the clerk's when you pay.

With these preliminaries in mind, let's move on to the six rules of buying at auction. I'll illustrate the rules with the story of the chain saw I bought for $9.

Rule number one: know your needs. I needed a chain saw. My ten-acre place has a three-acre woodlot, and another 3,000 acres of hardwood forest surround me. My three wood-burning stoves supply a large portion of the winter heat. I needed a chain saw but didn't have $250 to put into a good-sized new saw, and I wanted more capacity and ruggedness than a $100 minisaw could provide. The point to the rule is to avoid impulse buying at auctions, right from the start. Generally, impulse buyers end up paying more for less. At auctions, an unwary buyer can end up getting far less for far more than anywhere else I know. So, start right by disciplining yourself to know what you need when you read the auction ads.

Second: know the merchandise. This doesn't mean you have to become a manufacturer's representative for Homelite if you want to buy a chain saw. It means you should make some effort to discover the basics of the product. It is enormously helpful to know new models from old ones, good models from bad ones, and safe ones from dangerous ones. So I did some research. By talking to some folks who use chain saws every day, including a man who makes his living felling trees, I learned some valuable product information. I was ready to make intelligent decisions about brands, models, features, and the like. I knew the merchandise.

The third rule is related to knowing the merchandise: know the market. Find out how much the new product sells for and how it depreciates. This also requires a little research. I talked to the dealers, read classified ads, and generally shopped around. I discovered that I could expect to pay a retailer about $90 for a five-year-old saw in good working order. Now I was prepared to make a realistic auction bid.

Know your merchandise—original cost, present retail price, depreciation. Will it satisfy all your needs? If you're planning to buy a tractor, be sure to get there before the bidding begins, to start it up, look for oil leaks, and kick the tires.

The first three rules involve processes that occur before you get to the auction to bid. The last three involve decisions you must make at the auction. Once you have identified your needs, done some product research, and analyzed the market, go to the auction and inspect the merchandise. That means getting to the auction early. I read an ad in the local paper that listed a "Poland" chain saw among the items for sale. I was interested and showed up before the bidding began. The saw turned out to be a late model Poulan with a 20-inch blade. It was in good condition. I looked at it carefully, started it, and checked to make sure the blade was straight. I took the spark plug out and looked at the deposits on the electrodes. Remember rule four and inspect the merchandise.

Everything about the Poulan was fine, except the bidding. There were others interested in the saw. The bidding started at $50, I got in a bid at $60, and the price was up at $100 before I could nod again. I was tempted, but I stayed out after it passed my limit of $95. That is rule five: set a limit.

The limit is important because there is a psychology of auctions. The auctioneer, an agent for the seller, is trying to get the highest price he can for an item. He usually has a sound knowledge of what an item is worth. He tries to get the bidders to compete for the sake of competition and to lose sight of the intrinsic value of the item. The auctioneer hopes to make the chain saw a symbol of victory in the contest, rather than a tool for cutting wood.

Those old situation comedy scenes are accurate. People do get so involved in the bidding that they forget the worth of the merchandise. I saw it happen recently. I had gone to a farm auction to bid on some rolls of American wire. The wire was selling in the Sears catalog for $35 a roll. I had the page from the catalog with me. The auctioneer tried to open the bidding at $50 a roll, came down to an opening bid of $20, and when I left, the price was up to $40 a roll and still moving. You have to set a limit and stick to it. Otherwise, you are going to pay double—once for the merchandise and once for the fun of bidding.

Those five rules—know your needs, know the merchandise, know the market, inspect the merchandise, and set a limit—are adequate for most auction situations. The likelihood of disaster is minimal if you follow them. However, the chance of getting a fantastic bargain is also less than it might be. The final rule will permit you to seize a situation and make a score. It's simple: be flexible.

Don't abandon the first five rules. That's why I put them first. If you follow the first five, you will be adequately prepared to be flexible. It is the person who has learned flexibility without discipline who gets into trouble.

The conclusion to my chain saw story illustrates the importance of flexibility. While looking at the Poulan, I noticed an elderly David Bradley saw for sale. It had a 19-inch blade and didn't run. I looked closer. I'm not much of a mechanic, but I discovered part of the problem. There was no fuel line running from the tank to the carburetor. But there was oily sawdust around the blade and chain, and there was no rust anywhere on the saw. It was obvious that the saw had been running recently. The saw was heavy but well balanced and offered secure grips in all attitudes. I decided to bid up to $25 for it.

The auctioneer tried for a bid of $20 to open, but couldn't get it. I bid $5; someone else said $6; I said $9. I got it.

A piece of rubber gas line, a set of points, and some minor carburetor repairs, and the saw was running. It has been running ever since.

I got the saw because I was flexible and ready to run a risk. But it was a prudent risk, because I followed the rules of buying at an auction. The risk was calculated, based on a pretty good idea of what I was getting.

And now you are prepared to shop at local farm auctions. If you know your needs, know the merchandise, know the market, inspect the merchandise, set a limit, and are flexible, you will come out ahead. And you'll have a lot of fun at it, as well.

–2– Tools for Cultivation

The most important reason for cultivating is to prepare a firm seedbed. When seed is placed in the soil, the dirt should fit around it snugly, so that moisture is readily available to germinate the seed. If a seed is dropped among clods, it will just lie there until rain falls. If a seed is dropped among loose, partially broken clods, the seed may germinate and sprout, but then the seedling dries out and dies if rain doesn't fall.

A second important reason for cultivation is weed control. While cultivating for weed control, the soil benefits by being loosened for better aeration and drainage.

When to cultivate is usually the most difficult lesson for the novice gardener or farmer to learn. Soil moisture and temperature are the two gauges to use in determining the proper time to work soil—when the soil is fit, as a farmer would say. Of these two considerations, soil moisture is the more crucial—if soil is worked when it is too wet, especially clay soil, it will become too hard for plants to grow through easily.

HOES

MASTERING THE LOWLY HOE

by Hank Allison

Anybody who spends much time working a garden by hand will have a real need and appreciation for quality hand tools. The best part about buying good hand tools is that they don't cost that much more than cheap tools, and they'll last you a very long time. If you don't like your rotary tiller, you can still use it because you'll only need it a few times a year but if you don't like your spade, you have a real problem. When buying hand tools, look for quality and a piece that is of the proper proportions for you—something that will work with you not against you. Put on your work clothes and do some spading if at all possible before you buy the spade. It's just like buying shoes—if they don't fit your individual needs, you'll never use them, no matter how much they cost.

Doing battle with the weeds calls for the right tool, the right chopping method—and the right mental attitude. The right tool should be lightweight, of a handle thickness that's comfortable to you, and a length appropriate to your height. It should be just long enough for you to grasp almost at the end and still be able to stand nearly upright and chop. The longer the handle, the less your leverage on the blade. Keep the hoe sharp. A 45-degree edge slanting toward the handle will make efficient use of your labor and a longer-lasting edge.

The handle of a good tool is worth its weight in gold. Here we see two Bulldog tools flanking a standard hardware-store tool. Although all three are of D construction, the Bulldog gives you more gripping area, and room to maneuver your hand. The metal support and the rivet construction on the standard spade are subject to damage and weakening, while the split wood construction of the Bulldog is pinned for safety, stability, and long life. In addition, the natural split wood handle is more pleasing to the eye.

As for methodology, your aim is to destroy the root system. To do this without getting tired in the first half hour, tip your hoe blade to one side. Now chop an arc from one side of the row to the other, taking short, easy strokes and bringing your blade into contact with the ground as close to flat as you can. When each stroke stops, your blade edge should be about two inches under the surface and should have traveled about six inches through the soil. Now, on the way back to the right, move your arc forward about three inches and repeat. Instead of hitting the weeds head on and actually chopping them, you'll be slicing them off with the sharp hoe blade.

1) The pronged weeding hoe; 2) the Warren cultivating hoe; 3) the garden hoe; 4), 5), and 6) all-purpose garden hoes.
True Temper

The trick is to never take a swing that causes you real exertion. If you flail at that one big thistle, you'll run out of energy long before you run out of weeds.

Never take a swing that causes you real exertion. The reason for tipping the blade is to slide it into the ground with the least possible effort.

THE WARREN HOE

by Paul Koepke

Ever since primitive agricultural man forsook the pointed stick for more sophisticated cultivating tools, the hoe, in its various forms, has been found to be indispensable. No gardener's arsenal is thought to be complete without a standard garden hoe, and many have found the weeding, grubbing, and scuffle types useful on occasion.

Another type, the Warren hoe, has been unjustifiably neglected—in many areas it is almost completely unknown despite its practicality and remarkable versatility.

The Warren hoe was originally developed to make furrows for planting potatoes. Its unique design makes it admirably suited for this purpose. The blade is shaped like an arrowhead with a rounded tip and barbs, and in the standard model, it tapers throughout its six-inch length by curvilinear reduction from four and one-half inches at its base to the slightly rounded tip. In addition, the blade curves inward slightly toward the handle. It is longitudinally convex on the near surface and correspondingly concave on the obverse, with the thickness of the metal diminishing from one-eighth inch near the base to one-sixteenth inch at the tip. Mounted on the handle with the usual gooseneck found on the common garden hoe, it is canted inward at about 20 degrees from the perpendicular for greater efficiency.

This remarkable implement has capabilities far beyond the purpose for which it was designed. It can penetrate both loose and partially compacted soil with ease. Often, only one solid whack is sufficient to bury its head well below the roots of an offending weed, and a gentle tug will expose the interloper in its entirety. The pointed tip suits it admirably for pecking at the soil in confined spaces, while the absence of any cutting edge makes it possible for one to work the surface near the base of plants without danger of damaging any tender roots.

The Warren hoe is also an excellent furrowing tool to the depth of six inches, and when laid on its side with the point slightly depressed into the soil, it can be drawn parallel to a row of plants. It is also a well-balanced implement which lends itself readily to one-handed manipulation, leaving the other hand free to pick up and discard undesirable matter.

This excellent gardening aid has only two limitations: it is not an efficient breaker of stubborn clods, and it cannot cut. For those purposes the common garden hoe is without peer. But for quick, clean cultivation, easy furrowing, and delicate weeding, the Warren hoe is a champion.

SCUFFLE HOES

When seed farmer Rob Johnston thinks of cultivating, he thinks of a hoe for his vegetables—the scuffle or action hoe in particular. "It hoes when pushed as well as when pulled. The thin blade rocks back and forth slightly on the handle mounting so that the cutting angle is proper whether pushed or drawn. It is fast and effective on the annual weeds and works well on grass if the blade is kept filed. We were skeptical when we first noticed this hoe on the market, but we received one as a gift and liked it so well that we went out and bought another."

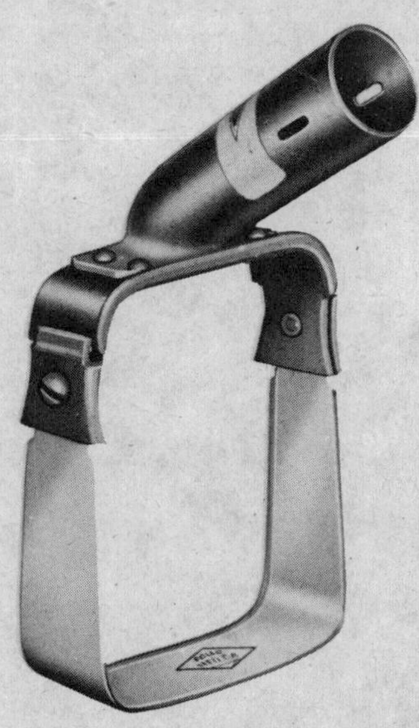

The Scuffle Hoe
Polar-Werke

THE LINCOLNSHIRE LONGHORN HOE

This tool was invented and developed in Lincolnshire, England, 300 to 400 years ago. "The pilgrim fathers may have used a hoe like this around Boston, U.K., before they sailed to America," suggests a manufacturer, David Tonge. Still used in Lincolnshire for larger gardens, small fields, odd corners, and headlands, it was originally used as a tool to fill the gap between the ordinary hand hoe and horse-drawn cultivators.

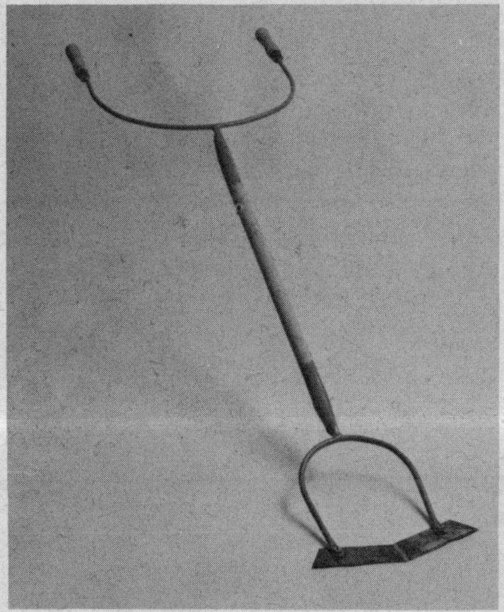

The Lincolnshire Longhorn Hoe

To use it, you stand in between the handles and push the hoe backward and forward while walking forward. The art of using it is to keep the blade one-half-inch deep in the soil while keeping the blade level. "A big selling point," says Tonge, "is that it enables one person to cover a lot of ground in little time. A fit and able man in a seven-hour day should be able to hoe four to five acres in 20-inch rows."

Oatsheaf Enterprises
Chapel Farm, Martin Dales
Woodhall Spa
Lincolnshire LN10 6XT U.K.

PRONGED WEEDERS

Most gardeners and small farmers have the need for a three-pronged hand weeder once in a while. They are useful in pulling out perennial grass in vegetable rows and in removing weeds between plants. "The best one that we have found is made by Mechanical Applications in Wiscasset, Maine," says Rob Johnston. "They call these tools Magic Weeders and they come in three handle lengths. They feature spring-steel prongs which have a better action in the soil than the stiff prong types."

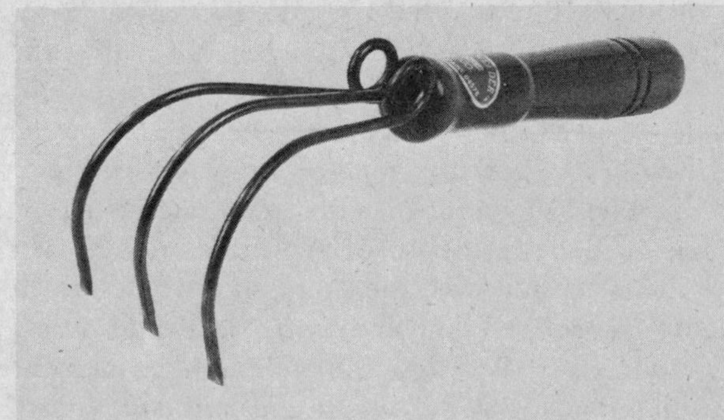

The Magic Weeder

SPADES

SPADING

To turn the soil over, a spading fork is usually better than a round-pointed shovel, though both are adequate.

To spade, dig a trench about the depth of the shovel blade or fork tines (the depth to which you can easily plunge a spade). The dirt dug out is put in the wheelbarrow and wheeled to the other end of the plot to be spaded. It will be used to fill in the last trench.

To spade, dig a trench about the depth of the shovel blade, put the dirt in a wheelbarrow, and save it to fill in the trench left after spading.

Next, simply dig another trench next to the first one, turning the dirt a spadeful at a time, upside down into that first trench. Tip the spadeful of dirt on its side rather than completely upside down. That leaves the plant residues and other organic matter that were on the soil surface at varying depths of the spaded dirt rather than buried completely at the bottom of the trench. The organic matter will rot faster that way.

Proceed across the garden in the same fashion, spading, turning, spading, turning. Don't be in a hurry and take too big a bite. Take care to keep the spading side of the trench straight up and down. In sod, the grass mat on top of the soil will make spading more difficult. When grass is still attached to unspaded sod by the roots, use a round-pointed shovel rather than a spading fork; the shovel will cleave the roots better. At the edges of the sod plot to be spaded, mark a line and then go along the length of that line with the shovel, jamming it down about four inches to slice through the grass roots. Then while spading, the shovelful along the edge will lift out easily. This will also clearly mark the edge of the area to be spaded.

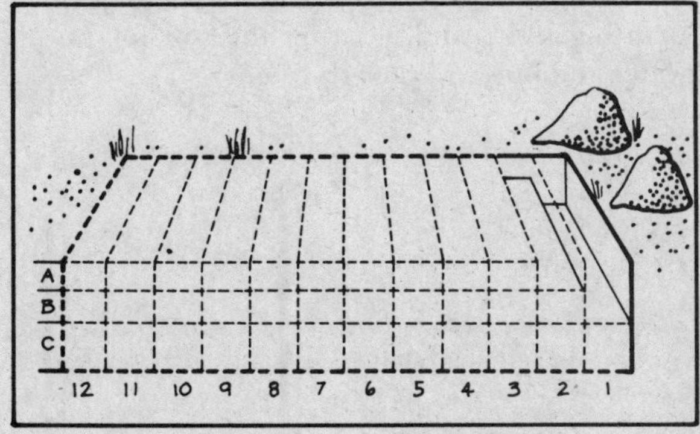

Triple spading is the ideal: the garden soil is carefully spaded and mixed. The top layer (A) is removed from blocks 1 and 2 and saved for eventual use in blocks 11 and 12. Soil is next removed from block 1B and saved for use in block 12B. Next, 1C is spaded to loosen and turn the soil, 2B is moved to cover it, and 3A is used to top off block 1. The sequence continues until the entire garden has been spaded. The process is laborious, and in practice is seldom done.

When the soil is turned over, give each spadeful a whack to crumble it, or stick the shovel or fork into it and twist. Either maneuver breaks up the clod a little and leaves the surface loose and friable.

If you are spading in the fall or early winter, leave the surface rough after spading. As is true with fall plowing, the rough soil surface will absorb and hold more water through winter and freezes will mellow it better. The soil will also dry out faster in spring. Work the surface as soon

When you're talking about working in the garden, it all comes down to how much strain you put on your back. Here we see a Bulldog spading fork in the foreground, and a standard spading fork in the rear. Notice how when the fronts of the tines are even, and the pivot points the same, the Bulldog gives you a full eight inches less bend to do the same work. Multiply that eight inches across a 25-by-25-foot garden, and you've saved yourself some mighty sore muscles.

as you can after spading, in spring or early summer, so that finer soil on the surface will hold soil moisture. Don't work the soil deeply, though, as that will only drag sod or other plant residues already spaded under back on top of the ground.

DIGGERS

The U-Bar Digger

A 50-by-50-foot plot of land can be dug to a depth of 18 inches in two hours with Eric Brunet's U-Bar Digger. Two handles support a bracket with very long digging tines. To use it, the prongs are forced into the soil with the foot, handles at arm's length. The handles are then pulled back toward the body and rocked back and forth to crumble the soil sitting on the tines. Leverage does all the work. This same action can be used to raise potatoes, turnips, and other root vegetables. No source is available at this time.

Eric Brunet and his U-Bar Digger.

The Grelinette

Similar to the U-Bar Digger is the Grelinette from France. The manufacturer claims it will work ten times faster than ordinary labor and is not as exhausting. "We say that it is a biological tool because it integrally respects the bacterial life in the soil and soil structure, both of which benefit cultivation. This is a new gardening tool offering a rational technique of manual labor to mellow the soil without turning it over."

Besides loosening the soil, the Grelinette can be used for digging potatoes and root crops, fertilizing tree roots without damaging them, planting leeks, and aerating the soil for proper water and nutrient penetration.

A. Grelin
73–Arkin
C.C.P. 2170–27
Lyon, France

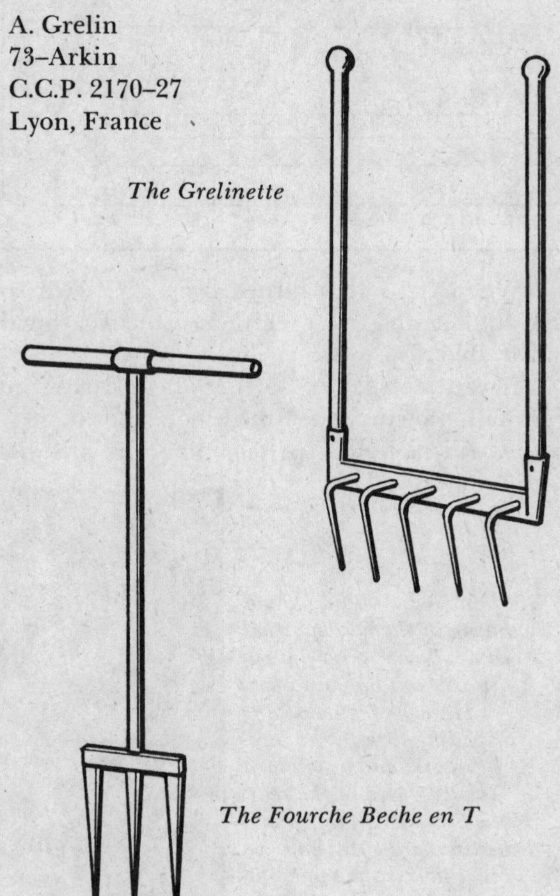

The Grelinette

The Fourche Beche en T

Fourche Beche en T

This is another French fork for working the soil without turning it over.

Association Culturelle
1 rue des Basses Boulangeres
77850 Heriey, France

ROTARY CULTIVATORS

Hoeboy Rotary Cultivator

Hoeboy is an unusual Danish-built rotary cultivator with 12 blades to penetrate and break up surface soil and lift it in layers to form an air-filled mulch conducive to bacterial action. A knife at the rear cuts through weeds and soil below the surface, causing roots to wither and die. The cutting depth is adjustable and is set so as not to injure lateral roots of garden plants. The compact 8½-inch width makes it easy to work narrow rows and close planting. Knife bars and cutter bar are of spring steel and bearings are of Etronax, requiring little or no lubrication.

Tradewinds, Inc.
P.O. Box 1191
Tacoma, WA 98401

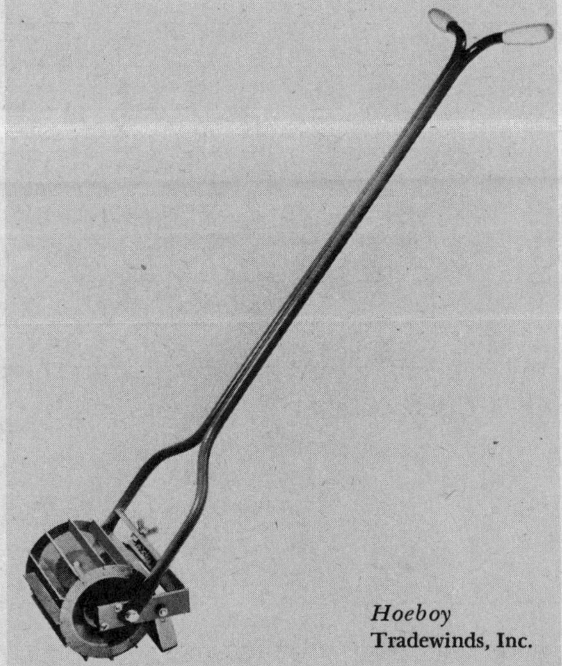

Hoeboy
Tradewinds, Inc.

Ro-Ho

The eight blades on this unit have 40 hoe points—20 angled right, 20 angled left—to give stirring action to the soil when the wheel rotates.

Ro-Ho
Rowe Enterprises, Inc.

Use one or more of the five cultivator shovels to match tillage needs. The scuffle knife cuts a layer to a depth of 1 inch.

Rowe Enterprises, Inc.
Galesburg, IL 61401

Garden Tender

This cultivator is similar to the Rowe Ro-Ho, but has a seed furrow-shovel/row marker attachment.

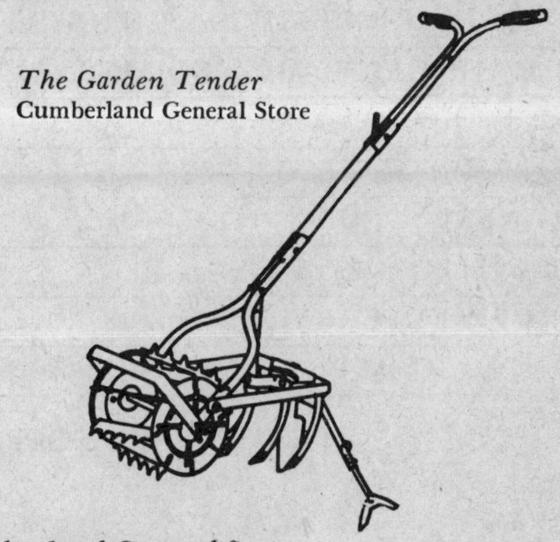

The Garden Tender
Cumberland General Store

Cumberland General Store
Rt. 3, Box 479
Crossville, TN 38555

Rotary Hoe Soil Pulverizer

Similar to the Rowe Ro-Ho.

Kumaon Nursery
Ramnagar
Nainital (U.P.) India

NORTH AMERICAN SOURCES OF HAND CULTIVATION TOOLS *

	HOES	SCUFFLE HOES	CULTIVA-TORS	SPADES	FORKS	SHOVELS	RAKES
AMES	X	X	X	X	X	X	X
BELKNAP, INC.	X		X	X	X	X	X
W. ATLEE BURPEE CO.			X				
CENTRAL TRACTOR	X		X		X	X	X
COUNTRYSIDE CATALOG	X		X		X		
CUMBERLAND GENERAL STORE	X		X	X	X	X	
FARM & FLEET	X	X	X			X	X
DEAN FOSTER NURSERIES	X			X			X
GLEN-BEL'S COUNTRY STORE	X		X	X	X	X	X
LEHMAN HARDWARE & APPLIANCE, INC.			X				
A. M. LEONARD & SON, INC.	X	X	X	X	X	X	X
BEN MEADOWS CO.	X					X	X
MONTGOMERY WARD	X			X	X	X	X
MOTHER'S GENERAL STORE CATALOG					X		
NASCO AGRICULTURAL SCIENCES	X		X	X	X	X	X
G. E. RUHMANN MFG. CO., INC.						X	
SEARS, ROEBUCK & CO.	X		X	X	X	X	X
SEYMOUR MFG. CO.	X						
STANLEY GARDEN TOOLS—U.S.	X		X	X	X	X	X
TRACTOR SUPPLY CO.	X	X		X	X	X	X
TRUE TEMPER CORP.	X	X	X	X	X	X	X
THE UNION FORK & HOE CO.	X	X	X	X	X	X	X

INTERNATIONAL SOURCES OF HAND CULTIVATION TOOLS

	HOES	SCUFFLE HOES	CULTIVA-TORS	SPADES	FORKS	SHOVELS	RAKES
AFRICAN HOE (PTY.), LTD.	X						
BULLDOG	X			X	X	X	
CEAF S.N.C. F.LLI SILETTI	X		X		X	X	X
THE CHILLINGTON TOOL CO., LTD.	X						

* Address for the companies listed in charts in this book can be found in the Appendixes A and B.

	HOES	SCUFFLE HOES	CULTIVA-TORS	SPADES	FORKS	SHOVELS	RAKES
COOPEXIM-CEPELIA	X		X	X		X	X
COSSUL & CO. PVT., LTD.	X						
ENGLISH TOOLS, LTD.	X			X	X	X	
FERFOR	X		X	X	X	X	X
FERUNION	X						
CG FUNCKE SOHN	X		X		X		X
HERRAGRO	X					X	
HILTON ENTERPRISES CO., LTD.						X	
HINDUSTAN ENGINEERING CO.	X		X			X	X
JENKS & CATELL, LTD.	X		X	X	X	X	
KUMAON AGRI-HORTICULTURE STORES	X			X	X	X	
KUMAON NURSERY	X		X		X		
KUMAR INDUSTRIES	X				X		
LASHER TOOLS (PTY.), LTD.	X			X	X	X	X
MOHINDER & CO. ALLIED INDUSTRIES				X			
NIKKO CO., LTD.	X		X	X	X	X	X
OY RETTIG-STRENGBERG, AB					X	X	
PEUGEOT	X		X		X		X
GEORGE PIKE, LTD.	X			X	X	X	X
POLAR-WERKE	X	X	X	X			X
SHW SCHWABISCHE HUTTENWERKE GMBH	X		X	X	X	X	
SCOVIL HOE CO.	X						
SELF-SUFF. & SMALL-HOLDING SUPPLIES	X			X	X		X
SOCIETE DES FORGES TROPICALES	X			X			
SPEAR & JACKSON TOOLS, LTD.	X		X	X	X	X	
STANLEY GARDEN TOOLS, LTD.	X		X	X	X	X	X
SYNDICAT DE L'OUTILLAGE	X		X	X	X	X	X
THE TATA IRON & STEEL CO., LTD.	X					X	
W. TYZACK SONS & TURNER, LTD.	X		X	X	X	X	
UBUNGO FARM IMPLEMENTS	X			X	X	X	
UNITED REPUBLIC OF TANZANIA			X				
VILHARD & CO.	X		X		X		
WOLF TOOLS FOR GARDEN & LAWN, LTD.	X		X	X	X		

Garden Weasel

Used to scarify the top layer of soil, the Garden Weasel is comprised of three pairs of eight-pronged metal wheels. The wheels are removable, and the unit may be used with one, two, or three sets for cultivating different-sized rows.

The Garden Weasel at work
Faultless Starch/Bon Ami Co.

Faultless Starch
Bon Ami Co.
Kansas City, MO 64101

THE WHEEL HOE

A real cultivation time-saver for small-sized farming operations is a hand-pushed wheel hoe. Essentially a multipurpose tool taking several attachments, it is useful for operations like weeding, hoeing, hilling, furrowing, cultivating, and even cutting roots. The three most popular attachments for accomplishing these tasks include: (1) the turn shovel or moldboard plow; (2) reversible shovel and (3) five-pronged weeder. Many other variations are available.

The wheel hoe with (top to bottom): shovel, five-pronged weeder, disc cultivator, and sweep.

Rob Johnston finds the six-inch-long blades to be the most useful attachment when caring for his vegetables. They run just below the soil surface as the hoe is pushed along and weed very close to small plants without throwing soil on them.

Supporting the attachments is a metal, tubular, or wooden frame with either a small or large wheel. The larger wheel makes pushing a bit easier, but a small wheel offers better control over the cultivating attachments. Most units have a straight handle frame bolted to the wheel. However, the overshot frame is advertised as being easier to push.

The wheel hoe is best put to work in the early stages of weed growth. It can be used for a continuous operation if one person pulls by rope while another pushes, but is most often pushed about two feet, pulled back, and pushed another two feet.

Double-wheel hoes are hard to find in North America since Planet Junior stopped making theirs, but they are well distributed throughout the developing nations. These units have a high arch connecting the two sides, permitting the operator to straddle a row of quite tall plants to cultivate both sides at once. A few models of single-wheel hoes will do all that the two-wheel models do except straddle tall (over eight or ten inches) plants, especially the erect plants like corn, reports Rob Johnston. "To straddle a row with the single-wheel hoe, the wheel is mounted to one side of the frame, instead of on center, and cultivating tools till each side."

When using wheel hoes for cultivation, rows may be sown as close as ten inches apart, showing a clear advantage over layouts which depend on a tiller for cultivation, necessitating wasteful, wide row spacing.

Care and maintenance are two important factors in determining the longevity and performance of any tool. It is important to remember the blade of a hand tool is its most important part. When purchasing a hand tool for cultivation, make sure that the blade is made of carbon or high-carbon steel so that it remains sharp and does not wear out quickly. It is important to keep the cutting edge of the blade sharp; otherwise too much power will be required to work it, and both the quality and total work done in a day will be reduced. The blade should be cleaned after use and a bit of grease applied to the cutting edge before storing.

Tom Ulich has spent many long hours using a wheel hoe on his small farm. He writes, "If I had to choose a single cultivating tool in addition to a hoe, it would surely be the Planet Junior No. 17 Wheel Hoe. These units are easily serviced and extremely durable. They may be used to cultivate any crop in row widths from eight inches on up. They work well on just about any type of good garden soil, and their ease, speed, and accuracy of operation are remarkable. A person in reasonably good physical condition can cultivate faster and more accurately with one of these hoes than with any rotary tiller I have ever seen. (I have cultivated an acre of crops in less than four hours with one of these hoes.) Furthermore, wheel hoes are about the most environmentally sound means of cultivating, besides being an excellent form of exercise. Everyone here on the farm finds using a wheel hoe extremely satisfying and pleasurable—even the children like it."

The Planet Junior No. 17 Wheel Hoe: The low wheel is more difficult to push but offers more control over the cultivating attachment.

NORTH AMERICAN SOURCES OF HAND WHEEL HOES

Planet Junior

It is available in either low- or high-wheel models. There is a full line of attachments including seeders and fertilizer drills. The high-wheel model has direct connection of handle to wheel. Low-wheel hoes place attachments right at the end of the handle for best control of the implement. The manufacturer can still replace parts for antique equipment.

Planet Junior Division
Piper Industries
P.O. Box 1188, Freeport Center
Clearfield, VT 84106

Cumberland

This model is constructed of 16-gauge tubular steel with painted, baked enamel.

Equipped with a 20-inch, sealed ball bearing wheel with rubber tire, handle grip, and 8-inch sweep. Designed to accept all standard implements for garden use. They also carry Planet Junior models.

Cumberland General Store
Rt. 3, Box 479
Crossville, TN 38555

Empire Garden Plows

A full line of attachments can be used on this high-wheel hoe with overshot frame and wooden handles. There's a straight frame model on the 18-inch, low-wheel model with a metal extension from wheel to attachment. The manufacturer can still replace parts for antique equipment.

Empire Plow Co.
Cleveland, OH 44127

Speedy Gopher

A 16-spoke, wide-rimmed, high-wheel hoe with a rear wheel allowing the operator to adjust the cultivating or furrow depth.

The Speedy Gopher Winona Attrition Mills

Winona Attrition Mills
1009 W. Fifth St.
Winona, MN 55987

Earthway Cult-A-Eze

Two wheels are provided for stability and easier operation of this unit. A 10- or 12-inch front wheel is followed by either the five-tine cultivator, slicing hoe, or furrow plow which in turn is followed by a small 5-inch wheel. The unit maintains adjustable depth settings from $1/8$ to 3 inches deep. Attachments slide and lock into place on the corrosion-resistant, heavy plastic frame.

The Earthway Cult-A-Eze with pronged weeder, blade, and shovel attachments.
Esmay Products, Inc.

Esmay Products, Inc.
P.O. Box 547, Maple St.
Bristol, IN 46507

ALMACO Hand Wheel Hoe

Two models are available with either 8- or 9-inch cutting blades. Both have a 14-inch guide wheel, hardwood handles, and a cutting depth adjustment.

Allan Machine Co.
P.O. Box 112
Ames, IA 50010

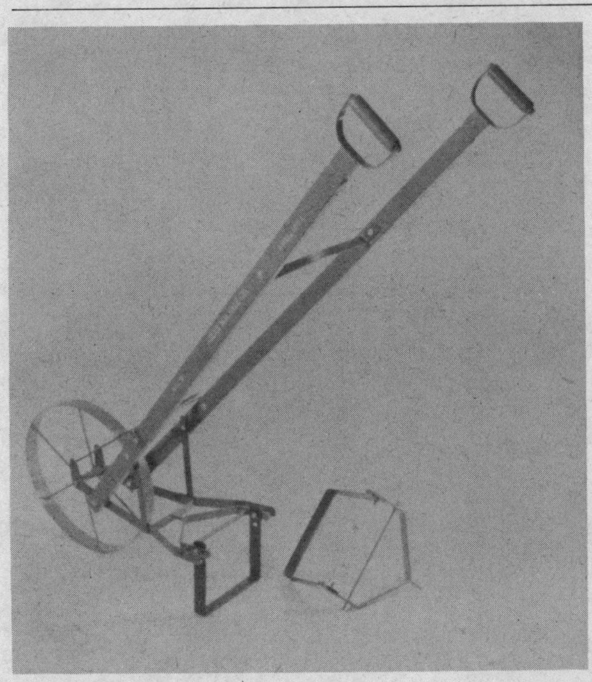

ALMACO Hand Wheel Hoe Allan Machine Co.

Hand Wheel Hoe

A full line of attachments is available for this high-wheel hand hoe.

Plow Mfg. Co.
Department MG
Bridgewater, VA 22812

Hand Wheel Hoe

You can get a full line of attachments for this high-wheel hand hoe.

Lambert Corp.
519 Hunter Ave.
Dayton, OH 45404

Distributors of Wheel Hoes

Distributors for these manufacturers of hand wheel hoes include the following:

Belknap, Inc.
P.O. Box 28
Louisville, KY 40201

Countryside Catalog
Rt. 1, Box 239
Waterloo, WI 53594

Farnam Equipment Co.
P.O. Box 12068
Omaha, NB 68112

Glen-Bel's Country Store
Rt. 5, Box 390
Crossville, TN 38555

Lehman Hardware & Appliance, Inc.
Box 41
Kidron, OH 44636

A. M. Leonard & Son, Inc.
P.O. Box 816
Piqua, OH 45356

Montgomery Ward
1000 S. Monroe St.
Baltimore, MD 21232

Mother's General Store
Box 506
Flat Rock, NC 28731

Nasco Agricultural Sciences
901 Janesville Ave.
Fort Atkinson, WI 53538

Sears, Roebuck & Co.
Farm and Ranch Catalog

INTERNATIONAL SOURCES OF HAND PUSH CULTIVATORS

Aspee APS-51 Hand Wheel Hoe

Hoe, plow, and cultivator attachments are available for this hoe. Weight: 7.5 kilograms.

American Spring & Pressing Works Pvt., Ltd.
P.O. Box 7602
Malad, Bombay 400 064, India

Single-Wheel Hand Hoe

Attachments for plowing, cultivating, harrowing, hoeing, opening and closing furrows, and hilling-up plants are available for this model. The frame is of pressed steel, and slots are designed for easy adjustment of attachments. Weight: 10 kilograms.

Cossul & Co. Pvt., Ltd.
Industrial Area, Fazalgunj
Kanpur, India

High Hoe

The High Hoe is strongly constructed, yet light and easy to use. The blades can be placed in a number of different positions for either center or side hoeing, and can be adjusted by simply undoing two wing nuts. The handles can be adjusted to three different heights for ease of use.

Highlight Engineering Co., Ltd.
Dunnington
Yorkshire, Y01 5LP, U.K.

The Jalo Hand-Pushed Cultivator with furrower, hiller (moldboard), cultivator tines, hoes, lawn aerator, and rake.
Jalo Engineering, Ltd.

Jalo Hand-Pushed Cultivator

This model can be used with one wheel (for cultivating between crop rows) or two wheels (for cultivating both sides of a single crop row). Attachments include plow, rake, ridging body, cultivators, and rotary pulverizer. It has a metal frame.

Jalo Engineering, Ltd.
Wimborne Industrial Estate
Mill Lane, Wimborne, Dorset, U.K.

Single-Wheel Hoe

Hoe, cultivator, plow, and rake attachments are supplied for this implement.

Kumaon Nursery
Ramnagar, Nainital
U.P., India

Thilot Hand Weeding Machine

This cultivator can be used with either one or two wheels. It is fitted with wooden handles and can be supplied with left- or right-handed plow bodies, cultivator tines, hoe blades, and a ridging plow—a low-wheel hoe.

Phyco b. v.
Postbox 79
Leusden–G, Netherlands

Hand Wheel Hoe

Attachments for furrowing, plowing, cultivating, and hilling are available for this low-wheel hoe.

A. J. Troster Landmaschinenfabrik
6308 Butzbach, Oberhess
Postfach 240, West Germany

Three-Tine Adjustable Hand Hoe

Union Tractor Workshop
8-B, Phase II
Mayapuri Industrial Area
New Delhi 110 027, India

Other Manufacturers of Wheel Hoes

CeCoCo
P.O. Box 8, Ibaraki City
Osaka Pref. 567, Japan

Danishmand & Co.
Karkhana Bazar
Lyallpur, Pakistan

International Mfg. Co. (Regd.)
Hospital Rd., Jagraon
Ludhiana, Punjab, India

Mohinder & Co. Allied Industries
Kurali, Dist. Ropar
Punjab, India

Self-Sufficiency & Small-Holding Supplies
The Old Palace, Priory Rd.
Wells, Somerset BA5 1SY, England

POWER CULTIVATORS

Soil Blender

This is an electric garden tool designed to dig 12 inches deep, mix soil, fertilizer, or compost from 1 to 9 inches deep, till 3 to 9 inches deep and 12 inches wide, hill 6 inches high on 18-inch centers, and cultivate 1 to 3 inches deep and 12 inches wide. A variable speed switch provides blade rotation from 0 to 125 rpm. It has a ¾ h.p. electric motor, direct gear, and chain drive. Weight: 33 pounds.

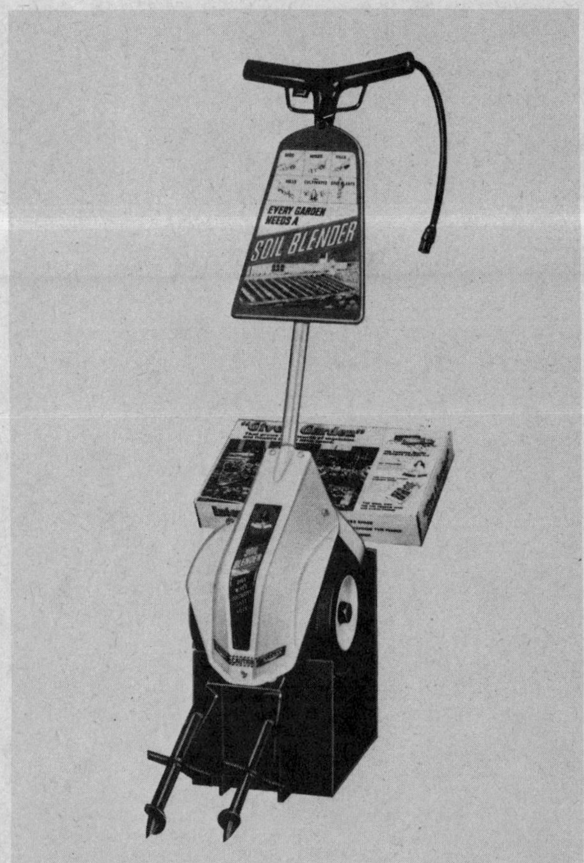

Soil Blender
Garden Maid Division, Detroit Tool and Engineering

Detroit Tool and Engineering
The Garden Maid Div.
P.O. Box 232
Lebanon, MO 65536

Derby Tiller Power Hoe

Designed for heavier cultivating work than you would want to approach by hand, the Derby Power Tiller consists of a single support tube with 32 guarded tine teeth at one end and a 1 h.p. gasoline motor at the other. Weighing 17 pounds, it gives a finely granulated deep till in one pass, working in 12-inch wide rows at depths up to 8 inches.

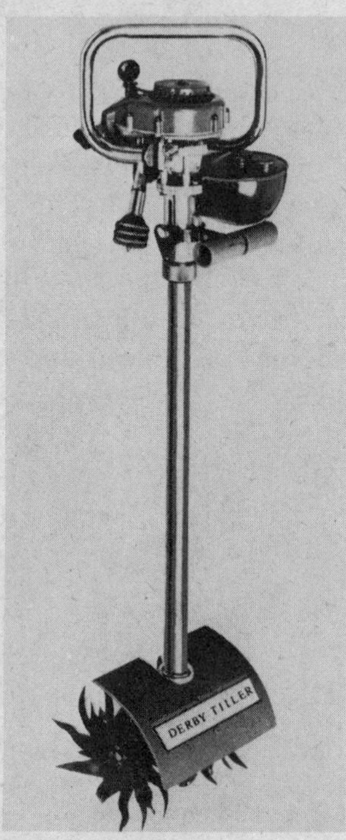

Derby Tiller Power Hoe Derby Tiller Co.

The Derby Tiller Co.
P.O. Box 21
Rumson, NJ 07760

A. M. Leonard & Son, Inc.
P.O. Box 816
Piqua, OH 45356

Bluebird

A gasoline engine powers this model's oscillating cultivator tines for an action which leaves an even layer of loosened soil without throwing soil on plants or damaging larger plant roots. Features include depth control and compact, fold-down handles.

Precision Valley Mfg. Co.
Box 9004
Springfield, VT 05156

Coleman Garden Plow

The Coleman garden plow is a one-row plow that facilitates plowing close to plants without damaging them. The cleated wheel has enough traction to enable slow and deep plowing. Attachments include a 12-inch sweep for cultivating, a two-prong fork for covering seed

The Coleman Garden Plow
Coleman Garden Plow Mfg. Co.

when planting, and extra attachments for breaking the ground, planting, and cultivating.

The engine is mounted in front for balance and easy handling, and adds weight to the cleated pulling wheel for better traction. The plow foot and depth wheel are adjustable.

Coleman Garden Plow Mfg. Co.
Rt. 8, Box 106
Dothan, AL 36301

The Carolina Plow

This is a one-drive-wheel unit powered by a 4½ or 5 h.p. engine mounted on a heavy steel and tubular frame. The tillage tool is located in front of the drive wheel and below the engine. Attachments include sweeps, turning plows, corn shovels, hillers, and cultivators. A smaller model is also available.

C. M. Products Sales Co.
Div. of Oneida Metal Products
P.O. Box 895
Rhinelander, WI 54501

EDKO Power Wheel

The compact EDKO workhorse incorporates a maintenance-free design on a balanced frame. The 5 h.p. engine with 6-to-1 gear reduction powers a chain-drive system to a 23-inch diameter lug tread tire. Liquid ballast is added for traction. Turn, corn shovels, and sweep plow are standard equipment for furrowing, hilling, and cultivating. The tool bar and handlebar are adjustable. Other attachments are available.

EDKO Power Wheel
EDKO Mfg., Inc.

EDKO Mfg., Inc.
2725 Second Ave.
Des Moines, IA 50313

PADDY WEEDERS

These implements uproot weeds and bury them in the soil. They work best in soils covered with a shallow depth of water and are readily available throughout Asia in different sizes to accommodate different row widths. One-row units are usually pushed by hand, but larger two- and three-row units are available with a power unit.

SOURCES OF PADDY WEEDERS

IRRI Push-Type Weeder
International Rice Research Institute

IRRI Push-Type Hand Weeder

This is a simple weeder equipped with two spiked wheels rotating in a supporting frame, the front of which forms a skid. The two rotors and skid are made from light sheet metal and are easily dismantled for cleaning and repair. The handle is made of wood. The leading skid serves as a depth control for the wheels. Build-it plans are available from IRRI for this simply constructed implement.

International Rice Research Institute
P.O. Box 933
Manila, Philippines

Paddy Weeder

This is a lightweight, all-steel weeder. It is best used on fields where 25 to 50 millimeters (1 to 2 inches) of water is standing. The rotary blades remove weeds and aerate the soil, thus encouraging crop growth. Weight: 5 kilograms.

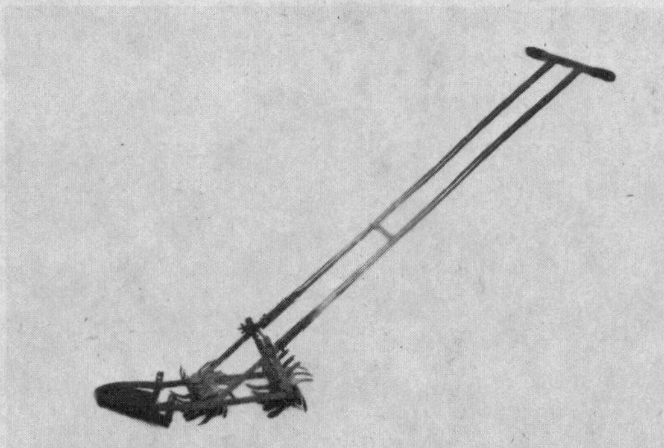

Cossul Paddy Weeder Cossul & Co.

Cossul & Co. Pvt., Ltd.
Industrial Area, Fazalgunj
Kanpur, India

Akshat Rotary Paddy Weeder

Cultivation by this implement between the rows of plants kills weeds and aerates the roots of the crop. It has a front skid and a tubular steel handle which is adjustable for different operators and soil conditions. It is available in two models, the AK-53, 150 millimeters wide and weighing 3.3 kilograms, and the AK-55, 90 millimeters wide and weighing 3.0 kilograms.

American Spring & Pressing Works Pvt., Ltd.
P.O. Box 7602
Malad, Bombay 400 064, India

Hand-Operated Paddy Field Weeder

The CeCoCo weeder is U-shaped with a float and two claw wheels, and it has a wooden handle which can be adjusted to suit the height of the operator.

It has a width of 150 millimeters to suit row spacing of 210 to 230 millimeters. Weight: 5 kilograms.

CeCoCo
P.O. Box 8, Ibaraki City
Osaka Pref. 567, Japan

Rotary Weeder Plan Number 16

Labeled photographs illustrate how a rotary weeder for row-planted rice can be locally built.

ITDG Paddy Weeder

Intermediate Technology Publications, Ltd.*
9 King St.
London WC2E 8HN, England

Bullock-Driven Wetland Puddler

Covering 3 to 4 acres per day, the Puddler is designed for quick and efficient preparation of paddy fields after first plowing. It reduces the number of plowings necessary and breaks up clods and lumps. The three angular, cast-iron hubs with four blades on each hub churn up the soil and leave fine particles on the soil surface.

Cossul Bullock-Driven Wetland Puddler
Cossul & Co.

* All Intermediate Technology publications can be ordered from International Scholarly Book Services, Inc., Box 555, Forest Grove, OR 97116.

Cossul & Co. Pvt., Ltd.
Industrial Area, Fazalgunj
Kanpur, India

Animal-Drawn, High-Clearance Rotary Hoe Plans

The rotary hoe is designed for weeding crops grown on paddy ridges at 75 to 90 centimeters spacing. It cultivates both sides of one ridge at a time and does not require straight and parallel ridges for efficient weeding. Cultivation is done by two gangs of four spider wheels, each having ten backward-curved tines. The rotary hoe can be used for weeding closer to the crop than sweep cultivators without causing apparent crop damage. Performance is good if weeding is carried out while the weeds are small, and the implement is designed to ride over stumps or other obstructions in improperly cleared land.

Intermediate Technology Publications, Ltd.
9 King St.
London WC2E 8HN, England

Japanese Puddler Plans

Illustrations for a multiaction paddy field puddling tool with Japanese design reveal a wooden frame. The 8-inch steel rotating discs, cutting knives, and rotating chopper blades are suitably designed for local construction.

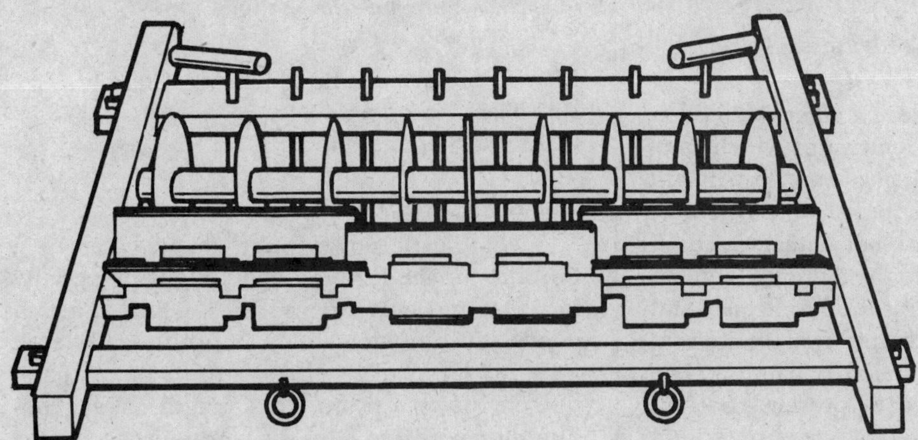

Animal-Drawn Japanese Puddler

Intermediate Technology Publications, Ltd.
9 King St.
London WC2E 8HN, England

IRRI Power Weeder

This three-row power weeder was designed by the International Rice Research Institute for use in lowland areas of developing countries. Many local manufacturers have adopted their design. Build-it plans are available from IRRI.

A Japanese manufacturer's verison of the IRRI power weeder adapted to light upland tillage requirements.
International Rice Research Institute

International Rice Research Institute
P.O. Box 933
Manila, Philippines

Mametora Rice Paddy Cultivators: Shan Shan MRT-3 and MRT-D

The MRT-3 is a three-row tiller with safety guards. The MRT-D is a cultivator which combines tilling and trenching work. It will till three rows at one time or trench one row in a "V" shape so that roots are not damaged. Both are lightweight, have adjustable handles, and are easy to maneuver. Tilling supplies oxygen and expels nitrogen gas which has generated from straw scattered in the paddies after harvest. The nitrogen must be expelled to prevent root rot and other damage.

A two-cycle, air-cooled, 2.2 h.p. gasoline engine is mounted on the handles where it balances the construction and places weight on the cultivating attachments. Model MRT-3 has a capacity for covering about an acre per hour while the MRT-D will cover the same area in 30 to 40 minutes.

IRRI Power Weeder
International Rice Research Institute

Mametora Agricultural Machinery Co., Ltd.
9-37 Nishi 2-chome
Okegawa, Saitama, Japan

Turtle Power Tiller

The Turtle power tiller was invented by a Filipino for the Filipino and designed especially for wet and waterlogged rice fields and fish ponds. It can mow, plow, rototill, and level. Power is supplied by either a 10 to 16 h.p. gasoline engine or a 6 h.p. diesel engine. Fuel consumption is 12 and 6 liters per 8-hour day, respectively. It has front-end drive and is 44 inches wide followed by a skid design body. Length: 55 inches. Capacity: 1.5 hectares in eight hours. (One hectare equals approximately 2.47 acres.)

Turtle Power Tiller
S-V Marketing

S-V Marketing
65 Commission Civil St.
Jaro, Iloilo, Philippines

FRONT-END TILLERS

A TILLER'S WORK IS NEVER DONE

by Gene Logsdon

After the leaves have been spread on the garden—along with the plant residues, horse manure, rock powders, and other soil amendments—it's time to get out the rotary tiller. The tiller chops them into the top eight inches or so of the soil where plant roots do their foraging and the humus and nutrients do the most good. The tiller is thus the organic gardener's basic humus-building tool, but it is also a lot more.

If you're approaching a weed- and shrub-infested or sodded piece of ground for the first time, intending to turn it into a garden, sample a small area with the tiller to make sure the machine has the muscle to do the job.

Neither front-end tiller nor rear-mounted model will do a good job of primary tillage on heavy sod or dense weed growth in soil that has not been cultivated in recent years. Don't expect the impossible from any tiller, even the heavier rear-mounted ones which generally chop up plant residues better than lighter front-end types.

A front-end tiller will bounce off hard, sod-bound earth just about the way it will bounce off rocks. A rear-mounted tiller won't exactly bounce, but it will lunge forward, jerking you with it. If you have no other way to work such soil, the secret, with either kind of tiller, is to go lightly over the surface repeatedly, skimming off only an inch or less with each pass—slow, hard work.

It's better to plow—or have someone plow—such soil in the fall, then work it in nicely the following spring with your tiller. Or, cover the area with deep mulch in the spring, and when that has rotted away together with the sod under it, then rotary till.

The rotary tiller earns its keep on the homestead by preparing garden beds in the spring, cultivating crops all summer long, and enriching the soil in fall with compost and cover crops.

You may be able to chop up and incorporate heavy plant growth like corn with a pass or two of your tiller, but really heavy, dense growth should be mowed with a rotary mower first. That makes the job much easier, because inevitably that dense green stuff will tangle and entwine in the tiller tines, and you'll have to get down and cut it out. A small amount of clogging can be cleared by reversing the direction of the tines while raising them just a wee bit above digging depth.

The kind of tines your tiller is equipped with—and how sharp they are—has more to do with clogging than whether the tiller is front- or rear-mounted. There are at least four kinds of tines: three-bladed chisel tines, four-bladed slicer tines, four-bladed slasher tines, and four-bladed bolo tines. Chisel tines are the cheapest, okay for cultivating, but they tangle the easiest if you try to incorporate plant residues with them. I wouldn't recommend chisel tines for organic gardeners. Slicer tines will dig from six to nine inches deep but will also tangle and clog where there is a lot of plant residue. Slasher tines are designed to cut and chop residue better with less clogging. They are longer than slicers (on six horsepower models) and will dig up to 11 inches deep. Bolo tines can be used on the bigger, six to eight horsepower tillers; these tines are heavier and wider and move more dirt per revolution, so you can move along at a faster speed. They are also less affected by clogging.

As you shop for a tiller, another choice presented is between gear-driven and chain-driven models. Gear-driven models are usually, if not always, combinations of belt and gear drives. A belt transfers the power from the motor shaft to the worm gear shaft, which then transfers power to the tine axle. Mathematically, the chain drive is more efficient since the transfer of power is more direct. Which is better? It's a toss-up in my opinion, as long as you are comparing models in the same price range. Chain drive will probably wear out quicker but is easier and cheaper to repair.

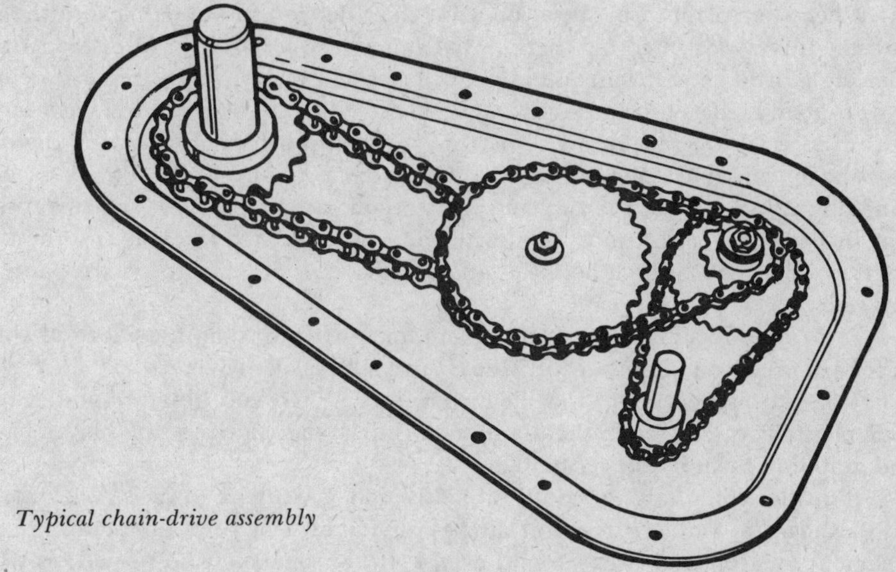

Typical chain-drive assembly

So let's pretend you have bought your tiller, and it's the first day of the gardening season. Preferably, your garden has been cultivated the previous year or was plowed the previous fall if virgin ground. You pick up a handful of dirt, squeeze it into a ball, press your thumb against it. If the ball crumbles apart easily, the earth is ready.

Don't try to see how deep the tiller will dig on the first pass—especially if you have plowed under sod. You don't want to drag those sod chunks back to the surface. Let your tiller dig only a couple of inches on the first pass. If you have the time, let the ground dry a bit before making a second pass. The second time, the tines will bite into the ground more easily and work the ground into a fine, crumbly texture. Dig at least six inches deep, and try for eight to ten, if possible. Set the brake bar at the rear of front-end tillers at a depth that will allow you to push it in and pull it out of the ground with ease, according to the depth you want to dig. Don't fight your machine; let the brake bar and the tines do the work. You push down, the brake bar holds the tiller back for digging; you let up, the tines propel the tiller forward. With gentle pressure between up and down, you allow the machine to inch forward slowly while it digs.

A rear-mounted tiller is even easier to handle. You set it for depth and speed; then all you have to do while the machine digs is guide it.

Work the ground the second time at right angles to the first pass if possible. You may need to go over the ground a third time to get a fine seedbed, but usually twice is enough, if your soil is in good condition.

After planting, your tiller becomes a weed cultivator. It can be used as a harrow for that first important cultivation of deep-sown seed (two to three inches) before the seed comes up, but when weeds are already germinating. This type of cultivation is tricky. You want to go over the ground very lightly, gently disturbing the soil surface without digging in to disturb the germinating seed. Skim very fast over the row, and you will kill many small weeds you can't even see yet. But don't try this technique on shallow-sown seeds.

As soon as your plants are above ground, you can start cultivating with the tiller between the rows. Unlike shovel cultivators, the tiller tines will not throw dirt onto the new plants and bury them, if you do not dig too deep. For cultivating, deep digging is not necessary anyway and can be harmful. If weeds are growing faster than your plants, however, and you must dig a little deeper to control them, you can buy special plant shields that fit on either end of the front-end tiller axle and prevent the dirt from falling on your plants (Sears has them). The hood on a rear-mounted tiller performs the same job.

When your plants are taller, you want the tiller to roll some dirt into the plant row, if possible, to bury the tiny weeds emerging there. That can save you hand weeding. So, without shields, you let the tiller dig a little deeper than you might otherwise, though not so deep as to cut into your plants' roots.

Front-end tillers can be modified quickly to cultivate between rows as narrow as six to eight inches or as wide as 26 to 30 inches. The narrowest width is achieved by taking the outer tines off completely and turning the inner ones around so the blades point inwards. Two intermediate widths can be attained by either leaving the two outside tines off completely with the two inside tines in regular position, or by replacing the outer tines with the blades pointed inwards and the two inner tines in regular position. Clip bolts, which hold the tines on the axle, are easy to remove, and the tines are easy to slip off the axle.

Remember to allow a few inches more for row width than the width of your various tine positions. If, for example, you intend to cultivate a swatch 26 inches wide, make your rows at least 30 inches wide—if not 32—to accommodate that 26-inch width. Why? You don't want the tines cutting too close to your plant roots; and when the plants grow taller, the whirling tine blades have a way of reaching out and grabbing them if you get too close.

If a tiller could talk, it would probably sigh, "A tiller's work is never done." Attachments turn it into a digger of garden irrigation ditches, or furrows, or rows for planting seeds. There's a hiller attachment for front-end tillers, too. I even know of someone who turned his tiller into a sidewalk edger by replacing one of the outside tines with an old plow coulter welded to a piece of pipe!

Tillers are handy for renovating berry patches and ripping out runners that are getting out of control. The tool is handy for pruning raspberry suckers growing out beyond the sides of the row where they don't belong. For cultivating or incorporating mulch under fruit trees in small orchards, the tiller is better than more cumbersome tractor machinery, and it is handier for cultivating under trellis wires between grapevines. The tiller is superb for running over asparagus beds in fall or spring to kill weeds and volunteer asparagus seedlings growing above the deep-set roots. Just don't dig more than three inches deep.

Some chicken farmers, who raise their flocks on litter, utilize tillers to mix and stir the old litter in place on the coop floor to speed the composting process. Tillers are handy to mix compost in large worm beds, too, before seeding with worms. In any raised bed, or confined greenhouse bed, the tiller is about the only power tool that can be utilized. Lighter models that can be lifted in and out of the beds without back sprains are preferable for this kind of work.

Care of the tilling parts is simple. Keep the oil bath around the worm gear at the specified level. On chain-driven models, the chain and bearings should be lubricated when and if it is necessary.

The motor, the heart and soul of your tiller, requires much more attention. Most walking, self-propelled tillers, if not all, are powered by air-cooled, one-cylinder, four-stroke engines—which, to mechanical amateurs like myself, simply means that they take oil in the crankcase and gasoline in the engine, and you do not mix the two as you do with two-stroke engines. According to Allen Brown, agricultural engineer at Purdue, a properly maintained four-stroke engine ought to give good service for at least five to eight years and probably longer. If an engine fails sooner than that, it usually means improper care. "A main cause of early failure is not keeping enough oil in the crankcase," he says. "Another is failure to change oil as often as recommended, and a third is using the wrong kind of oil."

Brown recommends changing oil every 25 operating hours—or sooner if very dirty conditions prevail. Use SAE 30 weight oil in summer and SAE 5w-20 or 5w-30 in winter (if you use your tiller in cold weather, which is not likely). If you can't get 30w, 10-30 will do. Do not use nondetergent oils with an API classification of MS, SC, SD, or SE.

Clean the air cleaner whenever you change oil, or more frequently. Neglect allows dirt to get into the cylinder and cause bearing failure. There are oiled filters, dry filters, and oil bath filters: follow the manufacturer's directions for your particular model.

Keep the whole motor clean. Don't let dirt and debris clog the cooling fin, as an overheated engine wears out faster.

An old motor can often be given new life by cleaning out the carbon buildup in the exhaust ports. Take off the muffler and you'll find the holes (usually three).

An important rule in keeping an engine running longer is never to run it at top speed for extended periods of time. There's rarely an occasion that justifies roaring around the garden at full throttle. You'll get finished at half-speed just as soon—and with better fuel efficiency. And your neighbors will love you, too.

Perhaps it is surprising to find coverage of the familiar front-mounted Rototiller in a book specializing in the hard-to-find. But surprisingly enough, there is a hard-to-find aspect to tillers which makes them an appropriate consideration for the farm tool collection, and that is versatility. Of course, the simplest models are strictly for tilling; they have front-mounted tines to break and cultivate the soil. But realizing the multipurpose potential of the little tiller as a power source, some manufacturers have produced attachments for a variety of operations. In North America, attachments are designed mainly for cultivation, while European models have a number of working tools for jobs like pumping and spraying.

TILLER ATTACHMENTS

Rather than discuss the many different tillers as power sources, we have decided to concentrate on attachments and their functions. A chart following the tool descriptions explains which manufacturer carries which tool. Manufacturers' addresses are listed in the index.

Tines

Tines are the blades of the Rototiller which do the actual soil tilling. Many manufacturers have coined their own names to represent their tines as unique. But actually, there are just a few basic designs that most follow.

Slicer—A medium-duty, short, knifelike tine.

Slasher—Similar to but more rugged and longer than the slicer, good for breaking up sod on virgin ground; cuts and chops plant residue with little clogging.

Chisel—Sometimes referred to as pick tines, good for rocky ground, clay, and hardpan. Clogs easily, not good for grasses or weeds.

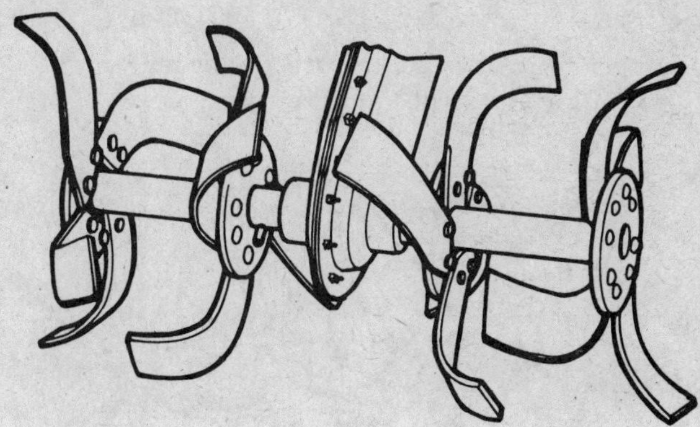

Chisel tines

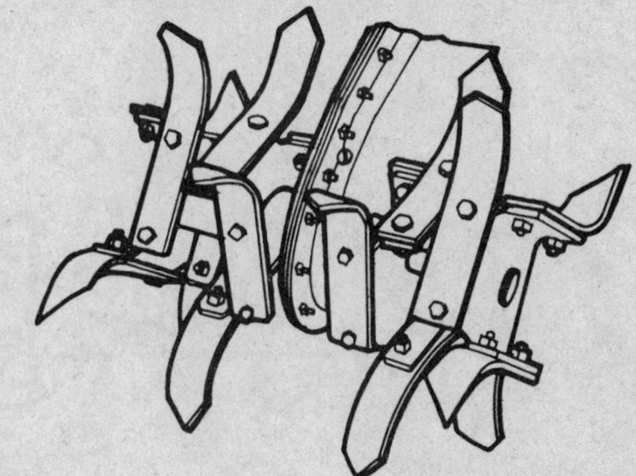

Slasher tines

Bolo—Heavy, wide tines good for normal cultivation and mulching without clogging with plant residue.

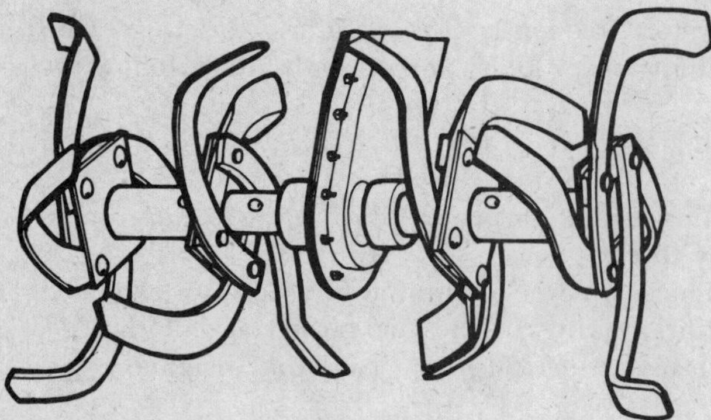

Bolo tines

Finger—Provides positive traction, good for cultivating and seedbed preparation.

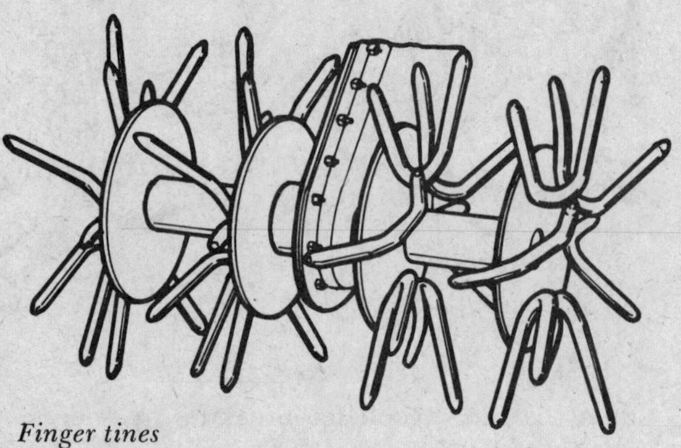

Finger tines

Til-Row

In place of tines, the til-row attachment builds rows, provides a prepared seedbed, and with the back plate removed, it converts to a cultivator. It can also be used to dig irrigation or drainage ditches.

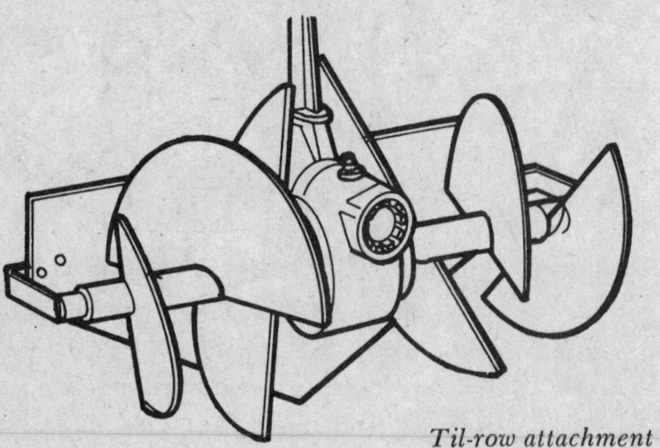

Til-row attachment

Cultivators

Cultivators appear with many different names and variations on a similar theme. Shovels, spikes, or spring-tooth tines are either fixed permanently on a frame or bolted to a toolbar, the latter being adjustable. Called either cultivators or harrows, they perform the function of removing weeds or preparing seedbeds by being pulled through the soil. Five-tine weeders, plow sweeps, and various hoe designs are available.

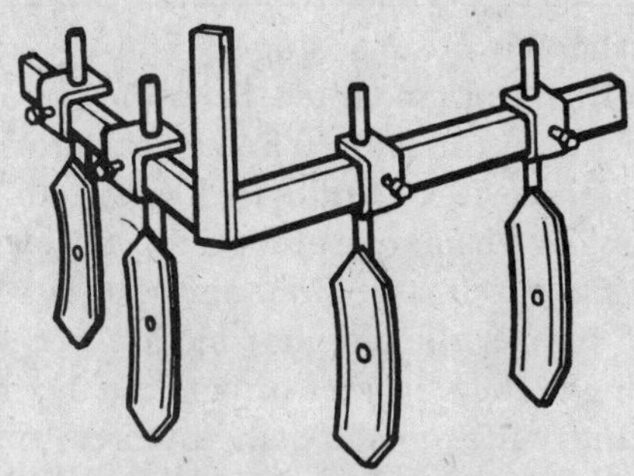

Cultivating shovels mounted on a toolbar

Plows

Small-power units have a limited amount of traction and power which limits their plowing capabilities as well. They do best at making furrows or hilling already-tilled soil. A furrow opener will dig a shallow trench for straight line or root crop planting which would otherwise

Hiller

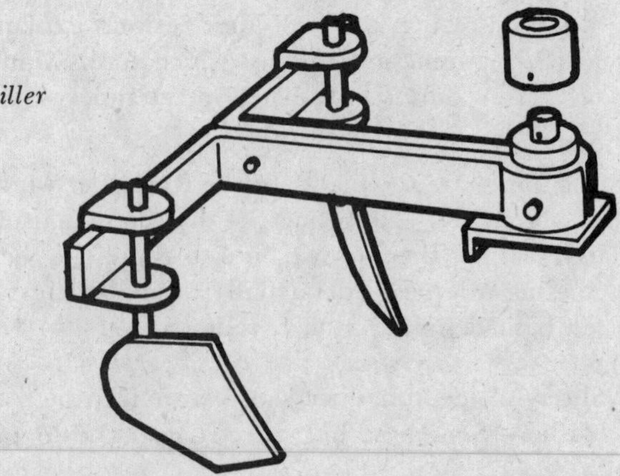

require digging holes. Hillers then fill in the furrow or hill-up around other plants.

It is worth mentioning that a hilling plow is actually one-half of a furrower. Some companies offer a furrower in two parts which, working together, furrow and hill separately. Furrowers are sometimes referred to as moldboard plows and hillers as turning plows.

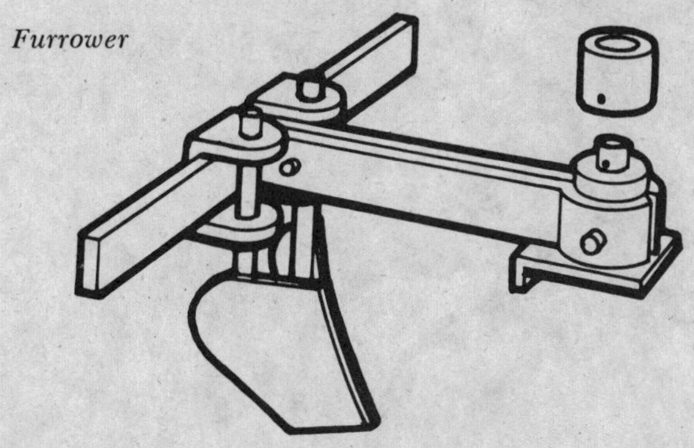

Furrower

A sweep plow is another kind of cultivating tool which makes a wide pass to cut weeds beneath the surface of the soil at a desired depth.

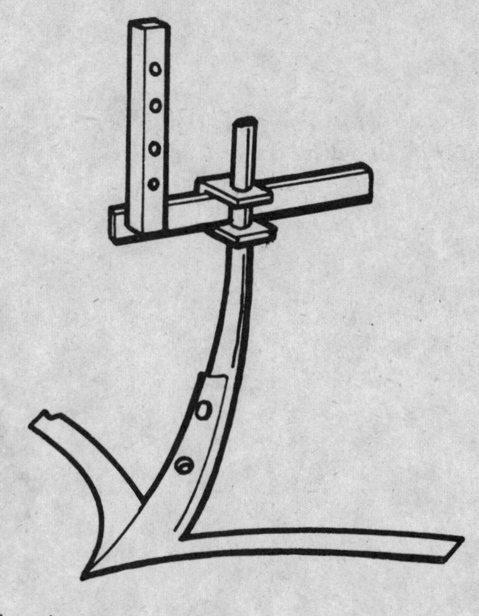

Sweep

Disc Shields

Sometimes called cultivating shields, side discs, or disc shields, these devices bolt onto the outside of rototilling tines to protect young plants from having soil spill over on them.

Disc shields keep soil from falling onto young, fragile plants.

Wheels and Tires

Most small tillers are sold with small semi-pneumatic or rubber tires which offer little traction. These are fine for rototilling since traction is provided by the action of the tines themselves. However, for plowing and cultivating, the extra traction provided by larger pneumatic or rubber tires or steel wheels is desirable. Tire chains, transport wheels, and wheel weights are also available.

Gilson Model 51104 compact chain-drive tiller with drive wheel and cultivator.
Gilson Brothers Co.

Small depth gauge wheels are provided with some attachments to offer support and depth guidance.

Plow Foot and Toolbar

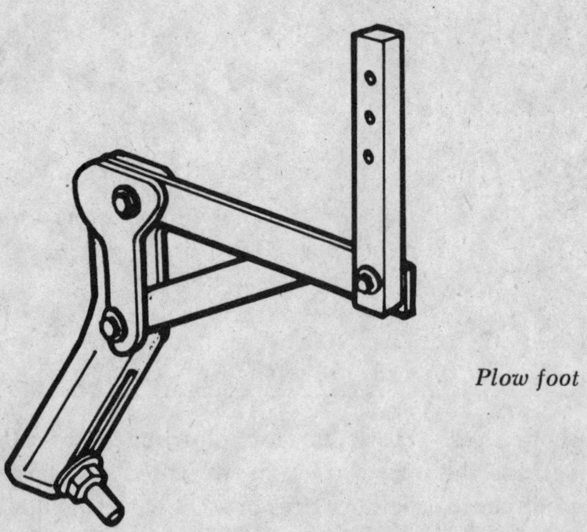

Plow foot

Some attachments mount directly onto the tiller frame, others to a toolbar or plow foot which is mounted to the frame. They offer a means of adjusting tool positioning for both width and depth of work. Bulldozing and snow-plowing blades appear with many of these models. Snowblowers are uncommon.

Mowers and Lawn Attachments

Mowers are uncommon to small, North American tiller models because the power take-off is usually limited to use with tiller tines. European models, however, are built with versatility in mind and have attachments for rotary, sickle bar, or spindle reel mowing. The listing of European models is meager here because most tillers are built to perform so many utility functions that they have been included in the two-wheel tractor section.

Some Unusual Tiller Attachments and Their Sources

See the Appendix for addresses.

Front–end carrier—Wolseley
Mulcher—Agria
Sprayer—Agria, Hako
Pump—Staub
Roller—Staub
Vine Guard—Auto Hoe
Shredder-Grinder—Roto-Hoe

THE GROUNDHOG: TILLER FROM A KIT

by Raymond Trull

After 14 years of hard work in gardening, my faithful tiller announced its imminent retirement with a chorus of grindings and rumblings and clouds of blue smoke.

What would replace it? In helping others in my gardening family, I'd used many well-known tillers, including Burns, Merry, Snapper, and Gilson. While most had good and not-so-good features, all were durable, hard-working machines. A tour of local dealers and an examination of gardening magazines made me itch to try every super clean, brightly painted new model on the stones, sticks, weeds, and dirty soil of my garden. There was nothing pretty about those tillers' prices—they had doubled in 14 years. To buy without carefully studying both quality and price was a foolish luxury I couldn't afford.

With attachments, many tillers convert to minitractors that plow, cultivate, rake, make planting ridges, harrow, and even move materials with a scrape blade. Could tillers be practical and efficient minitractors for gardens and small area crops? I wanted to know!

The Groundhog, by Heald of Benton Harbor, Michigan, is unique—it's sold as a kit. At $199.95 for a five horsepower, chain-driven model, it's at least $40 less than comparable preassembled models.

Fresh from the factory, the Groundhog is ready for assembly.
Raymond Trull

Groundhog's components are made by companies I recognized—engines by Briggs and Stratton and Tecumseh, chain drives by Parmi, and ground-working tools (a good variety) by Brinly-Hardy. More important, by assembling it, I should understand its internal workings and be able to repair it later. The goal—greater self-sufficiency!

Basic assembly included putting the transmission, frame, and tines together, mounting the engine, and attaching control cables and levers—a nine-hour job for this nonexpert fumblefingers. No tasks were strenuous or very complicated, but some required careful, patient work. A few wrenches, a screwdriver, and Heald's large drawings and careful directions kept the job moving.

With unexpected pride—it started and worked perfectly—I took the Groundhog to the garden for its first trial and my first surprise. At an engine speed just above idle, it cut six inches deep in garden soil undisturbed for six months. To make its task a bit tougher, I added extension tines for a 36-inch-wide cut. Although an inch of leaves and old stalks covered part of the area, the Groundhog easily maintained its tilling depth and forward speed.

A much tougher test came soon. When dozens of volunteer asparagus popped up among the berries and shrubbery, I wanted to add them to our skimpy parent bed. But before preparing the deep, fertile soil needed by asparagus, a thick sod of common Bermuda grass had to be removed. In the South Carolina Piedmont, Bermuda sod is a devil's brew of intertwined, tough surface runners and a thick underground mat of fibrous roots, usually yielding only to hours of toil with a mattock.

With its extension tines in place, the tiller bounced slightly each time its tines struck. But the Groundhog churned forward slowly, leaving a seven-inch-deep layer of soil and vanquished Bermuda sod in its wake. Three hours' labor was over in twenty minutes!

The Groundhog is an actor with many roles: replace the tines with deep-cleated wheels and it's a minitractor that works. Add a drawbar and make furrows with one plow or raised ridges with two plows in the furrower-hiller set. Replace them with the cultivator-scarifier set's four plows, and removing weeds and making dust mulches is safer for garden plants. Most of the weight of a well-

Optional equipment—here a front-mounted scraper blade and two kinds of rear plows —adapts the tiller for many chores.
Raymond Trull

balanced tiller is concentrated over its tines to make it dig easily and quickly. That's fine, unless you need to protect plant roots. With the Groundhog's culivator plows mounted at the rear drag bar and partially supported by the operator, plow depth is easily controlled.

Add a bit of imagination, and the Groundhog helps with many chores. Leaving two of the four cultivators mounted, I use it to rake together runners from our all-too-vigorous Japanese honeysuckle. (These make good mulch or a condiment for the compost pile when chopped with a lawn mower.) With the two plows still in place, the front-mounted scraper blade can be added for a gentle, mini-earth-moving machine. To flatten the ridge of an old crop terrace, I loosen soil with the cultivator plows and push it into position with the scrape blade. In addition, it smooths soil after potatoes are dug, distributes leaves and compost for tilling in, and spreads gravel. There are other applications and much more optional equipment.

Any problems with the Groundhog? One, due to personal preference. Rototilling with rear wheels in place—many users remove them—lifts the handlebars too high, even with the Groundhog's fine height adjustment. The solution? One extra hole in the wheel attachment rod brings handlebars down to just the right height.

In the minitractor disguise, the Groundhog runs out of traction and starts spinning long before its engine stalls. A better bite—with dual wheels or wider tires—would help in soft soil.

Overall, the Groundhog is a powerful, useful machine comparable to preassembled models. Its price, performance, quick and easy adjustments, and good design clearly recommend it.

I do have one strong opinion. Many gardeners underestimate a tiller's working ability. Except for turning under a heavy sod or green manure crop, a five horsepower, chain-driven Rototiller is not likely to be stumped when used correctly. Can a tiller with attachments provide most, if not all, soil-working power needed for a large garden and small area crops? Yes!

Heald, Inc.
Box 148
Benton Harbor, MI 49022

NORTH AMERICAN SOURCES OF TILLERS

FRONT-END TILLERS AND ATTACHMENTS	TINES—	EXTENSION SET	CHISEL	SLASHER	SLICER	FINGER	BOLO	FURROWER	HILLER	TIL-ROW	CULTIVATORS	OPT. WHEELS	SIDE SHIELDS	PLOWS	BARS & BLADES	MOWERS
AGWAY								X	X		X	X	X	X	X	
ALLIS-CHALMERS *																
AMERIND-MACKISSIC, INC.								X								
ARIENS		X	X					X		X	X	X	X			
ATLAS		X						X								
AUTO HOE								X	X		X		X			
BLACK & DECKER													X			
JOHN DEERE		X						X								
DERBY *																
EDKO				X		X		X			X	X		X	X	
FMC-BOLENS		X		X			X	X	X	X	X	X		X		
FORD *																
GARDEN MAID *																
GILSON		X	X			X	X	X	X	X	X	X		X	X	
HAHN								X								
HEALD								X	X		X	X			X	

* Tillers only

FRONT-END TILLERS AND ATTACHMENTS — TINES–	EXTENSION SET	CHISEL	SLASHER	SLICER	FINGER	BOLO	FURROWER	HILLER	TIL-ROW	CULTIVATORS	OPT. WHEELS	SIDE SHIELDS	PLOWS	BARS & BLADES	MOWERS
INTNL. HARVESTER	X														
MAGNA			X	X			X	X						X	
McDONOUGH (SNAPPER)						X	X			X	X			X	
MERRY		X	X		X	X	X			X	X		X	X	
MTD							X	X		X	X	X	X	X	
ROPER							X	X	X			X			
ROTO-HOE							X	X							
SEARS, ROEBUCK & CO.							X	X	X			X		X	
SENSATION						X			X						
SIMPLICITY	X						X								
TORO *															
MONTGOMERY WARD	X						X	X	X	X	X		X	X	

INTERNATIONAL SOURCES OF TILLERS

FRONT-END TILLERS AND ATTACHMENTS — TINES–	EXTENSION SET	CHISEL	SLASHER	SLICER	FINGER	BOLO	FURROWER	HILLER	TIL-ROW	CULTIVATORS	OPT. WHEELS	SIDE SHIELDS	PLOWS	BARS & BLADES	MOWERS
AGRIA-WERKE	X										X	X	X		X
HAKO-WERKE	X							X					X		X
ISEKI *															
MERCHANDISED GARDENING *															
SCHANZLIN										X			X	X	X
SOLO KLEINMOTOREN															
STAUB										X			X		X
WOLF TOOLS *															
WOLSELEY	X	X	X		X		X				X	X	X	X	X

* Tillers only

FMC-Bolens power unit and tiller with options: pneumatic tires, harrow, hiller and furrower, cultivator.
FMC-Bolens

The Gilson Compact Tiller requires a minimum of storage room. The same two wing nuts used to fold the handles are also used to adjust the height to suit the gardener.
Gilson Brothers Co.

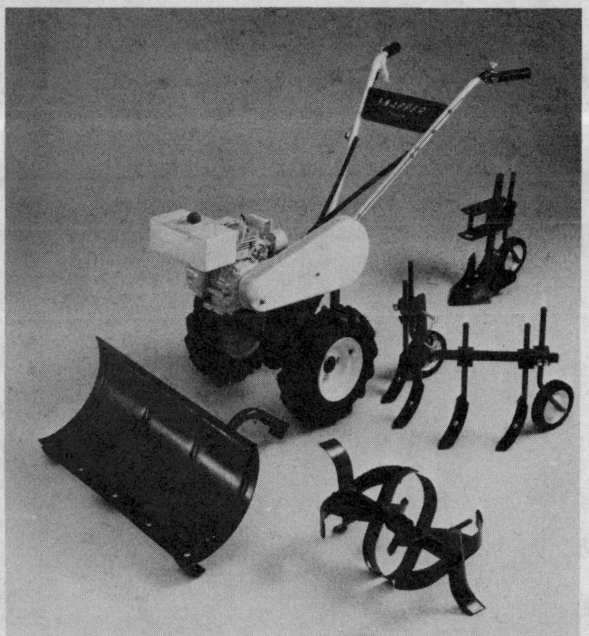

Snapper tiller with (counterclockwise) pneumatic tires, scraper blade, slasher tines, cultivator/harrow, and furrower.
McDonough Power Equipment

The Magna Chore Master with bolo tines
Magna Corp.

REAR-MOUNTED TILLERS

The rotary tiller is an excellent organic cultivating tool. It can take the place of plow, disc, field cultivator, and offset disc—and can be used as a weed cultivator too. The rotary tiller compacts the soil least of all implements. With the tilling blades mounted in the rear and the engine extending to the front, the result is a well-balanced machine which is easy to maneuver and which has efficient tilling capabilities. Rear-mounted tillers also have an excellent compost-shredding action, which is desirable when incorporating organic material into the soil. (Two-wheel tractors, discussed in chapter four, usually have rototilling attachments.)

But beyond tilling, it is quite common for a tiller to convert to a sickle bar mower or snowblower, or to have provisions for pulling a plow, trailer, or cultivator. Some tillers provide a power take-off (PTO) feature for powering a variety of attachments like pumps and sprayers, or even binders and reapers. These are discussed further in chapter four. Handlebars are usually adjustable to either side so the operator can walk beside the tiller rather than in a freshly tilled row.

NORTH AMERICAN SOURCES OF REAR-MOUNTED TILLERS

Troy-Bilt

The Troy-Bilt is a popular garden tiller, with several choices of model and horsepower. Attachments are available. Two forward and two reverse speeds are provided by the chainless, power train transmission with worm gear. Depth of tilling can be regulated to seven different levels while the machine is in motion, and the handles are adjustable as well. Attachments include a furrower (for trench composting) and a snowplow.

Garden Way Mfg. Co., Inc.
102nd St. & Ninth Ave.
Troy, NY 12180

Troy-Bilt
Garden Way Associates, Inc.

The Mainline Tiller *

by Howard Prussack

Mainline is a rotary tiller of high quality and multiuse adaptability. This versatile rear-mounted tiller helps fill the gap between single-use garden tillers and expensive tractors. The basic unit is an 8 h.p., cast aluminum block engine with Pearlite cylinders.

Pearlite is a graphitic process of cast-iron composition, the product being about 20 times the density of regular cast iron, reborable three times. It has an all-gear-drive transmission—no belts or chains. Its automotive design is completely ball bearing throughout, including both ends of the crankshaft.

The standard 8 h.p. power unit with tiller to the left, and the same power unit with gear-driven sickle bar to the right.
Central States Distributors

It is a 20-inch tiller with a heavy-duty cover completely enclosing the tines. There is separate engagement of wheel drive and tiller drive; so the tiller does not rotate (which saves wear and is safer) when transporting. The engine has a power take-off shaft to operate pumps, sprayers, and other attachments that are available, fifteen in all.

The BCS Company, which is in Italy, has been making this tiller since 1963, and it has been designed with the farmer and grower in mind—to take the heavy-duty use and do the different jobs that the attachments make possible.

The extra attachments which make the Mainline more useful for the small grower than any of the other tillers on the market include: a 44-inch sickle bar which can be mounted on the front; combination power hilling and furrowing attachment; a split-row tiller for strawberries and small vegetables; removable tiller so you can add a planter, tool bar, cart, or snowblower.

Mainline tillers come in 5, 8, and 10 h.p. models. BCS also manufactures commercial 16 h.p. rotary tillers which have optional grain binders and thresher attachments. In addition, they make riding tractors which are being imported into this country. The U.S. importer is BCS Mainline in London, Ohio, and the Natural Organic Farmers' Association has contacted them to become the New England distributor.

Central States Mainline Distributors
Box 348
London, OH 43140

* Excerpted with permission from *The Natural Farmer,* February 1977.

Ariens Rocket Tiller

In the same in-between league as the Troy-Bilt, the Rocket is a 7 h.p. tiller with two forward and two reverse speeds. The rear-mounted tines are 14 inches in diameter and till to a depth of 9 inches. Handles are adjustable for side operation, and the unit is available with attachments for extra-wide tilling and furrowing.

Ariens Co.
655 W. Ryan St.
Brillion, WI 54110

Ariens Rocket Tiller
Ariens Co.

The Mighty Mac 524-RT
Amerind-MacKissic, Inc.

Mighty Mac 524-RT

The Mightly Mac has an 8 h.p., four-cycle engine with a welded steel frame and a chain drive gear. Depth is determined by a manually adjusted drag control bar. Handles are fully adjustable, and speeds include one forward and one reverse. A furrowing kit is available.

Amerind–MacKissic, Inc.
P.O. Box 111
Parker Ford, PA 19457

Howard Gem

The Howard Rotovator Company specializes in heavier commercial tillers, both walking and tractor-drawn models. They call them rotovators. The larger hand-controlled Gem model is available in varying widths of 20, 24, or 30 inches. A smaller unit, the 350, comes in 16- and 23-inch widths. The transmission on the Gem has three forward and one safety reverse speed with a maximum forward speed of 2.82 mph. Each model is equipped with double wheels for added traction and a depth control wheel adjustable to 9 inches. The optional attachments and accessories include a furrowing attachment and pickline rotor.

E. C. Geiger
Rt. 63, Box 285
Harleysville, PA 19438

Howard Rotovator Co.
Box 100
Harvard, IL 60033

The Howard Gem
E. C. Geiger

Howard rotovators are distributed throughout the world: Australia, East Africa, France, Germany, Italy, New Zealand, South Africa, the United Kingdom, and Spain.

The Roto-Hoe Roto-Hoe Co.

Roto-Hoe

Roto-Hoes come with tillers mounted either in the rear or up front. A 6 h.p. Tecumseh engine powers the gear transmission with four forward speeds and one reverse. Attachments include a Cut-N-Shred shredder, a snowthrower, and a hiller-marker tool.

The Roto-Hoe Co.
Department 2
Newbury, OH 44065

Herter's Belgian Model 1100 Tiller

Modeled after a Belgian tiller but manufactured in the United States is the Herter Model 1100 rear-end tiller. The transmission is worm gear driven and powered by a 6 h.p., four-cycle engine. The machine has two forward, a neutral, and two reverse speeds. As a safety precaution, it cannot be locked in reverse. The eight-position depth regulator can be adjusted while in motion, and in the traveling position, tines are raised 2 inches above the ground. No attachments are mentioned. The manufacturer is the only distributor.

Herter's, Inc.
Waseca, MN 56093 or Mitchell, SD 57301

The Simar Morgan

The Morgan is made in Switzerland by the Simar Company and distributed in the United States. It employs a heavy-duty Swill 7½ h.p., one-cylinder, four-cycle engine to power its three forward and one reverse speeds. The unit's weight is 254 pounds. No mention is made of attachments.

Colt

Of German design, the Colt is a lightweight, rugged tiller for raised benches in greenhouses and outdoor cultivation. It comes with a 10 h.p. engine, an all-enclosed gear drive—no V-belts—and a single power-driven wheel for easy handling. The Colt and the Morgan are available from:

E. C. Geiger
Rt. 63, Box 285
Harleysville, PA 19438

The Simar Morgan
E. C. Geiger

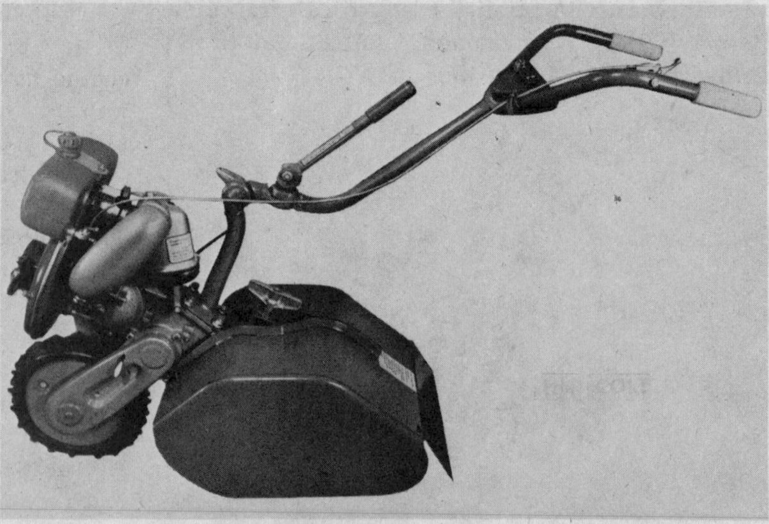

The Colt
E. C. Geiger

Mang Tillers

Weighing 503 pounds, the Mang Model 95 tiller is designed for heavy-duty tilling jobs encountered by landscapers and nurserymen. The overall width is 26 inches, but it only tills 15 inches at one time. The smaller, 380-pound Mang Junior has a tiller cutter width of 21 inches and is powered by a 7 h.p. gasoline engine. With both models, the strain and shock of the toughest tilling are distributed among the eight sprockets and the heavy-duty roller chain. The manufacturer reports that this feature is unlike most other tillers, where the strain is taken by only two or three gear cogs. There is one forward speed, no reverse.

Oregon Mfg. Co.
6920 SW 111th Ave.
Beaverton, OR 97005

Mang Model 95
Herb Fischborn

Mang Junior
Herb Fischborn

Yellowbird

This unit will rotovate or cultivate with oscillating power tines which cover a 16-inch width.

The Yellowbird Precision Valley Mfg. Co.

Precision Valley Mfg. Co.
Box 9004
Springfield, VT 05156

The Agria Model 2100 Agria-Werke

INTERNATIONAL SOURCES OF REAR-MOUNTED TILLERS

Agria Model 2100

A 7 h.p., two-stroke engine supplies power through one front wheel to drive this tiller. Hooded tillers are available in nine different working widths, and depth is adjustable. It is particularly suited for closely spaced rows. Three-speed tooth wheel gearing is shifted from the handlebar. Its weight is 80 pounds, and provisions are available for adding front weight. Attachments include a ridger, a leaf protector, and a cultivator.

Agria-Werke Gmbh
7108 Moeckmuehl
Germany

Buffalo Tillers

Three models are available. The 14 h.p. model weighs 335 kilograms, the 9 h.p., 235 kilograms, and the 7 h.p. model, 205 kilograms—

Tiller attachments come in varying widths, interchangeable for the specific requirements of each cropping situation. Hako

all without engine. All three have four-cycle, air-cooled, diesel engines, hand-cranked starting, and three speeds for both forward and reverse. With rotary tiller, capacities range from 1/4 to 1 acre per hour and with plow, from 1/3 to 2/3 acre per hour.

Three Farmers Machinery Co., Ltd.
No. 37 Min Chuan St.
Wu-Chi Taichun Hsien
Taiwan, Republic of China

CeCoCo Suzue Power Tiller Model LEC-50

Two types of engines are available: a water-cooled diesel with 6 or 7 h.p. or an air-cooled, gasoline engine with 6 to 8 h.p. There are six forward and two reverse speeds. Road clearance is a minimum of 178 millimeters, and it weighs 250 kilograms. Power take-off speeds are changeable with two or four steps. A safety device keeps reverse from engaging until the rotary blades have stopped. It has an adjustable handle.

CeCoCo
P.O. Box 8, Ibaraki City
Osaka Pref. 567, Japan

STATIONARY WINCH-POWERED CULTIVATION

Prior to the invention of the tractor, about the time of World War I, cable cultivation was the only form of mechanized agriculture for about 75 years, and this represented the first use of steam power for cultivation. Because the first steam engines were not self-propelled, a scheme employing a cable and windlass was used to get the plow from one end of the field to the other. The cable usually wound on a horizontal drum beneath the engine which was driven by bevel gearing from the engine shaft.

Though the most expensive initially, the most satisfactory implementation of this technique utilized two steam engines. One engine pulled the plow through the field while the other paid out slack cable and moved ahead into position for the next haul. As steam engines became lighter, it became more feasible to use them as tractors to pull implements through the soil, and the need for a cable disappeared. Today, cable cultivation is used on small, steep plots in France and Italy, and for plowing paddy fields in China. Agricultural engineering researchers recognize the winch as a significant tool worth developing in their quest for simply designed machines to satisfy the worldwide need for economical, energy-efficient field mechanization. Mechanical Engineer Stuart Wilson from Oxford outlines the reasons why.

"The three very considerable advantages of cable cultivation compared to conventional tractor use are:

1. Lower energy consumption due to elimination of both wheel slip and the energy needed to transport the prime mover.
2. No compaction of the soil, an increasing problem with large tractors.
3. Ability to plow in wet or slippery conditions.

The disadvantages include the need for two prime movers if the most effective method is used and the need for some sort of reversible plow."

Wilson continues, "However, in light of the fact that plowing is only a small part of the average tractor's use and that most of the remaining duties, especially road haulage, need much less than maximum power, there appears to be a case for evolving a design for a basic tractor of modest power which can be used in pairs for cable plowing when required, but is otherwise capable of performing a variety of lighter duties."

Three designs are on the drawing board to utilize winch cultivation: a pedal-powered Mechanical Mule, a two-wheeled tractor called the Snail, and a three-wheeled tractor, the Spider.

The Mechanical Mule

Designed by Rodale Resources, Inc., in Emmaus, Pennsylvania, the Mechanical Mule harnesses the power of the pedal to provide winch-pulling power for farm tilling tasks. The power unit seen in the photo on page 60 is positioned at the head of a row while a toolbar carrier is positioned at the foot of the row.

The Mechanical Mule

Mechanical Mule tool carrier with cultivator attachment.

As the operator of the power unit pedals, a high-test nylon or polypropylene line fastened to the tool carrier is reeled in and the tool carrier, guided by a second person, is pulled up the row.

When one row is completed, the helper walks the tool carrier to the foot of the next row, unreeling the power line as he walks. Simultaneously, the pedaler moves the power unit to the head of the next row. When everything is in place, the operation is repeated. This multipurpose implement can be used for plowing, subsoiling, harrowing, and row-making, as well as cultivating. Tools are quickly interchangeable for tending three rows at a time.

The tool carrier is light enough to avoid compacting the soil and narrow enough for minimal row spacing for intensive crop production. Such intensive cropping systems tend to reduce the need for frequent weeding, as the tightly spaced plants help to shade out the weeds.

Dynomometer tests reveal that an average man can exert a pull of 1,000 pounds with the aid of the Mechanical Mule. From a sitting position, the energy of the strongest human muscles, those of the thighs, is relayed through a bicycle crank mechanism to maximize leverage. With spacer bars on the uptake reel, the effective diameter is increased for reeling in several feet of power line with each revolution of the crank—the equivalent of high gear. For harder jobs, the spacer bar can be removed for reeling in only a few inches of line with each revolution of the crank—the equivalent of low gear. Pulling speed is reduced, but pulling power is about doubled.

The row-making tool simultaneously prepares three rows for planting 12 inches apart, facilitating intensive cropping systems.

Spacer bars on the uptake reel of the Mechanical Mule reel in several feet of power line with each revolution of the crank—the equivalent of "high gear."

In the interest of safety, to keep the crank from slipping backwards and the pedals from hitting the operator in the shins, a ratchet-brake mechanism was built into the unit. Depressing a clutch disengages the reel from the crank so the power line can be easily reeled out.

Rodale Resources Division
576 North St.
Emmaus, PA 18049

The Snail

The Snail, a primary cultivation device, was developed at the National College of Agricultural Engineering, Silsoe, Bedford, U.K., as a possible solution to the problem of cultivating hard, dry soil in developing countries during the dry season, so as to achieve early planting with increased crop yield the result, reports Peter Crossley.

The machine overcomes the energy constraints of human or animal power, is much cheaper than a large tractor and more efficient than a small one. The principle utilized is that of a self-propelled winch controlled by one operator, together with an implement mounted on a frame and controlled by a second operator. The winch unit is driven forward to the extent of its cable, drive is engaged to the winch drum, and the cable draws the implement towards the winch unit, which is prevented from moving backwards by a self-anchoring sprag.

The Snail
National College of Agricultural Engineering

In tests during the dry season in Malawi, sponsored by the Ministry of Overseas Development, the machine was found to work satisfactorily in most small farm conditions, and would be likely to be economical in areas where alternative cultivation methods were either unavailable or more expensive. It is designed to operate in hard soils and would not be technically satisfactory in wet land or in temperate areas.

The Spider

The Spider is a three-wheeled, self-propelled winch-tractor which evolved from the Snail and the Kabanyolo. In an article entitled "Are Small Tractors Possible?," * Peter Crossley reports that the Kabanyolo was an example of the "ingenious use of mass-produced components in a chassis which was designed to be manufactured locally from stock materials." He describes the Snail as an example of "a small, self-propelled winch, which provides a much higher draft force than a single-axle tractor of corresponding size and weight." When the limitations of these two units were clearly defined, efforts were directed at combining the best features of both in the design of the Spider.

Still in its early stages of testing, the Spider is being developed at the United Kingdom's National College of Engineering in Silsoe, England.

Crossley states that "the Spider consists of a fabricated chassis, on the front of which is mounted a 6.5 h.p. diesel engine, which drives the two rear wheels by means of a V-belt and

* *World Crops and Livestock,* May/June 1977.

The Spider
National College of Agricultural Engineering

chain reductions. In the center of the rear axle is a winch drum. Steering is tiller operated on a single front wheel, and the rear track is 1 meter wide."

"It was anticipated that light-draft operations would be carried out by direct traction with mounted implements at speeds of up to 4 mph, but that for high-draft work, the machine would be operated in the same manner as the Snail, by driving forward to the extent of the cable and then winching in the implement."

Now, even before testing has been completed on the Spider, plans are being drawn up for an improved design. Crossley continues, "The proposed design is that of a lightweight, three-wheeled tractor having 6.00 x 16 rear-drive wheels spaced at a 2-meter-wide track with a single 4.00 x 12 wheel at the front. The five kw. engine would be transversely mounted in front of the rear axle, the drive being supplied by a chain reduction. Further, enclosed chains would drive each rear wheel from the outer ends of the high-mounted axle, in the right-hand section of which would be mounted a winch drum. Good ground clearance and lateral stability would therefore be obtained. A sprag and guide roller device would act in line with the winch so that the tractor could be driven with the right-hand rear wheel in the furrow, in the conventional manner, for winched operations such as moldboard plowing. A patent has been applied for."

"No differential would be fitted, but as with the original Spider, either or both rear wheels could be engaged by means of dog clutches, thus allowing both wheels to be driven during light cultivation operations, or while moving forward prior to winching. In order to turn at headlands, the inner wheel would be declutched, allowing sharp turns to be made; a reverse gear would not be required. By adding a second primary chain and dog clutch, an additional forward speed could be provided for transport work."

"Although lightweight, the Spider would optimize its performance for low-draft operations by virtue of its axle characteristics and reasonably sized drive wheels. The track spacing and high ground clearance would allow it to work in ridges. During high-draft winching operations, the machine would work slowly but effectively, and with the addition of a second man on the implement, could undertake operations which no small tractor of equivalent size could attempt in poor traction conditions."

Such design work by the National College of Engineering is aimed at increasing the agricultural productivity in developing countries. One criticism of this final design is the complicated operation procedure. Present thoughts include considering a switch to hydrostatic transmission which would simplify operation, but increase cost and decrease efficiency.

UNIQUE CULTIVATION DEVICES

Kuranda Rotary Cultivator

The Australians have devised a cultivation unit which can be powered by any four-stroke gasoline engine to cultivate to a width of 14 inches. Other attachments are available for quick interchange of the engine, including a posthole digger and litter vacuum.

Kuranda Rotary Cultivator Kuranda Industries

Kuranda Industries Pty., Ltd.
42 Bank St., P.O. Box 26
Padstow 2211, Australia

The Friday Self-Propelled Power Hoe

The Friday Self-Propelled Power Hoe is a 9 h.p. tractor specially designed for hoeing around individual plants rather than only between rows. It is guided with individual turning brakes, thus leaving your hands free to operate the controls for the hydraulically powered hoe blades. Though specially designed with strawberry cultivation in mind, it is good for all row crops. It is particularly suitable for the organic farmer who would prefer to cultivate around individual plants rather than use herbicides.

Three different types of hoeing blades are furnished with each machine. An adjustable weeder will comb runners of young strawberry plants without damaging them while dragging out small weeds and leveling the ground. One hydraulic valve raises or lowers the cultivator, weeder, or hand hoes and also controls the fertilizer attachment.

The Friday Self-Propelled Power Hoe
Friday Tractor Co.

The 9.2 h.p., air-cooled engine powers one reverse and three forward speeds for a range of $\frac{1}{4}$ to 7 mph. Low rates of speed are necessary for thorough hoeing. The hoe has a 13-inch crop clearance and weighs 1,210 pounds. A fertilizer attachment and electric starter are available options.

The manufacturer claims that one man can cultivate, hoe, weed, and fertilize a whole acre in 2 hours. At this rate, he can assume responsibility for caring for 25 acres of strawberries.

Friday Tractor Co., Inc.
Hartford, MI 49057

PLOWS

Farmers through the ages have devised almost every conceivable type of soil-working tool—from nothing more than a tree branch dragged over the soil to level it, to sophisticated, spinning steel knives churning through the ground. Some inventions work; some do not. Some work better in certain soils than in others. Some work better in wet years than in dry, or vice versa. But be assured that whatever idea for tilling soil you may have, someone, somewhere, has the tool for it.

THE MOLDBOARD PLOW

The moldboard plow is the traditional power tool for opening or breaking the ground in preparation for planting. Characteristically, the moldboard, from which this type of plow gets its name, turns dirt completely over as the plow is pulled along, burying surface plant material and leaving soil bare, loose, and easily worked into a seedbed. Most moldboard plows have solid moldboards, though slotted moldboards are also made and used in some soils.

Some organic farmers think the moldboard plow is an undesirable tillage tool and put their faith in offset discs. This argument has been going on for over 50 years and won't be settled for 50 more. In the meantime, just remember that on a small, noncommercial

The only drawback of the moldboard plow is that it can cause greater erosion. The boy has his hand on the slicing coulter.

homestead, an old plow costing under $50 is adequate, while even the smallest, used offset disc, heavy enough to really chop up and incorporate crop residue and green manure into the soil, will cost you 10 to 20 times that much. The only drawback to the moldboard plow you will need to remember is that it can cause erosion. Don't plow steep slopes and don't fall-plow even gentle slopes with a moldboard plow.

Size is the first consideration when shopping for a used plow. For a two-bottom (two plows), 14-inch model, you need at least a 25 h.p. tractor, and 35 would be better. (The 14-inch measurement is the width of the furrow each plowshare makes.) A 15 h.p. tractor will pull a single 12-inch plow. (One of the editors of this book, Gene Logsdon, recommends not going smaller than a 14-inch plow for field work, but this is a matter of personal preference. He finds that the smaller plows aren't heavy enough to satisfy him, especially for turning under green manure crops.)

You may also have to decide between a mounted plow and a pull-type plow. Mounted plows attach to the tractor in such a way that

Coulters cut, moldboards turn the soil over, and a wheel to the rear adjusts the plowing depth.

The two-bottom plow does a good job on plots of ten acres or less.

Here the pull-type plow is in a raised position with its rear wheel completely off the ground.

they can be raised completely off the ground for ease in backing into tight corners of small fields or garden plots and in transporting them over the road. They are more difficult to attach to the tractor than are pull types, require a power take-off connection and/or hydraulic pump, and are more expensive.

Pull-type plows hitch and unhitch rather easily by comparison and are cheaper, but they are far less maneuverable. On some two-bottom pull-types, the rear wheel lifts completely off the ground when the plowshares are in the raised position. That's a desirable characteristic, since it lets you back the plow as easily as you can a two-wheeled trailer. When you cannot back up a plow, it is almost impossible to work small areas or tight corners where turning space is very limited.

The older two-bottom plows are all pull types and are perhaps a better buy for the money, even if they are a little awkward. Few of them are worn-out—they just become obsolete. A cog and gear mechanism powered by the revolving left wheel of the plow raises and lowers the plowshares when activated by pulling a trip rope. When you come to the end of the field, you tug gently on the rope and the plow lifts out of the ground. Another gentle tug and it drops into the furrow again. The tripping mechanisms probably wear out sooner or later, so you should check before you buy.

Most likely, the plow points will be dull, and you will have to get them sharpened or buy new ones. When you order new ones, you will need to know the name and model of your plow.

Check the two levers on the plow. Each lever raises or lowers the wheel closest to it. The shorter lever over the furrow wheel sets the depth of the plowshares, while the longer one levels the pitch of the two plows so that they plow evenly at whatever depth. Sometimes the levers are broken, cracked, or bent, especially the shorter one, from trying to adjust plow depth while the plows are in the ground. Always make the short lever adjustment with the plows raised. The long lever can be adjusted from the tractor while you are in motion.

The lever handles have a hinged piece which you squeeze against the main handle to lift the lever pin out of the slot that it's in. With the slot pin lifted, you can move the lever up or down. The lever pin may be rusted tight, or the spring that keeps proper tension on it may have become rusted or broken. All are fairly easy to repair.

Perhaps the most important point is to be sure each plow point is preceded by a coulter—the disc that slices off the soil which the moldboard will turn over. Coulters are easy to take

This is how to adjust the short lever for depth.

off of one plow and put on another plow: hence, they are easily lost. An old plow may cost only $10, but if the coulters are missing, replacements are liable to cost you $50 or more.

Next, check the condition of the moldboards and plow points. If the surfaces where the dirt slides are very rusty and pitted, you will have a difficult time getting the plow to scour. Dirt will stick to the steel, and the plow won't be effective. If there's only a little rust or shallow rust, it will wear off quickly when you plow, leaving the shiny, smooth steel surface necessary for good plowing. Better yet, an old plow that has been cared for will have its moldboards and plow points covered with a coat of grease or oil when not in use to protect against rust. Be sure you treat your plow surfaces to the same protection between plowing seasons.

A rusted moldboard may be reclaimed with fine sandpaper and rust remover, but if badly pitted, it will never scour very well. Look for another plow.

You want the plow to make even furrows, not every other one higher or lower. If the latter condition prevails on your plowed ground, keep changing the lever positions until the turned furrows all look level with each other. Remember that the right wheel runs in the furrow four to six inches lower than the left wheel if you are plowing four to six inches deep. So when you make your first pass across the field, there is no furrow for the wheel to run in, and therefore you need to adjust the plow depth lower. Otherwise, the front plow won't go deeply enough into the ground. On the second round, you will have to readjust, because then the one wheel will be in the furrow. Likewise, on your last round, when you are finishing a dead furrow, the other wheel will drop lower than normal, and you will have to adjust the depth again. If you don't, you will gouge out too deep a dead furrow.

Pull-type plows require a special clevis to attach them properly to the tractor drawbar. The clevis is first bolted to the tractor drawbar; then the tractor is backed up to the plow tongue, and the clevis is pushed into the hooded plow hitch until it latches—you can hear the click. If you are alone, with no way to lift the plow hitch up in line with the clevis so you can back the tractor into it, you will learn how to stop at just the precise distance from the plow hitch, get off the tractor, lift the hitch or push down on it, and force it into the clevis.

The reason for the somewhat complex hitching mechanism on a pull-type plow is to keep the plow from breaking should you hit a root or stone underground. When that hap-

The plow hitch is seen here just before it is coupled to the clevis.

pens, the jolt makes the hitch fly open automatically, and the plow, unhitched, stops immediately, saving many repair jobs.

For that same reason, don't tie the trip rope too tightly to the tractor seat. Loop it through a weak hook of wire so that if the plow comes loose, the rope will too. Also, leave plenty of slack in the rope so that it doesn't tighten up and trip the plow when you are turning at the end of the field.

Because of the way a plow works, you can't just root the soil up any way you please. A plow lifts the soil from one place and deposits it eight to twelve inches to the side of its original position. The ditch that is left is called a furrow. After the first pass across the garden or field, the furrow ditch is there to throw the dirt into from the second furrow and so forth. When you are finished plowing, you will have at least one furrow left over. This is called a dead furrow. Naturally, the first time you plow across the field or garden, you do not have a furrow already there. So the dirt turned over by the plow blade falls on the normal soil sur-

The Hertecant two-way, reversible plow attached to an Agria two-wheel tractor.
Willem Hertecant

face, leaving a ridge of dirt. This ridge is called a headland. The art of plowing demands that in subsequent years of plowing, you make your headlands fall where last year's dead furrows were, and last year's headlands then become this year's dead furrows. If you don't do that, your field will become less level every year.

Commonly, moldboard plows are one-way plows, but two-way plows are made, and they are often called hillside or reversible plows. A two-way plow has two sets of plows, one above the other. At the end of the furrow, the operator can flip the two over, so the top will swing down in plowing position and the bottom will swing up out of the way. He or she can then proceed to plow back in the same furrow just made, which would be impossible with a one-way plow. The two-way plow eliminates dead furrows and headlands and is very handy when plowing terraces or contours on hillside land.

For 14 and 18 h.p. garden tractors equipped with category 0 three-point hitch, the Brinly-Hardy 12-inch moldboard plow features an adjustable gauge wheel with scraper to control plow depth in varying soil conditions; a throwaway share for lower replacement costs, 11-inch adjustable coulter, and adjustments for landing and width of cut.
Brinly-Hardy Co.

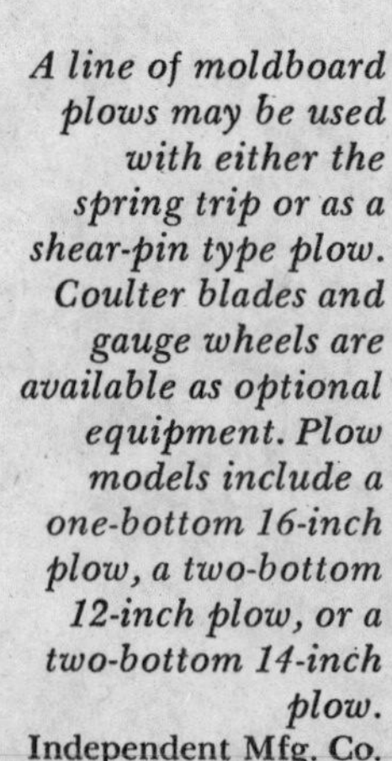

A line of moldboard plows may be used with either the spring trip or as a shear-pin type plow. Coulter blades and gauge wheels are available as optional equipment. Plow models include a one-bottom 16-inch plow, a two-bottom 12-inch plow, or a two-bottom 14-inch plow.
Independent Mfg. Co.

NORTH AMERICAN SOURCES OF MOLDBOARD PLOWS

	SINGLE-BOTTOM MOLDBOARDS	DOUBLE-BOTTOM (or more) MOLDBOARDS	REVERSIBLE MOLDBOARDS	SPARE PARTS & ACCESSORIES	DISC PLOWS
ALLIED FARM EQUIP. (KVERNELAND)		X			
BRINLEY-HARDY	X				
J. I. CASE		X			
CHROMALLOY FARM & INDUSTRIAL EQUIPMENT CO.				X	
CORSICANA GRADER & MACHINE CO.	X	X			
IMCO (INDEPENDENT MFG.)	X	X			
INTERNATIONAL MODERN MACHINERY, INC.	X	X			
SPEECO (SPECIAL PRODUCTS) available from TSC & CENTRAL TRACTOR	X	X			

INTERNATIONAL SOURCES OF MOLDBOARD PLOWS

	SINGLE-BOTTOM MOLDBOARDS	DOUBLE-BOTTOM (or more) MOLDBOARDS	REVERSIBLE MOLDBOARDS	SPARE PARTS & ACCESSORIES	DISC PLOWS
ACM EQUIPMENTS	X		X		
AGROMET MOTOIMPORT		X			
BEAUVAIS & ROBIN	X	X	X		
CECOCO	X	X			X
FISKARS		X			
FRANK'SCHE EISENWERKE				X	
GHERARDI JESI	X	X	X		X
W. HERTECANT	X		X		X
HUARD-VCF-SCM	X	X	X		
INDUSTRIAS METALURGICAS APOLO S.A.					X
KVERNELAND		X			
NARDI MACCHINE AGRICOLE	X	X	X		
PIERCE OF WEXFORD		X			
SYNDICAT DE L'OUTILLAGE AGRICOLE ET HORTICOLE				X	
TONUTTI S.P.A.	X	X	X		

THE CHISEL PLOW

Challenging the moldboard plow for the lead in farmer popularity, especially in hilly and dry country, is the chisel plow or the very similar field cultivator, sometimes called simply the digger. This plow consists of sets of curved tines or small shovels which dig up the soil to a depth of 12 to 18 inches, loosening and lifting it, but not turning it over like a moldboard plow does. The chisels are shaped in an arc, something like the letter C so that the point penetrates the soil ahead of the shank. Chiseled ground is not nearly as subject to wind or water erosion as moldboard-plowed soil. Some plant material remains on or near the surface to hold the soil in place.

Chisel plows come in several designs, either with twisted shovels or straight shovels. Straight shovels are usually two inches wide, while the twisted ones vary up to four inches wide. Twisted shovels tend to stir and mix the soil more than the straight type and are used when heavy plant residues need to be incorporated into the soil.

Most chisel plows demand big tractor power. A 13-foot chisel operating ten inches deep at five miles per hour requires 120 horse-

DIAGRAM SHOWING RELATIVE DEPTH OF PLOW

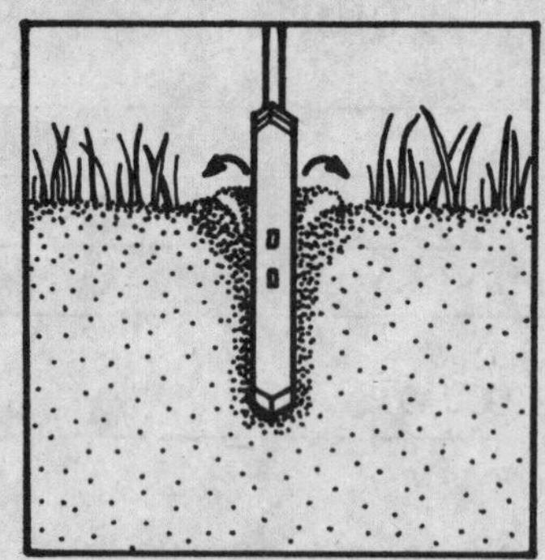

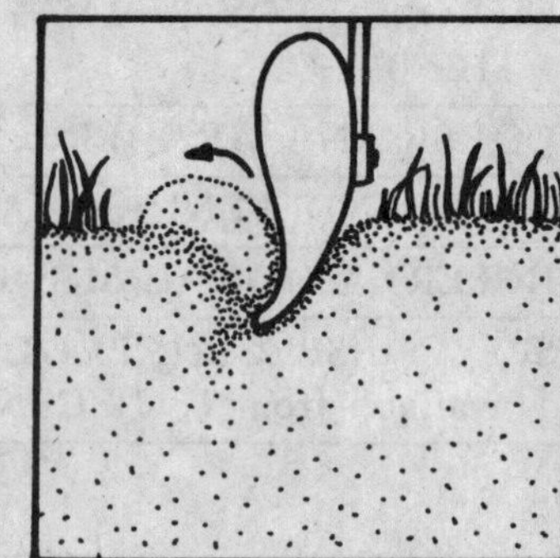

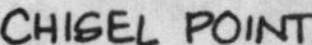

NOTE: ARROWS INDICATE SOIL DISTRIBUTION

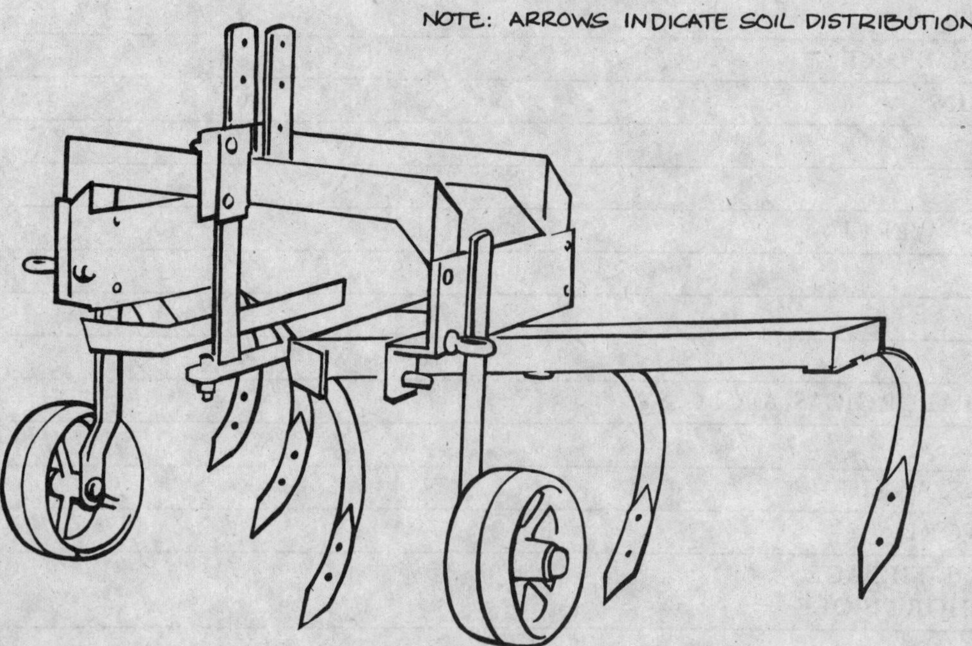

A chisel plow with depth wheels.

power. However, most chisel plows are put together so that you can remove individual blades (or shanks) to reduce the pulling load.

To avoid jamming plant residues in front of the blades, which can happen where surface trash (organic crop residue) is heavy, manufacturers have combined the disc and the chisel plow—a series of straight coulters in front of the chisels to cut up the plant residues. You don't have to use a stalk chopper or disc ahead of this kind of chisel. But it requires a large tractor to pull it.

The Cole 510 system for chisel disking with four springs, center spring, six discs, and a smoothing drag for category 0 and 1 three-point hitches.
Cole Mfg. Co.

FARMING ORGANICALLY WITH NO-PLOW TILLAGE

After 27 years of organic farming, the Mundt family in Michigan has developed a unique combination of green manuring and no-plow tillage to stop erosion and grow better crops. They're building humus, high-quality soil, on a sandy, hill farm. To incorporate the lush growths of sorghum-sudan grass, the solid-stand corn, and buckwheat, Bill Mundt uses a heavy, offset disc. It almost seems to work miracles in the sandy ground. Two passes, the second at right angles to the first, over a jungle of eight-foot-high sorghum-sudan, and the plants are incorporated into the soil, ready for a broadcast seeding of buckwheat or rye. After the seeding, another pass with the disc covers the seed, levels the surface fairly well, and firms the soil to sprout the seed. But still the ground is thick with chopped organic matter which reduces erosion to a minimum. The soil is so biologically alive that the rotting process of the incorporated leaves and stalks begins immediately. Each year the sand becomes richer in humus. "It works. The best proof I have is that I'm raising fairly good crops right over areas that were stone-filled gullies 30 years ago," says Mundt.

His other main cultivating tool is the field cultivator or chisel plow (some farmers call it a digger or chisel), which can be set deep to open up the ground. On grain stubble, sod, hay field, corn or bean fields after harvest, the chisel can be used as a primary tool to break the ground as well as plow it, but without turning it completely over on the surface and allowing easy erosion. Fall-chiseled soil can be gone over with a disc in the spring and planted. Two chiselings, the second at a right angle or bias slant to the first, can be planted with a drill, pulling a disc ahead of the drill. Or it can be broadcast-

To prevent loosened plant trash from chiseling the second time through, Bill Mundt uses "beavertail" ripper blades which are six inches wide—wider than regular chisels.

planted and covered with the disc. "For a plowdown crop, you don't need to have a smooth soil surface. Leaving it a little rough catches and holds moisture better," says Mundt.

When incorporating heavy trash, field cultivators are apt to plug up. "The first time through you're okay," points out Mundt. "But the second time, the loosened plant trash will collect in front of the chisels. To prevent that, I use what are called beavertail ripper blades. They are six inches wide—wider than regular chisels. What they do is throw dirt ahead of them in enough volume to prevent the jamming of plant material on the blades. You have to drive fast to get the proper action." If plugging still persists, or if you want to dig the ground so deep the tractor won't pull your field cultivator, you can remove every other blade and still do a fairly adequate job of primary cultivation.

Neither offset disc nor chisel is a machine for small tractors. "Figure you need five to eight horsepower for every foot of width of your tool," says Mundt. Since ten feet is about minimum width for standard American offset discs and chisels, you're talking about a tractor of at least 50 horsepower for the smallest models.

Mundt sometimes uses his chisel after the disc. "Where erosion is a bad problem, you can cultivate lightly with the disc a couple of times and chop the trash into the top layer of the soil. Then, with the trash on top to protect the soil, you can go deep with the chisel and open the ground without burying the top mulch."

Working with large amounts of plant matter can cause problems when you are cultivating weeds in row crops. Plant material collects on cultivator shovels. "High-clearance sweep shovels are one way around the problem," says Mundt, "but a better way I've found is the high-speed Danish cultivator. [His model is a Noble from Sac City, Iowa.] This row cultivator has narrow tines for shovels, and when pulled through the ground they shimmy and shake, avoiding buildups of plant debris and clumps of sod. I had no trouble even cultivating corn that I had planted in a field previously sown with orchard grass, which always leaves troublesome clumps of roots when you work it up."

The payoff? Very little erosion, low overhead, and satisfactory crops. "We don't get high yields," says Mundt. "We aren't interested in that. We're looking for quality. We're satisfied with 80 to 90 bushels of corn. We feed it to our milk cows and beef animals and believe they respond with better efficiency than if they were fed highly chemicalized, heat-dried corn. We don't even plant for high yields. I like a plant population of around 17,000 in 40-inch rows for corn."

The chisel and Danish cultivator are Mundt's alternatives for the moldboard on his highly erosive soil.

The Cole 510 system set for chisel plowing with four springs, center spring, and gauge wheels for category 0 and 1 three-point hitches.
Cole Mfg. Co.

SOURCES OF CHISEL PLOWS/SUBSOILERS

	CHISEL PLOWS (ass't. sizes)	GRAHAM PLOW	COMBINATION SUBSOILER/ CHISEL	SUBSOILER
BEAUVAIS & ROBIN, ETS.	X			
BOMFORD & EVERSHED LTD.			X	
J. I. CASE	X			
CECOCO				X
COLE MFG.	X *			
CORSICANA GRADER & MACHINE CO.				X
DELAPLACE, ETS.	X			
W. HERTECANT	X			
HUARD-UCF-SCM	X			X
INTERNATIONAL MODERN MACHINERY, INC.	X			
JEOFFROY MFG., INC.	X			
KMC (KELLEY MFG. CO.)	X			
KOEHN MFG. & DISTRIBUTING	X			
PLANET PLOWS, INC.		X		
ROYAL INDUSTRIES	X			
SEARS, ROEBUCK & CO.			X	
SOUTHEAST MFG. CO.				X
TAYLOR IMPLEMENT MFG. CO.	X			X
TRACTOR SUPPLY CO.	X			
UNITED FARM TOOLS	X			X
WIKOMI MFG. CO.			X	

* Available with planter attachment.

The Subsoiler

The chisel plow is not quite the same as a subsoil plow, sometimes called the deep chisel, or V-plow, though the actions of the two implements are now being combined into one machine. The subsoiler is a much heavier tool with narrow ripper blades that dig deeply into the soil to break up compacted layers for better drainage and root penetration.

The subsoil plow is a clear indication of the weakness of modern farming methods. It was designed to offset the negative effects of heavy

Years of moldboard plowing and use of heavy machinery have left this layer of hardpan which only the subsoil plow can penetrate. National Tillage Machinery Laboratory

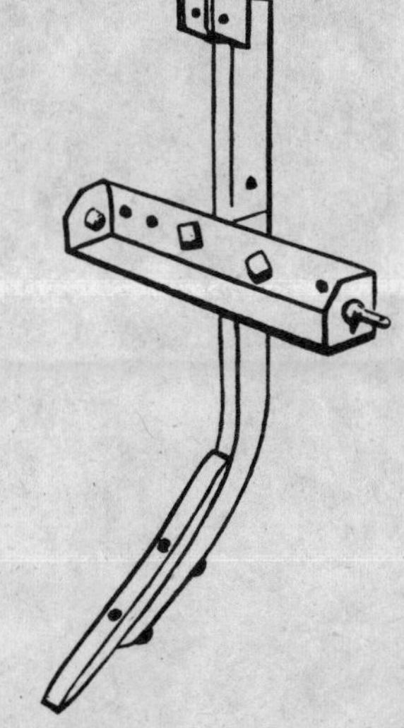

The subsoiler assumes the shape of the chisel, but it is a much heavier-duty tool which penetrates deeper as well.

farm machinery and the discontinuation of rotations of alfalfa and sweet clover, whose roots formerly penetrated into and broke up hardpan, a slatelike layer of soil 6 to 8 inches beneath the surface, caused by compaction from heavy machinery.

A cure for hardpan, though only a temporary cure, the subsoiler is a deep-penetrating chisellike plow which requires a tremendous amount of power to pull. A small-scale operator shouldn't plan to pull more than one subsoiling plow with a small tractor, and only a larger small tractor at that.

The Disc Plow and Offset Disc

Disc plows are a third type of soil breaker or sodbuster. The original kind, which was fashionable in the middle 40s, consisted of from two to six large, heavy discs, which when pulled at a slant, turned the soil over somewhat like a moldboard plow. Though still used in some areas, they are being replaced by the offset disc,

The narrow sections of this spike-tooth harrow are light and easy to lift for inspection.

The cement blocks increase cutting depth on this eight-foot, pull-type tandem disc harrow.

which resembles the conventional tandem disc, but is much heavier and is composed of only two gangs of discs positioned one behind the other at a bias to each other. (Tandem discs have four sets of gangs, two behind two.) At present, offset discs are very popular with farmers who have experienced erosion problems with the moldboard plow. What's more, the offset disc will incorporate rank, tall stands of green manure better than a chisel plow, and without plugging with crop residue.

The Disc Harrow

After a field is plowed and before it is planted, the soil has to be worked into a fine seedbed.

The standard tools for fining and leveling a good seedbed are the tandem disc and the spike-toothed harrow. The disc does the fining, and the harrow levels out the gouging marks of the disc. Hand tools in the garden do roughly the same operation when hoeing spaded soil into a finer texture and then smoothing it with a garden rake. Your hoe is the disc, your rake, the harrow.

If you can afford only one tool for this operation, make it a tandem-disc harrow. Old ones are common and often low-priced in the small 6-, 7-, or 8-foot widths. Yours should be wide enough to cover your tractor's tracks when pulling it. If the disc bearings are worn out, though, so that no amount of grease will get the blades rolling smoothly, look for another disc. There's usually one bearing for every two pairs of disc blades. Pump them full of grease and keep them that way.

Old disc blades are equipped with scrapers that are supposed to keep dirt from building up on them. On an old disc, they almost always will be bent out of position or loose. You may have to straighten and/or rebolt them. (Sometimes old bolts and burrs can be tightened, but more often they are rusted solid and have to be cut off and replaced.) Actually, if dirt is building up on your discs, nine times out of ten it means your clay soil is too wet for disking. When the soil is fit and the disc blades shiny—at least on their edges—dirt will seldom clog them.

Mounted discs, like mounted plows, are very nice for cultivating small plots and have the same advantages and disadvantages as the latter. Newer pull-type discs have rubber tires for transport and are raised or lowered to any desired depth by hydraulic pumps. If your tractor is equipped with hydraulic power, its potential usefulness is just about double that of a tractor not so equipped. If you are going to have to move your disc any distance on roads, you will need a fully mounted or rubber-tired disc.

Older discs can move from one field to another only on their disc blades, so the disc

Location of grease zerk on disc. Note the correct positions of the scrapers against the disc blades.

The crank for adjusting the slant of the disc blades. Below, the sliding tongue assembly may be moved back and forth to slant or straighten the disc.

gangs must be adjusted out of cutting position. A disc blade cuts and works the soil when it is slanted slightly sideways from the direction in which it is being pulled. The more slant, the deeper it digs. Moved out of slant completely, the blades roll along like wheels, barely cutting into the soil at all. On old discs, you can make the proper change from the tractor seat by means of a rope attached to a pin on the sliding disc tongue. With the disc hitched to the tractor, you pull the pin out of the slot it is resting in, drive forward, and the disc gangs straighten up. Release your pull on the rope, and the pin falls into another hole. To put the disc back in working position, pull the pin, back up slowly, and the sliding tongue assembly pushes the disc gangs back into slant position. Further adjustments can then be made by turning the crank above the disc tongue. The crank is intended to be turned from the tractor seat on most models, and it will turn much easier when the disc is actually moving.

No matter how much you fuss with your disc adjustment, getting the thing to leave a perfectly level swath is nearly impossible. If the front discs are cutting too deep in relation to the back, the center of the swath is too low, while the edges of the swath stay too high. If the back discs are cutting too deep in relation to the front, you have the opposite effect. The faster you go, the more this uneveness is accentuated. If you don't get your disc in good adjustment, you can just about ruin a field in a few years. The surface will look like the South Jersey surf.

Whenever possible, pull a harrow behind your disc for the finest leveling. (We say "whenever possible" because if you are disking heavy cornstalks, or wheat or bean straw, you can't utilize the harrow behind the disc. It would clog up with the stalks.) Small, two-section harrows of 8 to 10 feet in width are fairly easy to find and can be purchased for anywhere from $25 to $125.

The harrows you will find have levers that adjust the teeth from nearly horizontal to nearly vertical positions. For deepest digging, you set the teeth vertical. For dragging over ground where plant residues would clog the harrow, or for moving over lanes and uncultivated fields, set the teeth nearly horizontal. Someplace between the extremes is usually best for leveling ground behind the disc.

Harrows come in sections usually about 4 feet wide. The sections attach to a front drawboard beam which may be wood or steel. The beam, in turn, attaches to the back of the disc (or tractor or other soil-working tool) by means of a link-chain arrangement. The harrow sections connect to the drawboard beam by chain-link-type steel rings. On old discs, these are often missing or worn out. Or they are replaced by baling wire. Sometimes the hooks on the harrow or the drawboard beam to which the rings attach are broken off. All that's fixable, but know what you're buying.

The levers are about the only other parts of harrows that wear out. The notch pin may be rusted tight, or the spring may be, or both; or the rod that connects the notch pin to the handle may be broken. Broken levers require welding. If you are really short of cash or time, you can just ignore broken levers if the teeth are already set about right. Yes, broken levers sell cheap.

The Brinly-Hardy Model DD-1000 tandem disc harrow is equipped with four gangs, each having four 11-inch, heat-treated, steel discs. Gangs may be set at angles of 10°, 15°, or 20°, or moved horizontally. Width of cut is approximately 52 inches. The heavy-duty frame is designed to hold concrete blocks for additional ballast. This implement is designed for 14 to 18 h.p. garden tractors with category 0 three-point hitch. Weight: 182 pounds.
Brinly-Hardy Co.

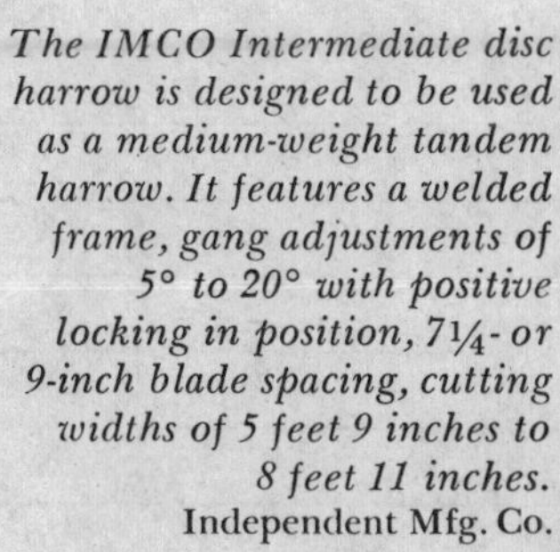

The IMCO Intermediate disc harrow is designed to be used as a medium-weight tandem harrow. It features a welded frame, gang adjustments of 5° to 20° with positive locking in position, 7¼- or 9-inch blade spacing, cutting widths of 5 feet 9 inches to 8 feet 11 inches.
Independent Mfg. Co.

Cultipacker

If clods are a problem in your spring-plowed soil, you may eventually want to add a culti-mulcher or cultipacker to your repertoire of tillage tools. And, in time, a small chisel plow and/or field cultivator will certainly be in order. But with plow, disc, and harrow, you're on your way. You should be able to handle up to 40 acres of diversified cropland with a 35 h.p. tractor, a two-bottom plow, an 8-foot disc, and a 10-foot harrow.

SOURCES OF HARROWS

	SPIKE-TOOTH HARROW	COIL-SPRING HARROW TINE	FLEXIBLE HARROW	SPRING-TOOTH HARROW	DISC HARROWS
ACM EQUIPMENTS	X				
BEAUVAIS & ROBIN ETS.	X		X		
BRINLY-HARDY CO.	X				X
BROWN MFG. CORP.					X
CECOCO	X				X
CENTRAL TRACTOR					X
EDWARDS EQUIPMENT CO.					X
FARNAM EQUIPMENT CO.			X		
FUERST BROS., INC.			X		
GHERARDI					X
W. HERTECANT	X				
HUARD					X
IMCO					X
INDUSTRIAS METALURGICAS					X
INTERNATIONAL MODERN MACHINERY, INC.					X
JOHN R. KOVAR MFG. CO., INC.	X	X	X	X	
MONTGOMERY WARD					X
NOBLE MFG. CO.	X	X	X		
PIERCE				X	X
SEARS, ROEBUCK & CO.					X
SOUTHEAST MFG. CO.	X				
SPEECO					X
TAYLOR IMPLEMENT MFG. CO.					X
TONUTTI S.P.A.	X				X
UNITED FARM TOOLS		X			
VASSAR CO.					X
WIKOMI					X

The Rotary Tiller

The rotary tiller can be used in place of a moldboard plow. Heavy ones for farm tractors and medium-sized ones for large, commercial, walking tractors are available, as well as the popular self-propelled garden tillers. The rotary tiller is probably the ideal tool for incorporating organic matter and avoiding soil compaction.

However, it is the nature of the tool that it can only move slowly across a field, and for that reason, it has not gained popularity on larger farms. When heavy stands of green manure have to be incorporated into the soil, the rotary tiller must usually be preceded by a stalk chopper or rotary mower to chop the plant material. Otherwise, rotary tiller tines will frequently entangle with crop residues.

In action, a rotary tiller among the vineyards as pulled behind the Holder A-18 tractor.

Holder

THE HOWARD ROTAVATOR

by Thomas J. Ulick

The Howard Rotavator is a fine tilling tool available for the small- to medium-sized vegetable grower. It allows you to prepare a seedbed in conditions which would be impossible for other types of tractor-powered or horse-drawn equipment, provides an incomparable seedbed, aerates soil, incorporates crop residues, and so forth. It very well may be used for cultivating, bed forming, and other operations, and may be coupled with planters or drills for one-pass tillage and planting. I have found objections that rotavators require excessive amounts of tractor power unfounded. I operate an 80-inch rotavator with a 45 horsepower, Ford 3000 diesel tractor on about two gallons of diesel fuel per hour. I can easily cover one to one-and-one-half acres per hour, and by making two or three passes am able to work 12 to 14 inches deep under most conditions. Howard Rotavators are distributed by a worldwide network of dealerships, a list of which can be obtained by writing: Howard Rotavator Company, Harvard, IL 60033.

Visible on this rotary cultivator are the three attaching points of a three-point hitch, the rotovating tines, and the power-take-off connection for hitching to a tractor PTO shaft. This is the Ferrari Super L rotary tiller.

Ferrari International, Inc.

THE SPRING-TOOTHED HARROW

The spring-toothed harrow is used principally as a soil leveler behind a disc, though it digs more deeply than the spike-toothed harrow. The spring-toothed harrow collects surface trash and plant material very easily and is therefore seldom usable in organic farming except after the moldboard plow.

HARROW IMPROVISATION

by Rob Johnston, Johnny's Selected Seeds

There is a tool often called a Scotch Harrow, a fencelike grid of chain, which is tractor-drawn to level a seedbed. Well, I'd wanted one for years but never felt we could afford it. Anyway, we now achieve just about the same effect by attaching a large old barn beam behind the disc harrow with a towing chain. The beam drags along behind the disc, leveling out high spots and filling in the ruts left at the edge of the harrow. If we need a really perfect seedbed for some delicate crop, we take time to go over the piece with a steel garden rake and have found it important to have one with an extra-long handle. This really gets it smooth and permits easy location of surface debris and stones.

The Cultimulcher

The cultimulcher or pulvimulcher is a combination of spring-tooth harrow and cultipacker—a set of cultipacker wheels in front and rear, with harrow tines in the middle. It is used (if at all anymore) to put a smooth surface of fine soil on recently plowed ground to prevent moisture from escaping in a dry planting season.

WEED CONTROL TILLAGE

Cultivating Blades

The old saying, "There are as many opinions on a subject as there are people thinking about it," holds fairly true for weed cultivators. There seem to be as many different kinds as there have been farmers who like to tinker. Some blades are shovel-shaped, some spear-shaped, some almost identical to the teeth of a spring-tooth harrow, some little more than narrow steel bars. All have some kind of spring or give to them. Spring-trip shovels will snap back out of the ground if they hit a root or rock that will not budge. The very narrow spring-tine cultivators, often called Danish tooth blades, vibrate and wiggle through the soil and seldom collect plant residue.

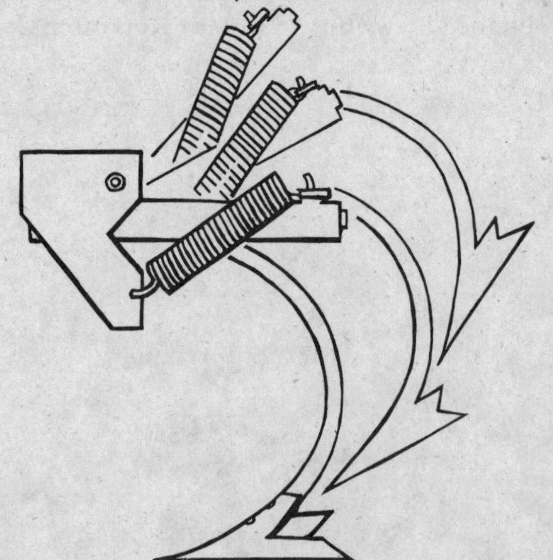

The "spring" in the spring tooth protects the tool when it hits a hard object.

The Wikomi one-row Vibrating "S" Tine Cultivator with an optional one-row shield. The vibrating characteristic allows the share to vibrate strongly sideways to churn the soil. It provides proper tine spacing with lateral tine spacing adjustment for 20- to 40-inch row spacing.
Wikomi Mfg. Co.

The rotary hoe is a special tool, consisting of several rows of pointed steel wheels, each about 10 inches in diameter. When pulled at a fairly rapid tractor speed, these wheels will dig out very small, germinating weed seeds without harming sprouted crop seeds if the latter are no more than an inch or two tall. The rotary hoe has become obsolete on farms where the use of herbicides predominates, but it is still an important tool on other farms, since the most important weed control is that obtained between the time a crop is planted and the time it is tall enough to cultivate with a regular shovel or tine weeder.

Rotary tillers convert to effective between-the-row cultivation, especially those with a faster gear than the one normally used for deep tilling. It should be set so it does not dig too deeply when cultivating weeds.

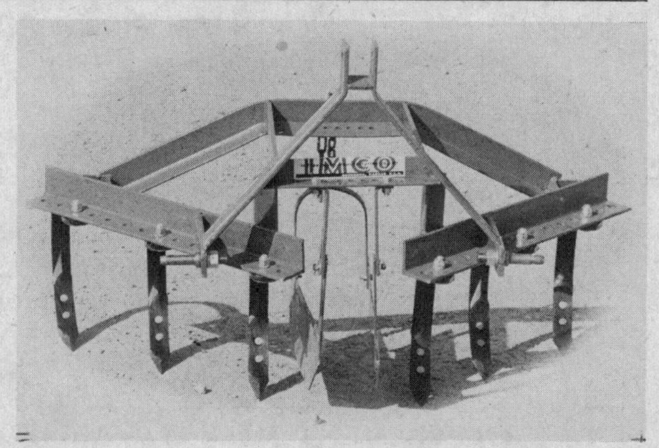

The IMCO one-row cultivator with reversible, heat-treated shovels. Heavy-duty spring tines and row shield are also available.
Independent Mfg. Co.

NORTH AMERICAN SOURCES OF CULTIVATORS

	CULTIVATORS	CULTIVATORS WITH VIBRATING TINES	DISC CULTIVATORS (ROLLING FENDERS)	ROTARY CULTIVATORS	TILLAGE REPLACEMENT POINTS
ALLIED FARM EQUIPMENT	X	X	X	X	
BRINLY-HARDY CO., INC.	X*				
CENTRAL TRACTOR		X			
EMPIRE PLOW CO.					X
GANTT MFG.	X				
GILMORE-TATGE MFG. CO., INC. (ALLIED)			X		
GILSON BROS.			X		
IMCO (INDEPENDENT MFG. CO.)	X				
MONTGOMERY WARD		X*	X		
NOBLE CULTIVATORS, LTD.	X				
ROYAL INDUSTRIES	X	X	X		
SEARS, ROEBUCK & CO.		X	X		
SPEECO (SPECIAL PRODUCTS CO.)	X	X			

* Models with planter bar hookup.

NORTH AMERICAN SOURCES OF CULTIVATORS

	CULTIVATORS	CULTIVATORS WITH VIBRATING TINES	DISC CULTIVATORS (ROLLING FENDERS)	ROTARY CULTIVATORS TILLAGE REPLACEMENT POINTS
TAYLOR IMPLEMENT MFG. CO. (ALLIED)	X			
TRACTOR SUPPLY CO.		X		
UTILITY TOOL & BODY CO.			X	
WIKOMI MFG. CO.	X	X	X	

INTERNATIONAL SOURCES OF CULTIVATORS

	CULTIVATORS	CULTIVATORS WITH VIBRATING TINES	DISC CULTIVATORS (ROLLING FENDERS)	ROTARY CULTIVATORS
ACM EQUIPMENTS	X	X		
AGRATOR INDUSTRIAL, S.L.				X
BEAUVAIS & ROBIN, ETS.	X	X		
CECOCO				X
DELAPLACE, ETS.	X			
GHERARDI S.P.A.	X			X
W. HERTECANT	X			
HUARD-UCF-SCM	X			X
INDUSTRIA METALURGICAS APOLO S.A.	X			
JUMIL, JUSTINO DE MORAES, IRMAOS S.A.	X *			
KUHN S.A.				X
PIERCE OF WEXFORD		X		
SCHANZLIN MASCHINENFABRIK GMBH				X
TONUTTI S.P.A.	X			
YANMAR DIESEL ENGINE CO.				X

* Models with attached fertilizer spreader.

-3- The Continuing Role of Draft Animals

FARMING WITH HORSES

by Wendell Berry

A team of horses, living off the hay and grain it helps to produce, is an embodiment of the life of the farm—which, under good care, is perpetually self-renewing. A team is therefore not only a much cheaper source of power than a tractor, but it is also a source that in the long run will be much more dependable. And whereas the wastes from a tractor's engine only pollute the air, a horse's bodily wastes will enrich the ground from which he feeds, thus significantly reducing the farmer's dependence on the fertilizer companies.

And horses, unlike tractors, can reproduce themselves. Many small farmers will find it possible to raise a pair of colts a year from a team of work mares. If the quality of the colts is good, and if the horse market stays favorable, the work team may earn considerably more than its feed bill, and thus provide the farmer with a year of free labor, plus some profit.

In the work itself, horses have certain advantages over tractors. They can be used safely on steep ground, where a tractor would be either dangerous or useless. A horse farmer can get into his fields more quickly after rain than can a tractor farmer. And horses do not pack the ground as much as tractors. It is generally acknowledged among the tobacco growers in my area of Kentucky that the work of horse-drawn cultivating plows has never been equalled by any tractor.

On the decline: as power equipment like this one-row corn harvester took hold, the significance of the draft horse began to fade. American Society of Agricultural Engineers

Beyond these practicalities, there is the satisfaction that one gets from working a good team. A tractor may be handy, always ready to use, untiring, enormously powerful; but it is not alive, and that is a great difference. To work all day with a well-broke and willing team is a pleasure as well as a job; it is a cooperative venture, a sort of social event. And when the day's work is finished, to stable the team and water and feed them well, or to turn them out onto good pasture, is a comfort and a fulfillment. Between a farmer and a team there exists a sort of fellow feeling that is impossible between a farmer and a tractor, and for me that rates as a considerable advantage.

Another thing I like about working with horses is their quietness. When you work with a tractor you hear nothing but the tractor; it is a kind of isolation. With the engine roaring in your ears all day, you lose awareness of the other life that is going on around you. With horses, unless you are using some noisy implement like a mowing machine, you hear the wind blowing and the birds singing and all the rest of the stirrings and goings-on of the countryside.

And so there is a good deal that can be said in favor of farming with horses. There are, in fact, a few widely scattered farmers who still do farm exclusively with horses. There are many more who keep a team or two for part-time use. And of course there are the Amish, for whom farming with horses is a community ideal and a way of life. Nevertheless, it would be irresponsible simply to recommend to anybody who owns a farm that he should sell his tractor and buy a team. There are difficulties

The draft horse farmer should be prepared to work a little harder physically than his mechanized neighbor. Here a team of blacks gets started on a morning's disking.

in the way; it is important that I should now mention them, and that interested readers should consider them with great care.

1. In many parts of the country a good team is difficult to find. And though a good team is less expensive than a good tractor, it will still be costly. At present the price of horses is high, and rising.
2. Most horse-drawn equipment has been out of production for many years. Some tractor equipment, of course, is fairly easily convertible for use with horses.
3. Horses are not standard. No two are exactly alike in looks, size, conformation, or disposition. It is therefore extremely unwise for an inexperienced person to attempt to buy a team on his own. I have said that a good team is a source of pleasure. It is now time to say that a bad one is a curse, a nuisance, a liability—sometimes a danger. Some horsemen will take pride in selling good stock and in satisfying their customers. Some will sell poor stock with extravagant praise.
4. Most important: It is not easy to work with and care for a team. It cannot be learned easily or quickly. A person who can drive a car can probably teach himself to drive a tractor in a short while. To learn to drive a team well, you need a teacher, and you need experience. An inex-

perienced teamster can easily injure or kill his team and can easily get injured or killed himself.

5. Obviously, then, a person inexperienced with horses who wants to farm with them is much in need of the advice and instruction of an experienced teamster whose intelligence and judgment can be trusted. And this brings us to the final difficulty: such people are getting scarce. The last generations that grew up working horses are dying out, and their knowledge is dying with them.

Fortunately, there are some experienced horsemen scattered over the country who have had these problems on their minds. And because of their efforts there begins to be some promise of help for the would-be or the novice teamster.

First, I want to mention, and recommend, *The Draft Horse Journal* (Route 3, Waverly, IA 50677), edited by Maurice and Jeannine Telleen. This magazine is an assembly point for all sorts of information about sales, breeders and dealers, suppliers of equipment, and other items of interest. There are articles on the history, breeding, and care of draft horses. And in the short time that I have been a subscriber, there has been an increasing number of articles on the use of horses for farm work. Anyone interested in farming with horses would find this magazine both a pleasure and a valuable investment.

In the Summer 1973 issue of the *Journal,* I was much interested to see an article which announced the first session of a Teamster's School to be held at Indian Summer Farm in Cabot, Vermont. According to the article, Ted Bermingham had undertaken to set up the school on his farm with the hope of preserving and passing on the knowledge and skill of "the last full generation of working teamsters." For this purpose Mr. Bermingham had rounded up a faculty of experienced horsemen to teach the disciplines of farming and logging with horses. Tuition was $150. This paid for all instruction, stall and board for a horse or team (if any), supper on Sunday night, and three meals a day, Monday through Thursday. Daytime instruction involved working at the chores of farming and logging. Study of the various tools and techniques always took place amid the practicalities of actual use. Students drove their own horses or horses furnished by the school under close supervision of the teachers. They also took part in the necessary stable work. The night sessions consisted of talks on such topics as horse husbandry, logging techniques, breeding, equine genetics, veterinary medicine, horse trading, and shoeing.

Mr. Bermingham and his staff are well aware, of course, that the teamster's art is complex and dependent upon experience, and that no novice could hope to become proficient at it in a few days. The school is meant to offer as full an introduction as possible to skills that the beginner can then practice on his own. There is no doubt that a few hours of work with an experienced teacher can save many hours of expensive and dangerous self-instruction by the method of trial and error. The students I talked to all believed that the school had been thoroughly worthwhile. So did their teachers—and so did I.

I hope that such schools will soon be undertaken in other parts of the country. They would be good for the draft horse business, and they would be good for farming.

The school was sponsored by the Draft Horse Institute, established in 1972 by Ted Bermingham, to collect and maintain the working knowledge of farming and using draft horses before it was lost. For information on the future sessions planned for coming seasons, you can write to Mr. Bermingham at Indian Summer Farm, Cabot, VT 05647.

POWER FOR FIELD WORK

by Joseph K. Campbell

What are the sources of power for field work in the world? According to the FAO (Food and Agriculture Organization of the United Nations), there are approximately 16.9 million agricultural tractors and 267.4 million horses, mules, asses, water buffalo, and camels in the world. Of course many of these animals are used for transportation, but a large proportion of them are used as draft animals. There are also estimated to be 1,200,000,000 cattle in the world. Most of the cattle are used for meat and milk, with only a few used as draft cows or draft oxen. The distribution of the animals is shown in Table I.

Table I DRAFT ANIMALS AND AGRICULTURAL TRACTORS

(in thousands) [a]

	CATTLE [b]	WATER BUFFALO	HORSES	MULES	ASSES	CAMELS	FARM TRACTORS [c]
NORTH & CENTRAL AMERICA	193,407	7	17,339	2,967	3,367	—	5,146.5
SOUTH AMERICA	212,444	166	16,837	5,934	5,410	—	525.4
AFRICA	151,396	2,280	3,567	2,140	11,235	9,624	379.5
EUROPE	135,363	433	6,115	844	1,584	—	7,000.6
USSR	109,122	427	6,749	2	501	253	2,267.
ASIA	356,439	128,455	14,085	2,267	20,000	4,233	1,137.5
OCEANIA	43,072	—	580	—	5	2	437.2
WORLD	1,201,243	131,769	65,272	14,154	42,101	14,112	16,893.7

a. Based on tables 102, 103, & 125 of the 1975 FAO *Production Yearbook*

b. Primarily for meat and milk

c. Sum of tracklaying and four-wheel farm tractors over eight developed horsepower and/or weighing more than 850 kilograms

What are the horsepower ratings of these various sources of agricultural power? Before answering this question, let's review the relationship of force, work, power, and energy.

The original source of the term "horsepower." The Implement Age, 1894

A force can be visualized as a pull or push which tends to move the subject being pulled or pushed. For example, a force of 250 kilograms may be required to pull a plow through the soil. In agriculture we refer to this force as draft and animals which pull loads as draft animals. Whether the plow is pulled a meter or a kilometer, the draft in this example remains two hundred and fifty kilograms.

The term work includes the dimension of distance. Work equals force times distance. The metric unit of work is the kilogram-meter. The English unit is the foot-pound. Note that work does not state the amount of time required to do a job. For example, to plow a hectare of land requires the same amount of work whether the job is done in twelve hours with a garden tractor or an hour with a large farm tractor. However, the power requirements will be very different.

Power is the rate of doing work. The faster the work is to be completed, the greater the power required. The unit of power in the English system is the horsepower. In the metric system power is measured by the kilowatt and metric horsepower. Horsepower is actually the rate at which a large draft horse can work. When the eighteenth century Scotsman, James Watt, was designing steam engines, he was faced with prospective customers insisting upon knowing the number of horses which could be replaced by a steam engine. So Watt experimented with some draft horses and determined that a horse exerting a constant 150-pound pull walked at two and one-half miles per hour. Watt called this amount of power one horsepower.

MAN AS A POWER SOURCE

From the food he consumes, a man develops horsepower, but only one-tenth is available for sustained useful work. The remainder is expended in life functions of the body. Thus, as an engine converting fuel to mechanical energy, we are about 20 percent efficient. Our muscles do provide some work overload reserve. For bursts of energy of less than a second, up to six horsepower may be expended. A rule of thumb for useful power for periods of four minutes to eight hours is mathematically expressed by:

$HP = 0.35 - 0.092 \log t$ (t is in minutes.)

For example, a man can put out one-eighth horsepower over four hours, but if he is putting out one-fourth horsepower he will last only about 12 minutes. The above rule of thumb assumes a 35-year-old male European laborer. A 20-year-old male will be able to generate 15 percent more useful work while a 60-year-old will generate about 20 percent less.

Man cannot compete successfully with engines or dumb animals as a source of power for constant-load repetitive jobs such as pumping water for irrigation. His low power output places him at a disadvantage. However, man has a unique brain and is well adapted for jobs with a low power requirement but demanding decision-making and dexterity of hand. For example, transplanting rice demands thought as well as dexterity—does the plant have sufficient roots? Is the spacing correct?

DRAFT ANIMALS

Oxen, water buffalo, horses, and mules are the primary draft animals. Camels and asses (donkeys) are more typically used as pack animals although they are used for pulling carts and tillage tools in some countries. Viewing the draft animal as a machine, we see that it can feed itself, maintain itself, be programmed for automatic control, and reproduce itself—four functions a tractor cannot perform. As a mechanism, the animal is a jointed framework held together with ligaments and muscles. The engine consists of the digestive organs while the products of combustion are removed by the excretory system. The brain and nervous system provide a control system with a memory bank, logic circuits, and feedback loops. Joints and moving parts have a sealed lubrication system. Protecting the mechanism is a covering of hide which is resistant to damage and self-healing as far as minor dents and scratches are concerned.

Unlike the farm tractor, however, draft animals can be purchased in a very limited range of horsepower, cannot be worked continuously, and continue to burn fuel when not working.

An FAO publication states that when used as draft animals, bovines have an energy efficiency of 9 to 10 percent and members of the horse family 10 to 12 percent. However, other experts state that horses have an efficiency of about 20 percent. The difference between investigators is probably due to the breed, type of feed, and whether the work was done by the test animals on treadmills or draft devices. As a reference point, the efficiency of energy conversion for gasoline and diesel engines is 20 to 35 percent.

POWER SUPPLIED BY DRAFT ANIMALS

ANIMAL	AVG. WEIGHT KG	APPROX-IMATE DRAFT KG	AVERAGE SPEED OF WORK KM/HR	POWER DEVL. H.P.
LIGHT HORSES	400-700	60-80	3.6	1.0
OXEN	500-900	60-80	2.0-3.0	.75
WATER BUFFALOS	400-900	50-80	2.9-3.2	.75
COWS	400-600	50-60	2.5	.45
MULES	350-500	50-60	3.2-3.6	.70
ASSES	200-300	30-40	2.5	.35
CAMELS	450-550	40-50	4.0	.67

Adapted from FAO Ag. Devl. Paper No. 91.

In general, a draft animal can pull approximately one-tenth of its weight. Horses provide a higher output than the other animals in relation to body weight. Just as an internal combustion engine requires high-quality fuel to perform well, an animal requires a sufficient amount of high-quality fuel to develop maximum power. The availability of fuel (feed) affects the choice of draft animal. Oxen, water buffalo, and camels can be thought of as low-octane engines able to perform on low-quality feed such as coarse forages while the horse can put out more power but demands higher-energy fuel in the form of grain. Asses and mules are intermediate on this fuel scale.

Like man, animals can, during a short period of overload, develop large bursts of power. A good pair of draft horses have been able to develop 20 to 25 horsepower for ten seconds while a yoke of good oxen have developed 20 to 30 horsepower over a distance of 100 yards. Compared to the power which a draft animal can produce over a six- to ten-hour day, the maximum power which can be maintained for five to 30 minutes is four times as great while the maximum power which can be exerted over a few seconds is 25 times as great.

Animals must receive periods of rest. In general, horses and mules can be worked eight to ten hours daily but should be given a break at noon. Adult oxen can be worked for six to eight hours although younger oxen or poorly fed animals may only work four hours daily. Water buffalos are worked approximately six hours per day. It is impossible to provide precise data for draft animals since performance depends upon an animal's individual characteristics such as breed, weight, sex, age, health, training, and feed quality.

Harness is the means by which the animal's effort is applied to the load. Poorly designed and ill-fitting harness not only reduces the available power but also causes the animal to suffer. When one animal cannot provide sufficient draft or power, a number of animals can be harnessed together as a team, but at a loss in individual efficiency. In general, if animals of equal strength are harnessed together as a team, the draft of a single animal working alone should be multiplied by 1.9 for two animals; by 2.5 for three; by 3.1 for four; by 3.5 for five, and by 3.8 for six. If six oxen are yoked together, the resultant draft will be double that of two oxen.

THOUGHTS OF A DESIGNER OF ANIMAL-DRAWN EQUIPMENT

by Jean Nolle

For several years, people have asked me: "Why do you invent new animal-drawn machinery when draft animals have almost disappeared? Why do you persevere in this misguided way when everything proves now that mankind is setting up his future on a highly developed technological base? What are your reasons for dedicating your life to the rescue of draft animals?"

Before I try to answer, I must first correct a mistake in the question. I do not dedicate my life to the rescue of draft animals, but to the development of the forgotten farmers.

That being said, I can explain that for 27 years, I have been involved in agriculture in almost all tropical countries. Since I was working alone, perhaps the modesty of my labor kept me safe from the noise around and allowed me to continue the same point of view for so long a time. Many developments have altered specific actions in machinery design, but there has been no deviation in my intentions.

I developed a new technology in matters of animal-drawn machinery for small agriculture for several reasons. The first was opportunity. In 1950 in Senegal, there were two large farms of 5,000 hectares each. They were set up to grow peanuts, and equipped with heavy-duty tractors and sophisticated implements. Both went bankrupt in 1954. The reasons were said to be climate, soil, plants, and human population.

Both of them were obliged to change their ways. At the first one, located in the Casamance region of south Senegal, the tse-tse flies prevented the use of draft animals so the farm continued its use of heavy-duty tractors, with the farmers using traditional hand tools.

The second, named Secteur de Modernization Agricole (S.M.A.) was located in central Senegal where tse-tse flies were unknown. As this farm was a state enterprise, the government decided to improve the animal-drawn machinery there. I was engaged by the S.M.A. from 1954 to 1958 with *carte blanche* to conceive, realize, experiment with and develop various animal-drawn machines.

I had to discover a formula that made possible the farmers' evolution from extensive methods to intensive ones. I had to find a solution to the width, the length, and the solidity of my future machines. I had to invent some ways to stimulate the curiosity of the farmers in order to make them understand without any teacher the laws of the interdependence between various farming operations.

It was quite a challenge to discover a single formula that could answer these diverse questions. However, it exists. Its name: polyvalence, or versatility.

To be successful in the tropics or with small-scale agriculture anywhere, a machine must be versatile. This adaptability is the strength of tractors with three-point hitches, and it applies to animal-drawn implements as well. In the design of agricultural machines, the main aspects of this versatility are the ability to adjust track width and the ability of the chassis to accept numerous implements. Next in importance is the means used to change the track and to attach the implements.

Single-purpose machines have their own chassis. Multipurpose machines, on the other hand, use the same chassis for many tasks. Of course, if the price of a multipurpose chassis is higher than that of several single-purpose chassis, the purpose is defeated. Likewise, if the device required to fit the various implements on the multipurpose machine is too complicated, farmers will not change them and the machine will be single-purpose anyway.

To meet these requirements, I had to design several chassis to meet the needs of farms ranging in size from two to 20 hectares. While the dimensions of the chassis varied, the hitching device was to be standard. At first, nuts and bolts seemed the simplest solution, but bolts require fixed holes in both the chassis and the tools, thereby limiting their versatility and ultimately weakening the chassis. Nuts and bolts are also subject to rust, and eventually require a hammer and chisel to remove them. In reality, the farmer rarely does this, and the machine becomes single-purpose once again.

My solution was to design a special type of U-shaped clamp. Each branch of the clamp is dug with a square hole, and the bottom of the clamp has an eye screw. Square holes are very helpful as they permit tools to be attached to any part of the chassis without drilling holes in the chassis.

NOLLE'S EQUIPMENT

Described below are some examples of Jean Nolle's ingenuity at designing multipurpose agricultural equipment for widely varying soil and cropping conditions. The emphasis on economy, ease of operation and maintenance, and versatility is consistent. Additional information on Nolle's machines may be obtained from the manufacturer, Mouzon S.A., 60250 Mouy, France.

Polycultor

The *polycultor* is an ox-drawn chassis adaptable to a wide range of cultivation implements. Designed by Nolle especially for farmers who need a small transport vehicle as well as a universal tool carrier, the polycultor features a hand lever for raising the implements and two handles on the toolbar for steering. The lift is connected to the toolbar by a chain for easy depth adjustment.

The Polycultor prepared for hoeing cotton in Uganda.
Jean Nolle

The toolbar is designed to carry from six to 12 cultivator tines. It can carry one or two ridgers, three markers for planting peanuts, a peanut lifter, and a grain drill. The single-bottom plow attaches directly to the axle with a stirrup clamp. Since it is fitted alongside the right wheel, the plow has its own lift. Uniform furrow width is obtained by the right wheel following the previous furrow. The farmer is seated in the middle of the chassis, beside the plow.

Another option is a 500-liter water drum, put in the same place the cart would normally be. Still another is a small mower, driven by the right wheel. The mower is mounted on the side of the platform cart, exactly in its pivot, so that it can be lifted for transport.

One of the chief obstacles preventing more widespread use of green manuring practices in Senegal and elsewhere in Africa is that the traditional moldboard plow with oxen is so difficult to keep in the ground with some of the newer, higher cover crops like sorghum. The stability and weight of the polycultor makes this much less difficult. The long stems are bent forward by the axle, so it is easier for the plow to cover them with earth.

Sine Hoe

Nolle's *polyculteur sine* (hoe) is built with a front bar, a rear bar, and a stirrup in between. This arrangement makes it possible to use the sine as a cultivator, with one short tine on the longitudinal toolbar and two short tines on the rear bar. For use as a hoe, three tines are attached to the rear bar, one long tine is placed in the middle, and two short tines are attached on the sides. The middle hoe is equipped with

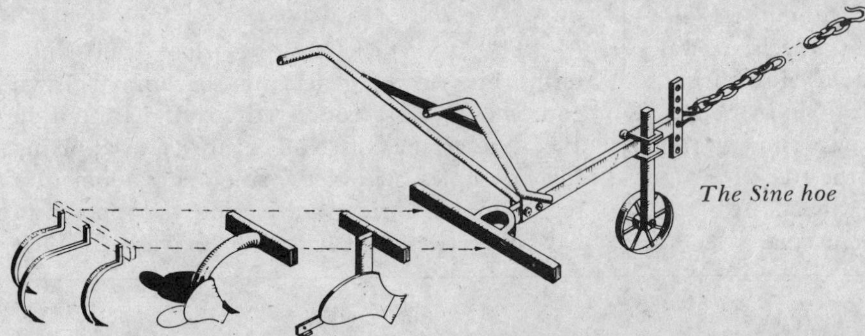

The Sine hoe

The Sine as a cultivator in Vietnam.
Jean Nolle

a duck foot sweep, and the sides with left- and right-hand side shovels.

The rear bar can be adapted to carry a furrow plow, a ridger, and a rigid tooth harrow. Disc and spring-tooth harrows can also be attached.

The width and length of the sine can be modified by means of clamp-on extensions, thereby making it possible to use the tool with two wheels or two skids, with one or two ridgers, with five tines instead of three, and other options. All in all, the sine is a fine example of a machine that is readily adaptable to the job at hand and the strength of the animals.

Saloum

Ranking in size somewhere between the sine and the polycultor, the *saloum* was designed for areas with soils too hard for the lighter sine to penetrate. The square chassis and two forward wheels make it possible to load the saloum with a bag of sand to achieve greater weight for plowing or cultivating in clay soils. The machine was also valuable for harvesting peanuts in heavy soils.

The Saloum
Jean Nolle

But the saloum was not without its disadvantages. With the two front wheels, it was almost impossible to steer effectively for hoeing. Since the wheels were not adjustable in height, it was also impossible to plow. Nor was it possible to adjust the width of the track.

For these reasons, Nolle abandoned the saloum and replaced it with the ariana.

Ariana

The *ariana* belongs to what Jean Nolle terms his second generation of animal-drawn equipment. First conceived in Afghanistan in 1961, the ariana was Nolle's answer to applying the principles behind the sine and saloum to a region in which ridge cultivation (as opposed to flat cultivation) and irrigation prevailed. What was required was a reversible plow that would place the final furrow alongside the field rather than in it. The ridge cultivation also required more clearance under the chassis.

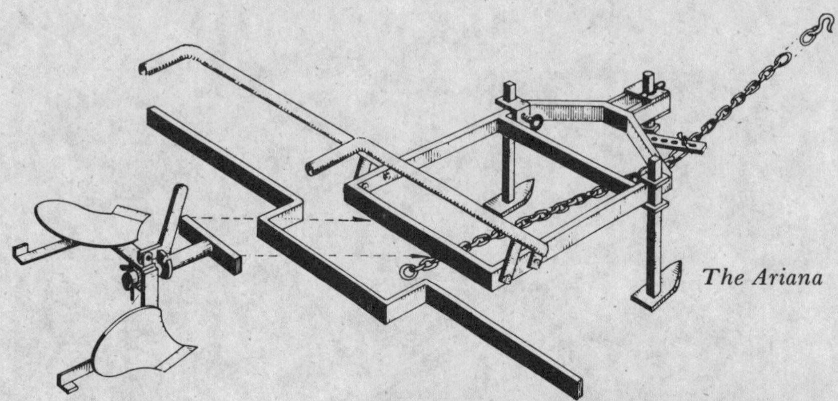

The Ariana

The Ariana preparing a seedbed with a cambridge roller and a spring-tooth harrow.
Jean Nolle

On Nolle's ariana, the two wheels for plowing are attached with clamps to the upright bars. Track width is adjustable from 30 to 70 centimeters. Besides the furrow plow and the reversible plow, the machine can be adapted with implements for ridging, cultivating, planting, fertilizing and peanut harvesting. For hoeing and all conventional cultivation work, the two wheels are replaced by a single wheel in the front center.

Tropicultor

Like Nolle's polycultor, the *tropicultor* is essentially a cart that is easily converted into a

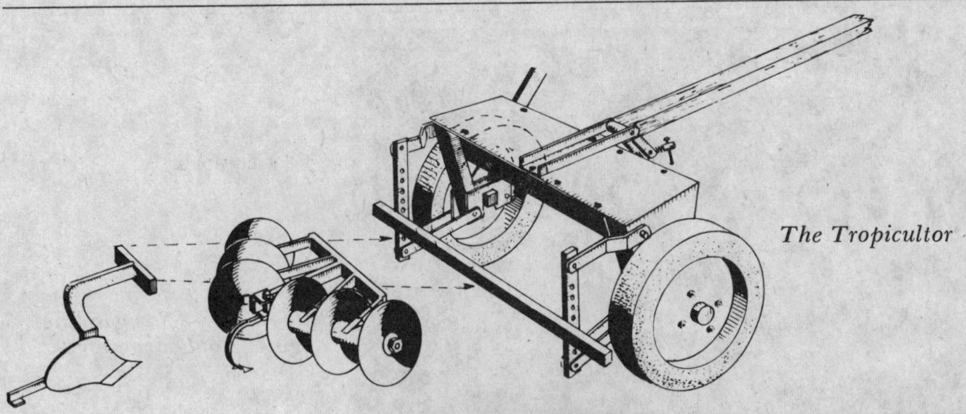

The Tropicultor

The Tropicultor plowing in Uganda.
Jean Nolle

multipurpose tool carrier. Unlike its predecessor, however, the tropicultor is adjustable for rows of varying width, and its chassis is made of two steel pipes making it high enough for use above growing crops.

The angle of penetration of the implements is controlled by an adjustment of the shaft. The ability to lock the toolbar in the low working position represents a real breakthough in the design of multipurpose tool carriers of this sort. It frees the operator from having to constantly lean down on the handles and devise crude weighting schemes for the cart. With a track width that can be adjusted from 60 to 160 centimeters, and a ground clearance of 65 centimeters, the tropicultor can work in almost any soil and cropping conditions. Like Nolle's other machines, the tropicultor offers various extensions and adaptors that permit it to function as a grain drill, disc harrow, mower, reversible plow, planter, and cultivator. All attachments are easily fastened to the toolbar with standard clamps and pins.

All told, the tropicultor will accept 24 different implements that make possible over 30 uses on the small farm. Such versatility greatly enhances the independence of the farmer using the device.

Avtrac

The *avtrac* was invented in 1961 by Jean Nolle in response to a request from the French Ministry of Agriculture to design an improved horse-drawn tool carrier similar to those he had introduced in Senegal. At that time there were a million-and-a-half draft horses in use in France, and the avtrac was essentially an attempt to design three-point hitch implements for draft

The Avtrac used in conjunction with an 8 h.p. gasoline engine to pull a manure spreader.
Jean Nolle

animals similar to those used with tractor-drawn equipment. There was no one making horse-drawn equipment in France at the time, and a serious shortage prevailed.

The frame of the avtrac consists of a wide transverse pipe, in the middle of which is fitted the support for the shaft. The machine can be pulled by one, two, or three animals, and the equipment used is the equivalent of that designed for 25 h.p. tractors. Each wheel support has a rear-mounted swinging drawbar to receive a standard toolbar or other implements. The third point is in the middle of the chassis.

For pulling a trailer there's a hook mounted on the toolbar. For the mower, manure spreader, and other powered implements, an 8 h.p. engine with PTO is mounted between the wheels.

Kanol

In the early 1970s, Nolle was called upon to develop animal-drawn implements for use in Latin America. Finding that his sine and ariana tools were often unsuited to the hard volcanic clays there, Nolle worked out a simplified version of his tropicultor that used hooks to attach the implements rather than clamps.

The main frame of the *kanol* consists of a shaft connected to a device that contains two levers—one for adjusting the angle of penetration into the earth and another to control balance. Implements are detached by simply lifting a hook.

The kanol carries two categories of tools: narrow tools that do not require wheels (one-furrow plow, subsoiler, peanut lifter, cultivator, ridger, etc.), and wider implements equipped with two wheels for stability (those used in conjunction with 150- or 170-centimeter toolbars and transport uses).

Latin American farmers experienced with the older Asian-type plows were quick to accept the kanol. Those already using a sine or ariana needed only to purchase the main kanol support and toolbar; all the attachments were interchangeable. With the addition of the hooks, it became even easier to change implements than with clamps.

THE EFFICIENT USE OF ANIMAL POWER

by Wayne Dinsmore

Editor's note: This material is excerpted from a paper presented at the annual meeting of the American Society of Agricultural Engineers, December 27, 1921, and published in the February 1922 issue of *Agricultural Engineering*. The information is still valid for small farmers today.

It has been found possible to drive teams 20 miles per day in a ten-hour day on various farm implements and to maintain this rate week after week. This allows two hours for driving to and from fields, hitching and unhitching, turning at ends, and occasional examination of collars. It requires that teams shall actually be in motion on productive work eight hours per day at an average speed of two and one-half miles per hour. When fresh, horses will exceed this; when weary, they will not equal it, but it is a practical standard, attained where sufficient horses or mules are used to permit steady driving, without stops to rest animals. Whenever teams require stops for rest, not enough power is being used. Put on another horse or a pair, or more if necessary, but add enough so that you can turn 20 miles of soil per day and not overdo the teams. The number of horses needed will depend on the hardness of the ground, the depth to which implements are cutting, the weather, and the age, size, and condition of the work animals used, so that each man must use "horse sense" and gauge his teams according to power needed.

Twenty miles of productive work daily means 5.6 acres plowed with two-bottom gangs, 14-inch plows; 24 acres double disked with ten-foot discs and trailer attachment; 70 acres harrowed with six-section harrows (five-foot sections) ; and as these soil preparation tasks are the ones requiring the most time, they also offer the greatest opportunity for cutting costs by increasing work done per day.

Disking is the greatest labor-saving soil tillage operation. On good farms it precedes and follows plowing. It pulverizes trash, kills weeds, conserves moisture and makes easier and better plowing. The 20-blade, ten-foot discs now available are usually drawn by six horses, but often need eight for steady progress, especially early in the spring when the horses are soft. One rule governs: Use "horse sense," and if you see the load is too heavy for the number of horses you are using, put on more, until there is enough power attached to allow the horses to walk at a good pace all day. You hire men to accomplish work, not to sit out in the field waiting for horses to rest and recuperate, and it is sound economy to furnish plenty of power, especially as one more horse, or a pair, will turn the balance between overload and ample power.

Plowing is heavy work, made worse by the general practice of crowding the horses too closely together and by failure to hitch on the true center of draft. On every plow, whether one-bottom or more, there is a point of hitch termed the center of draft and when the hitch is made at this point, the plow pulls with less exertion than when the hitch is made at a point more distant from the furrow. On a gang plow, two 14-inch bottoms, this center of draft is approximately 16 inches from furrow wall or 23 inches from the center of furrow when plows are cutting full, even furrows as they should. This means, therefore, that the eveners must be of such length, and the horses so hitched, as to give a straight forward pull over the true center of draft. This cannot be attained with four or more horses except by putting a horse or horses on plowed land, or by stringing the horses, so as to put the right-hand horse in the furrow and the others on solid ground. This causes the horses to pull the plows at great disadvantage, and the extra load thus created is called side draft.

Every farmer should recognize that it is just as easy to drive four, five, or six horses as it is to drive two, providing they are properly hitched; and the ease with which eight, ten, and even 16 horses are handled in the West by hired men who never before drove more than two or four is evidence, if proof be needed, that there is no real obstacle to multiplying the amount of work done per man per day. The size of the units, however, must depend largely upon the size of the farm. On a 100-acre farm, there are seldom more than 80 acres in tilled land, and four good horses are ample to operate such acreage. The implements purchased and the hitches used should therefore be based on a four-horse unit. This calls for six-foot discs with trailers (12-disc units), two-bottom gang plows of 14-inch bottoms and four-section harrows, together with seeders not over ten feet in length. Other implements should be proportionate. All these can be handled by four good horses, although if the ground is full of stones or ledges of rock, gang plows cannot be operated satisfactorily. Under such conditions, it is wise to use 14- or 16-inch walking plows with three horses, which are the oldest but most satisfactory plow units for use on such land.

On farms that have around 150 acres in tilled land, six good horses or mules will be needed. Here, with fields of 30 acres or over, six-horse units can be used on discs, plows, and harrows, which are the implements chiefly used in the preparation of the seedbed. It is in soil preparation that the greatest saving

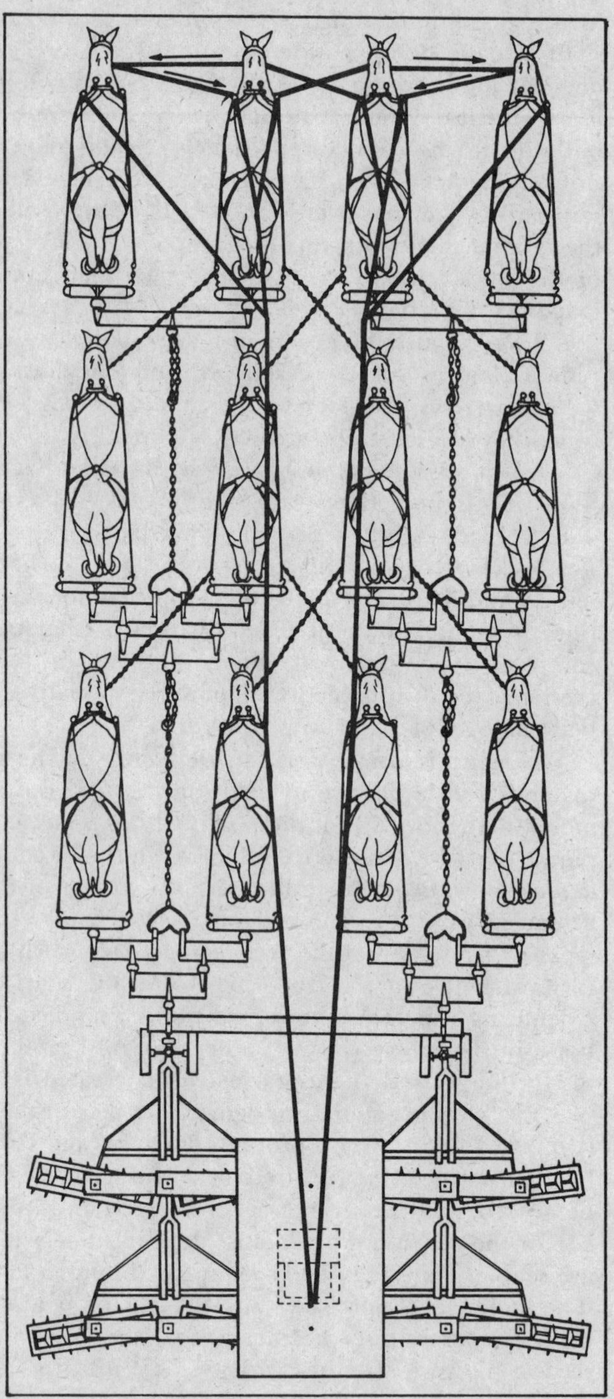

A hitch for twelve horses on two tandem disc harrows cutting all hoof prints except on turns.

A dimension drawing of tandem hitch for eight horses pulling a three-bottom plow to maintain a true line of draft.

in manual labor can be effected. One man, by using six-horse units wherever possible, can handle all the work on a farm containing 150 acres of tilled land, until time for corn plowing, thus cutting down the need for an extra farm hand to the months of June, July, and August—three months instead of six.

On larger farms of 400 to 1,000 acres, the use of 7- up to 16-horse units on various farm implements is both practical and desirable.

The great advantage about this seven-abreast or nine-abreast hitch is that it gives an absolutely straight pull over the true center of draft and the horses are back next to the plow and are so hitched and driven as to make it possible for anyone to handle the team very easily. The only disadvantage that can be charged against the hitches in question is the fact that they require three or four of the horses to walk on the plowed land. The actual experience of men who have worked these seven, eight, or nine horses abreast on plows shows conclusively that this objection has no serious weight. The strongest, toughest horses, best able to withstand the work, should be put on the plowed land and they will keep pace with the others so that no slackening in mileage per day will result. The details of these hitches are fully shown in the illustrations.

Three-bottom gang plows (14-inch bottoms) will turn 8.4 acres per day; four-bottom gang plows (14-inch bottoms) will turn 11.3 acres per day; two eight-foot discs hitched abreast with trailer attachments (double disking a strip 16 feet wide) will double disk 38 acres per day; an eight-section harrow (five-foot sections) lapping one foot each round, will harrow 94 acres per day, and the three seeders (one 12 feet and two 11 feet) will seed 80 acres per day.

So it was in 1922, and so it can be again now that the population of draft horses is increasing, along with the availability of equipment, as the following listings illustrate.

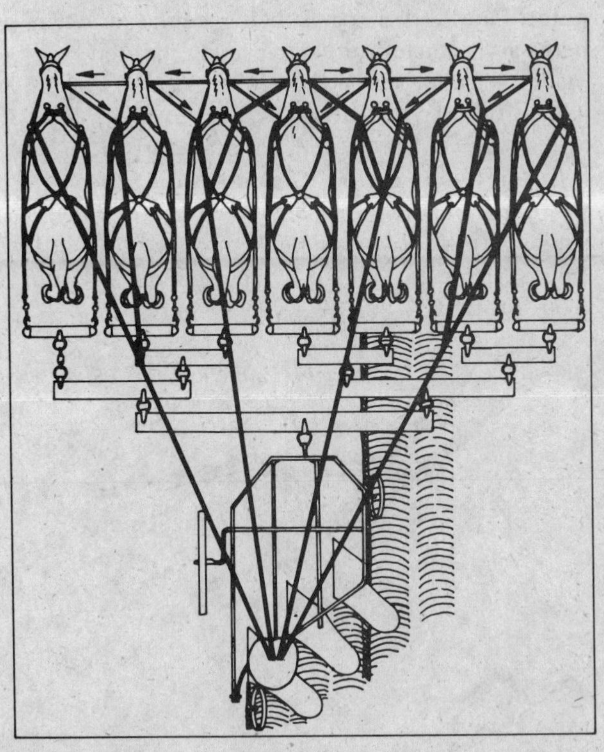

Seven-horse-abreast hitch for a three-bottom plow.

NORTH AMERICAN SOURCES OF ANIMAL-DRAWN EQUIPMENT*

Manure Spreaders

The Bowman Model K

The Bowman Model K comes with a 102- by 18-inch box made of heavy pine floor and 12-gauge steel sides. Apparently the only horse-drawn spreader currently being produced in North America, the Bowman features chain drive, wide paddle beaters that do a good job of breaking up and spreading lumps, and either steel or rubber wheels. Its capacity is approximately 90 bushels.

Bowman Model K
Bowman Mfg.
Hawkesville, Ontario, Canada

Plows and Cultivators

Planet Junior Number 8 One-Horse Cultivator

The venerable Planet Jr. comes with four 3-inch-by-8-inch cultivator steels, one 4-inch-by-8-inch cultivator steel, two 6-inch hillers, one 7-inch shovel, a level wheel, lever expander, and

* Listings of animal-drawn seeder/planter, threshing, winnowing, and cleaning equipment can be found in chapters five and seven.

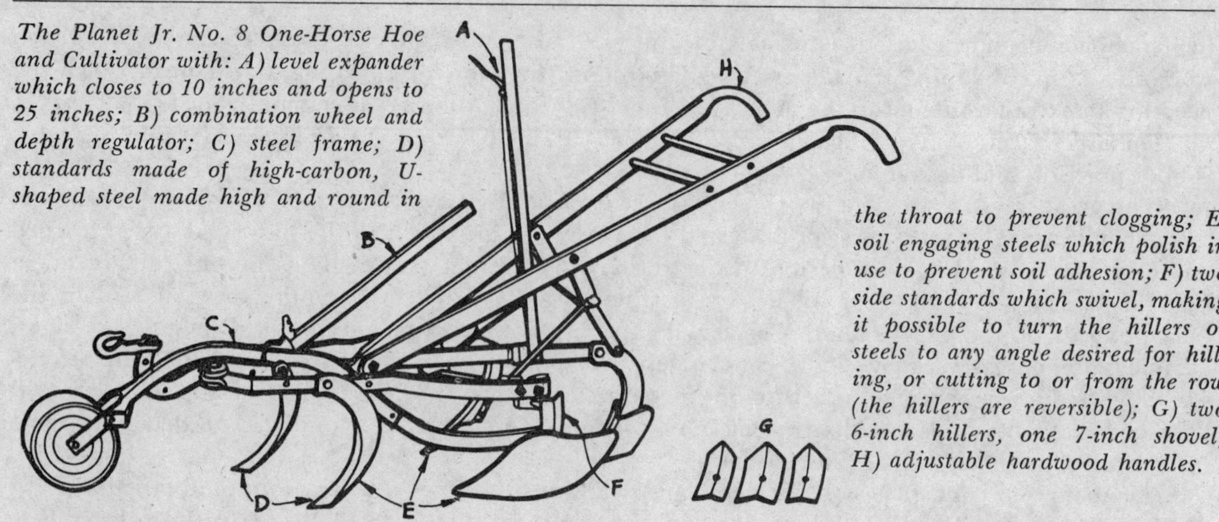

The Planet Jr. No. 8 One-Horse Hoe and Cultivator with: A) level expander which closes to 10 inches and opens to 25 inches; B) combination wheel and depth regulator; C) steel frame; D) standards made of high-carbon, U-shaped steel made high and round in the throat to prevent clogging; E) soil engaging steels which polish in use to prevent soil adhesion; F) two side standards which swivel, making it possible to turn the hillers or steels to any angle desired for hilling, or cutting to or from the row (the hillers are reversible); G) two 6-inch hillers, one 7-inch shovel; H) adjustable hardwood handles.

depth regulator. Its side standards have the virtue of swiveling to permit turning the hillers to any angle desired for hilling, or cutting to or from the row.

Planet Junior Division
Piper Industries
P.O. Box 1188, Freeport Center
Clearfield, UT 84106

The Reliable Model 60

The lightest draft plow of its type, the Reliable Model 60 does a good job of plowing in any kind of soil and in all conditions. The rear weight of the plow is supported by a rolling landslide which serves as the third leg of a triangular rolling support. Uniform depth and width of furrows is controlled by the front furrow master wheel.

The sulky seat is placed to one side, well to the rear, and low down so that the operator has all levers within easy reach. Right- and left-hand models are available in 14-inch and 16-inch models.

Reliable Model 60 Sulky Plow
D.A. Hochstetler & Sons
R.R.2,
Topeka, IN 46571

Cumberland General Store Plows

If you live in an area of the country where most horse-drawn equipment was abandoned and cut up for scrap around the time of World War II, you know that good pieces are hard to find. To help folks in this situation, the Cumberland General Store combs the countryside for used plows in good condition. These are then completely refurbished, with handles, points, and other parts being replaced where necessary. Each unit is cleaned, painted, and made ready for years of useful service. They are generally able to fill orders for turning plows, double shovel plows, and walking cultivators.

The Cumberland General Store also sells the Lynchburg Chilled Slat Moldboard Plow, a single-bottom plow designed for sticky clay soils where a conventional moldboard plow will not scour properly.

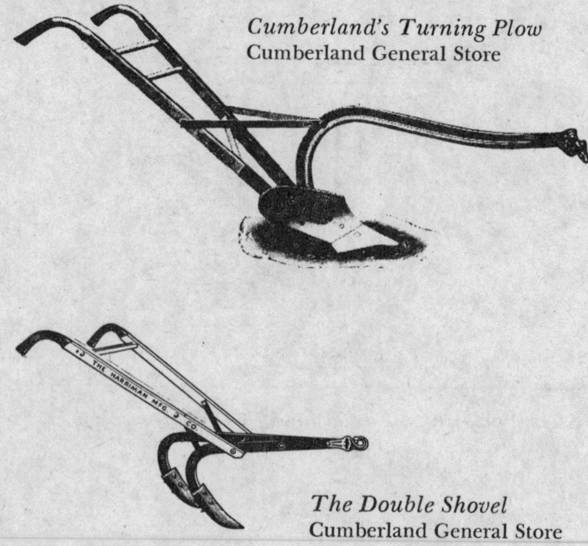

Cumberland's Turning Plow
Cumberland General Store

The Double Shovel
Cumberland General Store

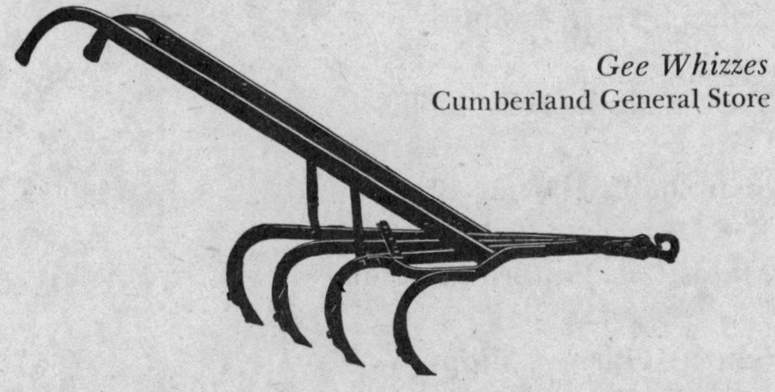

Gee Whizzes
Cumberland General Store

New oak plow handles and plow stocks are also offered. The stocks are of the type that will accept any kind or style of blade that takes a heel bolt.

Other pieces of horse-drawn equipment available through the Cumberland catalog are Ferguson single-row planters, Rex guano distributors, and Old Blue riding-type fertilizer distributors.

Guano Distributor
Cumberland General Store

Cumberland General Store
Rt. 3
Crossville, TN 38555

International Modern Machinery, Inc.

International Modern Machinery, Inc. manufactures this complete set of implements for the small farm where water buffalo, cows, or oxen are used instead of tractors. The set includes: plow, disc, harrow, row maker, cultivator, fertilizer and planter distributing unit, and a piece of equipment used for leveling and draining the field. This set of equipment will allow the world farmer to put in his crop within a six- to eight-day period rather than a forty-five-day period usually required when using his existing equipment and hand labor, leaving enough time for another crop.

International Modern Machinery, Inc.
P.O. Box 790
Beaumont, TX 77704

Manufacturers of Harness and Horse-Drawn Equipment

The Arthur Collar Shop
R.R. 2, Box 59
Arthur, IL 61911

Berlin Pad Shop
Eli B. Yoder
Rt. 5
Millersburg, OH 44654

Perry E. Bontrager
Highway 1
Kalona, IA 52247

Brubaker's Harness Shop
Wallenstein, Ont., Canada

The Country Harness Shop
Stillman Valley, IL 61084

Cumberland General Store
Rt. 3
Crossville, TN 38555

Lester Detweiler
Detweiler's Harness Shop
Rt. 1, Box 228
Hazleton, IA 50641

Diamond Tool & Horseshoe Co.
P.O. Box 6246
Duluth, MN 55806

George Edwards
Walpole, NH 03608

Art Eller
Eller's Harness Shop
Pierz, MN 56364

Freeport Harness Shop
Freeport, ME 04032

Roy Fritzges
St. Edward, NB 68660

Gavitt Mfg. Co.
230 7th St.
Macon, GA 31201

Glen-Bel Enterprises
Rt. 5, Box 390
Crossville, TN 38555

Hamburg Plow Works, Inc.
1021 S. 4th St.
Hamburg, PA 19526

Vaughn Huston
Box 155
Early, IA 50535

G.A. Kelly Plow Co.
Longview, TX 75601

King Plow Co.
887 W. Marietta, NW
Atlanta, GA 30318

Mast Harness Shop
Rt. 2, Box 169
Arthur, IL 61911

Frank McGrath
New Richland, MN 56072

Miller Harness Shop
Topeka, IN 46561

Paul I. Murphy
Box 307, 314 Park St.
Danvers, IL 61732

Raber's Harness Shop
R.D. 5
Millersburg, OH 44654

Aaron Ramer
25928 S.R. 119, Rt. 5
Goshe, IN 48526

Rocky Sabatino
Rockland, ME 04841

Bernard P. Samson
956 S. W. 12th St.
Forest Lake, MN 55025

Schrock Harness Shop
Rt. 1
West Union, OH 45693

Shanahan's Harness Shop
R.R. 2
Maidstone, Ontario, Canada

Smith's Harness Shop
P.O. Box 43
Shawville, Quebec, Canada

Daniel R. Stoltzfus
1902 Pioneer Rd.
Lancaster, PA 17602
Hickory single & double trees

Wagner Supply Co., Inc.
6—1st St. NW
Hampton, IA 50441

The Wagon Master
Rt. 1, Box 446
O'Fallon, MO 63366

Windy Hill Farm & Harness Shop
85354 Doane Rd.
Eugene, OR 97402

Wuis Leather Shop
2952 30th St.
Allegan, MI 49010

The Yankee Peddler
10318 Sagamore Rd.
Leawood, KS 66206

Cornelius M. Yoder
Rt. 2
Topeka, IN 46571

NORTH AMERICAN SOURCES OF RELATED EQUIPMENT

Wagonmakers and Wheelwrights

Cumberland General Store
Rt. 3
Crossville, TN 38555

Robert Faller
Whalan, MN 55986

Glen-Bel Enterprises
Rt. 5, Box 390
Crossville, TN 38555

Hoosier Buggy Shop
Rt. 2
Topeka, IN 46561

Southwest Wagon & Wheel Works
Box 738
Patagonia, AZ 85624

Blacksmith and Farrier Equipment

Buffalo Forges
465 Broadway
Buffalo, NY 14204

Champion Farrier Tools
Champion Blower & Forge, Inc.
100 W. Central Ave.
Roselle, IL 60172

Cumberland General Store
Rt. 3
Crossville, TN 38555

Diamond Farrier Tools & Horseshoes
Box 6246
Duluth, MN 55806

Enderes Tool Co.
P.O. Box 691
Albert Lea, MN 56007
Blacksmith's tongs

Fisher and Norris
301 Monmouth
Trenton, NJ 08609
Anvils

Glen-Bel Enterprises
Rt. 5, Box 390
Crossville, TN 38555

Heller Tool
Heller Drive
Newcomerstown, OH 43832
Farrier's knives and pincers

Milwaukee Tool & Equipment Co.
2775 S. 29th St.
Milwaukee, WI 53215
Anvils

P.F. Peddinghaus, Inc.
261 First St.
Palisades Park, NJ 07650
Anvils

Draft Horse Publications *

Draft Horse Journal
Rt. 3
Waverly, IA 50677
$6/yr. (4 issues)

The Draft Horse Primer
Maurice Telleen
Rodale Press, Inc.
Emmaus, PA 18049
$10.95/386 pgs.
A guide to the care and use of workhorses and mules.

The Evener
Putney, VT 05346
$6/yr. (11 issues)

Small Farmer's Journal
Box 197
Junction City, OR 97448
$8.50/yr. (4 issues)

Workshops

Draft Horse Workshop
Clarksburg, MA 01247

Hillcraft School of Horseshoeing
10890 Deer Creek Canyon Rd.
Littleton, CO 80120

Office of Continuing Education
North Adams State College
North Adams, MA 01247

* Subscription prices quoted for 1977.

INTERNATIONAL SOURCES OF ANIMAL-DRAWN EQUIPMENT

Ridgers

Kapas (Emcot) Ridger

The beam, moldboards, and handles of this ridging plow are made from steel. The moldboards can be fitted with extension pieces to increase the working width. Weight: 44 kilograms.

Cossul & Co. Pvt., Ltd.
Industrial Area, Fazalgunj
Kanpur, India

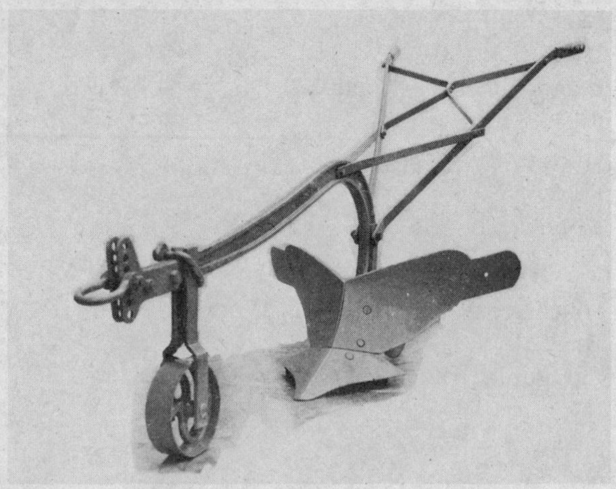

The Cossul Emcot Ridger Cossul & Co.

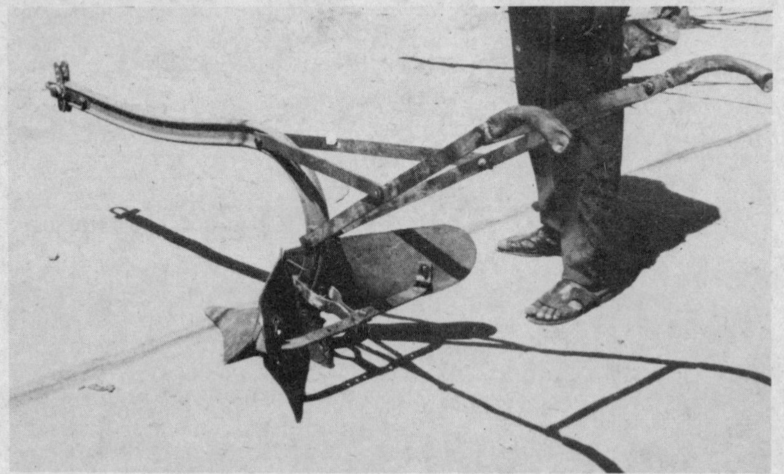

An Emcot Ridger Plow made by blacksmith Malun Ibrahim Musa of Funtua, Nigeria.

Emcot S30B Ridger

This all-metal ridging plow is fitted with moldboards which are adjustable for widths of 63 to 100 centimeters or, if the moldboard tailpieces are removed, widths of 51 to 74 centimeters.

The body is designed to form a wide-based, rounded-top ridge. The implement is generally pulled by two oxen. Weight: 49 kilograms.

John Holt, Agricultural Engineers, Ltd.
P.O. Box 352
Zaria, Nigeria

ITDG Plans for IDC Emcot Weeding Attachment

The weeding attachment designed at the Industrial Development Centre in Zaria for use with the Emcot ridger and one or two oxen consists of a frame which is attached to the Emcot beam and carries two weeding tines, set in front of the Emcot moldboards. The tool standards can be adjusted for height and width according to the row spacing. The weeding knives run close to the plants and dig deep enough to cut down the sides of the ridges. The sides of the ridges are remade by the ridger body following behind. Modifications to the frame were made to simplify manufacture without affecting the functioning of the attachment. Four examples of the modified attachment were commissioned from a local blacksmith and tested by Daudawa Settlement farmers during 1973. The weeding performance was good where the farmers had made uniformly spaced, parallel ridges.

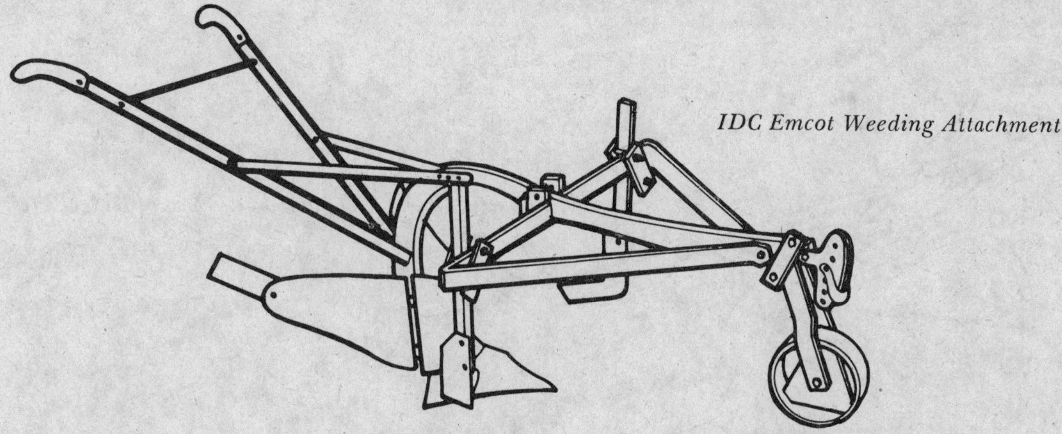

IDC Emcot Weeding Attachment

The Emcot ridger with weeding attachment was easy to control if the Emcot depth wheel was used, but Daudawa farmers do not normally use the wheel and were adamant in their refusal to use it during the trials. Without the wheel, the front of the Emcot beam tended to swing from side to side and the weeding tines swung with it, causing crop damage. This damage was reduced in a modification where the tines were set further back on the implement, but this was still not as satisfactory as using the wheel.

ITDG Report on the Dahomey Emcot Weeding Attachment

A very cheap and simple attachment to the moldboards of a ridging plow, designed and used with success for weeding in the northwest area of Dahomey, was constructed and tested. It was found to function well only in the sandiest fields in the Daudawa area. For the 1973 season, three pairs of Emcot moldboards with these weeding attachments were commissioned from a local blacksmith and sent for testing to Kafin Soli, an agricultural station 150 kilometers north of Daudawa. It was reported that the attachments worked well and seemed to be suitable for that soil type, which is sandier than that of Daudawa and similar to that of the northwest of Dahomey.

Close-up view of Dahomey moldboard extensions on an Emcot Ridger Plow.

Plans For Ox-Drawn Tie-Ridger/Weeder Implement (Attachment to Emcot Ridging Plow)

This attachment was developed by the International Development Center in Zaria, Nigeria to allow ridged row crops to be weeded by animal power rather than by hand. The plow, with weeding attachment, can be pulled by one or two oxen. Tool standards can be adjusted for height, and also for width according to the row spacing. The weeding knives should be run close to the plants without damaging the roots, and should dig deep enough to cut down the sides of the ridges. The ridges are re-formed by the ridger body following behind.

Adjustable-Width V-Drag Ditcher/Bund Former Plans

This implement, developed by the United States Department of Agriculture, can be used for making irrigation ditches, and also for con-

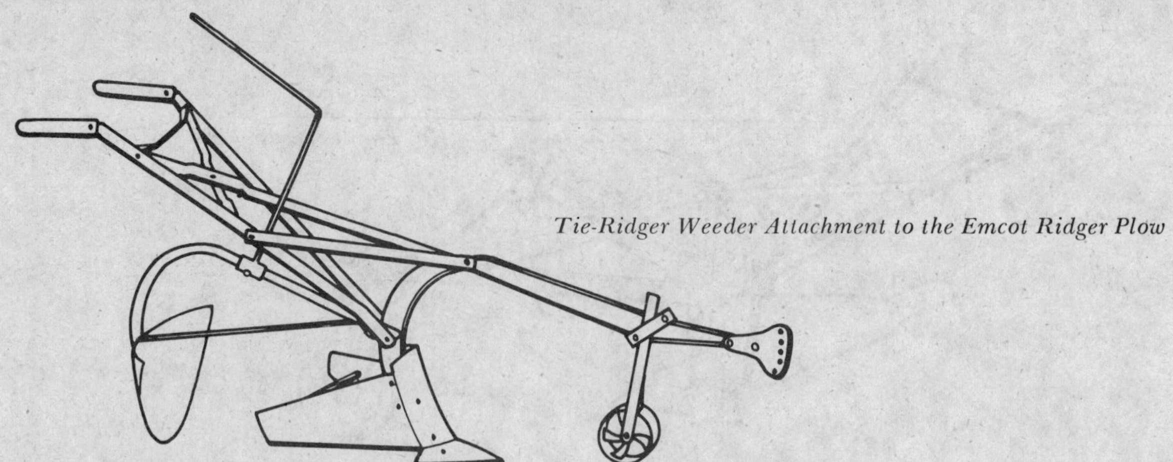

Tie-Ridger Weeder Attachment to the Emcot Ridger Plow

struction of low-height contour bunds for border irrigation. When making earth ditches, a furrow is first opened with a plow along the line of the ditch. The V-drag is then used with the runner board riding in the furrow bottom, the crowder board deflecting the soil sideways. When using the V-drag to construct contour bunds for irrigation, a plow is run down and back twice, throwing the soil into the border line. The implement is then run down the line, the crowder board pushing the soil into a ridge.

Sled-Type Corrugator/Irrigation-Furrow Former Plans

Designed by the United States Department of Agriculture, this implement can be used to make small furrows or corrugations for distributing water over a field. This implement can be used after the field has been broadcast seeded or before row-crop planting. The design can be modified to suit animal draft or tractor hitching as required.

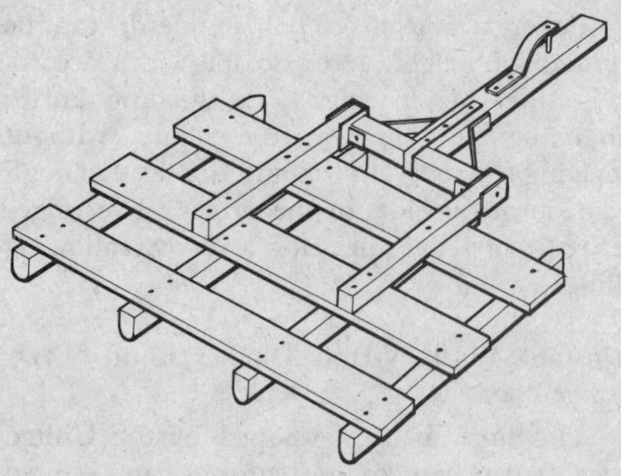

Sled-Type Corrugator/Irrigation-Furrow Former

All the above plans are available from:
Intermediate Technology Publications, Ltd.*
9 King St.
London WC2E 8HN, England

Bund Former

This is a simple labor-saving implement for forming bunds or ridges in the preparation of a field for irrigation. It is also used in dry farming areas to preserve moisture. On deep slopes bunds are made across to prevent washout during heavy rains. The main parts are a pair of collecting

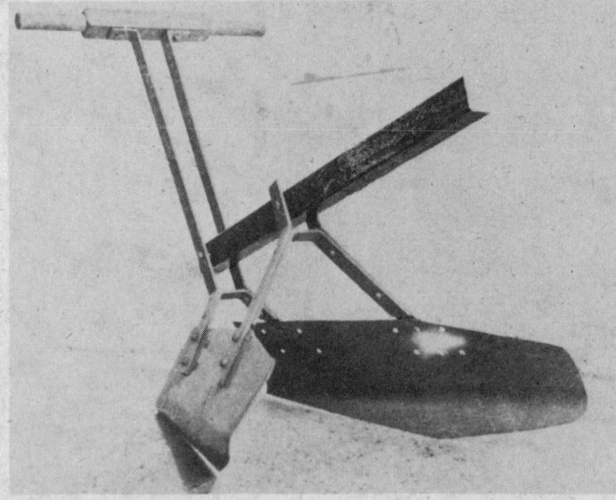

Cossul Bund Former
Cossul & Co.

* All Intermediate Technology publications can be ordered from International Scholarly Book Services, Inc., Box 555, Forest Grove, OR 97116

moldboards of steel. They are so fitted so as to collect soil and throw it on the center to make a bund. Size of bund and soil-collecting capacity can be increased or decreased by adjusting the moldboards.

Cossul & Co. Pvt., Ltd.
Industrial Area, Fazalgunj
Kanpur, India

Safim High-Wing Ridger

Wings adjustable from 400 to 760 millimeters width. Weight: 43.6 kilograms.

Massey Ferguson (South Africa), Ltd.
P.O. Box 677, Steel Road
Vereeniging 1930, South Africa

Vijay Ridger

A medium-size ridger designed especially for use in sugar cane. Wings are adjustable for different ridge sizes. Pulled by two pairs of bullocks, it can work at depths of 22 to 25 centimeters and make ridges at 60 to 90 centimeters spacing.

New Vijay Industries, Ltd.
Vishrambag, Sangli 416 415
Maharashtra, India

Ox-Drawn Ridger

Ubungo Farm Implements
P.O. Box 2669
Dar-Es-Salaam, Tanzania

The Vijay Ridger

An ox-drawn, one-row ridger/furrower

Delta (Bihar Type) Ridger

This is a long-beam ridging plow fitted with adjustable width moldboards. Weight: 40 kilograms.

Cossul & Co. Pvt., Ltd.
Industrial Area, Fazalgunj
Kanpur, India

Ridger Plow

Animal-drawn steel plow with wooden beam. Width of cut is 100 millimeters, depth of cut is 225 millimeters, draft 50 to 65 kilograms.

Rajasthan State Agro Industries Corp., Ltd.
Virat Bhawan, C-Scheme
Jaipur 302 006, Rajasthan, India

Ridger Plows

These ridgers are available with a long wooden beam or with a short steel beam and depth wheel. The moldboards are adjustable on both models.

Danishmand & Co.
Karkhana Bazar
Lyallpur, Pakistan

Care and Subhash Plows

These are general purpose, long-beam moldboard plows. They feature extra high clearance under the beam for work in weed-infested fields. The positions of the beam and handles relative to the plow body can be easily adjusted. Weight: 10.5 to 14.5 kilograms according to model.

Cossul & Co. Pvt., Ltd.
Industrial Area, Fazalgunj
Kanpur, India

Balwant Plow

A common type of Indian plow, made of wood with iron wearing parts. Pulled by a pair of small bullocks, it works to a depth of 15 to 20 centimeters and width of 22 to 25 centimeters. Weight: 42 kilograms.

New Vijay Industries, Ltd.
Vishrambag, Sangli 416 415
Maharashtra, India

Chota Plow

This plow has a long wooden beam and a steel moldboard. Pulled by one pair of small bullocks, it makes a furrow 8 to 10 centimeters deep and 10 to 15 centimeters wide. Weight: 18 kilograms.

New Vijay Industries, Ltd.
Vishrambag, Sangli 416 415
Maharashtra, India

Rajasthan Plows

Animal-drawn, left hand, steel moldboard plows with wooden beams. There are two models, No. 1 for medium and heavy soils, No. 3 for light soils.

	No. 1	No. 3
Width of cut	175 mm	150 mm
Depth of cut	75-125 mm	75-125 mm
Draft	70-80 kg	60-70 kg

Rajasthan State Agro Industries Corp., Ltd.
Virat Bhawan, C-Scheme
Jaipur 302 006, Rajasthan, India

Bose Super Plow

Single-furrow and two-furrow models available with either wooden or steel beams.

V.M. Thevar & Sons
Melur, Madurai Dist.
Tamil Nadu, India

Meston and Danish Plows

These are long-beam plows with inverting-type moldboards which can work to a depth of 150 millimeters and a width of 200 millimeters.

Danishmand & Co.
Karkhana Bazar
Lyallpur, Pakistan

Shabash and Praja Plows

These long-beam inverting-type moldboard plows are designed to be pulled by two bullocks. They plow furrows approximately 150 millimeters wide and 100 to 150 millimeters deep.

Sharda Engineering Works
105/661 D, Fahimabad
Kanpur 208 005, India

Vijaya (Victory) Plow

This is a strong, all-steel plow. A head wheel is provided to control the depth. It cuts a furrow 225 millimeters (9 inches) wide and 100 to 150 millimeters (4 to 6 inches) deep. Weight: 38 kilograms. Area covered: 0.3 to 0.4 hectares/day.

Cossul & Co. Pvt., Ltd.
Industrial Area, Fazalgunj
Kanpur, India

Dandekar Steel Plow

Moldboard plow with steel beam and forged steel share. It furrows 12 to 20 centimeters in width and 6 to 18 centimeters deep. Weight: 35 kilograms.

Dandekar Brothers (Engineers and Founders)
Sandli
Maharashtra, India

Safim Plows

These plows are available in VS models for general purpose plowing or IS models with higher clearance for use in trashy conditions.

Model	Cut	Weight
VS 8	200 mm (8″)	39.5 kg (87 lb.)
VS 10	250 mm (10″)	40.0 kg (88 lb.)
VS 12	300 mm (12″)	45.5 kg (100 lb.)
IS 12	300 mm (12″)	49.5 kg (109 lb.)

Massey Ferguson (South Africa), Ltd.
Steel Road, P.O. Box 677
Vereeniging 1930, South Africa

Walking Plow

Designed for light and medium soils. Comes in three sizes ranging from 24 kilograms to 31 kilograms in weight.

Agromet-Unia
Foreign Trade Enterprise
00-950 Przemyslowa 26
Warsaw, Poland

Walking Plow with Support Wheel

This horse-drawn walking plow is intended for use in light- and medium-cohesive soils in small fields and gardens. They are also recommended for plowing wedges and other intricate field shapes. Weight: 37 kilograms.

Agromet-Unia
Foreign Trade Enterprise
00-950 Przemyslowa 26
Warsaw, Poland

Swing Plow—Model V.B.

This moldboard plow is available with a front wheel or forefoot and with or without coulter, skimmer, or spare share. It comes in three sizes.

W. Hertecant
9200 Kwatrecht
Wetteran, Belgium

Two-Bottom Plows

Horse-drawn, double-furrow frame plows designed for light and medium soils. Frame is supported by two wheels. Weight: 96 kilograms.

Agromet-Unia
Foreign Trade Enterprise
00-950 Przemyslowa 26
Warsaw, Poland

Fixed Moldboard Plow

Pulled by one pair of bullocks, it plows a furrow 8 to 20 centimeters deep and 12 to 22 centimeters wide. Weight: 36 kilograms.

New Vijay Industries, Ltd.
Vishrambag, Sangli 416 415
Maharashtra, India

At 35 Plow

This plow consists of a one-piece forged beam, soil-engaging parts of heat-treated steel, steel handles, depth control wheel, and draft chain. Weight: 23.3 kilograms.

Sociète Des Forges Tropicals
B.P. 706
Douala, Cameroun

Moldboard Plow

Ubungo Farm Implements
P.O. Box 2669
Dar Es Salaam, Tanzania

Raja and Victory Plows

These are short-beamed, chain-drawn plows and can be supplied with wooden frame (Raja) or all steel construction (Victory).

Danishmand & Co.
Karkhana Bazar
Lyallpur, Pakistan

CF 000 P Plow

This ox plow has steel wearing parts. Working width is 25 centimeters; maximum working depth is 20 centimeters. Weight: 38 kilograms.

Siscoma
BP 3214
Dakar, Senegal

Punjab Plow

This is a heavy, short-beam plow designed to be pulled by two bullocks. It is capable of plowing a furrow 125 to 150 millimeters deep and 150 to 20 millimeters wide.

Sharda Engineering Works
105/661 D, Fahimabad
Kanpur 208 005, India

Turnwrest Plow

This ox-drawn turnwrest plow was specially developed for use across hilly slopes and for horticultural work where a level seedbed is important. It is normally fitted with two handles and a wheel, and is manufactured in two weights, 33 kilograms (73 pounds) and 40 kilograms (90 pounds).

The body is pivoted under the plow beam and locked in position by a lever.

ETS. A. Bourguignon
B.P. 17
26300 Bourg de Peage
Drome, France

Reversible Plows

Animal Draft Reversible Plow

Available with plain or ribbed moldboard and wooden or steel pipe frame construction.

CeCoCo
P.O. Box 8, Ibaraki City
Osaka Pref. 567, Japan

Turnwrest Plow

The turnwrest plows are capable of turning furrows either to the right or left. At the end of the furrow the plow bottom can be reversed by releasing the hook at the back of the breast, swinging the body under the frame into corresponding position on the opposite side, and

Hertecant Reversible Plow LEIE-9
Willem Hertecant

replacing the hook. The plow is supplied with a double steel handle, steel beam, cast breasts and self-sharpening cast-chilled shares. A headwheel is provided to give required depth. Available in different sizes from 150 to 250 millimeters. Weight: 43.0 kilograms.

Hertecant Plow—LEIE-9 Model

Characteristics of this model include a fixed beam and double handle; reversible elements on the rear; three easy adjustments for traction, depth, and angle correction; all wearing parts are interchangeable and skimmers are available as options.

Cossul & Co. Pvt., Ltd.
Industrial Area, Fazalgunj
Kanpur, India

W. Hertecant
9200 Kwatrecht—Wetteren
Belgium

Turnwrest Plows

A range of turnwrest or reversible plows is available from this company.

Cossul Turnwrest Plow Cossul & Co.

New Vijay Industries, Ltd.
Vishrambag, Sangli 416 415
Maharashtra, India

PLOW	POWER REQUIRED	WORKING DEPTH	WORKING WIDTH	WEIGHT
No. 1 (ill.)	4-5 pairs bullocks	20-25 cm	30-35 cm	96 kg
No. 2	3-4 pairs bullocks	15-20 cm	30-35 cm	86 kg
No. 3	1-2 pairs bullocks	13-15 cm	23-25 cm	55 kg
Vasant	1 pair bullocks	10-13 cm	15-18 cm	46 kg
Berar	1 pair bullocks	15-18 cm	15-20 cm	30 kg

Toolbars

Ox Plow

A two-handled plow fitted with wheel, hake adjustment, and knife coulter. It is made in four sizes, weighing from 51 to 113 pounds (23 to 50 kilograms). Attachments are available for ridging, sweep cultivation, and tined cultivation.

ETS. Techine
82400 Valence d'Agen
France

ETS. Techine Ox Plow

Tom and BM Plows

Three animal-drawn, single furrow, mold-board plows can be supplied, weighing 14, 22, or

23 kilograms. Single or double steering handles are available. Ridging and sweep tine cultivation attachments are available for these plows.

ETS. A. Bourguignon
B.P. 17
26300 Bourg-de-Peage
Drome, France

THE MOCHUDI TOOLBAR, THE MAKGONATSOTLHE

Editor's note: This report from the Agricultural Information Service in Botswana, Africa, describes a localized need and the development of an implement to satisfy it.

For a number of years the Mochudi Farmers Brigade has been working to develop and perfect a multipurpose farming implement suited to local conditions. The need for improved implements arises because those which are currently available for draft animals are not suited to the semiarid conditions of Botswana and are generally of poor design.

Farmers are often hindered when their equipment breaks down and they are unable to find a mechanic capable of making repairs. Some have tried planters but, due to poor construction, failed to get satisfactory results and concluded that planters are useless. Another common problem is an insufficient number of fit draft animals to perform operations in a reasonable amount of time.

Because of these and other constraints, many farmers continue with the traditional broadcast-plow method of cropping. Using this method, only fair yields are obtained even in years of above-average rainfall, and in poorer years, a total crop failure may result.

A farmer can only be successful in growing good crops if his equipment can cope with the work in the time available. It is essential to reduce, if not eliminate, the frequency of total crop failure and at the same time produce good crops in most years. In order to do this in a semiarid climate with erratic rainfall distribution, principles of conservation tillage must be applied.

By combining features borrowed from a number of existing implements and ideas gained from consultation with tillage experts from a number of universities in North America, the design of the present Mochudi Toolbar came about. When the implement was introduced to the public in April, 1973, it was given the local name, the *Makgonatsotlhe,* meaning "the machine which can do everything." The name is considered fitting, since almost any type of cultivation tool can be attached to it, and it can also be used for carting or transporting drums of water. By removing some of the components from the toolbar, a walking model can be obtained which allows inter-row cultivation when crops are taller.

The heavy angle iron frame of the Mochudi Toolbar is supported on two pneumatic tires which allow the frame to be lowered or raised mechanically for depth gauge control by pulling back on a lift handle. The frame will support a planter unit, fertilizer applicator, disc hiller/furrowers, sweeps for stubble mulching, and a transport cart.

Further information is available from:

Mochudi Farmers Brigade
Box 208, Mochudi
Republic of Botswana, Africa

Donkey Plow

This very simple, lightweight plow weighs 29 pounds (13 kilograms). It can be fitted with either a moldboard or a ridging body.

ETS. Techine
82400 Valence D'Agen
France

OD2 Ridger/Plow

This tool frame can accept either of two types of ridging body, or an adjustable moldboard plow. The frame is of lightweight but heavy-gauge rectangular section steel tube, and is all-welded. The handles are adjustable for height, and on the lister-type ridger the pitch of the body is also adjustable. Either a wheel

OD2 Ridger/Plow The Goodearth Group

or a skid is used for depth control. The slade and the steering fin are individually adjustable on all attachments.

Project Equipment, Ltd.
Industrial Estate, Rednal Airfield
West Felton, Oswestry
Salop SY11 4HS, U.K.

ST21 Plow/Ridger

The frame of this implement can be fitted with a moldboard plow body or with an adjustable-width ridging body.

Gebruder Eberhardt
D79 Ulm, Donau
B.P. 204, Germany

Three-in-One Implement

The frame of this implement is of steel construction. Attachments are supplied for moldboard plowing (three sizes are available), ridging, and hoeing. Two handles and a depth wheel are provided. The angle between the soil-engaging parts and the wooden beam can be easily adjusted by a screw mechanism.

The Goodearth Group
16 Asaf Ali Rd.
New Delhi 1, India

E.B.R.A. Omniculteur

This toolbar consists of a backbone-type frame and handles. Clamps allow fitting of a depth wheel, moldboard plow, and a ridging body, wide-sweep tine. Transverse frame extensions can be fitted to carry up to five rigid or spring-type cultivator tines.

E.B.R.A.
28 rue de Maine, B.P. 84
49009 Angers, France

Arara Multicultivator

This is a backbone frame toolbar with depth wheel and handles. The following attachments can be fitted by means of two bolts: moldboard plow; ridging plow; groundnut lifter; spring-tine hoe with three or five tines.

Siscoma
BP 3214
Dakar, Senegal

Unibar

This lightweight, multipurpose, animal-drawn implement was designed for use in the more arid areas of the tropics. It is made from square-section bar and square-section hollow tubing and is fitted with two skids for support. The tool can be used for plowing, ridging, ridge splitting, weeding, hoeing, rigid- and spring-tine cultivating, rotary cultivating, planting, row crop

Unibar with seeder attachments
The Goodearth Group

Unibar with two ridging plows
The Goodearth Group

lifting, and carting. Originally designed for farming on the ridge, it can be used as a single-row tool for inter-row cultivation up to a late stage in the growth of taller varieties of tropical crops.

Project Equipment, Ltd.
Industrial Estate, Rednal Airfield
West Felton, Oswestry
Salop SY11 4HS, U.K.

Heavy-Duty Unibar

This is a multipurpose, animal-drawn implement designed for heavier soils where extra weight is essential to maintain penetration. It can handle the full range of standard Unibar attachments apart from the transport cart and, in addition, a 20-centimeter-cut general purpose plow, a lister-type ridger, a two-furrow semi-digger plow, and a 1.22-meter-wide 17-tine harrow. Up to four units of a new design of roller/seeder can be fitted behind the harrow so that crops such as wheat, rice, and soy beans can be

Heavy-duty Unibar with a groundnut lifter
The Goodearth Group

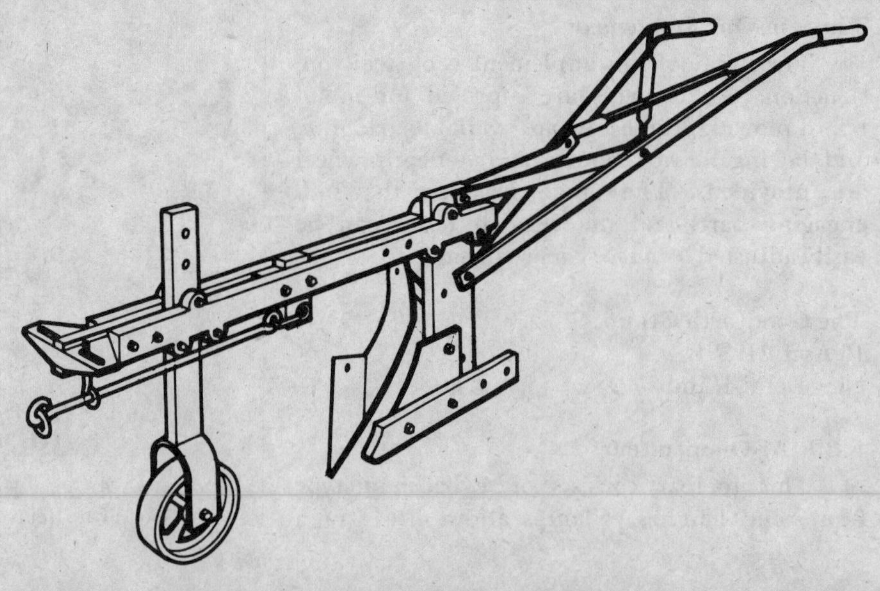

Chitedze Ridgemaster toolbar

planted in closely spaced rows. On this implement, the hitch and handles are fully adjustable.

Wide or narrow detachable V-pieces are used to carry the side stalks, to which various tools can be left assembled and merely bolted up to the frame when required. For plowing and ridging, the frame reverts to a width no greater than that of a conventional single-purpose plow or ridger.

Project Equipment, Ltd.
Industrial Estate, Rednal Airfield
West Felton, Oswestry
Salop SY11 4HS, U.K.

Chitedze Ridgemaster Toolbar Plans

This multipurpose tool bar is shown here and in plan views with a plow body attached, but a ridger or cultivator can also be fitted to the vertical beam. The unique design feature of this toolbar is that it combines lightness with adequate structural strength, the main parts being fabricated from rectangular, hollow-section (R.H.S.), mild steel.

Kabanyolo Ox Tool Frame Plans

This multipurpose tool frame is shown here and in plan views with a plow stem attached. When fitted with the Y-frame, it can be used as an adjustable-width, three-tine cultivator/weeder. The tool frame is fabricated from flat steel, angle iron, and round bar. A simple skid is used instead of a depth wheel.

Prototype Multipurpose Ox-Drawn Tool Plans

Designed specifically for the farmer growing crops on ridges, the share on this multipurpose tool is adjustable to four settings: approximately 40, 55, 70 and 85 degrees. On the comparatively heavy soils at Samaru, Nigeria, the share was used for ridging, splitting ridges, cross-tying, weeding, and breaking capped soils in the fur-

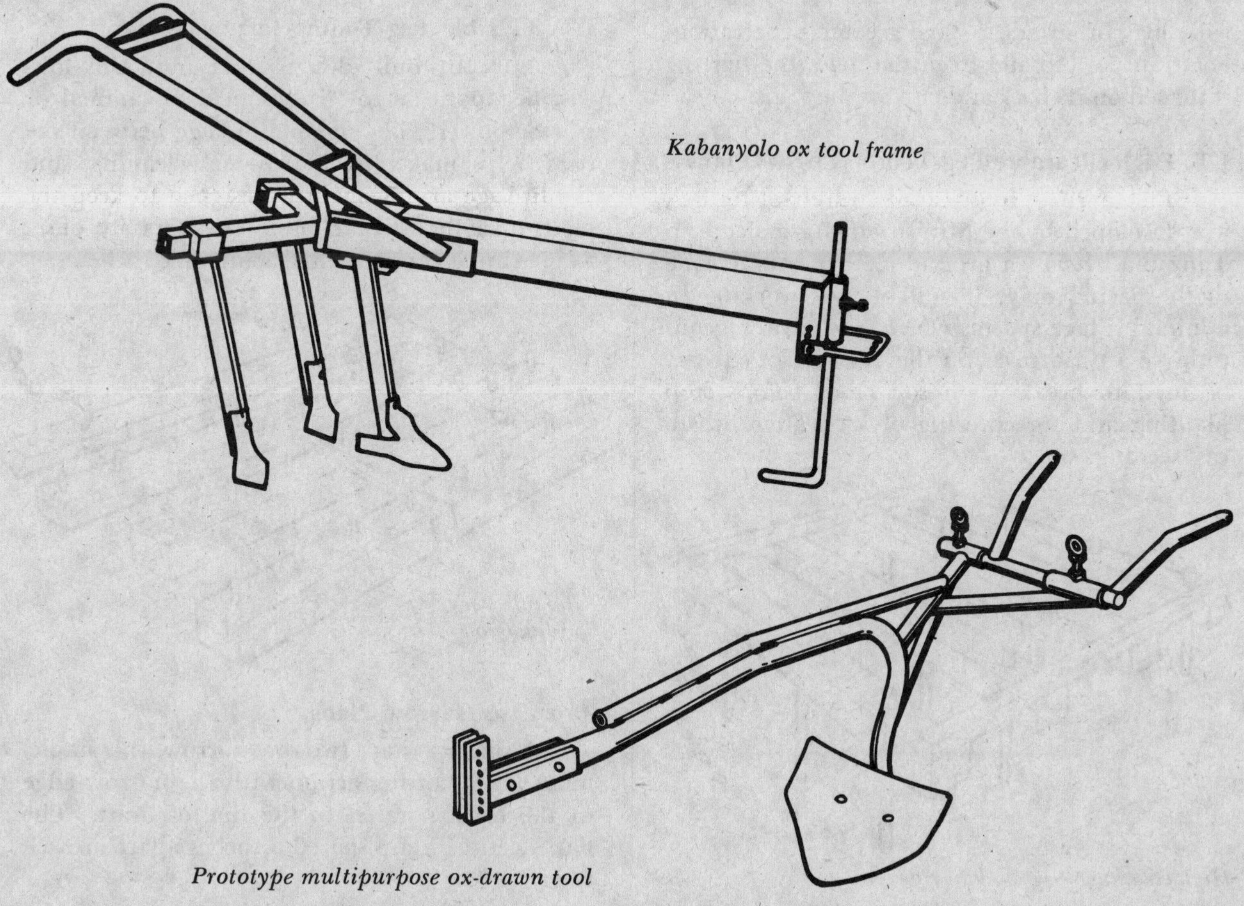

Kabanyolo ox tool frame

Prototype multipurpose ox-drawn tool

rows. The tool frame was designed with an offset beam to avoid blockage when lifting groundnuts. Though only a prototype, the design shows a considerable amount of ingenuity.

Above plans available from:
Intermediate Technology Publications, Ltd.
9 King St.
London WC2E 8HN, England

Harrows

I.T. Triangular Spike-Tooth Harrow Plans

Originally designed in India, the teeth of this harrow can be made of hardwood or mild steel. Tooth spacing can be varied to suit soil conditions by removing teeth for wider spacing or by drilling holes and inserting teeth for closer spacing. The harrow can be used for preparing a seedbed, after plowing, and for covering seed after broadcasting. The harrow can be loaded with logs or stones to give greater penetration. For transport to and from the field, the harrow is turned on its back and run on the skids.

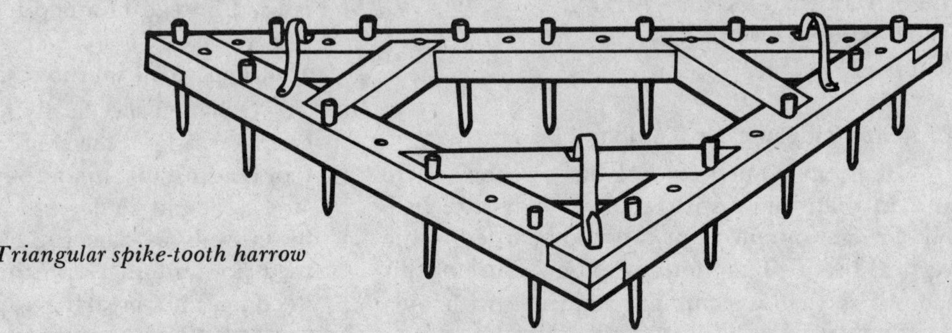

Triangular spike-tooth harrow

I.T. High-Clearance Peg-Tooth Harrow Plans

This harrow, constructed entirely of timber, was developed by the Ministry of Agriculture in Tanzania. Its high ground clearance and wide tooth spacing make it suitable for working in minimal tillage systems where it is advantageous to leave a trash cover on the soil surface. It can be used to break down soil clods before crop planting and for covering of seed after broadcast seeding.

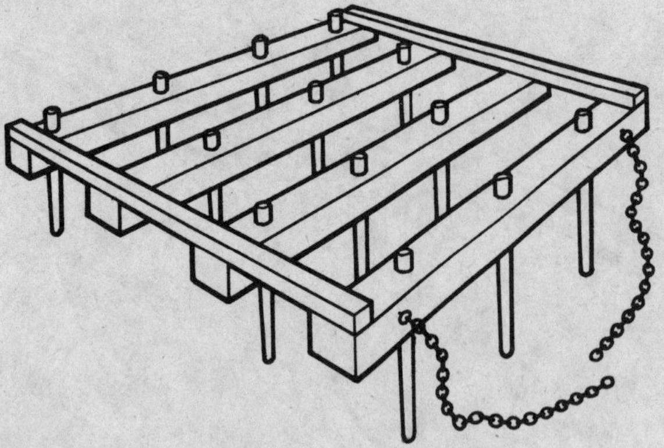

High-clearance peg-tooth harrow

I.T. Flexible Peg-Tooth Harrow Plans

A locally built design from Iran, this low-cost peg-tooth harrow is designed for animal or tractor power. The flexible linkage between the bars helps make the harrow self-cleaning, and the linkage arrangement is designed to keep the teeth upright while in use. The bars are offset to give an average tooth spacing of 2 inches.

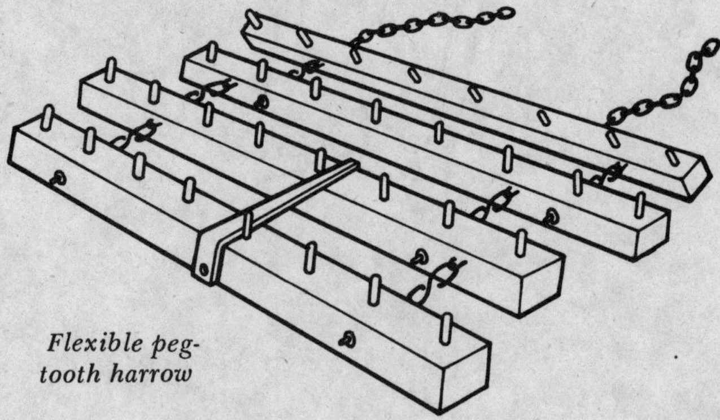

Flexible peg-tooth harrow

Japanese Harrow Plans

A simple, rigid, two-row harrow, this implement has a cutting action with the narrow edge of the teeth parallel to the line of draft. The flat, steel teeth are spaced 6 inches apart in each row.

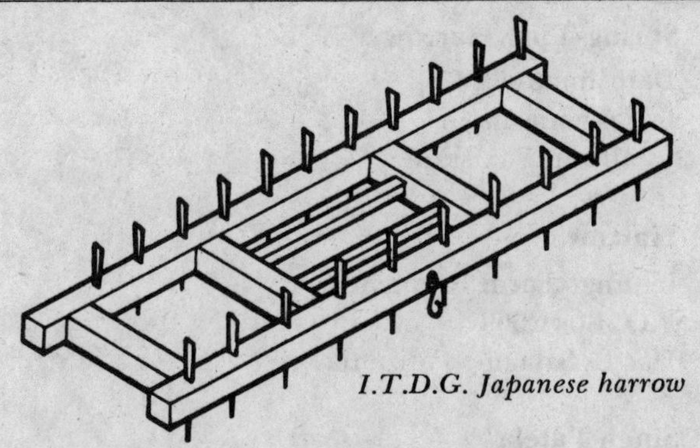

I.T.D.G. Japanese harrow

Above plans available from:
Intermediate Technology Publications, Ltd.
9 King St.
London WC2E 8HN, England

Allied Disc Harrow

This is a versatile implement for crust breaking and seedbed preparation. Six-disc and eight-disc models are available. The angles of the discs are adjusted by a hand lever and a seat is provided for the operator. The implement can also be used as a threshing roller. Working width: .80 meter. Working depth: 50 to 110 millimeters. Draft: 40 to 50 kilograms.

Allied Trading Co.
Railway Rd., Ambala City 134 002
Haryana, India

Cossul Disc Harrow

This is a versatile implement suitable for breaking clods to prepare a seedbed and also for puddling rice fields. It can also be used as a threshing roller. The discs are provided with scrapers. Weight: 6-disc model, 38 kilograms; 8-disc model, 92 kilograms.

Cossul & Co. Pvt., Ltd.
Industrial Area, Fazalgunj
Kanpur, India

Disc Harrow

Heavy-type, all-steel with six discs of 38-centimeters diameter. Adjustable. Fitted with seat.

Rajasthan State Agro Industries Corp., Ltd.
Virat Bhawan, C-Scheme
Jaipur 302 006, Rajasthan, India

Cossul Six-Disc Janta Disc Harrow
Cossul & Co.

SAECO Bullock-Drawn Disc Harrows

Fitted with six discs, each 41 centimeters in diameter, and a central cultivator tine. The angle of the discs is adjustable. This harrow comes complete with transport wheels. Weight: 104 kilograms.

Standard Agricultural Engineering Co.
824/825 Industrial Area B
Ludhiana A-141 003
Punjab, India

Peg-Tooth Harrow

This harrow is suitable for preparing seedbeds, for crust breaking or for covering seeds after sowing. The tooth angle can be adjusted by a lever. Skids are provided for easy transportation. Weight: 18-tooth size, 27 kilograms; 25-tooth size, 33 kilograms; 30-tooth size, 51 kilograms.

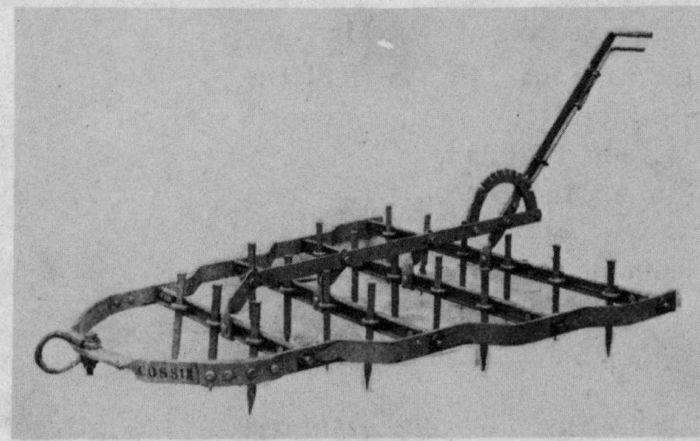

Cossul Peg-Tooth Harrow with 18 teeth
Cossul & Co.

Cossul Peg-Tooth Harrow with 30 teeth
Cossul & Co.

Cossul & Co. Pvt., Ltd.
Industrial Area, Fazalgunj
Kanpur, India

Disc Harrow Type PSP

This disc harrow is all metal and can be supplied with six to 12 discs with working widths of 2.5 to 7 feet (0.85 to 2.00 meters). In each case the angle of the discs can be adjusted, and the disc gangs are interchangeable so that discs can throw either inwards or outwards. The six- and eight-disc models can be increased to 8 and 20 discs respectively. Transport wheels and a central tine to work between the gangs can be supplied. A seat is supplied and scrapers are fitted to all discs. Weight varies from 327 to 463 pounds (147 to 208 kilograms).

ETS. Techine
82400 Valence D'Agen
France

Other Sources of Disc Harrows

International Mfg. Co. (REGD.)
Hospital Rd.
Jagraon, Ludhiana
Punjab, India

Kumaon Agri-Horticulture Store
P.O. Kashipur, Dist. Nainital
U.P., India

Mohinder & Co. Allied Industries
Kurali, Dist. Ropar
Punjab, India

Spring-Tine Harrow

Danishmand & Co.
Karakhana Bazar
Luallpur, Pakistan

Harrow

Ubungo Farm Implements
P.O. Box 2669
Dar Es Salaam, Tanzania

Singh Patela

This is a type of weeding harrow consisting of a 1.68-meter-wide wooden plank set in a steel frame and fitted with steel weeding hooks.

Rajasthan State Agro Industries Corp., Ltd.
Virat Bhawan, C-Scheme
Jaipur 302 006 Rajasthan, India

Soil Surgeon

This is an all-steel implement, 1.48 meter wide, with adjustable hooks which penetrate the soil to a depth of 100 millimeters and collect trash.

Rajasthan State Agro Industries Corp., Ltd.
Virat Bhawan, C-Scheme
Jaipur 302 006 Rajasthan, India

Spring-Tooth Harrow

This implement is suitable for tillage at depths to 150 millimeters (6 inches) and the action of the teeth loosens the soil. It is well suited to work in land which contains roots and stones. Depth of working is adjustable by a lever. Weight: 5-tine model, 40 kilograms; 7-tine model, 57 kilograms.

Cossul & Co. Pvt., Ltd.
Industrial Area, Fazalgunj
Kanpur, India

Fixed-Tooth Harrows

No. of Sections	Working Width	Weight
1	0.70 m	27.5 kg
2	1.40 m	56 kg
3	2.10 m	82 kg

ETS. Techine
82400 Valence D'Agen
France

Blade Harrow

All-steel construction with depth and blade angle adjustments. Available in 225 and 450 millimeter sizes.

Rajasthan State Agro Industries Corp., Ltd.
Virat Bhawan, C-Scheme
Jaipur 302 006 Rajasthan, India

Adjustable Harrows

The angle of the teeth is adjustable by means of a lever fitted to each harrow section.

ETS. Techine
82400 Valence D'Agen
France

Bar Harrow

All-steel or wooden-framed models are available.

Danishmand & Co.
Karkhana Bazar
Lyallpur, Pakistan

Harrows

Various patterns of chain and spike harrows are available.

Samuel Lewis & Co., Ltd.
Northfield Rd., Netherton, Dudley
Worcestershire DY2 9JD, U.K.

Animal-Drawn Harrows

Each section has 15 teeth arranged in five rows. The section weighs 19 kilograms and its working width is 70 centimeters. One or two sections can be used at a time.

ETS. A. Bourguignon
B.P. 17
26300 Bourg-de-Peage
Drome, France

Safim-Tined Harrows

Triangular harrow weight		19 kg (42 lb.)
Diamond harrow weight	2-section	64 kg (140 lb.)
Diamond harrow weight	3-section	97 kg (214 lb.)
Diamond harrow weight	4-section	131 kg (289 lb.)
Zig Zag harrow weight	3-section	118 kg (259 lb.)
Zig Zag harrow weight	4-section	157 kg (345 lb.)

Massey-Ferguson (South Africa), Ltd.
Steel Rd., P.O. Box 677
Vereeniging 1930, South Africa

Aitkenhead Flexible Harrows

Four types of tooth link are available. These harrows are suitable for preparing seedbeds, covering seeds and fertilizers with soil, spreading farmyard manure, and killing weeds in growing corn.

William Aitkenhead, Ltd.
Stamford Works, Lees, Oldham
Lancashire OL4 3DF, U.K.

Lister Big-Claw Harrows

These flexible chain harrows can be rolled up and easily handled by one man, the sections being of 1.22 meter width. Various link types are available for use on arable land and grassland.

R.A. Lister Agricultural, Ltd.
Dursley
Gloucestershire GL11 4 HS, U.K.

Cultivators

Safim Expandable Cultivators

Model S51 is adjustable from 24 inches (610 millimeters) to 42 inches (1,067 millimeters) wide. It is fitted with two reversible shares in front, two reversible moldboard hillers, a 10-inch (254 millimeter) sweep at the rear, and two spare shovels. Weight: 44 kilograms (97 pounds).

Also available: Safim Mahon 5-tine expandable cultivator equipped with four 3-inch (76 millimeter) reversible points, two hillers and one 10-inch (250 millimeter) sweep. Weight: 44.5 kilograms (98 pounds).

Massey-Ferguson (South Africa), Ltd.
Steel Rd., P.O. Box 677
Vereeniging 1930, South Africa

Ox-Drawn Cultivator

Ubungo Farm Implements
P.O. Box 2669
Dar Es Salaam, Tanzania

Adjustable Cultivator or Horse Hoe

The five-tine cultivator is useful for preparing seedbeds after plowing.

Danishmand & Co.
Karkhana Bazar
Lyallpur, Pakistan

Occidental Hoe

This is an all-steel, ox-drawn hoe weighing 17 kilograms. It is fitted with a main beam and furrow wheel. A variety of hoe blades or cultivator tines can be clamped to the beam.

Siscoma
BP 3214
Dakar, Senegal

PLOWS

Safim CS2 Cultivator

This is an easily handled, all-steel cultivator for use with small draft animals. Two adjustable shovels, 5½ inches (140 millimeters) and 7 inches (178 millimeters), are standard equipment. Weight: 31 kilograms (68 pounds).

Massey-Ferguson (South Africa), Ltd.
Steel Rd., P.O. Box 677
Vereeniging 1930, South Africa

Soil-Stirring Plow

Mohinder & Co. Allied Industries
Kurali, Dist. Ropar
Punjab, India

Lever Expansion Cultivator

This five-tine cultivator is constructed of steel and can be adjusted from 300 millimeters to 635 millimeters width. It is fitted with hardened steel tines and an adjustable depth wheel.

Sharda Engineering Works
105/661 D, Fahimabad
Kanpur 208 005, India

Adjustable Hoe

The frame of this implement, which takes five hoe blades or cultivator tines, can be adjusted for row widths of 0.40 to 0.70 meters. Depth of work is adjusted by a lever controlling the depth wheel. Width adjustment is made by a screw mechanism. Weight: 45 kilograms.

A simplified version with width adjustment by means of a clamp on the frame is also available.

ETS. Techine
82400 Valence D'Agen
France

Triphali

An all-steel three-row implement for intercultivation.

Rajasthan State Agro Industries Corp., Ltd.
Virat Bhawan, C-Scheme
Jaipur 302 006 Rajasthan, India

Akola Hoe

This is a long-beam, three-tined cultivator which can be adjusted from 275 to 375 millimeters width.

Sharda Engineering Works
105/661 D, Fahimabad
Kanpur 208 005, India

CeCoCo Animal-Drawn Cultivator

The working width of this cultivator can be easily adjusted and the blades remain parallel at all width settings. Weight: 21 kilograms.

CeCoCo
P.O. Box 8, Ibaraki City
Osaka Pref. 567, Japan

Cossul R.N. Cultivator

This is a three-tine cultivator, made of steel with long wooden beam and single handle. The shovels are made of high carbon steel and are reversible. The width can be adjusted very easily through holes provided in the frame. Depth can be adjusted by changing the height of the beam through holes provided for the purpose. Moldboard plow, ridger plow, and seeder/fertilizer attachment can be supplied as extras. Weight: 16.0 kilograms.

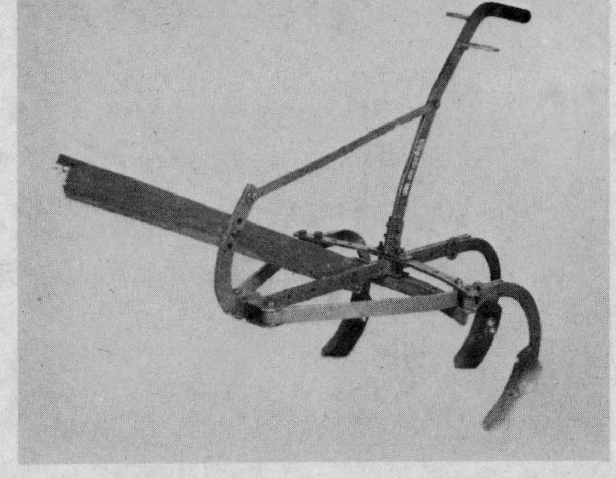

Cossul Bullock-Driven R.N. Cultivator
Cossul & Co.

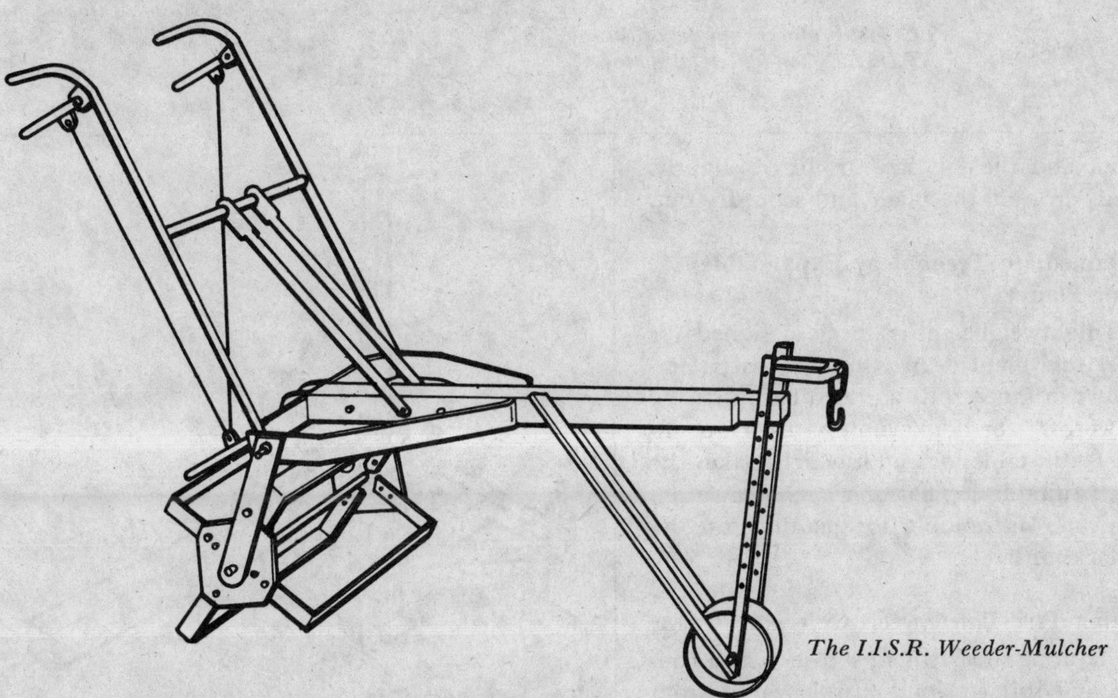

The I.I.S.R. Weeder-Mulcher

Cossul Lever Expansion Five-Tine Cultivator

This cultivator is designed for preparing seedbeds and for inter-row cultivation. The points are reversible. The width can be adjusted from 300 to 625 millimeters (12 to 25 inches) by means of a lever. Right- and left-hand moldboards and rear double-face shovel are available as extras for throwing soil against the roots of growing plants and for making shallow channels for irrigation. Weight: 35 kilograms. Both above units manufactured by:
Cossul & Co. Pvt., Ltd.
Industrial Area, Fazalgunj
Kanpur, India

The I.I.S.R. Weeder/Mulcher Plans
(Indian Institute of Sugarcane Research)

This animal-drawn, self-cleaning weeder is designed to destroy weeds, leave a mulch on the soil surface, and cover a lot of area per day. It can be used on most row crops with a spacing of 30 inches (75 centimeters) or more. The blade works at a depth of 2 inches (5 centimeters) below the surface. The weed roots are cut or

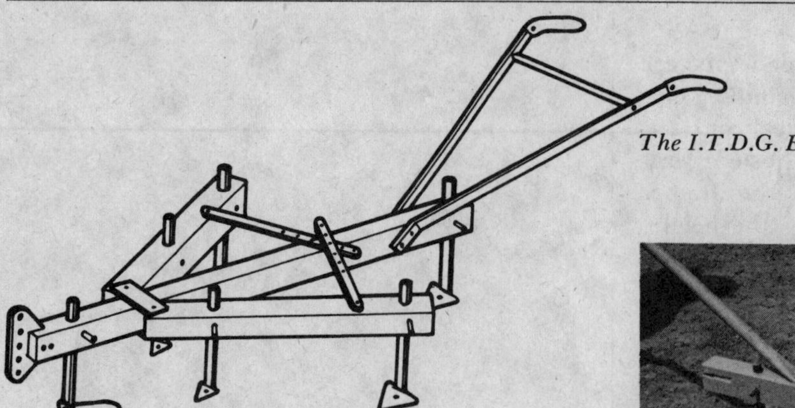

The I.T.D.G. Expandable Cultivator

The first prototype model of the I.T.D.G. Expandable Cultivator

pulled out and the soil layer is lifted slightly. The weeds drop off the blade and soon dry out.

The Intermediate Technology Expandable Cultivator Plans

This lightweight cultivator is designed for weeding crops planted in 70 to 90-centimeter-spaced rows in sandy soils and can be pulled by one or two oxen or donkeys. The tines are individually adjustable for depth which makes the implement suitable for flat or ridge cultivation. The cultivator is suitable for manufacture by village blacksmiths.

The Indian Five-Tine Sweep Cultivator Plans

Dry farming areas where soil moisture conservation and soil erosion control are essential will benefit from this implement. The tool standards are staggered to allow crop residue and cut weed growth to remain on the soil surface. This cultivator can be used for primary tillage, seedbed preparation, weed control, and inter-row cultivation. The rigid steel frame can be built with additional toolbars to permit greater trash clearance.

Above three plans available from:
Intermediate Technology Publications, Ltd.
9 King St.
London WC2E 8HN, England

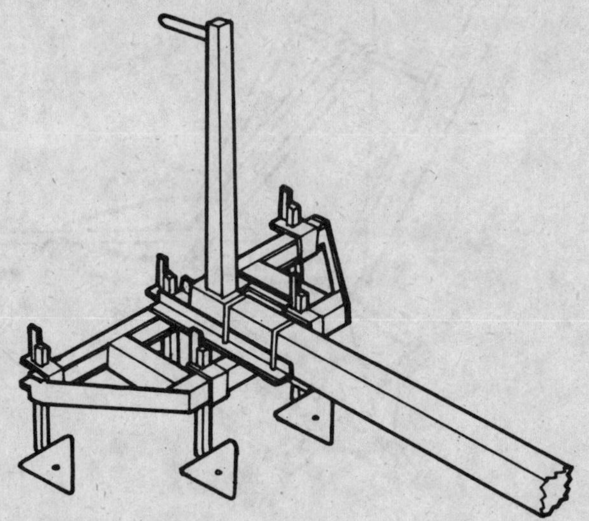

The Indian Five-Tine Sweep Cultivator

Manga Hoe

An adjustable-width cultivator available with 5 tines for donkey-draft or 7 tines for ox-draft. Extension bars are available to increase the width of the implement, in which form it can be used for row marking prior to planting.

S.A. Gard Pere et Fils
30500 Potelieres Par St. Amoroix (Gard)
France

Horse-Drawn Cultivator

Designed for spring cultivation following winter plowing, for cultivation of stubble, uprooting of quackgrass. Cultivating depth is controlled by a hand lever. Weight: 107 kilograms.

Agromet-Unia
Foreign Trade Enterprise
00-950 Przemyslowa 26
Warsaw, Poland

Multi-Purpose Potato Cultivator

Specially designed for potato cultivation, this combination three-purpose tool is supplied separately or combined with ridging, hoeing, and digging tools. The potato digger has a set of two guide wheels, the ridger, and an adjustable depth skid.

W. Hertecant
9200 Kwatrecht
Wetteren, Belgium

Miscellaneous Animal-Drawn Tools

Roller

This implement consists of two cylinders of 0.60 meters diameter. Available in two widths. Weight: 1.60-meter-wide model, 223 kilograms; 2.00-meter-wide model, 250 kilograms.

ETS. Techine
82400 Valance D'Agen
France

Wetland Puddler

It is designed for quick and efficient preparation of fields for paddy after first plowing. The three angular cast-iron hubs with four blades on each hub churn up the soil and leave the fine particles of it on the top surface. Weight: 39.5 kilograms.

Cossul & Co. Pvt., Ltd.
Industrial Area, Fazalgunj
Kanpur, India

Cossul Bullock-Driven Green Manure Trampler

Growing a green manure crop and burying it is a way of adding to the organic matter content of the soil. This implement is useful for trampling green leaves and stalks. It consists of four 250-millimeter (10 inches) diameter steel discs with cast-iron hubs mounted on a horizontal shaft. Blades mounted on the shaft help to cut the green material. Weight: 39 kilograms.

Cossul Green Manure Trampler
Cossul & Co.

Cossul & Co. Pvt., Ltd.
Industrial Area, Fazalgunj
Kanpur, India

I.T.D.G. Clod Crushers Plans

These are two simple and cheaply constructed implements which are used for reducing the size of clods in cultivated land prior to ridging up the soil. They are made principally of gum (eucalyptus) poles. Type 1 has roller gangs which are built from short pieces of pole

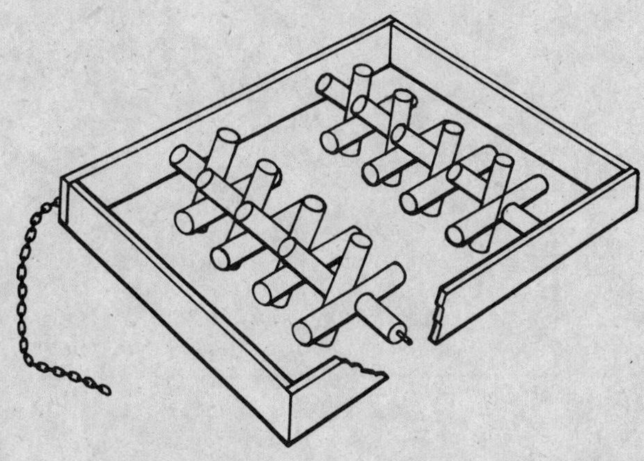

Clod Crusher, type 1

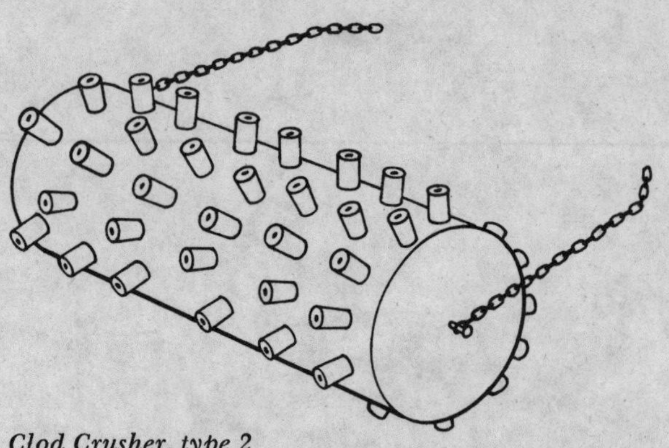

Clod Crusher, type 2

and rest at an angle of approximately 60 degrees to each other. The poles are mounted to provide a self-cleaning effect. Type 2 consists of short pole pegs attached in a staggered formation around the circumference of a single heavy log roller. Sharpened steel bolts are driven into the center of each end of the roller to which the draft chains are attached. A singletree is fitted to the roller chains.

I.T.D.G. Granule Applicator Plans

The granule applicator was developed as part of the Intermediate Technology Farm Equipment Development Project work program attached to the Institute of Agricultural Research of Ahmadu Bello University. A Planet Junior-based, hand-pushed seeder was fitted to an ariana toolbar and a simple direct-drive from a spiked wheel was used to replace the original bevel gears and shaft drive to the metering mechanism. Standard ariana soil-moving components were added to enable a ridge to be built and granules to be applied, either on the surface or incorporated into the soil, simultaneously.

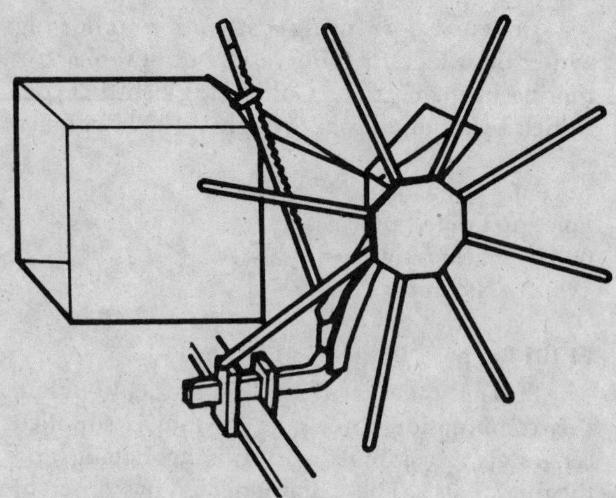

I.T.D.G. Granule Applicator

Intermediate Technology Publications, Ltd.
9 King St.
London WC2E 8HN, England

–4– Tractors

TWO-WHEEL TRACTORS

"Different levels of farm mechanization exist side by side in China," observes Ian Barwell in his report on the Chinese Two-Wheeled Tractor.* Barwell serves as a transport project officer with the Intermediate Technology Development Group based in London. He explains the different mechanization levels in terms of varying commune size (from 500 to 50,000 people), development, and farm machinery requirements. "At one and the same time, there is an increasing demand for conventional four-wheeled tractors, for two-wheeled tractors, and for draft animals such as horses and oxen for use in agricultural work."

Thousands of miles away, Gene Logsdon, an editor for *Organic Gardening* and *New Farm* in the United States, shows that a need for diversified, well-developed equipment is equally significant—even on a single, small farm such as his.

"When I figure my needs, I do not automatically figure that I have 20 acres to cultivate or even six, which is all the land I actually have in animal crops. Instead I look closely at that six-acre figure and ask myself: Of that total, how big an area will I ever have to plow (or disk, or weed, or plant, or harvest) in one day? The answer is usually one-quarter acre or less. That being the case, a quarter-acre is the size my tools need to be geared to."

"Actually, I'm overpowered with my ancient WD Allis-Chalmers tractor which has a horsepower rating of around 35. That's enough for quite a sizable little farm. My biggest plowing job takes me less than two hours. I only use my tractor's capability fully when I mow hay and pasturelands. My tractor would be just about right on an 80-acre farm if the 80 acres were devoted to the wide variety of food and fiber production typical of the self-sustaining homestead. Even on an 80, you should rarely *have* to work more than five acres a day. If, however, the entire 80 were given over to commercial fruit

* Material excerpted with permission from Ian J. Barwell. "The Chinese Two-Wheeled Tractor." *World Crops and Livestock*, July-August 1977.

The Kubota, a Japanese two-wheeled tractor.
Kubota, Ltd.

and vegetable production or any single specialty crop, you would usually need quite larger machinery to handle it."

Just as Gene Logsdon in North America is firmly convinced that many growers should look at single-axle tractors and tillers, so, too, are the Chinese. The two-wheeled or single-axle tractor has played a vital role in the mechanization of Chinese agriculture, reports Ian Barwell. Since much of the cultivated land is divided into very small plots for irrigation, the two-wheeled tractor works well in such small land segments. Besides, the two-wheeled tractor is a much cheaper unit to buy and run than a conventional four-wheeled tractor, and it also lends itself to production by a number of small- and medium-scale factories throughout the country.

Writes Barwell, "Ease of maintenance and durability are major considerations in the design of the tractor which can be used for plowing or rotary cultivation, and as a power source to drive other items of machinery. Attached to a trailer, it forms a simple means of transport and is extensively used in this role, both in rural situations and to carry goods and people from the countryside to the town and back again. Current annual production of the tractor runs into hundreds of thousands of units, and they are now being exported to certain other developing countries; both India and the Philippines are now producing similar machines. However, the tractor is not suitable for use in the very dry conditions prevalent in parts of Africa, because it does not have the tractive power required for cultivation in such circumstances."

A single-axle tractor hitched to a two-wheeled trailer for transport.
Ian Barwell

The tractor engine, he reports, has a power output of ten horsepower. The heart of the two-wheeled tractor is its rugged and durable single-cylinder, four-stroke diesel engine. Barwell continues:

"The engine, whose main block and crankcase are a single iron casting, has two other interesting features which simplify maintenance. It is water-cooled by means of an evaporative tank system mounted above the block. It is this feature which is responsible for the characteristic wisp of steam rising from the tractor when it is in use. Direct visual indication of the water level is achieved by means of a red button mounted on the end of a rod protruding from the tank and attached inside to a float. As the water evaporates, the rod falls until the danger level is reached, and the button drops out of sight of the tractor operator. A forced-circulation, oil lubrication system is used, and the oil is passed through a sight glass visible to the operator so that he has a continuous check on the flow of lubricant."

The Chinese have many uses for the two-wheeled tractor. It can be fitted with either a single- or a two-furrow plow which attaches to a bracket at the rear of the gearbox. The setting of the plow can be adjusted for height, for angle relative to the direction of travel, and for orientation of the blades themselves. The tractor can plow to a depth of 180 to 200 millimeters.

Using the power take-off at the rear of the gearbox, a rotary cultivator fitted with up to 16 blades can be attached. The rotor is shrouded by a canopy which helps to break up the lumps of earth, and the depth of cultivation is controlled by either a skid or a small-diameter wheel mounted behind the cultivator.

When plowing or cultivating, the operator may either walk along behind the tractor or sit on a seat mounted at the very rear of the machine. Steering is effected by control of the clutches engaging the drive to each of the wheels. The tractor is reportedly capable of working 0.1 to 0.15 hectares per hour.

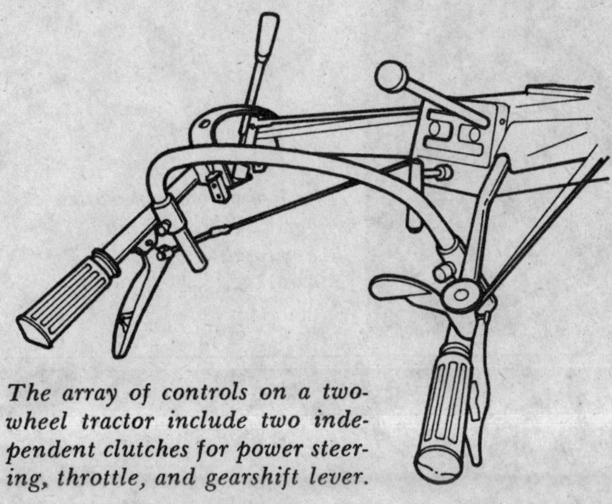

The array of controls on a two-wheel tractor include two independent clutches for power steering, throttle, and gearshift lever.

The tractor can be driven to and from the fields if a small castor wheel is fitted at the rear. However, when it is used for cargo or passenger transport the tractor is hitched to a two-wheeled trailer, and the driver normally sits on a seat at the front of the trailer. He can then steer the vehicle by means of the handlebar, and this obviates the need for the castor wheel. Maximum payload in the transport mode averages 1,200 kilograms.

Mounted on the end of the crankshaft alongside the grooved pulley described earlier is a large flywheel which doubles as a flat-topped pulley. Using this feature, the tractor may be used as a source of power to drive a range of items of agricultural and crop-processing equipment, through a flat-belt drive system. It could, for example, be used to power a water pump, an electricity generator, a flour mill, or a rice thresher.

SINGLE-AXLE TILLERS AND TRACTORS

A great variety of single-axle, sometimes called two-wheel, walking, or pedestrian tractors is available. The smaller models generally have a single-driven shaft which can be fitted either with rotary cultivator blades or with wheels for pulling trailers and trailed implements. Larger models often have a pair of driving wheels and an independently controlled drive for rotary cultivating. Engines usually run on gasoline in the smaller sizes and use diesel fuel in larger sizes. Transmission systems range from V-belt drive (with speed changing by means of stepped pulleys, and belt tensioning providing a clutch) to multispeed gear transmission with friction plate clutches.

Most manufacturers can supply a range of attachments for cultivation and transport work, and water pumps can usually be fitted, although it should be remembered that pumping is generally an arduous duty for a small engine. One maker supplies a threshing attachment with a rasp, bar-type drum, and concave.

Single-axle tractors have sometimes proved to be very successful in intensive agriculture on relatively soft soils which need thorough rotary cultivation—for example, in irrigated rice paddies in Asia or on market-gardening plots in Europe. They have been much less successful for relatively extensive agriculture on hard soils such as those in some savannah regions of Africa, where large areas have to be covered and tined cultivation is often more appropriate than rotary cultivation.

Like all small-engine-powered equipment, single-axle tractors require a good network of spare-part supplies, a high level of operator training, and regular maintenance, particularly in hot and/or dusty working conditions.

NORTH AMERICAN SOURCES OF WALKING TRACTORS

The Rokon Automatic Mototractor

At first glance, one can hardly take this stocky trail bike seriously as a useful farm implement. But after serious study, it is obvious that the Mototractor is a two-wheeled, two-wheel drive, dual-purpose power unit designed to handle all the usual farm chores with the same hearty determination of any tractor—while providing an expedient, rugged means of transportation as well.

A conversation with a Technical Assistance Official for Africa revealed that "the Mototractor could well be the sole piece of technology developed in the United States with significant implications for emerging nations. It is extremely strong and has few moving parts. In order to be useful, a farm tool must be able to till more land than the space it needs to turn around in, a problem with Western-oriented equipment.

The Rokon tractor crosses rugged terrain towing a heavy load.
Rokon, Inc.

"Unlike Far Eastern countries, labor is at a premium in Africa, not land. Without the help of a labor force, the farmer must rely on mechanization to get enough land prepared to feed his family and provide him with a cash crop. At the same time, he needs a means of local transportation and a way to get his produce to market—especially during the rainy season."

Rokon has designed the Mototractor to satisfy both needs. It has all the attachments of a small-farm, utility tractor—plow, cultivators, trailer, and spraying and irrigating equipment—is able to transverse two-foot streams, has wide tires for superior traction in mud, has a ten-horsepower gasoline engine and power take-off shaft, can climb 45-degree inclines, and has a maximum operating speed of 40 miles per hour.

In the United States, the Mototractor is widely used by engineers, foresters, and fire-

A third wheel provides added balance for plowing at slow speeds. Rokon, Inc.

fighters for rapid travel over rough terrain. The power take-off shaft will operate a pump for fire-fighting as well as many farm tools. Gearing ratios provide pulling power which has proved valuable in rescue operations. One ski resort in Vermont uses their Mototractor to climb mountains carrying workers, tools, and materials all year-round, as well as for rescue.

Rokon, Inc.
American Engineers & Manufacturers
160 Emerald St.
Keene, NH 03431

THE FORD DNT PEDESTRIAN TRACTOR, NOW THE INTEC

In 1964, Ford decided to develop a program designed to help solve the world food crisis while enhancing the reputation of the company and its farm products in developing nations. After a series of conferences with university and foundation experts and with representatives of governmental agencies, "Ford elected to design a tractor which would provide simple mechanization for small farmers at a price roughly comparable to a pair of oxen," reports Richard Dewey, Public Relations Manager for Ford Tractor Operations.

After five years of research and engineering Ford was ready to test marketability of their new model DNT—*D*eveloping *N*ations *T*ractor. Confidence in its powerful, reliable transaxle system, wheels designed for added strength and improved traction, the simplicity of the rope starter and push-pull metal clutch rod, and its basic rugged, durable design encouraged them to continue. As their news release announced, "The two-wheeled tractor is the first ever designed specifically to bring the benefits of modern farming technology to people on small farms in developing countries at a price they can afford to pay."

The INTEC's high ground clearance is an important feature in continuing mechanical cultivation late into the season.
Dowding Tool Products, Inc.

But "insurmountable logistical and social problems" terminated the effort. Dewey continued, "Getting spare parts to dealers posed no difficulty but getting the dealer to the broken-down machinery did. It just wouldn't pay any serviceman to spend three or four days trekking through the jungle in search of his customer. With attitudes as stubborn as they are, it's hard to convince village farmers that anything new, even appropriately scaled and designed machinery, will do the job right. They are skeptical of a tractor which runs on hard-to-get fuel and eventually breaks down into a pile of rusty nuts and bolts. Fuel for animals grows on trees and a worn-out ox can be eaten. There's real 'horse sense' in using animal-drawn equipment in developing countries."

The Ford people maintain that it was governmental philosophy which proved the greatest detriment to small tractor development. Their requests for governmental financing were rejected with the explanation that to make their agriculture efficient they must go big. Though peasant farmers expressed a desire for small farm machinery, their government felt it knew what was best—"big is best."

So goes the Ford DNT story, past history now—almost. There's a two-wheel walking tractor on the market now called the INTEC. It is really the old Ford DNT with a new name. Dowding Tool Products, Inc. of Springport, Michigan, took over where Ford left off. Tom Hanna, Product Engineer for Dowding describes the development of the INTEC tractor this way:

> Maurice Dowding, President of Dowding Tool Products, considered licensing the production and marketing of the discontinued DNT two or three years ago. Friends with overseas experience suggested that this product would supplement his metal stamping business and serve a need in developing countries' agriculture. Mr. Dowding was unable to secure Ford's active support for the venture, but on the other hand, received no objections since the tractor did not employ patentable concepts. After finding our own manufacturing sources and investing in tooling, our company was ready to market the INTEC tractor. INTEC was derived from intermediate technology, although this term is not usually attached to the trademark.
>
> Our emphasis is on rugged construction and ease of maintenance. The all-gear transmission is enclosed in cast iron and requires little attention. The seven-horsepower Briggs and Stratton engine has its own reputation for dependability and service organization. The tractor pulls the plow in difficult soils when properly weighted to 600 pounds.

Properly weighted and mounted with steel wheels for added traction, the INTEC is ready to disk harrow.
Dowding Tool Products, Inc.

> INTEC equipment will eventually encompass all steps of crop farming rather than just tillage. There have already been some additions to the DNT design. They include a power take-off, rotovator conversion package, one-meter-wide disc harrow, and a planter-fertilizer unit. Power take-off equipment under development includes a low-lift propeller irrigation pump capable of 800 gallons per minute at five-feet head. A sprayer, potato harvester, and mower are examples of future products.

INTEC Equipment Co.
Box 123, D.V. Station,
Dayton, OH 45406

BUILD—'EM—YOURSELF TWO- AND FOUR-WHEELED TRACTORS

Paul Davenport started building tractors over twenty years ago from parts he scrounged mostly from old Model A Fords. Now he says he is too old for that kind of work, but he still sells the plans for a two-wheel model with a two-and-one-half- or six-horsepower motor, and a four-wheeled, four-wheel-drive, six-horsepower model.

The feature Paul boasts of most is the ruggedness of his tractors. "These parts were originally designed to take the power of a 24-horsepower engine. With these small engines, they will last almost indefinitely." Some parts include a standard Model A transmission with three forward speeds and reverse, brakes for turning and handling, and regular wheels and tires (or implement tires).

You can build this four-wheeled, four-wheel-drive tractor from a Davenport kit.
Paul Davenport

The Davenport two-wheel tractor has a drawbar with a single pin for changing implements quickly.
Paul Davenport

The actual building cost is hard to estimate. It all depends upon how good a scrounger you are and how much of the work you can do for yourself. There is a certain amount of cutting, drilling, and welding you will need to do, or perhaps your local welder will have to help you out.

The plans illustrate a simple but practical drawbar which pulls from ahead of the axles for better handling. A single pin allows a quick change of implements. With the two-and-one-half-horsepower engine on his two-wheeled tractor, Paul can pull a nine-inch plow, eight inches deep in low gear. The four-wheeled unit can pull a 12-inch plow ten inches deep in light to medium soil. Flexibility in the center, keeping all four wheels on the ground, regardless of terrain, coupled with four-wheel drive gives this machine "sensational pulling power."

Paul's Tractor Co.
8520 Cherry St.
Fontana, CA 92335

Gravely Convertible Tractors

Gravely Convertible two-wheel tractors have an all-gear transmission separately powering both the wheels and the power take-off shaft for attachments. Models with 8, 10, and 12 h.p. engines provide power to match the job requirements and operate with forward, neutral, and reverse speeds. Attachments include sickle bar; rotary and flail mowers; a plow, sweeper, and blower for snow; a dumping trailer; and, for the garden, a furrower, cultivator, shovel, and rotary tiller.

This Gravely power unit has a rotary mower attached to the front, dual wheels for better traction, and a riding sulky with steering column.
Clarke-Gravely Corp.

Gravely Division of Clark-Gravely Corp.
One Gravely Lane
Clemmons, NC 27012

Ferrari

Ferrari carries three models of walking tractors with air-cooled diesel engines ranging from 7 to 21 h.p. The fuel injection system means there are no plugs, points, magneto, or carburetor. Direct gear-drive replaces the need for chains or belts. The middle range, 14 h.p. model has four forward and two reverse speeds, and power take-offs, each with two speeds. The tilling width is about 30 inches and the unit readily accommodates a sickle bar, snow blower, trailer, sprayer, plows, and even a table saw.

Ferrari with tiller attachment
Ferrari International, Inc.

Ferrari International, Inc.
6104 Avenida Encinas
Carlsbad, CA 92008

Ferrari S.P.A. Officine Meccaniche
42045 Luzzara
Reggio Emilia, Italy

Pasquali Walking Tractors

Pasquali Italian-made walking tractors come in many sizes, ranging from 7 to 18 h.p. All are equipped with a four-stroke, air-cooled diesel engine. The lower-powered models, from 7 to 14 h.p., have four speeds forward and two reverse; the higher-powered units have a sliding-type key gear with synchronizer operating twelve speeds—nine forward, three reverse—at a rate of 0.6 to 16 kph. All models have two power take-off shafts, the top one synchronized with all gearbox speeds and the bottom one with two independent speeds. The rotary tiller disconnects automatically when reverse gear is engaged, and the handles are completely adjustable.

Pasquali has the unusual attraction of offering over 70 attachments for its walking tractors. So extensive is their list of attachments that it takes a 200-page book to describe them all. All are available upon request through a dealer in the United States with the allowance of a twelve-week lead time.

The Pasquali Model 946
Pasquali U.S.A.

Pasquali USA
Verona, WI 53593

Pasquali: Macchine Agricole s.p.a.
Via Nuova, 30
Calenzano (Firenze)
Pama Calenzano, Italy

EDKO Walking Tractor

The EDKO tractor is constructed with a ¼-inch by 3-inch frame and 11-gauge handle with three-position adjustment. It is powered by a 5 h.p. gasoline engine with six-to-one gear reduction and recoil starter. It features two speeds forward with "dead man" reverse (1.25 mph). Low speed ranges from 1 to 1.75 mph, high speed from 2 to 2.75. It has a rugged chain-drive system with dual-split steel pulleys, and 11-inch ground clearance axle with rachet wheel. Wheel widths are adjustable from 17 to 23 inches on

The EDKO Chain-Drive Walking Tractor with toolbar and cultivators.
EDKO Mfg., Inc.

1-inch increments for each wheel. No tools are required to change the following attachments: 7-inch moldboard plow with coulter, disc, six-prong cultivator, furrow opener, 40-inch blade, wheel weights, and chains.

EDKO Mfg., Inc.
2725 Second Ave.
Des Moines, IA 50313

Haban Power-Trac V

The chain-drive transmission with one speed forward and reverse is provided only in the 5 h.p. size. The 3 h.p. model has no reverse. An attachment clutch acts independently of traction controls. Controls are mounted on handlebars of tubular steel. It has semipneumatic tires with 11-inch by 4:00 wheels. Both models feature 14-inch tines for tilling a patch 26 inches wide and 8 inches or more deep. Attachments for the 5 h.p. model include a variety of cultivator tools, a 22-inch-cut rotary mower, a 24-inch snow-thrower, and a 30-inch dozer blade for grading gravel and clearing snow.

Haban Mfg. Co.
2100 Northwestern Ave.
Racine, WI 53404

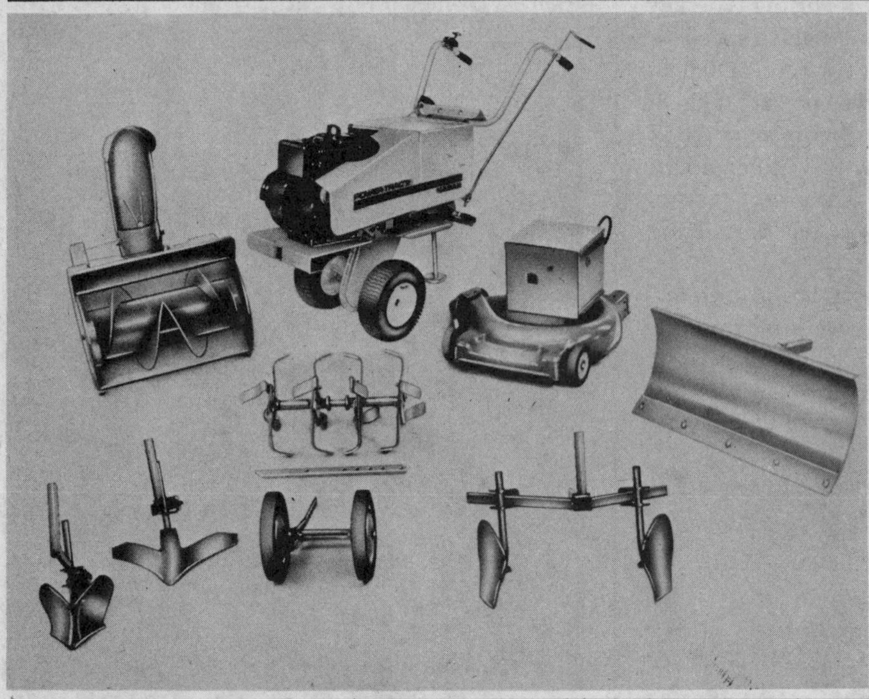

The Haban Power-Trac V with attachments: snow-blower, rotary mower, scraper blade, bolo tiller tines and depth bar, furrower, sweep, rubber tires, and hiller.
Haban Mfg. Co.

INTERNATIONAL SOURCES OF WALKING TRACTORS

Bucher M600

The Bucher M600 cutter bar mowers are specifically designed walking tractors for mowing and windrowing crops grown on the steep slopes of Switzerland. Three different mechanisms are available for windrowing; a trailer and sulky are also available. Special wheel extensions keep the mower upright when traversing a slope. The M600 is run by a 10 h.p., air-cooled gasoline engine, has three forward, one reverse speed, and weighs 320 kilograms. Other models are available ranging from 7 to 11 horsepower. At this writing, Bucher-Guyer is seeking a North American distributor.

Bucher-Guyer, Ltd. Engineering Works
CH-8166 Niederweningen
Zurich, Switzerland

AEBI AM Walking Tractors

AEBI tractors come in three models: the AM 8; the AM 15, with 15 h.p.; and the AM 75, with 10 h.p. All have four-stroke gasoline engines and mowing attachments. The AM 75 has a transmission with four forward and one reverse speed,

Bucher Cutter Bar Mower M200
Bucher–Guyer, Ltd. Engineering Works

The AEBI AM75 pulling quite a load uphill.
AEBI & Co.

a high-/low-speed option for the cutter bar and three forward and one reverse speed for the rear power take-off. Power can be linked to a trailer capable of a 900-kilogram payload; hence the unit becomes a four-wheel-drive machine. Other attachments include a sulky, hay turner, and rotary tiller. Operating in reverse, the AEBI AM 75 pulls a potato harvester which digs the potatoes, sifts the soil away from the tubers, and deposits them in a row on the surface of the soil.

AEBI & Co.
AG Maschinenfabrik
CH-3400 Burgdorf, Switzerland

Agria 6000 with weighted wheels for extra traction to pull a reversible moldboard plow.
Agria-Werke

Agria Model 2400 Walking Tractor

Agria Model 2400 walking tractors are available with either an 8 h.p., two-stroke or a 9 h.p., four-stroke gasoline engine. They have a six-speed gearbox, three forward and three reverse, and an independent power take-off shaft. The steel-tube handlebars are adjustable 180 degrees, and track width can be adjusted from 10.6 to 22.2 inches, depending upon accessories and row width. A wide range of attachments makes this unit Agria's versatile one. Attachments include a two-section, adjustable harrow, a two-piston spray pump, a water pump, a 31.5-inch spindle reel mower with seat, snow blower and plow, sweeper, rotary tillers with widths between 12.6 and 26 inches with or without duckfoot hoe, quarter-turn plow, reversible plow, ridger, cultivator, mulcher, sickle bar mowers of different working widths and fineness cuts, and a trailer with seat.

Agria Model 2700

Designed for power rather than versatility, the robust Agria 2700 walking tractor has a 13-h.p., four-stroke diesel engine with electric start. The nine-speed gearbox, six forward and three reverse, operates at rates between 0.7 and 12 mph. The upper power take-off shaft operates at two speeds; the bottom also at two but with the option of operating independently of the gearbox. The lower shaft stops automatically when reverse gear is engaged. The 270-kilogram unit is balanced for easy maneuverability when hoeing, tilling, plowing, and transporting. One unusual attachment is the sprinkler, complete with water tank. Agria is not represented in North America at this time and is seeking distributors.

Robust Agria 2700 with rotary tiller
Agria-Werke

Agria-Werke GmbH
D-7108 Moeckmuehl
West Germany

Moty Mule Universal

The Mule is a versatile mowing, tilling, hay-harvesting implement built for safe operation on steep slopes. It is available with either a two- or four-cycle gasoline engine or a four-cycle diesel engine. A floating axle adapts to rough ground conditions without transmitting jolts to the operator. The V-belt power transmission absorbs the shock when obstacles jam the cutting blade on the reciprocating mower. Front and rear power take-off shafts are provided to power a great variety of implement attachments which may be installed in seconds, thanks to a quick-disconnect arrangement. The rear power take-off can also be utilized to propel the shaft for a wheel-drive trailer. The unit weighs 150 kilograms, 100 kilograms without the mowing attachment, and operates in first gear at 4 kph, second gear at 10 kph and reverse at 3 kph. More than 25 attachments are available. Some of the more unusual ones include a grain-reaping attachment, push-on grinding attachment, hay-pushing rake, dibbling seeder with two-row arrangement, hay rake and tedder, hay rake with reversible rotation arrangement, and vineyard plow.

Moty-Werk, Landmachinenbau
8523 Frauental A./L62
Austria/Stmk

Kubota Versatiller

A heavy unit weighing 485 kilograms, the Kubota Versatiller has a continuous output of 9 h.p. and a maximum of 12. It operates at six forward and two reverse speeds and the tilling unit operates at four speeds. With a maximum traveling speed of 15 kph, the unit is powered by a rotary, diesel-powered, water-cooled engine with radiator. It tills a width of 60 centimeters, a depth of 19 centimeters with 20 blades, tilling at a rate of 1 hectare every ten hours. The Kubota puddles wet fields, tills, plows, harrows, and weeds. The power take-off provides a stationary 12-h.p. engine to drive belt-driven machines such as threshers, hullers, and generators.

Kerala Agro-Machinery Corp., Ltd.
Athani P.O. Ernakulam District
Kerala, India

Kubota, Ltd.
22 Funade-cho
2-chome Naniwa-ku
Osaka, Japan

Note: The Kerala Corporation is interested in marketing their products in North America but has no distributor at this time.

IRRI Power Tiller

The International Rice Research Institute has designed this 8 to 12 h.p. tiller with features especially for developing countries. The heavy-duty power tiller offers almost all of the features of the latest power tillers produced in the industrialized countries, yet it can be easily fabricated in developing nations at a fraction of the cost. The machine is well balanced and is equipped with steering clutches for easy maneuverability. The four forward and two reverse speeds can be shifted by using a simple main clutch control and gear shifting lever. Belts do not have to be shifted to change speeds. Used for cultivation on both upland and lowland conditions, the tiller can prepare 1.2 to 1.5 hectares of land per eight-hour day and can transport 600 kilograms on country roads. This rigid, heavy-duty machine is equipped with a water-cooled, horizontal-stroke diesel engine which transfers power through V-belts. Maintenance cost is kept low as most parts can be easily repaired in small machine shops, and many machine elements are readily available to developing nations.

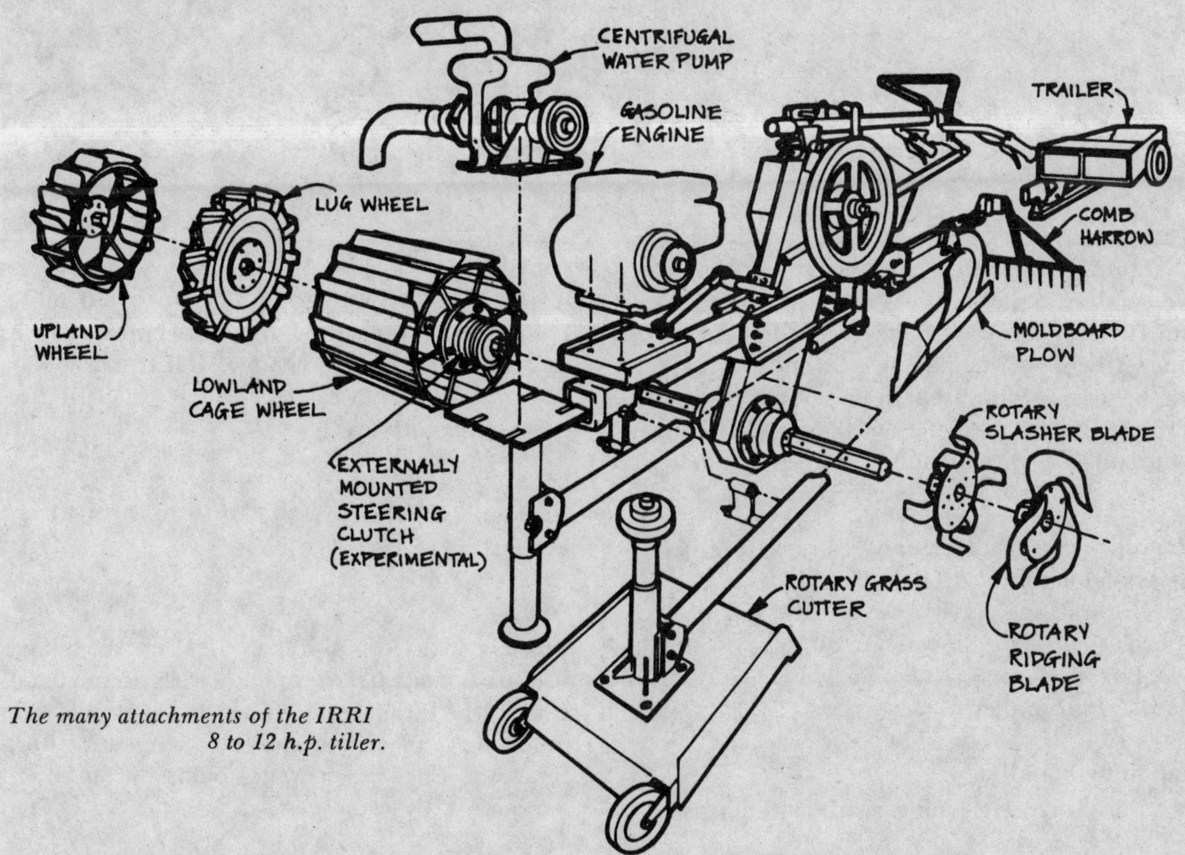

The many attachments of the IRRI 8 to 12 h.p. tiller.

The IRRI Power Tiller is seen here puddling a rice paddy while pulling the operator on a puddling sled. Notice the weight extending to the front to compensate for the weight of the sled and operator.
International Rice Research Institute

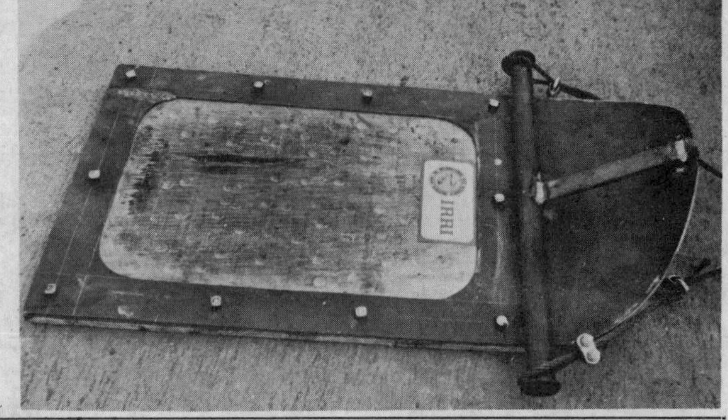

Not yet widely adopted, the IRRI puddling sled can be modified for construction with local materials for less than $20.
International Rice Research Institute

Simple to manufacture, the power tiller has five major assemblies: engine, transfer case, multispeed gear transmission, handlebars, and rotary tiller. All components, except the engine, can be easily fabricated in developing nations without special production dies and tooling. Consequently, production can be economical even with low market demand.

Manufacturers' addresses and construction plans are available from:
Agricultural Engineering Department
International Rice Research Institute
P.O. Box 933
Manila, Philippines

Hakorette Standard

The Hakorette comes with a 6 h.p. two-stroke engine, elastic three-stage V-belt drive transmission with three speeds up to 10 mph. High-traction capacity powers attachments which include rotovator, snowplow, trailer with 500-kilogram or ½-ton capacity, 8-inch plow, and a reel mower with seat.

Hako-Werke
2060 Bad Oldesloe
Postfach 1444, West Germany

Solo

The Solo combi-system is a single 4 h.p., two-stroke engine complete with centrifugal clutch which can be fitted quickly to any of the following implements: mower, rotary cultivator, generator, earth auger, water pump, or outboard motor.

Solo Kleinmotoren GmbH
7032 Sindelfingen 6
Postfach 20, West Germany

Bouyer Two-Wheel Tropical Tractors

Though they are made in France, these tractors are marketed solely (at present) in developing nations. They were designed in collaboration with CEEMAT (Center for Studies and Tests of Tropical Material), specifically to satisfy the demands of tropical cotton culture following a request of the CFDT (French Company of Textile). A spokesman for Bouyer explained, "It appeared to this company that a normal tractor was not able to work in cotton fields. In fact, it requires a simple machine to make eventual repairs very easy in areas far from economic centers, and a specific machine for cotton with a high clearance and an adjustable working width." They are able to work both in wet and dry cultures under hot climates.

Bouyer Walking Tractor with cultivator attachment. Notice depth adjustment and handlebar controls. Wheel weights are mounted to improve traction, and the extending frame in the front is a provision for adding even more weight.
Bouyer

Type 203

This is the smallest tractor made by Bouyer. It has a 5 h.p., four-stroke, air-cooled gasoline engine. The gearbox houses two speed ranges with two forward speeds each and two reverse speeds. There are two speeds for the power take-off shaft.

Type 334

Powered by a 6 or 7 h.p., four-stroke gasoline or diesel air-cooled engine, it has two ranges of three forward speeds and one range of three reverse speeds. There is one speed for the power take-off shaft.

Type TR

The heftiest of the Bouyer products has a four-stroke, air-cooled diesel engine available in either 9, 11 or 14 h.p. Special features for operation in a hot climate include an oil regenerator and oil bath air filter. There are two speed ranges for three forward speeds and one range of three reverse speeds. Three power take-off shafts operate at different speeds including one independent, one independent with clutch, and one driving the rotovator.

Bouyer supplies a wide range of attachments for use with all three tractors, though sizes differ. These include many variations of plows such as a reversible plow, universal hitch, rotovator, cultivators, toolbar frame for carrying hoes, potato lifter, four-row seeding drill, two-row drill seeder and fertilizer combination, spraying equipment and trailer reservoir, irrigation pump, sickle bar and rear rotary mowers-disc harrows, and many wheels for better traction in both wet and dry cultures. At the time of this writing, Bouyer is interested in establishing a distributor in North America.

Bouyer
B.P. 23
Tomblaine 54510, France

Sagisag Model A by Mametora

Any engine of a farmer's choice can be mounted on the basic engine frame. An overdrive clutch mechanism provides transmission efficiency when changing the all-gear transmission with 12 forward and six reverse speeds. Electric start and headlight are provided. The 16-blade rotary tiller tills 13 centimeters deep and 60 centimeters wide. The manufacturer claims a capacity of 2 hectares per hour with tiller; the plow attachment takes 75 minutes to cover the same area.

Tramat Mercantile, Inc.
747-749 Gandara St.
Sta. Cruz, Manila

Mametora Power Tillers MC

Three models are available from this company, no horsepower ratings are given. All have four-cycle, vertical, monocylinder engines with air cooling, two power take-off shafts, V-belt and gear-driven transmission with two forward and one reverse speed.

Mametora Power Tiller HMD

A 7 h.p. unit has all-gear transmission, eight speeds forward, four reverse and a four-cycle, 252-cubic centimeter engine. Attachments include a rotary plow, side and middle furrower, puddling wheel and rakes, power transmission pulley, and trailer.

Other models are available.

Mametora Return–Culti

The Return–Culti is the largest of the many walking tillers Mametora produces. It is available with either a 4.5 or a 6.5 h.p., four-cycle, air-cooled, gasoline motor, both units operating with two forward speeds and one reverse speed; however, the larger model has three forward speeds for the rotary tiller. The front-mounted rotary tiller has the unusual feature of operating both in forward and reverse, hence the name Return–Culti. Handles are adjustable 180 degrees in all directions, and the unit's low center of gravity makes it safe for working on slopes. It is most suitable for operations in mulberry fields, orchards, tea plantations, and vegetable gardens, and in addition to cultivation and weeding, can conduct various operations such as fertilizing, cutting stalks, and dislodging roots with a winch mechanism mounted on a frame. The Mametora power tiller Model HMD-25 is a 7 h.p. unit designed for plowing, rotary cultivation, side and middle furrowing, and paddy operations. Some of the more unusual attachments include a two-wheel carrier set for carrying compost and fertilizer, a special blade and cover for making trenches and a mulch dispenser for rolls of plastic. Weight: 97 kilograms without engine.

Above units manufactured by:
Mametora Agricultural Machinery Co., Ltd.
9-37 Nishi, 2-chome
Okegawa, Saitama, Japan

ISEKI Power Tillers

The Iseki Model KS500 is more than a tiller. Its four-cycle, air-cooled, 5 h.p. gasoline engine has six forward and two reverse speeds transmitting power through a gear-/chain-drive system. A few of its many attachments include puddling rotor and puddling rake, turn-wrest plow, ridger, power take-off pulley, auger-digger, as well as a rotary tiller. Another model, with the option of a two- or four-cycle, air-cooled gasoline engine weighs 180 pounds and operates a number of attachments also, including snow-handling and cultivating equipment. It has four forward and two reverse speeds; the main engine shaft is V-belt driven and the traveling section is driven by a gear-chain combination. The power take-off has two speeds.

Iseki Agricultural Machinery Mfg. Co., Ltd.
1-3 Nihonbashi, 2-chome, Chuo-ku
Tokyo, 103, Japan

Land Master Lion

The Lion is available with either a 7 h.p., four-stroke engine or a 6 h.p., two-stroke engine. Two forward and one reverse speed. Attachments include moldboard reversible or non-reversible plow, ridger, rotary cultivator, hoe, puddler, seeder, potato lifter, water pump (27,000 liters per hour, 7.6 meter head), and a thresher for rice and barley with a capacity of 140 kph.

Land Master, Ltd.
Sterte Rd.
Poole, Dorset BH15 2AF, U.K.

WB Power Tiller Model WB1-A

Powered by a four-cycle, single-cylinder, 8 h.p., air-cooled gasoline engine, Model WB1-A is made of heavy steel pipe framing and steel parts adaptable to local (Philippine) conditions with economical maintenance costs. Another unit is available fitted with a 10 h.p. engine. Accessories include moldboard plow, spiral plow, adjustable peg-toothed harrow, paddling steel cage wheel for wet plowing, paddling steel wheel for dry plowing with or without hub adaptor, wheel weight, pneumatic rubber tires, and rotary hoe with 12 blades. The company does export.

Warner Barnes Engineering
A Division of Warner, Barnes and Co., Inc.
2900 Faraday Street cor, South Expressway
Makati, Rizal, Philippines

Staub PPX

Staub offers a wide product line of different-sized tillers and walking tractors. The PPX is one of their most versatile walking tractors. It is powered by a 322-cubic centimeters, four-cycle, 7 h.p. diesel engine. The gearbox houses three forward and two reverse speeds which are controlled by means of a single lever which changes gears and locks the wheels in drive position. Two connections for power take-off are mounted in the rear. Handle assembly is adjustable to all positions and reversible for use with the cutter bar and certain other tools. Attachments include rotary cultivator, plow, toothed cultivator, harrow, trailer, cutter bar, rotary mower, advanced hoe, sower, scraper blade, brush clearer, pump, and saw.

Societe des Tracteurs et Motoculteurs Staub
25, Bd de Verdun
92402 Courbevoie Cedex, France

Honda Two-Wheeled Tractors

A range of models from 2 to 8 h.p. is available with attachments including plows, ridgers, rotary cultivators, and various types of puddling equipment.

Honda Motor Co., Ltd.
Tokyo, Japan

U 1200 Two-Wheeled Tractor

This tractor can be fitted with gas or diesel engines of 8 to 10 h.p. It has a gearbox with three forward and three reverse speeds, and a choice of six PTO speeds. Attachments include mower, rotary cultivator, plow, ridger, harrow, hoe, potato lifter, trailer, sprayer, and belt drive for stationary machines.

Iruswerke Dusslingen
7401 Dusslingen
Postfach 128, West Germany

Two-Wheeled Tractors

Six h.p. gas-engined and 12 h.p. diesel-engined tractors are manufactured, together with a range of attachments including plows, rotary cultivators, tined cultivators, mowers, trailers, and others.

Gebruder Holder Maschinenfabrik
7418 Metzingen/Wurtt
Postfach 66, West Germany

Krishi NV 700 Power Tiller

This machine has a 7 h.p. diesel engine and a four forward, two reverse speed gearbox.

Krishni NV700 Power Tiller Krishni Engines, Ltd.

Attachments include fixed and reversible moldboard plows, cultivators, disc harrows, puddling equipment, and others.

Krishi Engines, Ltd.
Sanatnagar, Hyderabad 18
A.P. India

FB 5 Motor Cultivator

The single-cylinder, 15 h.p. diesel engine has four forward and two reverse speeds. Attachments include rotary cultivator, plow, centrifugal pump, high-pressure spraying pump, and trailer.

Fratelli Baraldi s.n.c.
41010 Modena
Via Villanova, Italy

P.G.S. Diamante Tractor

Four-stroke gas or diesel engines of 7 to 10 h.p. are available with two forward and one reverse speed gearbox. Attachments include rotary cultivators, plows, ridgers, trailers, irrigation pumps, spray pumps, and pulleys. Larger two-wheeled tractors are also available.

P.G.S. S.p.A.
Cadeo, Piacenza
Italy

F.B. Motor Hoes

A range of one- and two-wheeled tractors from 5 to 14 h.p. with plowing, rotary cultivating, grading, mowing, pumping, spraying, and transport attachments are available.

Macchine Agricole F.B.
36040 Sossano
Vicenza, Italy

Bertolini Two-Wheeled Tractors

Diesel engines range from 8 to 21 h.p. Attachments include plows, rotary cultivators, trailers, irrigation pumps, and sprayer pumps.

Bertolini Macchine Agricole
42100 Reggio Emilia
Via Guicciardi 7, Italy

Goldoni Two-Wheeled Tractors

Gas- and diesel-engined models from 7 to 21 h.p. are available with plowing, cultivating, spraying, pumping, and transport attachments.

Goldoni S.p.A.
41012 Migliarina Di Caripi
Modena, Italy

CB 450 Tractor

Plowing, rotary cultivating, tined cultivating, and mowing attachments can be supplied for this tractor.

Mabec
27 Rue D'Orleans
92200 Neuilly-Sur-Seine, France

Allen Mayfield Tractor

The Allen tractor can be used with a mowing attachment, with a tool bar carrying cultivating tines, hoe blades, or ridging bodies, with a single furrow moldboard plow, or for pulling a trailer. Seven or 8 h.p. engines and three speed or three speed and reverse gearboxes are available.

Allen Power Equipment, Ltd.
The Broadway, Didcot
Berkshire 0X11 8Es, U.K.

Super U 70 Tractor

The Super U 70 tractor is fitted with an 8 h.p. engine and a four forward, two reverse speed gearbox. Individual wheel clutches facilitate steering. Attachments available include a mower, plow, rotary cultivator, and trailer.

Gutbrod-Werke GmbH
6601 Bubingen, Saar
Postfach 60, West Germany

"DEAR DETROIT, THANKS, BUT NO THANKS"

by Gene Logsdon

If American business is really interested in satisfying *my* needs, I haven't seen a whole lot of proof. I never needed or wanted these gas-hogging, chrome-laden, corner-lurching monsters Detroit built for me for so many years. For their error, our car makers had to watch Volkswagen take all that money away from them with an ugly little car Detroit thought Americans were too dumb to buy.

The tractor makers haven't learned their lesson yet, it seems. I don't doubt that those new 20 to 30 horsepower tractors that appear to be tailored to the homestead are worth $6,000, or at least have $6,000 worth of parts and labor in them. But many of the refinements on those tractors aren't necessary or affordable for the homesteader whose aim is not to generate cash profit from his food production. The tractor I need does not have to be a powerhouse that can do everything except brush my teeth. For instance, it doesn't need rubber tires. Iron wheels would be just fine and would never go flat. I'm not going anywhere with this tractor except back and forth across my little 20 acres, slowly. I don't need a dozen forward speeds. Two will be adequate—and one reverse. My tractor needs no expensive shock system. Any bumps on my place I intend to engage at one or the other of my two forward speeds—slow and slower. I do not need a bucket seat, cigarette lighter, twin-beam headlights, dashlight, radio, cab, high-capacity hydraulics, double-plate clutching, syncromesh gears, hydrostatic transmission, or power steering. All I want is something that will pull as much as three horses and just as quietly.

Can't American technology come up with a long-lasting, easy-running, air-cooled engine so we can dispense with radiators once and for all? A motor that chugs easily along like the old two-cylinder John Deeres would be wonderful. And speaking of old John Deeres, why can't my ideal tractor have an easily turned flywheel crank so I can dispense with high-priced batteries that always seem to be dead when you need them most?

Lastly, is it too much to ask for a tractor which even a mechanical simpleton like myself can take apart easily? I don't mind buying new parts for a piece of machinery if only I could replace them myself. It seems to me that a simple tractor that takes the place of three horses should come apart with any good set of wrenches so that you can get to any broken piece in less than an hour.

The real reason I haven't seen the tractor of my dreams might be that it wouldn't make enough profit for the manufacturers and dealers. Several years ago, I was involved in an article about how farm equipment companies were coming to the aid of underdeveloped (how I despise that word) countries. I don't know if anything came of their praiseworthy plans, but in the course of talking to one executive, he described to me what his company had in mind. They intended, he said, to build a low-cost tractor with a four to six horsepower engine that would still pull the tools similar to, but improved over, those which draft animals traditionally pulled (which our 15 horsepower lawn tractors won't pull). The tractor would be so simple and durable it would rarely need repair work, but when it did, even a mechanical ignoramus could fix it most of the time.

I gasped, genuinely impressed. "That's the kind of tractor *I'm* looking for," I exclaimed. "Why don't you sell it in the United States?" He laughed. No, Americans wouldn't buy that kind of tractor. Market analyses showed Americans buy for status and would reject a truly economical tractor, he said. Then, seeing disbelief written all over my face, he weakened in a moment of candor. "Actually," he said with a grin, "we're afraid to market that kind of tractor here. It might capture too much of the market where our more profitable models are doing nicely now."

Another aspect of the company's plans for a simple tractor was even more significant. The plans called for a very small tractor not only because of cost and simplicity of operation, but also so that it would not give one small farmer any competitive advantage over another. The idea was just to *replace* the farmers' present power unit—draft animals—not to make it possible to farm more land. The tractor was intended not as a machine for aggrandizement which would eventually put the land in the hands of fewer people and destroy the present social structure, but which would only relieve some of the toil of primitive farming, redirect more food from draft animals to humans, and improve production because the tractor implements work the soil better.

I don't know whether replacing hand and animal power with machine power is right for underdeveloped countries in the long run, but the thinking of the equipment company is revealing indeed, and certainly a step in the right direction. Someone evidently realized that what we have done in the United States might not be the best way to develop a country. The tractor never replaced the horse in this country; it replaced the farmer. The more powerful the tractor, the more farmers it replaced. At no time were the promises of the Machine God fulfilled except temporarily to the survivors in the get-big-or-get-out race. Each improvement in machinery meant more farmers out of business, so that today less than 5 percent of the United States' population produces the food and owns the land. What a shame.

The only practical solution I found was to look for an old run-down tractor and repair it. You know the old saying, "They laughed when I sat down at the piano." Well, my friends absolutely roared when I sat down under an old junk tractor and said I was going to make it run again. I can't blame them. As my wife would put it, I have just enough native mechanical ability to unlock a door—if someone turns the key for me.

But to tend my 20 acres, I had to have a small, farm tractor. Something that would pull a seven-foot sickle mower, or an eight-foot disc, or a two-bottom plow. Twenty-five horsepower would do just fine. And naturally I wanted a tractor that wouldn't cost much.

That meant finding a junk tractor and burying myself in grease and gasket glue for a month or two of weekends, a prospect I did not find inviting. But wasn't I the one who was always pointing out that the homesteader who could not be his own handyman and mechanic was headed for failure? It was time to practice what I preached.

Hydraulic improvisation

With a bit of ingenuity, tractors can be modernized like this old Farmall F-12. The owner installed a hydraulic lift system, covered the steel wheels, and now prefers this tractor over his many others for all his farming chores.

The used tractor market is a never-never land of intrigue and mystery, I soon discovered. In no sector of our economy does free-enterprise capitalism flourish so vigorously. Demand is the whole game. A tractor that ten minutes ago was worthless (which means priced under $300) suddenly rises in value to $950 because a couple of what the tractor salesmen refer to as hobby farmers showed interest in it.

In the horsepower range I was looking for, old Fords, Fergusons, Ford-Fergusons, and John Deeres with three-point hitches are in biggest demand right now. Such tractors in good running order will sell for over $1,000 (1975 price). Comparable tractors without three-point hitches go for around $700. If in poor shape, both kinds of tractors could be as much as $400 lower. So, for one of the less desirable models in poor shape, you might pay around $300 and put it in running order for as little as $200 more, not counting your labor. But even if you had to shell out another $200 for repairs, you'd still have a good bargain.

I didn't really need the convenience of three-point hitch equipment, so I decided on one of the less desirable old tractors. I selected a WD Allis-Chalmers made about 1950. For one thing, I could get it cheap, and second, the owner was an especially nice fellow who let me use his tools and helped me with the overhauling. Third, the WD is a fairly simple tractor to take apart and put together. Fourth, it has a reputation of running even for hammer-head mechanics like me. Fifth, the WD has a power lift system almost as convenient as the three-point hitch. And finally, the tractor has both a hand and a foot clutch, which gives you the equivalent convenience of live power take-off found on modern tractors.

My son and I have the tractor running well enough to work our wheat field and mow the fall pastures, and it only cost me $500. There's more work to be done, but I have all next winter for that and I figure I'm still ahead with my old junk. Before long it will be as good as new.

Old steel wheels are kept from the junkyard by bolting rubber treads over them.

But I'm not the only one who prefers the older models. "I farmed my 132 acres in my spare time for about 25 years with tractors in the 20 to 30 horsepower range," says Harrell Noble from Xenia, Ohio. "Mine were old tractors when I bought them, and I still use them. I don't think it makes much sense for a part-time farmer to invest $5,000 to $7,000 in a new tractor. On my kind of farm, plowing 1½ acres per hour with my older tractors seems more sensible than plowing four to six acres per hour at five to ten times the investment."

This old Farmall is like just another member of the family.

Noble's first tractor back in 1952 was an Allis-Chalmers WC, which with an old disc, plow, manure spreader, and row planter (the tools you almost must have at the start) cost him around $700. Next he bought an F-20 International (1939 model) so that both he and his son could work in the field at the same time. His third tractor, a rebuilt 1942 Farmall H, he still refers to as his modern tractor. He's had two more over the year—another F-20 made in 1935 and a Farmall M which would pull a three-bottom plow.

"One advantage of buying older tractors is that you can afford more of them," says Noble. "Having several tractors can be very handy. At haying time, for instance, you don't have to keep hitching and unhitching tractors. We could leave the mounted cultivators on the H, rather than having to take them on and off for other pulling jobs. We'd use the Allis-Chalmers to pull the mower, one F-20 to rake, and the other F-20 pulling the baler. With the hay all mowed, the Allis-Chalmers was free to pull the wagons back and forth from the barn to the baler in the field."

But having an extra tractor can repay its cost in more than just convenience. "One year, one of the tractors broke down when we had a lot of hay ready to bale. The repairman couldn't get it fixed until the following week," recalls Noble. "I quickly hooked another tractor to the baler, with still a third one free to haul the loads of bales to the barn. Just as we finished, a rainstorm struck and the weather remained wet for a week. Having that extra tractor saved 50 tons of hay, in those days worth $1,000. We literally paid for two of those tractors in one day."

Jerry and Jean Harper in Indiana also have two tractors, which they refer to as "His" and "Hers." "His" is a Farmall H, 1952 vintage; "Hers," a Massey-Harris of about the same age. The Farmall needed a complete overhaul when they bought it. Harper tore it down, took the head to a machine shop for valve grinding. He put in new pistons, rings, sleeves, rod bearings, and crankshaft bearings at a cost of about $100 plus labor.

When I was overhauling my WD Allis-Chalmers, after I got my tractor torn down, I found just about everything was worn out, so while new parts are still available from the company, I went whole hog and had a mechanic rebuild almost everything. Now I have a fairly new 25-year-old tractor at a fourth of the cost of a similar-sized new tractor. An additional benefit you sometimes gain from keeping up a vintage tractor is that it begins to accrue antique value after awhile. Restoring old tractors has become almost as hot a hobby as restoring old cars.

Another thing—get the service manual for your tractor if at all possible. On most makes, they are still available if the company is still in business. Extra-proper care is necessary for old tractors, and you just can't know everything you should do without the manual.

"By all means, get the service manual," seconds Bill Bennett in Wisconsin, who owns an older Ford 8N, the most popular homestead tractor of all. Manuals for most major models of tractors (Allis-Chalmers, David Brown, Case, Deere, Ford, International Harvester, Massey-Ferguson, Minneapolis-Moline and Oliver), both new and old, are available from I & T Shop Service, Technical Publications, P.O. Box 12901, Overland Park, KS 66212. Bennett began homesteading in 1972 on 40 acres. "About 37 acres were under rental contract to another operator the first year, so we could handle three acres with our big tiller," he says. "But when the 37 acres came out from under the rental, we knew we had reached beyond the tiller stage.

"Some folks opt for the big suburban garden tractors, mistakenly, I think. They are fine for a couple of acres, but not for a small farm—and they cost as much per pound as a Cadillac."

First, Bennett checked out the moderate-sized new tractors on dealer lots. "They are exciting machines with many improvements over older tractors, but cost at least $5,000—hard to justify on a not-so-commercial farm." So he started out on a quest for the simplest, cheapest, used rig in the real tractor category.

"We narrowed our search to the Ford models 8N, 9N, and 2N (depending on year of manufacture, 1939 to 1952); Massey-Ferguson models 20 and 30; the John Deere B; the Allis-Chalmers WD; the Farmall A, C, and H models; and the Case C and D. Fords seemed less rare than the others, so we tried to find one. Finally opportunity knocked. A machine repair shop in the township offered a shining 8N, overhauled, restored, repainted and guaranteed for $1,600. With it was a useful, hydraulically operated front-loader, said to be worth another $400. The tractor also had a two-range transmission, which means you can gear down and creep in difficult pulling situations. That provided eight forward speeds, as contrasted with the usual four on a model 8N—an accessory said to cost $200. So we figured the tractor was a good buy and have never regretted our purchase."

The earlier model, 9N (1939 to 1947) offers three forward speeds, while the 8N (1948 to 1952) has four. "You can't pull much of anything in fourth gear," explains Bennett, "but it allows you to speed up to twelve miles per hour over the road, handy for tooling over to the local garage for a tune-up."

Both these popular old Fords are rated at 23 horsepower. They are heavy and rugged and will handle a one- or two-bottom mounted plow, or an eight-foot disc, mounted or trailing.

New parts for old tractors are obtainable through the dealers who sell that make of tractor. New parts, even for older tractors, are not cheap. You can sometimes save appreciably by shopping the huge used tractor and junk tractor centers located all over the Midwest. Ask farmers or mechanics in your area for the supply centers closest to you. Some of them are: Worthington, MN 56187; Wenger's Farm Machinery, Inc., South Race St., Myerstown, PA 17067; Al Galloway, St. Johns, MI 48879; Willard Equipment Inc., St. Rt. 99N, Willard, OH 44890; and Central Tractor 1515 East Euclid, Des Moines, IA 50313. I've gotten parts at Willard. There are thousands of junked tractors there. It's a tractor restorer's paradise—or maybe nightmare. Dealers seem to have a pretty good idea of what they have in all that mess, so it pays to call ahead. But it pays to go looking in person, too.

"One place that sells the gamut of vintage tractor parts on a mail-order basis is the Tractor Supply Co., 7910 L Street, Omaha, NB 68127," says Bennett. "The company issues a big catalog annually and also has stores in farm towns in 27 Midwest states." Surplus Tractor Parts Corporation, P.O. Box 2125, Fargo, ND 58102, ships worldwide, and has a catalog available for $1.

An English-based company, the Vapormatic Company Ltd., P.O. Box 1, Budleigh Salterton, Devon, EX9 6JB, England, also specializes in tractor replacement parts for all major models. It has associate companies in several countries around the world, including Australia, Ireland, France, Holland, South Africa, Northern Ireland, and the United States.

Finally, where do you find the tractors? This is one time when the classified ads can be most helpful, especially in rural newspapers. Or even more especially, rural trading papers that are nothing but classified ads.

The second best place is at farm sales. Look at the sale announcements in your papers. Farm sales are usually on Saturday, and the notices always list the machinery to be sold several days to a week early. The third best place is at dealer lots. Even when dealers don't have the old equipment you need, they sometimes know where some is available.

I'm forever griping that the farm machinery manufacturers don't make tools to fit the two- to 20-acre homestead. But every time I wonder out loud "why don't they make such and such," sure enough I soon find out someone *is* making such and such.

Those of us familiar with the old Allis-Chalmers model G tractor remember its passing with tears in our eyes and terrible envy for those still lucky enough to have preserved one. The G is the ugliest tractor ever built; it looks like an arthritic spider trying to do push-ups. But there is no handier cultivating machine ever made for the large truck garden. It will turn sharp enough to turn itself inside out, and can be maneuvered (from the seat hovering over the plants) so easily that you could tickle the potatoes in their hills without harming them. No machine is designed to take attachments easier or can be repaired with less trouble. The G doesn't wear out—and the only way to get one is to inherit it.

The original Allis-Chalmers G: "The only way to get one is to inherit it."

But G lovers don't have to eat their hearts out any longer. There's a new small tractor on the market that looks and acts a lot like the old G. It's called Tuff-bilt, made by Tri-Tractor Manufacturing Co. (Rt. 1, Hwy. 19 North, Cumming, GA 30130). When I first heard about the tractor, the rumor going around said that the company was so small you could order your tractor in any color you wanted. "Well, that's not quite true," says Jerry Gravitt at Tri-Tractor headquarters in

Cumming. "That story got started because all the other machinery companies who wanted to sell the Tuff-bilt wanted it painted in their own colors. So we painted 'em orange, blue, or green depending on whom the order was for."

The tractor runs on a 16 horsepower, air-cooled, Lawson Tecumseh engine with all-gear drive and individual left- and right-hand brakes. It uses only about a gallon of gas an hour and has plenty of high clearance so you can cultivate over corn and other crops with ease. Cole and Brinly-Hardy tools fit the tractor, and there are all kinds of other attachments too—mower, 12-inch plow, 26-inch disc plow, cultivators—the works. The price is just under $2,800, which isn't bad considering that this is about all the tractor you really should need for handling 20 acres or so. "With a complete set of tools, you're talking about $4,200," says Gravitt, "which is quite a bit less than just the basic price on a regular small tractor."

Another company to bring back a version of the Chalmers G is John Blue with their Model G-1000. It's a bit larger and heavier than Tuff-bilt but the design is right there. With the engine mounted on the back, there is better traction and the front is left with clear visibility. Implements attached to the front let the operator watch with greater ease and drive with greater accuracy.

The Blue G-1000 had a slow start when it came out four years ago. "It was a novelty and folks were skeptical," reports Cecil Walker of their Bowling Green, Ohio, plant. But now it is really catching on with weekend farmers and garden folks—the garden implements are going with it. Surprisingly enough, sales have really taken off in Chicago.

Hefty has two models of the old-style G, a 27 horsepower, rear-mounted unit and the Hefty Hi-G. The Hi-G was particularly designed for nursery and agricultural applications where 36 inches of clearance and unrestricted visibility are required.

NORTH AMERICAN SOURCES OF MODEL G TRACTORS

Tuff-bilt

The smallest of the new G models available, the Tuff-bilt has a 16 h.p. engine for powering the liquid-cooled, hydrostatic transmission and two category O three-point hitches with 400-pound lifting capacities, front and rear. Implements available for use on the Tuff-bilt include front and rear cultivators, front attachment for the Cole No. 12 planter (page 204), disc harrow, three-point drawbar, 12-inch-bottom moldboard plow, 54-inch grader blade, a 26-inch disc plow and rotary mower.

The Tuff-bilt tractor—a lot like the Allis-Chalmers G.
Tri-Tractor Mfg. Co.

Tri-Tractor Mfg. Co.
Rt. 1, Hwy. 19 North
Cumming, GA 30130

Blue G-1000

The Blue G-1000 has a 16.8 h.p., water-cooled, four-cylinder gasoline engine. It has a Warner gear transmission with three forward speeds, and high and low reverse speeds. Hydraulic lift is standard but the live PTO is optional. The G-1000 can be operated with a single-row cultivator, 12-inch moldboard plow, 60-inch three-spindle mower, 6-foot single-section disc harrow, or a 5-foot spring-tooth or spike-tooth harrow.

John Blue Co.
P.O. Box 1607
Huntsville, AL 35807

Hefty Hi-G

A high ground clearance of 36 inches provides the Hi-G with its outstanding feature and its name. As is characteristic of all type G trac-

The Hefty Hi-G

The Hefty-G
Diana Branch

tors, its 27 h.p., water-cooled, gasoline or diesel engine is mounted in the rear, and the driver enjoys unrestricted visibility. A front-mounted, three-point hydraulic implement lift system or rear-mounted hydraulic furrowing bars support the ground-working tools. Its high ground clearance design is particularly suited for nursery and agricultural applications, but the high center of gravity makes it unsuitable for working on steep slopes. The selective sliding gear transmission has six forward and one reverse speed, providing a maximum forward speed of 13 kph. The 2- by 4-inch, welded rectangular steel tube frame is 82 inches high to the top of the steering wheel, has a 76-inch wheelbase, and weighs 2,440 pounds. A 12-volt electrical system operates a starter, generator, and four sealed-beam headlights. Available as optional equipment are a 540 rpm power take-off, live engine speed, front center power take-off, two-cycle, water-cooled diesel engine, variable tread widths as low as 4½ inches or up to 120 inches, single-row or multiple gang independent cultivator assemblies, rear hydraulic furrow and bar assembly, and rear drawbar kit.

Hefty Gw

Incorporating the same engine, transmission, and frame construction as the Hefty Hi-G, the Hefty Gw has a lower center of gravity with its lower, 19-inch ground clearance. The wide wheelbase straddles up to four rows or more of vegetables, reducing planting, cultivating and thinning time. It also has two specialized power take-off shaft outlets: one live at engine speed, one synchronized with ground speed. Optional implements include a 60-inch mid-mount rotary mower, single- and two-row cultivators, Danish fiber tine, spring-trip and spring-tine, double toolbar cultivator, midmount blade, and hydraulically controlled rear-mount furrowing bar with shanks. If you want the lower center of gravity of a Hefty but don't need the wider wheel base, a model called the Hefty G is available with a narrower wheelbase.

Hefty Tractor Co.
P.O. Box 188
Juneau, WI 53039

YE OLDE CHALMERS B AS HOMESTEAD TRACTOR

by John F. Sutton

If you're looking for a economical homestead tractor, you might consider one of the earliest of the utility-type tractors, the Allis-Chalmers Model B. This machine could be the workhorse tractor of today's homestead.

Rated at 20 horsepower, the B is considered a single-plow tractor, but depending upon soil types and conditions, it is capable of pulling a double plow.

While the B is a farm tractor in size, its power, workability, and durability make it superior to any of today's largest garden tractors, and its price, $150 and up, is a far cry from any other farm tractor or new 20-horse garden tractor.

A wide variety of attachments were produced for this versatile little tractor—mowers, cultivators, single-bottom mounted plows, and a rather unique two-way plow designed to allow plowing while traveling back and forth on the same furrow.

Don't limit yourself to mounted accessories. The B can easily pull a variety of manure spreaders, trailers, discs, drags, and planters. The power take-off will handle balers, blowers, rakes, and, best of all, the belt pulley will power feed grinders, saws, and small threshing machines, which are so handy in homestead and small farming operations.

Some of these tractors are equipped with a small hydraulic system capable of handling mounted plows, cultivators, and other assorted lightweight implements. For the most part, snow blades and manure buckets are homemade and thus of a wide variety.

Sutton on his old Chalmers B.

The B was introduced in 1937 as a lightweight general-purpose tractor; it is precisely this age factor which makes the B a very attractive tractor for the homesteader. Because of its age, the B often sells for less than $300 at farm auctions and between $300 and $500 through tractor dealers.

Even here in Wisconsin, where these tractors are highly prized by tobacco farmers, the prices remain low. Also, because of their age, they are simple machines and are economical to operate.

I prefer the hand start model, because of the simplicity of the mechanical workings of the tractor. The only concern with a hand start is the potential kickback of the cranking handle. Any indication of a backfire or kickback is a sign that it is time for maintenance.

At any rate, if you hold the crank properly (that is, with your thumb on the same side of the handle as your fingers), at most the flying handle may kick back and sting your hand, but there will be no broken bones.

Can you really homestead with the old Chalmers B? Absolutely! I have heard of people farming up to 80 acres with one B and a few attachments. My father-in-law farmed 280 acres, including up to 21 acres of tobacco, with a couple of Bs, an old Chalmers WC, and a good team—and with one of the Bs running the milking machines for 40 to 45 Jersey cows.

My wife, son, and I recently raised two organic acres of tobacco with our oldest B (hand start) doing all of the disking (no plowing) and all other soil preparations, planting, cultivating, and harvesting. And the old B could have handled more acres had we the time and fortitude.

Parts for all models are still readily available and inexpensive if purchased wisely.

THE CARE AND FEEDING OF TWO-CYLINDER JOHN DEERE TRACTORS

by Arnold Voehringer

The big, green, two-cylinder John Deeres of the pre-World War II years stand almost in a class by themselves as models of appropriate technology. They were built with one goal in mind—to perform the jobs for which they were intended as simply and economically as possible.

The two-cylinder John Deere is a fine example of form strictly following function. With its low compression ratio, it seems to run on just about anything. That little tank behind the main tank is for gasoline to start the tractor and warm it up. Then you switch to the main tank, which can contain kerosene, heating oil, or diesel fuel, as well as regular gas.

"No better tractor," says Arnold Voehringer of his vintage John Deeres. The 1936 and 1939 (styled) Bs seen here are adapted to a wide range of jobs on farms of all sizes.

The rugged elegance and almost primitive simplicity of design that are the trademarks of those machines that came out of John Deere's Moline, Illinois, shops are typified by features such as their flywheel starting system. While other manufacturers introduced fancy self-starters with batteries that went dead, and crank starters with their penchant for kicking back and breaking thumbs, John Deere opted for the big exposed flywheel, which almost always turned over on the first or second turn. The operator simply opens the petcock for each cylinder and pulls the flywheel (my wife can start our B with one hand) to top dead center, at which point the magneto fires and the tractor snorts to life.

The thermo-syphon cooling system bypasses the need for a water pump by capitalizing on that elementary law of physics that says hot water rises and displaces cold water in a closed system.

Another advantage of the old Deeres is the safety aspect of the hand clutch. When a foot slips off the pedal of a conventional clutch and the tractor lurches forward, the result is potentially catastrophic. Should the A or B with hand clutch jerk forward, it effectively pulls the clutch rearward and the tractor stops.

With their low center of gravity created by the horizontal engine, J.D.s are less prone to rolling over on hilly terrain. Also, with the engine closer to the rear axle, traction is improved. While this means the front end is correspondingly lighter, it can be correctd simply by the use of front-end weights.

But even beyond the hand clutch, the flywheel starter, and the interchangeability of parts, the old Deeres had something else going for them. They sounded right. It's a sound no one who is familiar with the unmistakable, sunup to sundown putt-putt of a two-cylinder J.D. going about its business on some hillside halfway across the county, or who has experienced the magnificent, unmuffled din of that engine set at full throttle for filling silo, is ever likely to forget.

With just two cylinders, there are fewer parts to replace and repairs are easy, even for the operator with very limited mechanical aptitude. With a peak rpm of 975, the John Deere A is a relatively low-revving engine, and is much less sensitive to exact tolerances than modern tractors. Just about everything that can go wrong can be fixed by anyone with a maintenance manual and some basic tools. Adjusting the clutch, for instance, almost invariably means an expensive trip to the

The hand clutch is a real safety plus, especially with young operators.

dealer with any modern tractor. All that's required to do the same job on an A or B are pliers and a ¾-inch wrench. Likewise for the carburetor adjustment. You just turn in the screw till you hear the pop, then turn it out until the black smoke appears. With the bearings, both the main and the connecting rod bearings are simple to adjust—a far cry from some of today's sealed roller bearings. The same simplicity applies to work on the steering, ignition, brakes, and any number of jobs that are major headaches with more sophisticated technology. Even the transmission, with its big, rugged gears and one-piece housing, is much less intimidating than its bewildering modern counterparts. Since the crankshaft turns parallel to the rear axle, not perpendicular as is the case with most later transmissions, the power is transmitted directly through the spur gears instead of around corners.

Unlike some other tractors of similar vintage, parts are still widely available for elderly J.D.s. The regional farm magazines regularly run ads from parts dealers. Many John Deere dealers still have parts on hand or can order them. The dealer is also the place to order a repair manual and parts book, both of which are worth their weight in gold if you do your own repair work.

This discussion is confined to the A and B models, since many more of them were made and, consequently, are still available. The two models were designed for two specific categories of farmer.

On my own hillside farm near Kempton, Pennsylvania, I use my 1936 B for mowing in the summer and sawing firewood in the winter, my 1939 B for cultivating, a 1947 A for disking, drilling,

"Just turn in the screw until you hear the pop, then back it off until the black smoke appears."

and spreading manure, a 720 diesel for plowing, baling, combining and picking corn, and a 1939 G for hayridges, secondary tillage, pulling wagons, and running a hammermill.

For the small farmer with five or ten acres and no more four-legged animals than, say, a horse and a goat or cow, the B is ideal. Unless it's a late model, big-piston B, or you have exceptionally loose soil, don't count on pulling more than a two-bottom, 12-inch plow. The A is a different story. You can run a 60-inch flail chopper, a baler, a combine, or a four-row front-mounted cultivator with an A. It may not get over the ground quite as fast as some of today's behemoths, but it's just right for most jobs on the small farm.

The big difference between John Deere's letter series (A and B) and their corresponding number series (60 and 50) is that the latter offers live hydraulics and live power take-off, a real asset when it comes to baling, combing, and corn picking. If you have live PTO and your baler starts to jam, you can pull out the clutch to stop the tractor without stopping the baler. Without the live PTO, the baler stops too, and once you stop a jammed baler, you'll never get it started again without unplugging it by hand. Three-point hitch attachments can be purchased for the A or B, enabling the operator to use the full range of newer implements.

The B started out in 1935 with a drawbar horsepower rating of nine and ended up in 1952 with a rating of 20. The A started out as a 16 horsepower drawbar tractor in 1934 and finished in 1952 with 26. Until the big tractors (40 horsepower and up) started to arrive on the scene around wartime, these tractors were generally regarded as *the* best source of power. Today, by virtue of their size and weight, they are often better-adapted to operations on the small farm than their streamlined modern counterparts.

Fortunately, many two-cylinder John Deeres in good condition are still available at sales. In the eastern U.S.A. (in 1977), Bs are bringing from $00 to $700, As about $1,000. The 50s and 60s are a little higher.

When sizing up old J.D.s at a farm sale, how do you tell a good one from a clunker? Here are a few easy checks:

1. Check the side play in the hand clutch. There is no grease fitting at the bushing, so unless a new bushing and pin have been installed (which you can usually tell), this play is a good indication of how hard the tractor has been used. Anything over three-inches play should be viewed with caution.
2. Check the play in the radiator fan. Again, three inches should be about tops, although I've seen four and five inches of play in tractors still being used daily.
3. Check the steering wheel play and the brake pedal side play. The left pedal may be a little looser, especially if the tractor has been used mainly for plowing with a conventional plow.

Flywheel starting beats cranking any day, the author reports.

4. Grab the flywheel and try to shake it. If it moves more than the slightest bit (.010 inches), steer clear.
5. Check for large leaks from oil, water, transmission, gear oil, and hydraulics. There should be no signs of oil in the radiator or water in the crank case.
6. Check the block and manifold for cracks. With two cylinder J.D.s, if you can't see the cracks there probably are none.
7. Check the rear-end housing. The best of the three types John Deere used is the Power-Trol, which allows the use of either a single- or double-acting hydraulic cylinder.

With so much to recommend them, what are the chances that John Deere might be prevailed upon to reintroduce a two-cylinder tractor in the 20 to 40 horsepower range? After all, the stock of parts around the country won't hold out forever. Not very likely, say J.D. marketing people, who argue that the largest of their current line of garden tractors and the smallest of the "Long Green Line" of utility farm tractors (the 36 horsepower 830) effectively overlap to serve this market. Maybe so, but speaking as one who has his doubts, I can see a legitimate case to be made for the two-cylinder as the tractor of the future.

THE BUFFALO

The Buffalo is an outgrowth of a little tractor Vern Schield invented in 1963 called the Self-Helper. It was developed to aid emerging nations in their transition from muscle to machine power. Self-Help, Inc., manufacturer of these tractors, is a nonprofit organization that only sells outside the United States.

The Waverly Tractor Company in Iowa modified the Self-Helper design to meet United States safety standards and now produces their model, the Buffalo, for sale here. They use recycled automotive parts to allow the Buffalo to compete in price with imported models. Vern Schield, inventor of the Self-Helper, makes these points about the Buffalo, "We have found that the Chevrolet differential used in 1955 to 1964 cars invariably outlasted its original application. When gears run together for 50,000 miles and still mesh within specifications, you know the differential was well

The Buffalo

designed. General Motors made millions of them and we only pick the best. In our application, it can last for years. Sure it helps America not to waste its waste, but most of all it helps us build a tractor you can afford. We have no reservations about guaranteeing everything we use."

The transmission is from a ¾-ton Ford or Chevy pickup. V-belts acting as a clutch make a two-to-one reduction from the 25 horsepower, air-cooled engine to the transmission. Except for a few later models, all American-manufactured combines and forage harvesters have such a V-belt drive from the engine.

Waverly Tractor Company's original intentions were to purchase a steering section from one of the manufacturers that make this type of equipment for small tractors. However, they found a Saginaw steering section which was standard on most General Motors cars, as well as Ford and Chrysler. It was easier to install and much heavier than the steering sections manufactured for this purpose. So, naturally, this was their choice.

Waverly Tractor doesn't fit any mold. The factory is in an old buffalo pasture, next to the shed where the first prototype now lives. The field testing is done by teenagers—nobody can break things faster than two kids competing. Everyone who works for the company wants to be there. Some employees have quit better-paying jobs to do so. Others have started cottage industries, working in their homes and usually furnishing their own equipment. Several partially handicapped people are turning out quality parts for the Buffalo. Schield feels that this, too, is a resource that should not be wasted.

Turning discarded materials into marketable products is not only a rewarding experience, but it is also good business. Seeking this combination has led Waverly Tractor into many interesting developments.

Waverly Tractor Co.
Sleeping Giant–Hwy. 3 East
Waverly, IA 50677

AFRICA'S OWN, THE TINKABI

Africa is proud to announce the arrival of its own tractor, the Tinkabi. With a name derived from the Siswati word for oxen, the Tinkabi was designed under the aegis of the Swaziland government and the National Industrial Development Corporation (NIDC) of Swaziland to give small

The Tinkabi with seeding attachment
National Industrial Development Corp.

farmers the opportunity to mechanize. As the NIDC theory goes, ". . . if [the] agricultural Third World is to develop, it is essential that a simple, low-cost tractor is made available to the farmer to increase his productivity and income."

The Tinkabi has many features not normally found on other tractors. Its front loading platform is capable of carrying 500 kilograms. The addition of a trailer brings the transport capacity to 2,000 kilograms. The heart of the tractor is an air-cooled, hand-started, twin cylinder, 16 horsepower engine which, under normal farm use, consumes less than 1½ liters of diesel fuel per hour.

A wide range of implements can be clamped to the toolbar assembly. Basic equipment like the plow, planter, cultivator, ridger, and harrow accomplish the usual agricultural tasks while additional features such as a sprayer, circular saw, hammermill, water pump, overhead sprinkler system for up to four hectares, sawbench, and electrical generator make a useful contribution to the general chores that are needed to be done around the farm on a daily basis. As of May 1977, Tinkabi will do all this for about $2,000.

With a front loading platform and trailer, the Tinkabi can transport 2,000 kilograms.
National Industrial Development Corp.

NORTH AMERICAN SOURCES OF FOUR-WHEEL TRACTORS

The International Cub Tractor

International Harvester has been making the Cub for over 25 years. It started out as an all-purpose farm tractor but has since gained popularity as a versatile implement for commercial situations: warehouses, loading docks, nurseries, and small airports. It has a 15 h.p., four-cylinder engine and hydraulic power for front-, rear-, and center-mounted implements. The offset front motor mounting improves visibility for front- and center-mounted work. The one-point fast hitch acts as a swinging drawbar to hitch or switch implements in a minute or less. The power take-off can be operated at three speeds to run a number of different implements

The International Harvester Cub
International Harvester Co.

with different power and speed requirements. Attachments available with the Cub include moldboard plow, cultivators, discs, earth and snowplows, rotary and sickle bar mowers. The Cub is also available as a compact model with an 18.5 h.p. engine. With lower clearance than the standard Cub, this unit is better suited for lawn and estate work.

International Farmall 140 Tractor

Capable of mounting attachments at the front, center, and rear, the Farmall is used most with front and center cultivation to take full advantage of the Culti-Vision feature, also available on the Cub. With no blind spot in front, you can see the ground rigs on both sides of a single row and control them precisely both horizontally and vertically. This tractor is widely used for cultivating tobacco, vegetables, and nursery stock. One size larger than the Cub, the Farmall employs a 25 h.p., four-cycle, water-cooled engine with four forward and one reverse gear.

International Harvester Co.
401 N. Michigan Ave.
Chicago, IL 60611

Power King Tractors

Power King, formerly known as Economy tractors, offers several models. Differing only in features—tire sizes and type of hitch—Power King tractors put a 14 h.p., four-cycle, air-cooled, gasoline engine to operate equipment for all sorts of tasks. A belt-driven power take-off on the front of the tractor operates the mower, tiller, and snowblower while the three-groove pulley behind the engine drives the sprayer and hydraulic systems. Other attachments include a full line of cultivating equipment: spring-tooth cultivator, heavy-duty cultivator, toolbar hiller-furrower, and rotary tiller, as well as a 5-foot sickle bar, trailer, sprayer, and seed-fertilizer spreader.

A Power King tractor with rotary tiller attachment.
Engineering Products Co.

Engineering Products Co.
P.O. Box 284
1515 E. Ellis St.
Waukesha, WI 53186

Ford 1600

Ford's smallest tractor outside of the lawn and garden category is their Model 1600 with a 23 h.p. diesel engine. With nine speeds forward and three reverse and many modern features, this unit transcends simplicity but is special because diesel tractors are not commonly found in the United States. This unit has attachments for many farm jobs: there are subsoilers, cultivators, harrows, mowers, rakes, scoops, cranes, post-hole diggers, loaders, seeders, and fertilizer attachments.

Ford Motor Co., Tractor & Implement Operation
2500 E. Maple Rd.
Troy, MI 48084

Ford Model 1600

Wheel Horse Series D

The 16 and 19.9 h.p. Wheel Horse tractors would fall into the lawn and garden category except for the fact that they offer a wide variety of attachments, making them more of a utility tool than an implement for lawn care. Some of the attachments include a 3-gallons-per-minute sprayer, log splitter, landscaping rake, rear-mounted garden blade, shredder-grinder, 4-foot side-mounted sickle bar, lug wheels, mowers, cab, and all Brinly-Hardy cultivating attachments.

Wheel Horse
515 W. Ireland Rd.
South Bend, IN 46614

Magnatrac

To date, Magnatrac is the only small-scale full-track crawler we have seen. The enclosed and protected tracking system with side panels and center idler wheels features No. A550 chain welded to 10-gauge interlocking steel shoes with over 10,000 pounds of ultimate track strength, and dual track tension springs for approximately 3,000 pounds of tension maintained on each track. The all-gear transmission with four forward and one reverse speed shifts like an automobile. It is powered by a 16 h.p., valve-in-head, cool-running, cast-iron (or 12 h.p. standard) engine. It can utilize over 30 attachments including the whole Brinly-Hardy line of farm and garden implements, both high- and low-lift loaders with either hydraulic or electric lift systems, a 42-inch snow and soil blade, a 42-inch snowblower, self-dumping bucket, 36-inch-wide manure fork, backhoe, and electric light kit.

Struck Corp.
Struck Lane
Cedarburg, WI 53012

Hefty-F and LNT

The Hefty-F is an all-chore power tractor with a 27 h.p., water-cooled, four-stroke, four-cylinder, gasoline engine with diesel option. A selective sliding gear transmission operates six speeds forward and one reverse for a maximum traveling speed of 8.5 mph forward. It has a live power take-off shaft at the rear of the tractor, a ground clearance of 19½ inches, weighs 2,200 pounds and has a 12-volt starter and generator and four sealed-beam headlights. Sharing the same specifications, the Hefty LNT incorporates the same components into a compact design for narrow nursery work. Its 38-inch overall tractor width is adjustable to 56 inches. An optional creeper gear unit is available to reduce ground speed to as low as $\frac{2}{10}$ mph for transplanting and for extra slow ground speed work. Optional implements include a 60-inch, midmount rotary

The Hefty-LNT
Diana Branch

mower, front-end loader, front-mounted snowblower, and all attachments accommodated by category 1, three-point hitches. Examples include chisel plows, one- and two-bottom plows, disc harrows, six-inch blades, one-row cultivators, field cultivators, 60-inch rotary tillers and a 60-inch rotary broom.

Hefty Tractor Co.
P.O. Box 188
Juneau, WI 53039

CPI Model AY

Custom Products makes a 14 h.p. tractor with a four-cycle, air-cooled, manual start engine. It comes with four forward and one reverse speed and has a steel channel frame with 60-inch wheelbase and 14½ inches of ground clearance. As optional equipment, the Model AY is available with head and tail lights, a hydraulic power take-off system with three-point hitch which operates the lift and all other tools requiring power. Accessories include a 50-inch rotary mower, snowblower, 54-inch rear leveling blade, a 44-inch, 16-bladed, double-disc harrow, six-sweep cultivator, rotary tiller, 12-inch single-row ridger, single-row planter, fertilizer hopper, transplanter, and tilt-top cargo trailer. Weight: 905 pounds.

Custom Products, Inc.
4232 Roosevelt Rd.
Stevensville, MI 49127

Belarus Model 250

Another air-cooled, four-stroke diesel tractor similar in size to the Ford 1600 is the Belarus 250. It has a standard three-point hitch with drawbar, rear PTO and side-mounted power shaft, eight forward and six reverse speeds. A full line of attachments and larger units is available.

Belarus Equipment of Canada, Ltd.
43 Goldthorne Ave.
Toronto, Ontario, M8Z 557 Canada

Belarus Machinery, Inc.
7075 W. Parkland Court
Milwaukee, WI 53223

The Belarus 250
Belarus Machinery, Inc.

NORTH AMERICAN SOURCES OF GARDEN TRACTORS

There are literally dozens of lawn and garden tractors which are available with attachments in North America for all kinds of large gardening and small farming tasks. Because they do not fall in the hard-to-find category we believe it will be sufficient to provide just a listing of manufacturers and their addresses. Contact a few of these sources. You'll be amazed at the attachments available.

Agway, Inc.
P.O. Box 1333
Syracuse, NY 13201

Allis-Chalmers
Box 512
Milwaukee, WI 53201

Ariens Co.
655 W. Ryan St.
Brillion, WI 54110

Avco New Idea
420 S. First St.
Coldwater, OH 45828

Belknap, Inc.
P.O. Box 28
Louisville, KY 40201

J. I. Case Co.
Outdoor Power Equipment Div.
Winneconne, WI 54986

Central Tractor, dist. by Weaver's Hardware Co.
RD 2, Lyons Rd.
Fleetwood, PA 19522

John Deere
Moline, IL 61265

Farm & Fleet
1600 E. Lincoln Hwy.
DeKalb, IL 60115

Farnam Sunrise Equipment and Supplies
P.O. Box 12068
Omaha, NE 68112

FMC Corp.
Outdoor Power Equipment Div.
215 S. Park St.
Port Washington, WI 53074

Ford Tractors
Ford Tractors Operations
2500 E. Maple Rd.
Troy, MI 48084

Gilson Brothers Co.
Box 152
Plymouth, WI 53073

or

3325 Orlando Drive
Mississauga, Ontario, Canada

Glen-Bel's Country Store
Rt. 5, Box 390
Crossville, TN 38555

International Harvester
Agricultural Equipment Div.
401 N. Michigan Ave.
Chicago, IL 60611

Massey Ferguson, Inc.
1901 Bell Ave.
Des Moines, IA 50315

Montgomery Ward
1000 S. Monroe St.
Baltimore, MD 21232

MTD Products, Inc.
5389 W. 130th St.
P.O. Box 2741
Cleveland, OH 44111

Roper Sales
1905 W. Court St.
Kankakee, IL 60901

Satoh
P.O. Box 5020
New York, NY 10022

Sears Farm and Ranch Catalog

Simplicity Manufacturing Co., Ltd.
500 N. Spring St.
Port Washington, WI 53074

Tractor Supply Co.
7910 L St.
Omaha, NE 68127

Wheelhorse
515 W. Ireland Rd.
South Bend, IN 46614

and your local hardware store.

INTERNATIONAL SOURCES OF FOUR-WHEEL TRACTORS

Finally realizing a market for the small utility farm tractor, many North American companies are distributing European and Far Eastern tractors, although they have not themselves undertaken to manufacture them. Those models readily available in North America but not manufactured there will be listed first.

Many of the larger agricultural machinery manufacturers in the United States, like John Deere and Massey Ferguson, are in the process of establishing arrangements with foreign manufacturers to build small tractors to their own specifications. As of fall 1977, arrangements were still being formalized.

The Holder Model A-18 Tractor

The Model A-18 was designed by the Gebruder Holder Company in Germany for use on hilly vineyard terrain, tree plantations, nurseries, berry farms—any situation requiring the combined features of maneuverability, stability, and power in a compact unit to operate in high-density plantings. Its 18 h.p., four-stroke, air-cooled, diesel engine claims to have the power of a 25 or 30 h.p. gasoline engine while consuming 1/8 the amount of fuel or less. Model A-18 comes with a standard three-point hitch and has the unusual feature of articulated, bends-in-the-middle, steering. Attachments available include a 31- or 39-inch rotary cultivator, an implement linkage for steep vertical lift, a universal implement carrier frame for plow and cultivating blades, a sickle bar, trailed spindle gang mowers, rollers, a trailer, seed and fertilizer spreaders, all varieties of rakes, and miscellaneous lawn equipment. Larger units are available.

Gebruder Holder
7418 Metzingen-Wurtt.
Postfach 66
West Germany

Tradewinds, Inc.
P.O. Box 1191
2339 Tacoma Ave. S
Tacoma, WA 98401

Pasquali U.S.A.

The Italian-built Pasquali is a 19.9 h.p. one-cylinder, four-wheel-drive, four-stroke, diesel tractor with articulated steering. Models with 24, 29 and 34 h.p. are also available. The transmission employs a sliding-type key gear with synchronizer supplying nine forward and three reverse speeds. The PTO has two speeds but it

Pasquali Four-Wheel-Drive Tractor
Pasquali U.S.A., Inc.

can also be synchronized with all tractor speeds. Supplied with both a two- and three-point linkage, the hitches can be raised with an independent hydraulic lift system. Implements available for use with the GBT Pasquali include a rotary tiller, front-mount mower, single- and double-bottom plows, cultivator, and side cycle mower. Pasquali offers a number of other PTO attachments—enough to fill a 200-page blooklet. These are discussed in the section on two-wheel tractors.

Pasquali Macchine Agricole
Via Nuovo, 30
Calenzano (Firenze), Italy

Pasquali USA
Verona, WI 53593

Satoh Beaver

The 15 h.p. Beaver is made in Japan. It has a two-cylinder, water-cooled, four-cycle, diesel engine and is available with either two- or four-wheel drive. A sliding selective gear transmission system offers six forward and two reverse speeds with a maximum speed of 7 mph. A power take-off shaft, live hydraulics, category 0 three-point hitch, sealed brakes, various warning lights, full lighting, and choice of tire tread are all standard. Optional equipment includes front chassis, front and rear wheel weights, rotary tiller with special two-point hitch, front power take-off, power take-off adaptor with guard, and hydraulic external adaptor plate. All standard category 0 implements can be fitted to this unit.

Satoh
P.O. Box 5020
New York, NY 10022

Satoh Agricultural Machine Mfg. Co., Ltd.
Hibiya Kokusai Building
2-chome, Uchisaiwai-Cho
Chiyoda-ku, Tokyo, Japan

Satoh Beaver

Kubota Models B6000, L175, L225, L285

Kubota offers four basic models, and variations, of two-, three-, and four-cylinder, liquid-cooled, diesel tractors with power output ranging from 12½ to 30 h.p. The three-point hitch fits all category one implements, and the PTO is located front, center, and rear with a ten-speed multirange transmission. Units are available with four-wheel drive and lug tire options. Kubota is made in Japan but dealerships are being widely established.

Kubota Ltd.
22 Funade-cho
2-chome Naniwa-ku
Osaka, Japan

Kubota Model B6000

Kubota Tractor Corp.
300 W. Carob St.
Compton, CA 90220

Yanmar

Another compact diesel tractor available with either two- or four-wheel drive, is the Japanese-built Yanmar. The engine has two cylinders, is water-cooled, and is a four-cycle unit available in either 13, 15 or 20 h.p. models. The constant-mesh/selective mesh gear combination provides six forward and two reverse speeds. A two-speed PTO accompanies the three-point category 0 hitch with hydraulic lift. The Yanmar can be operated with a rotary mower capable of covering 1½ acres per hour, a front-end loader and backhoe for the 20 h.p. model, a 30- or 42-inch rear-mount tiller (depending on the size of the tractor), and a full line of cultivation attachments—tandem disc harrow, moldboard plow, and one-row cultivators with either rigid or six Danish vibrating S shanks. Attachments are available through the Yanmar dealers but are not exclusive to Yanmar.

Yanmar National Sales Manager
Time-Life Building
303 E. Ohio St.
Chicago, IL 60611

Yanmar Diesel Engine Co., Ltd.
1-11-1, Marunouchi. Chiyoda-ku
Tokyo, Japan

Agrale Model 4100

A four-stroke, diesel, 16 h.p., air-cooled engine powers a seven forward and three reverse speed transmission, differential lock dry plate, spring-loaded clutch, and a power take-off with three engine speeds. The unit has a working weight of 1,100 kilograms, a ground clearance of 12 inches, and a 48-inch wheelbase. It has a hydraulic lifting system coupled directly with the front power take-off of the engine, governed by a controlling three-stage lever. Implements include a two-row seed and fertilizer drill, leveling blade, cargo transporter, coffee cultivator, cultivating harrow, and three-bottom moldboard plow.

Agrale S.A.
Rua Sinimbu, 1260
Caixa Postal, 1311
95.100 Caxias Do Sul, RS, Brazil

Iseki TX1300

Similar in design to the Kubota is the water-cooled, diesel Iseki. It has nine forward and three reverse speeds, three speeds on the PTO, and a hydraulic lift. Units with four-wheel drive are available, an important feature in small tractors. Often, a small tractor falls short in tractive ability before it runs out of power. Four-wheel drive increases traction by 50 percent, according to Iseki. A wide range of attachments is available for fertilizing, planting, ridging, puddling (rice culture in wetlands), mowing, tedding, mulching, and plowing.

Iseki Agricultural Machinery Mfg. Co., Ltd.
Overseas Dept.
1-3 Nihonbashi, 2-chome
Chou-ku, Tokyo, Japan

Agria 4800 Compact Tractor

Though universally applicable, the 4800 is designed to fill the gap between the range of operation of the two-wheel tractor and the commensurable four-wheel tractor in agriculture, nurseries, orchards, and vineyards. It is powered by a 19 h.p., air-cooled, four-stroke, single-cylinder engine with six forward and six reverse speeds, differential, and differential lock. Top speed is 10 mph. The rear power take-off is independent of gear speed. Track width is adjustable between 24.2 and 32.3 inches; its ground clearance is approximately 10 inches. Equipped with hydraulic lift and a 12-volt electrical system for starter, head and tail lights, and direction indicators. Weight: approximately 1,323 pounds. Implements and accessories include rotary tiller, wheel weights, spraying unit with its own 8 h.p., two-stroke gasoline engine with a 19.8 gallon capacity and high-pressure sprayer pumping 55 liters per minute, spring-tine cultivator adjustable from 80 to 125 centimeters, a six-disc harrow with working width of 43.4 inches, reversible plow, side reciprocating mower, four sizes of earth-boring augers, a two-part harrow with 70.8-inch working width, all-weather hood with front window, fertilizer-broadcaster in three sizes either ground-driven or driven by a power take-off connection, and 1,100-kilogram-capacity trailer. At the time of this writing Agria is seeking a distributor in North America.

The Agria 4800 Compact Tractor with reversible plow
Agria-Werke

Agria-Werke GmbH
7108 Moeckmuehl,
West Germany

Basak-12 Garden-Type Tractor

Weighted wheels are provided with this compact, single-cylinder, 11.2 h.p. tractor. It has three forward and one reverse speed and a mechanical command lifting system with three-point linkage. Attachments include a moldboard plow with a working width of 26 centimeters and working depth of 19 centimeters, a seven-tine or three-row cultivator, ridger, duck-foot cultivator, subsoiler, and sprayer.

Turkish Agricultural Supply Organization
P.O.B. 509
Ankara, Turkey

Bouyer Tractor Type TE

Made in France, the Bouyer Type TE is a tractor built for function and simplicity. An air-cooled, diesel, four-stroke engine with either one or two cylinders, it comes in sizes varying from 14 to 20 horsepower. Wheel tread can vary from 1.410 to 1.800 meters. The V-belt transmission provides two speed ranges, high and low, for three forward speeds and one range of three reverse speeds. A wooden front platform pro-

Bouyer Tractor Type TE
Bouyer

vides space for carrying a small load (500 kilograms maximum) without a trailer and provides a place for carrying extra weight in case more traction is required. The three-point hitch with hydraulic lift can be attached to a number of cultivation implements on a drawbar. A four-row seeder-fertilizer distributor is available along with a range of implements for tropical agriculture.

Bouyer Mototracteur MT-80

The MT-80 is a front-, two-wheel drive unit with articulated steering. The rear axle with seat mounting, the tropicultor, is separable from the main power unit. The front unit is powered with either an 8 or 10 h.p., air-cooled engine with special equipment for operating in tropical climates. The two-belt transmission operates a high and low range for two forward and one reverse speed. It is not clear whether or not the power section is designed for use without the tropicultor. However, it does appear that the tropicultor was designed to allow the power unit of a walking tractor to function with attachments for cultivation, plowing, and seeding larger than those of most walking tractors. It is equipped with a mechanical lifting device but no power take-off. Attachments include a subsoiler, a ten-inch moldboard plow, a spring-tooth harrow, a nine-tine chisel plow, and a three-row seeder.

Bouyer MT-80 with main power unit, tropicultor, and moldboard plow on a mechanical lift.
Bouyer

Bouyer
B.P. 23
Tomblaine 54510, France

TRACTOR ACCESSORIES

The PTO

Power supplied to farm equipment can come from the unit's own motor, a pulley drive from an independent motor, or by the power take-off shaft of a tractor. The power take-off (PTO) arrangement was introduced in the 1920s and has become the most widely utilized power source for farm work. Universal joint linkages between the tractor and implement have minimized the limitations the presence of a tractor imposes on the flexibility and maneuverability of this setup. The amount of use any one farm implement gets in a year does not usually justify the investment in a separate motor; so the PTO offers considerable savings in capital output here.

The flexible network of universal joints linking a PTO shaft to a hay baler.

The finger points to a power-take-off shaft on an old model tractor with a pull-type hitch.

Hitches

Machinery is called either pull-type (trailing) or mounted. Pull-type tools simply hitch to the tractor drawbar and are pulled thus by the tractor. Mounted tools attach to tractors in such a way that they can be lifted entirely off the ground for easy turning or transport to and from fields. Almost all mounted tools today use the three-point hitch arrangement pioneered by Henry Ferguson on the Ford and Ferguson tractors. (The Allis-Chalmers WD and WD-45 have their own hydraulic hitch arrangement which is somewhat different from the three-point hitch and will accommodate only Allis-Chalmers machinery built for it.) The three-point hitch (by which a tool hitches to two points on the drawbar and one above) makes hitching, transport of machinery, lifting, lowering, and depth adjustments relatively easy compared to older methods. Today, three-point hitches can be purchased and fitted to almost any tractor.

Pull-type tools are not to be ignored, however. If you are willing to give up some convenience, and especially if machinery does not have to be transported over the road, older implements can be used which offer a considerable saving. Three-point hitches and tools to fit them are in a higher price range than the same equipment in pull-type models.

Particularly when buying an older tractor,

Circled are the three points of attachment for a hydraulically powered lifting hitch.

a general rule to consider is to be sure that you know what equipment will or will not fit your tractor. The ideal is to buy your basic machinery—plow, disc, planter, mower, cultivator, and others—together with the tractor on which they have been mounted.

Many small tractors come equipped with three-point hydraulic lifting hitches which do not fit the many pull-type tools made for small farm and garden tractors. Brinly-Hardy makes the following adapters to convert three-point hitches into pull-type on 14 to 18 h.p., category 0 tractors.

A Frame Adapter With Sleeve Hitch

This unit was designed for adapting sleeve-type hitch implements for use on tractors equipped with category 0 three-point hitches. It is required for using Model KK-305 Planter-Fertilizer, TT-100 Toolbar and BB-363 Fork Lift Kit. Weight: 28 pounds.

Drawbar Attachment (For use with category 0 three-point hitch)

This unit includes cross-type drawbar and two adjustable support links for drawbar weight control. Use it for general-purpose trail-behind attachments. Weight: 18 pounds.

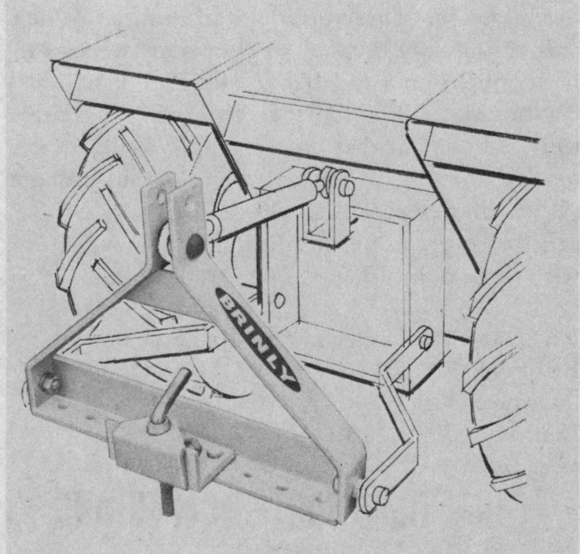

Model HH-1000 three-point A Frame Adapter with Sleeve Hitch.
Brinly-Hardy

The Toolbar

Rather than attaching each implement directly to a tractor, the toolbar allows the option of pulling many attachments at any desired spacing. When planting, both planters and fertilizer distributors can be utilized at the same time. Plantings can be made in irregularly spaced rows to make way for the tractor's tire

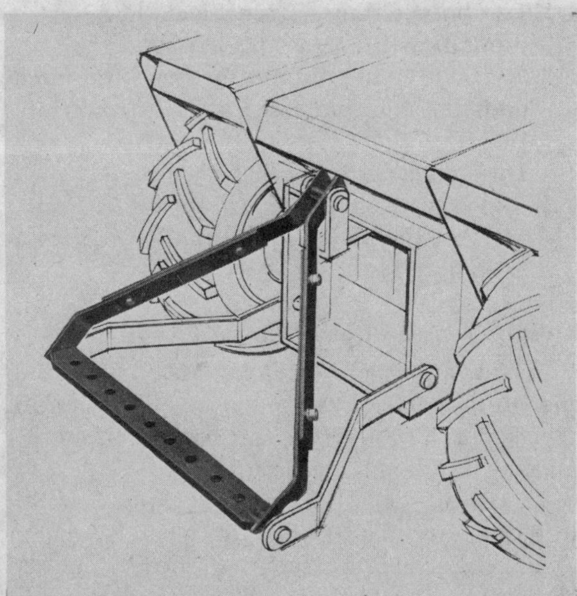

Model BB-370 Drawbar attachment.
Brinly-Hardy

tracks or for intercropping techniques. When cultivating, any number of chisels or sweeps can be mounted on a tool bar in any complementary combination. The tool bar also offers a savings in investment in that only a simple bar clamp is needed for the link between tool and tractor rather than separate hitching hardware, which can be especially complicated and expensive with three-point hitches.

The above three attachments are made by:
Brinly-Hardy Co., Inc.
P.O. Box 1116
Louisville, KY 40201

FARM TRANSPORT—CARTS AND WAGONS

Everyone is aware of the need for a utility transport vehicle on the farm, and their availability is certainly widespread. Rather than try to list a full range of sources for this kind of tractor attachment, we have chosen simply to cite examples of what is made and offer a few build-it-yourself plans. When selecting a trailer design, here are a few points to consider.

1. Capacity—both size and volume, can side extensions be added on, bought or built?
2. For hilly terrain, a long bed, low to the ground, with a wide tread is best.
3. The longer the distance between the hitch and the axle, the easier it is to back into places.
4. Do you need a trailer that can dump?
5. Match a trailer to your needs and to complement the power source pulling it with a maximum load.

Build-It-Yourself Dumper for a Pickup Truck

Tim Sanford of Alexander, Maine, was kind enough to send us these plans for adaptation to a pickup truck he has found useful. It simply involves building a platform to fit in the bed of a truck, but not fitted around the wheel wells. It must be free to slide out of the truck. A sturdy chain arrangement is attached to the front of the platform as illustrated, to which a fixed line will be attached. As the driver slowly goes forward, the platform and load will be neatly left behind but not in a dumping position. The driver then slowly backs up and pushes the load into a vertical position so the material slides off the platform.

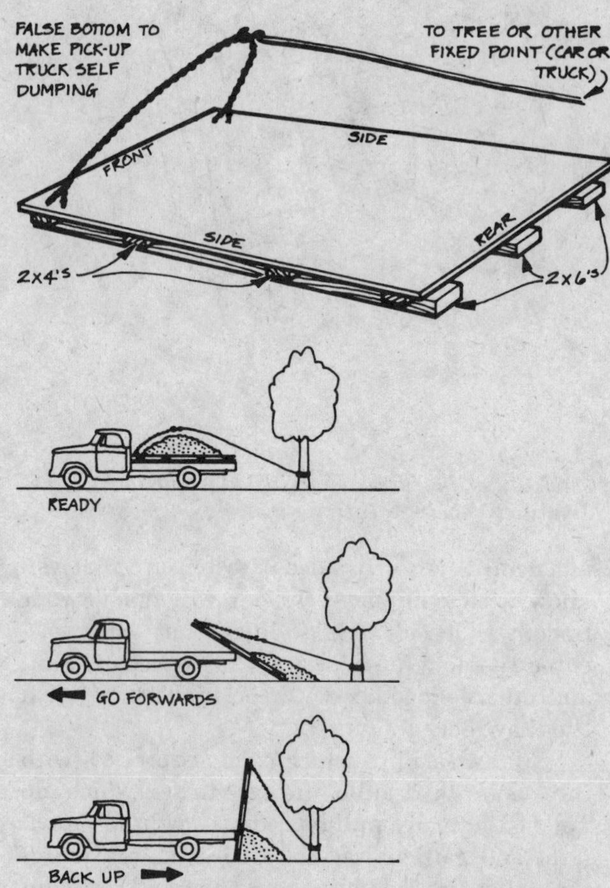

You can build this dumper from the Pickup Truck Dumper Plans described in the text.
Howard S. Berg

Pickup Truck Dumper Plans

Plans for a roll-out dump box are available for $3.75 (as of fall, 1977).

Howard S. Berg
3537 Concord Blvd.
Concord, CA 94519

ITDG Ox Cart Plans Utilizing Old Car Wheels

This cart uses the front wheels from an old car or lorry. Wheel mountings are cut off and welded to a box-section axle fabricated from angle iron. The cart chassis and body are constructed of wood, and all parts are bolted together.

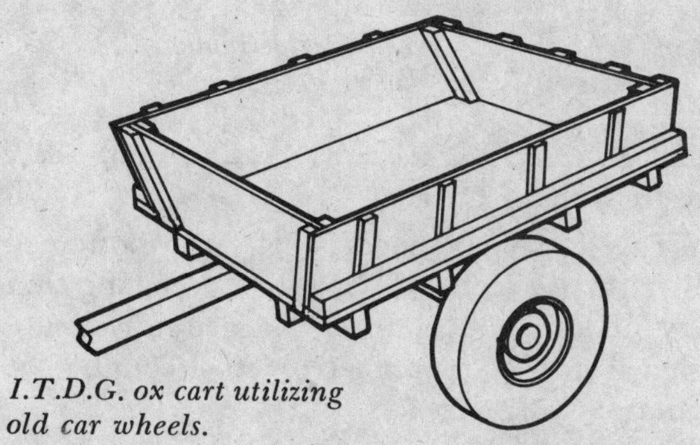

I.T.D.G. ox cart utilizing old car wheels.

ITDG Plans for Wananchi Ox Cart

Designed to carry a load of 1,400 pounds, this cart is pulled by two oxen. The wood-block axle bearings, each made of two pieces of wood, are oil-impregnated by soaking in hot oil, and the axle bearing hold is drilled centrally through the blocks. This bearing design facilitates ease of maintenance and renewal of the bearings by carpenters in rural areas.

I.T.D.G. Wananchi ox cart

ITDG Cart For One Draft Animal Plans

Designed to carry a load of 1,400 pounds, cart is pulled by one donkey or an ox. The wood-block axle bearings are oil-impregnated by soaking in hot oil before drilling and assembly. Both the front and back boards of the cart body are removable. The cart shafts can be made of tubular metal pipe instead of timber for extra strength.

All the above plans are available from:
Intermediate Technology Publications, Ltd.*
9 King St.
London WC2E 8HN, England

I.T.D.G. cart for one draft animal

Tractor Carryall Plans

Plans for a nonwheeled carryall bed to be attached by a three-point hitch to a hydraulic lift system of a tractor are available for a slight charge.

VITA (Volunteers in Technical Assistance)
3206 Rhode Island Ave.
Mt. Rainer, MD 20822

Heald's Hauler

Available as a kit, this quarter-ton utility truck features large flotation tires, sturdy tubular frame, and dump bed. The large, padded seat and bed tip open for easy access to the engine. The truck is powered by either an 8 h.p. Tecumseh or a 10 h.p. Synchro-balanced Briggs & Stratton four-cycle engine. A large Comet torque converter, forward and reverse transmission, number 40 chain, and differential axle complete the drive train. Hand-operated throttle and hydraulic disc brakes are standard. Lights,

* Intermediate Technology publications can be ordered from International Scholarly Book Service, Inc., Box 555, Forest Grove, Oregon 97116

The Heald Hauler
Heald, Inc.

speedometer, knob tires, and spark arrest muffler are options. The Hauler comes in easy-to-build semikit form with all parts furnished. The engine and transmission come assembled and are mounted on the welded and painted frame. The tires are mounted on the rims, so all that is required is to bolt the various parts together using an easy-to-follow step-by-step procedure. Construction time averages 6 to 8 hours.

Heald, Inc.
Dept. DTB, P.O. Box 1148
Benton Harbor, MI 49022

Bike Barrow

The bike barrow was designed by Jay Welsh at the Foundation of Self-Sufficiency Research Center, 35 Maple Avenue, Catonsville, MD 21228 as a simple pushcart to be built from recycled materials. The three-wheeled cart, built from two discarded bicycles, two-by-fours, and plywood can be maneuvered by one or two people. Plans presented in the May 1977 issue of *Rain* magazine are available by purchasing that issue.

Rain Magazine
2270 Northwest Irving
Portland, OR 97210

Fayette Trailer Carts

Fayette offers models of wide-bottomed trailer carts 4 feet wide by 6 to 8 feet long that carry up to 1,200 pounds. Rugged wheels are designed for transport across the country or around the corner.

Fayette Mfg.
Fayette, OH 43521

Garden Way Handcart

Three sizes with a wooden body are available as kits or finished carts.

The Garden Way hand cart
Garden Way Research

Garden Way Research
Department DTB
Charlotte, VT 05445

Economy Handcart

Plans are available for a cart with large wheels which converts easily to a garden tractor dumping cart. Tips on acquiring construction parts are also provided.

Economy Designs
Box 871, Dept. DTB
East Douglas, MA 01516

Vermont Ware

Two carts are available with 300-pound capacity and metal beds.

Vermont-Ware
Dept. 702-DTB
Hinesburg, VT 05461

Utility Trailer

A utility trailer capable of on-the-road travel is available in three sizes, all with a 1,200-pound capacity. The utility model weighs 389 pounds, has 24-inch removable side racks and a bed sized 102 x 55 inches. The bed tilts for easy loading of equipment.

Vann Industries
Clinton, NC 28328

ASSORTED TRACTOR ATTACHMENTS

A number of tools and implements for the small farm tractor are available for miscellaneous farm tasks which do not fall comfortably under one heading. We thought it would suffice to illustrate these implements with only one representative photograph and descriptive caption since differences between manufacturer's models are slight and because often the function is quite familiar.

A middlebuster, designed for the large garden or small farm, gives a full 12- or 15-inch cut. Two-row models are available, and both use a standard category 1 hitch.
Independent Mfg. Co.

Especially of interest to nurserymen and builders, a boxscraper or landscraper with its scarifier shanks assists in leveling and grading land.
Independent Mfg. Co.

Tractor-operated post hole diggers, or augers, make quick work of digging holes in most types of soil.
Independent Mfg. Co.

Scoops, attached to a tractor with a three-point hitch, can be used for pond and ditch digging, feedlot cleaning, and moving and dumping materials on the farm.
Independent Mfg. Co.

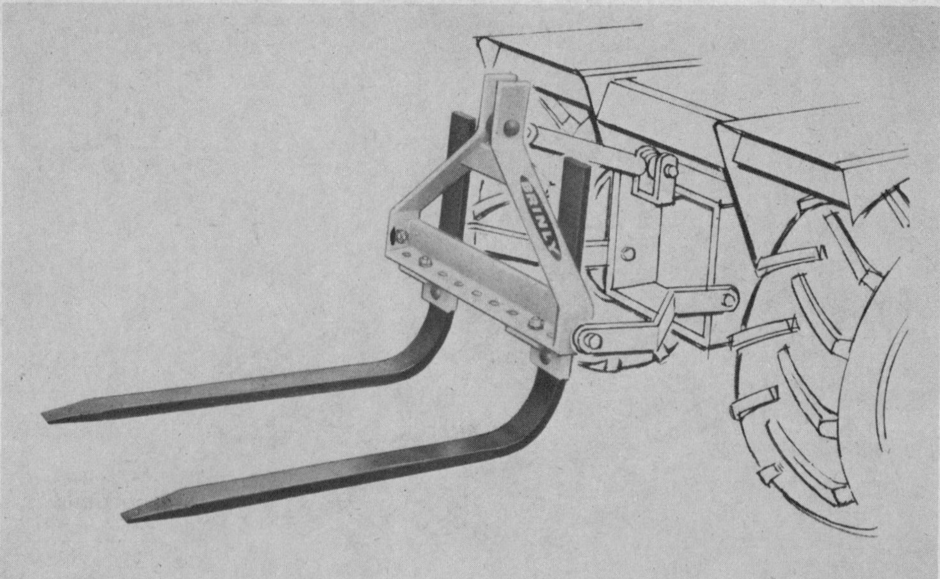

Forklifts, for lifting, hay handling, and short-haul transporting, can be valuable work savers.
Brinly-Hardy Co.

Rear blades, especially when they can be angled or reversed, can be utilized for a variety of tasks including landscaping, leveling, grading, and snow removal. Brinly-Hardy Co.

The Agria walking tractor with a hauling wagon, fully equipped for road travel. Agria-Werke

A boom crane is useful not only for lifting, but also for pulling fence posts, changing wagon tires, and even for some portions of a farm slaughtering operation. Wikomi Manufacturing Company

SHOULD YOU INVEST IN FOREIGN MACHINERY?

At the international level, attachments for two- and four-wheel tractors are not difficult to locate. Each manufacturer generally offers a full line of implements to fit his machinery, including even the unfamiliar power take-off tools for windrowing, harvesting, and pumping as explained in each chapter of this book. In North America, the latter are not always so easy to come by, but three companies do carry the basic tools required for plowing, cultivating, and seeding with small tractors. These include the Brinly-Hardy Co., Inc., P.O. Box 1116, Louisville, KY 40201; the Independent Mfg. Co. (IMCO), P.O. Box 300, Neodesha, KS 66757; and the Special Products Co. (SpeeCo), 15000 West 44th Ave., Golden, CO 80401. Many big-name manufacturers, who build tractors, carry a line of attachments from these smaller companies.

Europeans have all the tools they need for the small farm and they all attach to one power unit. For many implements, we have found no North American counterpart, but if available at all, chances are such counterparts will have their own motors. Certainly there are advantages to having one machine running while tending another, but consolidation provides the resources to afford a huskier power unit or other attachments.

Foreign manufacturers have shown considerable interest in marketing in North America, and from our vantage point, the prognosis for getting these tools into the hands of America's small farmers looks very good.

SOURCES OF ASSORTED EQUIPMENT FOR TRACTORS

	MIDDLEBUSTERS	SCARIFIERS (LANDSCRAPER)	POST HOLE DIGGERS/ AUGERS	SCOOP	LIFTER/CARRIER	BLADES	CARTS	ROLLERS	AERATORS	BOOMS
ALLIED						X				
ARPS DIVISION OF CHROMALLOY			X							
BEAUVAIS ET ROBIN, ETS.							X	X		
BRANTLY MFG. CO.			X							
BRINLY-HARDY					X	X		X		X
CECOCO					X	X	X			
CENTRAL TRACTOR				X						X
CONTINENTAL PRODUCTS			X							
CORSICANA GRADER & MACHINE CO.	X		X	X	X	X				X
GANTT MFG. CO.				X		X				
W. HERTECANT						X		X		
IMCO (INDEPENDENT MFG. CO., INC.)	X	X	X	X		X				

"Well sure," you say, "those tools are great for European farmers who have the manufacturer next door and can get parts and service with no problem. What about small farmers in the United States who can't wait to send for a part overseas?" Taking seriously the small-scale farming market and the skepticism against investing in foreign equipment, some companies (like Kubota and Pasquali, for instance) are setting out to solve that problem. For example, the Pasquali Company in Barcelona, Italy is establishing an arm of its company in Verona, Wisconsin called Pasquali U.S.A. Instead of passing through the hands of an importer, a distributor, and a dealer, all of whom handle a variety of products, Pasquali will serve as both importer and distributor and will handle only Pasquali products. They will stock every part that would be found at the manufacturing plant in Italy, so that a dealer need only send to them for a part and be assured of the same service as if they were dealing with a Detroit manufacturer. As for service, Pasquali U.S.A. is planning a training program for its dealers right at the manufacturing plant in Barcelona.

All this is great news to the small-scale farmer. Not only does it lend credibility to foreign products as worthwhile investments in the future in North America, but it stimulates the competitive spirit in our own free-enterprise system. We have had many requests for this book from United States manufacturers who are interested in new product lines. If the market reveals itself, many will jump at the chance to satisfy it. As we mentioned earlier, John Deere, Allis-Chalmers, and Massey Ferguson are contracting to sell Japanese-made intermediate tractors under their own names.

The ball is already rolling. There's no reason for this marketing approach to stop with tractors. Meanwhile, study the foreign alternatives as prospects of things to come.

	MIDDLEBUSTERS	SCARIFIERS (LANDSCRAPER)	POST HOLE DIGGERS/ AUGERS	SCOOP	LIFTER/CARRIER	BLADES	CARTS	ROLLERS	AERATORS	BOOMS
INTERNATIONAL MODERN MACHINERY, INC.		X	X			X				
K-W MFG. CO., INC.			X							
MONTGOMERY WARD				X						
PENGO CORP.			X							
PIERCE OF WEXFORD						X				
SEARS, ROEBUCK & CO.			X	X	X	X				X
SOUTHEAST MFG. CO.				X	X					X
SPEECO (SPECIAL PRODUCTS)						X				
TRACTOR SUPPLY CO.			X	X	X	X				X
THE VASSAR CO.		X	X	X		X				X
WIKOMI MFG. CO.				X		X				X

–5– Equipment for Seeding and Planting

The simplest hand-operated planters are the walking stick type, most suitable for planting seeds at wide spacings or for interplanting. They can be used in quite rough seedbeds so long as the ground is soft enough for the stick to be inserted.

A hand-pushed, wheeled seeder normally requires a well-prepared seedbed for easy penetration and uniform placement of seed as well as ease of operation. Two or more of these seeder units may sometimes be mounted on an animal-drawn tool bar.

After hours of back-bending labor, Don Green, a Michigan gardener, decided there was an easier way to put his seeds in place—to make an extension of his hand. Using the top part of a ½-gallon plastic container and a plastic tube used in a golf bag to protect the club shafts, he created a seed funnel. Total cost was 18 cents, and his device can be used to place rock fertilizers or shrubs or garden plants too.

The simplest animal-drawn seeders consist of a cultivator-type tine carrying a tube through which seeds are dropped by hand. These implements ensure that the seeds are sown in lines at approximately constant depth, but the spacing along and between the rows depends entirely on the operator's skill. Single-row and multirow versions are available. Most units are fitted with a reversible, adjustable marker.

Animal-drawn planter with mechanical seed-metering plates.

Animal-drawn seeders with mechanical seed metering are of two types.

1. Those planting several rows at close spacing are commonly used for grain crops in humid or irrigated areas.
2. Single-row machines are generally used to space seeds at wide intervals in drier areas.

Various mechanical seed-metering systems are used. A rotating brush or agitator controlling the flow of seed through an adjustable opening will handle most types of seeds with minimal damage, as will contrarotating soft rollers, but these mechanisms do not closely control seed spacing in the row. Fluted roller feed mechanisms give more accurate control of the overall seed rate per hectare but, again, do not control spacing in the row. Cell-wheel and perforated belt-metering systems can give very precise spacing of seeds, particularly those which are approximately spherical in shape. The metal cell wheel is more likely to cause damage to delicate seeds than the flexible perforated belt. Some seeders can be adjusted to plant bunches of seeds at wide spacings.

Many animal-drawn seed drills can also place fertilizers close to the seeds, where they may be more effective. Specialized fertilizer-spreading equipment is available.*

SEEDING

by Rob Johnston

To plant large seeds in large amounts, we generally use our two-row corn planter. However, most of our crops are small seeded, or planted in pieces too small to make setting up a corn planter practical. The implement which really comes in handy is our Planet Junior Number 300-A seeder. Planet Junior has been making hand garden implements for over 100 years, and the models have hardly changed. The 300-A has been made since the 1920s, and the current unit is nearly identical to the first ones made.

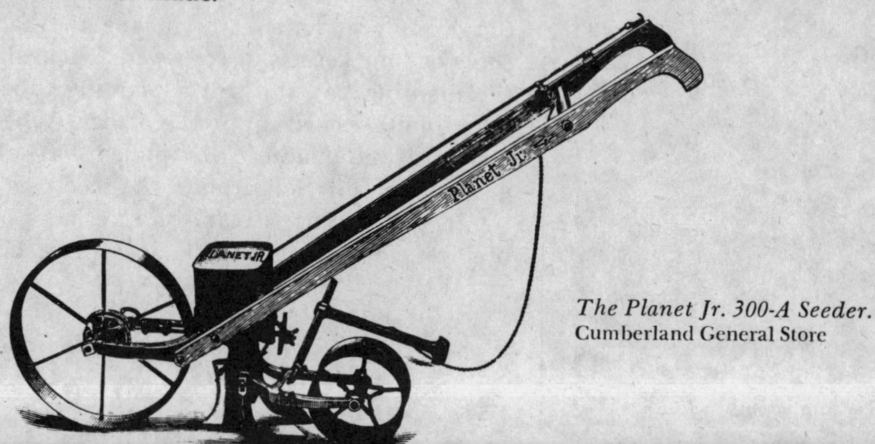

The Planet Jr. 300-A Seeder.
Cumberland General Store

We seed lettuce, beans, and everything in between. We could do just as good a job seeding by hand, but this is where the weather sets the rules. Here in Maine, considering the crops we're growing, we have to take full advantage of days with good planting weather. We might sow four crops with the hand seeder where we would have time to sow only one by hand. The unit is made of cast iron and steel and has enough weight (over 40 pounds) to roll with good momentum. Anyone who has tried to push a plastic seeder on less-than-perfect soil can appreciate this feature.

The seeding mechanism of the 300-A is simple. A small, fluted, feed wheel inside the hopper pushes the seed through a hole in the stationary seed plate; the seed falls into the furrow made with the depth-adjustable opening plow, is covered with a down-pressure-adjustable coverer, and firmed with a concave, rear packing wheel which leaves a slight ridge over the seed for easy sprout penetration. When changing from one seed to another or varying the spacing at which the seed is dropped, the seed plate hole size is changed (there are 39 different holes from which to choose).

Of course, we do a lot of seeding by hand, especially for our trials, where we may have 200 10- or 15-foot rows in a single trial. The time it takes to empty and refill the hopper on the Planet Junior seeder is impractical on these short rows of many different varieties. However, we often use the seeder to make rows for hand planting.

* Reprinted with permission from *Tools for Agriculture: A Buyer's Guide to Low Cost Agricultural Implements*, by John Boyd (London: Intermediate Technology Publications, Ltd.).

For the first row, we stretch a line between stakes and run the seeder along this line. The seeder has an adjustable row marker which marks the next row, so if we get the first row straight (easy when using a tight line), all the other rows in the planting will be straight too.

To make the furrows prior to hand sowing we use our Planet Junior garden plow, one of the high-wheel types that you find almost everywhere, which are made by numerous companies. I'm not sure about the other brands, but ours comes with three different-sized furrows. For large seed such as peas and potatoes, we use the moldboard plow attachment. After sowing the seed, the plow is run first down one side of the furrow, then back in the opposite direction down the other side, closing the furrow and covering the seed neatly and very quickly. It is certainly a whole lot faster than using a hand hoe. For small seeds such as carrots, we use the small cultivator tooth on the high-wheel plow and then cover the seed by hand during sowing.

HAND-OPERATED JAB PLANTERS

A hand-operated jab planter.

For at least a century, most of the corn in this country was planted with jab planters. Two variations on the same idea were built, but both of them are basically glorified dibble sticks. The lower steel blade of the planter was jabbed into the ground, and then, by moving the handles, three or four kernels of corn were dropped from the planting box through a planting tube into the ground opened up by the blades. When the point of the planter was pulled out of the ground, the dirt fell around the seed.

Even after these planters were more or less obsolete, farmers used them to replant hills of

Gene Logsdon demonstrating the use of the jab planter.

corn skipped by the horse-drawn planter.

Today, a jab planter can come in handy for interplanting. For example, if you have a row of corn up and growing and want to plant pole beans beside the cornstalks, the hand planter is just what you need. You can walk along the row, plant the seeds where you will, and not disturb the soil around the already growing corn.

Fancy new models of the jab planter are still available and are used in research plot planting. They are available from manufacturers and suppliers of seed industry equipment. Old, used jab planters are often available at farm sales. You might pay $5 for one, or you might pay $35—you can never tell at an auction.

NORTH AMERICAN SOURCES OF HAND PLANTERS

Jab-Type Hand Planter

The Allan Machine Company has three models of jab planters which are hand fed, spring operated, have a metal barrel, and will adjust to different planting depths.

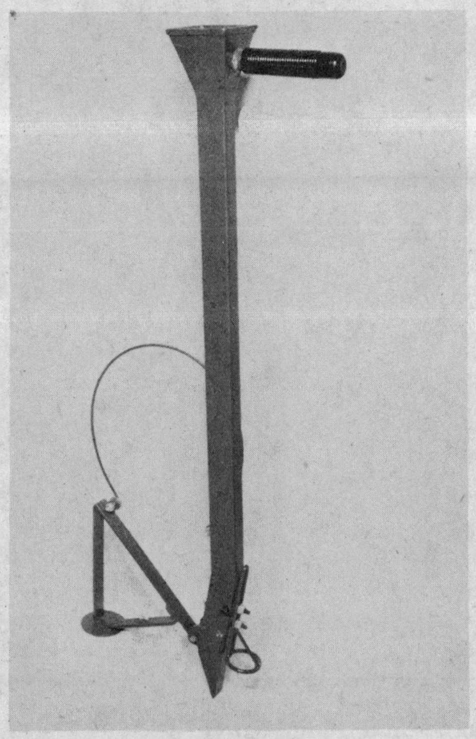

ALMACO Slim-Style Jab Planter model SHP-NBA
Allan Machine Co.

Model SHP-NBA

This is a slim-style unit and has a narrow, single barrel weighing 4½ pounds with a 1⅜-inch by ⅞-inch barrel opening.

Model HP-SBA

This is a single-barrel model which weighs 4 pounds and has a wooden back and a barrel opening of 2½ inches by 3 inches at the top.

Model HP-DBA

The third model has a double- or divided-barrel style and comes with a wood back.

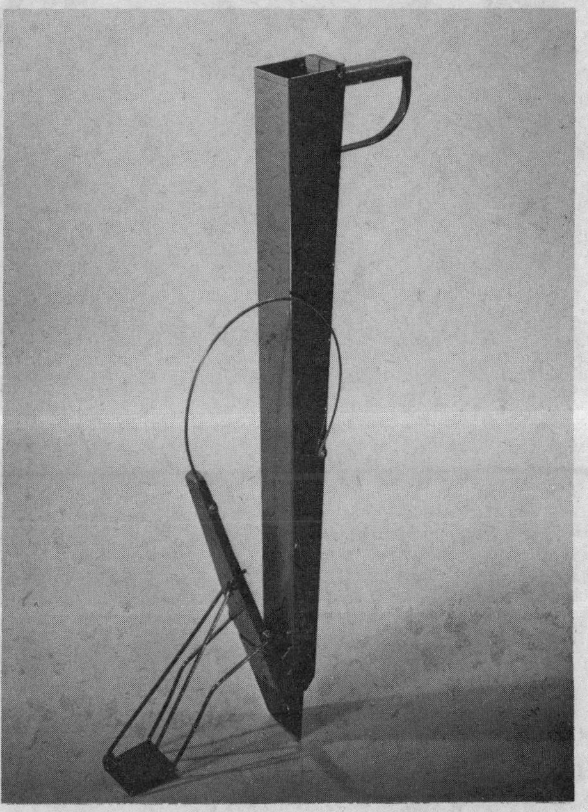

ALMACO Single-Barrel Jab Planter model HP-SBA
Allan Machine Co.

Allan Machine Co.
P.O. Box 112
Ames, IA 50010

Potato Planter

Made of lightweight, corrosion-resistant materials, this unit plants potatoes at adjustable depths. It has a one-year guarantee.

Hand Jab potato planter.
Esmay Products, Inc.

Esmay Products, Inc.
P.O. Box 547, Maple St.
Bristol, IN 46507

Jab-Type Hand Planter

Burrows offers two models, both made of sheet metal and hardwoods. A spring-operated, planting depth adjustment is provided. The 4-pound units are approximately 33 inches high and have an opening 2½ inches by 3 inches at the top of the barrel.

Burrows Equipment Co.
1316 Sherman Ave.
Evanston, IL 60204

Maquinas Agricolas
Avenida Brazil No. 232
Marilia, Brazil

The Plantmaster

To operate the plantmaster, you select one of a range of seed-metering discs according to the seed size, adjust the foot, place the unit on the soil, and depress the handle. A seed is automatically inserted into the soil. Up to 2,500 seeds can be planted per hour at a depth between 6 and 66 millimeters.

Vandermolen Corp.
119 Dorsa Ave.
Livingston, NJ 07039

Richmond Gibson, Ltd.
Salisbury Rd., Downtown Salisbury
Wiltshire, U.K.

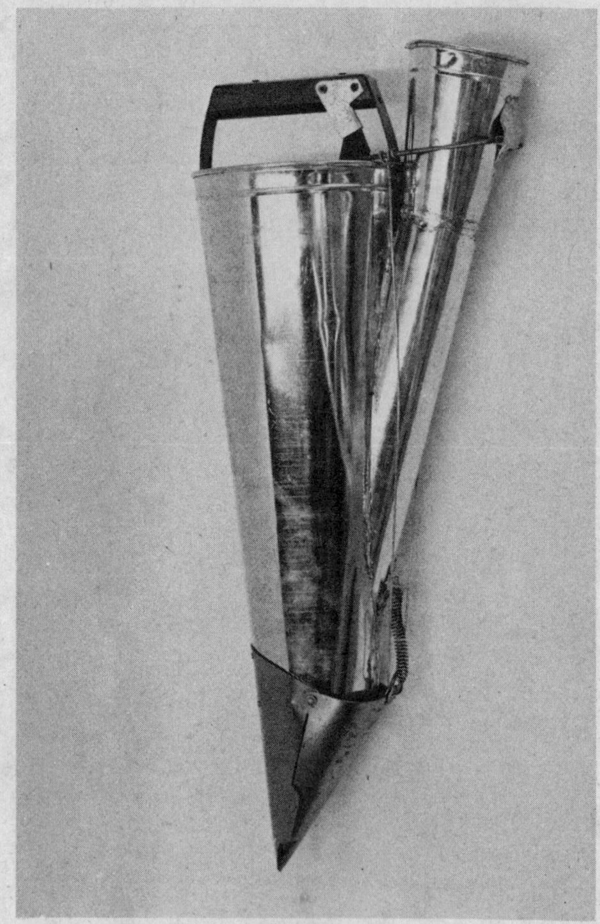

The Cumberland Plant Setter
Cumberland General Store

Cumberland Plant Setter

The Cumberland Plant Setter is a heavy

tin tank with a chute grooved and soldered to assure sturdy construction. High-carbon steel shovels with large, curved flanges rake the earth over the roots. It sets, waters, and covers tomato, tobacco, pepper, cabbage, sweet potato, strawberry, and other slip plants in one operation. Shipping weight is 12 pounds, height is 30 inches, and the diameter of the funnel chute is 4½ inches.

Cumberland General Store
Rt. 3, Box 479
Crossville, TN 38555

INTERNATIONAL SOURCES OF JAB PLANTERS

Hand Maize Planter

A single seed is placed in the soil automatically when the stick is inserted. It can be used with one hand and is suitable for small cultivation or experimental work. It weighs 0.5 pounds (0.2 kilograms).

Cossul & Co. Pvt., Ltd.
Industrial Area, Fazalgunj
Kanpur, India

Models PD, PCM, PC, PA

There are five variations of a basic two-handled, hand-powered, spring-operated jab planter.

Marila Industria E. Comercio Saszaki, Ltd.
Avenida Brazil, 232
Caixa Postal No. 196
Marila CEP 17.5000
Estado de Sao Paulo, Brazil

Hand-Operated Seed-Dressing Drum Plans

The object behind this drum was to build a seed-dressing device for village use, the design to be of fairly simple construction so that it could be made by local craftsmen.

The test drum used was an ordinary water tin of approximately 13 inches (330 millimeters) in diameter and 15 inches (382 millimeters) in height.

It was found that this drum had a capacity of 30 pounds (13.6 kilograms) of Chalimbana groundnuts, 35 pounds (15.9 kilograms) of soybeans or maize, and 38 pounds (17.2 kilograms) of fertilizer when filled correctly. In a durability test, a total of 1½ tons of fertilizer was mixed without signs of damage. The drum was also used for seed dressing of groundnuts and maize with satisfactory coverage performance and no apparent adverse effect on germination.

Intermediate Technology Publications, Ltd.*
9 King St.
London WC2E 8HN, England

THE HORN SEED SOWER

The simplest kind of broadcasting seeder, the Horn Seed Sower, consists of a reservoir which funnels seed into a long tube. The operator holds the tube, or horn, at the end closest to the reservoir, and with a skilled flex of the wrist, seed is flung out of the tube. It can be used to broadcast any seed to be grown in a solid stand and, in experienced hands, will result in a more even distribution of seed than would be achieved by hand alone.

SOURCES OF HORN SEED SOWERS

Horn Sower

This device sows primarily smooth grass or grain by swinging its horn back and forth. This sower spreads seed evenly from 30 to 40 feet at a rate determined by the adjustable feed gate in the base or tube joint and by rate of step. It comes with an 11-inch duck bag and an extension funnel attached to a tin distributing tube 22 inches long, 1¼ inches at the base and ¾ inch at the mouth. This sower has a capacity of ¼ bushel and a shipping weight of 1 pound, 8 ounces.

Cumberland General Store
Rt. 3, Box 479
Crossville, TN 38555

The Cyclone Seeder Co., Inc.
Box 68
Urbana, IN 46990

* Intermediate Technology publications can be ordered from International Scholarly Book Service, Inc., Box 555, Forest Grove, Oregon 97116.

Horn Sower with canvas bag.
Cumberland General Store

Horn Sower

This horn seed sower has a metal horn in three sections. It has an adjustable rate gauge and wire scatterer. The shoulder strap is also adjustable. It can be used for seeding grasses and small grains on any acreage. Its capacity is 1 peck.

Horn Sower
Cumberland General Store

Belknap, Inc.
P.O. Box 28
Louisville, KY 40201

Cumberland Country Store
Rt. 3, Box 479
Crossville, TN 38555

Glen-Bel's Country Store
Rt. 5, Box 390
Crossville, TN 38555

THE HAND-CRANKED BROADCAST SEEDER

A further refinement of the horn, the broadcast seeder hangs by a strap over the shoulder. Seed in the canvas bag or metal hopper flows through an adjustable hole in the bottom onto a distributing fan which is powered by a hand crank. The fan spreads the seed evenly over the ground. Adjustments let you alter your seeding rate to suit the crop. But remember that the speed with which you walk and turn the crank will also vary the seeding rate considerably. You have to learn to walk and crank uniformly and then match the seeder's adjustments to your motions. Cyclone and Universal are two popular brand names available from most hardware stores and country catalogs. Models are light- or heavy-duty, the former for sowing seed only, the latter for spreading fertilizer and lime. Don't try to spread fertilizer with the lighter models, though. Much larger broadcasters pulled behind a tractor and powered by a power take-off shaft are capable of extensive broadcast-planting coverage.

SOURCES OF HAND-CRANKED BROADCAST SEEDERS

Cyclone

This is a triple-gear, adjustable sower with a self-feeding, oscillating feed plate. Equipped with a wide shoulder strap, an 18- by 6½-inch hardwood base, and spring stop, it is 10½ inches in diameter and weighs 5 pounds. It broadcasts all kinds of seed and is readily available through mail-order catalogs and hardware stores.

Cyclone
Cumberland General Store

Little Giant

This is a seeder with a double-feed flow to sow any kind of seed to be broadcast. It has an automatic feed flow which can be adjusted for any amount of seed per acre. Features include a wide shoulder strap, a 7- by 14½-inch hardwood base, a four-section distributing wheel 10½ inches in diameter, and a self-agitating feed plate. The seeder has a capacity of ½ bushel and is readily available through mail-order catalogs and hardware stores.

Little Giant
Cumberland General Store

For more information on either of the above seeders, write:
The Cyclone Seeder Co., Inc.
Box 68
Urbana, IN 46990

Collapsible Hand Spreader

A rotary agitator whirls material out to cover up to a 15-foot-wide swath depending on the density and particle size of the material being spread. It comes with an adjustable spreading rate gauge, spring load, trigger action on-off switch, die-cast metal gears, and measures 10½ inches high with a 9-inch diameter.

Other Hand-Cranked Broadcast Seeder Models

Burrows Equipment Co.
1316 Sherman Ave.
Evanston, IL 60204

Cumberland General Store
Rt. 3, Box 479
Crossville, TN 38555

E. C. Geiger
Rt. 63, Box 285
Harleysville, PA 19438

A. M. Leonard & Son, Inc.
P.O. Box 816
Piqua, OH 45356

Mother's General Store
Box 506
Flat Rock, NC 28731

Sears, Roebuck & Co.
Farm and Ranch Catalog

Hand-Pushed Broadcast Seeder

Cyclone also has a hand-pushed, broadcast seeder-spreader which is popularly used for spreading fertilizer. It is accurate in ounces or pounds per 1,000 square feet. A tapered-edge spreader eliminates skips and double overlaps. It comes equipped with micro dial settings for light, medium, or heavy applications, 8-inch wheels, T-bar handle, and a galvanized steel hopper. This seeder is easy to find in any hardware store or country catalog.

Casoron Spreader

The Geiger Casoron is a rigid, rust-resistant unit weighing 6 pounds. The Casoron spreader can spread or seed at a rate of from 50 to 500 pounds per acre. The flat base keeps the unit from tipping while filling. An adjustable control varies the swath width from 3 to 12 feet. The unit comes with a wide shoulder strap and a lubricated gearbox, sealed for protection.

E. C. Geiger
Rt. 63, Box 285
Harleysville, PA 19438

Hand-Pushed Row Seeders

Small row planters mount the seed box on one or more wheels which not only carry the seed box but activate a disc or plate, as it is called, in the bottom of the seed hopper. As the plate moves around, it allows the seeds to fall through the planting tube into the soil at regular, uniform spacings. In the simplest type of row seeder available, for example, the Plant-Rite and Dial-A-Seed seeders, the wheel *is* the planting disc. The smallest two-wheel seeder with changeable discs for different planting intervals is the light Esmay seeder, which is regularly advertised and sold through catalogs and garden stores. A little larger and heavier, with a larger choice of planting depths and plates, are the Lambert, the Planet Junior, and one from Danville Manufacturing Co., Danville, IN 46122 (sold by Sears). There are probably others.

Lambert Corp.
519 Hunter Ave.
Dayton, OH 45404

Planet Junior Division
Piper Industries
P.O. Box 1188, Freeport Center
Clearfield, VT 84106

SOURCES OF HAND-PUSHED ROW SEEDERS

One-Wheel Seeders

With this unit, the wheel is the planting disc. It is sometimes called a Dial-A-Seed planter.

Countryside Catalog
Rt. 1, Box 239
Waterloo, WI 53594

Mother's General Store
Box 506
Flat Rock, NC 28731

Sears, Roebuck & Co.
Farm and Ranch Catalog

Wolf Tools for Lawn & Garden, Ltd.
Ross-on-Wye
Herefordshire HR9 5NE, U.K.

Two-Wheel Seeders

The lightweight version of two-wheel—one front, one rear—push seeders opens soil, spaces and covers seed, packs soil, and marks the next row in one operation. This unit usually comes equipped with six seed plates and an adjustable ground opener and row maker.

Burrows Equipment Co.
1316 Sherman Ave.
Evanston, IL 60204

Countryside Catalog
Rt. 1, Box 239
Waterloo, WI 53594

Esmay Products, Inc.
P.O. Box 547, Maple St.
Bristol, IN 46507

Farm & Fleet
1600 E. Lincoln Hwy.
DeKalb, IL 60115

Montgomery Ward
1000 S. Monroe St.
Baltimore, MD 21232

Sears, Roebuck & Co.
Farm and Ranch Catalog

American Spring & Pressing Works Pvt., Ltd.
P.O. Box 7602
Malad, Bombay 400 064, India

Before the development of a seed-metering device, this funnel seeder made hand seeding easier. One person would push as another rhythmically tossed seeds into the funnel.
Agriculture Canada

Heavyweight units are available from:

J. Gibbs, Ltd.
Stanwell Rd., Bedfont, Feltham
Middlesex, TW14 8ND, U.K.

Richmond Gibson, Ltd.
Salisbury Rd., Downton Salisbury
Wiltshire, U.K.

Lambert Corp.
519 Hunter Ave.
Dayton, OH 45404

Planet Junior Division
Piper Industries
P.O. Box 1188, Freeport Center
Clearfield, VT 84106

Polar-Werke, Engels & Sieper
Postfach 14 02 24/25
5630 Remschied 14, Germany

Project Equipment, Ltd.
Industrial Estate, Rednal Airfield
West Felton, Oswestry
Salop SY11 4HS, U.K.

Russel's (Kirbymoorside), Ltd.
The Works Kirbymoorside, Ltd.
York YO6 6DJ, U.K.

Sears, Roebuck & Co.
Farm and Ranch Catalog

Stanhay (Ashford), Ltd.
Ashford
Kent TN23 1PB, U.K.

Tanzania Agricultural Machinery Testing Unit
P.O. Box 1389
Arusha, Tanzania

A. J. Troster Landmaschinenfabrik
6308 Butzbach, Oberhess
Postfach 240, West Germany

Seeder Attachment

Offering versatility to the high-wheel cultivator, a seeder attachment opens the furrow, drops and spaces seeds, covers the furrow, and marks the next row. Six interchangeable seed plates make the unit able to handle seeds of all sizes.

Countryside Catalog
Rt. 1, Box 239
Waterloo, WI 53594

Montgomery Ward
1000 S. Monroe St.
Baltimore, MD 21232

Precision Garden Seeder

Constructed of corrosion-resistant materials, this push seeder comes with six seed plates for seed sizes ranging from radish seeds to corn and bean seeds.

Earthway Precision Garden Seeder
Esmay Products, Inc.

Burrows Equipment Co.
1316 Sherman Ave.
Evanston, IL 60204

Countryside Catalog
Rt. 1, Box 239
Waterloo, WI 53594

Esmay Products, Inc.
Dept. 70GP2
Bristol, IN 46507

Montgomery Ward
1000 S. Monroe St.
Baltimore, MD 21232

Sears, Roebuck & Co.
Farm and Ranch Catalog

Professional-Type Seeder-Fertilizer

This seeder has a heavy-duty construction for large areas. It seeds and fertilizes in one operation. A choice of seven different-sized discs plus two sprockets offers over 20 spacing and depth combinations. The seeder opens the furrow, plants, covers, fertilizes on both sides of the seed, and marks the next row. It holds 1 quart of seed and 15 pounds of fertilizer, and has a shipping weight of 80 pounds.

Sears, Roebuck & Co.
Farm and Ranch Catalog

Golden Harvest Garden Seeder

This seeder opens the soil, plants and spaces seeds, covers and firms the soil, and marks the next row in one operation. It comes with six seed plates that will handle most seeds and has rear-wheel drive. The Seeder Attachment can be ordered to fit the high-wheel cultivator with a 24-inch wheel and a slot attachment foot, or as a separate implement. The seèder weighs 12 pounds, the attachment alone, 11 pounds.

Farm & Fleet
1600 E. Lincoln Hwy.
DeKalb, IL 60115

Mother's General Store
Box 506
Flat Rock, NC 28731

Garden Seeder

This Garden Seeder opens the soil, spaces, plants, covers seeds, and marks the next row all in one pass. A drag chain covers the seeds ahead of the rear wheel which then packs the soil. There are six plates for versatility, and a kick-stand holds the seeder upright for filling the hopper. It has a shipping weight of 11 pounds.

Sears, Roebuck & Co.
Farm and Ranch Catalog

Planet Junior Number 4 Seeder

This seeder is available with or without cultivating attachments. With the attachments, it combines six tools in one:

1. an accurate hill-dropping seeder,
2. a rapid, continuous row seeder,
3. a light-running, single-wheel hoe,
4. a sturdy, single-wheel cultivator,
5. a furrower, and
6. a hand plow.

Shipping weight: 50 pounds.

Planet Junior Number 300A Seeder 7309X

This seeder is equipped with three interchangeable plates with a total of 39 holes giving ample adjustment for any variety of seed. It includes a K712 opening plow. Shipping weight: 55 pounds each.

Planet Junior Division
Piper Industries
P.O. Box 1188, Freeport Center
Clearfield, VT 84106

Almaco V-Belt Planter and Applicator

The V-belt planter is available as either a hand- or power-driven unit. It is manufactured for experimental agronomic work at universities and research stations. Features include a planter shoe depth adjustment, a 14-inch, wide-faced drive wheel, six interchangeable sprockets, roller chain drives, V-belt tension adjustment, V-type covering wheel, rubber-tired running gear, and adjustable handles. It is designed for use in planting test plots and in applying fertilizers, insecticides, and granular materials. Two models are available.

Allan Machine Co.
P.O. Box 112
Ames, IA 50010

ALMACO Endless V-Belt Planter-Applicator
Allan Machine Co.

English Seeders

Two types of seeder are available from this company, and each may be pushed by hand or mounted on a Unibar animal-drawn tool bar. The reciprocating slide-action seeder was designed mainly as a precision seeder for use with hybrid maize, but can also handle groundnuts and beans using the standard maize slide. The seeder drops two or three seeds at 45-centimeter spacing with fertilizer alongside. Slides with smaller holes are available to enable sorghum, millet, and delinted cotton to be sown. A simple reciprocating action, combined with positive ejection of the seed (by slide-actuated springs), ensures trouble-free operation. The use of graded seed is preferable. Seeds and fertilizer are kept separate throughout, so that burning of the seed does not occur.

The roller-seeder can be supplied as a two-wheeled, single-row machine for hand propulsion or ridge planting with an animal-drawn tool bar. Multirow tool-bar-mounted versions can also be supplied. The seed rollers can be drilled to suit the customers' requirements, allowing any spacing along the row up to a maximum of 1.65 meters. Seed ejection from the rollers is positive.

Project Equipment, Ltd.
Industrial Estate, Rednal Airfield
West Felton, Oswestry
Salop SY11 4HS, U.K.

Hand-Operated Sowing Machine

Union Tractor Workshop
8–B, Phase II
Mayapuri Industrial Area
New Delhi 110 027, India

IRRI Multihopper Seeder

This unit was designed by the International Rice Research Institute in the Philippines for sowing pregerminated rice. It can sow 50 kilograms of pregerminated seed per hectare in 5 to 7 hours. Pulled by one man, the single central ground wheel drives the metering tools. Row spacing is 25 centimeters. This seeder requires:

1. pregerminated seed,
2. good water control at planting time, and
3. good land preparation.

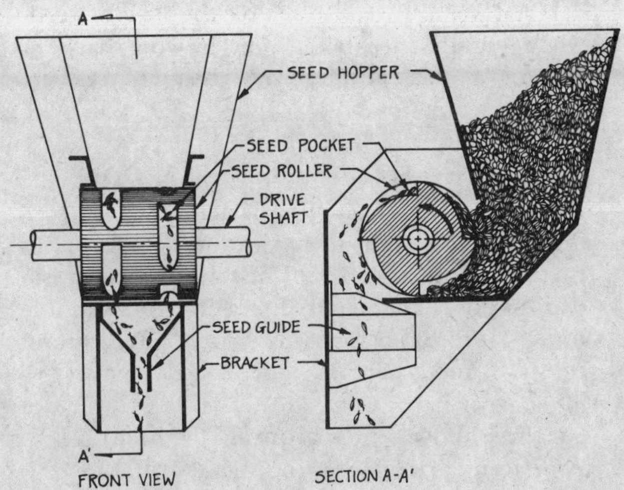

IRRI Multihopper Seeder

D. H. Farm Implements
Km. 1, National Hwy.
Roxas City, Philippines

International Rice Research Institute
P.O. Box 933
Manila, Philippines

Kalayaan Engineering Co., Inc.
4255 Emilia St., Makati
P.O. Box 655 MCC
Rizal, Philippines

Quinzy-Pacific
Pasong Tamo, Makati
Rizal, Philippines

Aspee APS-61 Seeder

This hand-pushed seeder can sow all types of seeds in thin lines by metering them through holes in a plate. It is suitable for light soils and incorporates a furrow opener and seed coverer. Weight: 15 kilograms.

Aspee APS-53 Hand Hill and Drill Seeder

Suitable for hill and line drilling of seeds in soft or dry soils, this seeder plants practically all seeds, big or small, in hill spacings of 10, 15, 20, 30, or 60 centimeters. It opens the furrow, drops the seed to the proper depth, covers it evenly, firms the soil over the seed, and marks out the next row in one operation.

A lever instantly shuts off the flow of seeds when handles are raised for drawing back or turning at the end of a row. Weight: 12 kilograms.

Aspee APS-54 Seed Drill and Wheel Hoe

This dual-purpose implement cuts the soil, drills seeds, covers them with soil, and packs them into the soil. The line-sowing mechanism drops seeds at the required spacing. It is suitable for small seeds such as wheat, rice, jute, linseed, mustard, and others. Weight: 15 kilograms.

All three above seeders are available from:
American Spring & Pressing Works Pvt., Ltd.
P.O. Box 7602
Malad, Bombay 400 064, India

Cottonseed Planter

This implement was especially developed for planting nondelinted cottonseed. Spacing between plant stands can be 17, 20, or 31 centimeters and six or seven seeds are planted at each stand. Alternative seed plates allow the machine to be used for planting other crops such as groundnuts, millet, maize, and sorghum. Weight: 39 kilograms.

E.B.R.A.
28, rue du Maine, B.P. 84
49009 Angers, France

Direct Seeder

A two-row hand-drawn machine for upland rice culture, with different feed rollers, it can be used for planting other seeds such as wheat, barley, maize, sorghum, and millet. Capacity of each hopper is 2.2 liters. Spacing between rows is adjustable from 150 to 360 millimeters.

CeCoCo
P.O. Box 8, Ibaraki City
Osaka Pref. 567, Japan

The Bean Drill

This single unit, thin-line drill is capable of handling all sizes of seeds, from the smallest up to peas and small beans. It sows at a predetermined depth with the row covered. The drill coulter is adjustable for depth, and the metal agitator ensures positive seed flow. Standard specifications include shut-off control, adjustable marker, and four seed plates giving 46 holes from 2.5 to 25 millimeters in diameter.

J. Gibbs, Ltd.
Stanwell Road, Bedfont, Feltham
Middlesex TW14 8ND, U.K.

Exel Hand Seeder

This push-type seeder unit is designed for drilling most types of vegetable seed on the flat. It is suitable for small market gardens where the seedbed has been well prepared. Twin rubber-tired wheels drive the mechanism, which consists of an aluminum cell wheel suited to the crop being sown. The hopper has a 2-pint (1-liter) capacity, and a simple seed coverer is provided.

Russel's (Kirbymoorside), Ltd.
The Works Kirbymoorside, Ltd.
York YO6 6DJ, U.K.

Hand-Pushed Seed Drill

This is a precision seeder in which seeds are metered through a perforated belt, resulting in minimal seed damage. Seeds which are approximately spherical (or pelleted into spherical pellets) can be drilled singly. Seeds such as lettuce or carrot can be distributed at an average of two seeds from each belt perforation. Group spacings can be arranged: two or three seeds 25 or 50 millimeters apart, followed by a gap before the next group of seeds. Double and treble line coulters are available to sow two lines of seeds 50 millimeters apart, three lines 25 millimeters apart, or three lines 38 millimeters apart. This device is suitable for nearly every type of seed up to the size of beans, peas, or maize. Two or more seeder units can be mounted on an animal-drawn tool bar.

Stanhay (Ashford), Ltd.
Ashford
Kent TN23 1PB, U.K.

Hand Seeder

A.J. Troster Landmaschinenfabrik
6308 Butzbach, Oberhess
Postfach 240, West Germany

I.A.R.I. Single-Row Seed-Cum-Fertilizer Drill

To operate this seeder designed by the Indian Agricultural Research Institute, one man pulls a rope attached at the front of the implement, while a second man steers.

Union Tractor Workshop
8–B, Phase II
Mayapuri Industrial Area
New Delhi 110 027, India

Semoir A Main

This hill drop seeder with 5-liter hopper capacity is driven by three sprocket wheels. Depth is adjustable on the shoe and the action of the press wheel is completed by two covering knives. Two models are available, one with row marker, weighing 25 kilograms, and one without a marker weighing 21 kilograms. Both are provided with 75 different seed plates.

E.B.R.A.
28, rue du Maine, B.P. 84
49009 Angers, France

Polar-Werke, Engles & Sieper
Postfach 14 02 24/25
5630 Remschied 14, Germany

Tanzania Agricultural Machinery Testing Unit
P.O. Box 1389
Arusha, Tanzania

Mini Nibex Planter

The Mini Nibex hand planter is for growers with up to 10 acres and will sow up to 2 acres in a day. The Nibex cup system includes 25 types of cups for different seeds—both natural and pelleted. This wide range makes it possible to be able to choose the most suitable

Mini Nibex Hand Planter
Nibe-Verken AB

cup for the desired drilling method. The seeding rate can be varied from 4 to almost 2,000 seeds per running yard—either thin-line or band-drilled in widths of 2, 2.5, or 4 inches (50, 65, or 105 millimeters). The cup system is largely unaffected by variations in seed size. To reduce the amount of seed required when sowing small and expensive seeds, a regulator-economizer insert is available for use in the seed-housing unit.

When a suitable drilling depth has been established and the seed distribution mechanism has been set for the desired number of seeds per yard, the Mini Nibex is ready for sowing. The coulter gives the furrow the correct depth, the cups distribute the seed in the desired way, the presswheel beds them down in the moist earth, and the coverers enclose them with loose soil.

Thirty-one seed-distributing cups are housed in this chamber, which is interchangeable to accommodate different seed sizes.
Nibe-Verken AB

Cups are easily switched for fast changes between seeds. The relationship between cup type, number of cup feeds per yard, and number of seeds sown per yard can be found in the detailed sowing instructions.

The seeder unit is mounted between two supporting wheels which are 4 by 16 inches, or 105 by 400 millimeters in diameter, and the bearing surfaces are perforated to prevent packing and crusting of the soil. Drive is from the front wheel via two chain transmissions. The changing sprockets offer 59 selections, from 3.5 to 86 cup feeds per yard. Drilling depth is progressively adjustable by means of two handwheels. Changeover is performed without tools.

Nibe-Verken AB
S–285 00 Markaryd
Sweden

CONE SEEDERS

Cone seeders have been an important development in equipment for research or experimental agriculture. Seed poured into a small funnel at the top of the cone is distributed evenly at the base when the funnel is lifted. The cone is geared to rotate one full turn in the plot length with a scraper deflecting the seed to the furrow opener. The cone base is roughened to prevent the seed from rolling.

SOURCES OF CONE SEEDERS

Craftsman Cone Seeders

Cones are available as single units or mounted in groups for installation on custom-built drills. They can be supplied with a 7- or 14-inch base diameter and with either knurled or plain base plates.

Craftsman also manufacturers a hand-pushed, single-row seeder with single- or double-metering cones. It has a three-wheel chassis with 12-inch, double-disc openers. Sprockets are available to adjust for row length. The two-cone model is used for simultaneous fertilizer or insecticide treatments during seeding.

Craftsman Machine Co.
61 Heaton
Winnipeg 2, Manitoba, Canada

Chain's Cone Planter

A planter manufactured by Chain Machine Company has four cone dispensers mounted on a 12 h.p. compact tractor. The cones are driven

Craftsman cone seeder for research plot work.
Craftsman Machine Co.

through a multiselection chain and sprocket drive from the rear wheel with selections for plot lengths from 4½ to 30 feet. The double-disc openers are hydraulically controlled and can be equipped with firming wheels and drag coverers. Two seats are provided for operators to load the cones.

> NOTE: This planter is referred to as a precision planter in the manufacturer's literature. This refers to the precision manufacture and not to precision planting, which requires a seed-cell planter and a short, controlled seed drop.

Chain Machine Co.
112 N. Kansas
Haven, KS 67543

The Swanson Planter

The Swanson plot planter, developed for small test plots for such seeds as soybean, sorghum and kenaf, uses a cone arrangement similar to the Craftsman cone. Sprockets are available for rows 3 to 32 feet long.

Swanson Machine Co.
20-26 E. Columbia Ave.
Champaign, IL 61820

A Norwegian Cone Seeder

The Oyjord plot drill has a single cone-type dispenser feeding a spinning divider which divides the sample into 2, 4, 6, 8, or 10 openings to correspond with the number of row openers used. The row length can be adjusted to any size between 13 and 49 feet. The drill is available with a three-point hitch or as a self-propelled model with a 4 h.p. engine. A planting rate of 60 to 100 plots per hour is claimed. Equipment for continuous drilling and press-wheels are optional extras. The cone dispenser differs from the Craftsman type in that the seed is guided around a fixed base by wipers and drops from a hole in the base.

Jens A Schou Mek Verksted
Drobak
Norway

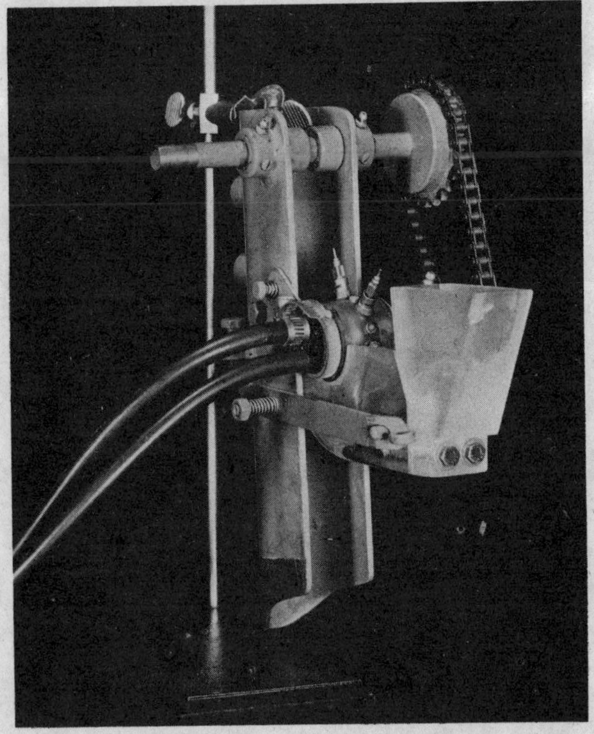

Suction-Spaced Seeder Agriculture Canada

Suction-Spaced Seeder

This plant seeder has been the inspiration behind many new types of planters. It was originally developed by Mr. L.G.I. Copp of the Crop Research Division, Department of Scientific Research, in Christchurch, New Zealand. It is a one-row planting unit, and mounts on a two-wheel tractor. Seed is picked up by vacuum through hypodermic needles on a revolving drum with a small vacuum pump.

W.A. Habgood, Ltd.
Lincoln, New Zealand

Soybean Planter

Originally developed by the Engineering Research Service of Agriculture Canada, this soybean planter for population studies is now available commercially in an improved form, making it suitable for repetition planting of large numbers of samples at different spacings. The original models used seed hopper bottoms mounted on a lightweight frame for adjustable row widths. Spacing within the rows was by sprocket and seed plate selection. Seed accuracy has been improved by using brush cutoffs and a smooth drop tube. The planter mounts on a four-wheel tractor.

Soybean Planter
Agriculture Canada

Mear Supply
327 Townline
Carleton Place, Ontario, Canada

Four-Row Plot Seeder

Seed is fed to the openers of this self-propelled seeder by either a V-trough belt or a fluted dispenser and a four-way spinning divider. It is designed for the exacting requirements of research plot experiments. Fertilizer may also be applied through a belt attachment. The four-row seeder pictured here is now obsolete because it was made to attach to a Bolens Ridemaster tractor, which is no longer being produced. However, models by other manufacturers are available. Plans are available from the Engineering Research Service, Agriculture Canada, Ottawa, Ontario K1A 0C6 Canada, and similar seeders are commercially available.

Four-row Plot Seeder
Agriculture Canada

Fabro, Ltd.
Swift Current
Saskatchewan, Canada

Mear Supply
327 Townline
Carleton Place, Ontario, Canada

Two Plot Drills

The first of these is a three-row planter employing two operators, one pulling and the other pushing, and using a seed cup to dispense seed to three row openers. The delivery rate is adjusted by a plate at the bottom of the cup. The cup is hinged to permit dumping of leftover seed.

Bill's Welding
South Grand St.
Pullman, WA 99163

Walter and Wintersteiger Plot Drill
Walter and Wintersteiger

The Walter and Wintersteiger plot drill is a three-wheeled, self-propelled model available with either a full-width or individual hopper seed box. Metering is done by a fluted wheel. The seed boxes have a provision for dumping unused seed. The machine can be purchased with three to eight row openers and with a two- or three-speed gearbox. Cultivating and spraying attachments are available.

F. Walter & H. Wintersteiger
4910 Ried im Innkreis
Frasch augasse 19, Postfach 124
Dimmelstrasse, Austria

Toothed-Wheel Seeders

Some European seed drills are suited to planting larger plots in that they are mounted on a three-point hitch and have a catch pan to collect seed when regulating the dispensers or when emptying the seed box through an unloading valve at each run. Individual runs can be shut off as desired, or hopper inserts can be used for seed separation in the box. The most common dispenser is a toothed-wheel metering device driven by a gearbox with up to 81 selections.

Manufactured by: Fiona, Denmark
Sold by: J.F. Farm Machinery
Exeter, Ontario

Manufactured by: P. Nordsten, A/S
Hillroed, Denmark
Sold by: G. White & Sons
London, Ontario

Manufactured by:
A.J. Troster Landmaschinenfabrik
6308 Butsbach, Oberhess
Postfach 240, West Germany

Plantox Drill

The Plantox drill is a machine mounted on a three-point hitch suitable for horticultural and forestry plantings. The five-row distributor is driven from the tractor PTO. All types of seeds can be planted in rows or wide beds.

Zijlstra en Bohuis NU
Beneden Westerdiep 105
Veedam, Holland

Finlay Plot Seeder

The Finlay plot seeder is a sophisticated semiautomatic machine for planting large numbers of plots per day. It uses cartridge loading and a false-bottom seed dispenser, and is available with one to nine row openers.

B. Forrest, Metal Patterns, Ltd.
749 Port Rd.
Woodsville, S. Australia

Svenska Plot Seeder

A plot seeder for sugar beet experiments, this unit meters a premeasured quantity of seed to a plot row and is available as one-row units.

Svenska Sockerfabriks Aktiebolaget
Betmekaniseringsavdelningen
Kavlinge, Sweden

Habgood Vacuum Planter

A vacuum pickup planter suitable for precision planting of any type of seed is available for tool bar mounting. A source of vacuum is required to provide suction to hypodermic needles mounted on a revolving cylinder.

W.A. Habgood, Ltd.
Lincoln, New Zealand

Mat-OSU Planter

The Mat-OSU planter was developed at Oregon State University for fertilizer trials. Commercial planters were found unsuitable for the precise planting required, so a vacuum pickup wheel was developed. It has been found suitable for grass, legume, cereal, flower, and tree seeds without grading the seed. Row spacing is adjustable from 12 inches to 6 feet. Fertilizer metering is by Cole top delivery hoppers. Fertilizer can be placed accurately at varying positions in relation to the seed.

Mater Machine Works
520 S. 1st St., Box 410
Corvallis, OR 97330

MacKey Plot Drills

The MacKey plot drills use a dispenser consisting of a base plate with grooves corresponding to the number of openers, and a seed tray with a press plate which slides along the grooves to deliver seeds to the seed tubes. The tray is geared to traverse its length over the plot length.

The hand-pushed model has one to three openers spaced at 6-inch intervals and can be geared for rows 40 to 80 inches long. One hundred 5-foot rows can be planted per hour. The power model has five openers and can be geared for 10- to 20-foot plots. Its capacity is 100 10-foot plots per hour.

Maskinfirma Tuland
P.O. Box 107
Landskrona, Sweden

A Seeder for Cereals

The N.I.A.E. spaced plant seeder was developed to replace hand dibbling of cereal grains for lattice-planted plots. The planter is cam operated to plant seeds 2 inches apart on a 6-inch row spacing. Holes are made by a series of dibblers, each consisting of a tube into which a plunger is inserted just before the tube enters the soil. The plungers are then raised and the seed is released from a preloaded, plastic seed magazine. A sowing rate of 500 rows per hour can be attained with a five-man crew. Twenty-three seeds are spaced in a 4-foot row. The planter is powered by a small engine with a 45:1 reduction box.

R.G. Garvie & Sons
2, Canal Rd.
Aberdeen, Scotland

SOURCES OF ANIMAL-DRAWN SEEDERS/PLANTERS

The Ferguson Planter

The Ferguson All-Purpose Planter is a one-row, team model planter with a duplex hopper and unique plate design. Shipping weight: 120 pounds.

Cumberland General Store
Rt. 3, Box 479
Crossville, TN 38555

A Two-Row Planter from India

Sowing depth is adjustable on this all-steel-constructed, two-row unit. Row spacing is adjustable from 175 to 450 millimeters.

Rajasthan State Agro Industries Corp., Ltd.
Virat Bhawan, C-Scheme
Jaipur 302 006, Rajasthan, India

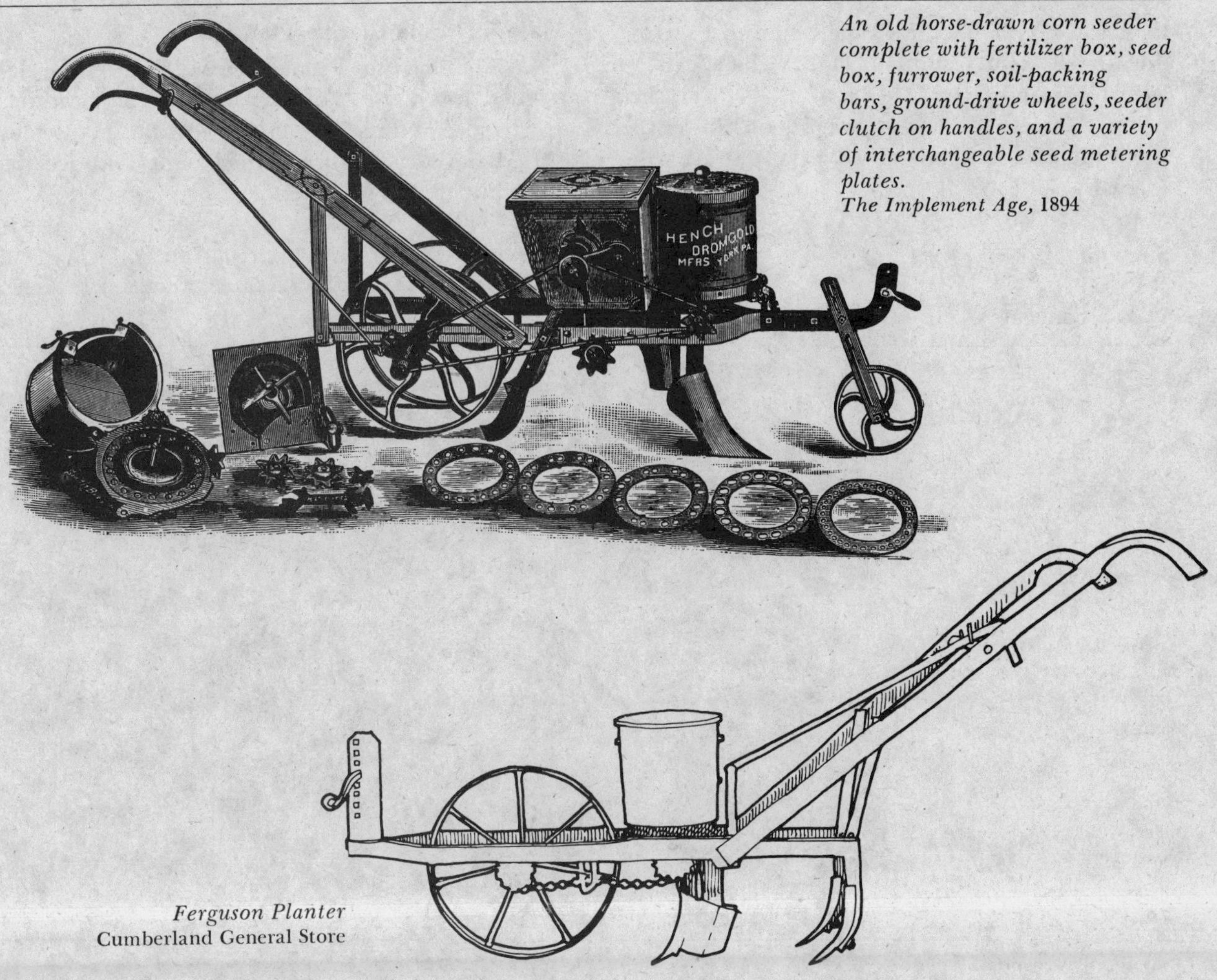

An old horse-drawn corn seeder complete with fertilizer box, seed box, furrower, soil-packing bars, ground-drive wheels, seeder clutch on handles, and a variety of interchangeable seed metering plates.
The Implement Age, 1894

Ferguson Planter
Cumberland General Store

Automatic Rabi Drills

Wooden-framed and all-steel models are available for sowing grain 20 centimeters between rows.

Automatic Kharif Drills

These are two-row drills for sowing seeds at wide spacings of 60 to 70 centimeters between rows. They are suitable for sowing maize, delinted cotton, and other seeds. Models with wooden frames or with all-steel construction are available.

Both the above types of drills are available from:
Danishmand & Co.
Karkhana Bazar
Lyallpur, Pakistan

Types ASD and RSD Seed and Fertilizer Drills

With working widths of 1.25 to 2.50 meters and row spacing adjustable from a minimum of 154 millimeters, this unit is fitted with a steerable front axle. Various types of furrow openers are available for different soil types. The fertilizer can be sown together with the seed or at the side of the seed rows, as required. This unit is available with either fluted roller seed metering or star wheel fertilizer metering.

A.J. Troster Landmaschinenfabrik
6308 Butzbach, Oberhess
Postfach 240, West Germany

Rice Seeder

This is a two-row seeder unit which can be fixed to the frame of the Occidental Hoe. The large-capacity hopper feeds the seed into a furrow dug by the two rear hoe blades, which can be adjusted to give row widths of 12 to 16 inches (.30 to .40 meters). Total weight, including the hoe unit, is approximately 100 pounds (45 kilograms).

Siscoma
B.P. 3214
Dakar, Senegal

Safaim Pitman Drive Planter

The Safaim Pitman Drive Planter is designed for maize planting but can be supplied with special attachments for cotton. It comes fitted with a fertilizer attachment and weighs 64.5 kilograms (142 pounds).

Massey-Ferguson South Africa, Ltd.
Steel Rd., P.O. Box 677
Vereeniging 1930, South Africa

Seeding ridges with animal-drawn equipment.

Super-Eco Seeder

This is an all-steel seeder unit with two large wheels driving the mechanism. Different plates or distributors are available for sowing groundnuts, millet, sorghum, maize, rice, and several types of vegetables. The unit is fitted with two handles, a furrow opener, coverers, a presswheel, and a row guide for marking subsequent rows. Total weight is approximately 82 pounds (37 kilograms), and the unit can be drawn by a single donkey or bullock.

Societe des Forges Tropicales
B.P. 706
Douala, Cameroun

E.B.R.A. SU 201 Animal-Drawn Seeder

This animal-drawn seeder is designed for use on the ridge or on the flat. The hopper has a capacity of 8 liters and the two front wheels

E.B.R.A. Animal-Drawn Seeder

are adjustable. Drive is through a series of sprockets which can be altered to vary the spacing in the row. Seed depth is adjustable on the shoe, and the unit is fitted with a presswheel and covering knives. A wide range of seed plates are available for planting the smallest to the very largest-sized seeds.

E.B.R.A.
28, rue du Maine, B.P. 84
49009 Angers, France

Seeder

Another animal-drawn seeder is made by:

Project Equipment, Ltd.
Industrial Estate, Rednal Airfield
West Felton, Oswestry
Salop SY11 4HS, U.K.

Automatic Seed-Cum-Fertilizer Drill

This drill is light in draft and is fitted with disc furrow openers. The row width is adjustable from 150 to 250 millimeters. A fluted roller feed mechanism is used. The three-row model weighs 95 kilograms and the five-row model, 110 kilograms.

Seed-Cum-Fertilizer Drill
Cossul & Co.

Cossul & Co. Pvt., Ltd.
Industrial Area, Fazalgunj
Kanpur, India

Maharashtra Seed-Cum-Fertilizer Drill
Maharashtra Tokan Yantra

Seed-Cum-Fertilizer Drill

This three-row drill has reciprocating plate metering mechanisms operated by a bell crank system from the land wheel. Row spacing is adjustable from 228 to 456 millimeters. Individual hoppers for each row allow the machine to be used for mixed cropping.

International Mfg. Co. (Regd.)
Hospital Rd., Jagraon
Ludhiana, Punjab, India

Maharashtra Tokan Yantra
Market Yard, Karad
Dist. Stara, Maharashtra, India

The Rajasthan Automatic Seed-Cum-Fertilizer Drill

This is a three-row machine capable of drilling small grain seed and fertilizer in one operation at an adjustable sowing depth.

Rajasthan State Agro Industries Corp., Ltd.
Virat Bhawan, C-Scheme
Jaipur 302 006, Rajasthan, India

Sisag Softroll Seeder Unit

Developed by the British National Institute of Agricultural Engineering, it will handle a wide range of seeds without fear of crushing or bruising. A pair of resilient neoprene rollers at the base of the hopper meter the seed (or fertilizer); metering is altered by varying the speed of the rollers. The unit can be adapted to feed a number of coulters, and is shown mounted on the rear of a tool bar.

Sisag Equipment Maccles-Field, Ltd.
Shoresclough Works, Hulley Rd.
Macclesfield, Cheshire SK10 2LZ, U.K.

Sisag Softroll Seeder Unit

Tanzanian Animal-Drawn Seed Drill

Ubungo Farm Implements
P.O. Box 2669
Dar Es Salaam, Tanzania

Allied Seed-Cum-Fertilizer Drills

Both two- and three-row models are available for sowing wheat, barley, maize, groundnuts, and rice seeds. A V-belt ground drive from the wheel drives the unit; seed rate is adjusted by a single lever, and the seeding mechanism is automatically engaged or disengaged when the tines are lowered or raised. Large wheels provide a low draft.

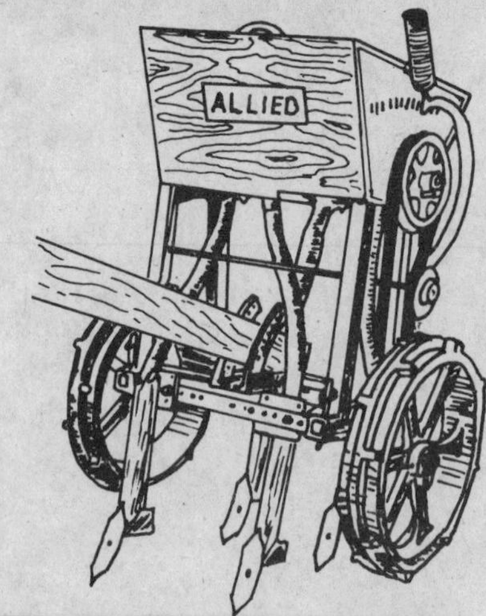

Allied Seed-Cum-Fertilizer Drill

Allied Trading Co.
Railway Rd.
Ambala City 134 002, Haryana, India

Single-Row and Three-Row Rice Seeder Plans

Plans for these seeders which originated in Zambia, are available from:

Intermediate Technology Publications, Ltd.
9 King St.
London WC2E 8HN, England

Jumil J-1 Planter

This planter, which also opens furrows and fertilizes, can be used on flat as well as mountainous terrain. It plants hard seeds such as corn and rice, soft seeds like peanut and castor bean, and cottonseed. Granulated, concentrated, or humid fertilizers can be used, or, if the soil is exceptionally fertile, the unit can be delivered without the fertilizer spreader.

Jumil
Justino de Morais, Irmaos S.A.
Rua Coriolano 380, Sao Paulo S.P., Brazil

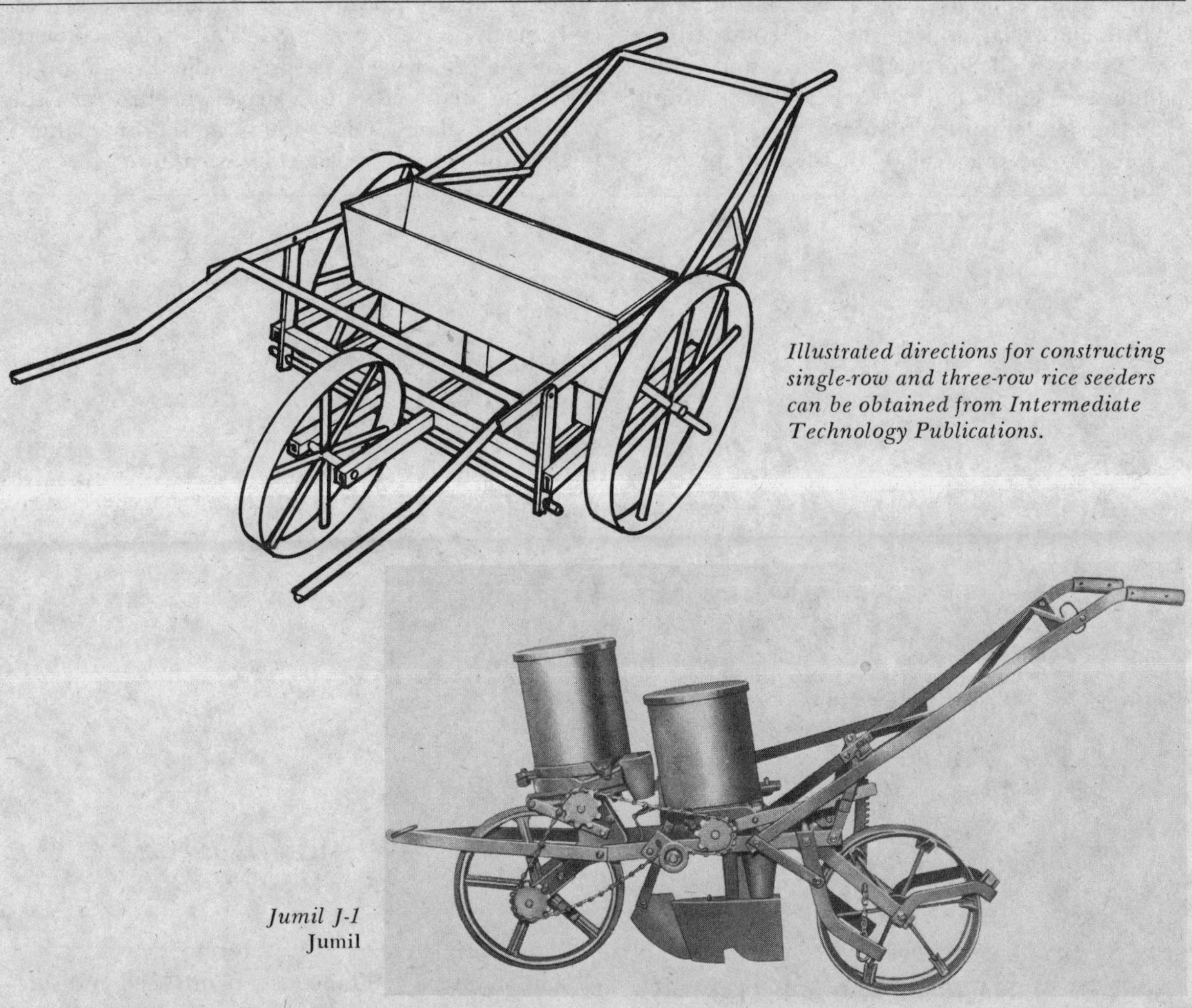

Illustrated directions for constructing single-row and three-row rice seeders can be obtained from Intermediate Technology Publications.

Jumil J-1
Jumil

TRACTOR-DRAWN UNIT PLANTERS

Many of the units described as hand-operated are also available with hitches for drawing by tractor. Larger, heavier planters, like the Brinly-Hardy (Louisville, KY 40200) and the Cole (Charlotte, NC 28200) are designed for tractor use only. The Brinly is for tractors with horsepower from 8 to 18, and the Cole for tractors on up to perhaps 15 to 25 horsepower. These seeders attach to three-point hitch arrangements or other hydraulic lift systems.

Larger and heavier commercial farm planters of great precision can now be purchased in single-row versions. The new planters, like those now available from all the large farm equipment companies like John Deere and International Harvester, are called unit planters. Each planting unit is powered by its own drive wheel, so many units can be used together. You will have to make your own hitch arrangement to attach one of these units to your tractor if it is not made for mounting on a tool bar. But the small commercial grower may find adapting a unit seeder well worth the effort, since these planters generally do a better job of planting than the smaller garden planters.

It may be practical, with the unit planters mentioned above, to go to a two-unit planter if you are row cropping more than four or five acres. The smaller Cole is a sort of unit planter, that is, two units can be put together quite easily. Old, obsolete, two-row planters originally designed for horses or smaller farm tractors also make fine tools for homesteaders with just a few acres to plant, but they are becoming scarce. Old four-row planters are now easier to find, but they are a little large for the typical homestead. However, you can modify one to a two-row model, or if you are mechanically equipped, you can take a single unit from a four-row or two-row planter and convert it to a single-row seeder. It means, on four-row models especially, converting the presswheel that presses the dirt on top of the planted seed, into a drive wheel to turn the planting plates. Older four- and six-row planters do not have a drive wheel for each unit.

Cole No. 12 Planter
Cole Mfg. Co.

SOURCES OF TRACTOR-DRAWN UNIT PLANTERS

Cole Number 12 Planter

Designed for the small farmer, the No. 12 is a garden planter with opening foot and three-point hitch for use with category 0 and 1 tractors. The planter simultaneously plants seed and side-dresses fertilizer. It has a single, inclined-plate seed hopper with a set of four seed plates for planting corn, large and small squash, small limas, okra, tomatoes, peas, and snap beans in hill or drill fashion. Other seed plates are available. A set of four distance gears for changing spacing is included. Fertilizer is placed beside the seed to prevent any fertilizer damage in germination. The galvanized, fertilizer hopper has a 40-pound capacity and a rate of application adjustable from 34 to 650 pounds. It will apply any dry fertilizer. An opening shank is included (sweep is not included).

Cole also offers a variety of hitches to mount the No. 12 planter to almost any tractor. These include International Harvester Models Super A, 140, and Cub tractors, both with and without fast hitch. They also have hitches for tool bar applications and for mounting the planter to other cultivators. All units are available worldwide.

The INTEC two-wheel tractor with a Cole No. 12 Planter attached. Often, equipment has applications even its manufacturer hasn't thought of.
Dowding Tool Products, Inc.

Cole's 210 Series

A lift-type, 50-inch carrier with category 1 three-point hitch and front and rear tool bars allow the farmer to simultaneously plant and put out fertilizer. He has the option to use either one or two fertilizer hoppers, one of four planter chassis, and three seed hopper options. Fertilizer is placed by two disc-side placers and run by a ground-drive wheel. Seed spacing, seed depth, and seed plates may be changed without special tools. A wide variety of plates is available for all seed hoppers. Cole also offers many attachments to fit a farmer's needs, such as gauge wheels, spring shanks, furrow openers, bed levelers, cotton attachments, and depth gauge extensions. Granular chemical applicators are also offered for both herbicides and insecticides.

Cole Economy 210 Series
Cole Mfg. Co.

Cole Mfg. Co.
1318 Central Ave.
Charlotte, NC 28299

Planet Junior Number 9192X Unit Seeder

Inside its own individual mounting cradle, this seeder unit is spring-suspended. This permits each unit to follow the contour of the ground assuring uniform depth of planting. It is suspended so that down pressure or lifting action is accomplished by actuating the tractor lift device. Units may be mounted in multiple-row applications at minimum-row widths of 9 inches, and are ground driven. Shipping weight: 56 pounds.

Planet Junior Division
Piper Industries
P.O. Box 1188, Freeport Center
Clearfield, VT 84106

Planet Jr. No. 9192X Unit Seeder
Piper Industries

ALMACO Cone-Type Nursery Seeder

This machine was developed specifically for planting small plots of corn, sorghum, soybeans, cereals, and other grain crops. These are seeder units which fit into the seed hopper box of commercial row planters like John Deere and International Harvester for planting nursery rows and space planting a large variety of seeds. This model has a cast aluminum base, 12½ inches in diameter.

ALMACO Cone-Type Nursery Seeder
Allan Machine Co.

Brinly-Hardy vegetable planter with row marker and fertilizer hopper.
Brinly-Hardy Co.

Allan Machine Co.
P.O. Box 112
Ames, IA 50010

Model KK-305 Vegetable Planter

A ground-drive unit for use in prepared soil, it is capable of planting seed as small as radish and turnip, as well as corn, beans, and peas. It opens the furrow and then drops and covers the seed at the desired spacing. It features a large-capacity seed hopper, a new float plate that allows the planter to follow ground contours, a new shovel-type opening foot, a new, larger, concave drive wheel which improves traction, reduces the possibility of skidding, and improves seed coverage. It is equipped with five quick-change seed plates, and 18 other seed plates are also available. Weight: 70 pounds.

Model KK-310 Row Marker and Model KK-320 Fertilizer Hopper (for use with the KK-305 Planter)

The KK-310 Row Marker helps maintain desired row spacing by marking next row as you plant. It is adjustable for different crop spacings. The KK-320 Fertilizer Accessory, when added to the KK-305 Planter, enables you to plant and fertilize in one operation. The rate of fertilizer flow can be regulated. Weight, Model KK-310: 10 pounds; Model KK-320: 20 pounds.

Brinly-Hardy Co., Inc.
P.O. Box 1116
Louisville, KY 40201

Ventura Large Seed Planter

This is a single-row planter which fits onto any tractor tool bar. The seed wheel revolves through the reservoir of seed, picks up one seed at a time, and deposits it into the planting opener. There are 12 different wheels for planting different-sized and -shaped seeds.

Ventura Mfg. & Implement Co.
1265 Commercial Ave., P.O. Box 1069
Oxnard, CA 93030

Jumil J-2 Unit Planter

Available with semiautomatic furrowers, this equipment furrows, sows, and fertilizes all in one operation at any required depth and spacing. The units themselves or the tool bar to attach them is furnished with three-point connections adjustable to any type or make of tractor. Discs are furnished to plant corn, cotton, rice, and peanuts. Special adapters are available for planting soybeans.

Jumil
Justino de Morais, Irmaos S.A.
Rua Coriolano 380, Sao Paulo S.P., Brazil

Jumil J-2 Unit Planter
Jumil

Gandy Row Seeders

Gandy makes a number of row seeder units with gear drives from a 12- or 6-volt electric motor or hydraulic motor drive. They have seeders for every major brand of farm equipment in all sizes.

Gandy Co.
528 Gandrud Rd.
Owatonna, MN 55060

Models 202-202F, 404-404F

The 202-404 planters for sowing cotton, corn, sunflower, melon, and sorghum seeds consist of separate T-63 sowing units which are attached to a rhomboid 2¼ by 2¼-inch tool bar. The units can be adjusted to a width of 16 inches to suit the required width between rows. The planter is made in three variations for two, four, or six rows. It is equipped with automatic markers fixed at a certain angle to ensure the creation of a prominent furrow that will mark the rows for the next pass. The marker works simultaneously with the elevation of the planter by the tractor operator. These markers can be set to suit different distances. The planter is equipped with front shovels mounted on a special front bar, to remove dry earth before sowing. Covering discs or shovels are optional. Other models are available, including those specially designed for planting sugar beets, vegetable seeds, onions, garlic, and peanuts, as well as multipurpose units.

Technohar Agricultural Machinery & Implements, Ltd.
New Industry Region, Petakh-Tikva
P.O.B. 225, Israel

Heath Precision Vacuum Planter

The seeds are picked up by means of a vacuum and held to the small holes in the plate, which is driven by the presswheel. An easily adjustable, graduated selector avoids doubling in case two seeds are picked up by the same hole. When each seed arrives near the lowest point, the vacuum stops abruptly; the seed is released and falls. The plate operates above the furrow opener and drops the seeds approximately 3 inches apart. The absence of mechanical handling means gentle treatment of the seeds, assuring maximum germination, which is especially important in beans. Planting depth can be easily controlled by a single handle which simultaneously adjusts the level of the two wheels. The fan is mounted on the tool bar and is connected to the tractor PTO which should be operated at 540 rpm. (A 1,000 rpm conversion kit is available.) The fan provides enough vacuum for up to 12 units. The vacuum's fine adjustment is controlled by the fan shutter, and a vacuum meter is connected to the fan. The planter is suitable for all row crops: sugar beets, cotton, corn, beans, sorghum, sunflowers, melons, watermelons, cucumbers, tomatoes, peppers, onions, cabbage, and broccoli, as well as coated seeds such as lettuce and carrots.

Features of the 925, as described by the manufacturer, include:

1. Precision planting with exact spacing.
2. Accuracy is maintained even at high speed; up to 50 seeds per second can be planted.
3. No grading is needed even with seeds of irregular shape and size.
4. No pelleting is needed for small seeds.
5. Changing the seeds or the seed plate and cleaning are very easy. The same seed plate is used for a variety of seed sizes.
6. A higher percentage of single seeds is dropped than with any other planter.
7. A zero pressure tire prevents mud from building up.

Seed spacings from 1.25 to 20 inches are easily obtained by changing a sprocket on the drive chain or the seed plate. The 925 is made up of unit planters. Up to 12 can be mounted on the heavy-duty tool bar with row spacings easily varied. The minimum spacing is 16 inches. The furrow openers are twin offset discs with a shoe to form the furrow. The discs cut away trash while the shoe firms and packs the sides and bottom of the furrow. Positive fin-type furrow closers are used. A furrow depth adjustment can be achieved without changing the level of the planter.

Heath Farm Equipment
125 S. Airpark Dr., P.O. Box 312
Fort Collins, CO 80522

ALMACO V-Belt Planter-Applicator

The V-belt planter-applicator can be supplied as a completely assembled unit, with mounting brackets in place of adjustable handles and rubber-tired running gear. The unit can be attached to power-driven equipment such as garden and riding tractors, or mounted on tool bars for single- or multiple-row planting or application of granular materials. Mounting brackets can be furnished which automatically adjust to the contour of the soil, thus assuring uniform depth of planting.

Certain parts of the planter-applicator such as the planter frame, V-belt pulleys and shafts, slanting, metal-covered hopper sides, metal apron, sprockets and drive chain, sliding gate, and smooth or ribbed-style V-belts can be special-ordered for different applications in mounting on power-driven equipment.

ALMACO V-Belt Planter-Applicator attached to the front end of a two-wheel tractor.
Allan Machine Co.

ALMACO V-Belt Planter-Applicator ready for mounting on a toolbar.
Allan Machine Co.

Allan Machine Co.
P.O. Box 112
Ames, IA 50010

Five ALMACO V-Belt Planter-Applicators mounted on a toolbar for planting five rows at one time.
Allan Machine Co.

Pneumatic Discharge Seeders

Dr. Giovanni Benati
37100 Verona
Via C. Battisti, Italy

Tanzania Agricultural Machinery Testing Unit
P.O. Box 1389
Arusha, Tanzania

Nibex Unit Seeder

The flexible Nibex system incorporates an original cup-distribution technique which is ideal even for planting irregularly shaped vegetable seed, which formerly was difficult or impossible to sow individually. The system includes 25 types of cups for most seeds, both natural and pelleted. This wide range makes it possible to choose a suitable cup for each desired drilling method. The seeding rate can be varied from four to about 2,000 seeds per running yard—either thin-line or band-drilled over a width of 2.5 or 4 inches (65 or 105 millimeters). The cup system is largely unaffected by variations in seed size, and seed cup discs are quickly interchanged for different crops.

The furrow is formed so that the seeds are immediately covered by a thin layer of moist earth. The coulter sideplates prevent dry surface soil from filling the furrow before the presswheel presses the moist earth into direct contact with the seeds. The furrow is next covered with loose earth, and conditions are now ideal for growth. The adjustable skid and the weighted presswheel allow a constant drilling depth to be maintained, even on loose and uneven surfaces.

The stainless steel coulter gives maximum wear resistance and prevents earth from sticking to it, even in wet conditions. Wheel brackets, seeder units, and marker brackets can be positioned anywhere on the beam, making the row spacing progressively variable from 7.5 inches (20

Nibex Unit Seeder
Nibe-Verken AB

centimeters) and upwards. (The rows can be brought closer together by attaching the unit sideways and driving back and forth in the same wheel tracks.)

Nibex unit seeders come in two- to twelve-row units; each unit has a 5-quart hopper capacity. Three-chain transmissions and a six-speed gearbox offer a choice of 18 settings. Normal operating speed is 2 mph; 3 is maximum. Depth is adjustable from 0 to 2 inches (0 to 5 centimeters). With 20-inch row spacing, a three-row machine will seed approximately 1.25 acres per hour.

Nibe-Verken AB
S–285 00 Markaryd
Sweden

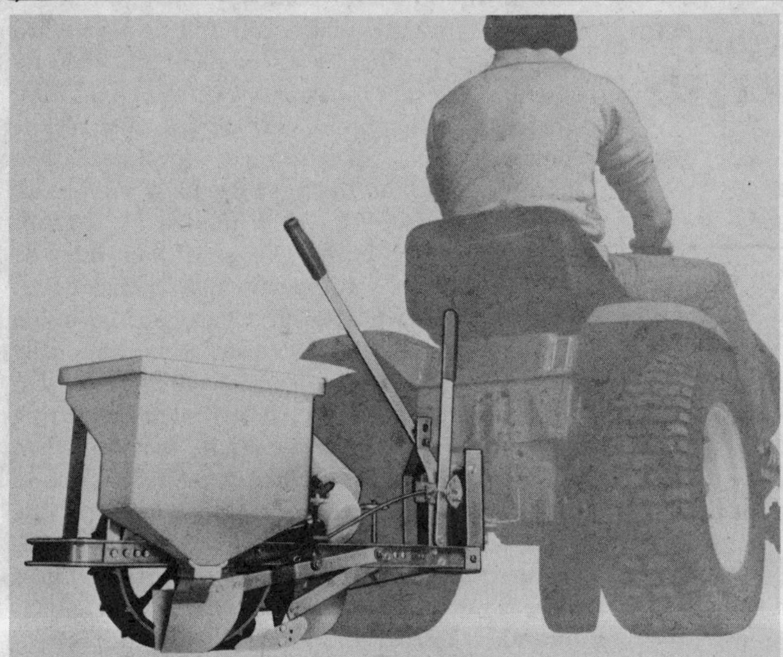

Esmay Unit Seeder
Esmay Products, Inc.

Seeder-Fertilizer Garden Tractor Mount

This unit was specifically designed for the truck farmer and larger home gardener. One pass opens the soil to the desired depth, seeds, fertilizes, and covers the seedbed. It attaches to standard hitching devices, category 0, three-point, drawbar, or sleeve hitches. Of corrosion-proof construction, it comes with seven seed plates which plant more than 20 common vegetable seeds.

Esmay Products, Inc.
P.O. Box 547, Maple St.
Bristol, IN 46507

GRAIN DRILLS*

* Reprinted in part from *Small-Scale Grain Raising* by Gene Logsdon. Rodale Press, 1977.

For planting seed in solid stands rather than in rows, a drill is used. For small acreages, however, you can often use small broadcasters much more efficiently, even counting the light disking or harrowing necessary to cover the seed. Generally speaking, the drill gives more precise planting depths than broadcasting and harrow covering and will result in better germination, especially if dry weather follows planting. The drill puts seed into the ground more or less continuously rather than depositing a precise number of seeds at precise spacings the way a row seeder does. It is used for cereal grains and grasses, and sometimes for soybeans if a solid stand is desired. Essentially, the drill is a long planting box with openings every six inches or so, from which planting tubes lead to the disc openers that run into the ground at planting depth. The discs open a shallow trench for the

DEALERS....

The McSherry Shoe Drill

IS A SELLER AND A WINNER.

WELL BUILT. WELL FINISHED.

SEND FOR CIRCULAR.

THE McSHERRY MFG. CO., Middletown, O.

A team of horses could plant 20 continuous rows of grain with this 19th century drill.
Farm Implement News, 1897

seed and close the trench on the seed after it falls. On old drills, a small length of chain drags behind each disc to aid in covering the seeds. The seeds are actually planted in rows, just inches apart, and when the grain gets to be about six inches high the plants grow together, giving the impression of a solid stand.

Normally, you can save quite a bit of money buying an old planter if it is still in working order. Be sure the planting plates come with it or can still be purchased. This is not usually a problem now because very cheap plastic plates are made to fit most planter boxes. In fact, the plates are given away by seed corn dealers when they sell a farmer his seed. The seed dealer wants a satisfied customer and the plastic plates he has are made specifically for the size kernels he sells—a different one for whatever plant population the farmer wants. But it is possible that on old and rare planters which you might find by chance, the plates wouldn't be a standard size. Before purchasing an old planter, it's always wise to make sure it has plates with it or find out where you can obtain new ones. Most of the common, older drills plant a swath of seven feet in one pass—about the right size for a homestead.

Seeding rates can be regulated by controls under the seed box. The seed box may be divided into two compartments, each side of which has its own control. Charts on the inside of the hinged box lids give instructions on setting the adjustments for different seeding rates. On old drills you will have to experiment by putting a measured amount of grain in the box, then planting a known, specified acre (or a portion thereof), and then see if the actual planting rate corresponds to what you have the drill set for. Compare and compensate accordingly. Those old cogs wear and may not work as precisely as they did when the drill was new.

Many drills, even old ones, have fertilizer

A single-point, tractor-drawn seed drill with fertilizer drill—about the right size for the small farm.

boxes just in front of the seed boxes. Unless they are well taken care of, the fertilizer boxes may be badly corroded or completely ruined. This will not necessarily stop you from using the drill, but you won't be able to fertilize as you plant. As another special feature, some drills have special smaller boxes for clover seed so that when planting spring cereal crops like oats, the farmer can sow clover right along with it.

SOURCES OF TRACTOR-DRAWN DRILL SEEDERS

Planet Junior 7135X Drill Seeder

A versatile planter with interchangeable seed plates for drilling vegetable seeds of all sizes. Special attachments are available for adapting the unit to field crops.

Planet Junior Division
Piper Industries
P.O. Box 1188, Freeport Center
Clearfield, VT 84106

Planet Jr. 7135X Seeder
Piper Industries

Hassia Model PS Plot Drill

The Hassia Model PS is a small plot drill with four, five, seven, or nine hoe-type openers. A fluted wheel meters the seed from either a single or a number of individual hoppers to isolate the runs. It is particularly designed for the precise nature of research work. The drill can be supplied with a tractor hitch, can be animal-drawn, or propelled by a 2½ h.p. gasoline engine. The centrifugal clutch on the motorized model enables the operator to set the

Hassia PS Plot Drill with gasoline engine: Front view
Rear view
H. J. Troster

accelerator to any walking pace. The unit is designed with even weight distribution for simple steering and handling.

A.J. Troster Landmaschinenfabrik
6308 Butzbach, Oberhess
Postfach 240, West Germany

MppD Monoseed Drill for Tubers

This unit is a hand-fed, double-drill, tuber-sowing machine. Sowing depth and row width as well as the depth of the covering layer are adjustable, by means of convex clutch discs. Fertilizer dispensers are optional extras, and the unit is attached to the tractor by a three-point hitch.

Fratelli Deidone, Macchine Agricole
C.C.I.A.N. 59212, Casella Postale 7
Villafranca DiVerona, Italy

Zita Sowing Machine With Fertilizer Distributor

Even when fully loaded, this machine is light enough to require only 1.6 h.p. to pull each drill (this model unit has seven drills). The seed tank is separated into two parts for seed and fertilizer, and each section can be regulated separately. The gear-type feeders for seed and fertilizer maintain a steady application rate independent of tractor speed. The Zita sowing machine can be operated by the tractor operator or by a second person sitting behind the unit.

Sons Ath. Zafiridi Industry of Machineries, Inc.
Langada 4.5 km. T.T.7
Stavroupolis, Thessaloniki, Greece

Hindsons Seed-Cum-Fertilizer Drill

Planting four rows at a time, all kinds of seeds can be precisely placed at a comfortable distance away from the fertilizer. The distance between furrows is adjustable with spring-steel tines. Construction of the unit was designed for simplicity, light weight, easy cleanability, and the drill can be pulled by most any tractor with a lift arrangement.

M/s. Hindsons Private, Ltd.
The Lower Mall
Patiala, India

Tye Soybean Drill

Not only for soybeans but wheat and other small grains as well, this drill is available in many sizes, the smallest is a two-row or 6.7-foot model. It is attached behind a tractor by a three-point hitch, has adjustable spacings, accurate seed metering, and positive depth control.

The Tye Co.
Box 218
Lockney, TX 79241

Tye Adjustable Drill, 80" model
Tye Co.

IRRI Multihopper Seeder

The IRRI Multihopper Drill Seeder for upland use is designed with a divided hopper for interplanting several crops simultaneously. It can be pulled by either a two- or four-wheeled tractor.

International Rice Research Institute
P.O. Box 933
Manila, Philippines

The multihopper seeder holds different kinds of seeds for interplanting crops.
International Rice Research Institute

The multihopper seeder being pulled by a two-wheel tractor.
International Rice Research Institute

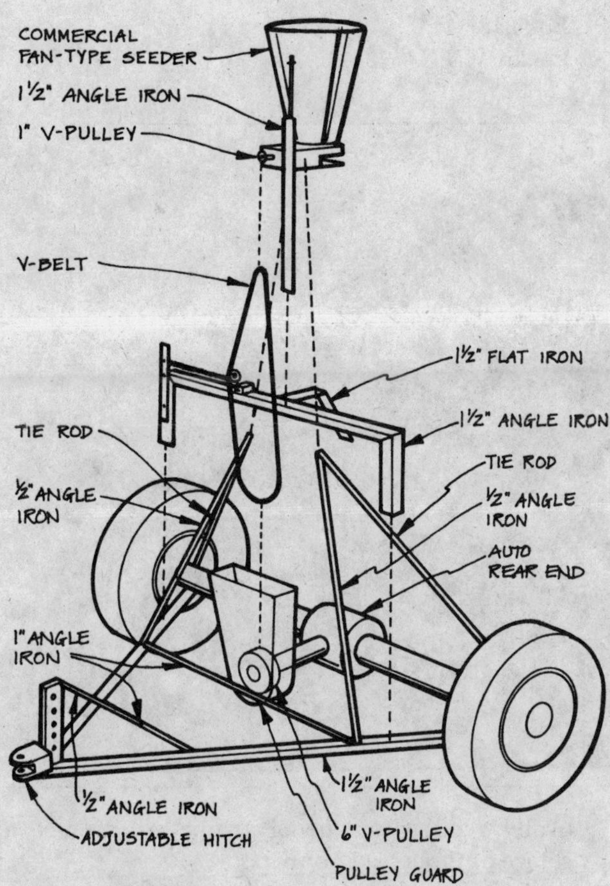

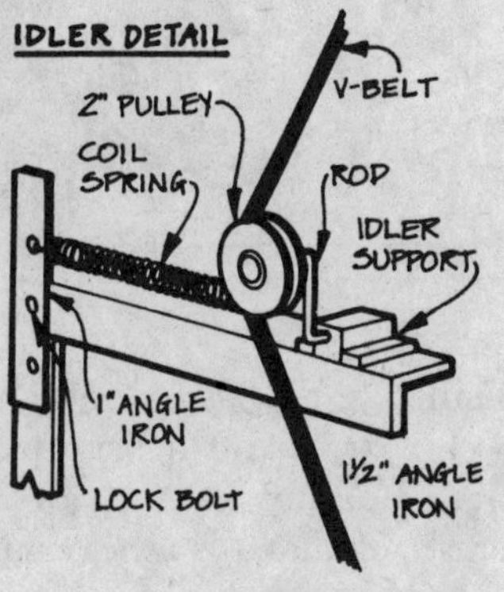

This basic design for a homemade seeder with hopper, idler, wheel assembly and hitch was developed by the Texas Agricultural Extension Service of the Texas A & M University System in College Station, Texas.

NO-TILL PLANTERS

Sometimes called a pasture renovator, the no-till planter is a seed drill with a special function. It is supplied with a disc and a shoe which allow it to slice the turf and plant a seed without first plowing and preparing a seedbed. Animals can continue to graze while new plantings of clover or grass get started. One farmer reports, "I get a lot of nitrogen this way and I get it where it counts." According to Dick Margulis, who writes advice for novice farmers in *Countryside,* "Good natural nitrogen in the plant means good natural protein for the cow. A farmer ought not to buy his nitrogen or his protein. His total farm cycle ought to handle the greatest share of this problem." Also, planting in existing sod is a very good practice to control erosion.

The Tye Pasture Pleaser

The Tye Pasture Pleaser is a compact three-point-hitch-mounted, no-till planting unit covering 80 inches, with disc units spaced 10 inches apart. It is a conveniently sized tool for seeding legumes, grass, or small grains in sod, permanent, or improved pasture. Drive is by a single, spring-loaded, front-running coulter. Each double-disc unit is preceded by a spring-loaded coulter blade. Each blade, as well as each disc unit and press-wheel, is individually hinged and spring loaded for work on uneven ground. The larger hopper is fitted with internally fluted seeder units for small grains as well as soybeans. The small hopper or grass box is fitted with externally fluted seeder units for dispensing grasses and legumes. Brackets are provided for adding suitcase-type weights to assist penetration of the coulters in hard ground.

The Tye Co.
Box 218
Lockney, TX 79241

Tye Pasture Pleaser
Tye Co.

Cole No-Till Planter

The Cole No-Till Planter has a double-disc seed opener which cuts straw and debris in the field, preventing trash buildup in front of and under the seed opener. Included is a heavy-duty swivel coulter—a chisel plow which automatically resets after being tripped. You get a choice of three seed hoppers:

1. Edgedrop with 1-bushel capacity
2. Uniplex with 1-bushel capacity and single, inclined seed plate

Cole No-Till Planter
Cole Mfg. Co.

3. Duplex with dual, inclined seed plates and 2-bushel capacity.

Fertilizer attachments which place fertilizer 4 to 6 inches deep in the slit opened by the chisel plow come with the ground-drive wheel and 250-pound capacity fiberglass fertilizer hoppers. Granular chemical applicators which put out herbicides or insecticides or both are also available. The planter also comes in four- and six-row models.

Cole Mfg. Co.
1318 Central Ave.
Charlotte, NC 28299

TRACTOR-DRAWN BROADCAST SEEDERS

Power to turn the mechanical rotating distributor of a broadcast seeder can be supplied either by power take-off from the tractor or by a ground-drive wheel. (The distributing mechanism is basically the same as that of the hand-cranked broadcast seeder, which we discussed earlier in this chapter.) With no power source, animal-drawn distributors rely on a gear drive from the ground wheel to the rotating wheel to rotate the distributor. The newest units are battery-operated so that the distributor can be attached to any moving vehicle, whether it's a tractor, jeep, or automobile.

SOURCES OF TRACTOR-DRAWN BROADCAST SEEDERS AND SPREADERS

Ezee Flow Model 105 Spreader

They call it a turf care model, but this 310-pound unit with a 7.7 cubic foot, 500-pound hopper capacity falls into the small farm category for us. With a 54-inch-wide coverage, this unit is ground driven and requires a minimum of 10 h.p. to pull it. The spreader is calibrated for seed as well as fertilizer distribution.

Ezee Flow No. 105 Spreader
Avco Corp.

Ezee Flow Number 113 Broadcast Seeder

With a 3-bushel (2-bushel extension available), galvanized steel hopper capacity, this 81-pound broadcast seeder spreads up to 36 feet. The spread is controlled from the tractor seat. The unit requires a minimum of 18 h.p., a three-point hitch, and a universal-joint PTO drive. Larger units are also available.

Ezee Flow, AVCO Corp.
First & Sycamore
Coldwater, OH 45828

Ezee Flow No. 113 Spreader with three-point hitch mounting and universal PTO shaft drive.
Avco Corp.

Wikomi Electric Broadcast Seeder

You can attach this electric seeder to your truck, jeep, or car—a tractor is not necessary, just a 6-volt battery. With a 1½-bushel capacity and an optional 1-bushel extension, you can plant 20 acres per hour. Larger units are available.

Wikomi Electric Broadcast Seeder
Wikomi Mfg. Co.

Wikomi Poly-Hopper Seeder-Spreader

A new product in their lawn and garden line, the 1-bushel seeder, 100-pound fertilizer spreader constructed of polyethylene fits most lawn and garden tractors and riding lawn mowers. It has a 12-volt electric drive, mounts on a rear drawbar, and weighs 28 pounds. Larger units are available.

Wikomi Mfg. Co.
P.O. Box 100
Litchfield, IL 62056

Sears Spreaders

The smallest unit Sears lists has a 1-bushel capacity. It bolts to a standard tractor drawbar and is powered with a direct drive PTO. It has an 18-gauge welded steel hopper and spreads a swath up to 50 feet wide. Weight: 37 pounds.

Sears, Roebuck & Co.
Farm and Ranch Catalog

Apolo Broadcaster

With a capacity of 400 to 450 kilograms, this fully adjustable unit operates from the power take-off shaft of a tractor. The recommended application speed is 7 to 12 kilometers per hour.

Industrias Metalurgicas Apolo S.A.
Carrera 50-2 Sur–189 Autopista Sur
Medellin, Antioqui, Colombia

Lely

Lely makes broadcasters for a tractor PTO with hopper capacities ranging from 8.5 to 156.4 bushels.

Lely
Box 1060
Wilson, NC 27893

Gandy

Starting with a 3-foot long, 1.6 cubic foot hopper, Gandy has tractor-drawn, wheel-driven spreaders for seeding or fertilizing.

Gandy Co.
528 Gandrud Rd.
Owatonna, MN 55060

106 Single Spinner

New Idea's smallest model spreader-seeder (No. 106) has a 12-gauge steel hopper capacity of 690 pounds and an effective spread width of 36 feet. Density of coverage ranges from 4 to 1,570 pounds per acre. It attaches to a tractor by a three-point hitch.

New Idea Seeder No. 106
Avco Corp.

AVCO Corp., New Idea Farm Equipment Div.
First & Sycamore
Coldwater, OH 45828

Diadem Precision Spinner Spreader and Seeder

Attached with a three-point hitch, the Diadem comes with 7-, 9-, or 12-bushel capacities.

Vandermolen Corp.
119 Dorsa Ave.
Livingston, NJ 07039

Gherardi Fertilizer Broadcaster

Although this spreader is suitable for most types of fertilizer, it was designed chiefly for high-concentrate, granulated, pulled, or semi-pulled fertilizers requiring a high degree of accuracy. Traveling speed can range from 3 to 16 kilometers per hour. Two sizes are available: a 75-kilogram model with a 300-liter capacity, and a 130-kilogram unit with a 500-liter capacity.

Gherardi
Officine Macchine Agricole Industriali
Jesi (Ancona) Via Gallodoro 68, Italy

Midjet

The Midjet is a small, tractor-drawn, broadcast seeder-fertilizer designed as a lawn tool, which hitches to a small garden tractor.

Champenois
Chamouilley
52170 Chevillon, France

PLANTING BY SYSTEMS

CHECK-ROW PLANTING

by Roger Blobaum

The check-row planter, an implement widely used on Corn Belt farms for more than 60 years, made possible the kind of mechanical weed control that many small farmers want.

The check-row planters, which disappeared along with work horses on most farms in the 1930s and 1940s, dropped seed corn in hills spaced about 30 inches apart each way. Their main limitation was that they could not be used on fields that were contoured or laid out in other ways that did not provide straight rows.

This checkerboard pattern made it possible to cultivate fields both ways, giving excellent results. This kind of cultivation threw dirt up around all sides of the corn hills and took out the weeds, both in and between the rows. It provided much better weed control than modern implements, which are unable to reach weeds between the plants in drilled rows.

The precise planting pattern was made possible by wire buttons spaced usually 40 or 42 inches apart on a check wire anchored with a stake at each end of the field. The stake had to be moved over by hand each time the planter came to the end of the row. The check wire passed through the planter as it moved across the field. The buttons tripped the plates in the seed corn boxes, dropping bunches of kernels in uniformly spaced hills.

Cultivators in that period had shanks that were guided by the farmer's feet. The shanks made it possible to guide the shovels around any hills that ended up slightly out of line in the checkerboard pattern. This arrangement was much more flexible than cultivators mounted on the tractors that were replacing horses on most farms.

The careful two-way cultivation made possible by check-row planting became less important when farmers began applying chemical weed killers. Fast-moving tractors and equipment that planted four or six rows at a time also helped bring about the switch to planters that drilled corn in rows and mounted cultivators that moved across these fields at much higher speeds.

The introduction of four-row check planters caused some problems. Scientists at Iowa State College in the early 1930s solved one of them—the tendency of these planters to pull check wires

The Check-Row Technique:

-.-.-.-.-.-.-.-.-.- check wire with buttons

——— marked guide for next row

xxxxxxxxxxx plantings

Checking

1. *After planting two or three rounds, stop and dig up about eight cross-rows to see if cross check is good.*
2. *If cross check is not accurate, adjust checkheads as necessary to correct cross check.*

Turning at Ends of Field

1. *Pull trip rope about nine buttons from the end. This will automatically release wire about seven buttons from the end.*
2. *Turn planter in position for planting the next two rows, stopping squarely over mark.*
3. *Move anchor stake behind runner on wire side. Set tension the same each time wire is moved.*
4. *Drive forward, keeping tractor straight over mark.*

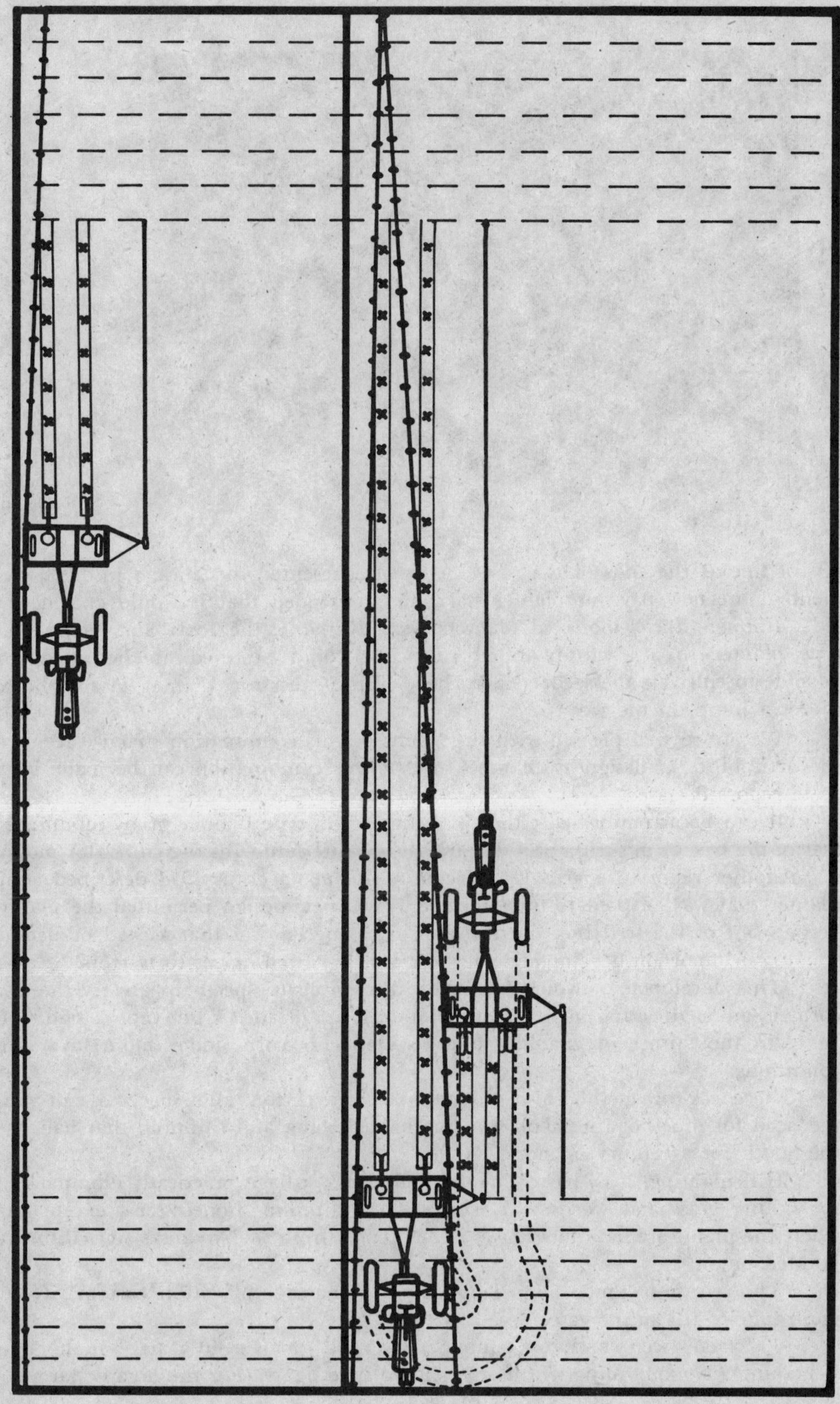

Parts of a check-row planter: 1) lever (arm); 2) seed hopper; 3) power lift control; 4) checkhead; 5) automatic release; 6) power lift clutch. Ron Krupicka

out of line at the ends of the rows. A report presented in Chicago in 1933 described the development of the new pay out planter stake and concluded that it would eliminate this problem.

Although tractor-mounted planters were available, the Iowa State experiments utilized a pull-type planter so a tractor-mounted cultivator could be used at the same time. This made it possible to cultivate the seedbed just ahead of the check-row planter, giving the corn a better chance to get a jump on the weeds.

"We are so well pleased with the results of this combination that we feel justified in suggesting the desirability of designing planters so that this combination can be made by the user," the Iowa State report declared.

"It can be accomplished either by using a pull-type planter or by mounting the planter on the rear of the tractor in such a way that it will not interfere with the cultivator mounting."

Another report prepared by a Deere & Co. manager in 1944 described a high-speed check-row planter that was adapted to tractor power. The new design permitted the planter to push the corn kernels out of the seed box instead of using a mechanism that kicked or batted them out. It was seen as an important development in the transition from horses to tractors.

"This development, which has made it possible to speed up greatly the operation of planting corn, is an engineering achievement of much significance," the report said. "It is of inestimable value to the farmer in enabling him to plant his corn under more favorable weather and soil conditions."

The check-row method also was used to plant cotton, allowing cross-cultivation and eliminating the need for much of the labor-intensive hand hoeing and thinning that had been commonplace in the South for a century or more.

"Hill planting, cross harrowing, and checkered tillage practically eliminate the hoe as a weapon for killing grass and weeds and render hand thinning unnecessary, except in an occasional hill where the plants are too numerous," a 1929 report from the Arkansas Agricultural Experiment Station pointed out.

"The release of much hand labor from the acreage of cotton customarily cultivated will afford more time to till an increased area."

We haven't seen check-row equipment around for over 40 years, but this equipment is certainly something anyone farming with horses should investigate. For the organic farmer, check-row planting is one way to completely devastate a population of weeds without the use of herbicides. Granted, fields cannot be as densely planted, but there is growing controversy over the importance of high-density planting, and with sparse plantings, there is more room for interplanting other crops like pumpkin and squash between the plants.

Back in the early 1930s, results reported in *Agricultural Engineering* * showed that production yields of cotton could be kept up by planting in the check-row fashion with more densely planted hills rather than distributing seed throughout the row with a drill, even with fewer plants per hill. Fueling the controversy is the escalating price of seed grains. Here are some sound arguments for check-row planting that were set forth in the article:

1. On bottom land, or on other lands of a high degree of fertility, cotton seems to produce as well when the plants are grouped in hills arranged for cross-cultivation as when the plants are distributed in rows.
2. Thickness of planting in hills appears to accomplish the same result in stimulating earliness as has been shown for close spacing in the drill.
3. No exact number of plants to the hills seems necessary. According to results, the number can range from two to six plants per hill or around 10,000 to 25,000 an acre. However, since the production was lowered less with 15 plants to the hill than with one plant to the hill, the stand maintained should be nearer the upper limits of the range of highest yields rather than toward the lower side of this range.
4. Hand thinning is unnecessary.

CHECK-ROW PLANTING ALIVE AND WELL IN NEBRASKA

by Ron Krupicka

Editor's note: Ron is Codirector with Dennis Demmel for the Small Farm Energy Project at the Center for Rural Affairs in Hartington, Nebraska. This story is about his uncle.

Louis Suchy, 72, has been farming his 320-acre, diversified farm near Niobrara, Nebraska all his life. He has always used a check-row planter for planting his corn. At first he used a horse-drawn check planter. Today, however, he uses a tractor-drawn, two-row, check-row planter he purchased at a local farm sale.

Louis' first step when planting with a check-row planter is to string a wire with buttons across the field from one end to the other. The wire is laid with just the right amount of slack so that it can be fitted in the guide located on the side of the planter. As the planter is pulled across the field, the wire passes through the checkhead and the buttons which are set every 40 inches on the wire trip a mechanism that turns the planter plate, allowing either two or three seeds to drop.

Louis has 16-hole plates in his planter which will drop three kernels to a button. But he feels that moisture is a limiting factor in his area and three kernels per hill would increase his plant population to the point where there wouldn't be enough water to supply all the plants. So Louis plants first two kernels, then three kernels in alternating hills. To do this, he has sealed up two holes on each plate by welding them shut.

To plant the corn, the planter is drawn down the row dropping two or three kernels in hills every 40 inches. After planting two or three rounds, the cross check is inspected by digging up about eight cross-rows to see if the check is good. If the check is off, the checkhead can be corrected by making the appropriate adjustments as explained in the instruction manual.

* Ware, J. O. The Hill Planting of Cotton and Checker Cultivation with Large Tillage Instruments. *Agricultural Engineering.* Vol. 11, no. 5, May 1930.

Louis Suchy with his check-row planter. Here he points to the trip mechanism which is engaged when buttons on the guide wire pass through the checkhead.
Ron Krupicka

Check-row buttons got their name when metal buttons like the one on the left were used years ago. No longer resembling a button, the head on the wire to the right acts as the tripping mechanism for newer models.
Ron Krupicka

The checkhead on a check-row planter. The buttons trip this mechanism releasing seeds in one spot.
Ron Krupicka

When the edge of the field is reached, the wire is disengaged and the machine is turned around in a figure eight, thus allowing planting as close as possible to the fence line. The wire is moved over two rows and the process is repeated back and forth across the field. The instruction manual states that six rows must be drilled for the end rows, but Louis' figure eight turn has reduced that to four. When he planted with horses, Louis said he could plant right up to the fence line and, as a result, there was no need to drill the end rows. Also, there was a seat on the horse-drawn planter so that the operator could manually trip the planter to drop the seeds.

Louis noticed that each year the extension service and equipment companies seemed to be promoting a different planting method. He felt that check planting started to decrease when the lister was pushed. When asked why he still uses the check planter, Louis simply replied, "Dad taught me how to cultivate." It is for the same reason that Louis has never been in his fields with herbicides. He has observed that if you don't follow up spraying with weeding, you will still have weeds.

Louis keeps his fields clean by cultivating three times. The first time he follows the planter, the second time he crosses the planter rows at a 90-degree angle, and the third time he follows the planter again because "otherwise it would be mighty rough picking!" He still picks his corn in the ear with a one-row cornpicker and then stores it in his corncrib.

His average yield over the years has been 50 bushels per acre, sometimes 60—without using any commercial fertilizer on his corn.

PLUG-MIX SEEDING AND EQUIPMENT*

Plug-mix is a method of seeding which incorporates crop seeds and water into a scientifically blended growing medium which is precision placed in the field with a type of jab planter called a hand plugger. Having ⅛- to ¼-cup of loose soil, the seed and compost-nutrient mixture cradles each hill to ensure a uniform, optimum environment for germination and for young seedlings to get off to a good start. It is particularly suited for extensive plantings of most small-seeded vegetable crops.

Advantages of plug-mix seeding over standard seeding methods:

1. A uniform, optimum environment in seed and young seedling zones is provided, along with an adequate, safe level of fertilizer readily available to the seedlings.
2. Plant stands are often better, and seed germination and plant growth are more rapid and uniform.
3. There is no compaction problem with the tilthy plug-mix soil.
4. Fertilizer salt damage during dry periods, and leaching of nutrients during top-water and rainfall are reduced.
5. Fertilizers and seeds are conserved by placement only where needed. This reduces the fertilization of competing weeds.
6. With the automatic plug-mix planter, an economical and successful method of seeding through mulch-covered beds is now available.

Perfecting the plug-mix method involved a joint research project between Cornell University and the University of Florida. Cornell worked on a soil blend while Florida worked on the design of application equipment. Cornell worked with chemicals, but you can arrive at a potent mixture of your own by blending compost, manure, and other organic nutrient sources.

* Reprinted with permission from Fort Pierce Agricultural Research Center *Research Report RL 1974-3*, by Norman Hayslip, Institute of Food and Agricultural Sciences, University of Florida.

AMOUNT OF SEED REQUIRED TO OBTAIN AN AVERAGE OF ABOUT FOUR, SIX, OR EIGHT SEEDS IN EACH ¼ CUP OF LOOSE MIX PER HILL

CROP	APPROXIMATE NO. OF SEEDS PER OUNCE [1]	AMOUNT OF SEED (OUNCES) FOR 4-CUBIC-FOOT BAG MIX		
		AVERAGE 4 SEEDS/HILL	AVERAGE 6 SEEDS/HILL	AVERAGE 8 SEEDS/HILL
BROCCOLI	9,000	0.8	1.2	1.6
CABBAGE	8,500	0.9	1.4	1.8
CAULIFLOWER	10,000	0.7	1.0	1.4

(Continued on next page)

CROP	APPROXIMATE NO. OF SEEDS PER OUNCE [1]	AMOUNT OF SEED (OUNCES) FOR 4-CUBIC-FOOT BAG MIX: AVERAGE 4 SEEDS/HILL	AVERAGE 6 SEEDS/HILL	AVERAGE 8 SEEDS/HILL
CUCUMBER	1,000	7.2	10.8	14.4
EGGPLANT	6,000	1.2	1.8	2.4
LETTUCE	25,000	0.3	0.4	0.6
OKRA	500	14.4	21.6	28.8
PEPPER	4,500	1.6	2.4	3.2
TOMATO	11,000	0.7	1.0	1.4

[1] James Edward Knott. *Handbook for Vegetable Growers,* rev. ed. New York: John Wiley and Sons, Inc., 1962.

A simple and inexpensive hand-operated applicator was constructed for use in early research trials:

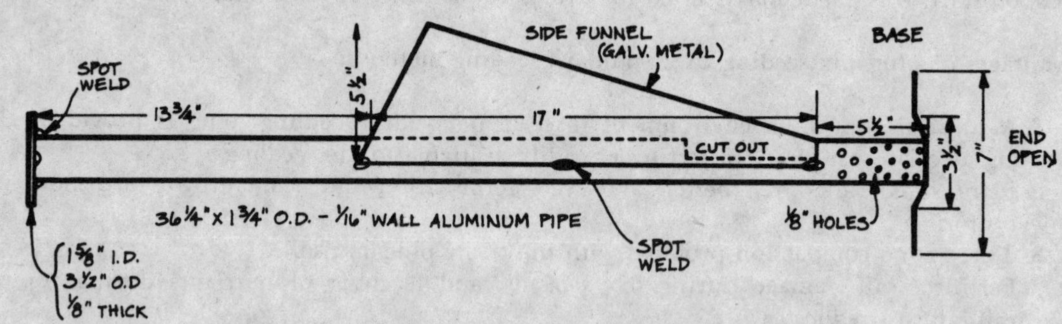

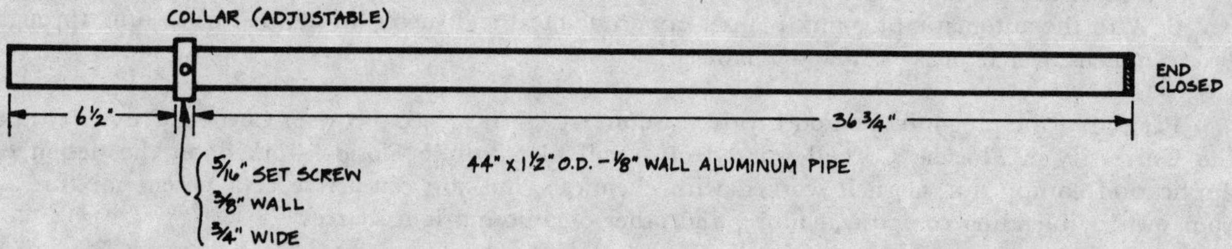

The pluggers were used by some growers with positive results, but high labor costs encouraged the development of an automatic planter.

Mechanical Plug-Mix Planters Number 900M and Number 900

The tractor-mounted automatic planter meters up to ½ cup of loose mix into revolving cups which deliver the mix to the planter pockets. The pockets pierce the soil and deposit the mix at fixed intervals. Presswheels can be mounted behind planter pockets to firm the soil from each side on unmulched beds. The unit works well without presswheels on mulch-covered beds, the pockets punching holes through the mulch as they deposit the mix. The toolbar-mounted planter has operated efficiently at a forward speed of 1 mph and is designed to plant at down-row spacings of 10, 12, 20, 30, 51, or 60 inches.

Mechanical Transplanter Co.
S. Central at U.S. 31
Holland, MI 49423

MECHANIZATION OF FARMING UNDER PLASTIC TUNNELS

Editor's note: This information is extracted from a letter written to the editor by Dr. Y. Alper, who is with the Institute of Agricultural Engineering in Bet Dagan, Israel.

The method of growing in low, plastic tunnels has become very popular in the Israeli agriculture over the last few years. Its main advantage is an early crop of fresh vegetables on the market. Our Institute started working on the mechanization of this method a few years ago.

The synchronized plastic mulching and planting machine was the first machine developed for this purpose. This unit, which seeds, mulches, and perforates the plastic above the seeds in one operation, is manufactured by a local company and is used commercially by farmers.

Low plastic tunnel cultivation is a popular technique for early crop ripening. Early ripening is achieved by this method not only by early planting, but also through the better microclimate conditions and the physical protection of the plants during their first stages of growth. The increasing use of this growing technique created a need for mechanical means to erect the tunnels.

The T-2100, which is fed by straight steel wires, forms the arches and places them into the ground in a continuous operation. The spacing between arches and their height are adjustable. The machine is pulled by a small-size tractor and ground-driven by its own wheels.

An automatic machine for farming and inserting wire arches into the ground was developed and field-tested during the 1976 season. Field-test results were very successful and some units were planned to be operated commercially in 1978.

A wire renewer which straightens used wires for reuse with an automatic inserting device was also built.

The development of these machines is a considerable contribution to the mechanization of growing in low, plastic tunnels in Israel; each of these machines can also be operated separately, according to local conditions.

The Kennco Plastic Machine

This plastic machine covers a formed bed with a 1.5-mil plastic. The machine simultaneously tucks and buries the plastic at the sides just under the outside corner of the bed to insure permanence throughout the crop. Plastic machines can be equipped with gas knives or nozzles to inject gas or liquid herbicides just prior to laying plastic on the bed.

Plastic-laying machines come complete with three-point hitch, seat, hiller blades, and aluminum end plugs. A larger, high-speed machine is also available.

Kennco Mfg. Co.
P.O. Box 1158
Ruskin, FL 33570

WINDFELL FARM: AN EXPERIMENT IN INTERMEDIATE AGRICULTURE

"We want to grow the highest-quality, best-looking organic produce possible and stay competitive with our chemically oriented neighbor," says Steve Talbott, of Banks, Oregon. To do this, he and his father are developing "a workable, efficient, small-scale family farm" that specializes in row crop vegetables. Affectionately named Windfell, the farm doubles as a home enterprise and an experiment in intermediate agriculture.

The key to the Talbott system is a transplanting machine called the Hydro-Synchron, invented and patented by the Talbotts, and a cropping system called Jetspeed. Jetspeed is the registered name for an integrated system of diversified row crop production, using high-quality facilities, machinery, and tools and an intermediate technology applicable to a small- or medium-sized operation, from 5 to 100 acres.

The system is neither capital-intensive nor labor-intensive, using both in an appropriate balance to maximize labor efficiency, provide a human scale in the process, and maintain as much as possible a diversity of tasks for workers. At the small end of the scale, the operation can be run by a family with seasonal help at harvest. At the other end, a sizeable outside payroll would be required. The Talbotts' system is ecologically sound, energy-efficient, uses the land intensively, adapts to highly diversified cropping, and they believe, is demonstrably profitable. Transplanting, as opposed to direct field seeding, is the key to Jetspeed.

During 1976 and 1977, research and development of all aspects of the Jetspeed transplant row crop system continued at Windfell Farm, some 70 acres located 24 miles west of Portland, Oregon. Windfell was advised that the soil, the slope, and the general conditions were not favorable for row crop production. The acreage had been in grain for years with mediocre results. But the Talbotts accepted the challenge and developed markets for their Biogold products in local communities and the city of Portland.

Long, straight rows of evenly spaced seedlings that require no thinning and a minimum of cultivation are the end product of the Hydro-Synchron, the key to the Talbott's planting system.

Some crops have been routinely transplanted by some growers for generations. The process is slow, often back-breaking and always inefficient, resulting in severe plant shock and mortality. Assuming an improved transplanter, the transplant system insures precise plant spacing and thus, maximum field population. Weeding and thinning problems are greatly reduced or even eliminated with good management, and maturity is more uniform so harvesting costs are reduced. The shorter period from transplanting to harvest means a more intensive and cost-effective use of the land. Talbott advises, "The figure on the bottom line is what counts."

To adopt a transplant system required either a reliable source of plants or a facility for producing them. Windfell developed the systems and the specialized equipment necessary to produce hardy plants that grow fast with stocky tops and strong, branching root systems. Their double-poly house is particularly well adapted to these techniques.

Thousands of seedlings get a good start and grow into hardy plants inside the Talbott double-poly house.

TODD Planter Flats with pyramid-shaped cells.

After investigating many different plant-growing systems, it was clear that the Speedling System was the one to adopt. In this system, the patented TODD Planter Flats with inverted, pyramid-shaped cells rest on aluminum T-rails. This promotes natural air pruning of the root system. The result is rapid branching and concentration of the root structure within the cell. Plants can be transplanted with virtually no shock and without interruption of growth.

The Jetspeed planting mix is composed of 50 percent peat, 50 percent vermiculite, bone meal, lime, dolomite, and several additives that have been found to produce the ideal transplants with strong, stocky tops, and quick-growing, widely branching root systems which can be easily pulled intact from the Speedling trays at an early date. The Talbotts found that for the small operator, mixing and tray filling can be done economically with hand labor and good organization. But they found that seeding without an efficient seeder was very time-consuming and costly. Hence the Digit-200 seeder.

The Digit-200 Plate Seeder
Gene Talbott

An ingenious invention, the Digit-200 seeder is simply a tray which sets on top of the 200-unit, cavity trays and has small holes placed exactly in line with where a seed should be deposited. A pile of seeds is scattered across the tray, one dropping in each hole. Excess seeds are gathered at one end. When the tray is lifted, one seed is left in each tray cavity and a thin layer of vermiculite is spread on top. With the Digit-200 seeder, six 200-unit trays can be planted per minute. Making such efficient

A short, powerful blast of fertilized water is the key to the transplanter. The four synchronized nozzles force water into the soil at designated spots as the tractor-pulled transplanter traverses the field. Through a braking system that allows the spray to remain stationary as the tractor continues its slow pace, the driver of the machine need only keep it on course. No stopping or restarting is necessary. As the holes are created, a new seedling is inserted by one of the riders who sits just behind the jet sprays.

use of hand labor, this simple tool exemplifies the kind of inventive work which is needed to develop an appropriate, intermediate, small-farm technology.

The indispensable key to success with the transplant system of row crop production is the transplanter. Experience illustrates that conventional transplanters were totally inadequate; so the Talbotts developed a completely new machine using the hydraulic jet principle. The result was the Hydro-Synchron, a fast, efficient, multirow implement that uses water jets to drill holes to receive the transplants. The drilled holes instantly fill with mud and water (together with a starter solution if desired), and the roots, hand-placed, are sealed deep in the muddy solution at any desired plant and row spacing. Three workers can transplant six rows of lettuce at the rate of about 8,000 plants per hour; wing units increase the planting capacity threefold.

Boxes of seedlings are placed directly in front of the three seats the riders occupy. Seedlings go from box to soil at a suprisingly unhurried pace considering the tractor maintains a constant crawling speed through the field.

Beyond planting, the Talbotts have other devices and techniques to complete their system. At Windfell, the main implement used in soil preparation is a Rototiller with a corrugated roller pulled in tandem for minimum tillage. Tillage is limited to the upper four inches of the soil. If the organic content of this layer is maintained, the open structure and fertility of the sublayers will be built continuously by a healthy biological population in the soil. Drip irrigation appears to be their only solution to a limited water supply.

Integrated pest control is an area of continuous investigation at Windfell. The availability of compressed air has facilitated experimentation with air-atomizing nozzles attached to the Hydro-Synchron for ultra-low-volume spraying. Numerous test programs are being conducted using some of the recent biological control methods.

For optimum population, the beds are five feet wide, six feet six inches on center and 500 feet long. Population is 2,550 plants per bed, with six rows nine inches apart and plants staggered at 14 inches apart in the row. The spacing is precise and each plant has exactly the same space to grow. It is estimated that with direct-seeded lettuce or celery, uneven spacing cuts the optimum field population by at least 20 percent. Add to this the approximately three-week longer growing period with direct seeding, and the dramatic difference in the two systems is clear.

But experience reveals another important factor with the Jetspeed transplant system—weed control. The rapid establishment of the crop canopy tends to smother weed growth. The beds shown were neither machine cultivated nor hand hoed—and no herbicides were used.

The Walker Harvester, another Talbott development, is a fine implement for assisting in field picking and packing of summer squash, cucumbers, tomatoes, and peppers. The machine is self-

Self-Propelled Walker Harvester
Gene Talbott

propelled and has a hydrostatic drive which is instantly adjustable to any appropriate speed, forward or reverse. A guidance wand keeps the wheels tracking in the spaces between the permanent beds. The two rear wheel cages are adjustable to accommodate various bed widths.

At Windfell, in order to insure a uniform, standard pack, summer squashes are harvested every day, beginning in June and continuing into October. The Jetspeed transplant system brings the crop to market early. Covering the beds with black plastic mulch and transplanting through the plastic will cut another two weeks off the time to market. Other experimental forcing systems are expected to bring the start of harvest even earlier. The grower with the earliest crop can quickly establish his market and command the top preseason prices.

For the small- to medium-sized grower, depending on the local market, diversification can be very important. The Jetspeed transplant system is particularly adaptable to the production of diverse crops side by side. Gross returns from just one lettuce bed were $404 (202-dozen heads at an average price of $2.00 per dozen). One acre consisting of 13 beds grossed $5,252. Under climate conditions at Windfell, a minimum of four and possibly five cycles per season may be obtained. The potential gross per acre is substantial!!

E.V. Prentice Machinery Co.
2303 N. Randolph Ave.
Portland, OR 97227

TRANSPLANTERS

Many crops are traditionally planted as small plants rather than from seed, either to extend the growing season by starting plants indoors, to avoid thinning, or to get more crops planted in one year. The Japanese have developed perhaps the most energy-efficient transplanting mechanism, which they use largely for rice and tobacco. It is a two-wheel tractor with an automatic steering mechanism which guides the tractor while one man feeds plants into the transplanting mechanism.

We in North America are familiar only with tractor-drawn units. They can plant from one to 16 or more rows at a time, with one or two people feeding the transplanter per row. Often, a water tank is mounted on the hauling tractor, and plants are watered with either a continuous or intermittent flow as soon as they are set and firmed into the ground. One unit just described makes the planting hole with a water spray. Additional equipment might include cultivators or a fertilizer distributor.

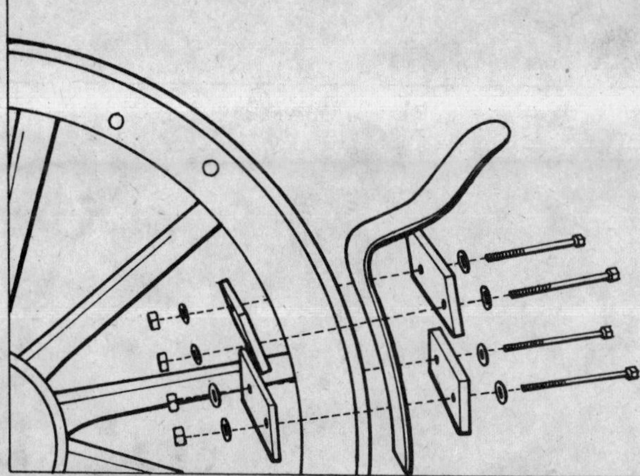

Here is a hint from Farm Labor Savers *suggesting that an extended cleat attached to a wagon wheel be driven across the field to automatically dig evenly spaced planting holes. Used in either wet or dry weather, it will save time and energy when a considerable number of plants or trees are being planted.*

A Semiautomatic Device For Planting Cassava Stem Cuttings on Ridges

From the Agricultural Engineering Department at Ife, Nigeria, G.A. Makanjuola reports the development of a mechanical device for planting cassava stem cuttings on freshly made ridges.

This device is a machine consisting of a disc ridge and semiautomatic planter which can be built as a multirow unit. It can be manufactured entirely locally (Nigeria) with the exception of the ridger discs and bearings.

A two-row ridger in operation, pulling a planter behind it with a pipe joint.

Investigations revealed that cassava stem cuttings can be successfully planted on an unridged field with the New Holland transplanter, but it cannot be easily modified to plant on ridges.

The newly designed planting mechanism consists of a disc on which are mounted three rubber pieces cut from 75-millimeter, flat belting material. These rubber pieces serve as hands for holding the stem cuttings in position as the cuttings are pushed into the newly made ridge.

When cuttings reach the erect position they are released. The hands are kept closed by means of a roller which moves along the surface of a curved member. The cuttings are prevented from slipping during the planting process by a combination of the grip of the rubber hands and stops welded toward the center against which the top of the cuttings bear as they are pushed into the soil.

The planter is pulled behind the disc plow and planting discs are mounted on shafts which are driven by chains directly from the implement land wheels. The sprocket on each of the land wheels is mounted on a sleeve which is bolted to the wheel hub. The sprockets on the planting disc shafts are mounted on a hub provided with a pawl and ratchet device which allows power transmission in one direction only. This is to make reversing possible. By varying the number of teeth on both sprockets, it is possible to alter the spacing along the rows. By moving the planting discs along their shafts and adjusting the center distance of the land wheels, it is possible to obtain different spacings between two adjacent rows.

The planting mechanism in operation.

The planting disc.

Ellis Transplanters

Deluxe models are available with positive gauge wheel drive. The operators place the plant at the right depth while the machine sets the plant in the furrow, waters the roots, and packs the soil around the roots and stem. Models are available with a one- to four-row capacity.

A continuous or intermittent water supply is available with all Ellis Automatic Transplanters. The system uses two valves mounted on the seat bar between the operators. One valve is used to adjust the amount of water applied per plant while the other shuts the water off at the end of a row and on at the beginning of the next.

D.R. Ellis Mfg. Co., Inc.
Box 246
Verona, WI 53593

Mechanical Transplanters

The Mechanical Transplanter Company has a number of models ranging in size from a one-row to a four-row unit which can be attached to any tractor drawbar with a single pin. Everything is adjustable on these units, including seats, footrests, plant spacers, and water valves. The Flo Check watering system turns water on and off at the instant of setting. Water is not lost between plants and the amount of water given each plant can be set by a wing nut adjustment control.

Mechanical Transplanter Co.
S. Central at U.S. 31
Holland, MI 49423

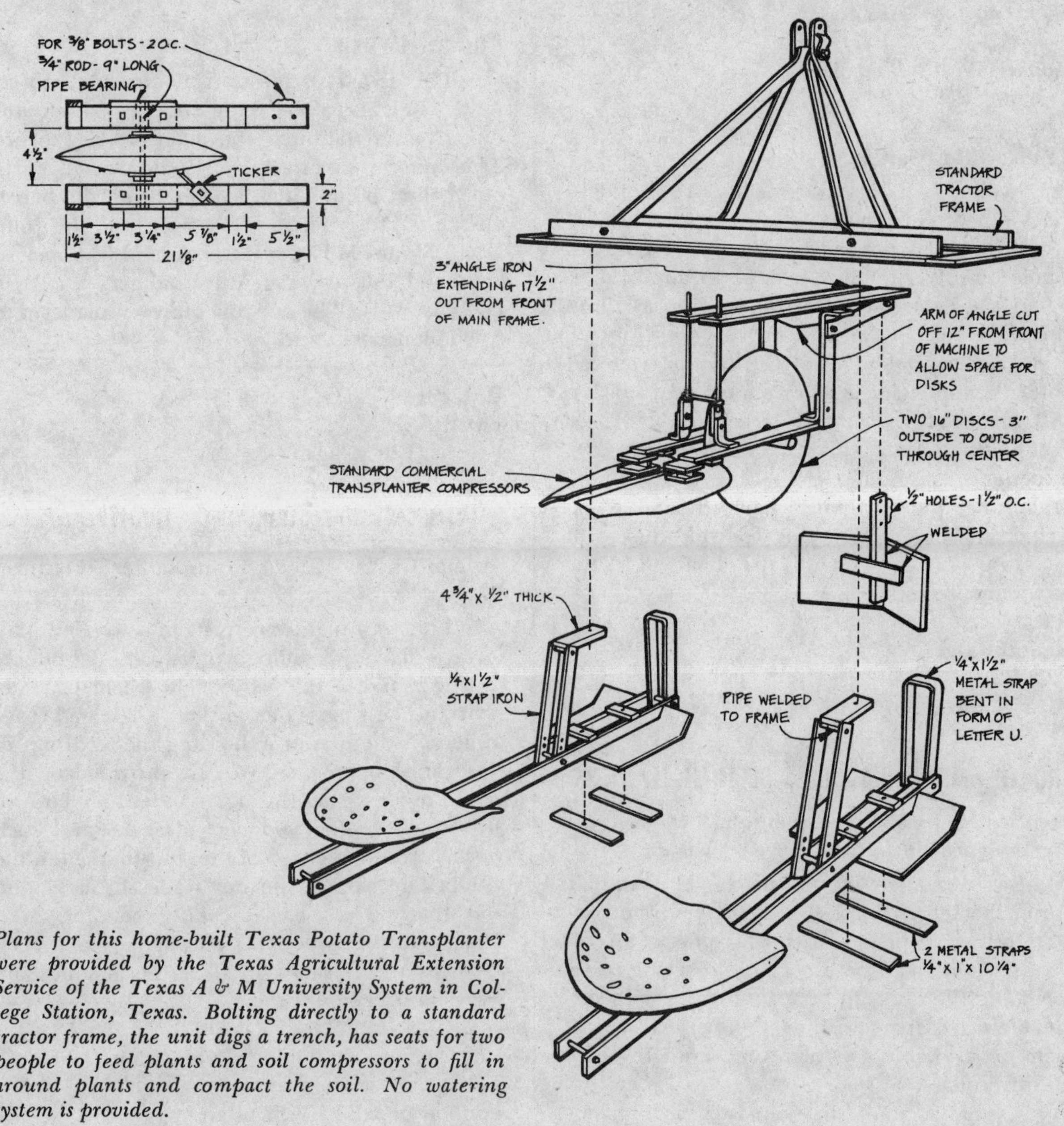

Plans for this home-built Texas Potato Transplanter were provided by the Texas Agricultural Extension Service of the Texas A & M University System in College Station, Texas. Bolting directly to a standard tractor frame, the unit digs a trench, has seats for two people to feed plants and soil compressors to fill in around plants and compact the soil. No watering system is provided.

Holland Transplanters

All Holland Transplanters have adjustable packing wheels, a Start-rite water valve, blunt- or round-point digging shoes, plant stands and plant boxes, plant holders, and back-rested seats as standard equipment. Available units range in size from a special one-row, one-seater unit for garden tractors, to eight-seated, four-row planters. They are available as either tractor-mounted or tractor-drawn units with or without watering tanks, cultivators, and fertilizer distributors.

Holland Transplanter Co.
Holland, MI 49423

Kennco Plant Setters

Available in one-, two-, or three-row models, the Kennco plant setter passes over a completed bed (with or without plastic covering), punches a hole for a plant and a stake (if required), then waters the hole completely, and allows a riding attendant to place a hothouse seedling or seedbed-grown plant directly into the watered hole. Attendants ride at a comfortable position with all plants and controls directly available for rapid but thorough plant setting in each row. Experience has shown that using this method, replanting due to young plant attrition is extremely minimal. Watering controls consist of metering valves and on-off valves handled by the attendant.

Kennco Mfg. Co.
P.O. Box 1158
Ruskin, FL 33570

NORTH AMERICAN SOURCES OF TRANSPLANTERS

Prentice Multirow Transplanter: Hydro-Synchron by Jetspeed

Just described in the article on Windfell Farm, the Jetspeed also has the diversity to convert from transplanter to boom sprayer to cultivator. The machine can plant from one to 18 rows, and the rows can be spaced as desired from 2 to 60 inches apart (with wing units). An attachment is available for planting through black plastic mulch.

A smaller unit, the Jetmaster, is a hand-pushed transplanter designed for planting two 3-foot beds at a time, at any desired spacing, with the same water-jet planting mechanism. Speedling transplants are set by hand by workers following the unit. A whole line of intermediately scaled tools and machinery is designed for a permanent-bed row-crop system.

E.V. Prentice Machinery Co.
2303 N. Randolph Ave.
Portland, OR 97227

Ellis Model 450

This is a one-row transplanter with three-point hitch and a 55-gallon barrel which mounts directly over the hitch and makes it easy to lift. The unit can be attached to some tractors without a three-point hitch, by mounting the barrel on the tractor. These tractors include the John Deere M and MT, the International C, Super A, Cub, and 140, and the Allis-Chalmers CA, D10, D12, and WD. The one-row unit will plant up to 5,000 plants per hour.

D.R. Ellis Mfg. Co., Inc.
Box 246
Verona, WI 53593

INTERNATIONAL SOURCES OF TRANSPLANTERS

Animal-Drawn Rice Transplanter Platform Plans

This transplanter consists of a wooden platform pulled by a buffalo or a pair of bullocks over the mud of the paddy field when it's ready for transplanting. Four workers are seated cross-legged on the platform, holding the seedlings in their laps. Special recesses are provided on the platform for extra seedlings. Under the platform are attached eight wooden markers, and each worker transplants two of the rows marked in the mud. The workers do not wade through mud and there is no back-breaking bending over. Transplanting is done in parallel rows, at least at twice the normal speed, as both hands are used simultaneously.

Intermediate Technology Publications, Ltd.
9 King St.
London WC2E 8HN, England

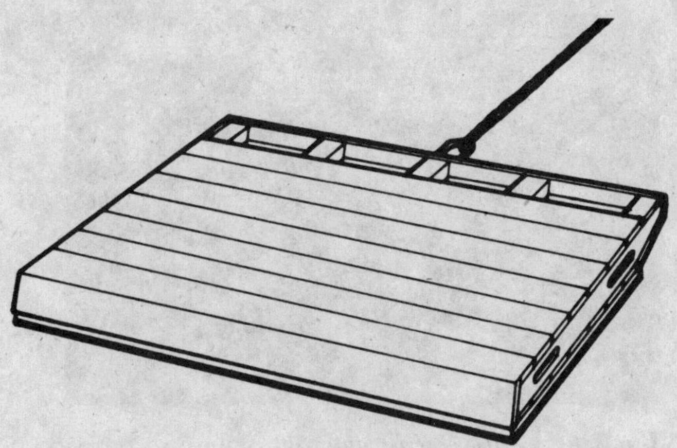

Animal-drawn rice transplanter platform.

Rau-Kombi Semiautomatic Potato Planter

This is available as a two- or four-row unit, one operator per row, tractor-drawn implement. It has spring-loaded adjustable covering discs, with a 50-kilogram capacity per hopper. Optional features include a track eliminator, sand plates for driving lugs, a coulter in front of the planting share, and an insecticide applicator. Weight: two-row, 242 kilograms; four-row, 463 kilograms.

Rau-Kombi Planter

This unit is suitable for vegetables, beets, tobacco, onions, strawberries, forestry plantings, and others. The press rollers do not act above the neck but below, at the feeder roots, closing the soil as required. It will plant two, three, five, or seven rows; spacing of plants along the rows is adjustable.

Hassia-Rau-Vertriebsgesellschaft
D 7315 Weilheim/Tech
Johannes-Rau-Strasse, West Germany

Hassia Automatic Potato Planter

The Hassia potato planter Model GLO is available for planting two and three rows at one time, with row spacing adjustable from 62.5 to 75 centimeters.

A.J. Troster Landmaschinenfabrik
6308 Butzbach, Oberhess
Postfach 240, West Germany

Hassia Automatic Potato Planter.
Hassia

Gruse Potato Planter

This planter has independent, front-mounted furrow openers that are adjustable for depth and float independently to facilitate an even planting depth. Two-row models will plant row widths of between 28 and 36 inches at a maximum speed of 5 mph. It is totally automatic.

RH Group Root Harvesters, Ltd.
Rengate
Peterborough PE1 5BD, England

Nardi Transplanter

This model automatically opens the furrow, places the plant, and firms the soil around it. A synchronized valve on the frame is operated by the planting disc wheel which measures the required amount of water for each plant. On request, the transplanter can be supplied with a fertilizing unit for surface spreading or depositing at a depth of 4 to 6 centimeters below the surface. Transplanting depth is adjustable, and the distance between plants can be adjusted by changing the gears on the drive wheels, changing the diameter of the drive wheels, or by changing the number of pincers. The unit is attached by a three-point hitch and is available with a special attachment for planting in offset rows.

Nardi Macchine Agricole
06017 Selci Lama
Perugia, Italy

Self-Propelled Tobacco Transplanter KC-6

Powered by a four-cycle, air-cooled, 2.3 h.p. engine, this two-wheeled walking transplanter plants all kinds of ridges and furrows—wide, narrow, high, or low—with tobacco plants at spacing intervals from 25 to 45 centimeters in circular or square holes. It can make sharp turns, so no additional turning space is needed. It requires a minimum labor input of one or two people for planting at a rate of 3 to 4 acres per day. The transplanter is self-propelled, with two speeds forward and one reverse. It has automatic steering; it will plant either before or after mulching with a nylon sheet.

Circle Tekko Self-Propelled Tobacco Transplanter KC-6
Circle Tekko Co.

Beet Transplanter BTP-2

The BTP-2 is used with a 35 h.p. tractor with a three-point hitch to plant two furrows at one time at a rate of 1.5 to 2 hectares per day. Its operation utilizes four or five people. Row spacing is adjustable between 550 and 700 millimeters; the planting interval is set at 225 millimeters. Standard attachments include two seedling pot separators, one seedling collector set, 30 seedling boxes, and one set of tools. The BTP-2 uses a new feeding-planting mechanism which guarantees reliable planting and easy adjustment. It comes with a special attachment for planting high furrows. A four-row unit to be pulled behind a 60 h.p. tractor is also available.

Circle Tekko Beet Transplanter BTP-2
Circle Tekko Co.

Both of the above transplanters are available from:

Circle Tekko Co., Ltd.
194 Izumicho, Takikawa-City
Hokkaido, Japan

Metamora Rice Planter MSP-2A

The MSP-2A plants rice seedlings that have developed from two to five true leaves. Seedlings may be raised in mats. A lever can be set for small (2 to 2.5 true leaves), medium (3 to 3.5) and large (4 to 5) seedlings, and also for the number of seedlings in each clump. The lever setting for planting intervals is adjustable in 1-centimeter steps between 12 and 21 centimeters. The seedling feeder is to the rear of the wheels, so that the operator has a good front view. Additional seedlings are set on two trays stacked on top. The trays can be reached from the operating position. Wheels are independently suspended so that the body is maintained in a horizontal position by operating the lever within easy reach. Two-wheel drive and a float for buoyancy assure easy travel across the paddy. Sharp turns can be made by operating side clutches which disengage one wheel as the other keeps moving. Seedlings are not injured by this planting. Planting depth can be varied by adjusting the float. The four-cycle, air-cooled, 3.5 h.p. engine operates the 83-kilogram unit at a capacity of ½ acre per hour as the operator walks along behind. Planting two rows at one time, 30 centimeters apart in clumps of three to five seedlings each, yields a density of from 50 to 90 clumps per 3.3 square meters.

Metamora Tobacco Transplanter

The operator walks behind the machine, feeding the planting mechanism with seedlings less than 22 centimeters high while steering. It will plant tobacco, cabbage, and Chinese cabbage. Adjustments you can make include the distance between seedlings from 25 to 41 centimeters (10 stages), the height of the ridge from 0 to 40 centimeters, the distance between wheels, and the inclination of the chassis. The air-cooled, four-cycle, 2.5 to 3.5 h.p. gasoline engine powers two forward and one reverse speed for planting at a rate of 1 acre every 3 or 4 hours.

Metamora Agricultural Machinery Co., Ltd.
9-37 Nishi 2–Chome
Okegawa, Saitama, Japan

Mizuho Suzue Rice-Transplanting Machine

The Mizuho plants two rows of either young or adult seedlings at a rate of approximately 2½ acres per hour without damage to the plant. Spacing is adjustable between plants, but row width is set at 300 millimeters. One person operates this gasoline-powered machine. A low center of gravity and the well-going straight faculty minimize the amount of attention the unit requires by the driver.

CeCoCo
P.O. Box 8, Ibaraki City
Osaka Pref. 567, Japan

–6– Harvesting Equipment

SICKLE, SCYTHE AND GRAIN CRADLE

The sickle and the scythe are the earliest forms of hand tools developed for harvesting a crop. Although their development can be traced back to around 2,000 B.C., they are still used in many parts of the world today for small-scale farming.

The scythe was developed from the sickle by lengthening the blade and adapting the handle in such a way that both hands of the operator can be used. The larger blade of the scythe increases the rate of doing work, while the longer handle is less fatiguing for the operator as he can stand upright when working. The scythe can be used for harvesting both cereal and forage crops.

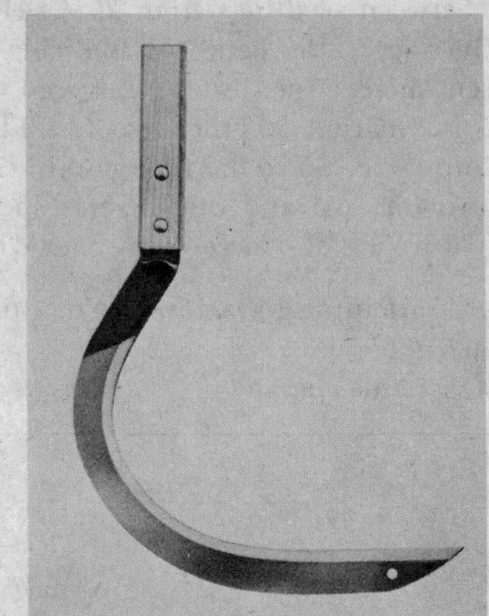

A common sickle. True Temper

BRING ON THE SCYTHE

by Drew Langsner

On a year-long trip, we found scythes in common use throughout Europe—from Turkey to France to Scandinavia. In modern Switzerland, Alpine farmers regularly scythe hay on slopes that are too steep for any machinery. Grazing cattle would lead to erosion. And if the grass is allowed to grow, winter snow clings to the long, dry blades until great weights accumulate, causing avalanches and loss of precious soil.

The Alpine farmers are very practical workers, so I was particularly interested in their technique for mowing. Watching a man and his teenage sons scything a very steep field gave me the impression of a functional ballet. The effort exerted was great, yet light and rhythmic all at once. About every 15 minutes work halted. The blades were quickly honed with a whetstone kept in a water-filled scabbard hung from each man's belt. With razor-sharp blades, mowing resumed until a small field, perhaps an acre, was cut.

One day our Swiss host informed me that the grass around his cheese-making hut was of sufficient growth for mowing into a small amount of fodder. Of course, I was quite anxious to try scything.

First he demonstrated his sharpening procedure. The edge of the blade must be so thin that it deflects when pressed against one's thumbnail. Lightweight grass-cutting blades come this way new. But after repeated honings, the thin edge section wears away, leaving a cutting edge too thick for razor-edge sharpening. Rethinning is done by pounding the blade with a hammer over a small stake anvil driven into a log. When the blade passes the thumbnail test, it is ready for honing.

That job is accomplished with the long, thin whetstone. The stroke used is very similar to knife sharpening—the stone is worked toward the edge with long, smooth passes at a very slight angle. The stone is dipped in water every minute or so to wash away accumulating grit that would contaminate its pores and hinder further sharpening. The test of an adequately sharp blade is in its

To begin a stroke, your trunk is twisted quite far to the right.

use. One should feel almost zero friction between the blade and the grass being cut.

For the proper mowing technique, legs are set rather apart, knees are bent a little, and the body cants forward at a slight angle for balance.

To begin a stroke, your trunk is twisted quite far to the right. The scythe is held so that the tang, the shank connecting the blade and handle, is just above the ground, at cutting depth. The blade tip is angled slightly upwards, but not much. The position of the tang regulates the cut. The slightly lifted tip is to help avoid hitting obstructions during the stroke. Finally, the blade is aimed so that it will cut a very thin swath with each stroke. The scythe is not a hacking weed chopper, but a fine cutting tool. In use, the blade actually slices along whatever is being cut. Each pass mows only a few inches in depth, perhaps six to ten inches, depending on the blade length.

The actual stroke involves using your entire body in a smooth, pivoting movement. Beginning at the right, swing in a full arc until your shoulders are turned all the way left. (This long, thin stroke actually cuts more grass than a short, broad hacking movement.) Then take a short step forward as the scythe is returned to the beginning position.

To mow a patch of grass, grain, or weeds, begin at the left edge and gradually work your way from one end to another. You can work up or downhill, but always go in the same direction. After mowing one swath, return to the beginning edge and mow a second swath one arc space to

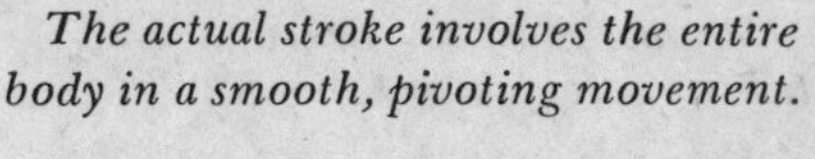

The actual stroke involves the entire body in a smooth, pivoting movement.

the right. Working in this fashion, your reapings will fall away to the cut side, not against standing growth in the following swath.

Several types of scythe blades and snaths (handles) are currently available in America. The standard blade, 30 inches long and made of fairly heavy steel, is suitable for cutting weeds and small grains. A shorter, even stouter blade is sold for clearing brush and briars.

The technique for using these scythes is the same as for mowing grass, but with extra vigor. These blades are generally not pounded thin or sharpened to such a high degree as grass blades. But they must be kept quite sharp to be effective. Standard blades are generally sharpened with a mill file or on a hand-turned grindstone. Work mainly on the bottom side of the edge. Many a frustrated mower has a blade sharpened on the upper edge. This creates a downward-slanting bevel that tends to run the scythe into the ground as it cuts. Always sharpen standard blades on the lower side first, then gently remove any wire edge that may form on the upper side. It is a good idea to finish up by honing with a hand stone.

Recently, thin, lightweight grass blades have been imported to this country. These blades are excellent for fine mowing work, but they are not suitable for cutting tough weeds. They are delicate; the fine edge is quickly dulled or nicked if run into the ground, a stone, or hidden debris.

Two styles of snaths, or handles, are on the market. The standard snath is made of bent ash and is quite heavy. These are rugged and suitable for use with standard and brush blades. Also available is a bent aluminum snath, which works quite well with the superlight grass blade. But aluminum snaths are too light for the more rugged work of cutting grain, coarse weeds, or briars. For such tasks, the extra weight of the ash snath creates a momentum that helps in mowing. Wooden snaths should be cleaned and treated, once or twice a year, with a mixture of two parts linseed oil to one part turpentine.

Some older hardware stores still carry scythes, especially in country districts. You might have to ask, as the last one ever ordered may be in the back storeroom.

Often scythes appear at auctions or yard sales. It is not too hard to clean up a mildly rusted blade. Be sure that the snath is not cracked, and that it has one, or preferably two, handles. (Snath handles are tightened by twisting counterclockwise.)

GRAIN CRADLE

The grain cradle is an improved scythe with a set of wooden tines above the blade that catch the wheat (or other grains) as the blade severs it on the forward swing. Mastering the art of the scythe and grain cradle takes coordination and practice. For a right-handed stroke, the left foot is placed one stride forward and the first stroke is taken with the blade nearly parallel to the ground. The trick is to keep the grain stalks laying all one way during the next four strokes. Before each consecutive stroke, the right foot comes forward one-quarter stride. After the fourth stride, the wheat on the tines is slid off into a neat pile at the farther reach of the cradle's forward swing, ready to be tied into a bundle.

A farmer is a proud person: proud of his tools and proud of the work he and his tools produce when working as one, together. And with good reason; it takes practice and skill to master a task. Like an old pair of shoes, the tool conforms to the technique its master employs—becomes molded to his style and uncomfortable in the hands of another. The skill and intimacy in the relationship between man and tool are reflected in the following article by Steve Taylor about mowing with a scythe and the rare people who have the skill to use it right.

Harvesting grain by hand with the help of the scythe and grain cradle. United States Department of Agriculture

BUILD-IT-YOURSELF GRAIN CRADLE

by Richard Weinsteiger

With new grain cradles impossible to find, and old cradles expensive and rare, here is an inexpensive way to convert a grass scythe into a functional cradle.

CONSTRUCTION

1. Start by obtaining a 30-inch-length by 3-inch-diameter piece of knot-free green hickory or ash. Remove the bark, using a drawknife and quarter the log. Shape the four pieces with the drawknife until they are approximately ¾ by ⅝ inches. Then, starting 10 inches from one end, taper the remainder to ⅜-inch diameter.
2. In order to bend these pieces to conform to the shape of the scythe blade, a jig has to be built using a 27-inch scrap piece of 2 x 4 and four pieces of 6-by-¾-inch dowel. Since all blades do not have the same arc, you will have to position the dowels accordingly. After the jig is built, place the four pieces in the jig and let dry for several days.
3. The upright or main support piece, also made from hardwood, is ⅝ by 1⅛ by 23½ inches. Drill four ⅜-inch holes 2, 8, 15 and 23 inches from the bottom. A shallow groove is filed across the grain ¾ inch from the bottom to accommodate the J-bolt. Drill a ¼-inch hole in the front face of the metal end cap of the scythe handle for the J-bolt. Make sure the hole is far enough from the center to avoid the blade clamp bolt.
4. Remove the pieces from the jig, apply resin to all outside bends and char with a torch to set

A grain cradle can be built to fit any store-bought scythe

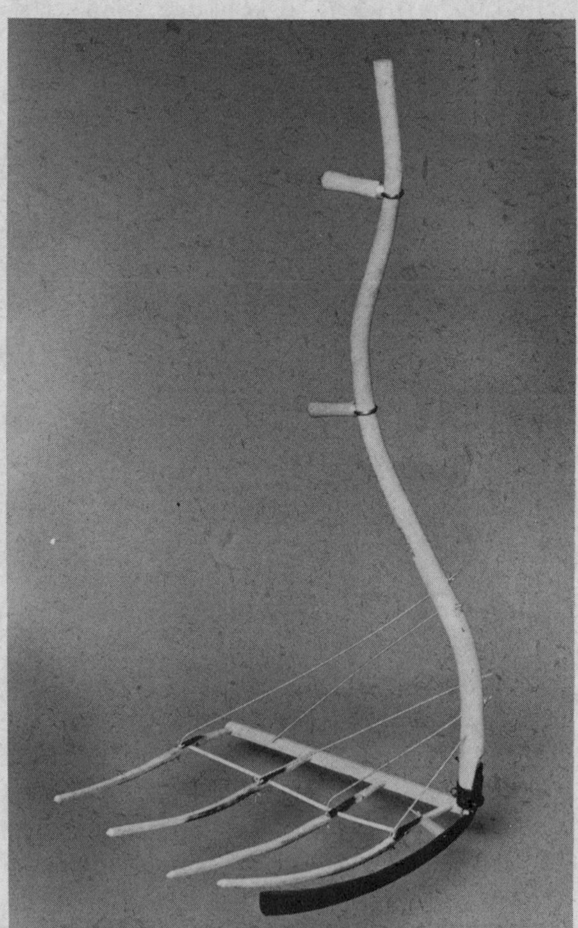

the bends. Then whittle 5/8 inch of the ends that are to fit into the upright to a 3/8-inch diameter. Drill a 3/8-inch hole vertically 7½ inches from the support end for a supporting dowel to slide through, and in each piece a 3/16-inch diameter hole horizontally 9 inches from the end for the supporting all-thread.

5. Now assemble the unit by inserting the J-bolt with the upright attached to the faceplate and tightening the nut. Insert the four bent pieces into the holes in the upright. Place the 5/16-inch-diameter by 23¼-inch dowel through the vertical holes of the bent pieces. Next, drill a 3/16-inch hole midway between the top two bent arms. Cut a 26-inch piece of 3/16-inch all-thread, and make a right-angle bend 1½ inches from one end. Insert this piece with the right-angle bend into the 3/16-inch hole at the top of the upright, and fasten with a washer and wing nut. Judging the angle by holding the piece of all-thread to intersect the handle, drill a 3/16-inch hole 16 inches from the end cap. Cut four pieces of all-thread 28½, 22, 17 and 14½ inches in length, and using the same method, attach to the handle 17½, 10, 8 and 7 inches respectively. Put wing nuts on both the inside and outside of the pieces that are inserted in the bent arms.
6. Cut a 2-inch piece of ¾-inch dowel, and drill a 3/16-inch hole through the center lengthwise. The same diameter hole should be drilled in the bottom bent arm and the blade approximately 4½ inches from the handle. Cut a 4-inch length of 3/16-inch all-thread, and peen one end so that it will not slip through the hole in the blade. Insert through the blade, dowel and arm, and fasten with washer and a wing nut. Using ¾-inch brads, fasten the dowels to the arms and upright. Then adjust the wing nuts on the arms and handle to align the arms with the blade, making sure to keep the arms in back of the blade edge.

The supporting all-thread strut is bolted in place with a wing nut.

The cradle's simple supportive network is adequately braced.

HAND MOWING: FEW HAVE THE SKILL TO SWING A SCYTHE—PROPERLY*

Story by Steve Taylor, Photos by Bob LaPree

Elwin Smith, herdsman on a large, East Washington dairy farm, gripped the handle of his scythe and at the starter's command went forth to mow the prescribed 50-foot course. Judges hovered around, measuring the swath he lay down in the lush green grass and clover.

When a half-dozen others had had their turn and the points and times were added up, Smith had won the Golden Scythe Award, symbolic of supremacy in the art of hand mowing in Sullivan County and other points east of the Mississippi.

The Sullivan County Dairy Herd Improvement Association (DHIA) has held its hand mowing championship every summer for the past 25 years or so. Anybody who thinks he or she is up to it can take a crack at winning a new scythe decorated with gold spray paint.

Elwin Smith, winner of the Golden Scythe Award. Neatness of stubble nudged him ahead of the others.
Bob LaPree

* Reprinted with permission from *New Hampshire Times,* 27 July 1977.

Elwin Smith calls himself an old-timer, and it's usually old-timers who win the Sullivan County DHIA's Golden Scythe. In 1977, Smith nudged out three dairy farmers by one- to three-tenths of a point, and all were veterans in the scythe competition. They were Fred Hall of West Unit, defending champ Horace Bascom of Charlestown, and Smith's boss, Hans Eccardt of East Washington.

A broiling July sun beat down on Charlie Stone's beautiful Meriden dairy farm, and the temperature hovered at 99 degrees in the meadow across the road from the cow barn. The veteran scythemen warmed up by taking a few swings at grass around the edges of the field and then set to work putting fine edges on their scythes with pocket-size sharpening stones. Then one by one they mowed the course.

The competition is scored on a combination of factors. Time over course is worth 15 points, width of cut 30 points, neatness of stubble 45 points, and completing course 10 points. Penalty points up to 10 can be assessed by the judges for spitting tobacco juice on the course or giving judges or bystanders lip.

Judges measure the width of his swath as Hans Eccardt finishes his course.
Bob LaPree

Elwin Smith was slower on the course, achieving 11 out of a possible 15 points. He ran well behind speed merchant Horace Bascom, who laid down his swath in two minutes, five seconds. But Smith picked up a total of 43 out of 45 possible points for neatness of stubble and that gave him the victory.

The swath where Smith had mowed looked like it had been cut with a lawnmower, so short was the remaining growth, and there weren't many places where the scythe had skipped and left little telltale manes of uncut grass.

Smith was repeating what he'd done at the DHIA field day back in 1959, winning the big prize, and darned if he didn't use the scythe he was given for the '59 championship to win in '77.

Later there was a competition for greenhorns, also known as dubbers or hackers. This was won by a Meriden area farmer-writer whose swath—like those of other contestants in his class—looked like it had been carved up with a hatchet.

After the competition, the veterans stood around and talked about their individual scythes. Eccardt had a European-style model with a straight handle. Stan Colby from Cornish praised his cherry snath. Elwin Smith savored a cold bottle of Miller beer Eccardt had sequestered in a clump of clover by the fence.

Then it was off to a picnic on the Stone farm lawn, with fiddle music by the Dave Levine

The competitors pose for the camera (left to right): Stan Colby, Elwin Smith, Fred Hall, Hans Eccardt, Horace Bascom, Dean Bascom and Bennie Nelson.
Bob LaPree

orchestra. Another hand mowing competition had been written into history, its participants and spectators well entertained at the sight of the vestiges of an ancient art.

Virtually every boy and man in rural New Hampshire knew how to swing a scythe a century ago. The skill was essential to family and individual survival, for it was the means by which the basic feed of livestock—hay—was harvested on the land.

Hand mowing as a skill exists today, but only among old-timers and a few younger men who probably have learned it working on a highway crew responsible for trimming roadsides.

Hay was harvested in July and August a century ago, and came all in one crop. Today, the first cutting is in the barn before July 4, and second and third cuttings come along later in the summer. That's because of the introduction of legumes such as alfalfa and trefoil, which have displaced timothy and other grasses, the old standbys for hay production in New Hampshire.

During the Civil War, many New Hampshire farm hands enlisted in the Union Army and marched off to fight. A similar development in other northern states stimulated the development of farm machinery to speed up and ease the task of harvesting hay in this area.

The first significant invention was the horse-drawn mowing machine, which was developed in 1847 but not perfected until well after the Civil War. The mechanical hay loader and the dump rake were introduced in the 1870s, and the pace of haying was stepped up considerably.

The need for skilled scythemen diminished steadily in the late nineteenth century, although many poorer farmers continued to put up hay using the old methods. These farmers kept alive the traditional methods and procedures.

Haying with scythe, hand rake, and pitchfork traditionally began on the first Monday after the Fourth of July.

Work began at dawn when several men went out to do barn chores and milking. While chores were being completed, Grandpa and the young boys would go to work on sharpening scythes in preparation for the day's mowing. The kids would have to turn the crank on the grindstone while Grandpa would start water trickling on the stone.

After removing the snath, or handle, from the scythe, Grandpa would grasp the blade in both hands and bear down on the stone. The stone would turn rapidly without resistance, but as the

Stan Colby sharpens his scythe with a whetstone.
Bob LaPree

pressure increased, the stone would slow to a drag. Periodically the edge would be tested with a thumb, and after 10 or 15 minutes the job would probably be done. To a youngster that would seem like an eternity, especially if there were two or three more blades to go.

After sharpening the blades on the grindstone, a whetstone, sometimes called a rifle, would give them an even keener edge.

After breakfast, the crew would assemble in the field and work would begin. The hired men would start off first, followed by Dad or whoever was boss. The boss would try to crowd the mowers ahead of him, and if he passed one or more of them in the advancing echelon, they were disgraced and had to retreat and pick up a new swath at the rear.

Behind the mowers would come young boys with pitchforks, spreading out the newly mown hay to speed up drying. Since hand mowing is such hard physical work, especially if the men were being pushed by weather or the boss to produce, mowing was usually done in the cool of the morning. The afternoon was devoted to raking up, tumbling, and loading the hay onto wagons for transport to the barn.

In raking, the crew would set out in reverse order of the morning arrangement, with the young boys leading with small rakes, and the stronger men bringing up the progressively larger mounds of hay into windrows. While one man fetched the horses and wagon, the others would tumble the hay, that is, arrange it in piles which could be forked directly onto the load and which presumably would stay intact through several handlings from field to mow.

Next would come the time to pitch hay. Strong arms would fork the hay onto the wagon, then fork it off the wagon at the barn, shove it up into the storage area where it would be mowed away. The following winter the hay was supposed to come out of the mow by the tumble as it had gone in, but likely as not, it came out with much grunting and groaning and not by the tumble.

The tremendous physical exertion required that large quantities of fluids be available in the field. Cider was one important beverage; some old accounts tell of rum; switchel is said to have been a popular refreshment. Switchel was a concoction of cold water, sugar, ginger, and vinegar, and those still around who have consumed it say it was more or less thirst quenching.

As late as the 1880s, there were purists who refused to adopt the labor-saving machines such as the mower and dump rake, often claiming the iron wheels spoiled the land. So they kept swinging their scythes. But as time rolled on, there came to be fewer and fewer farms where the hay was harvested by pure human muscle power.

Hand mowing is the same sort of rural skill as sheep shearing. It requires determination as much as anything. It also requires reasonable muscular condition and a fair measure of coordination. But once the essential rhythms and movements are mastered, it can be done with grace and smoothness.

A man who can handle a scythe as gracefully and efficiently as anyone in New Hampshire is Stanley Colby of Cornish, a retired agricultural extension agent for Sullivan County and now a town selectman and amateur historian.

Colby grew up on a river farm in Plainfield. His father declined to do hand mowing when Stanley approached manhood, and so the boy had to learn. Colby's grandfather, Albon Wood, instructed him on mowing by hand with a scythe and coached him for a year or two. Wood could mow all day long and hardly work up a sweat, Colby recalls. Colby is willing to coach greenhorns today, much as his grandfather did him a half century ago.

"There's not much to it. You just have to know how to mow, how to sharpen a scythe, and how to set the nibs." The nibs are the handles affixed to the snath, which is the curved handle of the tool. The scythe is the metal blade which does the actual cutting.

"You should set the nibs so they're comfortable and then hold the tool in a normal position close to your body. The tip of the scythe should then be at your left foot.

"Then you do it. You keep your heel down, stand up tall. If you bend forward, you'll be a basket case in no time," Colby advises.

Good scythes are hard to find these days. The ones made for the market today are typically imported tools. "Those rigs may be okay for Austria or some such place, but they're not much good for anything over here except maybe cleaning around a fence post or something," Colby snorts.

Many scythes on the market now are ill shaped and don't have enough steel to take and hold a good edge, and the handles are generally inferior. Colby likes a snath made of cherry, but it's impossible to find cherry snaths today.

The best method of finding a good scythe is looking around in old barns. A lot of scythes got stuck away up on beams years ago, and not many people have gone seeking them out for use since.

Most of the winners in the Sullivan County hand mowing championship over the years have brought their own pet scythes with them. Horace Bascom, Sid Clarke, Jesse Stone, and Colby have captured the title most of the time, and all of them did it with their own special tools.

Finding a good grindstone on which to set a scythe is difficult, too, Colby says. Most of the good stones have been appropriated by homeowners and antique fanciers for decorations. Once left to weather, old grindstones are worthless for sharpening scythes.

HARVESTING RICE

Rice is harvested in much the same way as other cereal crops. Care must be taken not to shatter the hull and risk losing some of the grain. Combines designed for wheat harvest (described later in this chapter), as well as sickles and knives, may be used for harvesting rice. However, tools designed by CeCoCo in Japan are specifically for rice harvest and are described as follows.

CeCoCo Hand-Pushed Rice Planter-Cutter

This is an adjustable, hand-pushed rice cutter which promises to make the work of men, women, or children five times faster than when using a hand sickle. A 20-inch wide cradle collects the stalks as they are cut.

CeCoCo Hand Rice Plant Cutter

This tool will reap slightly more than 1/10 acre per hour. The blade is easily detached for cleaning and sharpening. The operator uses both arms to power this tool and stands in an almost erect position. This technique is easy on workers and gives them the power to easily cut through stalks, even thick-cropped rice plants, leaving them grouped and ready for sheaves.

CeCoCo
P.O. Box 8, Ibaraki City
Osaka Pref. 567, Japan

NORTH AMERICAN SOURCES OF HAND HARVESTING TOOLS

	SNATHS	SCYTHES	SICKLES
AMES			X
BELKNAP, INC.	X	X	
COLUMBIAN CUTLERY CO.		X	
COUNTRYSIDE CATALOG	X	X	X
CUMBERLAND GENERAL STORE	X	X	
DEGIORGI CO., INC.	X	X	
GLEN-BEL'S COUNTRY STORE	X	X	
A. M. LEONARD & SON, INC.	X	X	
BEN MEADOWS CO.	X	X	
MOTHER'S GENERAL STORE	X	X	
NASCO AGRICULTURAL SCIENCES	X	X	
NORTHEAST CARRY TRADING CO.	X	X	X
G. E. RUHMANN MFG. CO., INC.			X
SEYMOUR MFG. CO.	X	X	X
STANLEY GARDEN TOOLS—U.S.		X	
TRUE TEMPER CORP.			X
THE UNION FORK & HOE CO.			X

INTERNATIONAL SOURCES OF HAND HARVESTING TOOLS

	SNATHS	SCYTHES	SICKLES
BULLDOG		X	X
CARALEL ENTERPRISE CO., LTD.			X
CEAF S.N.C. F. LLI SILETTI	X		X
ENGLISH TOOLS, LTD.		X	X
FABRICHE RIUNITE FALCI		X	X
FERFOR			X
HINDUSTAN ENGINEERING CO.			X
T. & G. HUTTON & CO., LTD.			X
JENKS & CATELL, LTD.			X
KUMAON AGRI-HORTICULTURE STORES			X
KUMAON NURSERY			X
KUMAR INDUSTRIES			X
LASHER TOOLS (PTY.), LTD.			X
OY RETTIG-STRENGBERG, AB	X		
GEORGE PIKE, LTD.	X		
PURMO PRODUKT	X		
SELF-SUFF. & SMALL-HOLDING SUPPLIES	X	X	
FRANZ SONNLEITHNER K.G.			X
SPEAR & JACKSON TOOLS, LTD.			X
STANLEY GARDEN TOOLS, LTD.		X	
SYNDICAT DE L'OUTILLAGE		X	X
W. TYZACK SONS & TURNER, LTD.		X	X
UBUNGO FARM IMPLEMENTS		X	X

CeCoCo Power Reaper

This is a lightweight tool designed to cut wheat or rice stalks at a rate of 1/4 acre per hour. It is made of steel pipe and is powered by a 1½ h.p., air-cooled engine.

All three above cutters are made by:
CeCoCo
P.O. Box 8, Ibaraki City
Osaka Pref. 567, Japan

Reciprocating Mower-Cutter

The reciprocating mower is a high-speed machine which has largely superceded the scythe for cutting grass and forage crops, even for small acreages. Cutting close to the ground, it is especially valuable for harvesting badly laid cereal crops. Avoiding the chopping and shredding action of forage mowers, reciprocating mowers do not disturb the kernel or separate it from its husk. Left intact, threshing and cleaning procedures can be saved until a convenient time after the crop is safely delivered to the barn.

The cutting mechanism of a reciprocating mower consists of a set of triangular-shaped cutting knives operating with a back and forth motion inside a guide shaped like a comb. It

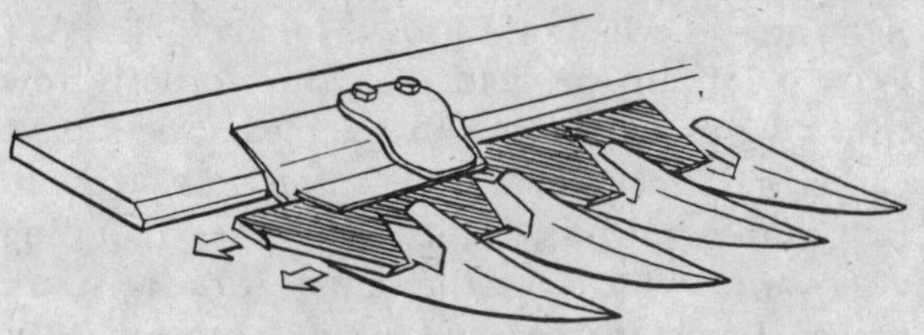

The cutting mechanism of a reciprocating mower.

can be either an animal-drawn or ground-driven machine, have its own power unit (motor mower), or be a front end or side attachment for a two- or four-wheel tractor.

When animal-drawn, the large land wheel rotating on the ground as the animal draws the machine forward provides the power to operate the mower knives through the gearbox and the pitman. For the tractor-drawn types, the power to operate the machine is obtained from the tractor engine. The tractor-drawn mower can be hitched to the tractor in a number of ways.

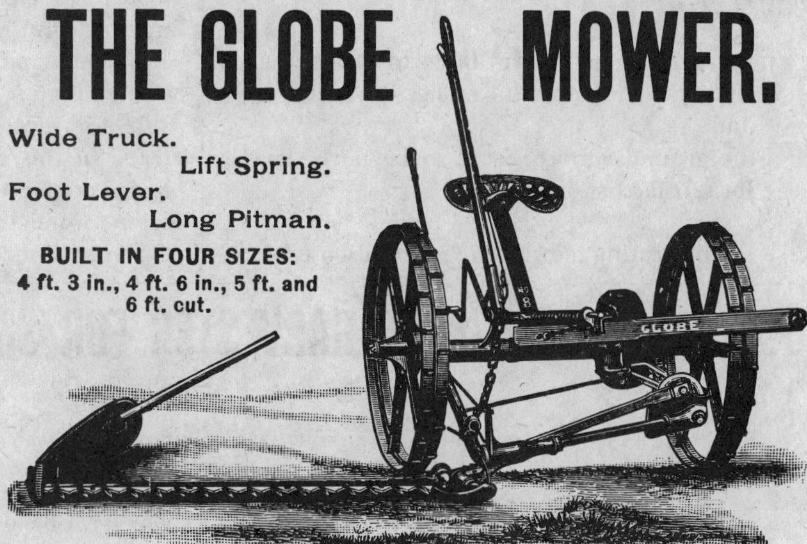

An animal-drawn, ground-driven mower with mechanical lift.
The Implement Age, 1894

a. The mower can be a trailing unit behind the tractor and the power to the reciprocating knives is then provided by the tractor engine through the power take-off (PTO) shaft.

b. The mower can be mounted on the tractor
   1. at the rear of the three-point linkage, and is then driven by the PTO shaft;
   2. at the middle under the main body of the tractor, and is then driven through the tractor belt pulley;
   3. ahead of the front steering wheels, and is then driven through the pulley mounted in front of the tractor engine; or
   4. ahead of the power unit, and is then driven through a power take-off shaft.

The Agria 4800 Tractor with a rear-mounted, side-operating reciprocating mower. The mower mounts on a three-point hitch with hydraulic lift and is powered by a rear PTO shaft.
Agria-Werke

In some recent models, the power to operate the mower knives is provided by the tractor's hydraulic system through a flexible coupling instead of the rather difficult mechanical arrangement of the power take-off shaft and universal joints or V-belts. The location of the hydraulically operated mower in relation to the tractor can be either at the rear, middle, or front, the last two positions allowing the tractor driver to supervise its operation with ease.

The main disadvantages of a reciprocating mower are:

a. the working parts are liable to rapid wear,
b. they are not successful in heavy vegetation, and
c. the ground surface needs to be fairly level for satisfactory operation.

Reciprocating mowers are generally used for light grasses which are grown for hay. The cut grass is left in the field in a thin, orderly row which helps it dry quickly. Some mowers have gathering attachments which direct the stalks to fall into windrows, which simplifies handling afterwards. Turning the grass with a swath turner helps further the drying process. But when harvesting some grains, there is a threat of losing the seed, so the crop is gathered right away and threshed soon after.

It is difficult and perhaps even unnecessary to draw a clear distinction between single-axle tractors and motor mowers because mowing attachments are available for some tractors, and cultivating and trailing equipment is often available for motor mowers. Many of the mowers listed in this chapter can be used for fodder or grain crops such as wheat. Rice, however, is often prone to shattering and is not suited to this type of machine.

A SEED HEAD HARVESTER FOR SMALL PLOTS*

by Rex L. Smith, Ph.D.

Editor's note: The lack of intermediate-scaled mechanization for harvesting small acreages of cereals encouraged us to adapt the following article from *Crop Science* into building instructions for a hand-carried, reciprocating harvester. Author Rex L. Smith originally published his article entitled "A Grass Seed Harvester For Small Plots" because "the seed harvester was helpful to my grass-breeding program and I wanted to share the information."

Seeds from small plots, especially those of species whose hulls shatter easily and whose seeds can be lost in the field, have been harvested mostly by hand because no suitable harvesters have been readily available. The increased cost of labor has made this practice expensive and, in our case, has restricted research because of insufficient seed quantities. The harvester described here was designed and built to reduce the cost and facilitate the seed harvesting of small plots of grass. It can reduce the time and labor requirements of hand cutting to one-fifth. The harvester is versatile and will effectively cut many species, including those producing small grains. In addition to harvesting seed, the cutter will also cut grass and legume forage samples.

The harvester consists of a Little Wonder gasoline-powered, 76-centimeter (30-inch) hedge trimmer (Little Wonder, Inc., 1028 Street Rd., Southampton, PA 18966), with a lightweight aluminum tray attached to catch the grass seed heads when cut. This hedge trimmer has two sharpened blades that reciprocate in opposite directions to give excellent cutting action; they can be easily resharpened with a file. As the gasoline motor is self-contained, there is no need for an expensive generator and no cord to manipulate. The harvester's overall weight is only 7.3 kilograms, so it can easily be held and operated by one man.

The aluminum tray was constructed of 0.5-millimeter aluminum sheet. Tray dimensions are 58

* Adapted with permission from *Crop Science,* vol. 13, 1973.

A researcher harvesting seed heads with a gasoline-powered hedge harvester and collection bin attachment.

A close look at the catch bin adaptation.

centimeters wide, 56 centimeters long, and 23 centimeters deep. The sides are sloped 45 degrees at the front to allow the cut material to fall back into the tray without interference. The front of the tray has a lip formed downward three millimeters over the front of the blade, and it is attached to the top of the blade by the four bolts. The rear of the tray is supported by the handle that is attached near the top of the tray side. This gives the tray a downward slope to the rear and facilitates collection of the cut material in the tray.

The handle is 50 centimeters long to permit the operator to balance the harvester by adjusting the position where it is held. It is constructed of thin-wall steel conduit with an attached six-millimeter-diameter rod which activates the hedge trimmer clutch when the handle is rotated. This retains the safety feature of the trimmer; both of the operator's hands have to be on the handles for the blades to function. The main section of the handle is constructed of 2.3-centimeter-diameter thin-wall steel conduit, with a short length of 1.8-centimeter-diameter conduit welded on the front end and inserted inside the original trimmer handle. Another short length of 1.8-centimeter diameter is welded on the rear bracket and inserted inside the rear of the main handle. Plastic wedges are used to give a good fit between the two conduit sizes. Our cost for the harvester was just over $100 when we built it in 1973.

The harvester is operated by sweeping it into the grass with the blade just below the grass seed heads. Cutting into a slight breeze is helpful in moving the harvested material into the tray, but not necessary. The tray empties completely when the harvester is tipped forward, and no cleaning is necessary when changing varieties. The harvested material is emptied directly into large cardboard boxes or onto sheets of canvas where it is dried before threshing.

Tea Leaf Harvester

Utilizing the same theory as Smith's seed head harvester, the Japanese have devised a machine to pluck leaves from tea bushes. Reciprocating cutters and/or spindle reel mowers cut the leaves which are collected in a bag. Electric or gasoline-powered units are made for one or two people, and they are mounted on rollers wheels or carried by hand. Some blades are curved for aesthetic round-topped tea bushes or hedges.

A two-person design harvests more at once and leaves an aesthetic round-topped bush.
Kobayashi Cutlery

The carefully guarded spindle reel mower snips tea leaves . . .

. . . and delivers them to a catch bag.
Kobayashi Cutlery

Kobayashi Cutlery Mfg. Co., Ltd.
1131–Horinoachi Kikugawa–Cho
Shigwoka–Pref. Japan

NORTH AMERICAN SOURCES OF FORAGE MOWERS AND HARVESTERS

Haban Sickle Mo

Made for operation from the power take-off shafts of 20 h.p. tractors or less, the Sickle Mo makes a 4-foot cut with a full 3-inch stroke of the blade. Power is governed by a convenient clutch lever which actuates the drive belt. A full-floating action to the self-adjusting cutting bar keeps the blade level close to the ground. A swing back device permits the bar to move back instantly upon hitting a solid object.

Haban Mfg. Co.
2100 Northwestern Ave.
Racine, WI 53404

Jari

Cutting bars on the Jari cut a range of 16 to 60 inches. It is a self-propelled unit available

Haban 48" Sickle Bar Mower for lawn and garden tractors.
Haban Mfg. Co.

with a snowblower attachment. Separate controls engage the wheels and power unit.

Jari Division, Year-A-Round Cab Corp.
P.O. Box 2075
Mankato, MN 56001

BCS Mainline Sickle Bar

Manufactured in Italy, the BCS Mainline is a 13 h.p., gear-driven reciprocating mower with a 44-inch cutting bar. Sickle guards and swathboard ends are available, the latter designed to windrow the cut material. This unit has attachments for roto-cultivation, plowing, ridging, riding, and a trailer for transport. The manufacturer also offers a larger unit, which is discussed in the section on binders and reapers.

Central States Mainline Distributors
Box 348
London, OH 43140

BCS Mainline Sicklebar
Central States Mainline Distributors

Ferrari

The Ferrari walking tiller is manufactured in Italy. The handle pivots 180 degrees, allowing the tiller to be removed and a sickle bar attached. In this position, the unit runs backwards.

Ferrari
6104 Avenida Encinas
Carlsbad, CA 92008

Kinco

This is a 38-inch-wide sickle bar with wide tracking for stability on hills. Individual wheel clutches provide a source of power for easy turning. The knife disengages for transport.

Kinco Mfg.
168 N. Pascal
St. Paul, MN 55104

The Seedburo Plot Cutter

Designed for experimental work on research plots, the plot cutter is an 18-inch sickle bar mower with a collection bin for catching cereal crops as they fall back after being mowed. It has a variable ground speed control and complements the use of the Seedburo plot thresher.

Seedburo Equipment Co.
1022 W. Jackson Blvd.
Chicago, IL 60607

Seedburo Plot Cutter
Seedburo Equipment Co.

INTERNATIONAL SOURCES OF MOWERS

Bucher M600

The Bucher M600 walking mower has a 10 h.p., gasoline engine and a three-speed and reverse gearbox. It can be supplied with a windrowing attachment, trailer, and extra-wide wheels for stability on slopes. Other models are also available.

Bucher-Geyer, Ltd. Engineering Works
CH–8166 Niederweningen
Zurich, Switzerland

Gebruder M 6

The M 6 walking mower has been designed for mowing in all types of terrain. It has a 6 h.p. engine with a two forward, two reverse speed gearbox. It is fitted with a fingerless cutter bar.

Gebruder Holder Maschinenfabrik
7418 Metzingen, Wurtt
Postfach 66, West Germany

Bertolini Mowers

Bertolini offers a 7 h.p. pedestrian and 14

Bertolini mower with only one wheel.
Bertolini Macchine Agricole

Bertolini 14 h.p. Riding Mower
Bertolini Macchine Agricole

h.p. riding mower. Both are suitable for cutting grass or grain crops.

Bertolini Macchine Agricole
42100 Reggio Emilia
Via Guicciardi 7, Italy

Schanzlin Mini Mower

This is a two-wheel pedestrian reciprocating mower.

Schanzlin Maschinenfabrik Gmbh
7831 Weisweil
Baden, West Germany

Freres SF8

This is a walking mower fitted with a 9 h.p. engine and a gearbox with four speeds forward and one reverse. Cutter bars of 1.10-, 1.27-, or 1.45-meter width are available. This mower may also be used to pull trailers and wheeled implements and to drive stationary machinery such as grinding mills.

Ets. Simon Freres
B.P. 47
50104 Cherbourg, France

Irus Power Mower

This mower has a 7 h.p. engine and can be supplied with cutter bars up to 1.40 meters wide, giving a work rate of 0.3 to 0.4 hectare per hour. A trailer, spraying, and pulling attachments are available for this two-wheeled power unit.

Iruswerke Dusslingen
7401 Dusslingen
Postfach 128, West Germany

MF-130

MF-130 motor mowers come with a 7 h.p. engine, two-speed and reverse gearbox. They are available with central or side-mounted cutter bar.

Macchine Agricole F.B.
36040 Sossano
Vicenza, Italy

M.R. Mower-Tractor

The steering handles on this mower can be set for driving in either direction. One direction is used for mowing and the other for rotary cultivating and trailer work. It is available with either an 8 h.p. gasoline or a 10 h.p. diesel engine. A special gearbox gives three forward and one reverse speed in both mowing and cultivating directions. Single-purpose mowers are also available.

S.E.P. Fabrica Macchine Agricole
Via Don Pasquino Borghi 6
42018 St. Martino In Rio
Reggio Emilia, Italy

AEBI

The Swiss AEBI two-wheel mower has a four-stroke, 10 h.p. gasoline engine with two forward and one reverse speed. It is specially designed for mountainous terrain, has 46-, 58-, and 66-inch cutting bars and a windrowing attachment which can be attached and removed without tools. (See walking tractor section for further details.) Various models are available.

AEBI & Co. AG
CH–3400
Burgdorf, Switzerland

The AEBI two-wheel mower.
AEBI and Co.

Bouyer

The Bouyer two-wheeled tractors have a lateral sickle mower mechanism with a mulch bar, but no windrowing attachment.

Bouyer
B.P. 23
Tomblaine 54510, France

Moty Universal and Gigant

The Moty Universal two-wheel tractor has a finger and double-acting cutting bar, 80 to 140 centimeters in width. Their Gigant four-wheeled, wide-wheelbase tractor will mow 5 feet at a time.

The Moty Gigant as a pedestrian mower with dual-wheel traction.
Moty-Werk

The Moty Gigant as a riding mower with four sets of dual wheels and a low center of gravity for serious work on hills.
Moty-Werk

Moty-Werk
8523 Frauental 62
Fernschreiber 3479
Steiermark, Austria

Hobby Models 80-2T, Elite 2T, Elite 4T

The Hobby is an extremely lightweight unit with an 80-centimeter-wide blade, adjustable cutting height, and optional two- or four-stroke motors. It is so lightweight, it is carried by the operator and simply lifted as mowing takes place. The larger Elite models have two wheels, one trailing the other. They are designed for smaller cutting jobs such as a small cereal plot would require.

Alpina
31015 Conegliano
S. Vendemiano (TV)
Casella Postale 44, Italy

Alpina North America
c/o Mr. H.J. Hutchinson
Box 313, Trail
British Columbia, Vir 466, Canada

Agria Motor Mower 300

Powered by an air-cooled, two-stroke, 5 h.p. gasoline engine, the Agria 300 has a fingerless, 1.20-meter-wide cutter bar, adjustable handlebars, and one forward and reserve gear. Iron traction rings are available as wheel extensions for stability on steep slopes. A snowplow attachment is available also. Weight: 105 kilograms.

Agria-Werke Gmbh
7108 Moeckmuehl
West Germany

WINDROWERS AND BINDERS

A windrow is a heaped row of cut vegetation. Grasses are raked into windrows to dry

Hand-tied sheaves are stacked in shocks to dry in the field.

before baling or storage. Delivering grain stalks neatly into a windrow as they are cut with a scythe and grain cradle facilitates bundling and eliminates the need for raking when harvesting by hand. Stalks are later tied into small bunches called sheaves which in turn are stacked and tied, butt end down, in larger bundles called shocks to allow grain heads to dry in the field.

In North America, hand harvesting has given way to a highly mechanized alternative, the combine harvester. This machine combines the cutting, gathering, threshing, and cleaning ac-

The Bucher M600 reciprocating mower with a windrower attachment.
Bucher-Geyer, Ltd.

tivities of grain processing into one large, expensive machine. It offers no practical alternative to hand harvesting for the small-holder in the size in which it is currently produced. However, in Europe, where homesteading has always been a way of life, a reciprocating mower with a windrowing mechanism is made to fit onto two-wheel walking tractors. Another attachment, the binder, has a rather complicated tying mechanism to carry out simultaneously the two operations of cutting a crop and tying it into neat and uniform sheaves. The binder basically consists of a reel to gather the crop for delivery to

The Bucher M600 with windrower at work.
Bucher-Geyer, Ltd.

The AEBI walking tractor with an attachment for turning or windrowing hay.
AEBI and Co.

the cutting mechanism, an elevating system of endless canvasses or a chainlike conveyor, and the binding mechanism which ties the cut material with a band of twine. Almost all of these parts are provided with adjustments so that a variety of crops can be harvested.

The binder has generally given way to the combine harvester for large-scale work. Until recently it was all but out of use in the United States except by conservative farmers of particular sects who have retained the old ways. But, recognizing a growing market for small-scale farming equipment, binders are making a comeback in North America.

A late 19th century reaper-binder.
The Implement Age, 1894

NORTH AMERICAN SOURCES OF BINDERS

Ottawa Single-Row Harvester

Developed to harvest single rows of standing or lodged cereal plots for research purposes, this harvester is a compact, two-wheeled machine designed specifically for plot harvesting, with proper balance and convenient controls. Lodged crops are picked up by a pair of oblique-head finger bar assemblies mounted at 30 degrees at the front of the machine. As the straw is straightened by the dividers, it is gripped by elevating belts, cut 6 inches above the ground, and elevated to a hopper large enough to hold the yield of two 18-foot rows of cereal grain. The

Ottawa Single-Row Harvester
Agriculture Canada

harvester can be turned in a 5-foot pathway without declutching. Two 18-foot rows can be harvested by two men in one minute, including the time for unloading and cleaning.

Craftsman Machine Co.
61 Heaton
Winnipeg 2, Manitoba, Canada

Winnipeg Plot Harvester

The Winnipeg research plot harvester is mounted on a standard 7 h.p. Gravely garden tractor. Modifications were made to the cutting bar to limit the cutting width to two rows seeded a maximum of 12 inches apart. Small wheels were added under the front end to raise the cutting bar to the desired height. The reel, driven from the front wheels, is adjustable horizontally and vertically. As the plot is harvested, the material is gathered in a pan and can be collected and tied by the operator. A small opening was left at the rear of the pan to facilitate cleaning between varieties. A bar was placed across the front opening of the tray, a few inches from the bottom to ensure that the reel will force cut material back into the pan and away from the cutter bar. With this machine, it is possible to harvest 1,000 rod rows daily without the back-breaking labor inherent in the old sickle method. Three men are required to operate this machine efficiently.

Machine Service & Repair, Ltd.
47 Landsdown Ave.
Winnipeg 4, Manitoba, Canada

BCS Binder

The BCS binder is a mass-produced farm machine from Italy which is mounted on the front of a European-style walking tractor equipped with a riding sulky. The tractor has a 9 h.p. engine, disc clutch, and a three-speed gearbox. The binder has a 54-inch wide cut and ejects the tied bundles to the rear. The crop remains in an upright position throughout the cutting and tying process. There is a provision for adjusting the size of the bundle, but not for tying height. Because the wheel tread is inside of the cutting width and the bundles are deposited on the stubble remaining where it was cut, adjacent plots are not disturbed. Optional equipment available from the factory includes a differential axle rather than the standard solid axle with wheel release, high-clearance axle, and electric starting. A mower attachment is included with the unit.

BCS Mainline Binder-Reaper
Central States Mainline Distributors

Ambassador Sales
Acton, Ontario
Canada

BCS Motofalciatrici
Viale Mazzini 161
Abbiategrosso, Milano, Italy

Central States Mainline Distributors
Box 348
London, OH 43140

INTERNATIONAL SOURCES OF BINDERS

Walking Harvester Binder

This self-propelled reaper and binder is suitable for harvesting wheat or rice. It is available from Suzue in three versions: 1-wheel, 1-row reaping; 2-wheel, 1-row reaping; 2-wheel, 2-row reaping.

Suzue Agricultural Machinery Co., Ltd.
144-2 Gomen-cho, Nankoku-Shi
Kochi-Ken 783, Japan

Iseki Model RS300

A single-row reaper binder, its 3.85 h.p., four-cycle, air-cooled, gasoline engine has two forward and one reverse speed. Paddies of all heights ranging from 60 to 120 centimeters can be efficiently harvested.

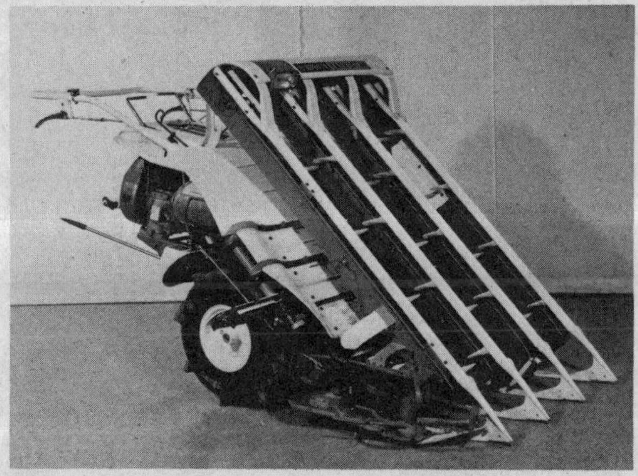

Kubota Harvester
Agriculture Canada

Iseki Agricultural Machinery Mfg. Co., Ltd.
1-3, Nihonbashi 2-chome, Chuo-ku
Tokyo 103, Japan

Models similar to the Iseki and Suzue binders for cutting and bundling rice and cereal crops are available from:

CeCoCo
P.O. Box 8, Ibaraki City
Osaka Pref. 567, Japan

Kubota, Ltd.
22 Funade-cho, 2-chome, Naniwa-ku
Osaka, Japan

CeCoCo binder for rice and cereal crops.
Agriculture Canada

Vacuum Blower Harvester

The vacuum blower harvester was developed by the Engineering Research Service, Agriculture Canada to quickly harvest two-row research cereal plots by cutting a minimum amount of material and transferring the cut material directly into a bag. Attachments at the front hold the cutter bar and act as a pivot for the gathering mechanism. It is supplied with a two-speed transmission and an air-cooled gasoline engine. All functions are adjustable.

Vacuum Blower Harvester
Agriculture Canada

Craftsman Machine Co.
61 Heaton
Winnipeg 2, Manitoba, Canada

Poynter Stripper Harvester

The Poynter pneumatic stripper harvester uses a comb to guide standing crops into a cylinder where heads are removed and threshed by the combination of impact from the cylinder and stripping through the comb. The chaff is removed by an air blast created by the cylinder. The straw is not cut. The unit is self-propelled and has a 24-inch swath extendable to 36 inches by additional crop fingers. The height of the comb is adjusted by a hand crank during operation.

The Poynter box stripper is similar to the pneumatic stripper except that all the stripped material is collected in an 8-cubic-foot box. This type of stripper is used in conjunction with a plot thresher to further thresh the collected material. The box stripper is normally hand-propelled, but it is also available as a power-propelled unit.

Poynter Products Pty., Ltd.
52 Greenaway St.
Bulleen, Victoria, Australia

Poynter Harvester
Agriculture Canada

Similar harvesters are also manufactured by:

Monier Metal Products, Ltd. (Quick Harvester)
749 Port Rd.
Woodville, South Australia

Winter Industries Products Pty., Ltd. (Waite Harvester)
41 Lairna St.
Athol Park, South Australia

The IRRI Stripper Harvester, which is currently being developed in the Philippines.
International Rice Research Institute

IRRI Stripper Harvester

Presently under development at the International Rice Research Institute, the six-row stripper harvester is a somewhat expensive, labor-replacing machine, particularly suited for countries like Japan where labor costs are high. In

The IRRI Stripper Harvester in a field trial.
International Rice Research Institute

North America, a machine like this might offer an alternative to the combine harvester.

International Rice Research Institute
P.O. Box 933
Manila, Philippines

COMBINE HARVESTERS

As the name implies, a combine harvester-thresher performs the multiple operations of harvesting and threshing a crop in a single pass over the field, the sequence of operations being cutting, conveying to the threshing mechanism, threshing, winnowing, cleaning, and finally, either bagging or delivering the grain in bulk to a bin, and from there to a trailer or truck alongside the machine. Because each of these separate operations are performed at the same time in a combine harvester, the resulting machine is necessarily complicated and expensive.

A combine can also be used either to pick up and thresh crops which have been previously cut and left in the swath, or as a stationary thresher for handling crops which have been cut and stacked. Separate headers, front end reaping mechanisms, are required for harvesting cereal and maize crops. Special attachments allow some combines to windrow or chop and scatter straw as well. Earlier models of combines were pulled by a tractor; the cutting and threshing mechanism was driven either by an auxiliary engine mounted on the combine or by the tractor engine through its power take-off shaft. Modern combines are self-propelled.

The losses from combine harvesting may be quite serious unless a constant watch is kept for signs of unsatisfactory threshing. Conditions may change from one hour to the next, and it may be necessary to vary the adjustments several times during a day for best results.

THE FIELD FOR THE SMALL, COMBINED, HARVESTER-THRESHER*

By W. M. Hurst

Editor's note: A 1935 look at the harvesting needs of the small farmer reveals that little has changed in the past 40 years or more.

* Reprinted with permission from *Agricultural Engineering,* June 1935.

The development and widespread use of the combine was retarded for over 75 years because farmers, grain dealers, and farm machinery manufacturers thought it would work successfully only on the Pacific Coast. After the practicability of the combine had been demonstrated in the Great Plains states, it was predicted that its use would be restricted to areas where large-scale farming was practiced in dry areas. The demand for combines for harvesting soybeans in the corn belt, the introduction of the one-man combine, and the windrow harvester again made possible a wider use of this type of equipment.

Few, if any, agricultural machines are more efficient in performing the work for which they are intended than combines. However, the cutter bar is designed for heading ripe, dry grain and the cylinder, for threshing such material. In harvesting soybeans in the South, it is necessary to cut the plants within two or three inches of the ground and to handle a large volume of tangled vines and green weeds. In combining rice in the South, it is also necessary for the machine to handle not only green (unmatured) straw and weeds, but also much more straw than is customary in harvesting wheat.

The combine is also one of the few machines which may be purchased as well as operated at a lower cost than the equipment which it replaces. It is not, however, sufficiently low in first cost to permit its use on thousands of farms where general-purpose tractors are used. A small, inexpensive combine of somewhat different design than those now on the market would, it is believed, be used on many small farms in the east, north central, and some of the middle and south Atlantic states for small grain, in the south Atlantic and east south central states for soybeans, alfalfa, and clover, as well as a stationary thresher for cowpeas and other legumes.

For wider use in states east of the Mississippi River, the following features appear to be desirable and, in some cases, essential for a small combine:

1. Capacity to cut a 5- or 6-foot swath
2. A threshing cylinder designed for a large mass of straw and vines; possible width of the cylinder the same as the width of the cutter bar
3. A reel of such design as to gently pull the crop back on the elevator without shattering
4. An overall width of the machine to be not more than 12 feet, or of such design that not more than 15 or 20 minutes are required to get the machine in condition for transporting from one field to another
5. Weight from 2,500 to 3,000 pounds
6. A maximum cost to farmers of $500
7. Suitability for small grain, soybeans, and other legumes
8. Drive by power take-off from a tractor
9. Possession of a means for quickly adjusting concaves and reel—preferably from the driver's or operator's platform
10. A flexible mounting—pneumatic rubber tires or springs.

NORTH AMERICAN SOURCES OF COMBINE HARVESTERS

K.E.M. Research Plot Combine Model SP 50

Available for about half the price of the smallest popular farm combines in the United States, the K.E.M. Research Plot Combine has a large-capacity cylinder and a wide range of speeds making it possible to harvest a wide variety of crops. This self-propelled unit employs a 17.5 h.p. gasoline engine and a hydrostatic ground drive with infinite speeds forward or reverse from 0 to 6 mph. The threshing mechanism utilizes a 15-inch by 27-inch rasp bar cylinder and an air and shaker sieve after cutting a 54-inch swath. The header is comprised of a sickle bar cutter and guards, a power reel with delivery to the cylinder by a 27-inch wide conveyor belt, and hydraulic lift.

K.E.M. SP 4000

Much larger than K.E.M.'s SP 50, this research plot combine has a 53 h.p., gasoline,

K.E.M. Research Plot Combine SP 50
K.E.M. Corp.

four-cylinder, Volkswagen engine. It has a 12-inch ground clearance, weighs 6,800 pounds (shipping weight), and has overall dimensions of 208 by 75 by 118 inches. The hydrostatic ground drive has two speeds for a traveling speed ranging between 0 and 12 mph. It comes with two adjustable sieves and a 27- by 80-inch straw rack. It can cut a width of 7 feet and has a 28-bushel-capacity grain tank. With grain and corn headers, it has multicrop versatility.

SP 4000 Combine
K.E.M. Corp.

Kincaid Equipment Mfg. Corp.
P.O. Box 471
Haven, KS 67543

ALMACO C-F Plot Combine

This combine, designed for research test plots of small grains, corn, and soybeans, is self-propelled by a 37 h.p. gasoline engine. Its hydraulic system powers the forward and reverse drives, the variable speed thresher, the lift on the header assembly, and reel and drive on the variable-speed reel. It has an underslung, self-cleaning, adjustable, concave rasp bar. The 51½-inch sickle bar cutter is accompanied by headers for small grains and corn which have bean saver snouts for soybean harvesting. It weighs 5,000 pounds, is 17 feet 6 inches long and 7 feet wide.

The ALMACO Plot Combine with a corn header.
Allan Machine Co.

Allan Machine Co.
P.O. Box 112
Ames, IA 50100

The ALMACO Plot Combine with a soybean header.
Allan Machine Co.

INTERNATIONAL SOURCES OF COMBINE HARVESTERS

CeCoCo Midget Combine

To thresh grain in a traditional fashion, men and women swing sheaves over their shoulders and beat them down into a tub, or they have buffaloes and oxen tread on them. These methods result in significant grain losses due to shredding, incomplete threshing, and a high incidence of grain damage.

The people at CeCoCo explain that "the need for a simple and efficient rice combine is essential. The shortage of labor has made it difficult to reap sufficiently fast, creating a bottleneck at harvest time. Furthermore, the loss and damage incurred by the traditional methods of harvesting and threshing could not be afforded in view of the rapidly increasing population and its inherent food problem."

To solve this problem, they have developed the CeCoCo Midget Combine. Their 6 to 9 h.p. unit with six forward and two reverse speeds is claimed to reap and thresh approximately 1 acre of rice, wheat, or barley per 8-hour day, utilizing an air current design. This is one modern machine which helps to improve the soil organically, since straw is left in the field to rot into humus.

CeCoCo
P.O. Box 8, Ibaraki City
Osaka Pref. 567, Japan

Iseki

Iseki manufactures two combine harvesters. Model HD660R has a 9 to 12 h.p., air-cooled, four-cycle gasoline engine and it is capable of covering 1.5 to 2.5 acres per 8-hour day. The harvesting mechanism employs a reciprocating mower for cutting and a Japanese type of thesher. It discharges the hay at intervals in fixed quantities to facilitate pickup. Their larger model, the Cosechadora HD 2000, has a 25 h.p., water-cooled engine which will harvest from 4 to 6 acres in an 8-hour day.

Iseki Agricultural Machinery Mfg. Co., Ltd.
1-3, Nihonbashi 2-chome, Chuo-ku
Tokyo 103, Japan

The Wintersteiger Kultraplant with a corn header.
Walter & Wintersteiger

The Kultraplant Pam 150-S

A self-propelled combine with a 63-inch cut, the Kultraplant is specially designed for small seed plots. The table, reel, and cylinder are comparable to a conventional combine, but seed is separated by air currents. The unit is powered by a Volkswagen engine and has three speeds forward and one reverse with a device to vary the speed in each gear. Cleanup time is claimed to be 1 minute. A 180-degree turn can be made in a pathway 20 feet wide, and the wheel tread is inside the width of the cut.

F. Walter & H. Wintersteiger
K.L., A–4910 Ried im Innkreis
Dimmelstrasse, Austria

The Wintersteiger Kultraplant with a bean header.
Walter & Wintersteiger

Hege Combine
Agriculture Canada

Hege 125

According to Agriculture Canada, the German Hege 125 differs from the Pam 150 in that it has straw walkers and a short cleaning sieve. A wide rubber belt is used to convey cut material to the cylinder; it does not have a reel. There are viewing doors to the screens and straw walkers. An overcapacity fan is used to blow the separating area clean at the end of each plot.

The cutting width is 49 inches, the total

length is 12.8 feet and total width, 51 inches. This combine is also powered by a Volkswagen engine with a combined four-speed transmission and variable-speed drive. It is possible to cut a plot 39.7 inches wide and 32.8 feet long in 1 minute, including the time to clean the machine. Models are being used at Oregon State and North Dakota State Universities in the United States.

Hans-Ulrich Hege
Saatzuchtmaschinen
7112 Domane Hohebuch
Waldenburg/Wiirtt, Germany

United States Parts outlet:

H & N Equipment, Inc.
Colwich, KS 67030

Garvie Plot Combine

The Garvie Plot Combine, developed by the National Institute of Agricultural Engineering in Great Britain, employs a canvas to convey the cut material to a rasp bar cylinder with a grate-type concave. Threshed grain falls through the concave to a conveyer belt which carries it to a grain pan. Straw is thrown into a collection bin and then removed by hand. The straw must be shaken when removing it to shake out any grain still in the straw. A special cleaner has been developed to further clean the sample.

The cylinder is direct-driven from a 7 h.p. engine. Wheel drive is by fixed displacement, double-volume, hydrostatic transmission to a single rear wheel, giving speeds of 1 or 3 mph in forward and reverse.

The total width of the machine is 4 feet 10 inches and the overall length, not including the reel, is 12 feet 3 inches. The driver sits at the side of the machine. Capacity is about 20 four-row, 10-foot plots per hour.

R.G. Garvie & Sons
2, Canal Rd.
Aberdeen, Scotland

Stationary Combines

Two makes of small European combines with 7-foot tables are available fitted with a large air compressor and nozzles located at strategic positions to make the combine self-cleaning. Also, extra rubber parts are fitted to the elevator flights.

Bolinder Mumktell
Eskilstuna, Sweden

W. Rosenlew & Co.
A.B. Engineering Works
Pori, Finland

Suzue Combine

Another combine to accommodate the average 3-acre Japanese farm is mounted on a walking tractor chassis and is available with wheels or tracks. The combine is unconventional in that air currents are used for the reel and for separation after threshing. Heads are cut off by contra-rotating rotary cutters at the front. Two threshing drums thresh the cut crop and deliver the material to the airstream in the cleaning section; the chaff and short straw is thrown out by a blower. The cleaned grain is then fed through an auger to a blower which blows it into a sack. The remaining stubble is cut into 5- to 6-inch pieces by circular cutters at the rear of the machine. A capacity of 1 acre per day is claimed. The combine is powered by a 9 h.p. kerosene engine and has a six-speed gearbox with a unique locking axle that gives good traction and maneuverability.

Suzue Agricultural Machinery Co., Ltd.
144-2, Gomen-cho, Nankoku-Shi
Kochi-ken 783, Japan

Sold by:

Nissho Canada, Ltd.
100 University Ave.
Toronto, Ontario, Canada

FORAGE CROPS

FORAGE HARVESTERS

The forage harvester has been developed fairly recently for collecting grasses or other forage crops from the field in their green stage to be used later for making either silage or artificially dried feed. Earlier models of a field forage harvester consisted of a stationary chopper-blower mounted behind a reciprocating mower or behind a pickup reel for collecting previously mown grass. Power to the chopper-blower was provided either by an independently mounted engine or through the power take-off shaft of the driving tractor. However, these models have now been largely superceded by the modern flail-type forage harvester where the mower unit or the pickup reel and the chopper-blower are no longer used.

The principle of operation involves flails, or blades, which are hinged on a shaft or cylinder which rotates at a high speed as the machine is being driven forward. The flails cut the stationary vegetation by impact, in a manner similar to a hand-operated grass slasher or a conventional rotary lawn mower. Rotating at high speed, they also act as a fan and provide a draft of air and the necessary momentum for blowing the cut material up through an elevated exit spout. The shape of the spout directs the cut material into a trailer at the rear with the help of an adjustable end flap. The height of the cut is regulated by adjusting the wheels on which the machine is mounted. Some flail mowers simply cut high grasses and leave them in the field to be raked or baled.

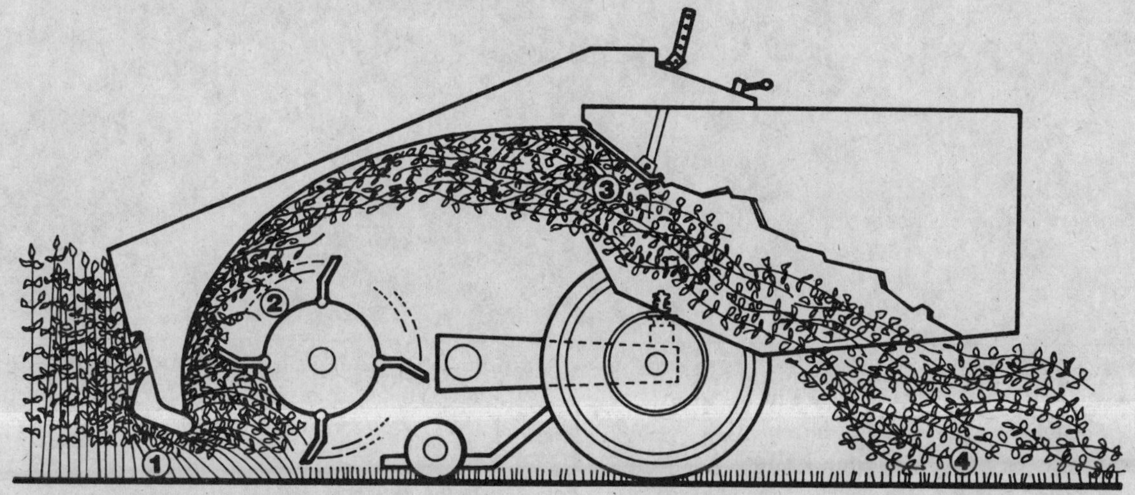

1. *The full-width adjustable crop deflector bends standing plants over so knives can cut stems close to the ground. Once cut, the stems are conditioned by repeated light contact with knife edges, ensuring uniform, effective conditioning and soft, palatable hay.*
2. *At a maximum speed, plants move up and over the rotor without further contact with the knives so the upper leafy portions of the plants are undamaged.*
3. *A deflector at the rear slows down the speed of the plants and also fluffs and directs the hay down to the rear.*
4. *Cut and conditioned material falls gently on top of the stubble into a loose, fluffy swath or into a neat windrow of your selected width and density, depending on shield adjustment.*

Avco Corp.

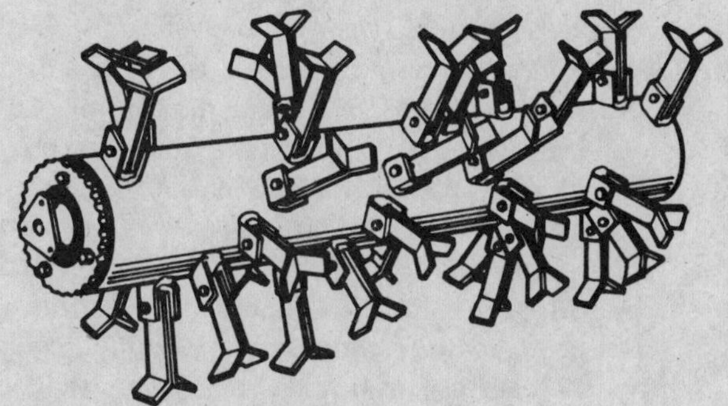

The Flail mower consists of a solid shaft with loosely hung, pivot-mounted blades rotating at high speeds. This creates a tremendous chopping action, pulling material in from the front, shredding it, and distributing it evenly over the field. The blades simply fold back when they strike rocks or debris, returning to a cutting position when the obstruction is passed over.

The modern forage harvester, built as a compact power take-off-driven unit, can perform the multiple operations of cutting, chopping, and loading green grass, dry hay, and other silage crops into a trailer in one pass over the field. It can also be used as an implement for the care of meadowland by cutting local concentrations of coarse grass and weeds, for distributing manure, and for removing molehills.

NORTH AMERICAN SOURCES OF FORAGE MOWERS AND HARVESTERS

Swift Current Harvester

The Swift Current forage plot harvester cuts forage material with a flail-type cutter and delivers it to a collection bin. The harvester is a two-wheel walking-type powered by a 7 h.p. engine. The width of cut is 24 inches, and grasses, legumes, or corn up to 3 feet high can be harvested. The sample box holds 6 cubic feet and is hinged so that it may be emptied by one person. An improved model is now available.

Swift Current Forage Harvester
Agriculture Canada

REM Mfg.
Swift Current
Saskatchewan, Canada

KEM Plot Forage Harvester

The Kincaid Plot Forage Harvester was developed for cutting crops when there is a need for weight data in research experiments. It is also used on small plots when crops must be harvested in a stationary thresher. Maneuverability is good, and steering is accomplished by use of two hydrostatic pumps. This enables it to be used in very small areas. The pickup reel is effective in lodged crops, and the pickup angle on the bats is adjustable by a rotating cam plate on the end of the reel. The collection box is easily dumped. Pickup reel, hydraulic header lift, header gauge wheels, and electric start are all standard equipment. It measures 56 inches by 49 inches by 156 inches, weighs 1,520 pounds, utilizes a conventional sickle cutting bar in 3-inch sections and uses an 8 h.p. engine for cutting a 54-inch swath.

Kincaid Equipment Mfg. Corp.
P.O. Box 471
Haven, KS 67543

Mott Model J-60

Model J-60 is a 60-inch, rear-mounted mower designed specifically for the Kubota L15 or other compact tractors (see chapter four). With a modified three-point hitch, it runs off a tractor power take-off with a 25 h.p. maximum. It can be used to mow lawns, and shred weeds for mulch, as well as cut up forage crops. A unit like this is particularly helpful to the organic farmer who wants to incorporate organic material into the soil with rototilling blades but who needs to have the crop residue finely chopped first to avoid clogging the tines. The mower will leave stubble ¾ to 3 inches high and cut a 60-inch swath. A triple-mower gang arrangement is possible for a swath of 10 feet 4 inches. This arrangement utilizes two self-powered trailer-type mowers with 8 h.p. engines.

Mott Model 18-60

Designed specifically for the front power take-off of the Bolens 1886 tractor, this front-end, 60-inch model employs hammer knife safety flails as the cutting tools on this unit. The knifelike flails have an edgewise cutting action which provides a cleaner cut and uses less power than conventional flail mowers. It is called a safety flail mowing system because, being lightweight and free swinging, the flails fold back when hitting an obstruction to absorb the force of impact and minimize the danger of objects being thrown by the blade.

Mott Model T38

A unit to be towed, the T38 cuts a 38-inch swath and employs an 8 h.p. engine. It attaches quickly to any tractor drawbar with a cotter pin.

Other units are available specifically designed for most major farm and garden tractors, including the Allis-Chalmers 616 and 620 and the John Deere 300 and 400 tractors.

The above harvesters are manufactured by:
Mott Corp.
500 Shawmut Ave.
Le Grange, IL 60325

Gehl FC72C Chopper

Gehl offers a wide range of large forage harvesters, and their smallest unit, the FC72C flail chopper, requires a 40 h.p. tractor or larger.

Gehl Co.
West Bend, WI 53095

Western Bear Cat Chopmaster

The Chopmaster requires the power of a two- or three-plow tractor for cutting a 6-foot swath of corn or cotton stalks and for mowing jobs. It operates from a 540 rpm power take-off shaft and fits any drawbar. Models are available with or without a blower, a discharge elbow, a cutter head, or an auger.

Westernland Roller Co.
Hastings, NE 68901

New Idea Cut/Ditioner

New Idea offers a 7-foot windrowing mower requiring a minimum of 40 h.p. as their smallest unit.

AVCO Corp., New Idea Farm Equipment Div.
First & Sycamore
Coldwater, OH 45828

Haban Flail Mo

The Flail Mo is designed for front mounting on compact tractors of 7 h.p. or more. Two sizes are available, a 36-inch size with 80 knives and a

Haban's 12 h.p. self-propelled flail mower, complete with riding sulky.
Haban Mfg. Co.

48-inch size with 120 knives. It will cut tall grasses and brush to a minimum height of 1 inch without throwing stones. Depending upon conditions, it can be operated at speeds from 1 to 4 mph.

Haban Mfg.
2100 Northwestern Ave.
Racine, WI 53404

INTERNATIONAL SOURCES OF FORAGE MOWERS AND HARVESTERS

Jumil JF-1

The JF-1 operates at a rate of 8 kph for an output of 15 tons per hour from a tractor's power take-off shaft. A 35 h.p. or larger tractor is required to power the unit.

Jumil
Justino de Morais, Irmaos S.A.
Rua Ana Luiza, 568 Cx, Postal 75
Batarais, Brazil

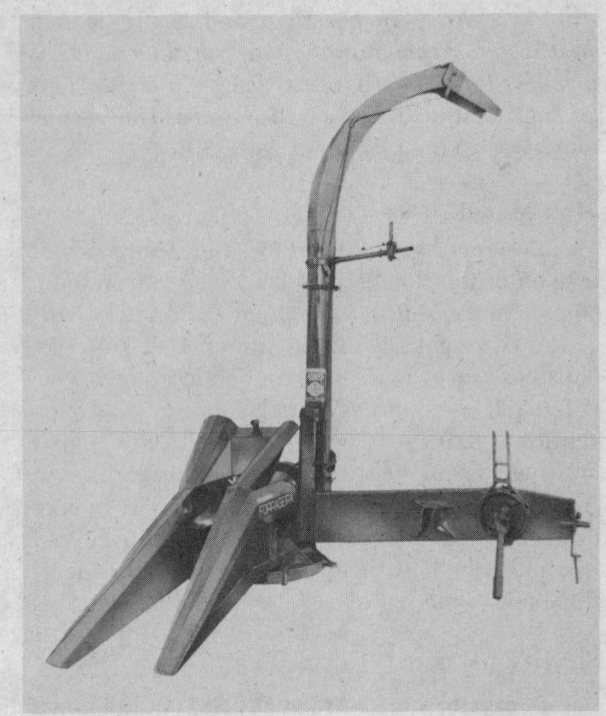

Jumil JF-1 Jumil

Hay harvesting in the late 1800s. The Implement Age, 1894

RAKING HAY

Once forage crops are cut and allowed to dry, they have to be gathered. The Rake Factory in Suffolk, England is still making hay rakes by hand, along with their handmade wooden scythe snaths. Wide, lightweight wooden rakes with long pegs for teeth are used for raking by hand. An early method of hay collection was a ground-driven, animal-drawn contraption with raking arms which carried hay up a primitive (but clever) type of conveyor and dropped it onto a wagon.

Today, baling is popular but most balers require the power input of a large tractor. However, one Italian manufacturer makes a baler attachment for a two-wheel tractor. They are Pasquali Macchine Agricole, Via Nuova 30, 50041 Calengano (Frenge) Italy. In North

America, you can write to Pasquali USA, P.O. Box 6235, Verona, WI 53716.

The Texas Agricultural Extension Service of the Texas A & M University System has developed detailed building plans for a raking attachment for the front end of a tractor. Made of wood, the rake becomes slick and slippery with use and glides easily across hay stubble. A hydraulic lift facilitates unloading hay onto a cart.

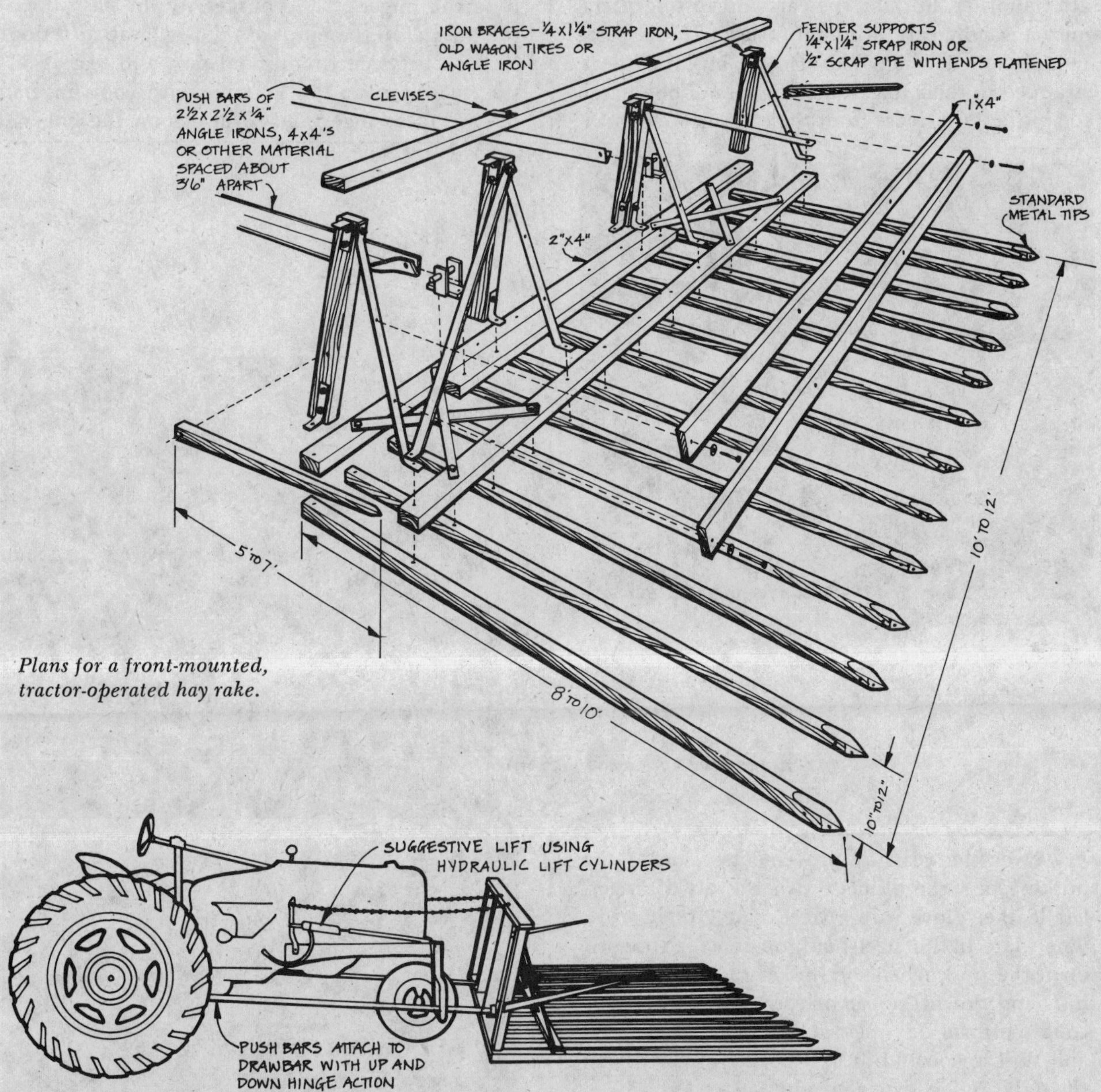

Plans for a front-mounted, tractor-operated hay rake.

HARVESTING CORN

Corn is grown as a row crop, and because its stalks are rather thick and tough when mature, specialized equipment is necessary for harvesting the crop by mechanical means. For small acreages under the peasant farming system, harvesting is still carried out by hand.

HAND HARVESTING

Corn Pegs

The easiest way to harvest corn by hand is to allow it to hang on the stalk until the plant is dead and brown. Then, move down one row after another, husking the ears and tossing them onto a wagon, cart, or pickup truck. In the past, farmers used many kinds of husking pegs strapped to their fingers or the palm of one hand to rip the husk loose from the ear with one swift downward motion. The original husking peg was a simple piece of wood or bone about ¼-inch in thickness, sharpened to a point at one end, and held in the middle joint of the fingers of the right hand. A string or leather thong held it to the fingers. The husker would slash open the husk with the point of the peg, grab a section of husk between thumb and peg, and tear it off the ear. You can do the same with your fingers, but it takes longer and is harder on the fingers.

Husking Peg.

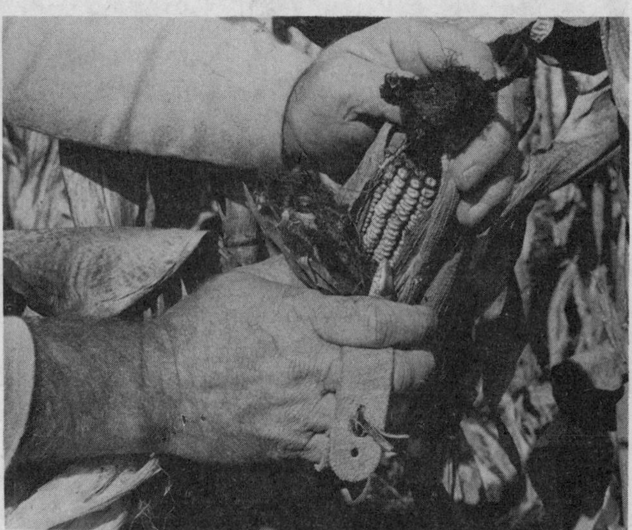

Stripping the husk away.

Over the years, improvements came to the husking peg, the ultimate being a sort of fingerless leather glove with a steel plate riveted to it. The plate had a steel hook on it which ripped open the husk when the husker ran the palm of his hand down the ear of corn. A good husker could perform this operation with amazing speed and skill and could husk a bushel of corn from the stalks in less than a minute.

Corn Knives

A simple tool called a corn knife, shaped like a sword or machete, is used to cut stalks about 4 inches from the ground. Some have long handles and serrated edges.

Corn Knife.

Chopping cornstalks with a corn knife.

NORTH AMERICAN SOURCES OF CORN-HARVESTING TOOLS

	CORN PEGS	CORN KNIVES	MACHETES & HARVESTING KNIVES
AMES		X	
BELKNAP, INC.		X	X
COLUMBIAN CUTLERY CO.		X	X
CUMBERLAND GENERAL STORE	X	X	X
GLEN-BEL'S COUNTRY STORE		X	
LEHMAN GOOD NEIGHBOR CATALOG	X		
A. M. LEONARD & SON, INC.			X
BEN MEADOWS CO.			X
MOTHER'S GENERAL STORE CATALOG			X
NASCO AGRICULTURAL SCIENCES		X	X
NORTHEAST CARRYING TRADING CO.		X	
SEYMOUR MFG. CO.		X	
THE UNION FORK & HOE CO.		X	

INTERNATIONAL SOURCES OF CORN-HARVESTING TOOLS

	CORN KNIVES	MACHETES & HARVESTING KNIVES
FERFOR		X
KUMAR INDUSTRIES		X
LASHER TOOLS PTY., LTD.	X	X
RALPH MARTINDALE & CO., LTD.		X
SHW SCHWABISCHE HUTTENWERKE GMBH		X
SELF-SUFFICIENCY AND SMALL-HOLDING SUPPLIES		X
SOCIETE DES FORGES TROPICALES		X
FRANZ SONNLEITHNER K.G.		X
SPEAR & JACKSON TOOLS, LTD.		X
SYNDICAT DE L'OUTILLAGE AGRICOLE ET HORTICOLE		X
UBUNGO FARM IMPLEMENTS		X
WOLF AND BANGERT WERKEUGFABRIK		X

MECHANICAL CORN HARVESTERS

Corn Binder

Rarely used anymore, a corn binder could still be handy on a homestead if one could be found in running order. Just as with grain, the binder cuts the stalks of corn with a small reciprocating sickle bar, then bunches and binds the stalks into bundles with an automatic tier. Binders were made for use with both horses and tractors, and some were powered by the tractor's power take-off.

Corn Picker

The commonly accepted colloquial name for the machine that replaced binders and the old method of harvesting corn is a corn picker. The picker strips the ear off the stalk as the machine moves down the row, husks the ear, and tosses it into a trailing wagon, leaving the stalk standing. One-row pickers are commonly available in the Corn Belt region of the United States and would suit many small homestead operations.

An old one-row, pull-type corn picker with a conveyor and PTO connection.

Mechanical single- or multiple-row pickers are equipped with snapping rolls to remove the cobs from the standing stalks. The power required to operate the machine is provided by the tractor's power take-off shaft, although self-propelled units or those mounted integrally on the tractor are also available. The machine is provided with a gatherer, or header, which guides the standing stalks in a row along a throat to the revolving, snapping rolls, where the cobs are pinched and snapped from the stalk. The cobs then drop onto an elevator system for conveyance to a trailer which is drawn beside or behind the machine. Most harvesters do not cut the stalks from the ground.

A simple, snapper type of corn harvester does not remove the husks from the cob, while a picker-husker is equipped with a husker attachment for removing the husks after snapping. A more recently developed machine is capable of shelling corn in the field after snapping and husking; another type can also shred the standing stalk after the cobs have been removed. Corn harvesters are generally classified according to the number of rows harvested and the way in which the machines are attached to the tractor.

SOURCES OF CORN HARVESTERS

New Idea One-Row Snapper and Superpicker

New Idea offers two corn pickers which can be operated with a minimum of a 35 or 40 h.p. tractor, with power to spare for pulling a loaded wagon behind. The picker removes husks but leaves kernels on the cob while the snapper leaves husks on as well. The picker weighs 2,400 pounds, the Snapper less than 2,000 pounds.

AVCO Corp., New Idea Farm Equipment Div.
First & Sycamore
Coldwater, OH 45828

New Idea Corn Harvester.
Avco Corp.

KMN Single-Row Corn Chopper Model MBJ

The model MBJ harvests corn as a forage crop at a rate of approximately 30 tons per hour when operating at a speed of 4.35 mph. Power is supplied by the power take-off shaft of a 30 h.p. or larger tractor. It is 8 feet long and weighs 860 pounds. A larger model, MB-37 is also available.

KMN Modern Farm Equipment, Inc.
12 Sullivan St.
Westwood, NJ 07675

Corn Combines

A corn combine is the same machine as a grain combine, but it has a different header and different screens. It picks, husks, and shells the corn in one operation. Just as many large American-manufactured combines are interchangeable for wheat and corn, so too are many of the smaller combines discussed earlier in this chapter.

ROOT CROPS

Root crops like potatoes, cassava, and sweet potatoes, which form their fruits under the soil, are usually grown in small acreages; so the high cost of specialized harvesting equipment is not justified by the amount of labor saved or the increase in output. However, a number of universal root-harvesting machines have been developed which can be used for a number of similar crops with only minor modifications to some of the parts. This way, the capital cost of the harvesting machine can be distributed over a number of crops, a particular advantage for the diversified organic farm.

The simplest and oldest implement for harvesting potatoes, still in use for small-scale work, is the potato-raising plow. A modified moldboard digger raises the potatoes from the ground onto prongs which sift the tubers from the soil.

The elevator-digger for potatoes carries a metal elevator chain composed of parallel links, which run on agitator sprockets behind the lifting share. The soil is shaken through the links of the chain web, and the potatoes are delivered partially clean at the rear of the machine in a narrow row ready to be gathered by hand. Taking the process one step further, some harvesters have another set of chains working either behind or at right angles to the first one to deliver the potatoes to an accompanying cart.

The most difficult operation in potato harvesting is the separation of stones and clods which are about the same size as the potatoes. It is necessary to follow harvesting with a step for separating the potatoes from the debris by hand. At this time, the potatoes are usually graded for size and quality.

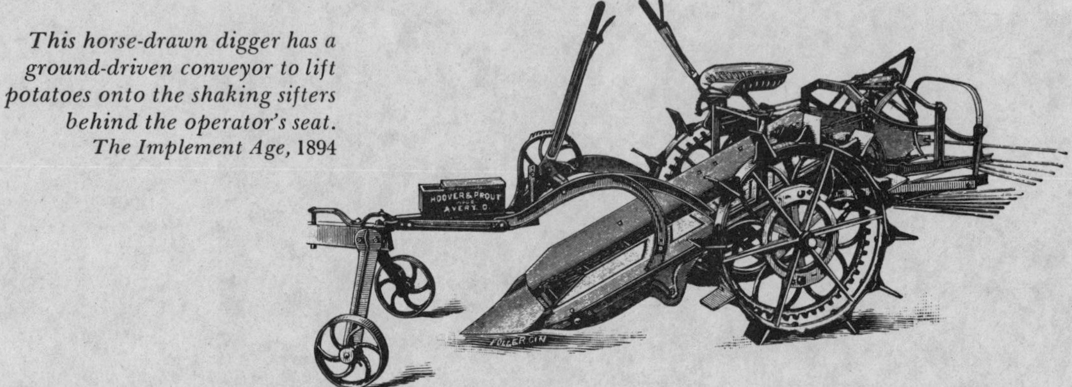

This horse-drawn digger has a ground-driven conveyor to lift potatoes onto the shaking sifters behind the operator's seat. The Implement Age, 1894

SOURCES OF HARVESTING PLOWS

I.D.C.-Bornu Groundnut Lifter and I.T. Groundnut Lifter Plans

The I.D.C.-Bornu Groundnut Lifter was originally developed in a joint USAID/Ministry of Agriculture project at Maiduguri for the savanna area of northern Nigeria. This tool was later introduced by the I.D.C.-Zaria for manufacture by local blacksmiths, and it was more recently adapted for local manufacture at the I.T.D.G. Project at Magoye, Zambia. The lifters have no sifting tines but were designed specifically for groundnut raising (peanuts and legumes).

Intermediate Technology Publications, Ltd.*
9 King St.
London WC2E 8HN, England

Hert Digger

Digging five times faster than a hand tool,

* Intermediate Technology publications can be ordered from International Scholarly Book Service, Inc., Box 555, Forest Grove, Oregon 97116.

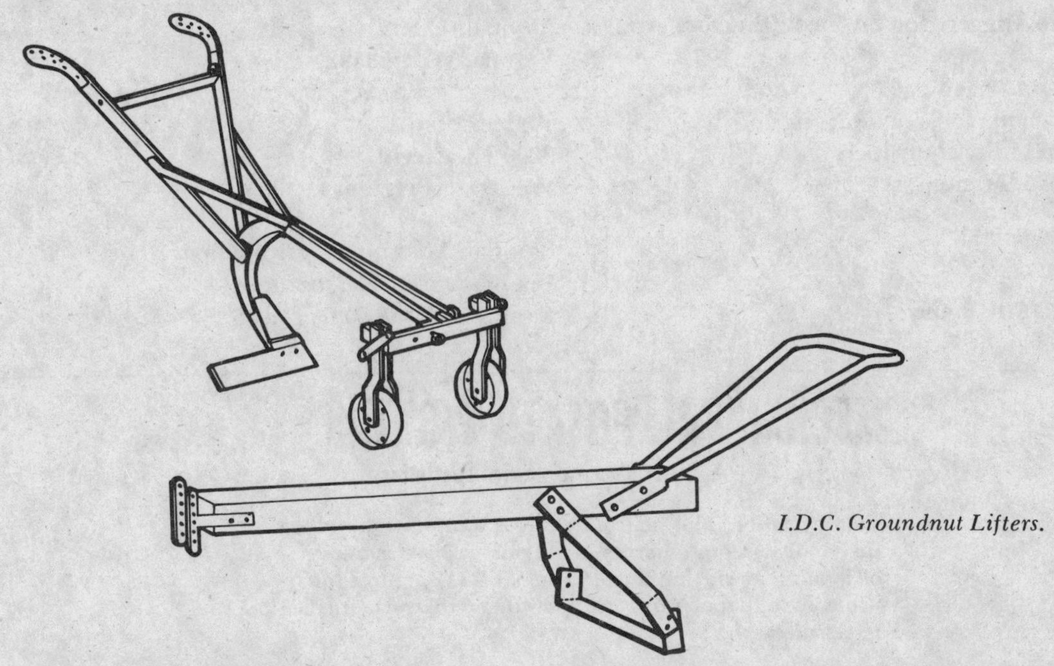

I.D.C. Groundnut Lifters.

The Hertecant potato-raising plow, mounted on an Agria two-wheel tractor.
Willem Hertecant

this digger is attached to a multipurpose main body. Other attachments include a hoe and ridger. The digging element weighs 37.5 pounds, the forecarriage 55.2 pounds. There is a choice of a single or double handle, made to order.

W. Hertecant
9200 Kwatrecht
Wetteren, Belgium

AEBI Potato-Harvesting Attachment

With their model AM 75 two-wheel tractor, AEBI offers a potato digger with a longsifting provision for rooting out potatoes and leaving them piled on top of the soil in a neat row. It is adapted for operation on a 35-percent slope.

AEBI & Co. AG
CH-3400
Burgdorf, Switzerland

AEBI Potato Harvester
AEBI and Co.

Other Potato Diggers for 2-Wheel Tractors Are Made By:

AMC Equipments
Bienvillers 6211 Fonequevillers
Boite Postale 5, France

Bouyer
B.P. 23
Tomblaine 54510, France

Pasquali U.S.A.
Verona, WI 53592

W. Hertecant
9200 Kwatrecht
Wetteren, Belgium

Pasquali Macchine Agricole s.p.a.
Via Nuova, 30, Calenzano
Firenze 50041 FI 082, Italy

MECHANICAL POTATO PICKERS*

by A. A. Stone and Eric Patterson

Editor's note: This article describes some of the old-time tools of potato harvesting. Looking back is a way of looking ahead for small farmers who recognize the value of old tools and can put them to work in a modernized way.

Before many years, the job of picking potatoes will be entirely a machine operation. Hand labor has been eliminated in nearly all of the other operations necessary to potato growing, and machines are even now on the market that eliminate the laborious job of hand picking.

Two types of mechanical potato pickers were used at the New York State Institute of Applied Agriculture at Farmingdale in 1929. These were picking machines only and had no sorting or grading attachment. Each of these machines employs a different principle.

In one, the potatoes are carried upward on the picker-elevator and emptied into bags at the rear of the elevator. While passing up the elevator, men on both side platforms must discard the vines, trash, and stones to prevent them from being bagged with the potatoes. The successful operation of this machine requires thorough separation at the digger, so that the load falling on the picker-elevator is reasonably clean. For best results, it should be used with a power-driven digger having a seven-foot main elevator, and either the usual vine turner and shaker or an extension elevator in the rear of the main elevator.

The other type was used for digging the entire crop on the Institute farm. The trash and vines are carried directly over the rear of the picker-elevator and dropped to the ground. The potatoes are picked off the long elevator by hand and placed in small conveyors at either side of the rear platform. Each side conveyor delivers through a two-way chute, permitting four bags to be carried.

The digger-elevator delivers its load directly to the main elevator of the picker. No vine turner or extension elevator is used on the digger. It was found that having a man on the digger to throw off the heaviest part of the vines and trash greatly lessened the work of the men on the picker.

No attempt was made to keep accurate figures showing the labor-saving or timesaving value of the machine, as the chief interest was in testing it from a mechanical standpoint. Various observers agreed, however, that it reduced the time usually required by 30 to 50 percent. The use of the picker made continuous digging possible, whereas with handpicking methods, the digging proceeds so much faster than the picking that the digger is kept idle much of the time waiting for the pickers to catch up. Digging proceeded at the rate of about two hours per acre.

There was an indication that some potatoes were bruised in passing over the picker. It was difficult to determine just where this bruising occurred, but it seemed to be on the main elevator of

* Reprinted with permission from *Agricultural Engineering*, September 1930.

One of the first mechanical potato harvesters built, though obsolete for large farms, still satisfies the needs of today's small farmer.

The best way to find an old forgotten tool is to scour the countryside and rummage through the weeds.

the picker, as potatoes passing up this elevator would occasionally be jostled, due to uneven ground, and would roll down the elevator, striking the bottom with sufficient force to cause the bruising. It was also noted that quite a number of small potatoes were left on the ground. These were believed to have sifted through the links of the digger-elevator. This was not considered a serious fault, as many growers prefer to leave such small potatoes in the field.

A tractor with a slow forward speed is necessary to use this picker. First or low speed was found to give the best results. It was necessary to idle down the tractor motor considerably in order to reduce the forward speed sufficiently. Where a traction type of digger is used, this reduction in forward speed would, in ordinary years, cause poor separation at the digger, but this year it made little difference. Probably an engine-driven or a power take-off-driven digger would be better than a traction digger for use with a potato picker.

THE TINKERING FARMER

Moving ahead by studying the past, Curtis Johns of Upper Sandusky, Ohio has built himself a small potato digger and he hopes to go into production soon. He fashioned it after a traditional design from spare and older parts to custom fit a category 0 or 1 three-point hitch on a tractor with 14 or more horsepower.

Johns' family and his daughter's family plant four or five acres of potatoes each year for their own personal use and a few more for sale. Such a large project called for something more than a potato hook with which to harvest, so he designed his own harvester. Johns is a tinkerer of the first degree, and the digger was by no means his first project. He has turned an old horse-drawn planter into a two-row corn planter and adapted a rotary hoe to the three-point hitch of his garden tractor.

The front blade of the digger is 15 inches wide to get the whole mound of potatoes and skims along under the ground. Potatoes slide up a drag chain onto shaking tines which sift the soil away. Then the potatoes roll back behind the digger onto the ground. The escalating chain and vibrating tines are powered by an independent 5 horsepower gasoline engine mounted on the rear end of the digger.

Curtis Johns' homemade potato digger.

Johns' digger at work.

One prerequisite of the digger is that it be used with a slow-gear tractor, one with a creeper gear if possible. Johns uses an Economy tractor; he is a dealer. In its lowest gear, the digger will harvest 300 feet of potatoes in 15 minutes. He is thinking of attaching a catch pan to collect the potatoes but, says Johns, "I prefer to let them fall on the ground and dry a little. They'll keep a lot better in storage."

Texas Potato Digger

Angle iron, discarded coulters or discs, an old road grader blade, some round metal bars, a few scrap steel plates, and a few bolts are all the necessary parts for building this potato digger. It attaches to a three-point hydraulic lift. The design originated at the Texas Agricultural Extension Service of the Texas A & M University System.

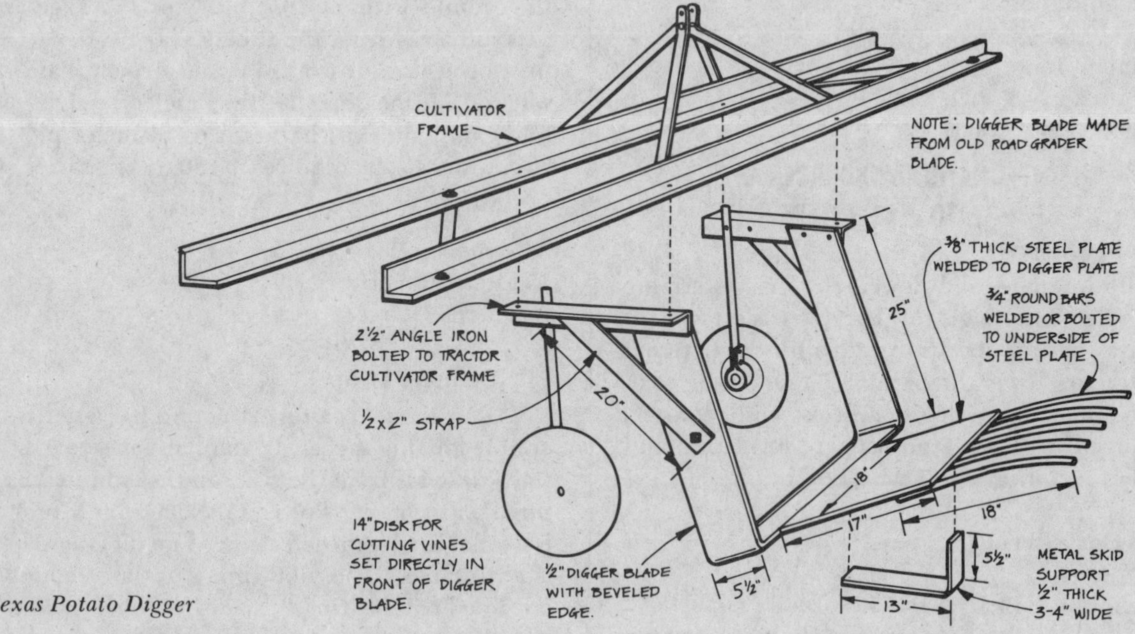

Texas Potato Digger

NORTH AMERICAN SOURCES OF POTATO HARVESTERS

P & S Digger

One-row, two-row, and wide-row, tractor-mounted, sweet potato diggers are available from this company. Mounted from a three-point hydraulic lift system, the depth is easily adjusted from the operator's seat. No additional supporting or gauge wheels are necessary. The one-row harvester can be pulled by a 25 h.p. tractor. A 26-inch wide digging shovel and shaker chain are used to insure lifting and cleaning of all potatoes in the row. Harvesters for grading by hand labor are also available.

H.S. Shoemaker & Son
Rayville, LA 71269

Dahlman Small Root Crop Digger

Suggested for use with a 25 to 40 h.p. tractor, this small root crop digger is used for harvesting potatoes, onions, beets, rutabagas, turnips, parsnips, sweet potatoes, carrots, and other bulb roots.

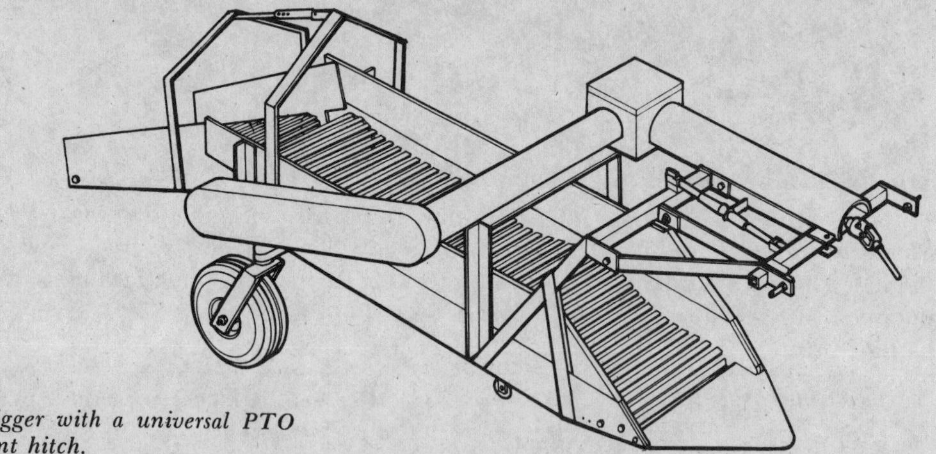

The Dahlman Potato Digger with a universal PTO connection and three-point hitch.

Dahlman, Inc.
540 Broadway S, P.O. Box 504
Braham, MN 55006

INTERNATIONAL SOURCES OF POTATO HARVESTERS

Turnill Diggers

Both single- and double-row harvesters are available. The single-row harvester is fitted with a V-drawbar for operation with a lift bar between the tractor lower limbs and PTO drive, combined pneumatic depth wheels, disc coulters (scalloped) with screw adjustment for depth, and 16- by 4-inch heavy-duty wheels.

Root Harvesters Ltd.
Fengate
Peterborough PE1 5BD, U.K.

Hellas Potato Extractor

The Hellas harvester extracts potatoes from the ground without any injury or blockage and sifts soil away from the tubers as they are carried up an elevator. It works in sandy, rocky, hard, or soft soil. It measures 1.4 by 3 meters, weighs 400 kilograms, and will harvest a 1,000-meter plot in 20 minutes. It requires a 30 h.p. tractor to pull it.

Altermon S.A.
15 Messogion Str.
Athens 609, Greece

Elli Deidone M Sp D

This model is a towed potato harvester with double-floating sieve. It handles one row at a time, unloads from the side, and is mounted by a three-point hitch. Power take-off from a tractor is by means of a carden shaft. The digging depth is adjustable. The vibrating parts are mounted on sealed ball bearings.

Fratelli Deidone Macchine Agricole
C.C.I.A.N. 59212, Casella Postale 7
Villafranca Di Verona, Italy

Agromet 2610

This unit digs potatoes from two rows simultaneously, cleans them on the lath conveyors, and lays them down in a narrow strip running along its side. High-efficiency performance on level ground as well as on slopes recommends this machine for farmers who grow potatoes on medium and medium-heavy soils.. It is equipped with a hydraulic system which steers its wheels, while a suspension frame prevents skidding on slopes and insures precise steering control. The construction element is a transversal conveyor with rubber-coated laths, belt, and side screen. Its working width is 125 centimeters; potato ridge spacing is 63 centimeters, and the working depth is up to 25 centimeters. The digger has an output of 5 hectares per hour and a power requirement of 14 h.p. The KEP-2 model is for light or medium soils, digs two rows at one time, and requires 25 h.p. or more to operate.

Agromet Motorimport
Foreign Trade Enterprise
Warszawa, Przemystowa, Poland

CeCoCo Potato Digger

This Potato Digger scoops up the buried potatoes with a digging blade. The mass of soil and potatoes is delivered to a traveling link elevator which is agitated up and down to sift soil through the links. A two-row type, powered by the PTO pulley of a 30 h.p. tractor, it has a capacity of 1.25 to 1.5 acres per hour and a working width of 1,240 millimeters.

CeCoCo
P.O. Box 8, Ibaraki City
Osaka Pref. 567, Japan

Hert Digger-Aligner Model PR-71

Designed for potatoes and sugar beets, the digger-aligner fits all tractors with a three-point linkage and a minimum of 15 h.p. It consists of a sturdy frame carrying the sieves which are actuated from the power take-off through connecting rods and link mechanisms. The unit handles easily on slopes of up to 18 percent. It digs and aligns two rows of potatoes at distances from 60 to 80 centimeters. A different set of sieves is necessary for sugar beets. Three rows of beets set at different distances will be dug and dropped together in one row.

Hert Digger-Aligner for Potatoes.
Willem Hertecant

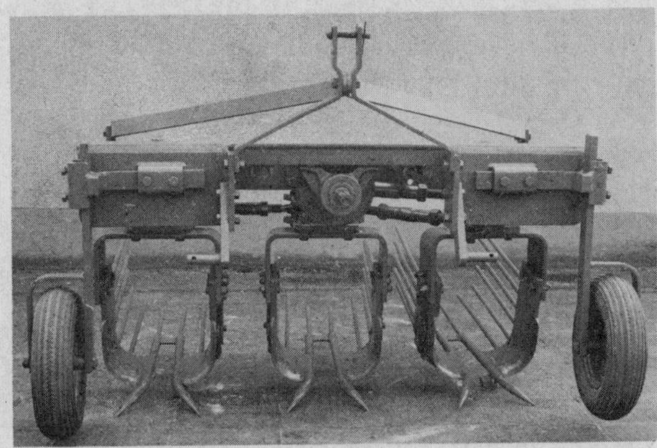

Hert Digger-Aligner for Sugar Beets.
Willem Hertecant

W. Hertecant
9200 Kwatrecht
Wetteren, Belgium

Champenois Potato Digger

The only design of its type seen as yet, this potato digger attaches to a tractor three-point hitch and power take-off shaft. A digging plate raises the potatoes from the ground and feeds them into a set of revolving tines. The tines flip the potatoes against a 1-inch soft mesh netting;

Champenois Potato Digger.
Champenois

the small stones and soil pass through, and potatoes drop in a line along the soil surface.

Champenois
Chamouilley
52170 Chevillon, France

HARVESTING NUTS

Anyone who owns several nut trees or has planted a small crop of groundnuts has no doubt been confronted with problems at harvest time. The equipment necessary for small enterprises simply is not readily available. Harvesting a nut crop may require hours of back-breaking labor to collect the nuts by hand or a substantial financial investment to purchase the large machinery designed for commercial ventures. We found only two devices which gather fallen nuts from under trees and spare the operator repeated bending over.

Stand-Up Pickup Pecan Gatherer

Designed to gather pecans and other nuts, this device has been in use since 1957. It is constructed of a spring-steel wire cage which can harvest nuts of many different sizes and permit the operator to remain in a standing position. Gathering occurs as the nuts are pressed between the wires of the cage, and when the wires return to their original position, the nuts are now contained within the cage. The nuts are released by catching the two punch-outs on the rim of a bucket and pushing forward. Should the wires wear out, replacements are available.

The Ray Griffith Co., Inc.
705 Sumrall Rd.
Columbia, MS 39429

Pecan Picker-Up-Er

Originally designed for pecan harvesting, this simple implement can be used to pick up most kinds of fallen nuts from the ground. The device is composed of a wire spring formed into a semicircle, with a long handle. Nuts are collected by pressing the spring onto the nut—the wires separate, then return to their normal position with the nuts inside. To remove the nuts, the tool is simply held upside down over a container.

H & K Co.
715 Camden St.
San Antonio, TX 78215

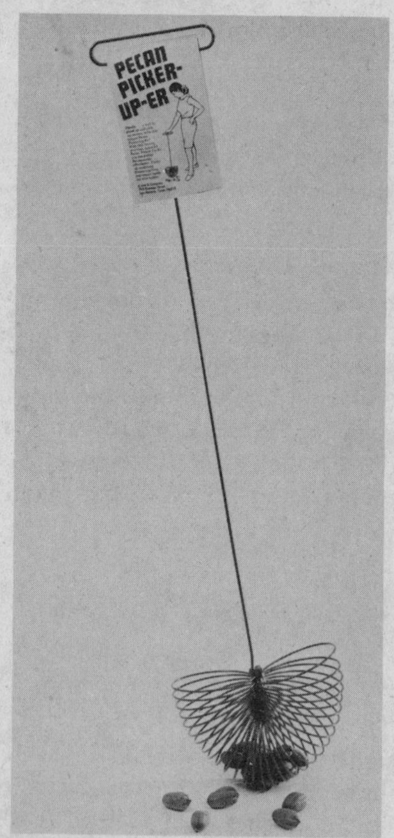

H and K Picker-Up-Er
H and K Co.

–7– Cleaning Grains and Seeds

After harvest, a grain, bean, or seed crop may need to be broken away from its stalk, separated from the inedible protective chaff, and cleaned of dust, dirt, and pebbles before it is ready for human consumption. The operations for completing these tasks are called threshing, winnowing, and cleaning. Grain to be used as seed proceeds one step further, through a separator. This process provides a product of uniform size and removes any misshapen seed which might not germinate.

In most parts of the world except North America, small-scale machinery for threshing, winnowing, and cleaning is available in abundance, especially in the Far Eastern countries. Until recently, a North American farmer had only three choices—using a primitive flail and hand winnower, antiques, or expensive combine harvesters which combine the harvesting and processing operations into one. We have uncovered numerous sources of tools to fill this gap, but most of them are foreign to the North American market. We can offer three points of encouragement, however:

1) Most manufacturers are willing to export to North America.
2) Many North American manufacturers have

The inscription "June 19, 1877. Try Me Once" should perhaps read "Try Me Once Again," as the value of old farm equipment is realized anew.

An old stationary thresher belt-driven from a pulley on the tractor power-take-off shaft.

An old stationary thresher in the field.
Dr. B. N. Ghosh

shown an interest in starting production on new tools and implements, given a market for their products.

3) The techniques are simple, and enough build-it-yourself plans are available for you to satisfy your own needs.

HAND THRESHING

The simplest method of hand threshing involves spreading a large, clean cloth (an old bedsheet is fine) on the floor of a barn or garage, laying a bundle of wheat on the sheet and beating it with an old rake, broom handle, or other appropriate club. The wheat heads do not have to be struck hard, for the grain will shatter out quite easily onto the sheet.

As another alternative, grain can be dislodged by allowing farm horses or bullocks to trample on unthreshed stalks. Threshing by trampling, however, is neither particularly efficient nor very hygienic, because of the possible contamination of grain from animal excreta.

In hand threshing, not every grain will fall out of the seed heads. But it need not go to waste. The bundles already flailed can be given to the chickens; they will pick out any grains missed, and the straw becomes their bedding. Each bundle of wheat will have a cup or two of grain in it. After several bundles are flailed, the corners of the sheet are pulled together, and the grain, chaff, and bits of straw are dumped into a bucket.

There are other alternatives to harvesting and threshing by hand, even for small-plot growers. Threshers and hullers are still very much used by the seed-processing trade, of course, but these machines are usually too expensive to be practical for homesteaders. But shredders will do a crude job of threshing grain in addition to performing their usual functions. Modifications, such as taking out every other blade or removing the screen completely, might improve the quality of the shredder's threshing work. The motor can be geared down so it will run the shredder more slowly. Wheat can even be threshed with a lawn mower, so long as a board is placed to one side to block the grain from being scattered too far by the blade.

ANIMAL-DRAWN THRESHERS

A fairly recent development in threshing by animal power that is much faster than trampling, is the Olpad thresher. It consists of some 20 serrated or ribbed metal discs arranged in three rows on a metal frame which is pulled by a pair of bullocks. A wooden beam or a suitable length of chain or rope can be used to hitch the animals to the frame. The output of the thresher is estimated to be four to five times that of a pair of bullocks threshing by trampling. Solid, cylindrical rollers and spiked wheel models are available, and ordinary animal-drawn disc harrows can also be used for this operation.

SOURCES OF ANIMAL-DRAWN ROLLER THRESHERS

Stone-Threshing Roller

This roller is tapered so that it can easily be pulled round in circles over the crop by the animals.

Dandekar Brothers
Engineers & Founders
Sangli, Maharashtra, India

Olpad Thresher

This unit has serrated discs 450 millimeters (18 inches) in diameter, and an angle iron frame. Discs are mounted on a steel shaft and cast-iron spools keep them in position. A seat with a back, footrests, and back and front guards are provided for the operator's safety. An extra raking attachment can be fitted for stirring straw during the threshing operation. This thresher is available in 20-, 14-, 11-, and 8-inch disc sizes.

Cossul & Co. Pvt. Ltd.
Industrial Area, Fazalgunj
Kanpur, India

Cossul Bullock-Driven Olpad Thresher
Cossul & Co.

Olpad Thresher

This model has 14 discs and transport wheels.

Rajasthan State Agro Industries Corp., Ltd.
Virat Bhawan, C-Scheme
Jaipur 302 006, Rajasthan, India

The Rasulia Bladed Roller Thresher Plans

This thresher is apparently suitable for all types of corn and similar crops, and could be made and used anywhere where bullocks are available and suitable local craftsmen and materials can be found. It has proved to be 60 percent more efficient than the traditional Indian method of using bullocks to trample the harvested crop.

Intermediate Technology Publications, Ltd.
9 King St.
London WC2E 8HN, England

TREADLE THRESHERS

Treadle-operated rice threshers are widely used in the Far East. Bunches of straw are held against a revolving drum and the grain is combed out by wire loop teeth. These machines are generally suitable for rice only and not for crops such as wheat, which require a more violent threshing action.

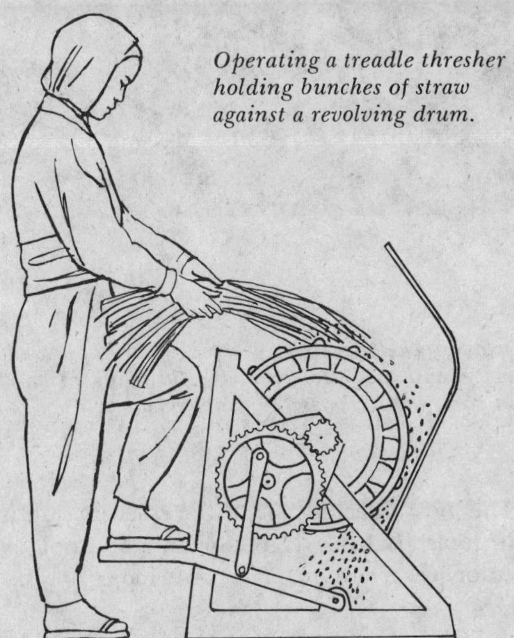

Operating a treadle thresher by holding bunches of straw against a revolving drum.

A FOOT-POWERED THRESHER FOR RICE, SORGHUM, OATS, AND OTHER SMALL GRAINS

by B. David Williams, Jr.

This type of foot-powered thresher is not new. Until more advanced mechanization became widespread in Japan and Taiwan, similar machines were found extensively on small farms in those countries.

Substituting bicycle sprockets and chains for the gear system provides a simple answer to the problem of gears. Bearings from the bicycle pedal shaft are also easily obtained and are adequate for both the drum and the large sprocket shaft. The only sophisticated tools needed to build this thresher are an electric welder and a drill press. Most of the operations can be done with simple hand tools.

Building plans are available for this treadle-powered thresher.
S.P.A.T.F.

Bicycle sprockets and chain replace a complicated gear system. Simple wire loops on the threshing drum knock grain from the stalks as the drum revolves.
S.P.A.T.F.

The most difficult part of the construction is the drum, but if done carefully, it can be made with simple tools. Balance is important, but not overly critical, as the drum spins at only 250 to 300 revolutions per minute. The wire loops on the drum are the teeth which strike the grain from the stalks.

* Reprinted with permission from *Appropriate Technology,* vol. 2 no. 2.

The thresher in operation—the cloth hood keeps threshed grain confined, and the drop cloth collects the kernels.
S.P.A.T.F.

This machine does not separate the chaff from the good grain. As in threshing by hand, the grain must still be winnowed. But the machine does speed up the threshing and is also effective on some tough grains such as sorghum, which often defies hand threshing.

Threshing is done by holding a bundle of unthreshed grain firmly in your hands, beating and twisting the bundle lightly against the drum (which revolves away from you), and throwing the bundle of threshed straw aside. The grains fall down onto a canvas or plastic sheet which is placed under the thresher.

The work of cleaning the grain will be a lot easier if you first put the threshed grain into a box with ½-inch wire mesh screen on top. This will remove many of the broken stems and longer trash.

Those who want a simple, engine-driven thresher can build a similar machine, but with a wider drum of 36 inches, a stronger shaft of ¾ inch, and a large pulley on one side. A three to five horse-power engine will be sufficient, and in this case, approximately 400 revolutions per minute would be best.

A 24-page fully illustrated booklet, "Do-it-Yourself Foot-Operated Thresher Plans," for construction, assembly, and maintenance is available from:

S.P.A.T.F., Office of Village Development
P.O. Box 6937
Boroko, Papua, New Guinea

A condensed version is offered by:
Intermediate Technology Publications, Ltd.
9 King St.
London WC2E 8HN, England

SOURCES OF TREADLE-POWERED THRESHERS

Peanut Thresher Plans

Five pages of fully dimensioned, illustrative plans with complete assembly instructions for a treadle-powered or bicycle-powered peanut thresher are available from:

Cumberland General Store
Rt. 3
Crossville, TN 38555

CeCoCo Light Foot Thresher

This machine separates the grain from paddy sheaths by eliminating the mud, sand, stone, pieces of metal, and other foreign substances contained in the paddy. It is portable and conveniently used in the paddy field at the spot where the crop is harvested. Rotary motion is caused by stepping on the pedal; revolution rate is increased by gears, turning the threshing drum at any required speed. Crops are threshed by placing them against the toothed revolving drum.

The number of pedal strokes ranges from 90 to 100 per minute; the approximate drum speed is 450 rpm. The thresher is capable of threshing paddy at 115 kilograms per hour. It measures 15 cubic feet. Net weight: 50 kilograms: packed weight: approximately 90 kilograms.

CeCoCo Treadle Thresher

CeCoCo
P.O. Box 8, Ibaraki City
Osaka Pref. 567, Japan

Pedal Thresher

This two-man pedal threshing machine can be used for either rice or wheat. Dimensions are 41 by 27 by 26½ inches. Weight: 62 kilograms.

Tien Chien Pedal Thresher
Tien Chien Enterprises

The thresher has a capacity of 500 kilograms per hour.

Tien Chien Enterprises Co., Ltd.
P.O. Box 20-18 Taichung
Taiwan R.O.C.

Pedal Thresher Model TAT-10

This unit can be operated by one or two people. Threshed grain is scattered on the ground so a pickup nylon net or grain box is recommended and is available as optional equipment. Dimensions are 75 by 100 by 70 centimeters. Weight: 61 kilograms. It is also available with a 3 h.p. gasoline motor.

China Agricultural Machinery Co., Ltd.
17 Nanking Rd. East, 1st Sec.
Taipei, Taiwan R.O.C.

Technology Consultancy Center Thesher

This pedal-powered rice and millet thresher is only in the prototype stage. The Technology Consultancy Center is also working on the development of prototype bullock and donkey carts, a winnower for pressing rice oil (60 percent efficiency), and a bellows pump.

Prototype pedal threshers at the Technology Consultancy Center.
Technology Consultancy Center

Technology Consultancy Center
University of Science and Technology
University Post Office, Kumasi
Ghana, West Africa

More Treadle-Power Threshers

American Spring & Pressing Works Pvt., Ltd.
P.O. Box 7602
Malad, Bombay 400 064, India

Cossul and Co. Pvt., Ltd.
Industrial Area, Fazalgunj
Kanpur, India

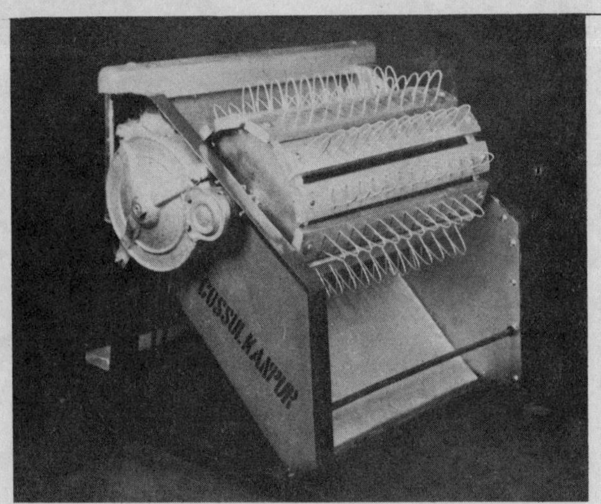

Cossul Treadle Power Thresher
Cossul and Co.

A.P. Rodriquez Agro Industrial Machineries
Bitas
Cabantuan City, Philippines

POWER-OPERATED THRESHERS

In a power thresher, the separation of grain from its stalk is carried out by passing the crop between a revolving drum and a stationary concave. The impact of the drum striking the grain against the concave beats the grain from the ears. In the shape of a half-cylinder, the concave forms a cradle below the threshing drum. It is either solid or grated and is always made of very strong wrought iron or heavy steel.

The revolving drum or cylinder carries a number of steel spikes or fine rasp bars as threshing teeth. Spiked teeth are often found in combines and threshers designed for rice processing. Because most small threshers are designed in rice-producing countries, they generally come equipped with spike-tooth drums which are not as efficient for threshing wheat. Rasp bar drums with fine-tooth spacings on the threshing bar are generally preferred for separating finer seeds from chaff. The threshing body of most modern combines comes equipped with a rasp bar, but both types of cylinders are usually available interchangeably.

Balance is an important factor. A thresher should be set on level ground with the drum carefully balanced to avoid vibration. If it's not level, the movement of grain across the width of the drum is uneven and threshing efficiency is impaired. The gap between the threshing drum and the concave is adjustable, depending upon the grain to be threshed. If the gap is too wide, the grain passes out of the machine with the straw, while too close a setting will break or bruise the grains.

Some small machines operate on a principle similar to the treadle rice threshers, with the crop being held against the revolving drum. But generally the whole crop is passed through the thresher. Spike-tooth drums are found particularly in Asia, where they are favored because they produce thoroughly crushed straw, or bhusa, which is fed to animals.

Threshers without cleaning equipment are often favored by small farmers because they combine high rates of threshing with low power requirements. They can often be driven from the power take-off (PTO) shaft of a two-wheeled tractor or by a gasoline or electric engine. Winnowing is done at the farmstead during slack periods. At this point, threshing is complete.

Plans for this build-it-yourself thresher may be obtained by writing to:
Organic Gardening
Readers' Service
33 E. Minor St.
Emmaus, PA 18049
Enclose a stamped, self-addressed envelope.

THRESHING SEED CROPS

by Rob Johnston

If the crop is small, we often use a homemade flail. For larger crops, we use a Universal Thresher made in Japan by CeCoCo (Central Commercial Company), P.O. Box 8, Ibaraki City, Osaka Pref. 567 Japan. While it is not built as ruggedly as a comparable domestically made machine, it gets the job done satisfactorily and costs a great deal less.

If you don't want to spend $1,000 for a thresher, which is what we paid for ours in 1974, the old models which still exist in this country are worthwhile, if they are in decent condition. In our area, the cost is between $200 and $500. These are usually large machines, powered by a gasoline motor or tractor power take-off with a flat belt. It is possible, however, to mount wheels on an old

Seedsman Rob Johnston threshing soybeans with his CeCoCo Universal Thresher from Japan.
Rob Johnston

thresher so the machine can be towed into the field for on-the-spot threshing. On the other hand, our CeCoCo thresher is small, weighing about 250 pounds, and can be carried short distances by two determined people. We went to a small bother of putting removable (bolted) wheels on one end, which aid in towing. This portable nature is a real plus for the Japanese machine.

The new American-made threshers are rather small units usually trailer-mounted and designed to thresh experimental plots in breeding and testing projects.

Catalogs which list such equipment include:

Burrows Equipment Co.
1316 Sherman Ave.
Evanston, IL 60204

Seedburo Equipment Co.
1022 West Jackson Blvd.
Chicago, IL 60607

NASCO
Ft. Atkinson
WI 53538

NORTH AMERICAN SOURCES OF POWER THRESHERS

VITA Thresher Plans

Volunteers in Technical Assistance (VITA) publishes a number of technical bulletins in response to requests for technical help from organizations and individuals in developing countries. VITA plans include a peanut (groundnut) thresher, soybean thresher, and Godavari rice thresher, as well as a set of guidelines for portable threshers. A complete listing of publications is available from:

VITA
3706 Rhode Island Ave.
Mt. Rainier, MD 20822

14-inch Plot Thresher
K.E.M. Corp.

14-inch Plot Thresher

The Seedburo plot thresher has a 14-inch wide peg-tooth cylinder and is completely self-cleaning. A straw puller is used to slow the material thrown from the cylinder and to meter it evenly into an air blast. Interchangeable screens are placed at the bottom of the air chute to further clean the sample. This thresher has a rasp bar cylinder with 52 teeth, and is mounted on wheels to be moved by hand. It measures 30 by 30 by 20 inches, weighs 200 pounds and is powered by a 3 h.p. gasoline motor (a ¾ h.p. electric motor is optional).

18-inch Bundle Thresher

This thresher is built with a coil spring axle for towing behind a vehicle. It is fully adjustable for small seeds and grains, including soybeans, and has 14-inch diameter cylinders, with eight rasp bars per cylinder. Two fans are used to assist in complete separation. It is powered by a 7.5 h.p. gasoline engine with a hand clutch, fully guarded for safe operation.

18-inch Bundle Thresher
K.E.M. Corp.

Both threshers are available from:

Chain Mfg. Co.
112 N. Kansas Ave.
Haven, KS 67543

K.E.M. Corporation
Box 471
Haven, KS 67543

Seedburo Equipment Co.
1022 W. Jackson Blvd.
Chicago, IL 60606

Small Bundle Plant and Head Thresher

A medium-sized, self-cleaning thresher, this model is suitable for efficiently threshing and air-cleaning single plants, small bundles (heads only) of cereal or grain crops, some types of legumes, and other crops for both yield and purity research experiments. Two styles of cylinders and concaves are available: overshot spiked-type (round or square, depending on the grain to be harvested) or overshot rasping bar-type. The thresher also comes with both styles of cylinders and concaves that are interchangeable on the same machine. It has a self-cleaning metering wheel, removable seed catch pan with recleaning screens, and an air blower. Its heavy-gauge metal housing is mounted on a channel iron frame with rubber-tired wheels and hand truck handles for easy handling. The thresher is approximately 34 inches long, 25 inches wide and 40 inches high. Weight: 190 pounds. Supplied with electric motor or gasoline engine.

Small Bundle Plant and Head Thresher with gasoline engine.
Allan Machine Co.

Small Bundle Plant and Head Thresher with electric motor.
Allan Machine Co.

Large Vogel Nursery Plot Thresher

Vogel plot threshers are one of the most popular makes because they self-clean completely in 8 seconds. The 20-inch-wide cylinder is the overshot type with spiked teeth or optionally equipped with rubber rub bars. The cylinder is fed directly from the feeding pan. A straw puller slows the flow of material from the cylinder and meters it to the shaker pan. A fan removes the straw and chaff from the grain as the threshed material passes over a tail rake. The seed is caught in buckets at the side of the machine. Power is supplied by a 9 h.p. gasoline engine. Approximate overall dimensions: 8 feet

Large Vogel Nursery Plot Thresher
Allan Machine Co.

long, 7 feet high, 40 inches wide. Weight: 1,350 pounds. This thresher has an all-metal construction, except for wooden fan blades and operator's platform.

Small Vogel Thresher

The Vogel head thresher is of the same basic design as the 20-inch Vogel thresher but without the shaker pan. The cylinder is 6 inches wide and is available with spike-teeth or rubber rub bars. Heads only are passed through the cylinder. Straw passed through the cylinder will not be removed from the sample if the straw pieces are heavier than the seed, as is often the case with forage. The thresher is self-cleaning within 3 seconds. It is powered by a ½ h.p. electric motor. Constructed of heavy-gauge metal, it is mounted on a coaster wagon truck for portability. Dimensions, including truck, are 15 by 38 by 46 inches high.

All-Purpose Nursery Plot Thresher

The Allan all-purpose thresher is used to thresh, separate, and clean samples of soybeans, wheat, oats, barley, flax, grasses, and other similar seed without loss. Construction is such that it may be easily inspected and cleaned between samples to prevent cross-contamination. Simple mechanical features permit fast adjustment of the cylinder blowers and shaker sieves to meet varying conditions of crops being threshed.

Standard equipment is an eight-bar, all-metal, rasp bar cylinder, five-bar adjustable concave, beater and straw puller, shaker pan with interchangeable no-choke sieves, adjustable catch pan, and two cleaning fans. A belt variator gives infinitely variable belt speeds to 2,000 rpm without affecting the speed of the shakers and blowers. Optional equipment includes rubber-faced rub bars.

The above threshers are available from:
ALMACO, Allan Machine Co.
P.O. Box 112
Ames, IA 50010

Burrows Equipment Co.
1316 Sherman Ave.
Evanston, IL 60204

Low-Profile Plot Thresher

Constructed with an eight-bar rasp bar cylinder and underslung grated concave, the low-profile thresher is hand fed from ground level. The stationary, towable machine was developed exclusively for threshing small and medium test plots of legumes, cereals, forages, and other

This low-profile plot thresher has a hydraulically operated unit for moving it as operators thresh row after row.
Allan Machine Co.

special crops. It comes with a galvanized metal shaker pan with choice of interchangeable no-choke sieves. With a 7 or 9 h.p. gasoline engine, the unit measures 113 by 40 by 57 inches and weighs 1,250 pounds.

LPT Stationary Thresher

Available in three types of overshot cylinders and concaves, each of which is interchangeable, the thresher will efficiently thresh a wide range of crops from small test plots up to ⅓ acre or larger in size. Cereal grains such as wheat, oats, barley, and sorghums; legumes including soybeans, cowpeas, and field beans; and forage crops such as grasses and sunflowers have been threshed without material loss of seed.

Its simple mechanical features permit easy changes of cylinders and concaves, no-choke sieves, varying cylinder speed, air blower, and seed catch pan to meet varying conditions for each crop being harvested.

Power to operate the standard-equipped thresher is provided by a 9 h.p., single-cylinder, four-cycle, air-cooled, gasoline engine with a rope-pull starter and hand-operated clutch take-off assembly.

The thresher, completely equipped, weighs approximately 1,375 pounds and measures 9 feet long, 5 feet wide, and 5 feet 6 inches high. It is light enough to be moved easily by workers in the field or towed behind a car, truck, or tractor from one area to another.

Researchers feed sheaves into the ALMACO-LPT Stationary Plot Thresher.
Allan Machine Co.

Both threshers are available from:
ALMACO, Allan Machine Co.
P.O. Box 112
Ames, IA 50010

Single-Head Plot Thresher

Single head selections can be easily threshed in this single-head plot thresher. A ribbed rubber roller threshes the head by a crushing action against a spring-loaded rough rubber concave. The concave is hinged to allow the roller and concave to self-clean. A fan is built into the bottom of the thresher to blow out the chaff. The cleaned sample is collected in a small drawer.

L.A. Mennie
1029 Manahan Ave.
Winnipeg 19, Manitoba, Canada

Single-Head Thresher

Single heads or the product of short rows are threshed with this machine. It is self-cleaning, enabling a large number of single heads or small lots to be threshed and cleaned rapidly. The heads are pushed through a funnel-shaped chute to a peg-tooth cylinder. The straw is not passed through. Chaff is thrown into the chaff receiver by the cylinder air blast. The cleaned sample is collected in a drawer at the base.

Bridge & Tank Western, Ltd.
Winnipeg 2
Manitoba, Canada

Kemp Stationary Plot Thresher

The Kemp stationary plot thresher has a spike-tooth cylinder that is 10 inches wide, with a 10-inch diameter base and a 7-foot long separating deck. The openings in the deck are varied in size to act as both a sieve and straw walker. Two blowers are used for cleaning. Unthreshed heads are delivered to a tailings drawer to be passed through the cylinder a second time. The thresher can be used for threshing many crops including clover and forage crops. Peas and beans are threshed by operating the cylinder in reverse.

Bridge & Tank Western, Ltd.
Winnipeg 2
Manitoba, Canada

Roller Thresher

Plant material contained in cotton bags can be threshed by passing the bags through the rollers of this thresher a number of times. Mixing and seed loss are eliminated but the material must be cleaned in a separate cleaning device. The rubber-covered rolls are 14 inches in diameter, and contrarotate differentially at speeds of 50 and 68 rpm.

Roller Thresher
Agriculture Canada

Machine Services and Repair
47 Landsdowne Ave.
Winnipeg 4, Manitoba, Canada

Swanson Plot Thresher

Developed to thresh a wide variety of crops, the Swanson plot thresher has a low profile for easy operation and inspection. A special air device gives precise air adjustments for efficient separation. The 18-inch-wide cylinder and concave are built to close tolerances to eliminate lodging of seeds within the thresher. The cylinder has a speed range from 450 to 900 rpm.

Swanson Machine Co.
24-26 E. Columbia Ave.
Champaign, IL 61820

Harmond-type Plot Thresher

The Harmond-type Plot Thresher has a rubber rasp bar overshot cylinder with a speed control and an rpm indicator. A feeder-beater is used to present the material to the cylinder. Cleaning is by air-assisted sieve action using an adjustable sieve. The thresher has been used on a range of materials from bent grass to pistachio nuts. The capacity is 30 pounds per minute of wheat straw and 10 to 20 pounds per minute of grass straw.

Mater Machine Works
Box 410
Corvallis, OR 97330

Labour-Ear Thresher Walter & Wintersteiger

Adapted from U.S. research models, these threshers were manufactured in the Philippines with the help of the International Rice Research Institute.

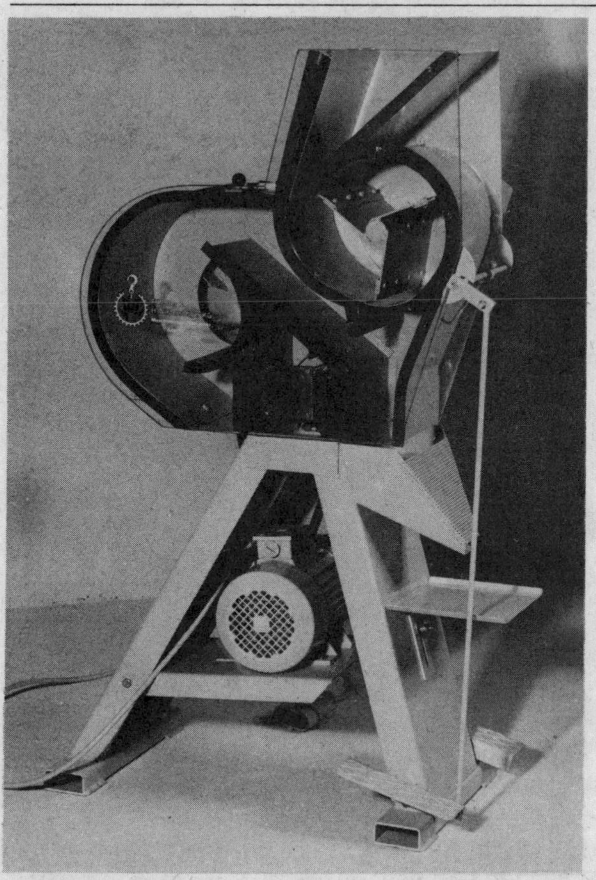

Vogel-type Head Thresher

Vogel-type Plot Thresher
International Rice Research Institute

INTERNATIONAL SOURCES OF POWER THRESHERS

Labour-Ear Thresher

The Labour-Ear thresher for single plants is unique in that it has a clear plastic side so the threshing and cleaning process can be observed. A hinged gate at the bottom of the cylinder keeps the material in the cylinder until threshing is completed. Chaff removal is by a suction fan with cleaned samples collected at an envelope chute. The unit is electrically powered and has variable speed pulleys for changing the cylinder speed. The thresher is claimed to be capable of threshing cereals, grasses, clover, and legumes.

F. Walter & H. Wintersteiger K.G.
4910 Reid im Innkreiss
Frosch allgasse 19, Postfach 124
Dimmelstrasse, Austria

2 TD Thresher

The 2 TD thresher has two threshing cylinders with adjustable concaves. The first cylinder does most of the threshing, while a second cylinder operates at a higher speed to shake and transport the straw during threshing. Cleaning is done by air currents. Straw and chaff are blown out at the top of a cyclone separator and the grain is collected at the bottom. The auxiliary air current necessary to blow the straw out of the top of the cyclone is shut off after each sample is threshed to drop any material held in the airstream. The thresher is powered by a 7 h.p. gasoline or electric motor.

Saat Und Erntetechnik
3440 Eschwege
Postfach 748, Germany

Garvie 14-inch Portable Thresher

This 14-inch-wide portable thresher is available with either a spike-tooth or rubber rub bar cylinder, and has a straw shaker and two cleaning sieves with an air fan. The machine is self-cleaning and can be inspected while it is running. It is powered by a 3 h.p. engine.

A typical Japanese thresher, similar to the treadle designs. This one is powered by a gasoline engine for a higher production capacity.
Agriculture Canada

Garvie Bench Threshers

Garvie bench threshers are available in 10- or 14-inch widths, with spike-tooth or rasp bar beaters and a variety of cleaning apparatus including a winnower, a cleaner (with up to three sieves or with a riddle case), and a fan.

R.G. Garvie & Sons
2 Canal Rd.
Aberdeen, Scotland

CeCoCo Portable Thresher

This is a lightweight, portable, and economical thresher suitable for small-scale rice and wheat growers. The all-metal construction unit is equipped with a 1.5 h.p. gasoline engine. It delivers unbroken grain at a capacity of 180 kilograms per hour.

CeCoCo Self-feeding Power Thresher

The CeCoCo Self-feeding Thresher is made for the purpose of threshing rice or wheat which is reaped as full stalks, gathered, and bound in sheaves. Paddy stalks to be threshed are placed on a feed table attached to the machine and are inserted continuously by hand in small quantities into the feeding end of the rotating chain. Inserted paddy straws are threshed while being shifted by the moving chain under the rotating threshing drum.

SPECIFICATIONS OF CECOCO SELF-FEED POWER THRESHER

Type	Capacity in paddy/hour	Power Required	Rpm		Dimension in mm			Net Weight	Gross Weight	Shipping Measurement
			Rice	Wheat	Height	Width	Length			
No. 1	500-1,000 kg	3-4 h.p.	570	670	1,380	1,010	1,350	150 kg	295 kg	60 cu. ft.
No. 2	400- 800 kg	3-4 h.p.	570	670	1,380	922	1,350	115 kg	255 kg	57 cu. ft.
No. 3	300- 600 kg	2-3 h.p.	570	670	1,374	842	1,350	90 kg	220 kg	54 cu. ft.

SPECIFICATIONS OF CECOCO POWER THRESHERS

Type	Capacity in paddy/hour	Power Required	Rpm		Dimension in mm			Net Weight	Gross Weight	Shipping Measurement
			Rice	Wheat	Height	Width	Length			
No. 1	300-1,000 kg	3-5 h.p.	720	750	1,046	1,070	1,287	144 kg	260 kg	60 cu. ft.
No. 2	approx. 350 kg	½-2 h.p.	530	630	1,090	875	1,370	80 kg	115 kg	35 cu. ft.
No. 3	approx. 450 kg	½-2 h.p.	530	630	1,090	950	1,370	95 kg	130 kg	38 cu. ft.
No. 4	approx. 500 kg	1-2 h.p.	530	630	1,090	1,000	1,370	100 kg	140 kg	40 cu. ft.

CeCoCo Power Thresher No. 1 Double Drum, No. 2, 3, and 4 Single Drum

These units are for long- or short-cut stems of rice, wheat, sunflower seed, and sorghum. The crops are fed by hand into the threshing chamber and a perfectly cleaned grain exits from the outlet on the side of the conveyor-elevator after being completely threshed. The machine is equipped with winnower, conveyor, thrower, and speed adjuster which controls the air velocity.

CeCoCo Universal

CeCoCo Universal Power Thresher Type T25H is capable of threshing various kinds of beans, pulses, rice, sunflower seed, and wheat by replacing the screen and V-belt between the pulleys of the threshing drum and winnower. Separation is adjustable and no winnowing is necessary. Second separation of grain and stalks scattered at the second outlet is also possible; therefore, complete separation can be made without waste. The interchangeable screen can easily be replaced according to the size of grain in order to prevent breakage.

CeCoCo Universal Power Thresher
Rob Johnston

SPECIFICATIONS OF CECOCO UNIVERSAL GRAIN THRESHER

Type	Capacity per hour	Power Required	Rpm	Size of Screen	Dimension in mm	Size of Drum	Net Weight	Gross Weight	Shipping Measurement
T25H	rice 500 kg	2-3 h.p.	550-600	750 × 595mm	1,100 H	756mmW × 364mmφ	115 kg	220 kg	80 cu. ft.
	wheat 500 kg		650-700		1,300 W				
	beans 1,500 kg	3-5 h.p.	250-550		1,500 L				

CeCoCo Bean Thresher

The CeCoCo bean thresher is made for threshing various beans and seeds of full length or short stalks. The materials are fed into the threshing chamber and threshed by a threshing drum with multiteeth. Only the pure and complete beans or seeds are carried by the screw conveyor to the vertical screw elevator, and then outside through the outlet of the elevator. Screens are easily interchangeable.

SPECIFICATIONS OF CECOCO BEAN THRESHER

Type	Capacity per hour	Power Required	Rpm	Dimension in mm			Net Weight	Gross Weight	Shipping Measurement
				Height	Weight	Length			
M	30 ares in soybean	2-3 h.p.	600-650	1,010	860	1,010	110 kg	160 kg	50 cu. ft.

CeCoCo Peanut Thresher

This machine will thresh peanuts from peanut plants harvested with vines. Care should be taken to give proper speed of revolution to the machine. If it is too fast, it will damage not only the husks but also the kernels. If it is too slow, it will mix stalks, because imperfect separation will retard the threshing efficiency.

SPECIFICATIONS OF CECOCO PEANUT THRESHERS

Type	Capacity per hour	Power Required	Rpm	Dimension in mm Height	Width	Length	Net Weight	Gross Weight	Shipping Measurement
No. 1	0.37 acre	2 h.p.	350	1,400	1,000	1,260	150 kg	280 kg	80 cu. ft.
No. 2	0.25 acre	1 h.p.	350	1,380	830	1,230	115 kg	200 kg	65 cu. ft.

The above threshers are manufactured by:
CeCoCo
P.O. Box 8, Ibaraki City
Osaka Pref. 567, Japan

Porta-fast Grain Thresher

This is a mini-size portable thresher for easy transport for in-field operation. With a built-in winnower and 5 h.p. gasoline motor, it has a capacity of 12 to 20 CAV per hour and 15 to 25 CAV per hour with an 8 h.p. motor.

Jamandre Industries, Inc.
88 Rizal St.
Iloilo City 5901, Philippines

Small-Capacity Motor-Driven Thresher Model TDG-400

Designed mainly for threshing rice and wheat, this machine adapts well to wet threshing work. The machine consists primarily of a main drum, auxiliary drum, feed chain, sieves, grain conveyor, winnowing fan, and a 5.4 h.p. electric motor. It can thresh 600 to 1,000 kilograms of rice or 350 to 750 kilograms of wheat per hour. It weighs 164 kilograms and measures 130 by 1,392 by 1,150 millimeters.

China Agricultural Machinery Import and Export Corp.
Tientsin Branch 14, Chang Teh Road
Tientsin, China

Thresher Models D710S, D610S, and D510S

The differences in Iseki's three models stem from the three different cylinder widths: 500, 400, and 355 millimeters, respectively. Its power requirements range from 0.7 to 4.5 h.p. for an output capacity ranging from 10 to 30 ares (one are = $\frac{1}{20}$ acre) per hour.

Iseki Agricultural Machinery Mfg. Co., Ltd.
2-1-3 Nihonbashi, Chuo-ku
Tokyo 13, Japan

Iseki Power Thresher
Agriculture Canada

Bel-500 Thresher

This unit was specially designed for stationary threshing and for cleaning corn and beans. It requires a 5 to 7 h.p. electric motor, or it can be run from a tractor's PTO. It will produce from 6,614 to 7,937 pounds per hour, tractor- or horse-drawn.

Laredo Cereal Thresher
Model Bel-500
Laredo

Laredo S.A.
Rua 1 de Agosto, 11-67-17.100
Bauru (SP) Brazil

TY-200

This unit threshes grains while separating leaves and roots from the grain with the powerful blower. It can be used with damp crops, weighs 120 kilograms, and measures 68 by 45 by 39 inches. It has an output of 1,000 kilograms per hour using a 5 to 6 h.p. motor.

Tien Chien Enterprises Co., Ltd.
P.O. Box 20-18 Taichung
Taiwan R.O.C.

Tien Chien Thresher
Tien Chien Enterprises

Agrima Rice Thresher Model TAP-20

This is a 3 h.p., gasoline engine thresher adapted from a treadle unit. It measures 55 by 120 by 68 centimeters and weighs 69 kilograms.

China Agricultural Machinery Co. Ltd.
17 Nanking Road, East, 1st Sec.
Taipei, Taiwan R.O.C.

Midget II Thresher

The Midget MKII is comprised of a basic

Alvan Blanch Midget II
Alvan Blanch Development Co.

rasp bar drum and concave, feed shute, and discharge cowl, and a collecting tray with a canvas shield. It requires 3 h.p. and can be driven by a gasoline or electric engine or tractor PTO. It weighs 280 pounds, measures 1 foot 11 inches by 4 feet 8 inches by 6 feet 3 inches and puts out up to 1,500 kilograms per hour of rice. Its other suggested uses include wheat, barley, oats, beans, peas, sorghum, maize, and millet.

Super Midget II

Requiring 5 h.p., this unit will put out up to one ton of rice per hour. Other larger units are also available.

Alvan Blanch Development Co., Ltd.
Chelworth, Malmesbury
Wiltshire, SN16 9SG, England

Alvan Blanch Super Midget II
Alvan Blanch Development Co.

Small-Size Automatic Thresher

This Indian thresher can be run by a 10 h.p. electric motor, 12 to 14 h.p. gasoline motor, or the PTO of a 14 to 20 h.p. tractor. Larger units are also available.

New Bharat Industries (Regd.)
Industrial Area
MOGA (Punjab) India

Power Wheat Thresher-Cum-Winnower

Fifteen h.p. is required to run this thresher with a 1.06-meter-wide drum for a capacity of 400 to 500 kilograms per hour.

Rajasthan State Agro Industries Corp., Ltd.
Virat Bhawan, C-Scheme
Jaipur 302 006, Rajasthan, India

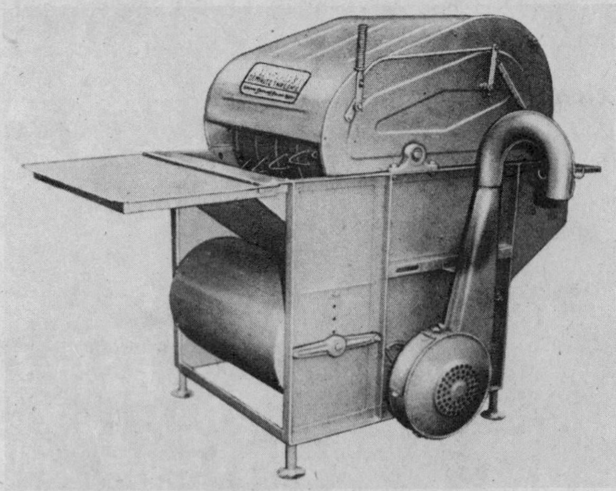

Akshat AK-58 Thresher
American Spring and Pressing Works

Akshat AK-58 Thresher

The Akshat AK-58 consists of a threshing

chamber, separator, dust-discharging device, and a grain-conveying and elevating mechanism. The threshing chamber contains a drum with fifty steel wire loops and a concave grill.

Stalks are held with both hands in a bunch, and the heads are inserted into the threshing chamber. The revolving drum combs out the grain, which falls through the grill into the winnowing chamber. Clean grain is raised by the elevator for bagging. The thresher requires 2 h.p. and can thresh 200 kilograms of rice per hour. Weight: 112 kilograms.

American Spring & Pressing Works Pvt., Ltd.
P.O. Box 7602 Malad
Bombay 400 064, India

Embee Power Thresher

This all-steel thresher is fitted with a threshing cylinder, grain auger, and elevator. The crop bundle is held in both hands and the heads are threshed between the loops of the rotating cylinder and the concave screen. The grain is separated from the chaff by a blower. The unit requires a 2 to 3 h.p. motor to put out 60 to 120 kilograms per hour of rice, or 100 to 150 kilograms per hour of wheat. Martin Burn also offers a conventional model thresher in which the complete crop is fed into the machine rather than just the heads.

Martin Burn, Ltd.
12 Mission Row
Calcutta 1, India

Wheat Thresher

The Wheat Thresher is designed primarily for wheat, although it will handle other crops. It is equipped with a winnowing fan and fills bags automatically. It has an output capacity of 200 kilograms per hour with a 5 h.p. motor.

Union Forgings
Sherpur, G.Y. Road
Ludhiana, Punjab, India

Model 42 Thresher

This simple thresher has no cleaning mechanism. It has an output of 1,300 to 1,600 kilograms per hour of straw and grain and requires approximately 2 h.p. to drive the machine. Larger models with cleaning mechanisms are also available.

Ets Cimon Freres
B.P. 47
50104 Cherbourg, France

ST-70 Thresher-Cum-Winnower

The ST-70 employs a rasp bar drum and concave to thresh rice, wheat, barley, beans, peas, maize, and other crops. It has an 18-inch drum which revolves at from 460 to 1,460 rpm for a wheat output of 1,500 to 2,000 kilograms per hour and a maize output of 3,000 to 4,000 kilograms per hour.

Vicon, Ltd.
Mudambai House, Lavelle Road
Bangalore-1, India

Jeco Threshers

Available in small and large sizes.

Jeco Engineering Co. (Regd.)
Near Shama Cinema, G.T. Road
P.O. Box No. 46
Gujranwala, Pakistan

Vogel-type Paddy Thresher

Similar to the Allan Vogel thresher described earlier, this unit is designed to yield grain of seed quality by avoiding damage to the grain. Damage to the kernel limits its germination capabilities. This machine has a 500-millimeter-wide drum, requires 10 h.p. to run, and produces 500 to 700 kilograms per hour.

Midget Rice Thresher

Similar to the Alvan Blanch Midget II thresher, this unit has a capacity of from 900 to 1,000 kilograms per hour. A 12 h.p. motor is required to run the 690-millimeter-wide drum.

A.P. Rodriguez Agro Industrial Machineries
Bitas
Cabantuan City, Philippines

THE AXIAL FLOW THRESHER

by The International Rice Research Institute

The widespread use of combines for harvesting and threshing crops in developed countries has led to a decline in the production and use of stationary threshers. Yet traditional methods are no longer suitable for threshing large quantities of rice, particularly in areas of multiple cropping. High-moisture paddy is difficult to thresh with conventional threshers available in the less-developed countries. The threshing output of the Japanese stripping-type thresher is generally low, and such machines are difficult to manufacture in less-developed countries. The International Rice Research Institute has developed the axial flow thresher for small- and medium-scale tropical farmers to use either through individual ownership or through contract threshing.

This machine can efficiently thresh rice, sorghum, soybeans, and other small grain crops over a wide range of grain moisture levels with low crop losses. The throw-in feed design and the axial movement of materials are distinguishing features of this machine. Separation and cleaning efficiency are excellent, and power requirements are low.

The thresher is mounted on two large wheels to provide good mobility on rough roads. It can be pulled easily with a power tiller or jeep, or it can be moved manually over shorter distances. A self-propelled version of the thresher has a motorized third wheel mounted on the front. The same seven horsepower engine provides power for threshing and transport. The self-propelled version is designed for custom threshing operations, which often require repeated movement of the thresher. When the ground is too soft to support the wheels, skids are available to attach to the underside of the thresher so that it can be pulled by animals.

The thresher can be powered by a seven to ten horsepower, air-cooled, gasoline engine. Power is transmitted through a series of V-belts to the five major components: the threshing cylinder, delivery auger, centrifugal blower, rotary screen, and aspirator fan. The threshing mechanism consists of a peg-tooth cylinder which rotates inside a full-circle cylindrical concave in two sections. The upper concave has spiral deflectors which move the threshing material axially between the threshing drum and the concaves.

IRRI Axial Flow Thresher
Union Tractor Workshop

This machine is well accepted and is gaining popularity among farmers across the Philippines. Twelve Philippine companies now produce the thresher. It is also being produced on a limited basis in Ghana, India, Indonesia, Pakistan, South Vietnam, Sri Lanka, and Thailand, and is being evaluated in Bangladesh, Guatemala, Peru, Korea, and Malaysia. The machine is being marketed for threshing soybeans and sorghum as well as paddy, and work is underway to adapt it for wheat threshing.

Engineering designs are available to manufacturers who are seriously interested in producing the thresher. Each request must be submitted on company letterheads with a history of the company and a list of available equipment, staff, capital structure, and product lines, along with tentative plans for production and marketing. Write to: The Agricultural Engineering Department, International Rice Research Institute, PO Box 933, Manila, Philippines.

An example of the IRRI-designed axial flow thresher is pictured here, manufactured by the Union Tractor Workshop in India.

7.5 Axial Flow Thresher

This unit was developed for small- and medium-scale farmers to use either through individual ownership or through contract threshing. This machine can efficiently thresh rice, sorghum, soybeans, and other small grain crops over a wide range of grain moisture levels. Distinguishing features of this machine include throw-in feeding, axial movement of materials, low power requirement, and excellent separation and cleaning efficiency. Paddy output is about 1 ton per hour when operated with a three-man crew and a 7.5 h.p. motor.

Union Tractor Workshop
8-B, Phase II, Maya Puri Industrial Area
New Delhi 110 027, India

The spike-toothed threshing cylinder of the Axial Flow Thresher.
International Rice Research Institute

Portable Axial Flow Thresher

The Portable Axial Flow unit has an output of 300 to 600 kilograms per hour of threshed paddy with a 5 h.p. engine. Two or three people are required to feed the machine, thresh, and bag the grain, and two men are required to move it. It has a multicrop capability for rice, sorghum, and other small grains. The unit weighs 105 kilograms with the engine, measures 96 by 76 by 138 centimeters, and uses about 1 liter of fuel per hour.

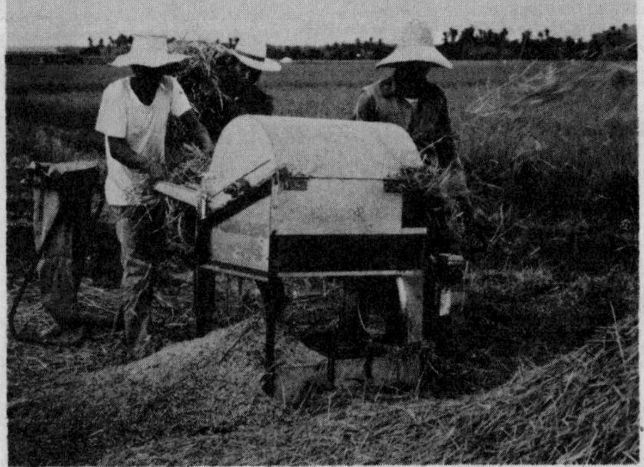

IRRI Axial Flow Thresher in operation in the field.
International Rice Research Institute

International Rice Research Institute
Box 933
Manila, Philippines

POWER DRUMMY THRESHERS

Drummy threshers usually incorporate 12

beaters inside a threshing drum to separate wheat from its hull. A winnowing fan attached under the machine separates straw from the grain but does not leave a cleaned grain; an average of 3.5 percent waste is left. There is no bagging arrangement with most of these machines, though adaptations can be made. The minimum power needed to thresh with a minimum amount of grain breakage is 470 revolutions per minute, as established by the Indian Council of Agricultural Research in New Delhi. At a lower speed, more breakage takes place.

SOURCES OF DRUMMY THRESHERS

Union Tractor Drummy Thresher

This is a very simple machine, particularly suitable for areas where farmers are being introduced for the first time to mechanical threshing. The threshing cylinder is the same as that on a complete thresher-winnower, but the threshed material falls directly onto the ground. A fan blows most of the chaff away from the grain, but some hand winnowing is still necessary.

Two sizes of threshers are available. The 75 centimeter size uses a 5 h.p. motor to produce 150 kilograms per hour and the 90 centimeter size uses a 10 h.p. motor for 250 kilograms per hour.

Union Tractor also has a full range of larger threshers and winnowers available, as well as the Pusa-40 Spike-Tooth Thresher, designed by the Indian Agricultural Research Institute, and the 4T-90 wheat thresher.

Union Tractor Drummy Thresher for the paddy.
Union Tractor Workshop

Union Tractor Wheat Thresher.
Union Tractor Workshop

Union Tractor Workshop is interested in establishing manufacturing facilities in other countries. Interested parties should contact Mr. Jagdish Chander.

Union Tractor Workshop
8-B Phase 11, Mayapuri Industrial Area
New Delhi 110 027, India

Power Threshers

U.P. State Agro Industrial Corp., Ltd.
Agricultural Workshop, Talkatora Road
Lucknow, U.P. India

Allied Drummy Thresher

Drum width on these units comes in five sizes ranging from 2¼ to 3½ feet, for an output of anywhere from 100 to 275 kilograms per hour. There are three 5 h.p. units, one 10, and one 15.

Allied Trading Co.
Railway Road
Ambala City 134 002
Haryana, India

Gepco Drummy Threshers

Gepco makes drummy threshers in three sizes. The 5 h.p. unit has a 76-centimeter drum and threshes at a rate of 180 kilograms per hour.

The 7½ h.p. unit has a 90-centimeter drum and a capacity of 300 kilograms per hour, and the 10 h.p. machine has a 105-centimeter drum and produces 450 kilograms per hour. Other units are also available.

Gepco Industries
Industrial Estate
Sonepat, Haryana, India

Drummy Thresher

Mohinder & Co. Allied Industries
Kurali, Distt. Ropar
Punjab, India

This machine is capable of threshing, winnowing, sieving, and bagging a variety of crops. Four people are required to operate this 3 h.p. unit to obtain a capacity of 300 to 500 kilograms per hour.

Jyoti, Ltd.
Baroda 390 003
India

Power Wheat Threshers

This Indian company manufactures threshers in a range of sizes, with or without winnowing mechanisms.

Khalsa Iron Works
2015 Railway Road
Narela, Delhi, India

Wheat Thresher

This small thresher is not fitted with a bagging mechanism and requires a power input of 5 to 7 h.p. Larger models and complete thresher-winnowers are also available.

New Bharat Industries
Industrial Area, Moga
Punjab, India

Saeco Power Wheat Threshers

The 90-centimeter (2½-foot) size has an output of 200 kilograms of clean grain per hour and requires 5 h.p. to run. Larger sizes are also available.

Standard Agricultural Engineering Co.
824/825 Industrial Area B
Ludhiana 141 003, Punjab, India

Hira Drummy Thresher

Four large drummy threshers are available from International Manufacturing. The drum sizes range in width from 24 to 42 inches. Power requirements vary from 3 to 10 h.p. for outputs of from 1,500 to 4,000 kilograms per hour. Complete combination thresher-winnowers are also available.

International Mfg. Co.
Hospital Road, Jagraon
Ludhiana, Punjab, India

WINNOWERS

The practice of winnowing consists of using air moving in a horizontal direction to separate grain from chaff or dust by allowing the mixture to fall vertically in a thin stream across the path of the airflow. The lighter chaff is carried farther by the moving air while the heavier grain falls nearer to vertical, with the material in between these grades occupying intermediate points according to their weight. This principle has been implemented by farmers for centuries in its simplest form, where the natural breezes in the open-air threshing yard are used. A fan can also be used, since it gives a steadier and more reliable air flow.

In a well-designed winnowing machine, the blast of air is produced by a fan rotating inside a suitable casing, while the material to be cleaned and graded falls vertically from a hopper held immediately above the fan outlet spout. In a combined winnowing and grading machine, after passing through the airstream the partially cleaned grain passes through a perforated shaker screen which retains the larger waste but allows the product to fall onto a second perforated shaker screen where small waste and dirt fall out. Finally, the product passes to the discharge chute. To achieve the maximum extraction of waste, the velocity of the airflow in the separation chamber can be adjusted over a wide range. The perforated shaker screens are usually se-

With the help of a fan or a good strong breeze, chaff is blown away as the heavier grain falls straight into the bucket.

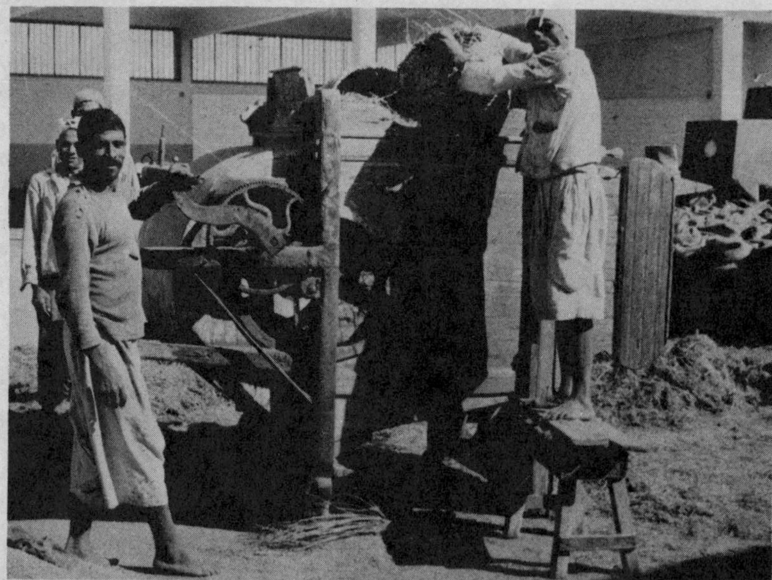

This hand-operated thresher was manufactured in this Egyptian village with locally available materials and craftsmen.
Dr. B. N. Ghosh

cured by spring clips which are manually released so that the screens can be easily removed for changing or cleaning. A range of screen sizes are available to deal effectively with almost all kinds of seed. The cleaned grain can also be delivered to bagging spouts by using a bucket elevator.

The quality of work done by a winnower is

limited, and it also suffers from the disadvantage of the dust nuisance, not only in the simplest machines but also in the more complex units. The remedy lies in making proper arrangements at the time of installation for the collection and disposal of dust in an effective manner. The usual method is to blow the dust and chaff into a large settling box provided with a wire-covered outlet.

Since much of the threshing in developing countries is carried out by hand or by using simple machinery as described previously, winnowing frequently has to be conducted as a separate operation and is often done by hand. The output of hand winnowing is approximately 45 kilograms of grain per hour. A hand-driven mechanical winnower can achieve outputs of between 200 and 1,200 kilograms of grain per hour and produce a very clean sample suitable for seed.

The simplest winnowers consist of hand- or pedal-driven fans without any sieves or separation devices. The other winnowers described in this section can be adjusted for different crops and can also be fitted with a range of metal sieves. For example, a special hand-powered rotating screen device is available for separating groundnuts from husk and dirt.

In developed countries, the winnowing process is usually incorporated into the function of the thresher. Hence, sources of winnowers alone are scarce in North America.

Prototype Pedal-Power Winnower

Most commercially available winnowing machines employ an electric motor or an internal combustion engine to drive the fan. These machines are too expensive for the small-scale farmer, and their capacities usually exceed his requirements. To meet the needs of the peasant

Dr. Ghosh's prototype pedal-powered winnower.
Dr. B. N. Ghosh

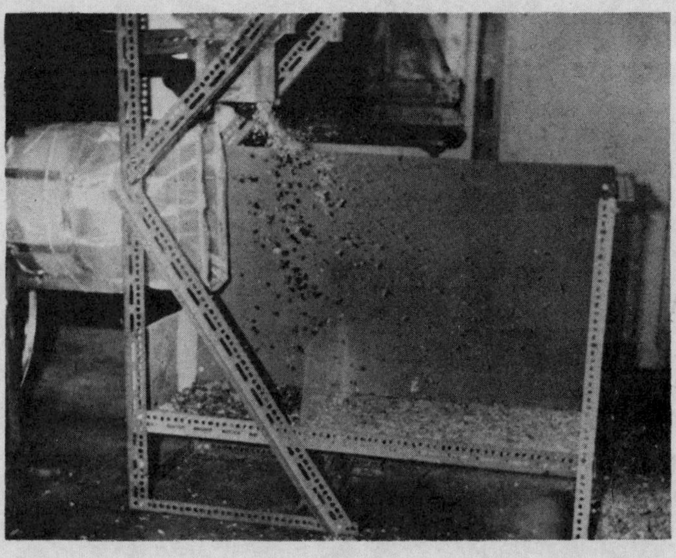

A demonstration of the pedal winnower in action. Notice that the larger, heavier matter falls first and that the lighter chaff is blown far away as the grain mixture falls from a hopper above.
Dr. B. N. Ghosh

farmer in India, an inexpensive winnowing machine which can be easily attached to and operated by a pedal bicycle (a vehicle which some peasant farmers already possess) is being developed by Dr. Biswa Ghosh.

An Old-Fashioned Winnower

This simple type of winnower predates hand-operated grain cleaners by a few hundred years. About the only improvement that has been made over traditional basket models is the addition of a screen to allow the fines, dust and dirt, to fall through. In use, the threshed grain is tossed into the air on a windy day—the wind blows away the chaff, dust, and the lighter seeds, the sand and smaller particles fall through the screen—and with any luck, what is left is cleaned grain. The sides are made of galvanized sheet metal, 8 inches high. The screen is galvanized and is riveted to the sides. Its size is 24 inches wide, and 24 inches deep (from front to back).

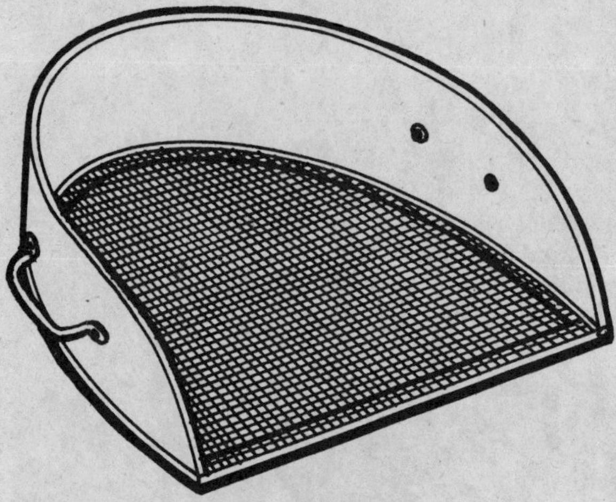

The AVI Winnower

American Village Institute
440 Meyers St.
Kettle Falls, WA 99141

Agrima Winnowers

Two models are available from this company, one made of metal and the other of wooden construction. Both can be operated by hand or with a small motor.

China Agricultural Machinery Co., Ltd.
17 Nanking Road, East, 1st Sec.
Taipei, Taiwan

Winnower

This firm offers a hand-driven winnower made of wood.

Self-Sufficiency & Small-Holding Supplies
The Old Palace, Priory Road, Wells
Somerset BA5 1SY England

CeCoCo Hand Grain Winnower Type A-1

This model is designed for cleaning paddy, hulled rice, wheat, barley, hulled sunflower seed, and any other grains or seeds.

With an output capacity of approximately 650 kilograms of hulled rice per hour, this unit separates cleaned grain from immature dead grain and chaff, husk, and dust. It is of all-steel construction. Weight: 300 kilograms.

CeCoCo
P.O. Box 8, Ibaraki City
Osaka Pref. 567 Japan

Hindson Seed Grader

This model comes equipped with an adjustable blower and two replaceable sieves. It has a capacity of 600 to 1,100 kilograms per hour with a ½ h.p. motor. Four sieve sizes are available.

Hindsons Pvt. Ltd.
The Lower Mall
Patiala, Punjab, India

Number 8 Winnower

This is a hand-powered machine constructed mainly of wood, but with metal moving parts and an oscillating bottom screen. It can be fitted with any of five 40- by 40-centimeter metal sieves for efficient screening of all kinds of grain, including wheat, barley, and maize.

R. Hunt & Co., Ltd., Atlas Works
Earls Colne, Colchester
Essex CO6 2EP U.K.

Hunt No. 8 Winnower
R. Hunt

An Indian Winnower

The air draft on this model is controllable, and you can replace the sieves as necessary. It runs on four ball bearings and is operated by hand.

Rajasthan State Agro Industrial Corp., Ltd.
Virat Bhawan, C-Scheme
Jaipur 302 006, Rajasthan, India

A British Winnower

This unit consists of a hopper, feed control slide, oscillating sieve assembly, and fan. It is available in two models with approximate capacities of 800 kilograms per hour and 1,000 kilograms per hour. Both models can be hand- or power-operated.

The Alvan Blanch Development Co., Ltd.
Chelworth, Malmesbury
Wiltshire SN16 9SG U.K.

Cycle Winnower

With a capacity of 1,500 to 2,000 kilograms per hour, this simple pedal-driven fan aids the farmer when natural breezes fail to blow. The blades have a span of 1,200 millimeters (48 inches) and are fitted onto a shaft running on two ball bearings. There are two freewheels in the gear train along with a flywheel. A seat is provided on this all-steel, 80,000-kilogram, framed unit. Enough air current is provided to keep four people winnowing at one time.

Cossul Cycle Winnower
Cossul and Co.

Cossul Hand Winnower

This hand-driven model has a capacity of 500 to 800 kilograms per hour, and will keep two people busy winnowing at a time. The blades are fitted to a post, and the unit weighs 25,000 kilograms.

Cossul Co. Pvt. Ltd.
Industrial Area
Fazalgunj, Kanpur, India

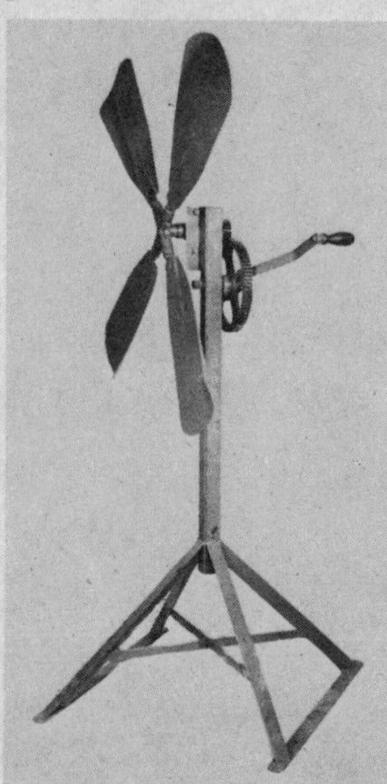

Cossul Hand Winnower
Cossul and Co.

The Winnower Kit

A winnower has been developed by the Overseas Liaison Department of the National Institute of Agricultural Engineering in England to meet the need for a hand-driven device for separating grain from chaff and groundnut kernels from their shells. The design is simple, and manufacture should be well within the capability of village craftsmen using normal hand tools.

The winnower consists of a frame supporting a feed hopper, separating duct, fan, and drive mechanism. The frame is made of ten wooden pieces bolted together. The hopper is formed by the two upper frame members, the top of the fan casing, and one side of the separating duct, which has a shuttered feed aperture level with the hopper floor.

The duct is of rectangular cross-section, roughly S-shaped, with a long vertical center part. The shaped sides are cut from thick plywood and the sheet metal front and back are screwed to the edges of the plywood. The fan is a plain paddle blade unit. The casing is constructed in the same way as the duct to which it is attached by a bolted, flanged joint. A six-blade wooden rotor is carried on a steel shaft running in plain wooden bearings bolted to the frame.

The drive is transmitted by bicycle chain from a crank and chain wheel to a small sprocket on the fan shaft. All the components are standard bicycle parts. The pedal crank and chain wheel are soldered to a steel shaft which runs in bearings bolted below the hopper. The small sprocket on the fan shaft is made from the ring of teeth from a bicycle freewheel pressed onto a wooden boss which is pinned to the shaft.

The following table summarizes the performance results of a prototype at an N.I.A.E. trial. Measurements of output were taken during short runs without stops for refilling the hopper. The rate of work over several hours may be lower, depending on the number of operators and their efficiency.

Crop	Crank Speed, Revolutions per Minute	Average Output Kilograms per Hour	% of Chaff or Shell Removed
Rice (long grain)	70-90	400	75-95
Groundnuts (North African)	84-94	250	83-99
Groundnuts (Gambian)	90	180	98

When the trial was conducted, researchers found that some of the rice samples contained short straw which could not be blown out. In the North Africa groundnut trial, the winnower's high crank speed gave a very clean result, but the Gambian groundnut trial yielded a poor sample, with 40 percent of the nuts left unshelled.

Overseas Department
National Institute of Agricultural Engineering
Silsoe, Bedford MK45 4HS England

A Dutch Winnower Kit

This kit offers the option of assembling the winnower after completing construction of the individual parts or assembling from a pre-assembled kit. This winnower is made of wood with metal working parts. Only the simplest shop tools are necessary for its construction.

Tool
Postbox 525
Eindhoven, Netherlands

CLEANING AND GRADING

Specially designed cleaning and grading machines can improve the quality of a sample grain to a considerable extent beyond the capabilities of the winnower. There are several reasons why such high-quality grain is desirable:

1) Grain required for seed purposes should be clean and uniform;
2) Removing weed seeds means that cultivation of the growing crop will be less costly;
3) An increased yield can be obtained from using cleaned and graded grains for seed purposes;
4) Seed-drilling machines perform better when clean and properly graded seed is used;
5) You can get better prices for graded samples;
6) Removal of insects and other foreign matter during cleaning ensures better and safer storage;

A hand-operated seed cleaner constructed entirely of wood. The crank powers a wooden-bladed fan for winnowing while screens in the foreground separate seed from chaff. Cleaned seed is deposited in a drawer below. No longer being made in the United States, these machines are easy to find at farm auctions but are now gaining in value as antiques. Construction plans are available from IRRI, Box 933, Manila, Philippines.

The hand crank, gears, and a peek at the wooden fan blades of an old seed cleaner.

7) Grain that is precleaned before drying improves the efficiency of the drying machine and produces a more uniformly dried sample.

In cleaning grain or seed, the main object is to separate all chaff, straw, weed seeds, broken and inferior seeds, dust, and other assorted rubbish from the sample. (However, some of this material can be a useful by-product with commercial value.)

Most machines used for cleaning also grade the grain according to size, shape, specific gravity, and/or weight of the seed. Seed cleaners commonly used on farms vary considerably in the quality of work done. The cleaner may be a very simple riddling or winnowing machine, or a complex dresser which employs a number of processes to treat or dress the grain. Some of the processes commonly used by seed cleaners are:

1) Screening over a sieve in order to remove stalks, stones, and other large roughage.
2) Separation by a blast of air, using either a winnowing or an aspirating device.

Two Methods of Cleaning and Grading Seed.

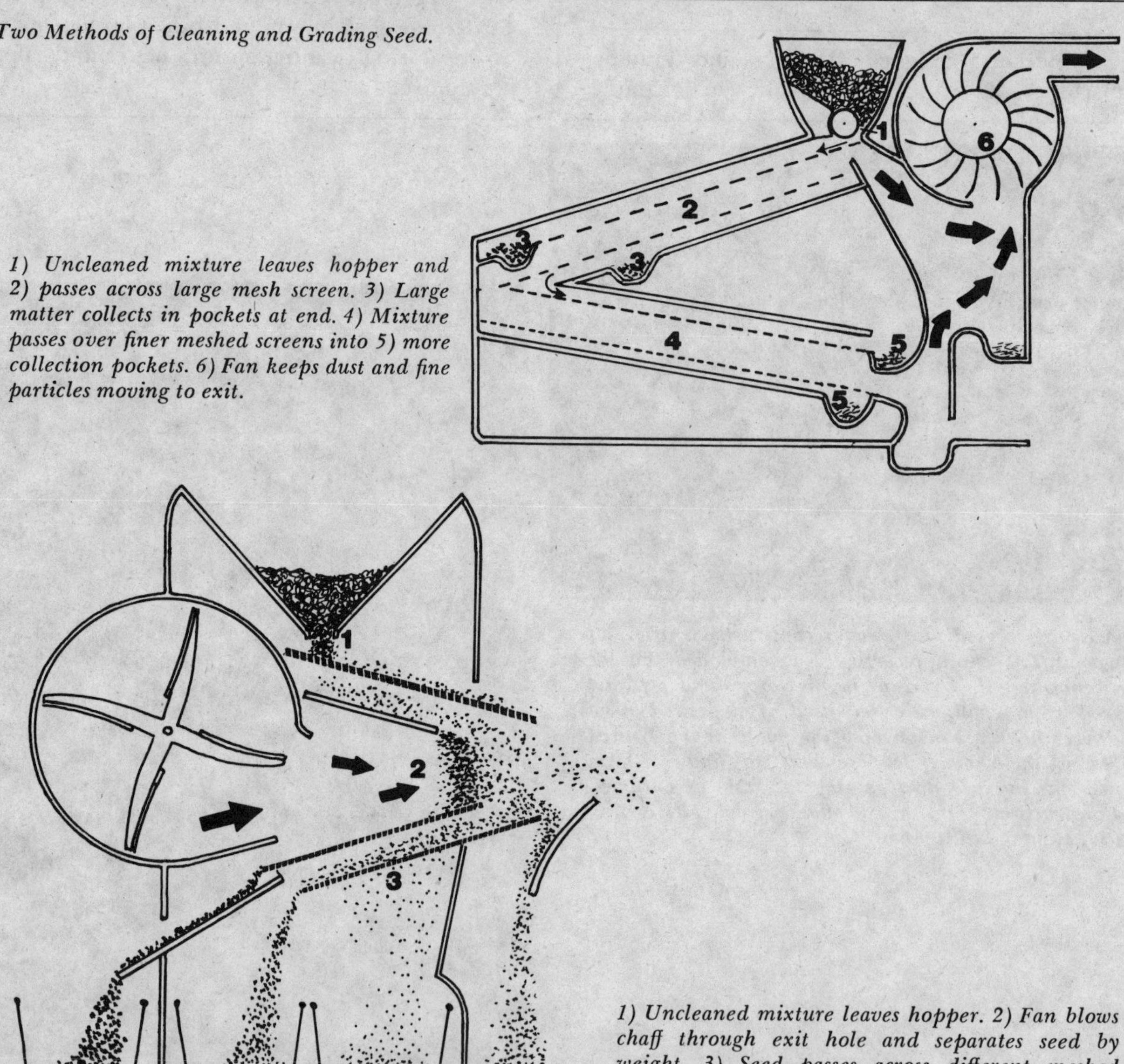

1) Uncleaned mixture leaves hopper and 2) passes across large mesh screen. 3) Large matter collects in pockets at end. 4) Mixture passes over finer meshed screens into 5) more collection pockets. 6) Fan keeps dust and fine particles moving to exit.

1) Uncleaned mixture leaves hopper. 2) Fan blows chaff through exit hole and separates seed by weight. 3) Seed passes across different meshed screening for four grades.

3) Rotary screens or nests of sieves usually separate the grain or seed into a number of samples according to width.
4) Indented cylinders or pockets are used to separate the sample according to length.

Some machines will simultaneously clean and grade a sample of grain or seed, while others will perform only one of these functions. They are grouped below according to the mechanism used for cleaning and/or grading.

OPERATING AND ADJUSTING CLEANERS AND GRADERS

Considerable skill is required to operate efficiently the various types of cleaners and graders that are available for farm use. Grain samples are variable and the correct setting for one particular sample may not be appropriate for the next sample. The following adjustments are usually available to properly set a machine for a given sample of grain:

1) The air blast can be adjusted by either regulating the fan blind or altering the speed of rotation.
2) The slope, length, and frequency of vibration of a machine can be adjusted to suit the requirements of a particular sample.
3) The sieves themselves are interchangeable for different sizes and types of grains.

NORTH AMERICAN SOURCES OF SEED CLEANERS

The Model 30 Burrows Seed Cleaner and Grader

This is a small-sized seed cleaner and grader, suitable for seed testing or cleaning small lots of seed. It has a small chaff or scalping screen on top and large cleaning and grading screens below. Standard equipment includes any four chaff–grading screens and any four double-grading screens. A suction fan removes chaff, and the screens remove large particles and damaged seeds. Its capacity for wheat and other grains is 20 to 30 bushels per hour. For clover and other seeds, it can process 2 to 10 bushels per hour. Shipping weight of this cleaner is 145 pounds. The screens weigh extra. This unit can be operated by hand or a ¼ h.p. motor. A bagging attachment is available.

Model 75 Burrows Seed and Grain Cleaner and Grader

This unit has a capacity of 60 to 75 bushels per hour when cleaning and grading wheat or other heavy grains, and 10 to 25 bushels per hour when cleaning and grading clover and other lighter seeds. This is a four-screen machine which has two separate shoes with two screens in each shoe. The scalping screens remove sticks, stems, pods, and other large particles; the grading screens clean the seed or grain and separate the cleaned seed into two grades when two screens are used. A high-speed multivane fan removes chaff and other light material. The Model 75 Burrows requires a ½ h.p. electric motor for use without an elevator. When a charging elevator is used with the cleaner, a ¾ h.p. electric motor is needed.

Burrows Heavy-Duty Double-Spiral Separator

This machine separates anything round from anything that is not round, according to the manufacturer. Vetch, peas, soybeans, pepper, rape, turnip, coriander, milo, mustard, and other round seeds are easily separated from wheat, oats, barley, flax, corn, screenings, rodent chips, etc. No power is needed. The Double Spiral separates by gravity to remove round seeds from oblong grains, screenings, or weeds.

The machine consists of two units of spirals which feed from the same hopper and deliver together at the bottom. At the top is a large hopper with an adjustable feed plate for each unit of spirals. The seed leaving the hopper runs over a cone divider which spreads the seed evenly to each of the five flights in each unit. Going down the flights, the round kernels travel at a much faster rate of speed than the other kernels. Their momentum increases until they run over the edges of the spirals, drop to the housing spiral and roll into a tray at the bottom of the machine. A single discharge chute is standard unless the double chute is specified. The double chute separates the round seed into two grades, portions of which can be controlled by adjusting levers.

The unit is built from galvanized steel, is set in a strong steel frame, and measures 77 inches high, 42 inches wide, and 22 inches deep. Its capacity is 10 to 50 bushels per hour (30 to

35 bushels per hour for soybeans). Shipping weight: 200 pounds. Available options include self-cleaning hopper, laboratory sample spiral (single, 5 feet by 20 inches, with two flights), heavy-duty single spiral (20 inches diameter).

Spiral Grain Cleaner Model 2825

As the screen and spiral rotate in this model, the spiral moves the grain over the screen. Because of the movement of the screen and spiral and the horizontal construction of the machine, the grain flow is completely controlled and distributed more effectively than in an operation depending on gravity. The spiral in the grain cleaner assures that the grain will be carried over the largest possible screen area. The result is thoroughly cleaned grain that dries faster to help eliminate spoilage. This cleaner is belt-driven for economical and reliable power. Easily interchangeable screens are available for most grains. The cleaner was designed for easy maintenance, and performance-tested to insure best results. Model 2825 is 24 inches in diameter and 6 feet long, with a capacity of 1,200 to 1,500 bushels per hour (for dry corn). It requires a 1 h.p. motor.

All the above cleaners are available from:
Burrows Equipment Co.
1316 Sherman Ave.
Evanston, IL 60204

Seedburo Cleaner

The Seedburow No. 464 seed cleaner is similar to the Burrows No. 30.

Seedburo Equipment Co.
1022 W. Jackson Blvd.
Chicago, IL 60606

Power-driven Seed and Grain Cleaner

This unit cleans and grades 2 to 10 bushels of small seed and 20 to 30 bushels of large grains per hour. It has a galvanized steel housing, smooth-action upper scalping or chaff screen, controlled-vibration lower cleaning and grading screens, and the suction of an adjustable airstream. Eight screens provide 12 different screening combinations. The cleaner requires little operating or storage space; it measures 23 by 38 by 40 inches high. It is shipped from the factory near Columbus, Ohio.

Spiral Separator
Seedburo Equipment Co.

Sears, Roebuck & Co.
Farm and Ranch Catalog

The Clipper for Sample Testing

The shoe of this model uses two 10- by 15-inch screens, one for top and the other for lower separation. The clipper also features a powerful blast fan driven by three step pulleys and controlled, adjustable shutters on air intake openings to provide intermediate air regulation. In

Clipper Seed and Grain Cleaner M-2B
Seedburo Equipment Co.

addition, it has a grain box and an air screening receptacle wth removable trays. This cleaner is operated either by a hand crank or by a 1/6 h.p. motor. The hand crank is furnished only if the motor is not mentioned on the order. Ten screens of the customer's choice and the cleaner drive pulley come as standard equipment. The Clipper Office Tester is 30 inches long, 15 inches wide, 23 inches high and weighs 45 pounds. Shipping weight: 90 pounds.

Clipper Hand-Testing Screens

Clipper Hand-Testing screens provide a liberal assortment of screens, enabling you to experiment with various separations and select the correct screens for each cleaning problem. For household use, you can use these hand screens to clean just as much as you intend to use. A storage rack is available.

Clipper M-2B

In this model, grain is fed to the hopper which spreads it evenly across the full width of the top screen. The top screen perforation is selected with large openings to hold up and scalp off large foreign matter while the grain drops through to the second screen. The lower screen is selected with openings slightly smaller than the grain. Dirt, splits, weed seeds, and im-

Clipper Seed and Grain Cleaner No. 27.
Seedburo Equipment Co.

mature kernels drop through this lower screen, and the clean grain discharges in the form of a curtain through the Bottom Air Blast Column. The bottom air is adjusted to remove any remaining lightweight trash or underweight kernels. This air separation is selective because the fan is precisely adjustable over a wide range. With a screen size of 24¼ inches by 22¼ inches and all-screen construction, this unit will clean up to 40 bushels per hour.

Crippin A-234, A-334 Seed Cleaners

The general construction and operation of the two-screen and three-screen models are similar. The first scalper on the three-screen model removes the largest trash and relieves the second scalper screen of this trash to provide more capacity and closer screening. In grading work, one more size can be obtained with this screen. All screens are interchangeable. With a 1 h.p. requirement, the Crippin Cleaner handles from 25 to 150 bushels of seeds per hour depending upon the stage of the seed.

These cleaners are available from:
Ferrell-Ross
1621 Wheeler St.
Saginaw, MI 48602

Nursery or Test Plot Threshers

These plot threshers, 14 inches standard or 18 inches heavy-duty, come assembled and ready for threshing small lots of grain such as sorghum, wheat, oats, soybeans, barley, and peas. Cylinder speeds are adjustable; the intake hoppers have baffles to prevent the grain from flying back out, and the air flow is adjustable for the type of grain being threshed. Both threshers have a secondary cleaning system that improves efficiency.

Maintenance is no problem: all pulleys, belts, and bearings are standard shelf items, and engine parts are easily available. Optional equipment includes a bagging spout and an extension hopper. Dimensions are 30 by 30 by 27 inches. The units weigh 200 pounds and require a 3 h.p. gasoline engine or a ¾ h.p. electric motor.

ALMACO, Allan Machine Co.
P.O. Box 112
Ames, IA 50010

Burrows Equipment Co.
1316 Sherman Ave.
Evanston, IL 60204

KEM Corp.
Box 471
Haven, KS 67543

Nasco Agricultural Sciences
901 Janesville Ave.
Fort Atkinson, WI 53538

Seedburo Equipment Co.
1022 W. Jackson Blvd.
Chicago, IL 60606

Lee Grain Cleaner

Lee's Model A Cleaner uses a waterless cleaning process, tumbling each grain kernel between a rotating stone wheel and a stationary wheel. Each kernel is polished, scrubbed, and the outer hull scoured away by the rubbing action of the stones, without disturbing the germ. Following the dry scrubbing phase, the grain passes through an air separator which removes fine particles of dirt, dust, chaff, and bee's wings, or loose hulls. With the cleaner properly adjusted, dirt and foreign matter amount to about 2 percent of the final product by weight. The cleaner uses a dual voltage ¾ h.p. single-phase motor to clean 150 to 200 pounds of grain per hour.

Lee Engineering Co.
2023 W. Wisconsin Ave.
Milwaukee, WI 53201

ALMACO Air Blast Seed Cleaner Allan Machine Co.

Air Blast Seed Cleaner

Designed for the precision work of research experiments, the Air Blast Seed Cleaner has two interchangeable screens with 1/8-, 1/4-, 3/8-, and 1/2-inch wire mesh openings, two seed catch pans, and a 180-cubic-feet-per-minute blower. It is made of wood; dimensions are 20 by 12 by 23 inches.

ALMACO, Allan Machine Co.
P.O. Box 112
Ames, IA 50010

Grain Cleaner

The AVI Grain Cleaner is patterned after the simple, efficient fanning mill cleaner-separator that was common around the turn of the century. This mill is designed for hand operation but may also be driven by any external power source. In operation, the threshed wheat is poured into the top hopper and is shaken through a series of screens which separate the grain from the dirt and chaff. The reciprocating action is accomplished by a cam and pitman arm attached to the camshaft. The fan itself is driven by a hand-operated sprocket and chain and essentially blows away all the chaff, dust, and lighter seeds. The cleaned and separated grain is ejected from a trough at the rear of the machine. All hardware is made of cast iron and steel. All screens are galvanized. The frame is of oak, and hopper and screen housings are of alder or maple. The fan is galvanized sheet metal, and is driven by a 6:1 ratio sprocket and chain assembly. The width of this cleaner is 28 inches, length is 42 inches, and height is 36 inches. Weight: approximately 125 pounds.

American Village Institute
440 Meyers St.
Kettle Falls, WA 99141

DICKEY
Fanning Mills.
Farm and Warehouse.
Of All Capacities.
Also TANK LUGS.
Band Fasteners for Tanks.
A. P. DICKEY MFG. CO., - Racine, Wis.

The Implement Age, 1894

The Mr. Pea Sheller shells all kinds of peas and beans—blackeye, purple hull, small crowder, cream peas, English peas, sweet peas, and the harder-to-shell limas and butter beans. Available from:
Mr. Pea Sheller
P.O. Box 29153-B
Dallas, TX 75229
R.E. Tenney & Associates

Plans for this pea and bean sheller are available from the Department of Agricultural Engineering, Cornell University, Ithaca, NY 14853. Ask for Agricultural Engineering Extension Bulletin No. 412.

Barley pearlers are becoming more generally available through homesteading catalogs. This one is manufactured by Seedburo Equipment Co.

INTERNATIONAL SOURCES OF GRAIN AND SEED CLEANERS

The N.I.A.E. Cleaner

The N.I.A.E. cleaner was developed for cleaning grain samples received from plot combines and threshers. As these samples often contain 60 to 70 percent chaff and straw, an air aspirator is used to remove this material first. The semicleaned sample then passes over a double sieve-cleaning riddle. Capacity is 25 samples per hour, based on samples received from the N.I.A.E. plot combine.

R.G. Garvie & Sons
2 Canal Road
Aberdeen, Scotland

CeCoCo Paddy Separator

Because of the different sizes, shapes, and degrees of maturity of grain, no rice huller can hull every paddy completely in one operation. Any attempt to hull all of a paddy will result in excessive breakage. When a mixture of hulled and unhulled rice is fed into the hopper or separator, it glides down along the surface of multistaged, inclined wire screen and separates the rice into four kinds: (a) completely cleaned, hulled rice, (b) unhulled rice, (c) unripened and imperfect rice, and (d) broken rice with mud, sand, or dust. It is also used for sorting the polished rice for grading. It is made of hardwood and can be dismantled and folded down for storing. Wire screens of different sizes are furnished to meet varying needs. It will separate paddies at a rate of about 70 bushels per hour and also grades brown rice.

CeCoCo
P.O. Box 8, Ibaraki City
Osaka, Pref. 567 Japan

Heid Saat 6

The Heid Saat 6 seed cleaner produces unadulterated seed grain from all kinds of large and small seeds, such as wheat, rye, barley, oats, pulse, clover, vegetables, linseed, millet, and colza. The machine is of compact, all-steel construction and its design combines all the standard elements used in conventional seed cleaning: coarse sieves, sand or grading screens, air sifter, and trier cylinder. Suitable screens and indent cylinders are available for all varieties of crops. The Heid Saat 6 is equipped for drive by either electric motor or a handwheel. Weighing no more than 150 pounds, the machine can be trundled from place to place like a wheelbarrow by a single person. It has a 0.4 h.p. requirement and an output of 300 pounds per hour.

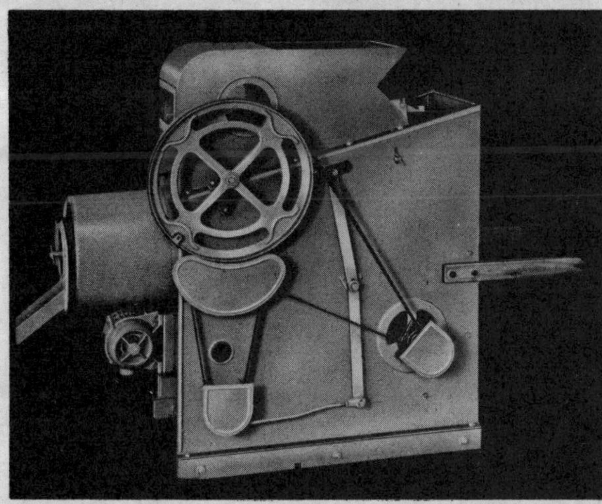

Heid Saat 6
Heid Ag

Heid Ag
Postfach 147
A-1015 Wien Austria

CeCoCo Bean Separator and Grader

This machine will automatically separate and clean beans from dust, grit, stone, mud, sand, seeds, or any other foreign matter and classify them into three grades—small, medium and large—by means of interchangeable screens. Of wood construction, the separator is available in four sizes:

Type	Hourly Capacity	Power Required
No. 1	50-60 bushels	½-1 h.p.
No. 2	40-50 bushels	¼-½ h.p.
No. 3	8 bushels	Hand
No. 4	12-16 bushels	¼ h.p.

CeCoCo Bean Cleaner and Separator

This unit is specifically for use with the red bean and other round-shaped beans. The input funnel is equipped to regulate an even flow of beans to the first separating device, which removes impurities, husks, and dust, and onto the second separating plate, which removes imperfect or immature beans. There are provisions for adjusting the machine to fit the specific bean being cleaned.

CeCoCo White Rice Cleaner

Using the difference in weight between grains and the accompanying impurities, this machine will separate rice from dust, sand, stone, grit, and other foreign substances. The machine is light; the heaviest of the four models weighs 110 kilograms. Also, it requires only $1/12$ to ½ h.p. to operate.

CeCoCo
P.O. Box 8, Ibaraki City
Osaka, Pref. 567 Japan

IRRI Power Grain Cleaner

The Power Grain Cleaner uses rotary screens in conjunction with an air blast. This combination simplifies the design and permits extended exposure of a tumbling mass of grain to air, resulting in improved cleaning.

It is ideally suited for tropical countries and was designed particularly for rice mills, farms, warehouses, and experimental stations. The grain is cleaned by means of two concentric cylindrical screens. The inner screen retains large impurities but lets the grain through.

Power grain cleaner with 1.6 to 2.5 ton per hour capacity.
International Rice Research Institute

Smaller impurities like sand, dust, and weed seeds pass through the outer screen. This cleaner has an adjustable air opening for quality cleaning and an adjustable feeding rate. The three pulley settings result in approximate cleaning capacities of 1.6, 2.0, and 2.5 metric tons per hour by powering with a 1 h.p. electric motor.

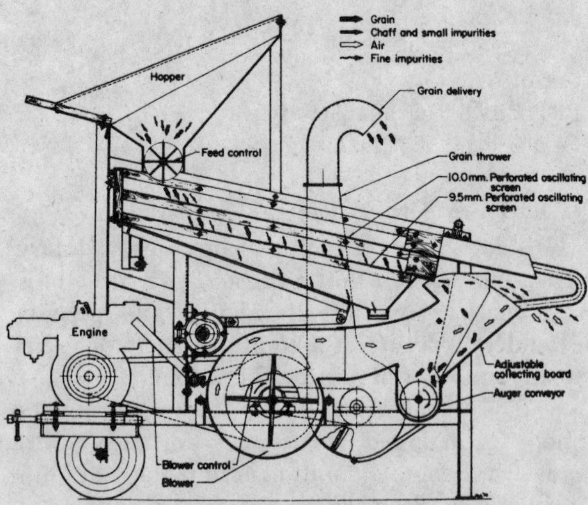

Sectional View of Oscillating Grain Cleaner
International Rice Research Institute

International Rice Research Institute
Box 933
Manila, Philippines

Hindsons Seed Grader

This grader has a manually fed hopper with a 66-kilogram capacity. It has one high-speed electric blower run by a 1 h.p. motor. Two sieves can be used at one time, and four sieves are provided with the unit. Screens are available for almost all crops.

Hindsons Seed Cleaner
M/s. Hindsons Pvt. Ltd.

M/s. Hindsons Private, Ltd.
The Lower Mall
Patiala, Punjab, India

Improved Portable Grain Cleaner

The International Rice Research Institute has released an improved and simplified model of the small, oscillating grain cleaner for manufacture which has a 1-ton per hour capacity. It includes a 12-millimeter plywood body attached to a light-gauge angle iron frame and legs. An integral, eccentric drive and blower arrangement provide for both screen oscillation and air discharge to aid the grain cleaning. It is equipped with a small motor. Construction plans and sources of machinery are available from IRRI.

Improved Portable Grain Cleaner
International Rice Research Institute

International Rice Research Institute
P.O. Box 933
Manila, Philippines

Oilseed Thresher

This thresher, designed for a variety of oilseed crops such as safflower, flax, sunflower, and others, cleans by means of a straw walker, sieve, and fan combination. Spring-loaded crushing rolls and variable cylinder speeds from 200 to 1,200 rpm are used. The Engineering Research

Oilseed Thresher
Agriculture Canada

Service at Agriculture Canada found this to be one of the best research threshers because it will also handle a number of other crops, from field beans to alfalfa. It is, however, expensive to produce, and is not available commercially. Interested parties should contact:

Engineering Research Service
Agriculture Canada
Ottawa, Ontario, K1A OC6, Canada

Forage Plot Thresher

This small-capacity thresher, which cleans by means of a straw walker, sieve, and special aspirator fan, uses a radial rubber rub bar against a rubber mat for hard-to-thresh forage plants. The plans are available from the Engineering Research Service of Agriculture Canada, but only on microfilm. Inquiries about possible manufacture should be directed to:

Engineering Research Service
Agriculture Canada
Ottawa, Ontario K1A OC6, Canada

Forage Plot Thresher
Agriculture Canada

Rotary Corn Thresher Plans

This guinea corn threshing machine, designed and built by the Intermediate Technology

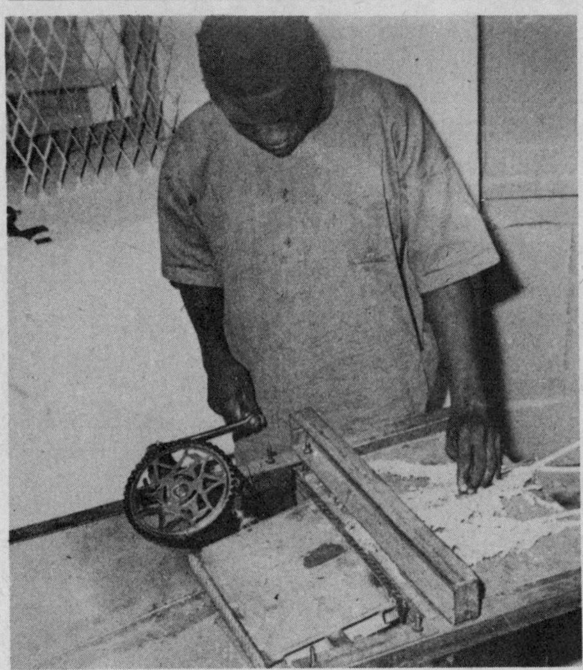

Rotary Corn Thresher

workshop in Zaria, Nigeria, utilizes a bicycle crank and pedal as its main components. Plans are available from:

Intermediate Technology Publications, Ltd.
9 King Street
London, WC2E 8HN, England

Small-Scale Seed Cleaner

Farmers have been inventors for hundreds of years. As long as there are jobs to be done, individuals like Tim Sanford of Alexander, Maine, will be devising easy, inexpensive tools like his seed cleaner.

The cleaner, which uses a vacuum cleaner, a plastic snap-cover pail, a funnel, and a mailing tube, can clean over 100 pounds of seed per hour, though we wouldn't recommend it for anyone with over 1,000 pounds of seed to clean. "It works quite well, but not perfectly, for wheat and our seeds," Sanford explains.

To operate the seed cleaner, a steady stream of the grain to be cleaned is poured into the funnel. If it clogs, a thin stick will unclog it.

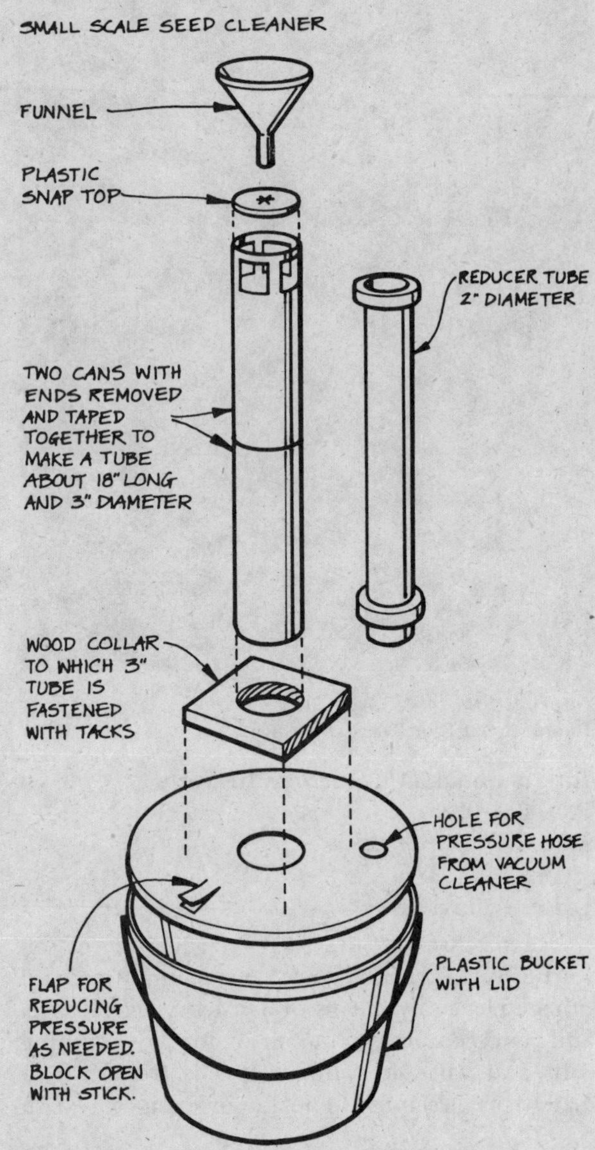

Adjust the airspeed (the vacuum should be blowing into the bucket) so the good seeds (the heavier parts) will be just heavy enough to escape being blown from the chaff holes at the top and will fall to the bottom. The inner tube (Sanford uses a cardboard mailing tube) can be made smaller to get more force from a vacuum cleaner with low pressure.

–8– Processing Equipment

GRINDING AND CRUSHING EQUIPMENT

In processing a crop for either human or animal consumption, it is generally necessary to reduce its size by either grinding or crushing it. This process is useful for correct feeding of livestock, since it increases the digestibility or palatability of the crop and also facilitates mixing it with other constituents of the feed. There are three basic kinds of mills used to crush or grind the harvest: (1) burr mills with either stone or steel burr plates, (2) roller mills, and (3) hammer mills. Before it is stored, the ground material is usually graded by sieving, as different sizes of material are used for feeding the various farm animals. For example, a coarser mixture is used for beef cattle, sheep, or laying hens, and a finely ground feed is more suited to high-producing dairy cows and young chickens. Oats, owing to the presence of fiber in the husk, are usually ground to a fine state for poultry feeding.

According to W. C. Krueger, author of an article entitled "Basic Principles Involved in the Design of the Small Feed Grinder," which appeared in the July 1927 issue of *Agricultural Engineering*, "the problem of feed reduction has always been of vital interest to farmers. From the time of the first horsepower burr mills to the largest present-day attrition mills, the progress in mill development has been towards faster, cheaper, and more economical grinding. Custom mills operated by waterpower or steam supplanted the use of the individual horse-operated mills. The development of the gas engine, however, resulted in a revival of the individual farm mill, improved and reduced in cost by this time."

Krueger goes on to explain that with the coming of electrical power to villages and country towns, custom feed-grinding enjoyed a brief revival. The new attrition mills produced a feed of better quality than that ground in farm mills, and farmers once again brought their feed crops into town for grinding. Later, when electricity was available to everyone, even rural dwellers, farmers began investing in electric motors to run their own mills.

Today, most milling is done right on the farm. The self-sufficient small farmer needs a mill which will serve a variety of functions involving both the household and farm. He should seek long-term economy and durability while satisfying his every milling need.

A burr mill is generally a better choice than a hammer or roller mill if you will need to do fine milling for household flour. Hammer mills are quite popular on the farm for grinding animal feed, but they do not produce a uniform grind, and are therefore not appropriate for milling flour. They are rugged and can grind different kinds of dry material at one time into different textures. Probably the most expensive mills to buy, yet the cheapest to operate, are the roller mills. They put out a good-quality feed, produce little waste, have a high-production capacity and require little power.

SMALL GRINDING UNITS

Many kitchen-scale grinding units are available for grinding both feed and household flour. Their output is considerably lower than that of mills specifically designed for farm use, but their versatility makes them worthy of consideration when only a few animals are kept on the farm.

Domestic mills are either hand-cranked or run by a small motor. Metal burr grinding plates are suitable for grinding and cracking grains, hulling some seeds, splitting peas, grinding coarse cereal, and making flour of a degree of fineness acceptable for bread. For a pastry-fine flour, stone mills are best. They can be used only with dry grains and seeds of 12 percent moisture or less. Moist seeds have a tendency to glaze the stones. If this happens, passing very hard winter wheat or very dry corn through the stones at their widest setting will clean the glaze away.

A cast-iron, steel burr mill disassembled to show feeding auger, stationary burr plate and interchangeable burr plate on auger.

Grinding pastry-fine flour with a stone burr combination hand mill.

But these mills are not made for certain jobs, and the manufacturers' guidelines should be followed carefully.

The most versatile type of mill is called a burr/stone conversion. One plate is a stationary burr which cannot be removed. The operator has the choice of interchanging a stone or burr for the other plate. A fine flour can be obtained from the burr/stone combination while the burr/burr combination will crack grains, handle oily seeds, and make nut butters.

Most electric mills designed for small-scale household use have stones. Often a hand crank is available in the event of a power failure.

SOURCES OF HAND MILLS*

All-Grain Mills

The H-1 Metal Burr plate mill is designed for cracking cereals; Model H-10 has stones and burrs. The grooved stones are designed for slow turning and will grind fine flour the first time through.

* For specifications and more detailed information on 75 household grain mills, write to *Organic Gardening* Readers' Service, 33 E. Minor St., Emmaus, PA 18049.

All-Grain Distributing Co.
3333 South 900 East
Salt Lake City, UT 84106

BH Grain Mill

This mill has a cast aluminum body with a chrome steel auger. Its artificial, adjustable stones will grind fine flour or coarse cereal.

Agri Resources
RR 3, Napanee
Ontario, K7R 3K8 Canada

Corona Burr Mill

This cast-iron burr mill grinds one pound of cereal per minute. It is adjustable for fine flour (which must be run through several times) or coarse cereal. The Corona Stone Mill with two stones is available for grinding fine flour the first time through. A conversion mill is also available.

Natural Health Appliances
P.O. Box 169
Meclean, Australia 2463

R & R Mill Co., Inc.
45 West First North
Smithfield, UT 84335

Village Equipment Suppliers
P.O. Box 2172
Lea, Papua, New Guinea

Red Chief Feed-Grinding Mill

The Red Chief, which can be used with all small grains and is especially recommended for poultry feed, grinds 1 to 2 bushels per hour. Spring tension regulates the fineness of ground material. Triplex and flat steel burrs are used in the process. The mill fastens to a box or barrel.

Cumberland General Store
Route 3, Box 479
Crossville, TN 38555

S.A.M.A.P. Cereal Grinder

Also designed for specialized milling of very dry grains, the S.A.M.A.P. Cereal Grinder is a vertical-axis mill using natural stone granules embedded in stabilized magnesite cement. Fineness of grinding and the rate of grain feed between the stones are adjustable. Controlling the rate at which the grain is fed is a unique feature to the S.A.M.A.P. mill which allows the operator to determine the difficulty of his grinding stroke. The weight of this unit is 19¼ pounds (8.75 kilograms). (See photo on page 337.)

Miracle Exclusive, Inc.
16 West 40th Street
New York, NY 10018

S.A.M.A.P.
B.P. Horbourg Wihr
68000 Colmar, France

Stone Miller

The AVI Stone Miller grain grinder is specifically designed to make it easy to grind wheat into fine flour in one grinding. It should be pointed out, however, that what is gained in ease is lost in speed. Although primarily designed for hand power, this mill can be efficiently run with an external power source. It is made of reinforced cast iron with gears providing a 2:1 reduction for easy grinding. The 18-pound, 16-inch diameter flywheel handle drives an auger which feeds grain between two 5-inch stones. The stone separation is adjustable and the hopper holds 4 pounds of grain. Total weight: approximately 55 pounds.

Red Chief Mill
Cumberland General Store

AVI Stone Mill

The American Village Institute
440 Meyers St.
Kettle Falls, WA 99141

Little Gem Hand Mill and Juicer

This is an adjustable cast-iron, stone, hand mill. Turn the handle to the left to grind grain, to the right to make juice.

Little Gem Mills
23655 S.W. Francis
Beaverton, OR 97005

O.B. (Quaker City) Steel-Stone Grinder

This model has two sets of metal burrs—coarse burrs for cracking grains and grinding oily grains and seeds, and sharpened burrs which grind flour from oily grains that would clog stone grinding surfaces. This company also carries the Victoria stone-burr combination mill. (See photo on page 337.)

Sterling H. Nelson & Sons, Inc.
525 South 500 West P.O. Box 1296
Salt Lake City, UT 84110

Victor Stone-Burr Mill

This cast aluminum and durable plastic mill has a stone grinding surface and a stainless steel screen to sift flour to a uniform texture. Pulleys are available to attach the mill to a motor.

Victor Mfg. Co.
8141 4th SW
Seattle, WA 98106

Little Ark Hand-Electric Stone Mill

This mill is designed to grind all dry grains and should not be used to regrind flour previously ground or to grind damp grains. It can be motorized, but the stones should be set at 150 rpm or less to avoid damaging them. A 1/3, 1/2, or 3/4 h.p. motor can be used.

Retsel Corp.
Little Ark Division
McCannon, ID 83250

SOURCES OF ELECTRIC MILLS

All-Grain

The All-Grain has a turbine-cooled air mechanism. The silicon carbide stones are placed horizontally inside a metal housing. There is a five-year unconditional guarantee on the mill, your choice of a 1/3, 1/2, or 3/4 h.p. motor, and the stones. (See photo on page 337.)

All-Grain Distributing Co.
3333 South 900 East
Salt Lake City, UT 84106

Lee Engineering Company Mills

This firm offers either fully adjustable grind or fine grinding mills. An automatic mechanism feeds the aluminum oxide grinding stones. The polyethylene hopper holds approximately 4 pounds of grain. Grinding rates for the 1/6 h.p. mill are 3 to 5 pounds per hour of fine flour, 20 to 25 pounds per hour of coarse meal. Rates for the 1/4 h.p. mill are 6 to 10 pounds per hour for fine flour, 40 to 45 pounds per hour for coarse meal.

1) Victoria Combination Hand Mill. 2) All-Grain Power Mill. 3) Marathon Uni-Mill. 4) S.A.M.A.P. Hand Mill

Homestead Industries in California once made this power transfer unit to adapt their mill to pedal power. It is no longer available commercially but the technique is simple enough for the tinkering miller to duplicate. A wheel secured against the rear bicycle tire transfers power to a pulley which can operate any mill whose driving mechanism can be fitted with a pulley and run with a V-belt.

Lee Engineering Co.
2023 W. Wisconsin Ave.
Milwaukee, WI 53201

Marathon Uni-Mill

This unit has a particle board cabinet with a ½ h.p. motor and a direct-drive handle for manual operation. The adjustable stones have a shear-slice grinding action which grinds 1 pound of flour per minute and 2 pounds of cereal per minute. (See photo on page 337.)

The Grover Co.
2111 S. Industrial Park Ave.
Tempe, AZ 85282

The Harvest Mills Mill

The spring tension on the stones in this mill prevents them from locking due to the heating of grinding, and it absorbs the shock from foreign materials entering the grinding area. The mill has a $\frac{3}{4}$ h.p. motor with a 1-year guarantee, stainless steel hopper and drawer, and an oak cabinet. It produces flour at a rate of 60 to 70 pounds per hour. A hand-crank adapter is provided.

KBL Enterprises
3471 South West Temple
Salt Lake City, UT 84115

Excalibur

This mill has a $\frac{1}{2}$ h.p. capacitor-start motor with a $\frac{3}{4}$ h.p. motor optional. The $\frac{3}{4}$-inch birch cabinet is standard, but other woods are available as options. The 5- by 1-inch stones are fed by a 7-cup capacity hopper producing 42.1 pounds of fine flour per hour.

Excalibur Products
57711 Florin-Perkins Rd.
Sacramento, CA 95828

Golden Grain Grinder

The stainless steel inserts on this model crack the grain before it enters the stones, producing less grit in the flour and less wear on the stones. The self-cleaning stones produce up to 40 pounds of flour per hour. A $\frac{3}{4}$ h.p. motor and hand crank are provided.

Golden Grain Grinder
Division of Kuest Enterprises
Box 110
Filer, ID 83328

Little Gem Mill

A $\frac{1}{3}$ h.p. motor gives the Little Gem a grinding rate of 25 pounds of fine flour per hour and 100 pounds of coarse meal per hour. The mill comes with a hand-conversion kit and birch cabinet.

Little Gem Mill
23655 S.W. Francis
Beaverton, OR 97005

Miller Boy Mill

On this model, a $\frac{1}{3}$ h.p. motor powers the tungsten-carbide shears which cut the grain before it is fed into the stones. The mill will grind approximately 36 pounds per hour. Two cabinets are available with different bin capacities.

The Miller Boy Mill seen here has been modified from electric to pedal power. The pedal power unit, called the Energy Cycle, is a product of Rodale Resources Division, Emmaus, Pa.

Magic Valley Industries, Inc.
405 Highway 30
Filer, ID 83328

Mil-Rite Stone Mill

The 5-inch adjustable stones of this mill are powered by a 1/4 h.p. motor, for a grinding rate of 12 to 15 pounds per hour. Hand conversion is provided. The model carries an unconditional 2-year guarantee.

Romper Stone Mill

This mill grinds 3 pounds of flour per hour. Hand conversion is available.

R & R Mill Co., Inc.
45 West First North
Smithfield, UT 84335

Great Northern Flour Mill Kit

The tools needed to assemble this mill include a hammer, screwdriver, wrench, nails, and glue. The kit includes milling stones with a mounting arbor, ready-to-finish birch cabinet pieces, a Dayton 1/2 h.p., 3,450 rpm capacitor-start motor with cord and switch, a 17-cup capacity flour pan; a 6-cup capacity grain feed funnel, and all the necessary hardware and instructions. The stones are guaranteed for 10 years, and can be converted to hand- or bicycle-powered operation.

Great Northern Distributing Co.
325 W. Pierpont Ave.
Salt Lake City, UT 84101

FARM-SCALE MILLS

Burr Mills

The hand-operated grinding stone, the earliest grinding device used on the farm, somewhat resembled a mortar and pestle in form. It consisted of two pieces of stone roughly cut in the shape of flat discs. The top disc was rotated by hand over the stationary bottom disc, and the material to be ground was fed through the space between the two discs. The old-time grist mill driven by water, wind, or mule power is a good example of a mechanized version of the grinding wheel.

The modern burr-stone mill is a further development of the grinding wheel and is often referred to as an attrition mill, meaning a mill which grinds by friction. The burr mill consists of two disc-shaped stones with burrs or grooves cut into their grinding faces. The grain is fed at the center of the stones and is cracked without crushing as it passes toward the periphery. The stone discs have generally been replaced by chilled, cast-iron plates (hence the name plate mill) with corrugations or projecting cutting edges cast into the rubbing surfaces.

The stone plates of the Moderne Mill with grooves cut on their grinding faces. The pattern is designed wide and deep for cracking near the center where grain is first fed into the mill and gradually shallows to reduce the grain to a fine flour.
Renson Et Cie

The space between the plates is controlled by a spring-loaded, spacing screw, and the plates are usually corrugated on both sides to make them reversible. When starting a plate mill, the grain feed is blocked off and the spring pressure relaxed, leaving the plates at their coarsest setting. Once the mill is rotating at normal speed, the grain is fed into the mill. The plates are gradually forced together by tightening the spring until the desired texture is obtained.

This kind of mill is best suited for grinding meal and flour for household use since it grinds the finest and loses none of the whole grain. When set correctly, the tight hulls on barley and oats will come off in stone grinding. The ground material comes out as a flour and crushed hull mixture. The hulls, which now resemble flakes, can be sifted away. Steel-burr plates grind the entire kernel, making separation of hulls and grain much more difficult. Small, hand-operated barley pearlers are available to shatter the hull away from the kernel before the grain is milled.

Among the weeds, a power-take-off burr mill about to be sold at an auction.

The main advantages of a burr or plate mill are relatively low speeds of operation (around 1,200 rpm), better adaptability for grinding texture than hammer mills, uniform grade of grinding, and fairly low power requirement. This is the farm mill best suited for kitchen use, since it grinds the finest and loses none of the whole grain. Disadvantages of a burr mill include: fast-wearing plates, the possibility of equipment being damaged by foreign objects like stone or metal fragments, a relatively high power requirement for finer grinding, and the possibility of damaging the plates when operating the mill empty, unless the pressure between the plates has been released.

NORTH AMERICAN SOURCES OF BURR MILLS

C. S. Bell Number 2 Hand Model

For dry grinding only, the No. 2 Model Hand Grist Mill can grind all dry, small grains, shelled corn, beans, peas, coffee, and even dried bones. The cone burrs are easily adjusted for a fine or coarse grind. The mill is furnished with a counterbalanced crank to help ease operation and allow a capacity of approximately 25 pounds

Bell No. 2 Hand Burr Mill
C.S. Bell Co.

per hour depending on the material being ground.

C. S. Bell Number 60 Model Power Mill

For dry grinding only, the No. 60 Model Power Mill is designed for grinding all small grains, shells, roots, bark, and salt. The unit is available with a set of coarse, fine, and extra fine grinding burrs to be operated by a 1 to 2 h.p. electric motor. A 3 h.p. motor is recommended for extra fine grinding. Depending upon the material being ground, the fineness of the grind, and the size of the motor, this mill has a capacity of 100 to 300 pounds per hour. Shipping weight: approximately 52 pounds.

Bell No. 60 Power Mill
C.S. Bell Co.

C. S. Bell La Milpa

La Milpa is a large, power grist mill which can handle wet or dry grinding of grain, soybeans, bananas, wheat, and tortillas at a rate of up to 1,400 pounds per hour. The 6-inch steel alloy burrs are adjustable for coarse or fine grinding and are fed with a large feed worm for maximum capacity. A 5 h.p. motor is recommended for hard-to-grind material to maintain high capacity; however, a 3 h.p. motor will do the job. Ready for shipment, the unit weighs 110 pounds without the motor.

C.S. Bell La Milpa Power Mill
C.S. Bell Co.

The above three models are available from:
C. S. Bell Co.
P.O. Box 291
Tiffin, OH 44883

Speed King Cracker

Incorporating 14- to 16-inch burrs powered by a 5 to 10 h.p. motor to yield a 2 to 5 ton per hour capacity, the Speed King Corn Cracker cracks and grinds shelled corn, small grains, and other grindable granular products. Shipping weight: 450 pounds.

S-Crusher

Slightly larger than the Speed King Cracker, the Speed King S-Crusher can be driven with a 5 to 20 h.p. motor to yield a capacity from 2 to 15 tons per hour. It is designed for grinding and cracking ear corn and small grains, and for size reduction of other grindable products.

Both these units are made of cast-iron components with adjustable burrs. The product is

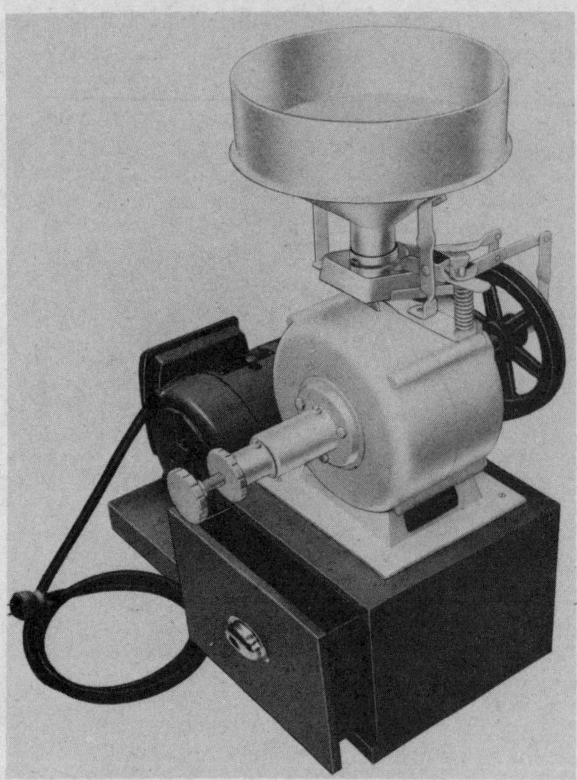

The Meadows 8-inch Stone Burr Mill
The Meadows Mill Company

cut rather than impact-ground, to eliminate undigestible particles.

Winona Attrition Mill Co.
1009 W. Fifth St.
Winona, MN 55987

Meadows Household 8-inch Stone-Burr Mill

Stones housed in cast iron are machined male and female for a precision fit. This mill is available with a wooden base and receiving drawer or mounted on a steel stand for bottom discharge into a bag. Eight-inch diameter stones are made of natural granite. Dry, free-flowing, small grain enters the mill at an adjustable feed-flow rate which requires no attendance.

Meadows Mill Co.
North Wilkesboro, NC 28659

INTERNATIONAL SOURCES OF BURR MILLS

Dandekar Mills

Dandekar offers four vertical grinding mills employing 12- to 18-inch natural kurund stones for dry milling. The motor requirements range from 5 to 8 h.p. for capacities of 200 to 350 pounds per hour.

Dandekar Brothers
Sangli, Maharashtra
India

CeCoCo Hand Grinder Type D

This model is made of metal, with easily adjustable burr plates for fine or coarse grinding.

CeCoCo Hand Grinder Type D

It is adaptable for grinding flour from all kinds of grain and other materials such as rice, buckwheat, soybeans, and even fried fish! It has a grinding capacity of from 5 to 50 kilograms per hour, a hopper capacity of 10 kilograms, and a gross weight of 40 kilograms.

CeCoCo
P.O. Box 8, Ibaraki City
Osaka Pref. 567, Japan

Diamant Domestic Mill

As with all burr mills, the Diamant is suitable for grinding any kind of grain, coffee, spice, or sugar, in wet or dry form. It is easily dismantled for cleaning without special tools and comes with a selection of plates for milling different materials. By hand, its output for grinding grains is approximately 70 kilograms per hour. The handle is mounted on a large flywheel to ease operation. A groove in the flywheel supplies the option of operating this mill with a V-belt connection to an electric motor. The features of the Diamant mill typify the different features available on most hand mills.

A.B.C. Hanson Company A/S
Hauchsvej 14
DK-1825 Copenhagen V, Denmark

IN-TEC Equipment Co.
Box 123, D.V. Station
Dayton, OH 45406

Dunia Hand-Operated Grinding Mill

This small, hand-operated plate mill is constructed of all-welded steel and has been designed in Africa for grinding maize, wheat, coffee, and other foodstuffs. The front cover can be removed for cleaning and inspection by unscrewing three wingnuts.

Ndume Products, Ltd.
P.O. Box 62
Gilgil, Kenya

Gaubert Mini-Grinder

This French mill is designed for crushing wheat, barley, corn, millet, and coffee. It mounts on a table or workbench with two screws and has a 350-millimeter diameter wheel with a handle for manual operation; the flat wheel rim will accommodate a belt drive to a small electric motor. This mill has interchangeable 90-millimeter grinding wheels made of cast iron. An adjustment screw varies the separation between the wheels to provide for coarse or fine grinding.

Gaubert Senior and Junior 170 Mills

The Senior 170, a standing mill, offers an hourly production of 150 to 400 kilograms, depending on the fineness of the grind. It operates at a speed of 450 rpm, and contains 300-millimeter emery stones. The bearings are fitted with interchangeable self-lubricating bronze rings. Options for this model include a 3 h.p., 1,500 rpm electric motor or bearing, and a mounting for tractor drive. A smaller model, the Junior 170, with a reduced hourly production, is also available.

Gaubert Senior Mill
Ets. A. Gaubert

Gaubert Junior 170
Ets. A. Gaubert

Ets. A. Gaubert
16700 Ruffec
23 Rue Gambetta 23, France

Atlas Hand Grinding Mill

The Atlas Grinding Mill is suitable for grinding all types of dry grains, rice, coffee, spices, and some industrial products. It is made of cast iron and will grind from 7 to 9 kilograms

Atlas Grinding Mill
R. Hunt

per hour, depending on the fineness of the sample required and the speed at which the handle is turned. It is suggested that if a very fine sample is required, the meal be first ground coarsely and then ground again with the grinding plates at their closest setting.

Manufactured by:

R. Hunt & Co., Ltd.
Atlas Works, Earls Colne
Colchester, Essex CO6 2EP, U.K.

Distributed by:

Self-Sufficiency & Small-Holdings Supplies
The Old Palace, Priory Road, Wells
Somerset, BA5 1SY, U.K.

Superb Mill

The Superb burr mill is suitable for grinding all types of cereals. Its 270-millimeter plates are powered by a 5 h.p. motor for an output ranging from 230 to 270 kilograms per hour.

E.H. Bentall & Co., Ltd.
Maldon CM9 7NW
Essex, U.K.

Amuda Domestic Mill

Designed to be driven by a ½ h.p. motor, the Amuda Domestic Mill can grind all cereals finely at a rate of 18 kilograms per hour and kibble at a rate of 50 kilograms per hour.

Amuda Flat Plate Mill Number 1

A spring mechanism allows the plates to open and avoid damage if any hard substance enters this burr mill. It is designed for grinding all cereals, beans, spices, cocoa, coffee, and wet or dry corn. The rate of feeding the material to be ground into the milling chamber can be adjusted by regulating the shaker feed mechanism.

Both the Amuda mills are available from:
Rajan Trading Co.
P.O. Box 250
Madras 600 001, India

Diamant Vertical Mill

The Diamant Vertical mill employs stones of special composition available in 300-, 400- and 500-millimeter diameters for grinding dry cereals. A continuous feed flow from the hopper provides constant grinding. Diamant mills can be operated with motors ranging from 2 to 10 h.p. for outputs from 100 to 650 kilograms per hour. Another model, with steel-burr plates, has an output of 300 kilograms per hour with a 5 h.p. motor and 1,100 kilograms per hour with a 15 h.p. motor.

A.B.C. Hansen Comp. A/S
Hauchsvej 14
DK—1825 Copenhagen V, Denmark

Moderne Mill

The Moderne Mill has an agitator feed from a 35-liter capacity hopper into its 300-millimeter diameter grinding wheels. It has a screw adjustment for fineness of grinding. Its output ranges from 200 to 300 kilograms per hour when powered by a 4 to 5 h.p. motor. (See photo on page 339.)

Renson Et Cie
B.P. 14
59550 Landrecies, France

Type S Cereal Breaker

The Type S Cereal Breaker is suitable for crushing maize, rice, barley, beans, and poultry or cattle feed. It can be turned by hand or by a ¼ h.p. motor for a capacity of 40 to 60 kilograms per hour.

CeCoCo Feed Grinder

The Feed Grinder is an ideal machine for grinding corn, oats, soybeans, green peas, and wheat, and also for coarsely crushing fish meal and shells. Grinding plates are adjustable for either coarse or fine grinding. The double-faced grinding plates are reversible and interchangeable.

CeCoCo
P.O. Box 8, Ibaraki City
Osaka Pref. 567, Japan

R2 Grinding Mill

This model's 210-millimeter diameter, vertical millstones powered by a 2 h.p. motor provide an output of fine grist at 110 kilograms per hour for wheat, 80 kilograms per hour for barley, and 90 kilograms per hour for oats.

Iruswerke Dusslingen
7401 Dusslingen
Postfach 128, West Germany

CeCoCo Multipurpose Grinder Model FG-61

The Star brand FG-61 feed grinder is designed to meet almost every grinding requirement. It will uniformly grind all types of dry grain such as wheat, oats, and barley, as well as peas and shelled corn, to any desired grist. The adjustable grinding plates are reversible and interchangeable. Two to four h.p. are required to operate at a capacity of from 8 to 13 pounds per hour. The unit weighs 132 pounds.

CeCoCo
P.O. Box 8, Ibaraki City
Osaka, Pref. 567, Japan

Roller Mills

The ruggedness of a roller mill makes it the most expensive to purchase of the three types available. Grain is mashed between two serrated rollers which operate with the same action as a clothes wringer, so that the teeth on one roller fit the space between the teeth on the other. One roller is usually fixed and the other can be moved to adjust the clearance between the two.

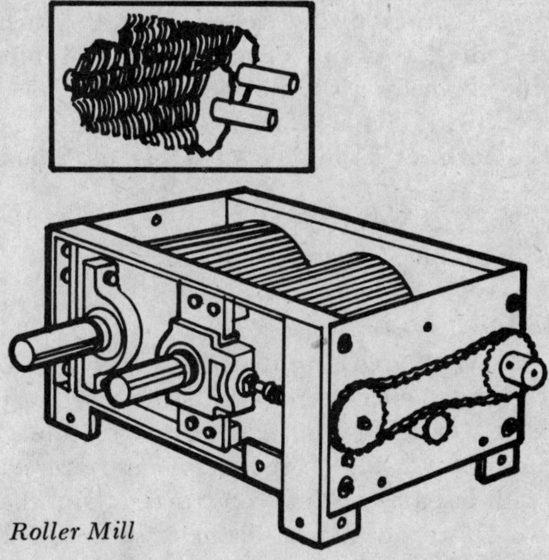

Roller Mill

Roller mills are inexpensive to run and have a high capacity per horsepower because they reduce particles less than other mills. This mill's low power requirement does not provide it with the power to start with even a few kernels between the rollers—it must be completely clean to work. Its function in preparing animal feed is merely to break the hard, outer seed coat of a grain to make digestion easier and more complete. This process provides an important advantage over hammer mills, in that it keeps the percentage of fines (small particles, powder, and dust) to a minimum, producing less waste.

Grain can be hulled, cracked, crushed, or ground with a roller mill; the better models are even capable of producing a fine flour. Special crushing rollers will handle any kind of grain, wet or dry, and can be used to chop green corn and barley for making silage.

SOURCES OF ROLLER MILLS

Stationary Roller-type Feed Mill

The roller-crushing action of the Sears mill

minimizes dust waste. Two heavy-duty rollers (6 inches long, 9 inches in diameter) run on self-aligning ball bearings. This mill allows crimping or crushing of hard grain shells and makes feed more palatable than grain which is finely ground. It has a large 19 by 23½-inch, 16-gauge steel hopper. The hopper height, 32 inches, facilitates loading. The mill is furnished with a motor mount bolted to a stand and a 16-inch V-belt pulley. The overall measurement is 22 by 34 by 32 inches high. Requiring a 2½-inch motor pulley, this mill operates with a 4 h.p. gasoline engine or a 1½ h.p. electric motor for a capacity of 15 bushels of oats, 50 bushels of cracked corn, or 35 bushels of wheat per hour.

Sears, Roebuck & Co.
Farm and Ranch Catalog

W-W Roller Mills

The W-W roller mill handles any type of small grain: shelled corn, oats, barley, sorghum grains, or wheat. It crimps, cracks, or crumbles, depending upon the degree of fineness desired. This mill has a heavy-duty construction, and the chilled, white-iron, 10-inch diameter rolls do not chip or peel and can be regrooved when necessary. A single control wheel handles all the adjustments. Roller sizes vary from 6 to 36 inches in diameter. Optional accessories are available.

Burrows Equipment Co.
1316 Sherman Ave.
Evanston, IL 60204

Grain Rollers

Particularly of use in raising goats, cattle, and sheep, the Gaubert grain rollers come with two equal cylinders 300 millimeters in diameter and 130 millimeters in width. The grain-feeding mechanism is mounted in self-lubricating bronze rings powered by a 3 h.p. motor driving through a set of double pulleys and two V-belts, or through a one-flat, three-ply belt. Grains are rolled without crushing at a rate of 200 to 400 kilograms per hour, depending upon the grain.

Gaubert S.A.R.L.
B.P. 24 16700 Ruffec
France

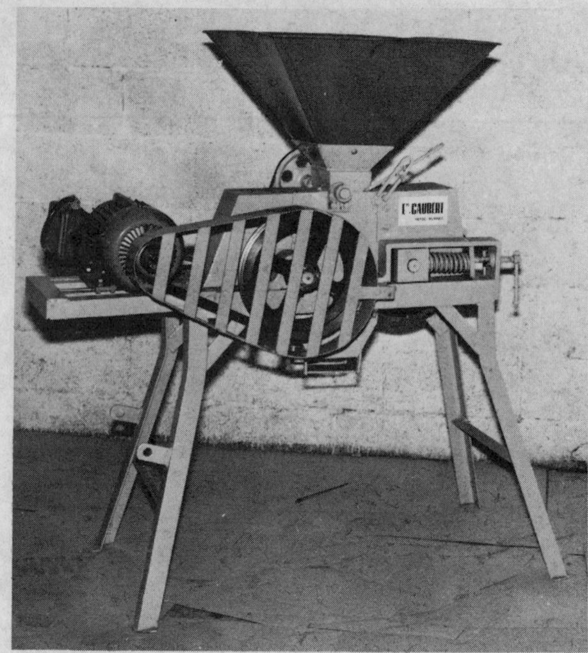

Gaubert Roller Mill
Est. A. Gaubert

6 by 6 Single Roller Mill

This 1 to 2 h.p. mill has solid white-iron rollers which are available without a corrugated surface for flaking, or corrugated for chopping, cutting, or crumbling. Its capacity for milling dry corn is 180 bushels per hour and 140 bushels per hour for high-moisture corn. Many other models are available in larger sizes.

Roskamp 6 by 6 Roller Feed Mill
Roskamp Manufacture Inc.

Roskamp Manufacture, Inc.
616 Grand Blvd.
Cedar Falls, IA 50613

BearCat Grain Roller Mills

BearCat Roller Mills are available in a range of sizes between 5 and 30 h.p. and a number of power arrangements: stationary-mounted with electric motor drive; trailer-mounted with PTO drive; and stationary-mounted with PTO drive. An elevating auger feeder is available as an accessory. Rollers are one of three sizes: 10 by 12, 10 by 18, or 10 by 24 inches. BearCat also carries large hammer and burr mills.

Westernland Roller Co.
Hastings, NE 68901

Hammer Mills

The hammer mill is most often used today to grind feed for livestock and poultry. Instead of having burrs for the grinding process, the hammer mill employs rows of free-swinging, steel flails whirling at high speeds with an action similar to that of a leaf shredder. The impact of these hammers reduces the particle size. The screen under the hammers controls the fineness of the ground feed; the finer the mesh, the finer the feed. Hammer mills will grind all kinds of feed, even mixed grains, ear corn, and hay.

Large units are generally driven by the power take-off shaft of a tractor. A unit which requires 20 h.p. to drive produces 10 to 20 hundredweight of ground material per hour. The smaller hammer mills are popular for farm production of animal feed and concentrate mixes, and they are usually operated by an electric motor. The actual capacity depends on the rate of feeding, the speed of the hammers, the amount of power available, the kind of material being ground, fineness of grind, size of screen mesh, and the size of the mill. The capacity of a hammer mill for a given fineness and horsepower

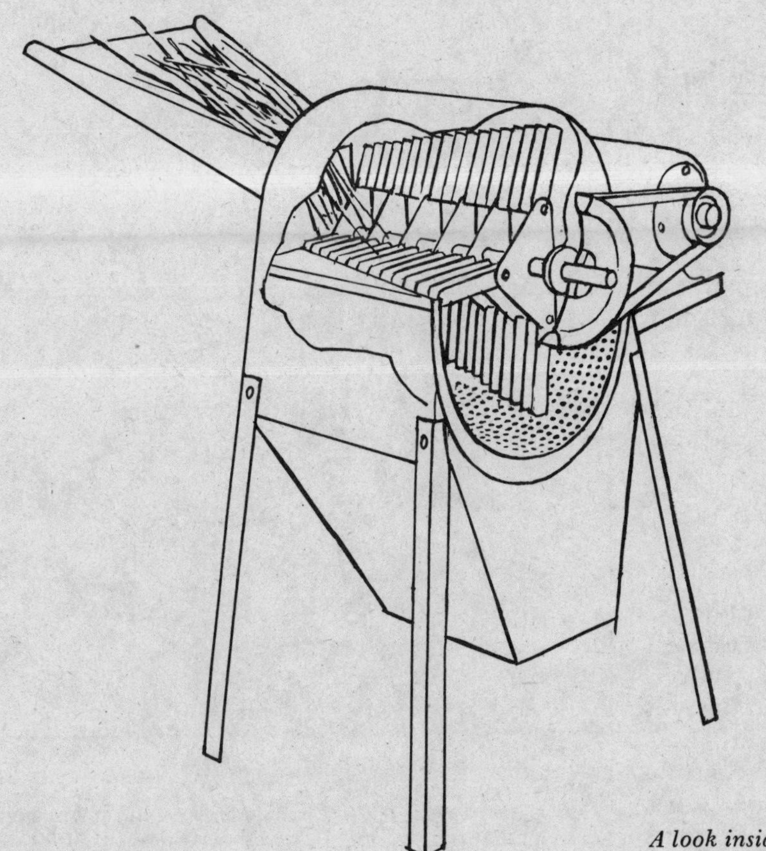

A look inside a hammer mill.

is ultimately limited by the size of the grading screen.

The main advantages of a hammer mill are its simple construction and low replacement cost for spare parts, availability in a large range of sizes, durability of hammers combined with no reduction of efficiency during their lifetime, and there is little chance of damage from hard foreign objects like stones or from empty running of the machine. The main disadvantages are an initial high cost, high power requirements, inability to produce a uniform grind, and production of a high percentage of fines.

Though a hammer mill will not produce a uniform grind, some people feel that it produces a satisfactory flour if a fine enough screen is used during milling and the material is sifted afterwards. Hammer mills are used for a number of other functions besides grinding feed—primary seed cleaning, for example. The C. S. Bell Company has successfully used their hammer mill for such homestead tasks as processing garbage for compost, grinding wood and bark for mulch, and even shredding paper for worm-farm bedding.

NORTH AMERICAN SOURCES OF HAMMER MILLS

Sears Hammer Mill

The Sears 10- and 17-inch hammer mills offer rapid handling of any dry feeds such as wheat, oats, barley, ear and shelled corn, as well as roughages like hay and stalks. With 60 hammers, the 10-inch mill runs from a 10 h.p. tractor power take-off (PTO). The larger 17-inch mill requires a 15 h.p. PTO to operate its 80 hammers.

Sears, Roebuck & Co.
Farm and Ranch Catalog

Meadows Number 5 Hammer Mill

The Meadows No. 5 hammer mill is designed for farm and specialty use. It has a V-belt drive to 24 hammers from a 5 to 10 h.p. motor. The screen measures 9 by 17 inches, and the unit employs a 4-inch fan. Shipping weight is approximately 280 pounds. Meadows also manufactures three other mills with horsepower requirements ranging from 20 to 65.

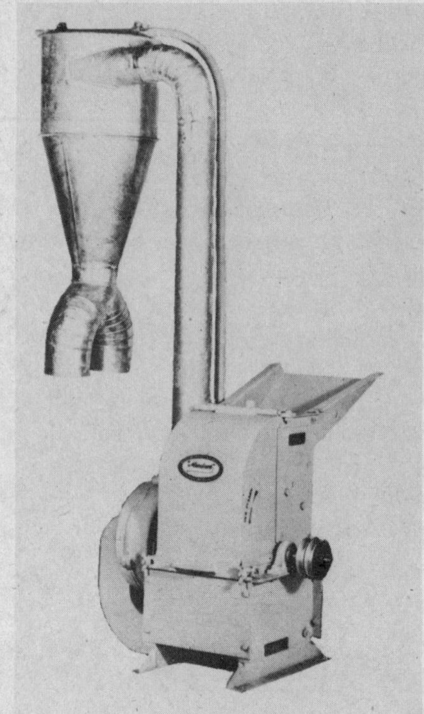

The Meadows Mill No. 5 Mighty Marvel, requiring 5 to 10 h.p. The Meadows Mill Co.

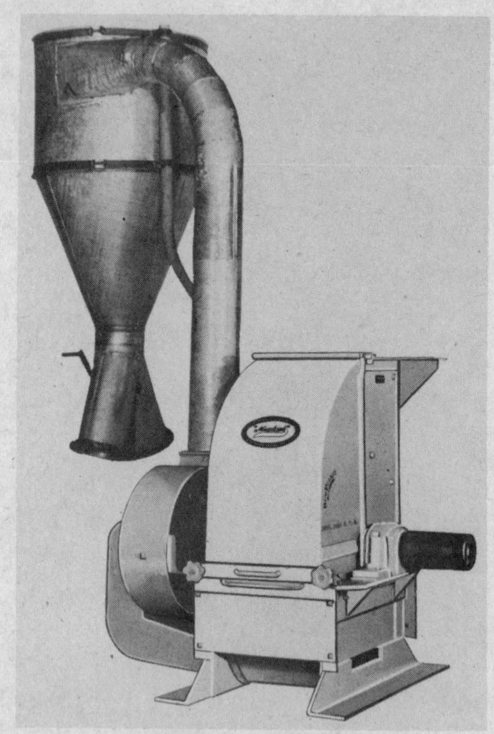

The Meadows No. 25 Trojan hammer mill requiring from 20 to 65 h.p. The Meadows Mill Co.

Meadows Mills Co.
West D St.
North Wilkesboro, NC 28659

C. S. Bell Hammer Mills

The Bell hammer mills are available in three sizes: No. 10, with a 6-inch width; No. 20, which is 9 inches wide; and No. 30, which is 12 inches wide. All are available with or without feed table; some have a blower discharge, others a bottom discharge. All models perform a variety of tasks.

C.S. Bell No. 10 Blower Hammer Mill
C.S. Bell Co.

C. S. Bell Co.
P.O. Box 291
Tiffin, OH 44883

Viking Electric Mills

The Viking electric mill's hardened steel hammer blades, which are mounted directly on the motor shaft, turn 3,600 times a minute within the full-circle screen, converting the grain kernels to correctly sized ground feed.

Viking mills are available in 1, 7½, 21, and 51 h.p. motor sizes and can mill a range of perforations from 1/16 to ½ inch. Capacities vary according to the items being milled, the perforation size, and the size of the motor. The 1 h.p. unit can mill 375 pounds per hour with a ⅛-inch mesh screen.

C.S. Bell No. 30 Bottom Discharge Hammer Mill.
C.S. Bell Co.

Burrows Equipment Co.
1316 Sherman Ave.
Evanston, IL 60204

Seedburo Equipment Co.
1022 W. Jackson Blvd.
Chicago, IL 60607

W-W Hammer Mills

W-W hammer mills have a Star Cylinder design that functions as a flywheel to reduce power requirements without sacrificing capacity. Special heat-treated reversible hammers, hard surfaced, always maintain a cutting edge. This mill is available in a range of sizes up to 150 h.p. The screens, which are easily changeable, are available with perforations ranging from 1/32 to 2 inches. As an option, this mill can be provided with a dust collector and a 20-foot pipe (without bagger). Gooseneck models are available where floor space is limited. Pulleys, sheaves, master baggers, feed tables, PTO drive, and direct motor drive can also be obtained.

Burrows Equipment Co.
1316 Sherman Ave.
Evanston, IL 60204

Model MG Hammer Mill

The Model MG hammer mill has a 15-inch wide throat and can be powered by a 5 to 30 h.p. motor. It is used to pulverize or reduce a wide variety of industrial materials including chemicals, plastics, grain, and dyes. It is also used as a finisher to smooth out a mixed product before bagging or final delivery. Direct-drive or belt-driven, this hammer mill can be mounted directly over the inlet or discharge point of a horizontal or vertical mixer in order to pulverize material before mixing or to smooth out mixtures after they are blended.

The Duplex Mill & Mfg. Co.
Springfield, OH 45501

Jacobson Models 66 and 88

Models 66 and 88 laboratory-size pulverators are belt-driven to provide a choice of grinding characteristics. They can be arranged to discharge into a bin, conveyor, or sack. Cast aluminum and steel construction assures resistance to corrosive materials. Featuring easy cleaning and a quick screen change, Models 66 and 88 have rigid hammers and adjustable feed gates and are available in two sizes, $3/4$ and $1\frac{1}{2}$ h.p.

Jacobson's new lab model Full Circle Pulverator hammer mill, Model 66-B.
Jacobson Machine Works, Inc.

Jacobson Models 120 and 160

The Models 120 and 160 utility pulverators are generally used for moderate-capacity installations of a wide variety of free-flowing materials. Of standard welded-steel construction, they are also available in stainless steel, if required. The feed hopper is equipped with a slide gate for controlled feeding. These mills are available in either belt- or direct-drive, and with power requirements ranging from $3/4$ to 200 h.p.

Jacobson Machine Works, Inc.
2445 Nevada Ave. North
Minneapolis, MN 55427

Speed King Hammer Mills

Speed King hammer mills are high-capacity, impact grinding machines which come in seven sizes. They have hinged hammers and screen sizing. Other features include changeable wear plates, feeders, auger discharge, blower and pneumatic discharge, and other special features to suit the customer's needs. Horsepower re-

Winona No. 1008 Hammer Mill
Winona Attrition Mill Co.

quirements range from 1 to 5 for capacities from 12 to 100 cubic feet per hour.

Winona Attrition Mill Co.
1009 W. Fifth St.
Winona, MN 55987

INTERNATIONAL SOURCES OF HAMMER MILLS

CeCoCo Model HM-10, Type S

The power requirement for the model HM-10 ranges from 7.5 to 10 h.p. to provide an hourly capacity of 650 kilograms of corn or 500 kilograms of dried hay. Type S requires a 1/4 h.p. motor to yield 40 to 60 kilograms per hour of crushed cereals, beans, and most other material going into animal feeds.

CeCoCo
P.O. Box 8, Ibaraki City
Osaka Pref. 567, Japan

Hammer Mills Model MF

This model comes with three screen sizes: 100, 120, and 150 millimeters, for three units with a combined power requirement ranging from 20 to 70 h.p. The smallest unit has a capacity of 200 to 300 kilograms per hour for cereals.

OTMA Hammer Mill Model MF
OTMA

OTMA
06018 Trestina Di Citta Di Castello (PG)
Italy

Vulcano Mini

The Vulcano Mini can work with knives or hammers or both. It is mounted on a column, has three fastening points for hitching to a tractor, and is available with an electric motor option. With a minimum power requirement of 15 h.p., it will mill from 500 to 1,500 kilograms of grain per hour. Larger models are also available.

F. Lli Deidone
Villafranca Verona
via a. messedaglia, 20, Italy

Funcor Fodder Grinder

This unit is specially designed for grinding many types of materials for a more complete use of animal foods. It grinds both green and dry fodders, corn cobs, oyster shells, straw, grains, and other feed materials. The unit calls for 5 h.p. and is available with either a tractor PTO link or a diesel engine. Milling size is adjustable and capacity varies accordingly.

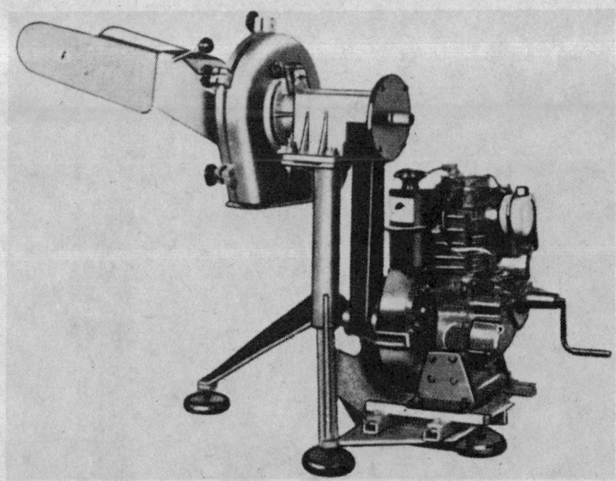

Funcor Fodder Grinder with Mounted Motor
Funcor Maquinaria Agricola

Funcor Hammer Grinder

This is a 5 h.p. machine for grinding and milling all types of grains.

Funcor Combined Grinder

This machine combines the operations of

Funcor 5 h.p. Hammer Grinder with Tractor PTO Connector
Funcor Maquinaria Agricola

Funcor Combined Grinder with Tractor PTO
Funcor Maquinaria Agricola

the Fodder Grinder and Hammer Grinder, and it can mill all kinds of grains, green and dry fodders, corn cobs, bagasse, and straw. It also has a 5 h.p. motor.

Funcor Hammer Grinder Model-A

A feeding hopper on this model can be adapted for grinding dry fodder. This larger unit has an 8 h.p. requirement. It grinds all types of grains and dry fodders, is provided with a collector-bagger cyclone, and can be joined to one or two mixers for the complete preparation of the compound fodder.

Funcor Hammer Grinder Model A with Gasoline Motor
Funcor Maquinaria Agricola

The above mills are manufactured by:
Funcor Maquinaria Agricola
Elorrio (Vizcaya)
Spain

Nogueira Disintegrator

The Nogueira Disintegrator is a versatile machine, useful for either dry or green products. It cuts sugar cane, grass, boughs, roots, and tubercles; grinds corn with husk and cob, rice straw, corn stalks, and all sorts of grain. It can produce coarse, medium, fine, and extra fine cornmeal without heating the meal. It is available in three sizes with electric motors ranging from 5 to 10 h.p., and will produce cornmeal at rates ranging from 60 to 200 kilograms per hour.

Irmaos Nogueira S.A.
Avenida Ipiranga, 1071—10 Andar
Salas: 1001/4, Sao Paulo, Brazil

Tonutti Models 70, 100, 120, 150, and 200

Tonutti makes five models of hammer mills of differing power requirements and capacities. They are all designed to handle corn cobs, barley, and grains. They can be powered by electric motor or tractor PTO.

Tonutti s.p.a.
Remanzacco
33047 UD 063, Italy

Dandekar Pounding Machine

This unit is designed for pounding, not grinding, for the specific purpose of maintaining flavor in pulverized, pungent dry spices. No detailed specifications were available in English.

Dandekar Brothers
Shirajinajar Factory Area
Sangli, Maharashtra, India

Jumil Model 6 Hammer Mill

The Jumil Model 6 is constructed of sheet metal and is powered by a 10 h.p. electric motor. The top part of the disintegrator is removable, which facilitates changing sieves and checking and changing knives and hammer rotation. Available equipment includes three types of sieves—one type for regular cornmeal, one for corn grits, and one for whole grains. Large, perforated sheets are used when chopping sugarcane, and a smaller sheet is used when pul-

Dandekar Pounding Machine
Dandekar Brothers

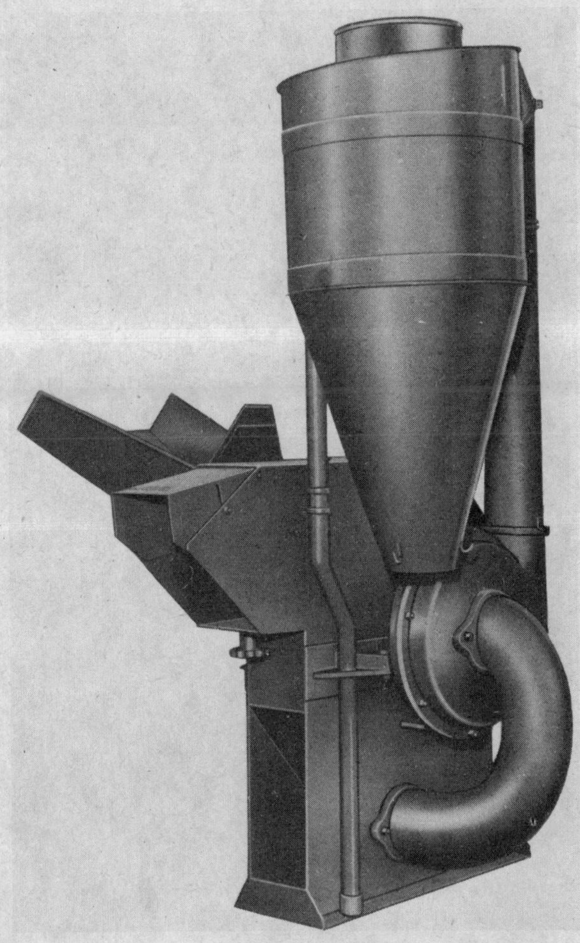

Jumil Hammer Mill
Jumil

verizing. The extra-reinforced flywheel, welded directly to the shaft, has two chopping knives and four hammers, and is made from a special steel to chop or pulverize as required. The machine pulverizes dry materials such as corn stalks with cobs, corn cobs with or without shucks, manioc, soybeans, and other dry fodders. It also pulverizes green fodders such as sugarcane, sorghum, pumpkins, and napier grass.

Justino De Morais, Irmaos S/A
Industria, Comercio e Importacao
Rua Ana Luisa, 568, Batatais-SP, Brazil

Champenois Hammer Mill V300

This French mill has a capacity ranging from 300 to 400 kilograms per hour for grains.

Champenois V300 Hammer Mill
Champenois

Champenois
Chamouilley
52170 Chevillon, France

JUICE PRESSES

Homemade fruit juices, fruit butters, cider, vinegar, wine, brandy—these are all good reasons for including a juice press on the list of tools that belong on a small, self-sufficient farm. Designs for juice presses consisting of five basic components—grinder, press, framework, juice-funneling system, and catch basin—are available from various companies as plans, kits, and fully constructed units. Use of the juice press need not be confined to that short time in autumn when cider appears on roadside stands. Fresh cider can be made as long as your supply of apples lasts in cold storage. Outside of apple season, the juice press is ready to go to work just as the blueberries, strawberries, cherries, peaches, and pears come into season to make fine homemade juices, jellies, and wines.

The single most important element in juice extraction is the efficiency of the grinding mechanism in turning the fruit into pulp. For maximum yield, every cell should be crushed. The press itself is only responsible for squeezing the juice from ruptured cells and does little to whole fruit. For this reason, grinders can be acquired separate from the pressing mechanism and framework.

A sharp, stainless steel-bladed roller is needed to cut through the tough skins of apples and chop them into pulp. Softer fruits like grapes and berries require less chopping. The squeezing action of cast-iron, ridged rollers does an adequate pulverizing job on these softer fruits. Both hand-operated and motorized crushing rollers are available. The best hand grinders have a flywheel and a three- or four-to-one gear ratio for the handle to give momentum to and take the rough spots out of the stroke.

The pressing plate can be driven by a hand-cranked press screw, a hydraulic jack, or even a car bumper jack. It is important that the framework of the press be rugged, and it is usually made of cast iron or rigidly constructed hardwood. After the fruit is crushed, the pulp is wrapped in cheesecloth and placed either inside a framework of vertically arranged wooden slats or on press trays composed of horizontal slats. The pressure exerted by the press sends the juice through the grooves in the framework to an exiting funnel.

Small Home-Built Juice Press *

This small juice press can be constructed from fairly easy-to-find discarded materials, the most important of which is an automobile bumper jack to act as a pressing mechanism. No grinder is provided on this unit, but apples may be satisfactorily pulverized with a kitchen food grinder before pressing.

Three pounds of ground fruit can be pressed at one time. Wrapped in cheesecloth, the pulp is placed inside a strong-framed press box. Routered grooves lead to exit holes which allow the juice to drain to a pan below.

MATERIALS NEEDED

Wood

1 piece 2 x 12 x 4 feet	or	**Bench:** 1 piece 2 x 12 x 36 inches **Press:** 1 piece 1½ x 7¼ x 8 inches (act. meas.)
1 piece 2 x 4 x 10 feet	or	**Legs:** 4 pieces 2 x 4 x 11 inches **Uprights:** 2 pieces 2 x 4 x 34 inches
1 piece 2 x 4 x 8 feet	or	**Crossmembers:** 4 pieces 2 x 4 x 19 inches **Mounting blocks:** 2 pieces 2 x 4 x 6 inches
1–2 feet x 4 feet sheet ¾ inch ext. plywood	or	**Juice box:** 4 pieces 8 inches x 9¼ inches
1 piece 1 x 1 x 2 feet	or	**Cleats:** 2 pieces 1 x 1 x 11¼ inches 2 pieces 1 x 1 x 10 inches

Hardware

16d nails
Glue
8d nails
6d nails
3–4½″ x 5⁄16″ bolts w/nuts
8–5⁄16″ ID fender washers
4–6″ x 5⁄16″ bolts w/nuts
Enamel paint

Miscellaneous

1 bumper jack

Construction:

1. Cut a 36-inch length of 2 x 12 and four 11-inch lengths of 2 x 4. Using 16d nails and glue, fasten the 2 x 4 legs to the bench.
2. Cut four 19-inch lengths of 2 x 4 for jack support crossmembers. Fasten one to the bottom of the bench, against the front legs. A narrow face of the 2 x 4 should be against the bench bottom, a broad face against the legs. Use glue and 16d nails, driving the nails through the support into the legs, and through the bench into the support. Using a short 2 x 4 as a temporary spacer, locate the second lower support crossmember and glue and nail it in place. Then remove the spacer.
3. Construct the box. The press can have a plywood box, but you can construct yours of 1 x 10 material. Cut four 8-inch by

* Reprinted from *Build It Better Yourself,* by the editors of *Organic Gardening and Farming* (Emmaus, Pa. Rodale Press, Inc. 1977).

Bumper Jack Juice Press

9¼-inch pieces of ¾-inch plywood, then glue and nail them together, using 8d nails, forming the juice box.

4. Place the box in position, centered on the bench between the supports. Scribe a line on the benchtop around the inside of the box. Remove the box, then drill three rows of ½-inch holes through the bench. You must locate the rows of holes so they penetrate the bench in front of, between, and behind the supports. The juice will run out of the box through these holes. To speed that process, a crosshatch pattern of grooves should be routered into the bench within the confines of the box. In doing this, be sure not to damage your router bit on the nails you've driven into the bench to secure the jack support crossmembers. Now replace the box and toenail it in place with 6d nails. Cut two 11¼-inch and two 10-inch lengths of 1 x 1 stock and using 6d nails, fasten them to the bench around the outside of the box.
5. Modify the bumper jack. The jack shaft socket in the base must be cut off so the shaft will pass through the base. Then the ratchet mechanism must be welded to the base, so the base moves up and down the shaft with the ratchet mechanism. A welding shop can do this work quickly and inexpensively.
6. Cut two 6-inch lengths of 2 x 4. With a backsaw and chisel, cut a groove across the center of a broad face of each to accommodate half the thickness of the jack shaft. The two blocks are then sandwiched with the end of the shaft between them, as shown. Drill a 5⁄16-inch hole through the three-piece

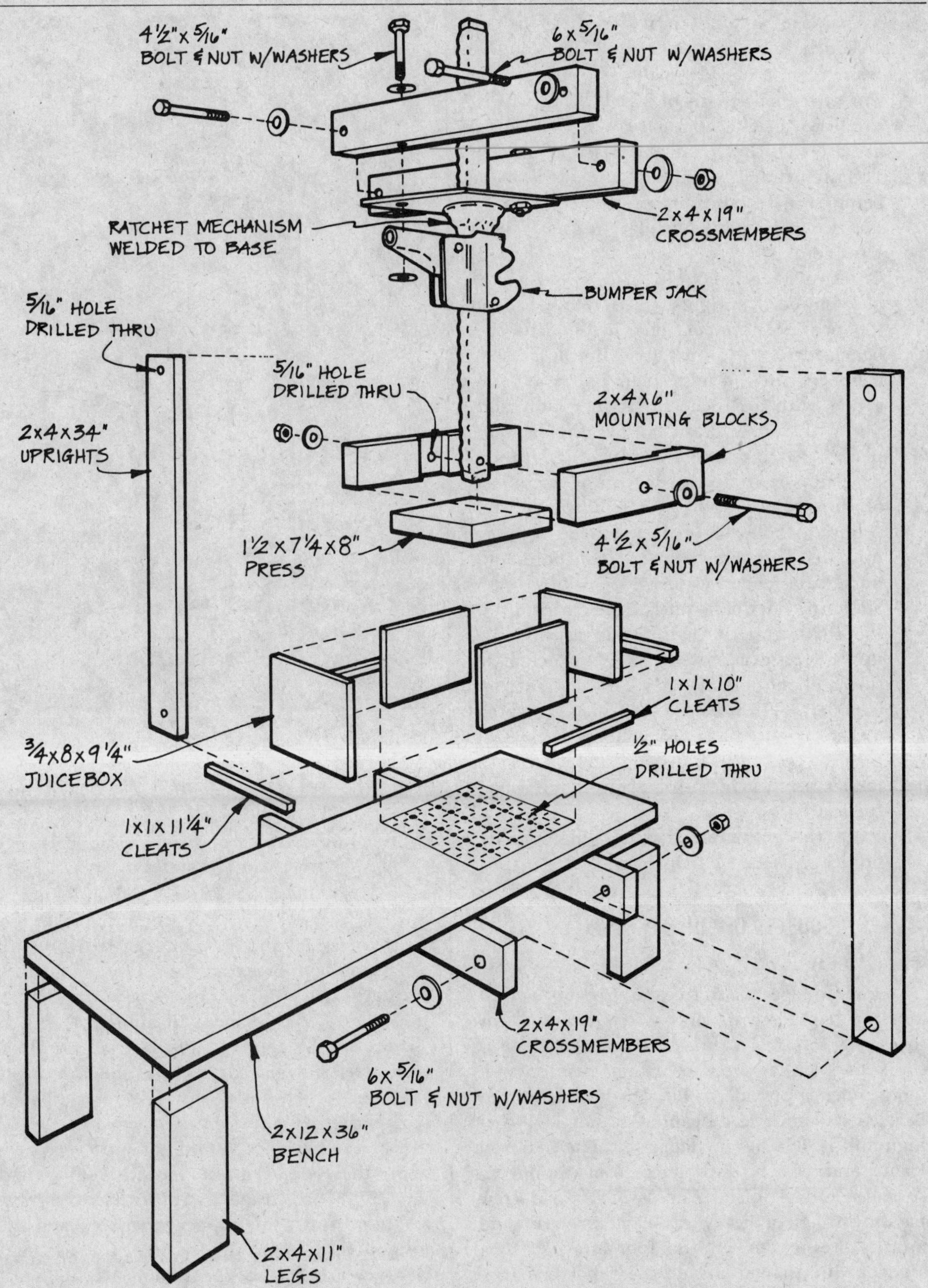
4½" x 5/16" BOLT & NUT W/WASHERS
6 x 5/16" BOLT & NUT W/WASHERS
2 x 4 x 19" CROSSMEMBERS
RATCHET MECHANISM WELDED TO BASE
BUMPER JACK
5/16" HOLE DRILLED THRU
5/16" HOLE DRILLED THRU
2 x 4 x 34" UPRIGHTS
2 x 4 x 6" MOUNTING BLOCKS
1½ x 7¼ x 8" PRESS
4½ x 5/16" BOLT & NUT W/WASHERS
1 x 1 x 10" CLEATS
¾ x 8 x 9¼" JUICEBOX
½" HOLES DRILLED THRU
1 x 1 x 11¼" CLEATS
2 x 4 x 19" CROSSMEMBERS
6 x 5/16" BOLT & NUT W/WASHERS
2 x 12 x 36" BENCH
2 x 4 x 11" LEGS

assemblage and fasten it together with a 4½-inch by 5⁄16-inch bolt. Use fender washers on each side of the assemblage.

7. Cut an 8-inch length of 2 x 12, then rip it to the width of a nominal 2 x 8, that is, an actual 7¼ inches. Nail this piece to the 2 x 4s fastened to the end of the jack shaft, being sure to position the wood grains of the two parts perpendicular to each other. Use 16d nails.
8. Cut two 34-inch lengths of 2 x 4, for the jack support uprights. Slip one between the two crossmembers on each side of the bench, drill a 5⁄16-inch hole through crossmembers and upright, then bolt them together with a 6-inch by 5⁄16-inch bolt and nut with fender washers. Set the jack in place, then take the two remaining upper jack support crossmembers (cut at the outset of the project) and, after drilling the appropriate holes, bolt them to the support uprights. Use 6-inch by 5⁄16-inch bolts and nuts with fender washers.
9. Slide the jack-base/ratchet mechanism up the shaft until it seats firmly against the upper crossmembers. Drill a 5⁄16-inch hole through the metal base and each crossmember. Then secure the metal jacking mechanism to the crossmembers with 4½-inch by 5⁄16-inch bolts and nuts, with a fender washer included against the wood surface.
10. Paint the entire press with a high-quality nonleaded enamel paint.

SOURCES OF JUICE PRESSES

The AVI Cottager

The Cottager is a simple, heavily constructed tabletop fruit or wine press. It is designed for squeezing soft fruits, but it is only efficient if the fruit is either sliced or ground beforehand. No grinder is provided. The hardwood tub has beveled staves for easy cleaning, stands 11 inches high and is 9 inches in diameter. The cast-iron frame and oak base produce a maximum in strength and rigidity. The ¾-inch press-screw passes through a heavy cast-iron crossarm and applies pressure to an iron foot attached to a wooden disc that fits inside the tub. The base is 11 inches square, height is 21 inches, and the weight is 30 pounds.

AVI Cottager

The AVI American Harvester

The American Harvester double-tub cider mill is a hand-operated mill capable of doing both pressing and grinding at the same time. The double-tub feature becomes a practical advantage when you're processing a large number of apples. The quantity of apples processed depends on the speed of the operator(s). Experience has shown that two people can produce as much as 30 gallons in one hour (that's the current record), but ordinarily, two people working at a steady pace should not expect to produce more than 80 gallons of cider in an average day.

The basic frame is constructed entirely of oak, the tray and hopper of maple and alder, respectively. All joints are dadoed (rectangular grooves are cut in them) and cross-bolted for

AVI American Harvester

structural rigidity. The hardwood tubs are 12 inches high and 13½ inches in diameter, and have beveled staves for easy cleaning. The press-screw is 1½ inches in diameter; the grinder housing is all cast iron. The grinding cylinder is laminated hardwood with inserted stainless steel teeth. A 16-inch flywheel and 3 to 1 gear ratio accompany the handle. Overall size is 22 inches wide, 36 inches long, and 45 inches high. The press weighs approximately 200 pounds.

The Villager

The Villager is a single-tub cider or wine press with the same basic frame and press-screw assembly as the double-tub model. It has been specifically designed as an all-purpose fruit press which is capable of grinding and squeezing a variety of fruits, including apples. The grinding attachment is mounted directly over the tub, allowing the pulped fruit to be squeezed in place. The large bevel-staved tub holds about a bushel of pulped apples and will yield from 1 to 3 gallons per press (depending on the kind of apples used). The handle is a heavy flywheel with direct drive attached to the grinding shaft. The overall size is 18 by 22 by 42 inches high. Weight is about 125 pounds.

AVI Villager

The above three presses are available from:
American Village Institute
440 Meyers St.
Kettle Falls, WA 99141

Rolling River Presses, Inc.
Dept. 499, 5 Ranch Rite Rd.
Yakima, WA 98901

Berarducci Brothers

Berarducci Brothers are manufacturers, exporters, and importers of Italian specialty equipment for the kitchen. Their product line includes a variety of electric and manual fruit crushers and both hydraulic and press-screw fruit presses, for example:

Superior Electric—A 1/4 h.p.-driven mill for grapes. The roller is of cast aluminum, 9 inches by 4 1/4 inches. Weight: 100 pounds.

Ontario Electric—A 1/4 h.p.-driven mill for apples, pears, and plums. Roller is cast aluminum, 5 3/4 inches by 17 inches. Weight: 75 pounds.

Erie Electric—A grape crusher with 10 by 3 1/2 inch cast aluminum rollers. It is driven by a 1/4 h.p. motor. Weight: 37 pounds.

Michigan—A manual press with all red oak frame and hopper, and double-aluminum rollers; handle-driven for grapes. Weight: 25 pounds.

Erie—A manual press with all-aluminum hopper, sharp teeth-type aluminum single-roller mounted on an aluminum frame, and red oak hardwood cross handles; handle-driven for grapes. Weight: 21 pounds.

Superior—A manual fruit crusher with all red oak wood frame and hopper, double-aluminum rollers, and adjustable bearings for spacing rollers; flywheel-driven for grapes.

The six sizes of hydraulic fruit presses are constructed of selected red oak hardwood to purify and not taint the delicately flavored juices. All cast-iron parts are machine finished for easy operation and painted with a heavy, blue, acid-resisting enamel. The diameter of the pressing plate varies from 16 to 25 inches, according to the size of the model. Its capacity for crushed pulp ranges from 150 to 800 pounds.

One press-screw press is available with a ratchet system handle, 11-inch diameter press plate and 3/4-inch diameter press screw. It weighs 30 pounds and has a capacity for 60 pounds of crushed pulp.

Berarducci Brothers Mfg. Company, Inc.
1900 Fifth Ave.
McKeesport, PA 15132

Fruit Press

The Colonial-style grinding unit of this fruit press has stainless steel cutters mounted in a 4-inch wooden roller with a 12-inch diameter flywheel. A bushel of apples can be ground in 15 to 20 minutes. Pressing 3 gallons of cider takes only 3 minutes. The fruit press stands 4 feet high, and is made of hardwoods, spruce, and exterior plywood. Attached to the press, the grinder will drop fruit pulp directly into the pressing tub, or it can be removed and bolted to another support. This way, two people can work together, one grinding and the other pressing. The press plate is driven by a 1-inch diameter, threaded steel press-screw. The unit comes unassembled.

Cumberland General Store
Rt. 3
Crossville, TN 38555

Farnam Sunrise Equipment & Supplies
P.O. Box 12068
Omaha, NE 68112

Garden Way Research
Charlotte, VT 05445

Good Nature Fruit Press

Good Nature Products offers three sizes of hydraulically operated fruit presses. The hydraulic jack employed can apply 6,000 pounds of pressure and will retract itself with one turn of a valve, unlike the old press-screws which had to be cranked backwards before starting a second batch. The familiar slotted tub of other models is replaced in this one with several layers of slotted, flat wooden racks between which cloth bags full of pumice are squeezed. The racks insure that no drop of juice has to force its way through more than one inch of pulp, whereas the old tub presses required that juice travel through as much as 10 inches of packed fruit pulp. This press yields about 3 or 4 gallons of juice from each bushel of apples. The grinder design incorporates a rotating drum with short, stainless steel blades that shave apples gradually as they rotate, forcing the pulp through a narrow slot from which a coarse applesauce emerges. The drum is turned with a hand crank, electric drill, or 1/4 h.p. electric motor. Available models

The Goodnatured Fruit Press
Good Nature Products, Inc.

include a 130-pound press with a capacity of 1 to 5 bushels for a maximum output of 60 gallons per hour, a 110-pound press with a capacity of 1 to 2½ bushels for a maximum output of 30 gallons per hour, and a 55-pound table press with a 1-bushel capacity for an output of 12 gallons per hour.

Good Nature's electric grinder is self-feeding, has all stainless steel parts, grinds up to 30 pounds of apples per minute, and is powered by a ½ h.p. electric motor. It can be used to grind or shred any fruits, vegetables, or cheeses. The company's manual grinder is hand crank operated, but may be automated with an electric drill. The polyvinyl chloride drum with stainless steel blades will grind almost any fruit or vegetable.

Good Nature Products, Inc.
4879 Old Buffalo Rd.
Warsaw, NY 14569

Hand Crank Hopper Kit

This kit includes a precut oak frame, crushing roller, and all the hardware you need, ready for assembly.

Hand Crank Hopper Kit
MacKay's Wood Products

Portable Hand Crank Press

This press is of the oak stave barrel-type. The grinder is positioned directly over the press tub and is manually operated with a gear reduction crank. The press is hand cranked also. The

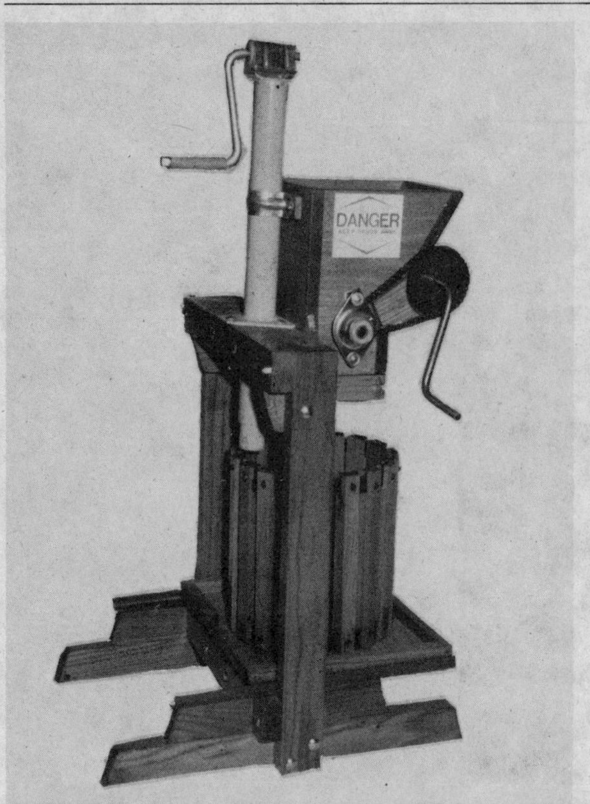

MacKay's Portable Hand Crank Press
MacKay's Wood Products

unit is 18 inches wide, 22 inches long, and 35 inches high: Weight: 60 pounds.

Electric Press Models A223 and A203

Complete and ready to run, this press is supplied with either one or two oak drums. A ¼ h.p. electric motor drives the grinder. The press is hand cranked. This press is 18 inches wide, 29 inches long, and 30 inches high. Weight: 100 pounds.

Commercial Press

This press replaces the stave press barrel with a 17-inch oak press rack. It has a high-speed, six-knife cutter head in the grinder which is powered by a 1 h.p. electric motor. Thirty-inch, heavyweight, nylon cloths are provided to contain the fruit pulp during pressing. Pressing is done by a 3,000-pound hydraulic jack. Model C1K1 comes with six press cloths, seven oak racks and one oak cheese form. Model C2K2 comes with 12 press cloths, 13 oak racks and one cheese form.

MacKay's Electric Press
MacKay's Wood Products

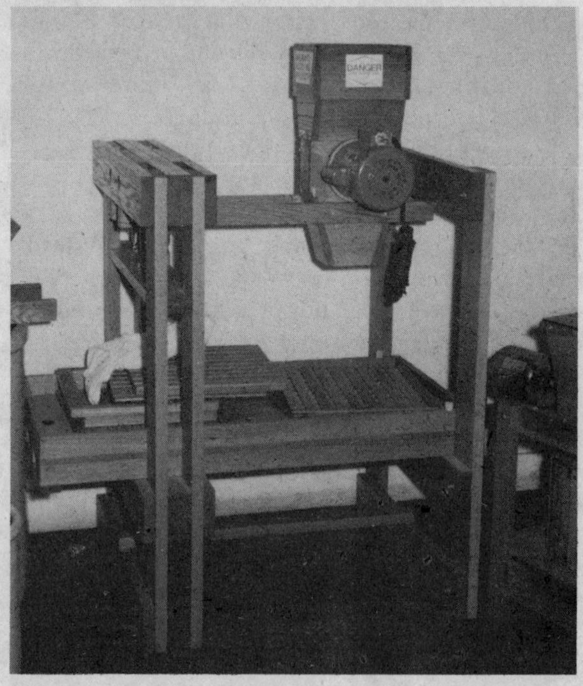

MacKay's Commercial Press
MacKay's Wood Products

The above four presses are manufactured by:
MacKay's Wood Products
10th and Taylor Ave., P.O. Box 1023
Bellingham, WA 98225

Bell's Hand-Turned Crusher

This press has a finished hardwood hopper and sides with cast-iron cutter, side mounting plates, and a counterbalanced crank. A perforated screen allows apples and fruits to be ground to the proper size. The grinder will process approximately 90 pounds of apples per hour. The 24 by 13 by 13-inch grinder is easily disassembled for easy cleaning. Shipping weight: 38 pounds.

Bell's Fruit-Wine Press

This press is constructed of cast iron and white oak (a wood that is favored because it will not impart any undesirable taste to the juices.) It has a vertical-slat press tub and hand-operated press-screw. Shipping weight: 35 pounds.

Bell's Hand-Turned Crusher
C.S. Bell Co.

Bell's Fruit-Wine Press
C.S. Bell Co.

Both presses are manufactured by:
C. S. Bell Co.
170 W. Davis St., Box 291
Tiffin, OH 44883

Sears' Hand-Turned Fruit Crusher

This model comes with cast-iron crusher teeth, steel crusher screen, and oak hopper and sides. It holds one peck of apples and measures 24 by 9½ by 13 inches.

Sears, Roebuck & Co.
Farm and Ranch Catalog

Five-Quart Fruit Press

Of cast-iron and hardwood construction, this press has a capacity of approximately 5 quarts. It has a vertical-slat tub and hand-operated press-screw. Shipping weight: 24 to 25 pounds.

Belknap, Inc. (distributor)
P.O. Box 28
Louisville, KY 40201

Glen-Bel's Country Store
Rt. 5, Box 390
Crossville, TN 38555

Sears, Roebuck & Co.
Farm and Ranch Catalog

Cumberland's Fruit Crusher

For grapes, berries, cherries, and other soft fruits, excluding apples, this crusher has an oak frame and an 18½ by 18-inch hopper which holds 30 pounds of whole grapes. Its two stationary rollers are made of aluminum. Shipping weight: 25 pounds.

Fruit Crusher
Cumberland General Store

Apple Crusher

The machined claw-cut teeth on this press work well to extract juice from all kinds of fruit, especially apples, which are difficult to grind. A selected hardwood 18½ by 17-inch wide hopper with a 45-pound capacity feeds a 32 by 16½-inch cast aluminum roller. The handle operates on a 17-inch diameter flywheel.

Apple Crusher
Cumberland General Store

Cider Press

Constructed of red oak for purer juice and for strength, this press weighs approximately 90 pounds and can hold 250 pounds of crushed apples. Its cast-iron parts are machine finished and painted with acid-resisting enamel. The press stands 43 inches high, and tub size is 12 by 18 inches.

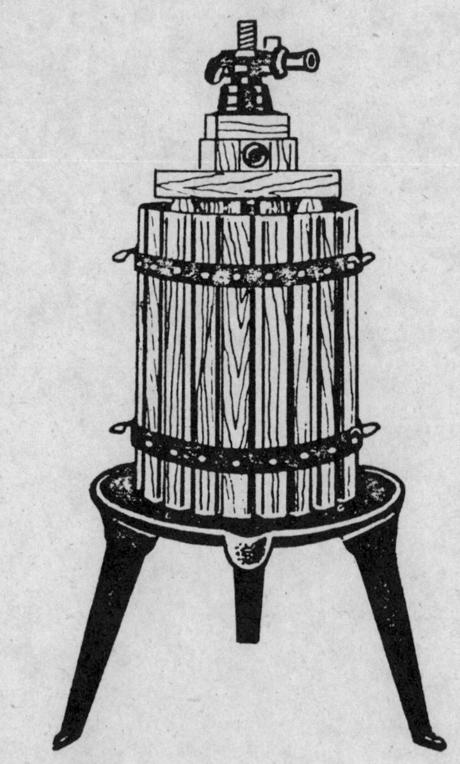

Cider Press
Cumberland General Store

Kits

Cumberland also carries a fruit grinder kit and a cider press kit. Both kits contain plans, and all the hardware necessary for building. No lumber is included.

The above four presses are available from:
Cumberland General Store
Rt. 3, Box 479
Crossville, TN 38555

Day Equipment

Both electric and hand-operated presses are available from this company for use in roadside stands and small orchards. Graders, press racks, cloths, labels, filters, pasteurizers, picking bags, cutters, and all the accessories needed for a small operation are also available.

Day Equipment Corp.
1402 E. Monroe
Goshen, IN 46526

Hydraulic Cider Presses, Palmer-Style

These presses are specially suited to roadside stand and orchard use. A full line of accessories is available.

Orchard Equipment & Supply Co.
Conway, MA 01341

Wine, Fruit, and Cider Press Plans

Plans for a wooden-framed, slat-sided, oak, basket-style press with a hand-cranked press-screw are included in a catalog from New Jersey. An electric drill and router are required to build the press, but no other special tools are needed. Instruction plans only are provided.

Dorsay Poor Man's Catalog 3
240 Kinderkamaca Rd.
Oradell, NJ 07649

Mearelli Presses

Mearelli offers a full line of hand-operated and electric fruit crushers, hydraulic, vertical-staved presses, and hammer mill-type electric crushers. Units range in size from models appropriate for the home and small farm to large commercial applications, with a full range of sizes in between. Mearelli also offers accessories for all your wine-making needs, including wood kegs, wine pumps, and bottle corkers.

Manual Fruit Crusher

This manual crusher, available in either wood or iron, has roller supports and gears enclosed in cast iron. Five sizes are available in iron, ranging in weight from 28 to 45 pounds. Three sizes are available in wood, ranging from 30 to 39 pounds.

Iron Manual Crusher
Mearelli S.P.A.

Motored Crusher

Two models of this powered crusher are available, with either monophase 0.5 h.p. motor weighing 56 kilograms, or three-phase 0.5 h.p. motor weighing 59 kilograms.

AM Motored Crusher
Mearelli S.P.A.

PVD/15 Manually Operated Stemmer-Crusher
Mearelli S.P.A.

PVD/15

This model is a manually operated stemmer-crusher, with a removable screen for maintenance. Weight: 60 kilograms.

Lever Press
Mearelli S.P.A.

Lever Press

This lever press comes in fourteen sizes ranging in weight from 17 to 750 kilograms.

Hydraulic Press on Wheels

Utilizing a hydraulic jack, this press operates with glycerine oil and attains pressures of 350 to 400 atmospheres. Eight models are available, ranging in weight from 160 to 830 kilograms.

At this time, Mearelli is interested in locating distributors for its products in North America.

Mearelli S.P.A.
Trestina (pg)
Italy

Hydraulic Press on Wheels
Mearelli S.P.A.

CORN SHELLERS

Feed mills grind cobs and kernels together for cattle feed, but hand- or power-operated shellers are required to separate the kernels from the cobs before the corn can be ground into meal for people and for most other animals.

Several manufacturers produce small, hand-operated shellers which can be clamped onto a board or the edge of a box or barrel. Larger shellers are turned by a handle, by pedals, or by belt drive from an engine or electric motor as required. Large power-driven maize shellers are often fitted with cleaning fans and screens to separate the grain from husks, dust, and spent cobs.

Hand Corn Sheller

Appropriate for shelling small amounts of a wide variety of corn, this hand sheller is especially desirable for shelling seed corn because it does not break off the germ ends of the kernels. It is similar to the sheller described in the following article.

Burrows Equipment Co.
1316 Sherman Ave.
Evanston, IL 60204

Cumberland General Store
Rt. 3, Box 479
Crossville, TN 38555

Nasco Agricultural Sciences
901 Janesville Ave.
Fort Atkinson, WI 53538

A MAIZE SHELLER FOR EVERY HOUSEHOLD*

by Dr. D. J. Hilton

Senior Lecturer, Dept. of Mechanical Engineering, University of Nairobi, Kenya

One type of hand sheller currently sold in parts of Africa is made from a metal tube, with internal ribs set in the direction of the cylinder axis. The sheller is held in one hand while the other hand pushes the maize cob into the tube with a twisting action. The internal ribs strip the kernels from the cobs, and the kernels fall out the bottom of the tube. This sheller, which is now being made from an aluminum casting, has been found to have two disadvantages. First, the ribs are too numerous and tend to become clogged with grain. Second, the sheller is really only suited to one diameter of cob. Where both traditional and hybrid varieties are grown, therefore, it is not capable of stripping all cobs satisfactorily.

I have overcome these difficulties by redesigning the tube sheller and incorporating two novel features. At the same time, the cost has been lowered by a change of material.

The tube of the new sheller is constructed from a short length of 2-inch diameter rigid, polyvinyl chloride water pipe. This is a readily available material in industrial centers in most countries. The ribs are made from the same pipe, cut into thin strips, and glued together in stacks of three or four. For glue, a polyvinyl chloride solvent is used which is supplied for use with polyvinyl chloride water pipe by all distributors. Four such ribs are then glued to the inside of the tube at 90-degree intervals. This placement allows the ribs to reach the core of the maize cob, and still leaves enough space between them to allow the grain to drop through. The two novel features I introduced are as follows:

1. A slit is made along the tube to allow it to expand when very large cobs are being stripped. This is made possible by the elasticity of the material. Residual stresses in the material, as a result of the pipe extrusion process, ensure that the tube normally remains well closed.
2. One of the four internal ribs is positioned higher up the tube than the other three and this is the rib which does most of the stripping. It is found that this feature results in an easier stripping action than when four ribs strip off the grain simultaneously.

The performance of the new maize sheller is quite impressive and a dry cob can be stripped in about 5 to 7 seconds. This compares very favorably with the performance of other designs, though

* Reprinted with permission from *Appropriate Technology*, August 1976.

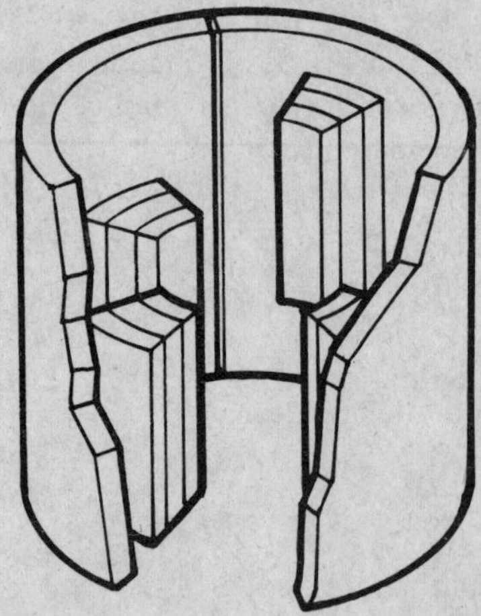

A cutaway view of a PVC sheller with a slit in one side for expanding with the size of the cob.

it is accepted that the vigorous wrist action involved could not be maintained for prolonged periods. The tools required for manufacturing this sheller are minimal; they consist of a hacksaw, small clamp or vice, and sandpaper. The cement used is a standard polyvinyl chloride solvent which produces a very powerful bond, provided the surfaces are free of grease.

The material cost including normal waste is low, and each sheller takes around 1 to 1½ hours to assemble by hand. The product is beginning to sell in a few areas on a trial basis and indications are that demand will be considerable when the product is given a little promotion.

A SIMPLE MANUAL MAIZE-SHELLING DEVICE*

by Professor A. S. Rana

Head of the Department of Agricultural Engineering
and Land Planning, University of Dar-es-Salaam

In many developing countries, most of the maize (corn) is produced by small subsistence farmers, and whatever little surplus is available is sold at the market. The subsistence farmers in many countries in Africa grow only a few hectares of maize, and these are often intercropped. The yields in general are low, about 1,000 kilograms per hectare. Under these conditions all the shelling is done by hand, and the following methods are generally used:

1. With bare hands, holding the cob in the palm with four fingers, a person removes the grains one by one with the movement of the thumb. The shelled corn is consumed or sold as is without cleaning or grading.
2. Rubbing a shelled cob on a cob to be shelled is faster than the first method but is more tiring and requires skill and practice. It is not very suitable for maize with a high moisture content, as the grains are sometimes bruised and the shelling rate is low. The shelled grains are used as in the first method.
3. This method involves putting the husked cobs in a bag and beating them with a stick while turning the bag. Later on, the cobs and grains are taken out of the bag and cobs are picked. Any grains remaining on the cobs are taken off by hand as in the first method.
4. There are some variations of this method, but basically, the cobs are spread on a raised platform made of sticks and bamboo poles, with small gaps between the adjoining pieces. The spread cobs are beaten with a stick; the shelled grains fall through the gaps; the remaining grains on the cob are removed by hand.

* Abridged from *Appropriate Technology,* vol. 2, no. 1, May 1975.

Maize shelling is not a labor bottleneck for the small producer, especially if he is only growing for home consumption. The family sits together in the evening and shells maize by hand, while talking for a few hours. One evening of shelling is sufficient for a week's supply of corn. Most of the maize being brought to the market by the peasant farmer is shelled by one of the four methods described above.

For larger producers, such as those who grow corn to feed their livestock as well as themselves, these simple shelling methods aren't sufficient. The following device has been found to be, on the average, about three times more efficient than the methods described above.

The shelling section consists of U-nails (also called staples) arranged on a wooden board in a way that will facilitate the smooth rubbing of the maize to be shelled. Various arrangements of fixing the U-nails on the wooden board were tried. The best results have been obtained by fixing the U-nails in two rows parallel to each other 1.9 to 2.0 centimeters apart, and 2.5 centimeters between the nails within the row.

HAND-CRANKED CORN SHELLER

A manual cranking handle, sometimes accompanied by a flywheel, powers this simple but effective corn sheller. A compression spring adjustment enables the sheller to adapt to the size of each cob as it enters the feed opening. Husked corncobs are forced by hand into a feeding device which delivers the cob between one stationary and one rotating, toothed, cast-iron shelling plate, and are held in place by spring-loaded stripping claws. The action of the rotating plates causes the cob to rotate in a spiral fashion against the teeth, with the kernels flying off as it feeds through. After shelling is completed, the bare cob follows an ejection path automatically and makes way for the next cob to follow directly, as soon as the operator can feed it into the opening. The least expensive models clamp directly to a fence or tub side while the sturdier, generally faster models come inside a wooden or metal housing. Many come with an attachment for shelling walnuts.

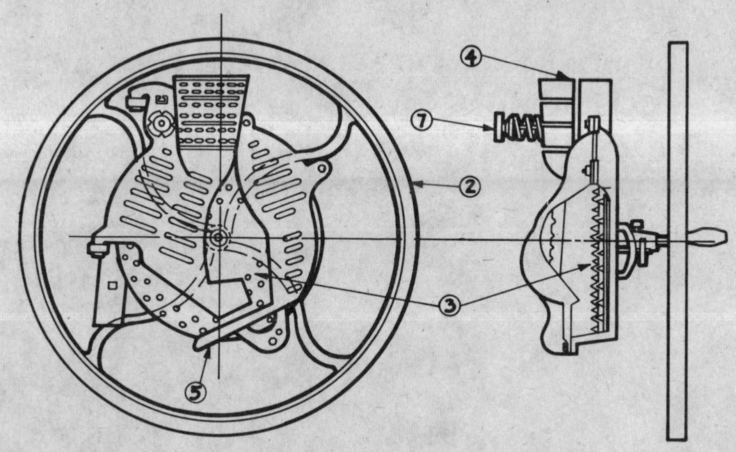

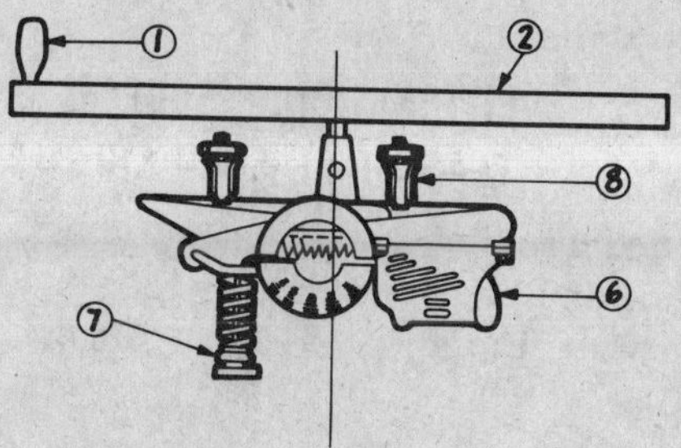

Hand Crank Corn Sheller: 1) manual handle, 2) power pulley (flywheel), 3) shelling disc, 4) corn inlet, 5) shelled corn outlet, 6) shelled cob outlet, 7) compression spring, 8) clamps.

NORTH AMERICAN SOURCES OF CLAMP-TYPE CORN SHELLERS

C. S. Bell Co.
P.O. Box 291
Tiffin, OH 44883

Burrows Equipment Co.
1316 Sherman Ave.
Evanston, IL 60204

Cumberland's Red Chief with unshelled corn entering at the top and shelled corn exiting at the bottom.
Cumberland General Store

The ribbed cone in the middle of the C.S. Bell Corn Sheller is an attachment for shelling walnuts.
C.S. Bell

Cumberland General Store
Rt. 3, Box 479
Crossville, TN 38555

Glen-Bel's Country Store
Rt. 5, Box 390
Crossville, TN 38555

INTERNATIONAL SOURCES OF CLAMP-TYPE CORN SHELLERS

Allied Trading Company (India)
Railway Road, Ambala City 134 002
Haryana, India

CeCoCo
P.O. Box 8, Ibaraki City
Osaka Pref. 567, Japan

Cossul & Co. Pvt., Ltd.
Industrial Area, Fazalgunj
Kanpur, India

Dandekar Brothers
(Engineers & Founders)
Sangli, Maharashtra, India

R. Hunt & Co., Ltd.
Atlas Works, Earls Colne
Colchester, Essex CO6 2EP, U.K.

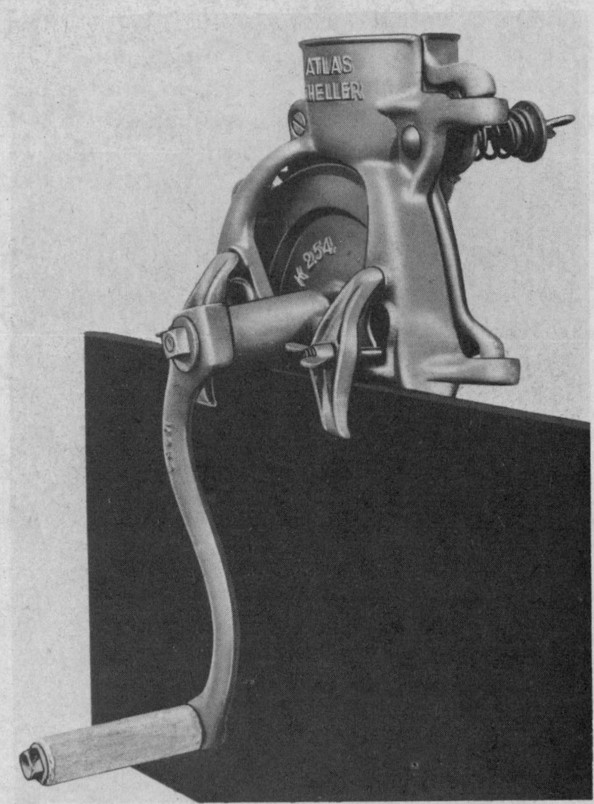

The Atlas Sheller secured to a vertical board as one might attach it to a fence.
R. Hunt

Ernest H. Johnson (Pty.) Ltd.
Box 7536
Johannesburg 2000, South Africa

Ransomes, Sims, & Jeffries, Ltd.
Nacton Rd.
Ipswich, IP3 9QG, U.K.

SOURCES OF OTHER MANUAL CORN SHELLERS

AVI Corn Sheller

This sheller has all-metal parts of either cast iron or steel. The housing frame is constructed of oak, and the remainder of the sheller is alder or maple. The flywheel is 21 inches in diameter and is mounted on a ¾-inch steel shaft. The sheller's dimensions are 12 by 30 by 42 inches, and it weighs approximately 125 pounds.

The AVI Cornsheller, showing the hand crank and corn exit. On the other side of the sheller, a large flywheel gives each stroke momentum.

American Village Institute
440 Meyers St.
Kettle Falls, WA 99141

Rotary Corn Thresher Plans

Fully illustrated instructions for building a corn thresher are available from ITDG. On this model, drive is supplied by converting a bicycle pedal and sprocket system into a hand crank.

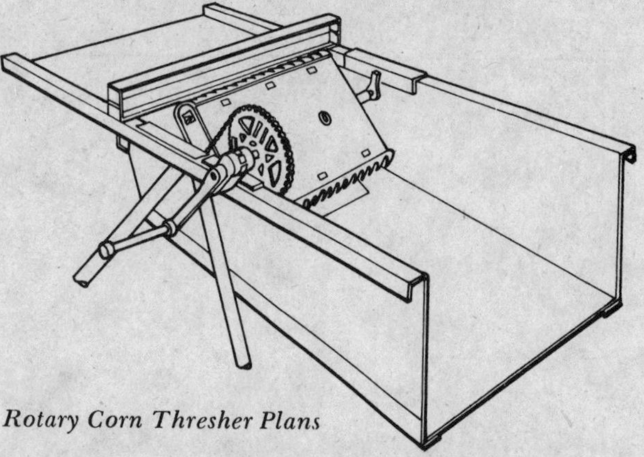

Rotary Corn Thresher Plans

Intermediate Technology Publications, Ltd.*
9 King St.
London WC 2E 8HN, England

CeCoCo Sheller Type Number 4

Sheller No. 4 is treadle-operated and attached to a stand with driving gears, flywheel, and pedal. The body is made of cast iron, the stand of angle iron. Its capacity ranges between 300 and 350 bushels per hour at a standard rate of 250 revolutions per minute. Shipping weight: 75 kilograms.

CeCoCo
P.O. Box 8, Ibaraki City
Osaka Pref. 567, Japan

NORTH AMERICAN SOURCES OF POWER CORN SHELLERS

Burrows Corn Sheller

Burrows' Model 22 is the smallest of three available shellers with aspirator and cob blower. Operable with either a 10 or 15 h.p. motor, it will yield a capacity of up to 400 bushels per

* Intermediate Technology publications can be ordered from International Scholarly Book Service, Inc., Box 555, Forest Grove, Oregon 97116.

hour. The 8-inch diameter cob pipe can be up to 100 feet long with up to 45 feet of vertical pipe left. Height of the sheller is 4 feet. Models are also available to be run with 25, 30, 40, and 50 h.p. motors.

Burrows Equipment Co.
1316 Sherman Ave.
Evanston, IL 60204

Haban Number 101-007 Husker-Sheller

The Haban No. 101-007 Husker-Sheller is made to shell corn of any variety or size. Corn is fed into the machine at a comfortable height of 32 inches. A corn thrower is used to elevate the shelled corn into a truck or storage container. This model is available on wheels or as a stationary unit with a power take-off drive. It requires a 15 to 25 h.p. gasoline or 5 to 7 h.p. electric motor.

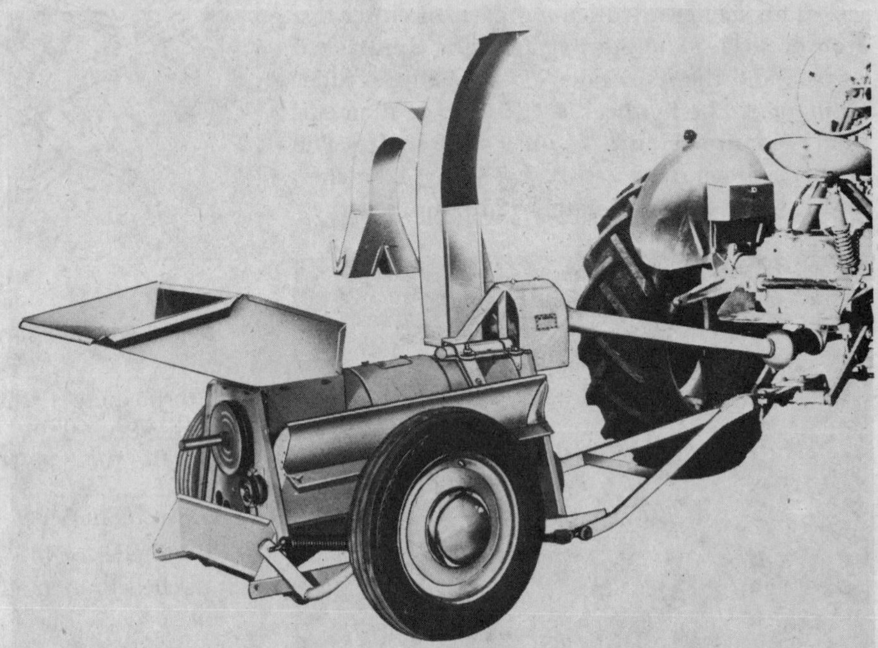

Haban No. 101-007 Husker Sheller, complete with two wheel trailer.
Haban Mfg. Co.

SHELLING CAPACITY IN BUSHELS PER HOUR

Condition of Corn	Moisture Content of Corn (Percent): 17 Percent and Less	17 to 25 Percent	25 Percent and Greater
Clean corn (no husks)	350 to 500	250 to 350	200 to 250
Corn with 50 percent husks	250 to 350	200 to 250	150 to 200
Corn with 100 percent husks	200 to 250	150 to 200	100 to 150

Haban Husker-Sheller

Haban's smaller unit, powered by a 6 h.p. gasoline or 2 h.p. electric motor, also handles all types and sizes of corn. It separates husks, cobs, dirt, and dust. Feeding height is 33 inches.

Both shellers are made by:
Haban Mfg. Co.
Racine, WI 53404

Sears Husker-Shellers

Until 1978, Sears offered a three-point hitch

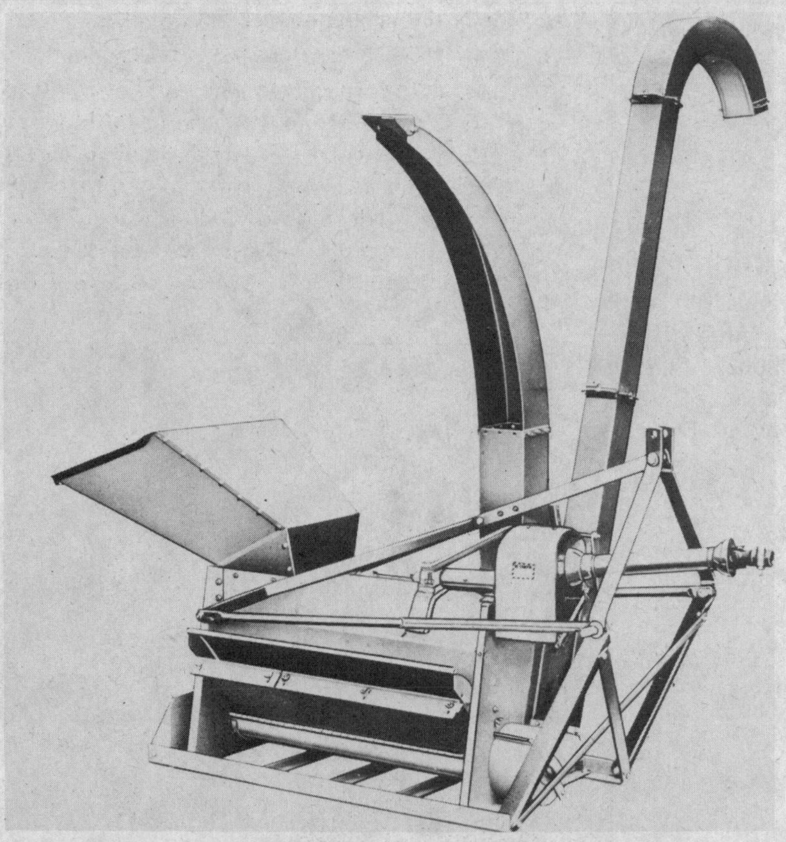

Haban No. 101-005 Husker Sheller, complete with 3-point lift.
Haban Mfg. Co.

and pull-behind husker–sheller operated off a tractor's power take-off shaft. It could strip husks, extract cobs, and separate and clean shells of most types of corn. The sheller was constructed of 36 by 27 by 56-inch-high, heavy-duty galvanized steel units with low, four-way adjustable hoppers for convenient loading. The cob stacker pipe discharged husks and cobs at many positions. A large cleaning fan and sieve with controlled air blasts cleaned shelled corn three times. Sears discontinued its sheller for lack of demand, but they may return it to the market if a demand reveals itself!

Sears, Roebuck & Co.
Farm and Ranch Catalog

INTERNATIONAL SOURCES OF POWER CORN SHELLERS

Cossul Hand and Power Maize Sheller

This one-hole, spring-type sheller can be operated by hand, yielding 100 to 200 kilograms per hour, or by a 1 h.p. motor supplied with a belt pulley, yielding 200 to 300 kilograms per

Cossul Hand and Power Maize Sheller
Cossul & Co.

hour. The unit is of all-steel construction, weighs 94 grams, and has a built-in cleaning fan.

Cossul & Co. Pvt., Ltd.
Industrial Area, Fazalgunj
Kanpur, India

CeCoCo Corn Sheller Type Number 2

Operated by hand, this sheller yields 100 to 150 kilograms per hour; with a ½ h.p. motor, it puts out 250 to 300 kilograms per hour. This machine has a flywheel and can be attached to any box or barrel. It measures 24 by 10 by 7 inches.

CeCoCo Corn Sheller Type Number 3

This sheller has a 2 h.p. motor and yields 750 to 1,125 kilograms per hour.

CeCoCo
P.O. Box 8, Ibaraki City
Osaka, Pref. 567, Japan

Allied Power Maize Sheller

This sheller has a winnowing fan which separates the corn kernels without breaking them. A 5 h.p. motor is required to run the machine.

Allied Trading Co.
Railway Rd., Ambala City 134 002
Haryana, India

Dandekar Power Maize Sheller

This company offers a 5 h.p. machine which shells up to 1,500 kilograms of corn per hour, and separates the dust and chaff from the grain.

Dandekar Brothers
Sangli
Maharashtra, India

Unitrac Maize Sheller

The Unitrac shells corn by a rolling action at a speed of 600 rpm. It has a shelling capacity of about 2 tons of grain per hour with a 10 h.p. motor.

Dandekar Power Maize Sheller
Dandekar Brothers

Union Tractor Workshop
8B Phase II, Mayapuri Industrial Area
New Delhi, 110 027 India

Laredo Corn Shellers

Laredo's Model MDL-900 is a powerful sheller which produces 3,600 to 6,000 kilograms of shelled corn per hour. It can be operated by a 15 h.p. electric engine or an 18 h.p. diesel/gasoline engine.

Model MDL-500 is attached to a tractor three-point hitch and powered either by the power take-off shaft or by a stationary engine. It will generate 3,000 to 3,600 kilograms per hour with a 5 to 7.5 h.p. electric motor or with an 8 to 10 h.p. gasoline/diesel engine.

Laredo Models S.A. Industria E. Comercio
Rua 1 de Agosto M-67
17.100—Baru(SP) Brazil

Power Maize Sheller

This sheller has an output of 100 kilograms

per hour when driven by a 1 h.p. motor or engine. Shelling gaps are adjustable.

Rajasthan State Agro Industries Corp. Ltd.
Virat Bhawan, C-Scheme
Jaipur 302 006, Rajasthan, India

Ransomes Power Maize Sheller

This is an all-steel-construction sheller with a belt-driven winnowing fan. When driven by a ½ h.p. motor, it has an output of 300 kilograms per hour.

The Ransomes 4A

The Ransomes 4A is manufactured for small farmers in developing countries. Husked ears of corn are shelled individually on both sides of a rotating, toothed, shelling plate as the cobs are forced past the plate by rotating, feeding drums. Spring-loaded stripping claws hold the ears against the shelling plate while shelling takes place. The spring tension and the size of the opening are adjustable. Below the shelling mechanism is a cleaning shoe where corn is cleaned and graded. Three screens are provided for the sheller: a 19-millimeter round-hole upper sieve, a 10-millimeter grading sieve, and a 5-millimeter lower sieve to remove chaff. The cleaning shoe is oscillated by a crank pin.

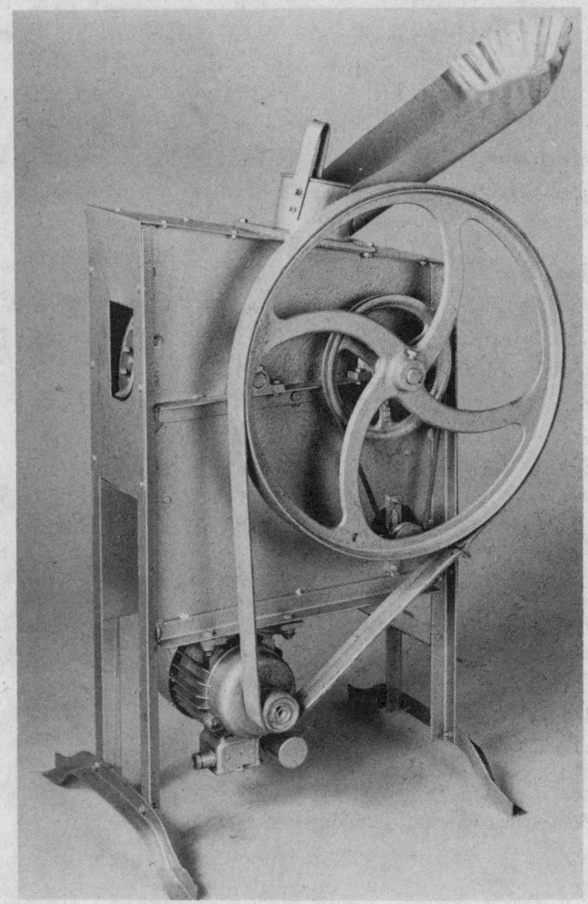

Ransomes Power Maize Sheller
Ransomes, Sims and Jefferies, Ltd.

Ransomes 4A Sheller, modified for experimental work.
Agriculture Canada

Moon Sheller

This unit consists basically of a shelling cylinder fitted with renewable pegs. A powerful fan at the bagging point removes flakes, silks, and dust from the corn. This sheller can strip 2,700 to 4,500 kilograms of kernels an hour from husked cobs. It requires 4 to 6 h.p. to maintain a speed of 6,000 rpm. Weight: 200 kilograms.

Cobmaster Sheller

Specially designed for the smaller farmer, the Cobmaster sheller is available with a choice of hand, pedal, or motor drive. Husked cobs are hand-fed from a hopper into two feed holes with adjustable rubbing pads. The internal cleaning fan gives a flywheel effect and will blow light refuse out the front of the machine. The crop falls through the bottom of the machine. Maximum output with a ½ h.p. motor is 750 to 900 kilograms per hour (1,600 to 2,000 pounds).

The Cobmaster Sheller
Ransomes, Sims and Jefferies, Ltd.

The above four shellers are manufactured by:
Ransomes, Sims, & Jefferies, Ltd.
Nacton Works
Ipswich IP3 9QG U.K.

Jumil DM-30

For a production capacity of 30 sacks per hour, this corn sheller-thresher can be operated either as a stationary unit or attached to a tractor power take-off and hydraulic lift system. Shelled corn is obtained without crushing the kernels.

Jumil
Justino de Moraes, Iramos S.A.
Batatais, S.P. Brazil

Jumil DM-30
Jumil

SILAGE CUTTERS AND CHOPPERS

CHOPPING SILAGE BY HAND

One way of providing succulent animal feed throughout the year is to cut or chop grass, hay, straw, root crops, or forage crops into small pieces and convert the material into silage. Stored in a silo, anaerobic acid fermentation converts green fodder into succulent feed, a form in which it can be stored through the year.

For small acreages where only one or two animals are to be fed, a simple method of hand chopping can be used to prepare green fodder for storage. All you need are a butcher's knife and chopping block. Hold a bundle of material in one hand and chop against the block with the other. Output and efficiency of this method is low, of course, and the work is tedious. Some foreign companies have devised hand-operated equipment to make the job easier.

A typical hand-operated silage cutter consists of a feed trough with or without conveyor rollers. At the end of the trough, straw is gripped between two toothed rollers which feed it over a shear plate. A pair of rotating knives mounted on a hand-cranked flywheel chops the feed into short lengths. Two men are required for the operation—one to turn the flywheel and the other to feed the machine.

For this cutting tool to function efficiently, it is important that the knives be kept well sharpened, and a few spare sets of knives should be available for regular changing. Even more important, you must keep the correct bevel on the cutting edge (instructions should be provided by the manufacturer). Finally, the knives should be adjusted so that they lightly touch the mouth of the machine over its full width.

SOURCES OF HAND-OPERATED SILAGE CHOPPERS

Dandekar Hand-Operated Chaff Cutter

This implement cuts chaff into 1-inch (25 millimeter) segments.

Dandekar Brothers
Sangli
Maharashtra, India

Silex Chaff Cutter

This machine also cuts chaff into 1-inch (25 millimeter) segments.

Ernest H. Johnson (Pty.) Ltd.
Box 7536
Johannesburg 2000, South Africa

Ajanta Silage Cutter

This implement has two blades and runs on ball bearings. The worm gear drive can be set to either of two fodder-cutting lengths with segments ranging from 5/8 inch (15.9 millimeters) to 7/8 inch (22.2 millimeters). The output for dry fodder is 200 to 250 kilograms per hour and 250 to 300 kilograms per hour for green fodder.

Ajanta Ensilage Cutter
Mohan Singh Harbhajan Singh

Mohan Singh Harbhajan Singh
G.T. Road, Goraya 144 409
Distt. Jullundur, India

The shear-plate of a silage cutter, and the pair of knives mounted on the hand-operated flywheel.
R. Hunt

Simplex Silage Cutter

This model has 7½ inch by 2¾ inch knives, and a large flywheel.

R. Hunt & Co., Ltd.
Atlas Works, Earls Colne
Colchester, Essex CO6 2EP, U.K.

Renson et Cie Grass Cutter

This unit has a cast-iron body and base plate with semisteel gearing. Four adjustable blades are mounted on a 450 millimeter hand-cranked flywheel. It weighs 13 kilograms and cuts 3-millimeter segments.

Renson et Cie
B.P. 14
59440 Landrecies, France

Poultry Feed Cutter

This unit is similar to a small chaff cutter and is fitted with a 425-millimeter diameter flywheel.

Ernest H. Johnson (Pty.) Ltd.
Box 7536
Johannesburg 2000, South Africa

Chaff Cutter

This all-cast-iron, manually operated chaff cutter runs on two ball bearings and employs a flywheel.

Rajasthan State Agro Industries Corp., Ltd.
Virat Bhawan, C-Scheme
Jaipur 302 006, Rajasthan, India

POWER-OPERATED SILAGE CUTTERS

The feeding mechanism of the power-operated silage cutter does not differ much from the hand-operated type, although the cutting mechanism itself may differ a bit. Two types of cutting heads are available, a cylinder type and a flywheel type. In both cases, a fan is provided for blowing the cut material into a silo through a vertical blower pipe. A power-operated silage cutter performs three functions—feeding the material into the blades, cutting, and elevating material into a storage bin.

The capacity of a silage cutter depends on the width and height of the throat, length of cut, number of knives, and speed of operation. One-half inch is an average length of cut, but this can be regulated by the speed of the apron and feed rollers. Faster feeding results in longer cuts while slower feeding will give correspondingly shorter cuts.

SOURCES OF POWER-OPERATED SILAGE CHOPPERS

Nogueira

This model cuts all kinds of forages into lengths varying from 4 to 32 millimeters. It will throw the cut product to a height of 10 meters while the adjustable outlet allows it to be deposited in any preselected place.

Irmaos Nogueira S.A.
Rua 15 De Novembro, 781
Caixa Postal, 7
Itapira, Est. Sao Paulo, Brazil

Atlas

Fitted with forward, stop, and reverse action and controlled by a safety stopping lever, the Atlas comes supplied with two pairs of change wheels which will cut a range of lengths from 1/4 to 3/4 inch. The output for 1/4 inch lengths ranges from 7 to 15 hundredweights per hour, depending upon the blades used.

R. Hunt & Co., Ltd.
Atlas Works, Earls Colne
Colchester, Essex CO6 2EP, U.K.

Laredo Chopper

This unit works coupled to the three-point hitch of a tractor or powered by a stationary engine—electric or fuel. It is a combination hammer mill–silage chopper capable of producing from 220 pounds of fine corn flour to 2 tons of chopped grass in an hour.

Laredo
Rua 1° de Agosto
11-67—17.100
Bauru (SP) Brazil

Tien Chien Silage Chopper

The Ta-Yu Silage Cutter and Potato Slicer is treadle-powered but can be operated with a 1/4 to 3/4 h.p. motor. It weighs 84.6 kilograms, measures 27 by 34 by 39 inches, and produces at a rate of approximately 300 to 500 kilograms per hour.

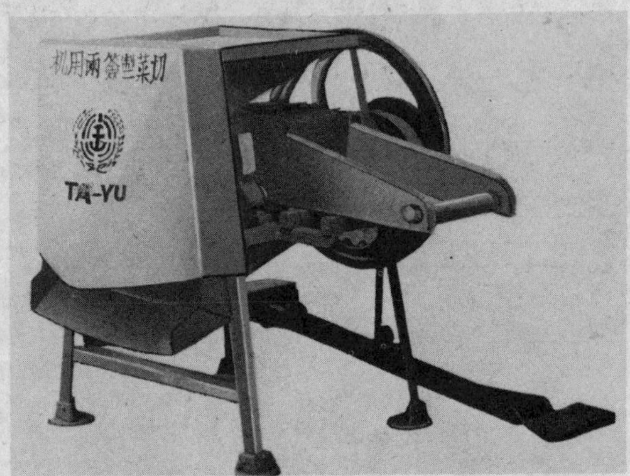

Tien Chien Treadle Power Ensilage Cutter and Potato Slicer.
Tien Chien Enterprises

Tien Chien Enterprises Co., Ltd.
P.O. Box 20-18
Taichung, Taiwan, R.O.C.

CeCoCo Chopper

The chopping length of this unit varies from 9 to 51 millimeters utilizing a 2.5 to 4.0 h.p. motor. It has a capacity of up to 4.9 tons per hour.

CeCoCo Chaff Cutter

This power unit comes in four models ranging in power requirement from 1/4 to 2 h.p. for output capacities of 300 to 800 kilograms per hour. The cut is freely adjustable, and the blades are made of sheer steel for long-lasting sharpness.

CeCoCo Silage Cutter

The silage cutter is designed to blow chopped material into a high storage space. The

Many of the early power-operated silage cutters received their power from a V-belt and pulley arrangement from a tractor power-take-off shaft. This model has a conveyor for delivering ensilage to a high bin or into a wagon.
The Implement Age, 1894

SPECIFICATIONS OF THE CECOCO SILAGE CUTTER

Power Required	rpm	Capacity ton/hour Corn	Capacity ton/hour Straw	Cutting Length in millimeters	Net Weight
5-6 h.p.	800	6.0-8.0	1.8-2.3	10, 16, 22, 32, 41, 76	265 kg
3-4 h.p.	770	3.5-4.5	1.3-1.7	same	180 kg
2-3 h.p.	770	2.5-3.5	0.9-1.3	6, 13, 19, 32, 54, 85	145 kg
1-2 h.p.	750	1.5-2.5	0.9-1.1	13, 22, 35, 64, 102	115 kg
1-2 h.p.	750	1.0-1.5	0.8-0.9	8, 21, 38, 110	100 kg

knives are easily removed for sharpening and the shear-cutter-bar has double cutting edges which can be reversed when one side is worn out.

CeCoCo
P.O. Box 8, Ibaraki City
Osaka, Pref. 567, Japan

ROOT AND VEGETABLE CUTTERS

The root and vegetable cutter is a very simple tool for slicing potatoes, turnips, sugar beets, carrots, and other root crops into small pieces suitable for animal feed or compost. It is not designed to handle branches or heavy brush. In practice, the hopper is filled with semihard fruits or vegetables which are then sliced and shredded by the action of a heavy, cast-iron wheel with a number of small cutters attached to it.

SOURCES OF ROOT CUTTERS

A.V.I. Root Cutter

The 18 inch, cast-iron disc of this hand-operated cutter is mounted on a 1 inch diameter shaft. Cutter teeth are of a heavy-gauge stainless steel. The basic frame is made of oak, the hopper of alder or Western maple. The unit weighs approximately 75 pounds and measures 40 by 24 by 36 inches.

American Village Institute
440 Meyers St.
Kettle Falls, WA 99141

The AVI Root Cutter

Polish Hand-Operated Root Cutter
David Scott

Hand-Powered Root Cutter, Series B

This unit is made of cast iron, has a cutting cylinder measuring 200 by 380 millimeters, and has a flywheel diameter of 600 millimeters for a hand-powered operation. Weight: 100 kilograms.

Renson et Cie
B.P. 14
59550 Landrecies, France

Hand-Operated Root Cutter

Of Polish manufacture, this machine is hand operated and has an output of 500 kilograms per hour. At the base of the hopper are a pair of concave discs facing each other, each with 26 short, curved blades projecting from the surface. The crank is on a flywheel which helps rotate the cones at a slow, steady speed. The hopper can hold 22 kilograms of harvested roots, and guide plates ensure that they are pressed by their own weight against the moving blades. As the discs are rotated, the blades gouge out short chips which then drop through the opening below the discs.

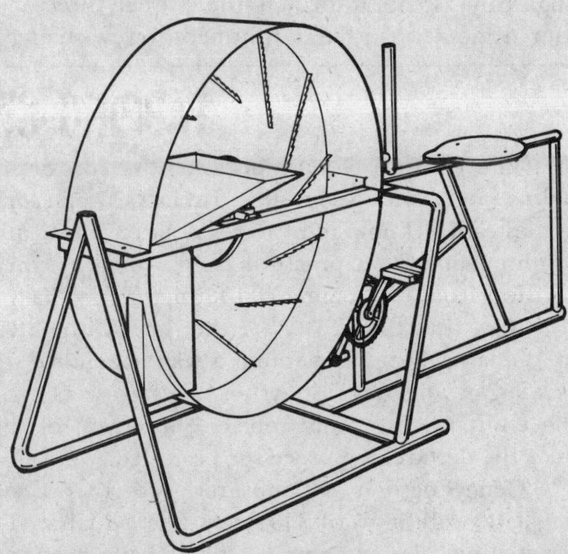

The Intermediate Technology Development Group designed this pedal-powered cassava grinder for use in their work at Zaria, Nigeria. London-based Intermediate Technology Publications carries the plans.

United Nations Division of Narcotic Drugs
Palais Des Nations
Geneva, Switzerland

SORGHUM AND SUGARCANE PRESSES

Pressing the juice from nonwoody plants like sorghum and sugarcane requires only simple tools and yields a sweet extract which can be processed for use as table sugar. The most common technique for pressing sorghum and sugarcane involves passing the stalk between two rollers, similar to the rollers on an old wringer washing machine. The weaker units require passing the stalk through a number of times, or splitting or pounding the material with a hammer before pressing.

If you're interested in improvising to build your own press, you may want to consult a book called the *Lik Lik Buk* from Papua, New Guinea (available from VITA, 3600 Rhode Island Avenue, Mt. Rainier, MD 20822). It illustrates a simple two-man sugarcane crusher that has no gears but has an adjustment screw at the top. Sugarcane is passed through the crusher three or four times, with the adjustment screw being tightened each time. The rollers are made of four-inch galvanized pipe, eight inches long; shafts are one-inch mild steel, and bearings are of hardwood. The top pair of bearings slides up and down depending upon the thickness of the stalk. Another unit has preset, spring-loaded rollers which require no further adjustment.

This setup may sound suspiciously like an old wringer washer to you, but heed this word of warning from the *Lik Lik Buk:* "If you think you can crush effectively with an old clothes mangle or wringer, you're wrong. Save yourself the bother. The springs aren't strong enough and if they are, the rollers might break."

SOURCES OF SUGARCANE AND SORGHUM PRESSES

Hand-, animal-, and engine-powered crushers are available for crushing sorghum and sugarcane. For convenience of the drive layout, it is usual to employ vertical rollers in animal-powered crushers and horizontal rollers in hand- and engine-powered machines. Hand crushers are normally used only for domestic purposes and extract a rather small percentage of the sap. Animal- and engine-powered crushers can employ higher crushing pressures and obtain better extraction percentages.

TAPPING SWEET SORGHUM

The tedious, old-fashioned production of sorghum syrup is rather like an old soldier: it keeps fading away but never dies. In fact, sweet sorghum may be making a comeback. Gardeners and homesteaders know it provides a tasty substitute for store-bought sweeteners. They also think that sorghum may be a practical cash crop they can grow for a sideline income without too much competition from big commercial farmers, since harvesting is still a process done pretty much by hand.

Now that the USDA (at the Agricultural Research Service Food Crops Utilization Research Lab in Weslaco, Texas) has found a way to remove starch from sweet sorghum so that it can be made into raw sugar, and not just syrup, small growers are bound to get even more interested. Experts say that the United States could replace 30 percent of the sugar it now imports with its own sorghum sugar, once the destarching process is perfected.

Gene Logsdon of Ohio grew two rows of sweet sorghum last year, each about 150 feet long, to see how well it would grow in the North. "I'm interested in it strictly as a northern source of sweetening," he explains. "I don't have bees yet, and only two maple trees large enough to tap. I wanted another alternative to buying sugar."

Drew Langsner in North Carolina looked more at sorghum's possibilities to add income to his homestead. "We were told that we could make up to 120 gallons of molasses per acre which could be sold direct to customers for as much as $12 a gallon," he says. "Moreover, the plant has few insect enemies here and is not critically affected by blights. Also, not only do you get the syrup, but the seed heads and leaves can be used for livestock feed."

Actually, sorghum in some areas can produce a good deal more molasses than what the Langsners

Sorghum is planted the same time corn is, about one to two inches deep. Begin cultivating right over the row two days after planting, when the weeds are beginning to germinate, but the sorghum is not yet up.

were shooting for—three times that amount. Or it can produce a good bit less and sell as low as $5 per gallon, depending on supply and demand. But any way you look at it, with a little luck and a normal crop, sweet sorghum ought to gross at least $1,000 per acre and maybe as much as $2,000 per acre—or enough money left over after expenses to repay you fairly well for the hard work involved.

The Logsdons didn't know precisely when to harvest their sorghum for juice, so they relied on advice from Amish farmers who grew it. The farmers said to wait until the seed heads had turned from green to reddish brown, when the seeds are past the milky stage, but still soft. However, the stalks didn't have to be cut immediately at that stage. Any time from then on was okay, so long as the harvest was finished before hard frost hit the plants.

At any rate, the first harvest step is stripping off the leaves, a job that's more easily done when the stalks are still standing. Wear gloves and just slide your hands down the stalks, knocking off most of the leaves. It doesn't hurt for the stalks to stand stripped of their leaves for a week.

"Stripping the leaves off is drudgery," says Langsner, "especially when, as in our case, many of the stalks have fallen over. We bind about half the stripped leaves into bunches to dry for winter livestock feed, and the rest we let fall on the ground for mulch."

Next, the stalks are cut and the seed heads lopped off. The Logsdons just cut the stalks with a corn knife as they do corn and pile them in bundles beside the row. Then they carry the bundles to the pickup truck, whack off the heads from an entire bundle with one blow of the corn knife, and load the stalks on the truck.

The seed heads should be spread out in the barn for drying, then stored for feeding. They need not be threshed except for grinding into flour. Rolling a seed head vigorously between the palms of your hands will easily thresh out the grains. But the seed heads can be fed directly to chickens, rabbits, and other livestock.

From their half acre, the Langsners harvested 102 bushels of seed heads—or roughly about 30 bushels of seed. That much nutritional energy bought at the feed store in the form of conventional grains would cost at least $100, so the seed alone may justify the labor involved.

Finding a press, if you don't have one, is not as difficult as it might seem, even in the North. They're still around—just keep asking. Gene Logsdon found at least three within easy driving distance of his place, but had you asked him two years ago, he'd have said there were none. Once you haul your stalks to the press, don't worry if the man can't get yours pressed and boiled down right away. The canes can lie two weeks without any noticeable loss of juice.

Many presses are now powered with motors, but a surprising number are still turned by horse or mule—the animal walks in a wide circle, pulling a sweep that turns the gears that make the rollers run. The operator shoves the stalks through the rollers, which squeeze the juice into a waiting barrel through a screen. The crushed stalks fall to one side in a pile. They can be used for mulch or composting, or even fed to cattle as silage if laced with some of the syrup skimmings produced during the boiling-down process.

A sorghum cooker can be built at home. The farmer who boils the Logsdons' sorghum made his own cooker—a cement fireplace about eight feet long and two feet wide, with a ten-foot chimney at one end and a roof overhang to protect the cooker from rain. The fire is built near the open end of the fireplace, and the draft pulls the heat evenly under the cooking pan and out the chimney.

"The pan can be a very simple affair made of 2-by-8 inch boards for sides and ends and a sheet metal bottom," says one expert, "the whole pan should be about six feet long and two feet wide to fit nicely over the fireplace. Don't use galvanized metal, because the zinc coating on it might react adversely with the acids in the syrup."

SOURCES OF SUGARCANE PRESSES

CeCoCo Hand Sugarcane Squeezer

Employing three rollers to do the squeezing, this unit can be powered by hand or by a ½ h.p. motor for a production capacity of 115 kilograms per hour of cane. CeCoCo also manufactures larger cane mills with capacities ranging from 6 to 15 tons of cane per hour.

CeCoCo
P.O. Box 8, Ibaraki City
Osaka Pref. 567, Japan

Kumar Cane Crusher

This is a vertical three-roller sugarcane crusher which can be driven with one pair of animals. Its capacity falls between 300 and 350 pounds of cane per hour (136 to 158 kilograms per hour). Two other units with higher capacities are available—the Karmat and Kamal vertical three-roller crushers.

CeCoCo Hand Sugar Cane Squeezer

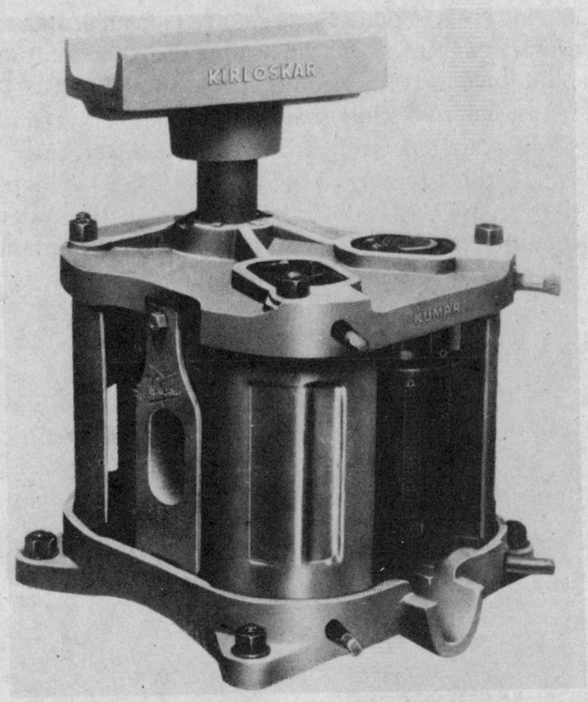

Kumar Cane Crusher

Kumar Industries
Edathara Post, Palghat District
Kerala State, South India

Konya-a Cane Crusher

This is a horizontal crusher designed to be operated by a 4 or 5 h.p. motor. It has a crushing capacity of 800 to 1,000 pounds per hour (365 to 455 kilograms per hour). Higher capacity units with three or five rollers are also available.

Kirloskar Brothers, Ltd.
Udyog Bhavan, Tilak Rd.
Poona 411 002 India

Raja Horizontal Sugarcane Crusher

With a crushing capacity of 1,500 to 1,700 kilograms per hour and a juice extracting capacity of 1,300 to 1,600 liters per hour, this machine requires a 5 to 7½ h.p. motor to run it.

Raja Trading Co.
P.O. Box 250
Madra 600 001 India

Nogueira Sugarcane Crusher

Constructed of rust-resistant iron, the Nogueira crusher can be powered by a 2 h.p. electric, 5 h.p. gasoline, or 3 h.p. diesel engine. The 95 by 165 millimeter rollers are designed for

Nogueira Sugarcane Crusher
CIMAG

self-feeding so that the cane does not have to be forced through the rollers. Adjustments and maintenance on the 125 kilogram unit are simple. It has a production capacity ranging between 300 and 400 liters per hour.

CIMAG, Comercio & Industria De Maguinas Agricalas LTDA.
Rua Padre Rogue n.° 1.840
Mogi-Merim S.P., Brazil

SEED OIL PRESSES

Pressing oil from seeds requires much more force than what's needed to press cane or sorghum. Prior to pressing, the seeds are ground or mashed and often heated in water until the water boils. Some oil may have collected on the surface of the water; this should be skimmed off and saved. The ground, cooked seed mash is then put in a cloth bag and pressed. A second boiling and pressing could yield a bit more oil.

Unfortunately, we have not been able to locate any sources of oil presses presently under manufacture in the United States, although many people are seeking such units.

SOURCES OF OIL PRESSES

***Lik Lik Buk* Press**

The Papua, New Guinea *Lik Lik Buk* (distributed by VITA, 3600 Rhode Island Avenue, Mount Rainier, MD 20822) pictured this oil press design as a build-it-yourself suggestion for villagers. It was designed as a sturdy unit which will exert a great deal of pressure on a small

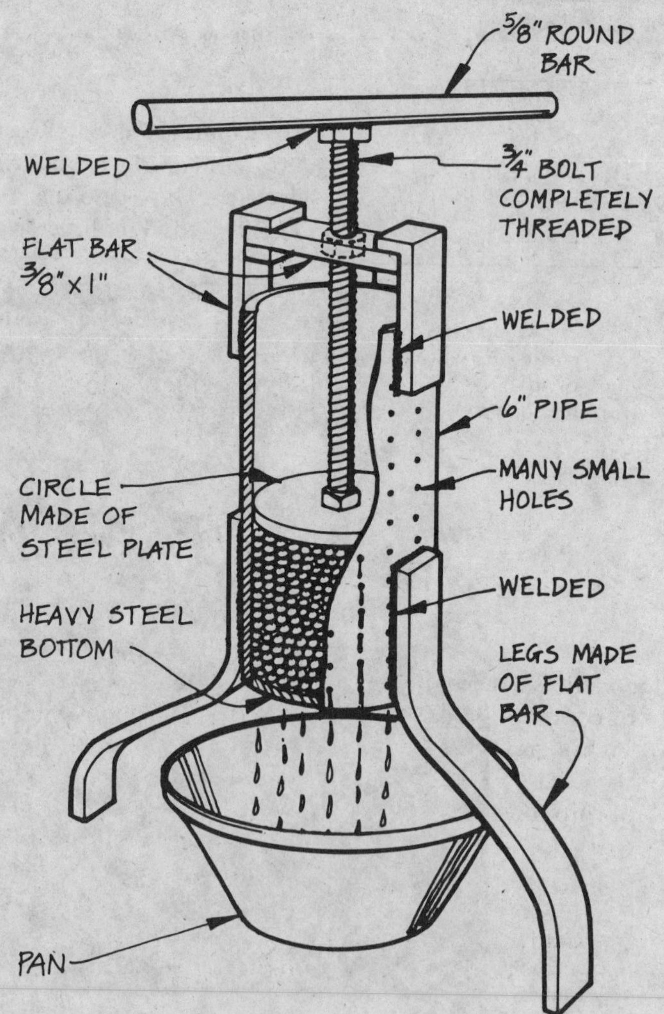

Hand Oil Press

amount of seeds. Reducing the capacity raises the amount of pressure generated for any given torque on the operating arms and downward thrust of the piston.

CeCoCo Oil Mill

CeCoCo provides equipment for all stages of the oil-expelling process. A Seed Scorcher is used for drying the product, to reduce its moisture content to 4 or 5 percent. The oil expelling is done by tightening a screw worm, either by hand or motor. Finally, a filter press is used for filtering the raw crude oil through filter cloths and papers. This system works for many kinds of beans and seeds including rape, mustard, sesame, cotton, and sunflower seeds, and palm pericarp, peanuts, castor beans, and dried coconut, or copra.

SPECIFICATIONS FOR CECOCO OIL MILL MACHINERY

Machine's Name	Type	Capacity per hour	Power Required	Rpm	Dimension in mm			Net Weight	Gross Weight	Shipping Measurement
					Height	Width	Length			
Crusher	AA	600 kg	2 h.p.	1,400	560	395	640	75 kg	115 kg	10 cu. ft.
Seed Scorcher	L	5 bu.	1 h.p.	150	1 ft. × 4 ft. ϕ Vessel			436 kg	633 kg	57 cu. ft.
	S	3 bu.	½ h.p.	150	1 ft. × 3 ft. ϕ Vessel			115 kg	160 kg	31 cu. ft.
Oil Expeller	H-3	3-6 kg	Hand	Proper	520	260	600	27 kg	43 kg	4 cu. ft.
	New 52	45-55 kg	3 h.p.	300	630	520	1,000	150 kg	200 kg	14 cu. ft.
	New M	120-140 kg	5 h.p.	350	700	560	1,050	170 kg	220 kg	22 cu. ft.
	H-54	150-180 kg	7½ h.p.	600	700	700	1,250	430 kg	520 kg	31 cu. ft.
	HX-200	250 kg	10 h.p.	450	980	800	1,920	880 kg	1,080 kg	90 cu. ft.
	C	600-800 kg	15-20	1,000	1,180	960	3,000	3,600 kg	4,000 kg	120 cu. ft.
Filter Press	A	12 gal.	½ h.p.	170	7″ × 7″ × 10″ chamber			125 kg	175 kg	9 cu. ft.
	B	40 gal.	1 h.p.	200	12″ × 12″ × 14″ chamber			340 kg	500 kg	25 cu. ft.

When inquiring about an oil mill plant, please let CeCoCo know: (a) name of raw material to expel oil; (b) desired capacity per hour or 24 hours in raw material; (c) how you will use the oil produced; (d) whether you need group-driven or individual-driven equipment: if motor driven, also specify phase, voltage, frequency, current, and other details.

CeCoCo
P.O. Box 8, Ibaraki City
Osaka Pref. 567, Japan

Table Oil Expeller

Four models of oil expellers are available from S. P. Engineering. Two presses, each with a 3 h.p. motor, yield 30 or 40 kilograms per hour, and two with 5 h.p. motors yield 50 or 55 kilograms per hour. All four units operate at 450 rpm.

S. P. Engineering Corp.
P.O. Box 218, 79/7 Latouche Road
Kanpur, India

COFFEE PROCESSING MACHINERY

Coffee cherries, the ripened fruit of the coffee shrub, each contain two coffee beans. Two different techniques are utilized to remove the covering and pulp to produce clean coffee beans, the desired product.

The wet process begins with the pulping of the fruit by a pulping machine or pulper. Additional operations involving fermentation and washing may be needed to remove the pulp residue that remains. The seeds are then dried in the sun or in driers, until the moisture content has reached 12 percent. The seed parchment is then removed in additional mechanical operations.

The dry process begins with the drying of the ripened fruit, either in the sun or driers. When the fruits are dry, hullers are used to remove the seed coverings. Graders are then used to separate varieties, sizes, and shapes of coffee beans offering a standard of sale.

SOURCES OF COFFEE PULPERS

IRIMA-67 Disc Coffee Pulper

This small machine pulps the coffee by squeezing the cherries between the rotating disc and the fixed pulping chop. The disc is of smaller diameter than standard and carries bulbs on one face only. Normally, the disc has cast-iron bulks of No. 75 pattern suitable for Robusta and Arabica coffees. Alternative discs can be supplied for use with Arabica and Liberica varieties.

The capacity of the machine is 594 to 792 pounds (270 to 360 kilograms) an hour of ripe coffee cherries, which should be fed into the machine with water on the same day as it is picked. The machine weighs 55 pounds (25 kilograms).

IRIMA-67
John Gordon

DG Disc Coffee Pulper

The DG coffee pulper is a single-disc machine which employs pulping bars and a pulping disc. The bars are straight, with a renewable steel edge, and are fitted with a cam device for ease in setting the chop relative to the disc. It has an index to enable the setting to be found again easily, and the chops are readily removable for cleaning.

DG Disc Coffee Pulper
John Gordon

For treating Robusta and Arabica coffees, copper discs No. 75 or cast-iron bulbed discs No. P75LC are available. For other varieties, copper discs only are supplied, No. 71 for Liberica and No. 77 for coffees allied to Liberica but slightly smaller, or for large Arabica.

The machine can pulp up to 1,540 pounds (700 kilograms) of ripe coffee cherries per hour.

They should be fed to the pulper with an abundance of water on the same day as they are picked. The DG pulper has a net weight of 294 pounds (133 kilograms).

Estrella Coffee Pulper

This is a cylindrical coffee pulper, which squeezes the coffee cherries between the rotating, embossed cylinder and the fixed breast. It is made in two models. In one, a stirrer is fitted in the hopper, which has no stone trap. In the other, the hopper has a stone trap but no stirrer. In both models, the distance between the breast and the cylinder is adjustable. The machine is suitable for Arabica and Robusta coffees, but not for Liberica. It can pulp up to 594 pounds (270 kilograms) of ripe coffee cherries an hour depending on type and condition. The coffee should be pulped the same day as it is picked and fed to the machine with water. The machine with stirrer weighs 103 pounds (47 kilograms) and without stirrer, 85 pounds (38 kilograms).

Estrella Coffee Pulper
John Gordon

MTOTO Coffee Pulper

This small coffee pulper is intended for use on small plantations but is also useful for treating the first crop on larger plantations. It is of the cylindrical type. The machine is suitable for Arabica and Robusta coffees, but not Liberica, and can pulp up to 100 pounds (45 kilograms) of ripe coffee cherries each hour. The cherries should be fed into the machine with water on the day they are picked. The working surface of the breast is machined, and the iron barrel has a renewable embossed cover.

MTOTO Coffee Pulper
John Gordon

A different version of the MTOTO called the Starlet Major is available without a stirrer but with a stone trap.

The machine weighs 34 pounds (15.5 kilograms).

All the above pulpers are available from:
John Gordon & Co. (Engineers, Ltd.)
196a High St.
Epping, Essex, England

Atom Coffee Pulper

This pulper is suitable for Arabica and Robusta coffees, but not suitable for Liberica coffee. Its output of ripe cherry pulp is 55 kilograms per hour. Weight: 15 kilograms.

McKinnon Number 1 Disc Pulper

This model is fitted with ball bearings, cast-iron disc, flywheel, and handle for hand operation.

Both models available from:
William McKinnon & Co., Ltd.
Spring Garden Iron Works
Aberdeen, AB9 LDU, U.K.

Baby Pulper

The Baby Model No. 2 yields 127 kilograms per hour and No. 2½ yields 254 kilograms per hour. No. 2½ is hand-operated and can be supplied with a flywheel grooved for V-belt power drive.

Sunbeam Pulper

This unit is power-driven with an output of 550 to 650 kilograms per hour when driven by a 1 h.p. engine.

The above models are manufactured by:
E. H. Bentall & Co., Ltd.
Maldon
Essex, CM9 7NW, U.K.

SOURCES OF COFFEE HULLERS AND SEPARATORS

Engelberg Huller Company carries two sizes of coffee hullers and separators. These ball- or roller-bearing machines will hull coffee in the whole (coco) cherry or parchment form, separate and discharge the hulls, and deliver cleaned coffee beans.

Model No. 1 has a capacity of 1,600 pounds per hour for pulped coffee, and uses 10 to 12 h.p. Model 0, using 15 to 18 h.p., has a capacity of 3,400 pounds per hour. This larger model is also available with tight and loose pulleys.

Engelberg Huller, Co., Division
U.S. Route 11, P.O. Box 277
Factoryville, PA 18419

Number 5 African Huller

This model's output of clean coffee from dry cherries is 114 kilograms per hour. Output of clean coffee from parchment coffee is 127 kilograms per hour.

Power required is 5 h.p. The No. 5 weighs 216 kilograms. Larger models are also available.

E. H. Bentall & Co. Ltd.
Maldon
Essex, CM9 7NW, U.K.

Number 10 Africa Coffee Huller

This coffee huller can be conveniently operated by hand power and is ideal for small-scale farmers. It is normally fitted with two handles but it can also be supplied fitted with a pulley 229 millimeters in diameter by 76 millimeters wide, requiring 1.5 h.p. The machine can shell dry cherry coffee and also parchment coffee. It will treat Arabica, Robusta, and Liberica varieties,

No. 10 Africa Coffee Huller
John Gordon

although with hand power, dry cherry Liberica coffee is too difficult to shell. The machine is fitted with two adjustable hulling blades, a feed slide and a weight to regulate the pressure on the discharge door, all of which are adjustable to obtain optimum performance. A perforated plate, which is easily detachable for cleaning purposes, is fitted to the bottom of the machine. Dust and small flakes of shell pass through it. The coffee is delivered shelled but mixed with large flakes of shell; it should be winnowed afterward.

Dry cherry Arabica coffee can be shelled at the rate of 48 pounds (22 kilograms) of clean coffee an hour, and parchment Arabica coffee at the rate of 79 pounds (36 kilograms) an hour. For Robusta, these outputs are about 30 percent more, and for Liberica about 30 percent less. The machine has a net weight of 95 pounds (43 kilograms).

Bukoba Coffee Huller

This small huller is designed for shelling dry cherry coffee, but it will also shell parchment coffee. Its use is indicated for small-scale farmers, and as a sampling machine for larger mills.

Bukoba Coffee Huller
John Gordon

The machine is strongly constructed and has no adjustments. The coffee is simply fed to it and the handle turned. The shelled coffee is discharged mixed with the shells and dust and must then be winnowed and sieved. Dry cherry coffee can be shelled at the rate of 20 pounds (9 kilograms) of clean coffee an hour. Parchment coffee can be shelled at the rate of 60 pounds (27 kilograms) an hour. The coffee must be quite dry and crisp when fed to the machine, which is not suitable for the treatment of Liberica coffee. The net weight of the machine is 29 pounds (13.5 kilograms).

Limprimita Coffee Sheller
John Gordon

Limprimita Coffee Sheller

This is a small huller which is very useful in coffee-cleaning mills and also to those coffee buyers who purchase parchment or dry cherry coffee. According to the manufacturer, the advantage of this model over other sampling machines is that any quantity from one bean to several kilograms can be shelled rapidly, completely, and safely.

A ribbed roller operates in conjunction with an adjustable, flexible block. The lightest pressure consistent with good performance is applied by adjusting this block. The roller is turned before the coffee is fed into the machine, and this should be done gradually and evenly. The coffee is discharged mixed with the loose shells, and should then be winnowed. The machine should be fixed firmly to a table. It is 17 inches (43 centimeters) high and its net weight is 29 pounds (13 kilograms).

The above hullers are manufactured by:
John Gordon & Co. (Engineers, Ltd.)
196a High St.
Epping, Essex, England

SOURCES OF COFFEE GRADERS

Congo Coffee Grader

This little grader is especially suitable for use in an installation of small, hand-driven coffee hullers. Its output is 110 pounds (50 kilograms) an hour. The cylinder is composed of a perforated plate with two sets of perforations, thus giving three grades. The grades may be determined to suit the requirements of the planter, and about 2 pounds (1 kilogram) of coffee should be sent to the manufacturer when passing the order to make sure that the most suitable perforations are provided. The perforated plate is easily detachable. With spare plates of different perforations, it is possible to treat several varieties of coffee in the same machine. Plates are available with three perforations, thus giving four grades, but the output is less. The shafts are mounted in ball bearings.

Congo Coffee Grader
John Gordon

A larger grader of the same design, having a capacity of 495 pounds (225 kilograms) an hour, is also available, and can be supplied for hand power or complete with small electric motor. The small grader weighs 187 pounds (85 kilograms), the larger, 495 pounds (225 kilograms).

John Gordon & Co. (Engineers, Ltd.)
196a High St.
Epping, Essex, England

MAPLE SUGARING EQUIPMENT

Equipment for collecting and processing maple syrup is so very specialized that all the necessary implements can generally be obtained from the same source. For collecting, there are plugs, sap bags, collection tubs, and buckets. Evaporators and skimmers are used for processing, and for the small commercial venture, there is a need for molds, cans, bottles, and filters.

Instead of itemizing the tools and accessories available from the different companies, we recommend you send for their fully illustrated catalogs. Instruction books are available for the novice maple sugarer from these companies:

G. H. Grimm Co., Inc.
Box 130
Rutland, VT 05701

Leader Evaporator Co., Inc.
25 Stowell St.
St. Albans, VT 05478

Small Brothers, Inc.
P.O. Box 160
Dunham, Quebec JOE 1MO, Canada

Les Specialites Techniques De Valcourt, Inc.
746 rue St. Joseph, C.P. 68
Valcourt, P.Q. JOE 210, Quebec, Canada

Down to a science: Ralf Clark and Fred Behringer of Waterford, Connecticut, keep the wood stacked high a year ahead of time to dry, use it as a barrier against the weather, and have the system arranged with pulleys so that their sugaring project stays a one-man job.

GOLD IN THE TREES

by Bruce Mays

Two years ago, my neighbor and I devised a system that yields three gallons of maple syrup every year from a total investment of under 12 dollars. If we can do it, anyone can. Boiling your own maple syrup is surprisingly easy. And when that syrup is free, boiled during the first hint of spring in your own backyard, you know you're living well.

Sugar sap is manufactured by maple leaves all summer long, then stored for the winter in the roots. The following year, that sugar supplies a ready-made energy reserve to the growing tree until new leaves are able to photosynthesize their own. During the first thaws of spring, the roots must move that sap through the trunk to the branches. Only if conditions are right, only if the sap is racing like an elevator between the roots and branches, can the tree be bled. Warm, sunny days draw the sap from the earth. Freezing nights pull it back down. That combination is essential; any other locks the sap motionless in one spot or another. In the South, or by late spring, there are no freezing nights that will gather the sap to the roots. But don't despair. If you live in sugar country and the season is right, there is no mistaking it. Morning ice will cover the bark, and by afternoon, the branches will sweat with glistening sap.

The first step in sugar production involves drilling holes through the bark. A general rule of thumb calls for the holes to be drilled no closer than one foot apart in a waist-high circumference around the trunk. Each year the holes should be shifted three inches to one side or the other, making sure no new holes are above or below the old. Since sap flows only through the newest growth directly beneath the bark, the holes should be angled upward no deeper than three inches toward the center of the tree. Tap primarily the southern face: sunlight coaxes a quicker flow. The standard drill bit is 7/16 inch; hardware store taps are made with that size in mind.

A tap is nothing more than a stiff pipe plugged into the hole that funnels the sap out of the tree. Any tubular, soft piece of wood will do. My own yard abounds with one-inch diameter sumac trees. Once the branches have been cut into six-inch lengths, it is a simple matter to ram a red-hot straight iron through the spongy pith. All that remains is to whittle one end of the shaft to a taper and drive the tapered end into the tap hole like a bung into a barrel of wine. The sumac will swell with the first run of sap, sealing the tap tightly against each hole. Professional buckets are made of

The top shaft should be tapered at one end and driven into the tree at an angle. It is best to have a covered collection can.

galvanized steel, come complete with a hood to keep out unwanted rain and snow, are very handsome, and cost $4 each. For that price, I can empty ugly homemade buckets every time it rains or snows. A friend of my neighbor's gave him three dozen unused number ten tin cans—for free. Any large container will do, of course. The tin cans were simply the most convenient for us. I have seen plastic gallon milk jugs and unused paint-stirring cans used with great success. By punching a hole on each side near the top and looping a length of wire between them, we produced three dozen collecting buckets in less than an hour. And when we hung the buckets from our homemade taps, the fit was extraordinary. Forty-nine-cent taps stick out only about an inch from the bark; our homemade variety extends five inches from the trunk, far enough to direct sap into the very center of each bucket. By carving a small notch near the end of each tap, the collecting cans were safe from even the strongest breezes.

Our total investment so far was nothing. By the second week of March, our taps carried clear sap in a stream, filling each two-quart can within hours. And if you hate the thought of all that boiling, stop there—maple sap in place of water makes the most exquisite tea and coffee you've ever tasted.

If you do boil it, there are a few considerations to prepare for before you begin. If you have a job during the week, you will probably want to boil only on the weekends. That means storing your daily collections for at least six days. Twenty-gallon trash cans with plastic liners are about as large a storage container as you want to get and still be able to move them easily.

Now, however, you must keep the sap cold during the week. Left by itself, on a warm day, collected sap soon clouds to a bacterial soup. The easiest solution is to keep the trash cans in daylong shade. Each night, a skim of ice will form to protect the sap during the following day. And when warm weather still threatened to melt the ice and spoil the sap, we simply froze some fresh sap overnight in milk cartons and floated the chunks of ice in the cans. As long as even a small ice cube remained until dark we knew we were safe.

After eight days of collecting we were ready to boil. Once again, we were in a potentially expensive situation. From every 40 gallons of sap, 39 gallons of water must be evaporated. That takes a tremendous amount of heat. The only realistic way for a home maple boiler to produce syrup is to cook the sap over an outdoor wood fire. Our three gallons of syrup demanded about two cords of wood.

Four years ago, I used an old ten-gallon lobster pot for the actual boiling. For someone with only a few maple trees, this is fine. But remember, it takes 40 gallons of sap to produce one gallon of syrup, and the evaporation rate of that excess water is a direct product of the size of the pot. Water will evaporate only from a surface in contact with the air; no amount of heat can alter that fundamental rule. Anyone planning to produce more than a pint of syrup in less than a lifetime of boiling will be forced to use a professional evaporator. We were, and now I know we were right.

From every 40 gallons of sap, 39 gallons of water must be boiled off. Three gallons of sap call for about two cords of wood.

Don't let the word professional scare you. It means simply a very large pan. The smallest of them, like ours, is about five feet long by three feet wide and ten inches deep. That is enough to hold 50 gallons of sap and presents an evaporating surface of 15 square feet—a twenty-fold improvement over my lobster pot. Fancier, more expensive evaporators have baffled compartments to route the finished syrup away from the new sap, inlet spigots and outlet faucets, and mysterious coils winding along the bottom. But beyond all that finery is still the simple physics of a larger evaporating surface. My neighbor found our small, used pan in a local newspaper for $10. Five dollars each, and we had made our last expenditure.

It remains only to get the fire underneath the pan. In our case, that meant piling used bricks in a three-sided structure 18 inches high, making sure that the edges of the evaporator pan would sit snugly on the inner brick wall. I suppose the bricks should be cross-stacked for maximum strength, but by the time we set the pan, leveled it out, poured in the sap, and stoked two cords of wood, our neat rectangle was something of a shambles anyway. The real trick is to concentrate as much of the heat uniformly onto the pan while still allowing enough air into the blaze to keep it burning hot. That meant removing a stray brick for ventilation here and there, sticking an old stove pipe from the back end as a chimney, maybe sealing the gap between the evaporator and the bricks with mud. Generally, though, it meant just watching the fire at all times to balance its needs.

There are some things to be remembered during your boiling day. If the boil slows, the evaporation rate decreases. Too much heat in one spot tends to melt the solder holding the pan seams together. You have to work on the furnace a little to prevent those annoyances. We slanted a dug pit towards the rear of our rectangle and tried to keep most of the burning wood near the bottom. The heat then tends to climb up the slope towards the mouth of the furnace and disperse somewhat evenly across the bottom of the pan.

Be sure to add fresh sap steadily throughout the boiling. Too much cold sap all at one time will quench your good boil and slow the evaporation rate. Each time new sap is added, a scum will rise to the top. Skim these impurities from the broth with a slotted spoon.

Finally, the sap will taste distinctly mapley. Since our three gallons of syrup made a dangerously shallow layer in the pan, we found it prudent to remove the syrup from the fire when it was obviously brown and sticky-sweet, but still too thin for good syrup. This meant boiling the last few gallons in pots on the kitchen stove, but that way you can watch the syrup more carefully as it thickens. Books will tell you to dip in candy thermometers, or to measure the specific gravity and weigh the sugar content. At that point, the usual rolling boil is replaced by a kind of brown foam that sudses above the syrup. Syrup at just the right stage will cling to the spoon like thin taffy as it cools.

Your new syrup should be poured through muslin or felt at least once to pick up stray flecks of ash left by the fire. If you're planning to store the syrup for longer than a few months, be sure to fill each container right to the top while still hot and cap it immediately. When the syrup cools, it will hold the cap down with vacuum and never spoil. Pint or quart mason jars are perfect for this, but old bottles or food jars—anything with a sealing lid—can be used. If the syrup ever does cloud, simply boil it again and rebottle it. In a cool spot it should keep for years.

By the end of the day everyone is exhausted. Last year we began at six in the morning and were still sitting in a freezing drizzle at eleven o'clock that night. In between, a half ton of sap was poured by cupfuls into the steaming evaporator, the fire was tended, new sap was collected, and spare wood split.

And yet every winter I am restless for sugaring season. By late February, I swear I can smell the sweet air from other boilers. There is something very special about this first outdoor project of the year, something very satisfying about using your hands and brains to produce such an indecently delicious syrup.

NUT SHELLERS

GROUNDNUT DECORTICATORS

Groundnuts, peanuts for example, have fibrous cellulose shells which need to be removed prior to consumption. The task requires a rubbing-stripping action and a method for cleaning. Most hand-operated decorticators do not do this and so require a separate winnowing step.

SOURCES OF MANUAL DECORTICATING EQUIPMENT

Handy Groundnut Decorticator

Built from steel and cast iron, the Handy is simple to operate and easily transported. Nuts are placed in a receptacle and the operating handle moves forward and backward, rubbing the nuts against spiked rustlers and the shelling grid. Kernels are not separated from the shells after decortication with this device.

Harrap Wilkinson, Ltd.
5 North Phoebe Street
Salford M5 4EA, U.K.

R. Hunt and Company Groundnut Decorticator

The distance between the galvanized, heavy mesh screen and the rubbing bars on this unit can be adjusted to accommodate a variety of sizes of nuts. Four different sizes of screen are available for this hand-operated sheller.

R. Hunt & Co., Ltd.
Atlas Works, Earls Colne
Colchester, Essex CO6 2EP, U.K.

CeCoCo Model 300D Peanut Sheller

In this model, revolving beaters shell the peanuts, and kernels are separated from the shells by a screen and fan. Output is 40 to 50 kilograms per hour, and kernel breakage is 2 to 3 percent.

CeCoCo
P.O. Box 8, Ibaraki City
Osaka Pref. 567, Japan

Groundnut Sheller

A hand-operated groundnut sheller is available from:

Ubungo Farm Implements
P.O. Box 2669
Dar Es Salaam, Tanzania

Hand-Operated Groundnut Decorticator

For more information write to:

Dandekar Brothers
Sangli
Maharashtra, India

Hindsons Treadle Power Groundnut Decorticator
M/s. Hindsons Pvt., Ltd.

Hindsons Groundnut Sheller

This is a foot-operated, portable device designed to quickly separate nuts from their shells. The balanced flywheel eases operation, and the blower separates shells from the nuts. Maximum output of the unit is 441 pounds per 8-hour day.

M/s. Hindsons Private, Ltd.
The Lower Mall
Patiala, India

SOURCES OF POWER-DRIVEN SHELLING MACHINERY

CeCoCo Peanut Sheller

In the CeCoCo sheller, threshed and cleaned peanuts are shelled by a revolving beater mechanism. After being run through the machine, unshelled and shelled peanuts are separated with a fan and screen. Unshelled nuts should go back in the implement until shelling is complete. Breakage of kernels is between 2 and 3 percent. Four model types are available using 1, 2, or 3 h.p. motors and with outputs of 120 to 420 kilograms per hour depending on the model.

CeCoCo
P.O. Box 8, Ibaraki City
Osaka Pref. 567, Japan

Harrap Wilkinson, Ltd. Automatic Groundnut Decorticator

Nuts to be shelled are placed in a hopper at the top of this machine. The nuts pass into a beater chamber by means of a ribbed feed roller; the rate is adjustable. Rotating, flexible beaters break the shells, and a blower mechanism separates the shells so that only the kernels are in the delivery chute. Wilkinson's No. 2 machine has a 1½ h.p. motor and an output of 254 to 406 kilograms per hour.

Harrap Wilkinson, Ltd.
North Phoebe St.
Salford M5 4EA, U.K.

Dandekar Brothers Groundnut Decorticator

Dandekar Brothers manufactures four types of power-driven decorticators. Type A needs a 5 h.p. motor and has an output of 80 (180 pound) bags per (12 hour) day. Type B requires a 6 h.p.

Dandekar Power Groundnut Decorticator
Dandekar Brothers

motor and will produce up to 100 bags a day. Type C is powered by a 7 h.p. motor and will shell up to 120 bags per day, and Type D uses a 10 h.p. motor for a maximum output of 200 bags per day. The hopper is on the upper part of the machine. Nuts pass from there into an opener cylinder where the shells are broken and separated from the kernels. The shelled nuts fall on the ground to be collected.

Dandekar Brothers
Sangli
Maharashtra, India

SINGLE NUT NUTCRACKERS

New Dynamic Nut Cracker

Designed to crack any size nuts except hickory nuts or hard-shell walnuts, this sheller locks and cracks them automatically. Kernels and shells fall out for rapid repeats, and the safety shield protects the operator from flying shell particles. This electrically operated device requires 110 volts and 60 cycle alternating current. The cracker is guaranteed for 1 year, and has an estimated life of 10,000 pounds of nuts.

L.H. Powell
8647 Wingate Drive
Dallas, TX 75209

Texas Native Inertia Nutcracker

Made of oak and aluminum, this device will

Texas Inertia Nutcracker
R.P. Industries, Inc.

crack any type of pecan, Brazil nut, filbert, almond, macadamia, and English or California walnut. The cracker operates by placing the nut between two sockets, pulling the safety shield over the nut, pulling back the knocker stick, and releasing it. The kernel is left in the sockets, and the shell falls away from it. The tool is guaranteed for 1 year, and can crack up to 30 nuts in a minute.

R.P. Industries, Inc.
610 W. Johnson St., P.O. Drawer 10938
Raleigh, NC 27603

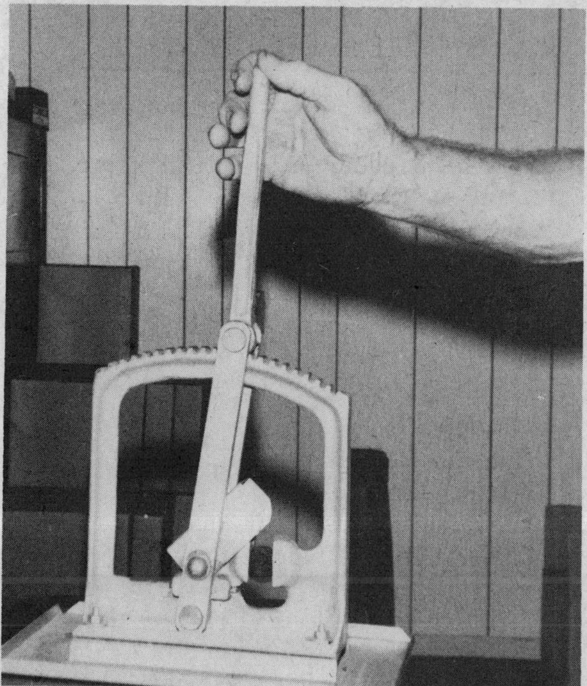

The Potter Walnut Cracker
Fred Klingensmith, Inc.

Potter Walnut Cracker

This device cracks walnuts one at a time. Heavy-duty crackers are also available.

Fred Klingensmith, Inc.
Sapulpa, OK 74066

RICE HULLING

Similar to wheat, rice grows with a bran layer and an outer hull covering the kernel. For the grain to be edible, the hull must be removed in the hulling process. An unnecessary second step, polishing, removes the bran and the germ, and along with them, much of the grain's B-vitamin content. Rice that is hulled but unpolished is called brown rice. Both the hulling and polishing processes require a milling action, often by two rollers rubbing the kernel between them. Most hullers are designed for power operation, but a few hand-operated models are still being made.

SOURCES OF RICE HULLERS

Java Hand-Powered Rice Huller

This is a small machine intended for the grower of small quantities of rice paddy, and for domestic use. It replaces a model called the Paddy Pounder. Paddy can be shelled at a maximum rate of about 30 pounds (14 kilograms) an hour, but the capacity may vary considerably depending on the type of rice and its condition. The machine has three adjustments controlling the feed, the discharge, and the hulling knife. A perforated plate allows dust to escape, and the machine can be opened easily for cleaning. Strongly made, its net weight is 23 pounds (10.5 kilograms), and it is provided with holding-down screws and spanners.

John Gordon & Co. (Engineers, Ltd.)
196a High St.
Epping, Essex CM16 4AQ, U.K.

Java Hand-Powered Rice Huller
John Gordon

CeCoCo Two-Man Rice Huller

Two men operating the hand levers will rotate this huller at 3,500 to 4,000 rpm, hulling

250 kilograms per hour with 90 percent hulling efficiency. Net weight: 60 kilograms.

CeCoCo Two-Man Rice Huller

CeCoCo Hand Rice Polisher Type E

Operated either by hand or by a 1/4 h.p. motor, the Type E Polisher will polish unhulled rice that has already been dried and winnowed. Capacity is 10 to 15 kilograms per hour by hand, and 30 kilograms with a motor. Weight: 22 kilograms.

CeCoCo Hand Rice Polisher Type E

CeCoCo Hand-Hulled Rice Separator and Sorter

Constructed of steel and easily dismantled for storage, the four models of this sorter have capacities ranging from 20 to 32 bushels per hour. Hulled rice is fed into a hopper, and while sliding across the surface of the piano-wire screen, it will separate into whole hulled rice, unhulled rice, unhulled paddy rice and immature rice, mud, and sand. It may also be used to sort polished rice for grading.

CeCoCo Hand-Hulled Rice Separator and Sorter

CeCoCo
P.O. Box 8, Ibaraki City
Osaka Pref. 567, Japan

Amuda Rice Hullers

These power-driven machines can be used as hullers alone or supplied with polishing attachments. Three models are available, requiring 5, 12, or 15 h.p. They will hull rice from the paddy or shelled rice. From the paddy, the smallest huller will produce 36 to 45 pounds of cleaned rice; the middle, 136 to 204 pounds; the largest, 250 to 295 pounds per hour. When using shelled rice, production capacity is a little less than double those amounts per hour.

Rajan Trading Co.
P.O. Box 250
Madras 600 001, India

Grantex Rice Hullers

Three sizes of Grantex hullers are made. The smallest, requiring 5 h.p., produces 80 to 100 pounds of polished rice per hour. The amount is doubled if shelled rice is being polished. The two larger models utilize 12 and 15 h.p., respectively; they produce 300 to 450 and 500 to 650 pounds per hour. The two larger models can

Grantex Rice Huller
Lewis C. Grant, Ltd.

produce five separate products directly from the paddy: white rice, coarse meal, fine flour, bran, and husk. Optional extras include polishers, aspirators, fans, drive units, and reciprocating sieves.

Lewis C. Grant, Ltd.
East Quality St., Dysart
Kirkcaldy, Fife, KYI 2UA U.K.

Iseki Rice Polishers

The Iseki Model JE25 is an automatic, cabinet body machine. Horsepower required to operate the polisher is 4 to 5, and 300 to 350 kilograms of rice can be polished per hour. The manufacturers recommend combined use with a rice huller, but state that it can also be used as a rice-hulling and -polishing machine. Three larger models are available, either in cabinet or strip enclosures. Efficiency ranges from 300 to 1,000 kilograms per hour. None of the Iseki models include their own power units.

Iseki Agricultural Machinery Mfg. Co., Ltd.
1-3, Nihonbashi 2-chome, Chuo-ku
Tokyo, 103 Japan

CeCoCo Automatic Rice Hullers and Combinations

CeCoCo, with its wide variety of all types of machines, offers seven automatic rice processors, with many sizes of each type. Their automatic hullers feature rubber rollers, which they claim will increase output recovery of hulled rice 15 to 20 percent. They also recommend that rubber-rolled rice be stored and shipped as brown rice, with any polishing to be done at the destination of the shipment to avoid deterioration of the product.

1. Rubber Roll Rice Huller: The original model consists of a hulling head and installation bed. Separation of brown rice and husks is necessary. Seven models are available, ultilizing 1 to 10 h.p. or V-belt drive; capacities range from 500 to 4,000 kilograms per hour in paddy.
2. Combination: Three models, with or without suction husk exhaust, are offered. The basic unit includes a huller and husk winnower. The suction exhaust model is recommended for use in buildings. The three sizes utilize from 2 to 5 h.p., with capacities ranging from 500 to 2,000 kilograms per hour.
3. Automatic KL-A: This self-contained unit includes hulling head, winnower, double elevator, separator, and rice elevator. The smaller model requires 4 to 5 h.p. and produces 600 to 700 kilograms per hour; the larger requires 5 to 6 h.p. and produces 1,000 to 1,200 kilograms per hour.
4. Automatic AM and ME: These are miniaturized versions of the complete unit, suitable for a single farmer or a group of farmers. The one-body construction includes huller, winnower, and separator.

Three larger rubber roller units, having hourly capacities of 1,200 to 4,000 kilograms, are also available.

CeCoCo
P.O. Box 8, Ibaraki City
Osaka Pref. 567, Japan

Nogueira Rural Rice Mill

The Nogueira Rice Mill husks and polishes rice, then separates polished rice, husks, rice bran, and broken rice. It will utilize a 3 h.p. electric motor, a 6 to 9 h.p. gasoline motor or a 5 to 8 h.p. diesel-oil motor. Production capacity is approximately 2 sacks (60 kilos or 132 pounds) per hour. The cabinet is metal and weighs 236 kilograms.

CIMAG: Comercio e Industria de Maquinas Agricolas Ltda.
Rua Padre Roque no.° 1,840, Mogi-Mirim S.P.
Brazil

Genuine Engelberg Combined Rice Huller and Polisher Number 3

Powered by flat belt-drive pulley, this 3 h.p. machine will, in a single operation, hull, scour, and polish rice as it is received from the thresher. An optional built-on exhauster is available to carry away chaff and dust.

This item is suggested for small mill operators or larger growers. The No. 3 has a capacity of 80 to 100 pounds of rough rice per hour, and two larger models are capable of up to 700 pounds per hour.

Genuine Engleberg Huller Number 4

Similar in design to the No. 3 Rice Huller and Polisher, the No. 4 does not contain the polisher attachment. Two larger models of hullers are also available.

Engleberg Huller Co. Division
P.O. Box 277
Factoryville, PA 18419

–9– Tools for Adding Organic Matter to the Soil

To the practitioners of today's chemical agriculture, a fertilizer is a substance that has a measurable quantity of at least one of the major nutrients required by growing plants. The most widely used chemical fertilizers are those which contain three primary plant nutrients: nitrogen (N), phosphorus (P), and potassium (K) in varying combinations.

Organic growers, on the other hand, rely on natural fertilizers to maintain and replenish all the elements in their soil that are necessary to plant growth. They view soil fertility as a broader, more complex concept which involves not only specific plant nutrients, but also organic matter, the living organisms present in the soil, and the very structure of the soil itself. To them, humus content and tilth are important aspects of soil fertility. Unlike those farmers who employ chemical fertilizers to supply their crops with specific nutrients in forms that are readily available, organic farmers use a variety of natural materials to maintain and improve overall soil quality. In this way, soil fertility and health are improved even as crop yields increase.

Direct application of livestock manures has been the farmer's traditional approach to return-

Mule-Drawn Manure Spreader
Reading Eagle, Lancaster County, Pa.

ing organic materials to the soil. Originally, manure was spread over the soil surface from a cart, with a many-tined pitchfork called a manure fork. Then came the development of the manure spreader, a horse-drawn cart with a ground-driven set of chopping blades in the rear. Manure fed into the blades was chopped into small pieces and evenly distributed onto the field.

SOURCES OF MANURE SPREADERS

Most manure spreaders made today are designed for pulling behind large tractors beyond the scope of this book. They are easy to locate through most agricultural equipment dealers. Farm auctions are the best source for smaller units in North America.

Uebler Mini

One company to appear with a mini manure spreader, requiring only the power of an 8 to 12 h.p. tractor, is Uebler. Their smallest model has a capacity of 18 bushels which it distributes under power from its own 4 h.p. gasoline engine or a power take-off shaft. Their next size larger has a 50-bushel capacity.

Uebler Mini Manure Spreader
Uebler Manufacturing Co.

Uebler Mfg. Co.
Vernon, NY 13476

New Idea

The smallest manure spreaders put out by New Idea are a 138-bushel model with the combined chopping action of a cylinder and paddle, and a 146-bushel, single-beater model.

AVCO, New Idea Corp.,
Farm Equipment Div.
First & Sycamore
Coldwater, OH 45828

OrBilt Manure Spreader

The main beater of this spreader is made from heavy channel iron. These channels are welded around the beater pipe in two opposing spirals. This beater will tear apart the toughest manure, whether it is from a feedlot or pen, even if it is frozen. Strings don't catch or hang on this beater as they do on others. A lower-splash blade beater has the specific purpose of breaking up and scattering both liquid and clumps. This lower beater is particularly useful if you are spreading on a hay field or some other place where large lumps could smother patches of a crop.

The sliding pusher and false front endgate move as one unit to the rear of the box. The speed is controlled from the tractor seat by a variable flow, hydraulic valve. The pusher, replacing the traditional conveyer apron, is the heart of the entire machine. Part of the hydraulic cylinder is enclosed by the center housing

OrBilt Manure Spreader
O'Reilly Manufacturing

of the sliding pusher; the other part extends out over the tractor hitch. The entire inside of the box is lined with tough plastic. Manure does not penetrate or stick to the plastic, nor does it freeze to plastic as it does to wood or steel.

O'Reilly Manufacturing
Rt. 3
Goodhue, MN 55027

Prototype Material Spreader

Charles E. Fox, of Jonesboro, Louisiana, has invented a spreader wagon that hitches to a tractor and distributes material such as pulverized chicken fertilizer, sawdust, or ground bark. It is a two-wheeled cart with a series of arched platforms in its bed that funnel material onto a conveyor belt, and then through a gauging or measuring device. The gauge limits the amount of material laid per foot. The belt can be disconnected for transport. Mr. Fox is currently seeking a manufacturer for his spreader with the help and guidance of the Raymond Lee Organization. His invention, covered by a patent application pending in the United States Patent Office, is designed primarily for organic farmers.

Charles Fox
Rt. 3, Box 77
Jonesboro, LA 71251

Raymond Lee Organization, Inc.
230 Park Ave.
New York, NY 10017

COMPOSTING

Manure spreaders are still a necessary tool on the organic farm, but increasingly they are being used to spread composted manures and other organic wastes. Composting is the biological process of decomposition during which wastes are broken down into their basic chemical parts and made ready to be used again in building another plant. The product is called humus.

With the proper microorganisms present in the soil, humus will evolve by simply applying organic wastes to the soil surface. However, composting speeds the process, and by following a basic composting recipe, a more-balanced nutrient fertilizer is produced.

COMPOSTING AS A MANURE MANAGEMENT SYSTEM

by Richard Thompson

Editor's note: Richard Thompson was born and raised on his present farmstead, consisting of 300 acres outside Boone, Iowa. He graduated from Iowa State University with a B.S. in Animal Husbandry and an M.S. in Animal Production.

Composting, in my opinion, is a sensible, practical, economical way to deal with animal waste on the farm. My reasons for starting to compost followed the same pattern as my reasons for changing to organic farming back in 1967, namely—problems.

Back then I was on a continuous corn program, applying chemical N-P-K, herbicides, and insecticides. The fences were removed from between the fields, cattle were brought in and confined to barns and lots.

We live in a low, flat area so the barns and lots needed to be cemented. This situation brought about all kinds of sickness in the cattle. It seemed like it was just one thing after another. I got to the point where, out of frustration, I said, "There has to be something better than this." In the spring of 1968, we stopped using all chemicals and started putting fences back, so the cattle could have limited pasture. The cropping system was changed to a corn-soybean-corn-oats-hay rotation.

Even with all-chemical N-P-K added to the continuous corn program, I had to dispose of all the manure from the cattle and hogs. Note that I say dispose of, not use. The manure was hauled out of sheds and lots during the winter and early spring, and applied to frozen, plowed fields that were often covered with snow. This was a very poor utilization of the nutrients, especially the nitrogen content in manure which would turn into ammonia, dissipate in the air, and be completely lost. Also the raw manure would move with the melted snow and end up in creeks and rivers, polluting our water supply.

After I stopped using the artificial N-P-K, the corn yields stayed at 120 bushels per acre for the next seven years. The corn yields, previously, were about the same, averaging 120 bushels per acre.

My yields, on the organic program, were oats: 70 to 80 bushels, soybeans: 35 to 45 bushels which, I felt, were good and also competitive with the neighbors. The hay fields also seemed to improve each year. After about seven years of organic farming, the field of corn following soybeans dropped to the 80- to 90-bushel range. The cornfield following hay remained in the 120-bushel range. The profit on the 80- to 90-bushel yield would probably be okay, since the expenses per acre were $40 to $50 lower than those of the neighbors on chemical methods. However, I felt with all this manure and only 80 to 90 bushels, something must be wrong. This was where composting came into the picture.

Composting is a way of turning a liability into an asset on the farm.

In the spring of 1975, we decided not to spread the manure on frozen ground during the winter. The manure was pushed up into large piles in the yards during the winter. On June 5, we started to clean out these piles and haul to our compost site on the edge of the hay field. This manure was cold and had large chunks of ice in it.

A bacteria starter was spread on the manure piles in the yard, loaded in the spreader, and taken to the compost site located centrally between our farmstead and the neighbors'.

The spreader needs to be power take-off-operated so it will unload in a stationary position. When the manure builds up to the beaters, the spreader is moved forward about one foot and the rest of the load is unloaded in this fashion. I feel the ideal pile is about eight feet wide at the bottom and four feet high. In two days' time we saw a miracle happen. This cold, frozen manure which had a temperature of about 30 to 40 degrees heated up to 140 degrees, and steam was coming out of the top of the windrows. I feel that, in my situation with all the manure off concrete, I need the added bacteria to get the action started, as little earth was combined with the manure. We tried some windrows without bacteria and the action was very slow.

One of the important keys to good composting is moisture content. This should be in the 40 to 60 percent range. If the manure is wetter than 60 percent, it will take more turnings with the spreader to get it dried down. If the manure is too dry, water needs to be added. Generally, I take some wet manure and mix it with dry manure and this usually comes out about right. Much has been written about carbon-nitrogen ratios in composting; they should be 20 to 30 parts carbon to one part nitrogen. For the farmer, I think this means simply that what creates a good environment for livestock will make good compost. If cattle or hogs are kept clean and dry with bedding, the carbon-nitrogen ratio will be excellent.

My windrows were turned by reloading the spreader and unloading to make a parallel windrow. The windrows need to be turned until the temperature stays below 100 degrees. However, if it is time to spread on fields, incomplete compost that is still steaming can be applied to fields and disked in the same day. We initially applied four tons of compost per acre in fall after the soybeans were combined and bean straw was stacked. The N-P-K analysis of the compost was 2-1-2.

This year I bought an Easy Over compost-turning attachment for my tractor. With this attachment

I can now turn the more than 500 tons of compost I'm making in an hour, as opposed to the two days it took using the stationary manure spreader and loader. I attach the turner to the hydrostatic PTO of a tractor, and use another tractor to slowly move it along through the windrow.

Before getting the turner, we were somewhat lax about turning our piles, since it took so much time. During the growing season it was often impossible to find the time to give two days to turning compost. Now, time is not a problem. If composting had a drawback, it was always because of the amount of time it took to turn. Turning time is no longer a problem for farmers, thanks to the turner.

Although the turner costs five to six thousand dollars, I still think it's a good investment. On a family farm, time is often the critical commodity, and the turner frees a lot of time. I don't think every farmer should own a turner, and as long as there is one in your area, you can hire it for custom work. The turner is easy to transport on the highway, so moving it is no problem. In fact, we now use ours to do our own composting, in the sewage sludge composting operation my son has set up, and a neighbor uses it to compost chicken manure.

As I stated before, we are dealing with raw, wet manure when we start to compost, so we locate our compost site away from farmsteads. When composting starts, the odor changes to a musty smell and isn't noticeable over 40 rods away from windrows. The fly problem is eliminated when the temperature starts to rise, and these temperatures will also kill weed seeds and harmful pathogenic organisms. As I mentioned before, the compost is applied to my field following soybeans. The planting of corn that followed the soybeans was where we were having the yield reduction problem. Last year, we applied 300 tons of finished compost to the fields. The time required to turn 300 tons three times was 30 hours using two people. This year I'll produce more than 500 tons of compost, with not more than eight or ten hours of labor. The yield response from compost was very encouraging, producing a strong 100 bushels per acre in a dry year. This yield was equal to the corn yields of neighbors who used chemical methods.

SOME SPECIALIZED EQUIPMENT FOR COMPOSTING MANURE

Editor's note: Dennis Demmel of the Small Farm Energy Project in Hartington, Nebraska has supplied much of the information used in this report.

Nebraska is a state that can be said to be blessed—or plagued—with a variety of organic wastes. Its large communities are burdened with paunch manure from slaughterhouses as well as sewage sludge and garbage. Huge piles of dry manure in feedlots or other animal confinement facilities can mean serious dust and odor problems.

In a report in *Farm, Ranch, and Home Quarterly* (Fall, 1977), agronomy professor Leon Chesnin of the University of Nebraska foresees solutions in the near future. His report is entitled "Composting Converts Waste into Valuable Resources," and he writes that "there is a way all of these wastes can be converted into valuable resources—*composting*." One reason for his optimism is that specialized equipment has been developed to handle large volumes of wastes. Some of this equipment is now in use at the University's Mead Field Station.

The Roscoe Brown Corporation of Lenox, Iowa has supplied a Brown Bear integral auger tractor to the University of Nebraska. The unit is used in composting feedlot manure, paunch manure, sewage sludge, and crop residues.

According to the manufacturer, the Brown Bear can mechanically aerate 3,000 cubic yards per hour—working directly into and parallel with the windrow. In describing the machine's auger speed, the company notes: "By simply changing sprockets, the speed of the auger can be increased to 180 revolutions per minute or more for more aggressive boiling action in the organic waste." The Brown Bear is manufactured by the Roscoe Brown Corporation, P.O. Box 48, Lenox, Iowa 50851.

Edgar Wuebben of Cedar County, Nebraska had a Compost Field Day at his farm last August to demonstrate his home-built compost-turning device. The turner is built from discarded materials,

The Brown Bear Integral Auger Tractor

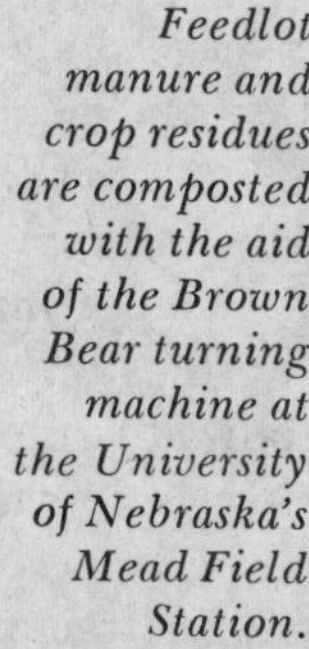

Feedlot manure and crop residues are composted with the aid of the Brown Bear turning machine at the University of Nebraska's Mead Field Station.

including a gearbox, tool bar, and silage-unloading auger. The auger is used to aerate, break up, and mix the pile. Afterwards, a tractor loader is used to repile the materials.

Wuebben has been keeping daily records of the temperatures within the compost at 50 different points along his 500-foot windrow. The records have indicated that the temperatures of the pile rose substantially after each turning and also following rains that occurred between turnings. The increase in temperature following a rain would indicate that the moisture content of the compost wasn't adequate for optimum bacterial activity.

Edgar Wuebben's home-built compost turner.

Wuebben's compost turner in action.

A sample of the finished compost was taken to an Omaha laboratory to be analyzed with the following results:

Moisture	34.80%
Nitrogen (N)	0.80%
Phosphorous (P_2O_5)	0.62%
Potassium (K_2O)	1.17%
Organic Matter by Combustion	14.40%
pH	7.3
Total Organic Carbon	8.5 %
Carbon-Nitrogen Ratio	10.6

A tractor-powered, turning machine built by the Mehlaf Machine and Manufacturing Company of Freeman, South Dakota is used to turn compost at the rate of 400 to 500 tons per hour. This unit is used by Town and Country Park, Inc., in Sioux Falls, South Dakota, which processes sewage sludge, paunch manure, and stockyard pen wastes.

At the McGinley-Schilz feedlot in Brule, Nebraska, a specially designed machine aerates the windrowed manure. The compost is made under contract with the Colorado-Nebraska Compost Corporation owned by Jack E. Martin and Lester R. Kuhlman of Sterling, Colorado. The machine, known as the Scarab, was developed by Fletcher Sims of Canyon, Texas.

"About 20 tons of raw manure to the the acre would have to be applied to equal the benefits derived from two tons of compost," says Martin.

"It's turned our feedlot waste problem around. Instead of manure being a nuisance, it's a valuable asset," Schliz was quoted in an *Omaha World-Herald* article.

SOURCES OF COMPOSTING EQUIPMENT

The Cobey Composter

An Ohio feedlot has effectively used the Cobey Composter for processing animal wastes. This unit is a diesel-powered, self-propelled machine which straddles the windrows.

Manufactured by:
Eagle Crusher Co., Inc.
Rt. 2, Box 72
Galion, OH 44833

The Easy Over Composter

Another composting machine was developed by the late Elton Schaeffer of Menno, South Dakota "out of his own necessity." The machine has knives similar to those of a garden tiller, for lifting material up and back into the windrow. One-half of a compost windrow is taken with each pass of the machine, compared to the full windrow taken by larger machines. The operation, according to Schaeffer, is best accomplished with a hydrostatic-drive tractor for slower ground speed.

Schaeffer's machine now has the commercial name of Easy Over, and is distributed by:

General Corp.
322 S. 16th St.
Philadelphia, PA 19102

The compost turning machine used on the Elton Schaeffer farm at Menno, S.D., for composting manures brought to the farm from the local livestock sales barn.

Schaeffer's composting machine has tines similar to those of a garden tiller, to lift material up and back into the windrow.

Accelerator Compost Bin

This 34 by 36 inch circular bin is made up of green, rigid, polyvinyl chloride interlocking and sliding panels. Waste is added through the top of the bin which has an inflatable cover to repel rain. Ventilating holes in the panels allow for ventilation while helping to hold in heat and insulate.

Rotocrop (U.S.A.) Inc.
P.O. Box 237, 58 Buttonwood St.
New Hope, PA 18938

Farnam
Dept. HB957, P.O. Box 12068
Omaha, NE 68112

Rotocrop Accelerator
Rotocrop (U.S.A.), Inc.

Compostumbler
Gardening Naturally

The Earthmaker and Compostumbler

This compost bin is arranged on a stand which allows the drum to be rolled in place. It holds more than 14 bushels of raw, organic waste and retains liquids.

Gardening Naturally
Rt. 102
Stockbridge, MA 01262

Garden Way Mfg. Co., Inc.
102nd St. & Ninth Ave.
Troy, NY 12180

Global Services, Inc.
P.O. Box 185-A, College Park
Lewisburg, PA 17837

Hand-Operated Mini-Composter

The steel blades of this composter grind vegetable refuse, bush clippings, vines, roots, and weeds up to a 3/8 inch diameter. Measuring 15 by 10½ by 8 inches, it clamps to any flat surface. The cast-iron cutter is manually operated.

Sears, Roebuck & Co.
Farm and Ranch Catalog

Cassaplanta
Dept. 123, 16129 Runnymede
VanNuys, CA 91406

SHREDDERS

Today's shredder-grinders are better than they've ever been—thanks largely to 20 years of organic gardening experience contributed and shared by a multitude of backyard growers. They're also more available in greater variety—some larger and more powerful, and some more compact—but all are designed to do a specific gardening job better.

The type of shredder you buy should depend on the kind of gardening operation you run, the size of your place, and the kind of organic materials you're going to feed through it. A good shredder will handle all kinds of garden wastes and residues without clogging, and it should be easy to move around, which means you can take the tool to the work—to the compost pile, the garden row, or the pile of wood chips that were dumped at the end of your driveway.

Today, there are two main types of shredders: the low center of gravity shredder-bagger with its big-mouth hopper, and the classic stand-up shredder-grinder designed to handle a greater volume and variety of materials.

Many combinations of accessories and functions are now available in one machine. The once-reluctant gas engine has been made a lot more dependable and easier to start. You can also find electric-powered shredders which are a lot quieter, easier to start, and also free of fumes. But they have to stay closer to the house and there is always the danger of playing around with electricity outdoors on the damp ground.

Many shredders, both low-profile baggers and the bigger grinders, are equipped with a chipping fixture which is usually a rotating knife that operates through a side slot and can

To keep a shredder from clogging, it's sometimes best to remove the screen, especially when shredding wet, soggy leaves.

handle branches up to two or even three inches thick. The MacKissic, Roto-Hoe and Lindig machines are three models with this feature.

Then there are the shredder accessories or attachments that fit onto a small riding tractor or a walking power unit that also functions as a rotary tiller, a mower, a chipper, a snowblower, or even a dozer blade.

Overloading any machine will result in jamming and stalling it. This especially holds true for the shredder whose job it is to chop up fibrous, damp, or wet materials and then eject them through a screen or grid. We recommend working with as large a screen as possible—the 1¾ inch screen on the Lindig is excellent. Gilson, W-W, and Roto-Hoe offer a grating of rods or square roller bars which seem almost jam-proof. Another solution to the problem is the Winona's "wet mat rack" which encloses only half the shredding chamber.

If you're shredding with very wet, soggy, and rubbery leaves, here's a sure way to eliminate frustration and loss of time—remove the screen. Without it, the action of the cutters chops the leaves into a satisfactory aggregate which can be used either for compost or mulch. If you're working with a shredder-bagger, you may find it speeds up the task to remove the bag. You'll also find it's a good idea to deposit the aggregate immediately in the compost pile or the planting row.

You may also find that a clutch, either centrifugal which depends upon the speed of the motor to actuate it, or one that is manually operated, helps avoid jams. This calls for alert operation of the machine, but it can save a lot of time spent clearing out the inside of your shredder.

Check the wheels on the shredders you are considering. They should have at least a pair, rugged and rubber-tired, and placed so they will comfortably and safely support the machine when you move it. Some of the larger models

FOUR TYPES OF CUTTING MECHANISMS

Three-Cutter Rotary System

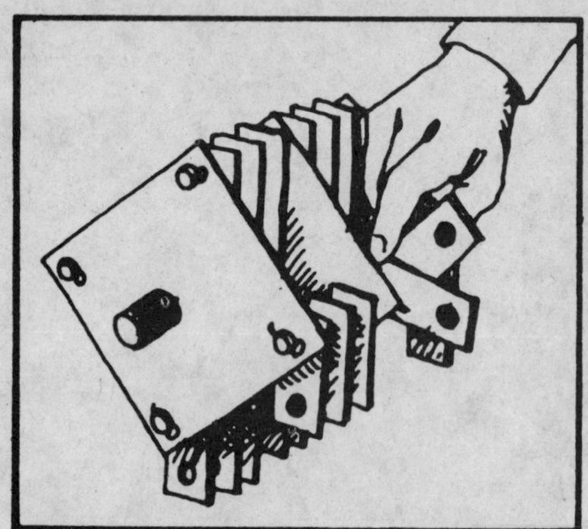

Hammer mill Unit

Rotary Blades with Frame-Mounted Knives

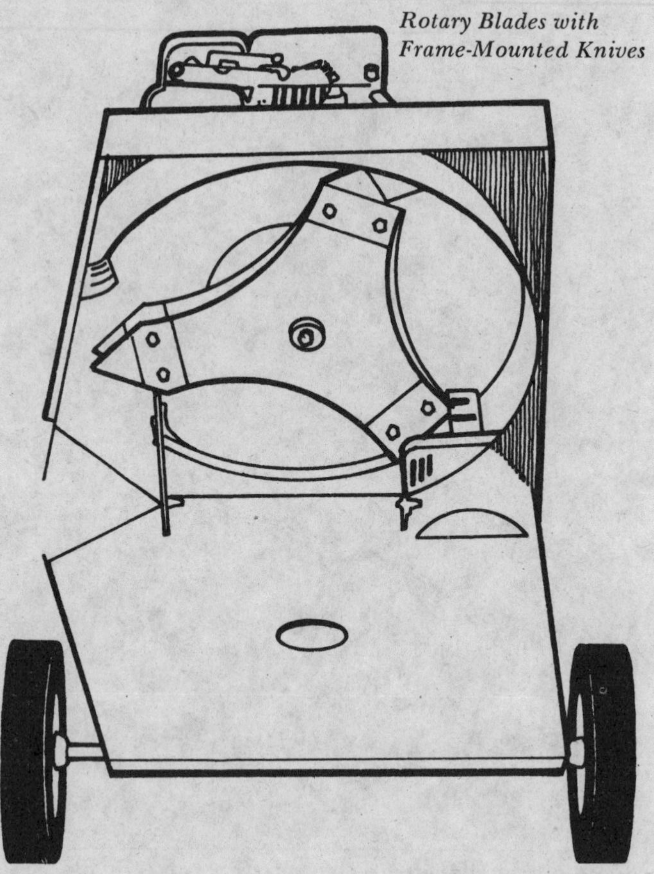

Rotary blades that whirl through stationary knives mounted on the frame chop and fling the mass of particles out the side vent.

Another time-tested system is a series of knives rigidly mounted in a revolving horizontal shaft. The fabble plates and a screen tend to hold the material against the cutting action of the blades.

Rigidly Mounted Knives on Horizontal Shaft

come with three wheels, and some with four. Make sure the machine you are thinking of buying handles easily and comfortably.

One of the most sensible gardening arrangements we've ever seen was at the Golden Acres Farm in lower Bucks County, Pennsylvania, where a double track of sturdy rails was erected over and along a series of compost bins. A king-sized shredder was mounted on the rails and traveled from bin to bin, depositing its aggregate as it went.

There are three or four basic systems for reducing and mixing your organic wastes. Hammer mill tempered steel flails revolve freely on a rotating shaft, and so have the ability to absorb shocks from hitting stones. There also seems to be a minimum of blockage in the mixing chamber caused by wet materials. Sets of hardened steel teeth or knives, fixed rigidly on a revolving shaft, work in combination with interior baffle plates and the bottom screen, which tend to keep the material in contact with the knives. The smaller shredder-bagger machines work with a series of two or three rotary blades similar to a lawn mower's. In some models, these whirling knives pass between stationary cutters that are part of the frame or chassis to achieve more complete cutting. The turbulence created by the rotary blades also whirls the aggregate out through the vent, which permits you to deposit it right where it is needed—either in the compost pile or in the planting row.

Any matter that is organic and compostable can be reduced to a workable aggregate or mass in your shredder. You will find that there is plenty of material on your home grounds to keep your shredder and you busy for a series of weekends, particularly in the late summer and fall. There are the weeds, the grass clippings, the crop residues, and the leaves. Add to these local benefits the contents of your garbage pail; it combines well with just about anything.

Next, there are the wood chips from the local road department, sawdust from the neighborhood lumberyard, and corncobs from the nearest feedmill (if you can get them ground). All of these varieties of cellulose are fine for mixing with the garbage. Working with unground corn cobs, though, can be tricky. The tough cobs have a habit of flying back up out of the hopper, right at your head. Some gardeners have reported that a thorough soaking (up to a week) of the cobs softens them and makes shredding easier.

No garden chore is easier or pleasanter than shredding dry, autumn leaves. But if your leaves have wintered over and are tough, wet, and rubbery, feed them into the shredder in very small handfulls which are followed by dry sawdust, and again, be prepared to work without a screen.

TYPES OF SHREDDERS AVAILABLE

Think over your shredding needs carefully before you begin to shop for a machine. There are many different shredders on the market today, and rather than trying to list them all, we've decided to describe the basic types available and give some examples of each type. Keep in mind that models change from year to year, and be sure to investigate all the features of the models you're considering.

Large Shredder-Grinders

Most of the shredders in this group comprise the classics of the industry—the Amerind-MacKissic, Gilson, Lindig, and W-W. To them should be added the Royer, the Ariens, the Roto-Hoe, the Hahn-Eclipse and the Winona, all of which feature the larger machine in their wide-ranging lines.

Four-Wheel Shredder-Grinder

In general, these shredder-grinders are designed for the 1- to 5-acre place in the country, although you may be perfectly happy with one of these bigger machines on your suburban ½ acre. You'll find that they can handle a greater diversity of materials than the shredder-baggers and also a greater volume. And, thanks to their rugged framework and wheels, it's a lot easier than you would think to roll them out into the garden or up to the compost pile. It's also good to be able to report that shredders last for years with very minor repairs (made easily by the local dealer), so their cost can be amortized over quite a period.

Amerind-MacKissic Model 12-P is a 6 h.p. combination log chipper and shredder-grinder. In addition to handling conventional organic composting materials including corncobs, it reduces logs up to 3 inches to wood chips. Model 9-P is powered by a 4 or 5 h.p. engine and works through a series of 24 free-swinging knives. Power take-off units are available for many popular small estate tractors.

The 6 h.p. Gilson Chopper features nine, square, rotating cutter bars instead of a screen, which are ideal when you're grinding wet, soggy, fibrous materials. Cutting action comes from three sets of rotating double-edged knives—12 cutting surfaces. The gravity-feed hopper is king-sized—almost 17 by 17. The Chopper is belt-driven with an idler clutch.

The Lindig Concho is also available with an electric motor or a 5 or 7 h.p. engine. It offers a wide range of grinding screens from ¼ inch to 1¾ inch. A side-vented brush and wood chopper feed directly into the mixing chamber. The cutting and shredding unit is a series of free-swinging hammers. The steel frame is supported by three wheels, one up front which pivots plus two in the rear.

The 8 h.p. Roto-Hoe Cut'n Shred heavy-duty shredder-mulcher includes a side-feed which leads directly to three knives passing by a hardened block. We have used this feature to shred long, tough corn stalks, and found it did a good job. Built of 12-gauge steel, the frame sits on four wheels and has a long tow handle for easy mobility. The steel bar grate is wide-spaced to reduce jamming.

The Royer 8 is a specially designed machine whose endless shredding belt is lined with tempered steel cleats mounted in rows. Models 8, 10, and 12 are electric or gas powered with a capacity that ranges from 5 to 12 cubic yards per hour of soil, peat, and other organic materials. Many municipalities use the larger models for shredding prior to composting them. This is a well-made machine designed for blending, potting, and soil compost mixes.

In addition to a conventional screen, the W-W Model 62-G offers a grating of six rods and rollers for use when shredding wet materials.

The Royer Shredder

Powered by a 5 h.p. engine, it works through a series of tempered, hammer mill flails and can handle all conventional organic materials up to 1½ inch tree trimmings, small bones, phosphate rock, tin cans, and bottles. Optional grinding screens handle corn, wheat, or milo.

The Winona Model JR-AW comes mounted on four wheels, but Model JR-S can be mounted on a garden tractor or over the compost pit. The Winonas are electric or gas driven and have changeable racks including a wet mat rack for gummy materials which is a short screen covering only half the mixing chamber. Powered by a 2 h.p. engine, it works through a cutting unit comprising 16 hinged knives.

Lickity Chipster

The Chipster has an 8 h.p. gasoline-powered feed roll, a clutch to disengage the feed roll, a hammer mill-type rotor, shredding screen, and chip direction head. There are two wheels for convenience in moving, but the Chipster is not to be hauled as a trailer. The brush feed chute is 16 inches wide and 13 inches long with an opening to the rotor that permits feeding branches up to 2 inches in diameter. The self-feeding roller, located at the end of the chute, feeds the branch into the hammer mill-type rotor where it is shredded, screened, and dropped on the ground in front of the Chipster. If the dynamically balanced, hammer mill rotor should become overloaded, the powered feed roll will automatically stop until the overload has been cleared and then will automatically start again. Weight: 215 pounds.

Lickity Chipper Model PTO-5

The Brush Chipper utilizes the power takeoff of a tractor. The PTO model is equipped with wheels, tires, and tubes as standard equipment. It can be towed to the job at normal highway speeds behind any vehicle. The feed chute can be folded up and the blower discharge chute adjusted to make towing easier. The PTO model is equipped with a pin-type hitch coupler. The hammer mill rotor handles limbs up to 5 inches in diameter at a rate of 50 feet per minute.

A.M. Leonard & Son, Inc.
P.O. Box 816
Piqua, OH 45356

Diadem Brush Chipper

The Diadem Chipper will handle up to 3 inch diameter limbs. Brush self-feeds through the chipper and is converted into small chips in just a few seconds. Small brush can be processed in bundles at a time. It is constructed of heavy-duty plate steel with a 6 gauge (5 mm.) engine deck and a solid cylinder rotor. Imbedded in the solid rotor are two 0.4 inch thick cutting knives of specially hardened chrome vanadium steel. The wheeled Diadem is 30 inches wide; it can be taken anywhere for on-the-job brush disposal. All tires are fully pneumatic. You can choose from a three-point hitch PTO and 8, 10, and 12 h.p. models.

Vandermolen Corp.
119 Dorsa Ave.
Livingston, NJ 07039

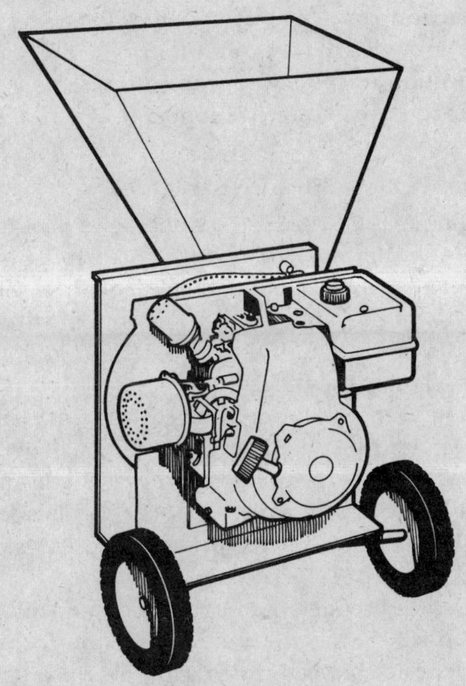

Top-Vented Shredder-Bagger

Top-Vented Shredder-Baggers

A top-vented, compact shredder-bagger will throw a stream of chopped aggregate into the garden or compost pile. The Hahn 3½ h.p. Mighty Compact and International Harvester 35P are in many ways identical. They are low-profile, with wide-mouth, gravity-feed hoppers and a pair of wide-set, rubber-tired wheels for extra stability plus mobility. Both models feature hammer mill cutters and optional baggers.

Free-swinging, hardened steel hammers, a large feed hopper, and an adjustable discharge chute are built into the low center of gravity-feed McDonough Snapper. Model 30-S has been designed to handle leaves, bush trimmings, tree prunings up to ½ inch thick, and cornstalks. It is powered by a 3 h.p. engine with centrifugal clutch and belt drive.

A large (22 inches wide) drop chute for raking in leaves and other lawn debris plus a side-mounted chipping opening for branches are features of three top-vented shredder-baggers that are almost identical in design. They are the Columbia Model 654-4, the Jacobsen No. 50080, and the MTD No. 244-650. Powered by a 5 h.p. engine, each machine features a three-stage cutting action consisting of a single, flat reversible blade, nine flail knives, and four cutting fingers. In addition to the novel drop chute, these shredders each have extra-wide hoppers.

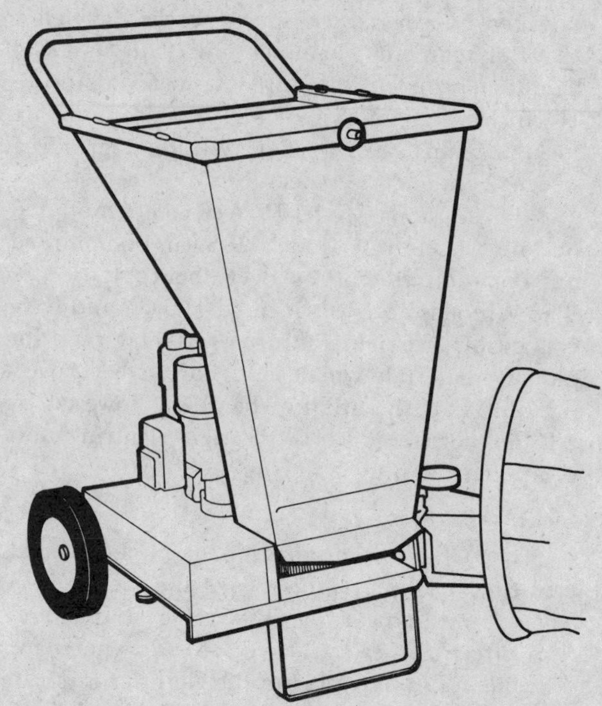

Bottom-Vented Shredder-Bagger

Bottom-Vented Shredder-Baggers

The Atlas, Cross, Kees, Roper, and Sensation models, while more or less identical in appearance—wide, low-set hoppers, each with a set of sturdy wheels, and engines mounted directly over the cutting units—are somewhat different in the features they offer.

The 5 h.p. Atlas does its cutting with three steel blades plus eight shear bars which permit it to cut wood up to 1 inch thick. Blade drive is direct from the engine. A poker rod has been built into the hopper for breaking up twigs and vines.

Cross shredders come in two models, the 3½ h.p. 4365, and the 5 h.p. 4650. Both shredders deposit chopped material in a bag and feature a sweep-in hopper that makes lawn cleanup easy. Power goes direct from the engines into the double-bladed rotary cutters.

The Kees Kom-Pak also has a rake-in hopper, an optional extra. Its steel cutting blades will handle wood up to 1 inch on the 5 h.p. model or ¾ inch for the 3½ h.p. Three bags are packed with each machine.

The 3½ h.p. Roper works with two high-speed blades to chop up leaves, twigs, and vines. It is worth noting that the accompanying Roper photos show it handling corncobs. The 6 h.p. model depends on triple cutting blades plus breaker bars in the chopping chamber. There is a fixed steel deflector on the discharge chute for directional control of the shredded matter. Bags are also available.

Power in the Sensation Eager Beaver goes directly from the engine to the double set of reversible blades without belts or chains; a safety clutch has been designed to protect the engine against shocks. The Eager Beaver dismantles easily for transport by car, thanks to large-diameter hand knobs.

The Sears 8 h.p. Super-Shredder resembles a rotary mower with its engine mounted directly over the three high-speed cutting blades. Shredded particles—leaves, vines, twigs, and garden debris—are vented at the bottom in a bag. The wide-mouthed but shallow hopper may be lowered for raking and sweeping in of lawn debris. Five bags are included.

The Toro comes in two models, 3½ and 5 h.p. Each features a big, slanting, gravity-feed hopper with a pusher rod to handle the material. The engine sits directly over the cutter blades—two in the smaller model and three in the larger—which work in conjunction with the shredding bars at the bottom vent. An optional bagging kit is available.

SOURCES OF SHREDDERS

The following companies all market several different models of shredding machines:

Allis-Chalmers
Outdoors Leisure Products Div.
1126 S. 70th, P.O.B. 512
Milwaukee, WI 53201

Amerind-MacKissic
Box 111
Parker Ford, PA 19457

Ariens
111 Calumet & 655 W. Ryan St.
Brillion, WI 54110

Atlas Tool & Mfg. Co.
5151 Natural Bridge Ave.
St. Louis, MO 63115

Bolens Div. FMC Corp.
Urban/Suburban Power Equipment Div.
215 S. Park St.
Port Washington, WI 53074

Columbia
P.O. Box 2741, 5389 W. 130th St.
Cleveland, OH 44111

Gilson Brothers Mfg. Co.
Box 152
Plymouth, WI 53073

Hahn, Inc. Agricultural Products Div.
1625 N. Garvin St.
Evansville, IN 47717

International Harvester
401 N. Michigan Ave.
Chicago, IL 60611

Jacobsen Mfg. Co.
1721 Packard Ave.
Racine, WI 53403

F. D. Kees Mfg. Co.
Box 775, 700 Park Ave.
Beatrice, NB 68310

Lindig Mfg. Corp.
Box 111, 1877 W. County Rd. C
St. Paul, MN 55113

Magna American Corp.
Box 90, Hwy. 18
Raymond, MS 39150

McDonough Power Equipment, Inc.
Macon Rd.
McDonough, GA 30253

MTD Products, Inc.
Box 2741, 5389 W. 130th
Cleveland, OH 44111

Red Cross Mfg. Corp.
Box 111, 124 S. Oak
Bluffton, IN 46714

Roof Mfg. Co.
1011 W. Howard St.
Pontiac, IL 61764

Roper Sales Corp.
1905 W. Court St.
Kankakee, IL 60901

Roto-Hoe & Sprayer Co.
100 Auburn Rd., Rt. 87
Newbury, OH 44065

Royer Foundry & Machine Co.
158 Pringle St.
Kingston, PA 18704

Sears, Roebuck & Co.
925 S. Homan Ave.
Chicago, IL 60607

Toro Co.
8111 Lyndale Ave. S
Bloomington, MN 55420

Winona Attrition Mill
1009 W. Fifth St.
Winona, MN 55987

W-W Grinder Corp.
2957 N. Market St.
Wichita, KS 67219

W-W Grinder Model 5-20-4
W-W Grinder Corp.

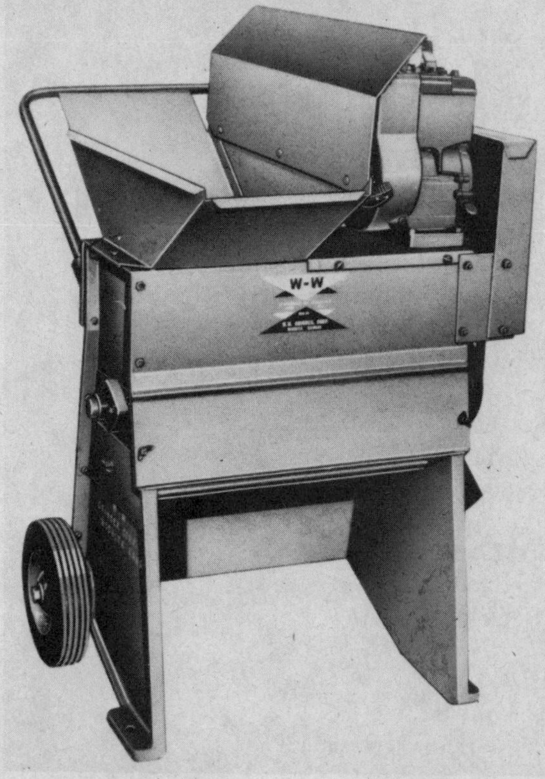

W-W Grinder Model 2 + 62
W-W Grinder Corp.

W-W Grinder Economy Model A
W-W Grinder Corp.

MULCHING

Mulching is an important technique employed by the organic farmer for maintaining weed control, retaining of soil moisture, and increasing the amount of organic matter or humus present, hence improving the soil's tilth. Specially adapted lawn mowers are good for chopping grasses and weeds for mulch on a small scale. But we know of only one source of equipment for applying mulch on a serious scale.

SOURCES OF MULCHING EQUIPMENT

Rotary Mulching Mower

Manufactured by:
FMC Corp., Outdoor Power Equipment Div.
215 S. Park St.
Port Washington, WI 53074

Rotary Mulching Mower Conversion Plans

Plans for converting a lawn mower are available from:
Dorsay Poor Man's Catalog 3
240 Kinderkamack Rd.
Oradell, NJ 07649

Wayne Peters
Rt 2
Meadville, PA 16335

Rotary Mulching Mower Conversion Parts

The parts needed to convert a lawn mower are available from:
Better Life Enterprises, Inc.
1462 John St.
Whiting, IN 46394

Friday Straw Spreader

Originally designed for strawberry culture, the Friday Straw Spreader has the potential of being an important tool for the organic farm. Lack of mechanization for the mulch-spreading process has discouraged many organic farmers from utilizing mulch to its fullest potential. The 36 by 100 inch straw spreader mounts on a trailer or wagon and is powered by a crank start, 18 h.p., two-cycle engine (electric start optional). It can be adjusted to mulch on or between rows at a rate of about 1 acre per hour, governed by tractor speed. A hydraulic drive option utilizing a tractor hydraulic system or PTO pump can be provided. Shipping weight: 640 pounds.

Friday Tractor Co., Inc.
Hartford, MI 49057

The Friday Straw Spreader
Friday Tractor Co.

SLUDGE

While supplying the farmer with a source of plant food, applying organic wastes to the soil in the form of sludge offers a solution to the problem of finding an outlet for human waste products. Special equipment to pump, store, transport, and apply sludge to farm lands is in the early stages of development as the technique slowly gains credibility as a multipurpose solution to land fertility and waste disposal problems.

EQUIPMENT FOR INCORPORATING SEWAGE SLUDGE AND ANIMAL MANURES INTO THE SOIL

by Charles H. Reed

Professor of Agricultural Engineering, Rutgers University, New Brunswick, New Jersey

For centuries, man has applied animal manures and human sewage to the soil to improve crop production. The principal technique was to spread it on the land and then work it into the soil.

With the expanding population, depletion of our natural resources, and intolerable pollution of the atmosphere and hydrosphere, there is an urgent need for techniques to recycle biodegradable wastes into the upper horizon of the soil where they are degraded and utilized, resulting in a beneficial effect upon the environment.[1] Bohn and Cauthorn state, "In summary, compared to air and water, the soil has a vastly greater potential for waste disposal and transformation . . . and it has the capacity to absorb far more material than it can produce or than is added to it." [2]

The incorporation of wastes directly into the soil is superior to surface spreading because there are no odors, no opportunity for flies or other pests to feed or breed, no runoff or surface erosion of wastes, and the wastes are placed in the best possible media for immediate degradation to plant nutrients and utilization by plants. These techniques conform to the concept of land treatment as defined by Stevens et al.:[3]

> Land treatment is any of several methods of waste water treatment and sludge application which consider the qualities of land, waste water, and sludge in the design of facilities. Land treatment conveys the reciprocal, beneficial relationship between the land and the waste. Most such facilities are designed to produce valuable end products, such as green crops and pure effluent as a result of the treatment processes.
>
> Land treatment differs from land disposal, a term used to describe any method which applies sewage, raw or treated, to the earth; and land application, a term used by EPA [Environmental Protection Agency] to describe all methods of waste water disposal associated with the ground, that is, sewage farms, land treatment, septic systems, and underground disposal.

The design of an effective land treatment system and the selection of appropriate equipment necessitates the consideration of many factors, some of which are outlined below:

1. Wastes to be incorporated into soil:
   - Kind and previous treatments.
   - Physical and chemical properties, i.e., percent solids (wet basis) and rate of production (daily, weekly).
2. Storage available or required. Transportation.
   - Distance to sites.
   - Mode of.
3. Site characteristics or limitations.
   - Acreage.
   - Topography.
   - Existing vegetation.
   - Soil characteristics.
   - Ground water. (Depth, quality).
   - Location of human habitation. Distance. Prevailing wind.

4. Climatic limitations.
   - Temperature. Duration of frozen soil.
   - Rainfall. Seasonal, normal, and extreme variations.
   - End product desired. Crops to be raised, use of land, etc.

Irrigation of sewage sludge and effluent is receiving considerable attention at this time.[4,5] Only thin slurries with low-solid contents can be irrigated. Because of the high water content (more than 95 percent as it comes from the digesters), conveyance to disposal sites by pipeline may be the only practical transportation system. Storage structures at the sites will be required during periods of subfreezing temperatures, frozen impervious soil, saturated soil, and other periods of shutdown. Unless thoroughly digested, surface applications of sewage sludge may generate odors and attract flies. Any surface applications are susceptible to surface runoff. There is a possibility of soil clogging and waterlogging when sewage sludge is irrigated.[3,6] Also, there may be damage to foliage when large quantities of sludge are repeatedly sprinkled on plants. There will be large power requirements. The aerosol effect may limit high-pressure irrigation on some sites.

Irrigation of effluent containing only dissolved solids can be managed without many of the above disadvantages of sewage sludge, and may be considered for irrigation of crops or ground water recharge when needed. The limiting factor usually is the amount of water which can be added to the soil at different seasons of the year; that is, ice buildup or saturated soil.

Composting is an ancient technique of recycling biodegradable wastes. Modern techniques and equipment have been developed to compost balanced mixtures of biodegradable wastes including sewage sludge, animal manure, and solid wastes. See *Compost Science,* Vol. 13, No. 3, May-June 1972, for information on General Motors' Terex-Cobey Composter. These techniques are relatively expensive and may generate some localized odor. Well-cured compost can be spread on the land without attracting flies, is not as susceptible to surface runoff as is noncomposted waste, and is an excellent soil conditioner. An outstanding advantage of compost is that it can be readily stored in piles at low cost without nuisance until an appropriate time for application in the soil.

Land spreading is the most ancient method of utilizing both human and animal excreta. When plowed or disked immediately after application, it is an effective method of incorporating it into the soil. When large quantities are involved, this may be the most economical, but if not properly treated, it will not be the most sanitary technique.

The ridge-and-furrow technique might be considered a surface method of application unless covered immediately. The furrows can be made on the contour or slightly sloping to permit the water to filter into the soil. Ridge-and-furrows on the contour have been used experimentally at the New Jersey Agricultural Experiment Station as a low-cost winter storage. Aerobic conditions should be maintained in and at the bottom of the furrow.

Equipment has been developed which will incorporate wastes directly into the soil, either in one or two operations by Sub-Sod-Injection or Plow-Furrow-Cover.

Sub-Sod-Injection (SSI) equipment is available which will inject any slurries that will flow by gravity or under pressure through a six inch diameter hose two feet long. Animal manures with up to 20 percent solids and sewage sludge with up to 10 percent solids can be injected by gravity into the soil at the rate of 400 gallons per minute in a band up to two inches thick and 28 inches wide and from six to eight inches beneath the surface without turning over the soil. The injector has a standard category two, three-point hitch with a spring-trip release for passing over subsurface objects. It is comparable to a two-bottom plow in weight and durability. This equipment is not yet available commercially, but can be assembled from existing components.

The Plow-Furrow-Cover (PFC) method is the most adaptable of any of the previously mentioned techniques. Equipment is available, or can be assembled from manufactured components, to incorporate directly into the upper eight inches of the soil up to 300 tons per acre of biodegradable wastes, ranging from thin slurries (septic tank pumpouts) to semisolids (sewage cake). PFC leaves the soil plowed and ready for disking and seeding. Two types of equipment will be described for PFC: one for 25 percent solids or less, and the other for greater than 25 percent solids.

One of the two recently developed pieces of equipment was assembled by Agway, Inc., of Syracuse, New York. The first one was used at the University of Connecticut in a research demonstration project to study the effect of incorporating septic tank pumpouts into the soil. In this project more than 100,000 gallons of slurry were incorporated into the soil in two months. The capacity of the tank is 800 gallons. A nine inch auger with ample hydraulic power from an auxiliary hydraulic pump on the tractor, and 12 inch as well as six inch valve openings will unload much heavier solids than would the previous prototypes. The highest limit of solids content which it will unload has not yet been determined. This equipment will not unload low-moisture sewage cake, semisolid animal manures with bedding, or caked poultry manure reinforced with feathers. A gooseneck tongue is built permanently into the tank to provide easy maneuverability of either a 16 inch single-bottom moldboard plow or a sub-sod-injector which is mounted on the three-point hitch of the tractor.

A second unit, constructed in 1973, is identical, except that it has a capacity of 1,500 gallons, a nine inch ribbon auger, and a slurry spreader on the rear. This unit has not yet been field-tested. The augers, valves, and spreader are powered by the hydraulic system on the tractor.

To plow-furrow-cover, a 16 inch single-bottom moldboard plow is mounted on the three-point hitch of a standard farm tractor. A slurry with up to 25 percent solids can be deposited into a six to eight inch deep plowed furrow. Immediately after deposition, and in the same operation, the plow covers the waste and opens the next furrow. With properly adjusted equipment, one and one-half to two inches of slurry can be completely covered. This is approximately 170 to 225 tons of slurry per acre. A well-formed furrow, 16 inches wide, seven to eight inches deep and 400 feet long with one and one-half inches of slurry, contains 500 gallons, or approximately two tons. PFC leaves the soil well plowed and ready for disking and seeding. The equipment has been designed to operate at three miles per hour and unload up to 200 gallons of slurry per minute. The axle of the trailer is adjustable so that the trailer is offset, permitting the right rear trailer wheel to travel in the newly formed clean furrow.

A combination transport and field unit was assembled by a tank on a four-wheel-drive, 1½-ton truck chassis with flotation tires. It is equipped with a hydraulic pump, controls, and a category two, three-point hitch. The tank has a capacity of 500 gallons. With a 12 inch ribbon auger in the bottom of the tank and a 12 inch diameter valve, semisolid animal manures with up to 30 percent solids, and sewage sludge with up to 20 percent solids have been unloaded. Because the hydraulic power is limited, the full performance capabilities of the 12 inch auger have not been determined. A spreader can be installed on the rear for land spreading.

A ridge-and-furrow opener can be mounted on the three-point hitch of the tractor or mounted on the tongue of the trailer. This consists of right-hand and left-hand moldboard plows bolted together on the same trip-release beam. The 12 inch opening in the center of the trailer tank permits a high-capacity application of semisolids into the furrow. Presently the furrows are closed or covered in a second operation.

The best equipment field-tested to date at the New Jersey Experiment Station, for unloading semisolids and cake with more than 25 percent solids, is a New Idea Flail Spreader. It can be adjusted for a wide range of surface applications, which are plowed under in a second operation. A conveyor similar to the one on a forage wagon is being adapted to this spreader to convey the waste into a furrow for PFC.

International Harvester sells an attachment to convert one of their heavy-duty manure spreaders into a self-unloading forage wagon. At this time it has not been demonstrated for unloading a gummy, sticky semisolid into a furrow.

There should be no difficulty to adapt either of these pieces of equipment to PFC for either one or two operations. Plans are underway at the New Jersey Agricultural Experiment Station to make these adaptations.

There are outstanding advantages in handling dewatered sludge with a solids content of 15 percent or greater.

1. As solids content increases, volume and weight decrease. For example, to inject one ton of solids in a 5 percent solution, 20 tons of slurry must be handled; for one ton of solids in a 15 percent solution, 6⅔ tons; and only 3⅓ tons if a semisolid with 30 percent solids, dry-weight basis.
2. It can be stored in contoured furrows or piles on well-drained sites to be incorporated into the soil when weather and soil conditions are optimum.
3. It can be transported in regular dump trucks without leakage on the highway.
4. Sludge with a solids content of 15 percent represents the minimum solids content which can be incorporated into the soil by PFC at the rate of 40 tons dry-weight equivalent per acre in one application: that is, 2.27 inches of depth in the furrow can be completely covered. Greater rates of application can be achieved in one operation if the sludge contains less moisture and more solids, and also because greater depths can be covered in the furrow. This rate of application represents the performance capabilities of the equipment and not necessarily the optimum or safe amount which the soil can tie up, degrade, and recycle. Smaller quantities can be applied.

In order to utilize the continuous output of sewage treatment plants, daily PFC applications at the desired annual rate may be made in contiguous strips or furrows, resulting in the entire plot receiving the total annual treatment. At any time when there is sufficient area of contiguous strips of plowed ground, it may be disked and seeded to the crop appropriate for that particular season. After some forage crops, that is, hybrid Bermuda grass, have been established, one or two applications can be made annually by PFC or SSI without replanting. For maximum recycling and utilization of nutrients from the sludge, crops should be raised on and harvested from the treated sites when mature or at the end of the period of their maximum assimilation. Numerous crop management plans and rotations are possible, depending upon the sites and the end product desired.

REFERENCES

1. Meadows, Dunella H.; Meadows; Randers; and Behrens. "The Limits to Growth." A report for the Club of Rome's project on the Predicament of Mankind. New York: Universe Books, 1972.
2. Bohn, Hinrich L., and Cauthorn. "Pollution: The Problem of Misplaced Waste." *American Scientist*. Vol. 60, Sept.-Oct. 1972, pp. 561-565.
3. Stevens, R. Michael; Elazar, D.J.; Schlesinger, Jeanne; Lockard, J. F.; and Stevens, B. A. "Green Land-Clean Streams," Center for the Study of Federalism, Philadelphia, Pa. 1972.
4. Hinesly, Thomas D., and Sosewitz, Ben. "Digested Sludge Disposal on Crop Land." 41st Annual Convention Water Pollution Control Federation. Chicago, Illinois, Sept., 1968.
5. "Recycling Sludge and Sewage Effluent by Land Disposal." *Environmental Science and Technology*. Vol. 6, No. 10, Oct. 1972.
6. Reed; Murrman, S.C.; Kortz; Rickard; Hunt; Buzzell; Carey; Bilello; Buda; Guter; and Sorbor. "Wastewater Management by Disposal on Land." Special Report 171, Corps of Engineers. Cold Regions Research and Engineering Laboratory, Hanover, N.H., 1972.

SOURCES OF EQUIPMENT TO ADD ORGANIC MATERIAL TO THE SOIL

Big Wheels

Big Wheels is a 1,600-gallon tank truck used for distributing sludge in either surface or subsurface applications. It is not built for road transport; it must be used in conjunction with sludge transport systems. For surface application, sludge is sprayed from the rear of the truck. For subsurface application, soil-slicing coulters precede chisel-plowing tines to cut a narrow path for application hoses. Injection is possible at adjustable depths usually between 6 and 9 inches. Furrow coverers are available but are usually unnecessary.

Big Wheels, Inc.
I-57 and Rt. 9
Paxton, IL 60957

Big Wheels—a coulter/chisel combination to dig the application channel.
Big Wheels, Inc.

Sludge leaving the outlet under pressure hits the deflecting cover . . .

. . . and sprays a wide pattern behind the truck for surface application.

DTS-100 Stationary Manure Pump Unit

This is a stationary unit comprising the HSP-100 electrically driven screw pump as well as the delivery pipe with three-way valve and mixing nozzle. It is mounted on a supporting rail made of channel sections which should be fixed permanently at the place of pump installation. It is possible to mix the manure in tanks, to pump it over from initial tanks to main tanks, to pump over from the tank to the water cars, and to deliver from the tank directly to the sprinkling system, when the area to be sprinkled is nearby the farm. The unit can be used with even very dense liquids for which no other pump can find application. The stationary unit is best suited for large pumping jobs.

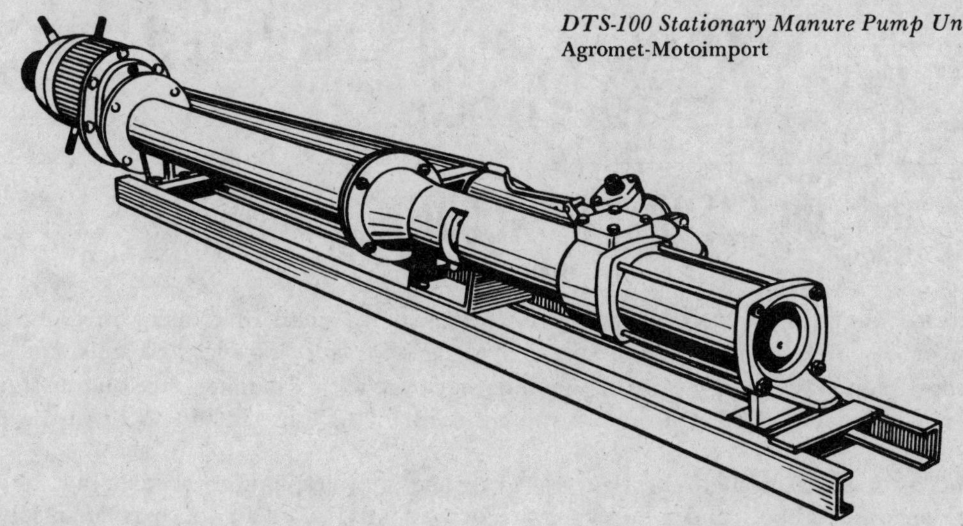

DTS-100 Stationary Manure Pump Unit
Agromet-Motoimport

Specifications:	
Delivery of pump	—40 meters over 3 hours
Pressure of pump	—100 m H 0
Speed of pump	—560 rpm
Electric motor	—type SZJVe-64 b
Total weight	—897 kilograms
Depth of tank	—3.5 meters

It will deliver at a rate of 40 cubic meters per hour.

Agromet-Motoimport
Foreign Trade Enterprise
00-950 Warszawa, ul.
Przemyslowa 26, Poland

–10– Woodlot and Orchard Management

TOOLS FOR THE WOODLOT*

by Jim Ritchie

For most homestead timbering purposes, you will need to make a small investment in tools: a lightweight chain saw or bow saw, an axe, at least two steel wedges for splitting logs and rails, and a sledge to drive the wedges. You may prefer a splitting hammer: a sledge with a hammer face on one side and a wedge-shaped splitting blade on the other; once you get the hang of using it, this tool can speed up timber chores.

You may also find a use for a machete, brush hook, grub hoe, mattock, power circular saw, and bucksaw. Other, more specialized tools and equipment are occasionally called in for particular jobs around the homestead, but unless you use a specialized piece of equipment enough to justify the investment, you may want to borrow or rent, rather than buy.

Handling wood with a peavy.

* Reprinted from *Trees for the Yard, Orchard, and Woodlot,* edited by Roger B. Yepsen, Jr. Rodale Press, 1976.

All woodcutting tools should be kept sharp and out of the rain. Well-maintained equipment is not only easier to work with, but safer as well. A sledge or axe that is loose on the handle is a hazard both to the operator and to fellow workers or bystanders. A dull axe blade may bounce or glance off the log and into a human limb.

SAWS

For most homestead work a lightweight chain saw with a 14 or 16 inch cutter bar is sufficient. You can buy heavier, more powerful models if you need to do a lot of heavy work. But by notching and undercutting with smaller saws, you can fell trees up to three feet in diameter. If you've never operated a chain saw, try out two or three different models and sizes. Also, consider the availability of parts and service before you buy.

Chain saws aren't for everybody. Many people object to the cash investment, the stink or the noise, or the gas and oil consumed. You may prefer to work with a crosscut saw—either the two-man variety (if you have a steady helper) or a one-man saw. The rhythmic sound of a crosscut has a soothing quality, something that certainly cannot be said of a chain saw.

Two-man saws are typically six to seven feet long and have cutting teeth alternated with drag teeth to remove sawdust from the saw kerf (or slot). These saws are made of high-quality steel and are too limber and springy for handy operation by one man. However, it is possible to use a two-man saw by

The proper stance at a sawhorse.

yourself if you remove the handle from one end and support that end of the saw with a slender, limber stick cut to just the right length. Poke the stick into the ground at the midpoint of the saw's travel, on the opposite side of the log (or tree) from the sawyer, and tie the upper end of the stick to the saw where the handle was removed. The stick then supports the saw so the blade doesn't flop and wobble. It's not as handy as a sawing partner, but it works.

One-man crosscut saws are shorter, about five feet in length, and are made of heavier metal than two-man crosscuts. They are not as likely to buckle when pushed and pulled from one end.

Because of the chain saws's great popularity, manual crosscut saws have all but disappeared from some areas—even in regions of heavy timbering. And, as with most steel products, prices have climbed rapidly in the past few years. To find a used saw, check classified ads in local newspapers and visit a few farm sales. (Often you can also find reasonably priced axes, sledges, wedges, files, and other timber equipment at these sales.)

For lighter work, a bow saw or bucksaw is more convenient than a crosscut. These have two- or three-foot saw blades stretched in a metal or wooden frame, hacksaw fashion. They're ideal for bucking off cordwood cuts, limbing, and other light timber work and can be used to fell smaller trees. They also come in handy for pruning fruit and ornamentals.

With all saws, power or manual, the condition of the cutting teeth has a big influence on the condition of the sawyer at the end of a day's work. There's an art to filing and setting saw teeth, and no two timbermen file a saw the same way. You'll need a good, clean file—about a number ten bastard flat file for crosscut saws. Chainsaw chains have teeth of various sizes, so you'll need to buy a file to fit your particular saw. Bow saw blades can be easily replaced.

You'll also need gauges to show the length and set of the saw teeth. (Turn the saw teeth up and sight lengthwise along the blade or chain; the angle of the cutting teeth from the plane of the saw blade is called the set.) For cutting fibrous wood, such as green oak or hickory, you'll need to set a greater angle than normal into the saw's teeth.

Older circular saws, like this PTO-run model, often appear at farm sales and auctions.

For clearing brush and small trees from land to be cultivated, a wheel-mounted circular power saw can come in handy, particularly if you're clearing large areas. These saws are fast and effective in cutting top growth. Some models are self-propelled but shouldn't be used on steep slopes.

AXES

A good single- or double-bitted axe is a necessary homestead tool. Keep the blade sharp on the job with a small pocket whetstone.

Some woodsmen prefer to use a double-bitted axe, with one blade honed sharp and the other allowed to dull slightly; the dull blade serves well for grubbing out roots and cutting off sprouts below ground level, while the sharp blade is never used for such rough work.

Leaving one blade slightly dulled gives a measure of protection when chopping among limbs that might catch the axe and divert your swing. If the axe glances into your leg or foot (an occurrence to be avoided at all costs) at least you have an even chance that the dull blade will make contact.

HOMESTEAD USES OF TIMBER

A homestead woodlot can provide shelter, fuel, tools, equipment, and outbuildings—depending on the size of the woods, the kind of trees grown, and the imagination and skill of the landowner.

FIREWOOD

Trees are most often cut for burning. Even if you cut timber for other purposes, you'll find that much of your firewood supply—perhaps all of it—can come from the leftover portions of the harvested trees.

Wood varies in heating value with species used and the degree of seasoning. Wood that has been allowed to air-dry for a year or more after cutting has a moisture content of 20 to 25 percent and will burn better and produce more heat per unit of wood than freshly cut, green wood. Also, dried wood does not deposit as much creosote on flue walls, lessening the chance of a chimney fire.

The best firewood burns steadily but not too quickly, produces a lot of heat for the amount of wood used, and burns cleanly with little creosote deposit and little ash. The table below gives the heat equivalents of the most common firewood species (based on air-dried wood) as compared with fuel oil. The heat values are given in millions of Btu's (British thermal unit—the amount of heat required to raise the temperature of one pound of water by one degree Fahrenheit) per cord of wood.

Softwoods generally make poor firewood. They burn too quickly, produce relatively little heat, and often give off unpleasant odors. For example, air-dried red pine has but 12.8 million Btu's per cord as compared with 24 million Btu's per cord of white oak.

HEAT EQUIVALENTS OF WOOD, BY SPECIES

Wood (1 standard cord)	Available heat of 1 cord of wood (Btu's)	No. 2 fuel oil (gallons)
Hickory, shagbark	24,600,000	251
Locust, black	24,600,000	251
Ironwood (hardhack)	24,100,000	246
Apple	23,877,000	244
Elm, rock	23,488,000	240
Hickory or butternut	23,477,000	240
Oak, white	22,700,000	232
Beech, American	21,800,000	222
Oak, red	21,300,000	217
Maple, sugar	21,300,000	217
Birch, yellow	21,300,000	217
Ash, white	20,000,000	204
Walnut, black	19,500,000	198
Birch, white	18,900,000	193
Cherry, black	18,770,000	191
Tamarack (Eastern larch)	18,650,000	190
Maple, red	18,600,000	190

continued on next page

HEAT EQUIVALENTS OF WOOD, BY SPECIES

Wood (1 standard cord)	Available heat of 1 cord of wood (Btu's)	No. 2 fuel oil (gallons)
Ash, green	18,360,000	187
Pine, pitch	17,970,000	183
Sycamore, American	17,950,000	183
Ash, black	17,300,000	177
Elm, American	17,200,000	176
Maple, silver	17,000,000	173
Spruce, red	13,632,000	139
Hemlock	13,500,000	138
Willow, black	13,206,000	135
Pine, red	12,765,000	130
Aspen (poplar)	12,500,000	128
Pine, white	12,022,000	123
Basswood	11,700,000	119
Fir, balsam	11,282,000	115

WHAT TO LOOK FOR IN AN AXE

by Ken Bernsohn

1) Head weight. This varies from a pound and a half on some Hudson Bay or Tomahawk models to over six pounds. Traditional wisdom suggests that the heavier the head, the more effective the axe. There's more weight behind the cutting edge, so gravity can help it on its way. The theory proves out when felling trees, splitting wood, or chopping logs so they'll fit your fireplace. Too light an axe can make you feel ineffective. But that heavy head can also be a hindrance when you're limbing trees, grubbing out saplings, or just turning dead branches into firewood for a campfire. For these uses a 2½ pound head works better, letting you control exactly how the head lands while it's on the way down.

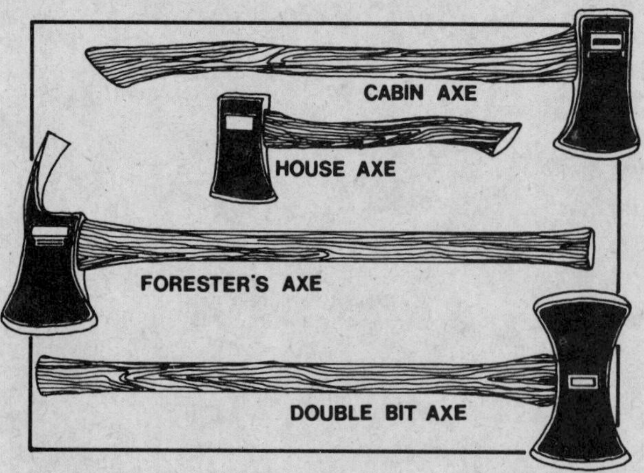

The other obvious aspect of weight is that gravity can help your axe down only after you've hoisted it up against gravity. A six pound axe is a quick way, at first, to hurt yourself more than you hurt the log. If you're going to be using an axe for a living, or intend to build a log home, you might consider one. If you're using your axe, like most of us, as an adjunct to a chain saw, or for both limbing and felling, you'll find a four pound head is far more comfortable to live with, providing enough wallop to go through a log without harming you and enough control to make limbing easy.

2) Head shape. Double-bitted axes reek with the romance of the North Woods. They're also practical because one edge can be razor-sharp for fine work, while the other can be blunter and stand an occasional nick when used for splitting logs or grubbing. However, you do not want one when starting out with an axe. I live in an area where the main industry is logging, and almost every home has an axe, yet I've seen only

three experts use double-edged blades. The droop-nosed Tomahawk is even less popular because of its excessively curved face and bantam weight.

If you're interested only in felling, a very narrow blade is right. An axe intended for a bit of felling, splitting, limbing, and grubbing will probably be best with an edge about 4½ inches from top to bottom.

3) Steel. Some axes have steel so soft you'll have to almost continually sharpen them, touching up in the midst of each tree or log. Others are so tough that you need a grindstone to sharpen them, pausing every minute or less to plunge the axe head into cold water to make sure it keeps its temper. The ideal axe head is between these extremes, soft enough to let you manicure it in the field when it gets a little dull, hard enough that this won't be necessary too often. If your choice is between the two extremes, get the soft one and take along a file and stone.

4) Handle length and style. A handle less than two feet long will cramp you, forcing you to prop up whatever you're chopping on a high platform. You'll also find that the short handle means less power behind each swing. A straight handle makes sense only on a double-bitted axe.

These are the only sure things about length and style. When people made their own handles, each man worked out for himself what was best for him. I find an axe with a 2½ foot handle is usable, and a model that's a yard long is best. But that's probably influenced by the fact that I'm six feet, five inches tall. I also would prefer to have more of a ball end on the bottom of the handle (the foot) to help stop any tendency to slip or twist. But that's me, not you. To find out what suits you, you've got to take each axe off the rack, hold it across your body for feel, and make a few practice swings. Sure, it's a good way to feel a little foolish, swinging at invisible trees in a crowded store on a Saturday. But it's better to feel a little foolish on a Saturday than feel a lot foolish when you go back to get a different axe a few Saturdays later.

HOW TO SHARPEN YOUR AXE

The odds are that when you buy your axe it will need sharpening. Step 1: Immobilize the head by putting it in a padded vise. If you're outdoors or don't run a workshop, you have two options. One is to lean the head against a stump or something else far more solid and stable than your knee. This is the traditional way, with the blade up, which I used until Gary Champagne saw me using it. He pointed out that, since you file into the edge of the axe, there was nothing to stop me from running my fingers into the edge. Gary's method is to lay the axe flat on a stump or table with just a quarter-inch of edge showing over the side. Now when you file into the blade, your fingers will hit the side of the stump or table before the steel, thanks to the angle you'll be filing at. Step 2: Use a full-size metal file, preferably with a wooden handle,

When sharpening the axe, use a full-size metal file. Make sure you do not sharpen the edge only, but work back one inch.

working back from the cutting edge. Make sure you do not just sharpen the edge itself, or you'll end up with a wide V that gets wider with time, making your axe less and less effective. Instead, sharpen a full inch back from the edge so the taper is gradual. Wear gloves. Step 3: Finish off with a whetstone. Trying to do the whole job with a stone will wear your patience thin long before the edge gets that way.

HOW TO CHOP DOWN A TREE

Put your axe in a safe place and walk around the tree, studying it. Are there any large branches that will cause problems? How thick is the tree? If it's more than 1½ feet in diameter, chopping with an axe will be a workout. Consider borrowing or renting a chain saw if you have several large trees to be removed. Does the tree lean? Most do. The easiest way to fell a tree is to chop so it'll follow its natural bent. If the tree shouldn't fall in the direction it's leaning, you'll have to do extra work.

The best way to change the direction of the fall is to tie a weight to a rope and throw it toward the top of the tree, snagging some branches before the rope falls back to earth. Bring the weighted end around the tree, so you're holding both ends with the tree in the middle of the loop. (This will take a few tries; if the tree is firmly rooted and easy to climb, like most apple trees, consider using your feet instead of your pitching arm to get the rope in place.) Now tie one end of the rope around the base of another tree that's roughly in the direction you want your tree to fall.

Haul on the rope, and you'll find it's easy to sway the tree. Have someone else tie your end onto another tree base so the three trees and the rope make a V, with the point being the one you're cutting. If it's hard to sway the tree, or if the tree's rough, have a few friends help. Do *not* tie the second rope to a truck and use it to pull the treetop! The tree will probably either snap in the middle or pull out by the roots, falling on the truck or on you.

Another, less sure way is recommended only for trees with moderate lean when you want to change the angle of fall less than 45 degrees. Let's assume the tree is leaning south. Chop your first notch, the one that determines the fall, on the west. Make the second cut, the one that actually topples the tree, from the northeast. The tree will twist as you make this cut and fall more toward the west. How much more will depend, of course, on how much it was leaning in the first place. This is faster than the rope trick, but far less precise, as our phone and power companies will attest.

When you go back for your axe, pick it up so your hand is on the handle right against the base of the head. Now you can control it, which you can't if you carry it over your shoulder or swing it by your side. This way there can't be a problem if your dog rushes up or if you trip.

Remember: an axe is more dangerous than a gun. You can unload a gun, but an axe, even one with a leather sheath, is always ready to do damage.

That's why you should look about carefully when you get to where you'll stand while cutting. If there's anything around that might deflect the blade, like low bushes or low branches, clear away the obstruction. Make sure children, advice-giving adults, and animals are well beyond the place where the tree might hit if it falls where you don't want it to. Stand at a right angle to the side where you'll make your first cut, with the axe going in on the east if you want the tree to fall that way (unless you're correcting a twist).

With your right hand at the base of the head, thumb against the metal, left hand at the bottom of the handle, make your first swing, letting your right hand slide as you swing. It should go straight in, waist high. Your second swing goes in higher, cutting down toward the first. How much higher? It depends on how thick the tree is. If you make your blows right on top of each other, as though driving in a nail, your axe will soon get stuck.

By making a wide kerf, as the notch is called, this problem is eliminated. And even when the kerf is six inches wide, a slight twist with your right hand as the axe lands will pop out a broad, flat chip each time to clear a space clean down to your bottom cut. Alternating blows, straight in and down, continue until you're about two-thirds of the way through. This will again vary, depending on the tree. Do not go more than three-fourths of the way through. You may have a winner of a tree that leans a lot and needs only a one-third cut before the shifting of the top or the sound of a creak tells you you've done more than enough.

Listening for the sounds of the tree and glancing up to see what the top is doing every few swings will help you pace yourself, instead of chopping as though each minute costs you money. High speed only costs you energy.

On a wide tree, work your way across the full diameter, cutting a chip from the far side, then one from the near, then as many as necessary in between to keep your line straight.

When you feel "just a couple more whacks will be enough," stop, walk to the opposite side, looking up while doing so, and start your second cut. On a narrow (six-inch-wide) tree this can be about four inches higher. On one a foot in diameter it should be about eight inches higher. Unless you're cutting sequoias, 1½ feet would be maximum.

The tree will fall before you chop all the way through. So watch and listen as you chop. Pause, lean on the tree a little, long before you've cut enough, just to see if the tree agrees with your judgment.

HOW TO LIMB A TREE AND LOG IT

When the tree falls, a lot of it will still be in the air. Stand with the tree between you and the first branches you'll be cutting, working from the bottom to the top.

Some people do both felling and limbing holding the axe like a baseball bat. I don't like this method for felling, but for limbing, the baseball or golf club grip works fine. Cut away from your body, working only on the far side of the tree. Then go around to the other side and limb the one you were standing on first.

If you're working with a large tree, you'll reach a point where branches hold the trunk five feet or so into the air. To log into approximate eight-foot lengths, go back to the base.

About eight feet from the bottom step onto the trunk, plant your feet at least 2½ feet apart. Have someone hand you the axe and chop from the side, with the axe going between your legs that are safely out of the way. If you had stayed on the ground chopping from the top down, the tree would eventually bend, making further chopping impossible. Make a deep notch on one side, then turn around and work from the other side. Once again, you should stop before chopping through. Standing with one foot on each half of the trunk when the ends break and the log shifts is not a good idea. After you're two-thirds of the way through, you can continue from the ground with the wide kerfs you've cut, giving your axe room even when the trunk bends at the hinge you've been making. When the tree has had a few of these eight-foot lengths cut out, you'll find the limbs are now easier to reach, and the eight-foot sections you've cut can be moved around to let you get at any branches holding up trunk sections.

HOW TO SPLIT A LOG INTO FIREWOOD

Wait until you feel tense and frustrated. Then go out and prop up an eight-footer across another, or even across a few so that a two-foot section sticks over the end. Cut it off. A bow saw is the best hand tool for this, since it'll leave you a flat end that's important later. If using an axe, make that first cut straight in and chop toward it, gradually turning the log so each piece you cut has one flat end. Then move the log you cut farther along and do it again and again, until you have a stack of two-foot lengths.

In cutting hardwoods—trees that once had leaves—you'll find the going a lot easier if you cut while the logs are still green. This isn't as important with softwoods, but again it makes the work a little less.

To split the wood, look for cracks in the log. Stand one up on a stump and drive your axe into the biggest crack. Some people pick up the axe and log together at this point. But the log will twist on the axe. The log may fall off the axe onto you. The log may come back with your axe and keep going, as though propelled with a throwing stick on your backswing. Instead, I pry the axe loose, reset the log, and whack into the same spot. Three or four whacks and you'll have most logs in half. Depending on the diameter, you may want to split it again, and possibly again.

If the log is as big around as the potbelly stove, the method you've just read doesn't always work. You may find it best to drive a wedge (which can be a genuine wedge or a battered axe head you picked up at a junk shop) into the top of the log, using a sledge. Using the back of your good axe for this can stop it from being your good axe, so use the sledge. Then lay the log on its side and use your axe to drive toward the crack the wedge started.

HOW TO DAISY A LOG

by Lewis Weeks

When a piece of wood is too large to be halved or quartered with an axe, daisying is called for. To daisy a big hunk of wood efficiently is a pleasing experience both mechanically and aesthetically. As you move around the chunk, backing away from the last cut, you split off a three- or four-inch deep piece from the outside of the chunk. If your cuts are clean, each piece will fall away from the center of the chunk and lie flat on the ground. When a complete circuit has been made, there will be the petals of your daisy, facing out from the center. Pile the petals, and go around again and again until you have reduced your big piece to half or a quarter of its original size.

STORING YOUR AXE

When you are done using your axe, take a hefty swing at your chopping block and leave the axe imbedded, assuming you'll return the next day. If you won't be chopping for a few days, bring the axe inside, wipe it off with an oily rag, and put it away. Storing it behind a bookcase or workbench will make sure it doesn't cause problems.

This sounds as though using an axe is a lot of work. It is, especially at first, when you forget to wear gloves and raise blisters. But it's satisfying work that you will enjoy in several ways. It removes you from the majority of folks who rely on store-bought logs to fuel their stoves, since in many areas the state forest services have areas open for those who want to cut their own firewood. It gives you a justified sense of self-sufficiency as you gain skill. And it makes your evening fire a matter of pride, something far more enjoyable than it would otherwise be.

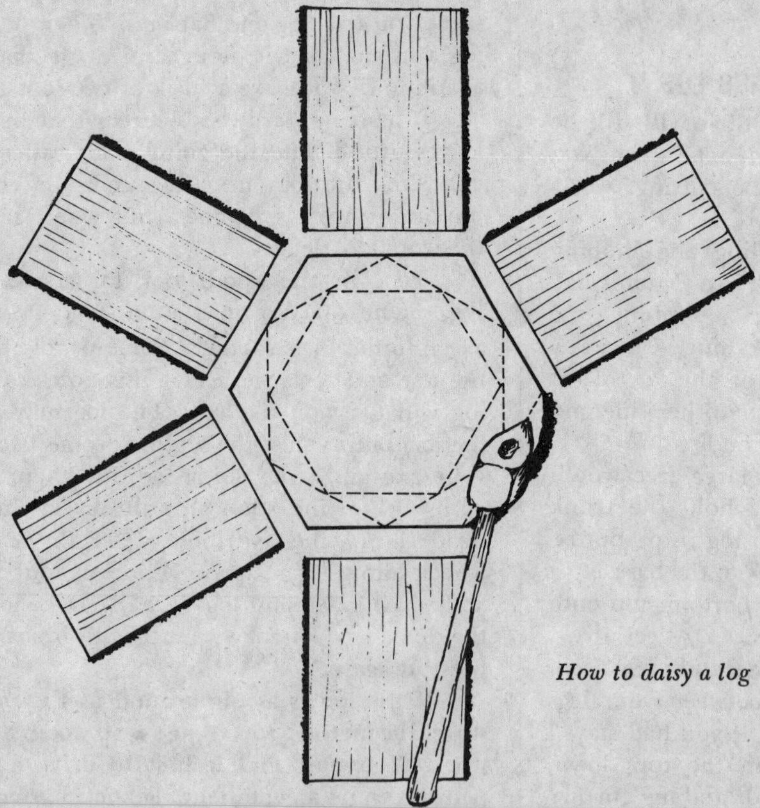

How to daisy a log

WOODLOT EQUIPMENT

The following manufacturers and suppliers deal in forestry equipment of all types and sizes. If you are looking for peaveys, cant hooks, grapples, axes, shears, or machetes, try the following:

Snow and Nealley

Manufacturers of "Our Best" line of forged tools for loggers and lumbermen (pulp hooks, cant dogs, pickaroons, etc.) along with some real specialties—bush hooks, grab hooks, and tell-tale rods.

Snow and Nealley
155 Perry Rd.
Bangor, ME 04401

Glen-Bel

The Glen-Bel catalog features a full line of hand tools for woods work, including shears (Wiss, Belknap, Cyclone, and Blue Grass), pruning saws, bow saws, pike poles, timber carriers, and all types of axes and hatchets.

Glen-Bel Enterprises
Rt. 5
Crossville, TN 38555

Tree-Trimming Tools

Stanley offers a good variety of hydraulically operated tree-trimming tools, from pole chain saws and tree pruners to circular saws and weed eaters.

Stanley Hydraulic Tools
13770 S.E. Ambler Rd.
Clackmas, OR 97015

Friend

The Friend catalog features a full line of hand and power pruning equipment—shears, anvil pruners, lopping shears, pole tree pruners, telescoping saws, and more.

Friend Mfg. Co.
Gasport, NY 14067

Bartlett

A comprehensive line of tree-trimming equipment is offered by this company.

Bartlett Mfg. Co.
3003 E. Grand Blvd.
Detroit, MI 48202

Sandvik

This firm offers a complete line of pruning saws, bow saws, and hand saws.

Sandvik, Inc.
Saws & Tools Division
1702 Nevins Rd.
Fair Lawn, NJ 07410

An Assortment of Woodlot Tools

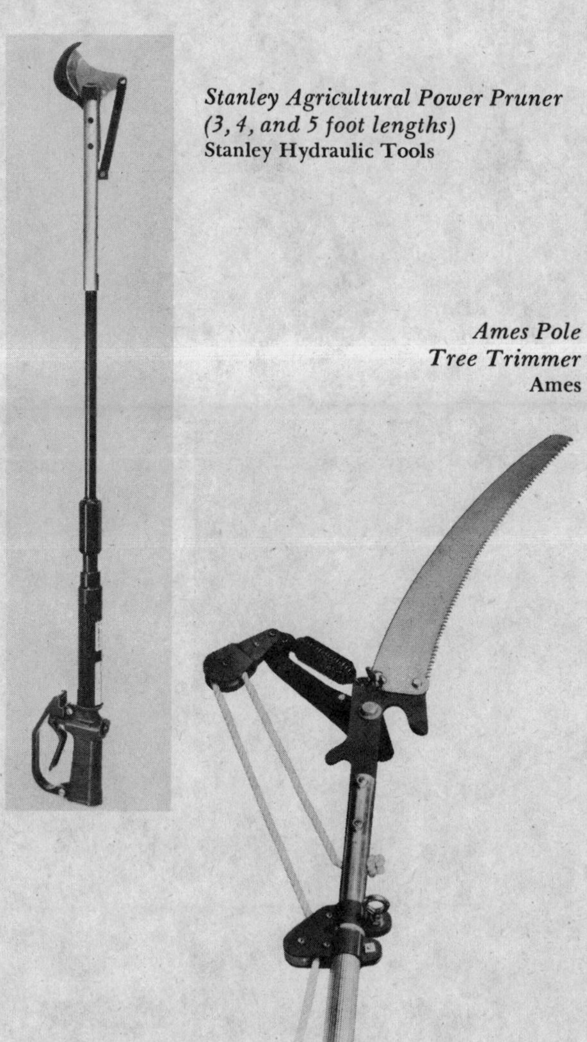

Stanley Agricultural Power Pruner (3, 4, and 5 foot lengths)
Stanley Hydraulic Tools

Ames Pole Tree Trimmer
Ames

Stanley Agricultural Long-Reach Circular Saw (overall length, 5 feet)
Stanley Hydraulic Tools

Ames Brush Hook
Ames

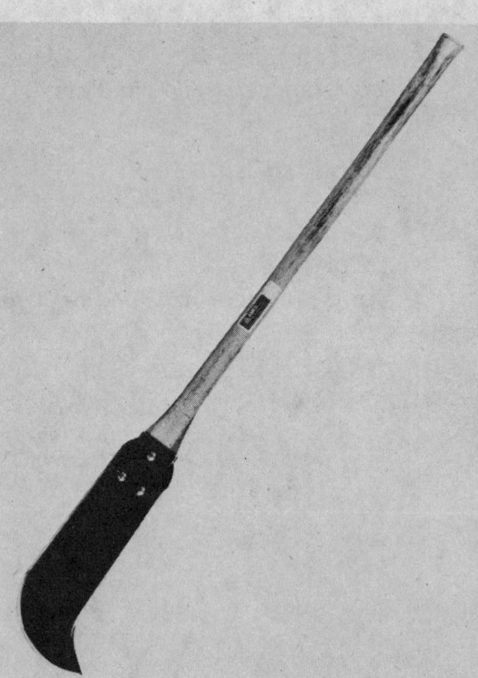

Ames Ditch Bank Blade
Ames

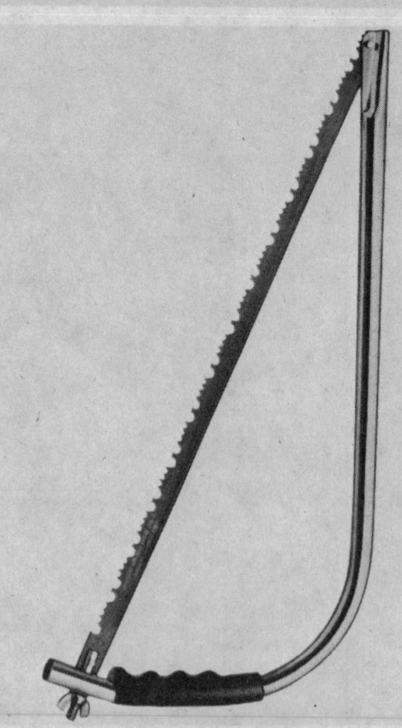

Ames Bow Saw
Ames

Woodsman's Pal Brush-Clearing Knife. Note the two cutting surfaces.
Oley Tooling, Inc.

Survival Equipment Co.

This company manufactures an especially helpful lightweight, machete-type tool for efficient land-clearing with minimum fatigue. It features a concave design with a blunt toe at the end of the cutting edge to minimize the risk of injury from a missed stroke.

Woodsman's Pal Brush-Clearing Knife
Survival Equipment Co.
Oley Tooling, Inc.
Oley, PA 19547

Cumberland

Pruning knives and saws, lopping shears, and budding and grafting knives are among the forestry-related equipment of various manufacturers listed in the Cumberland catalog.

Cumberland General Store
Rt. 3, Box 479
Crossville, TN 38555

Leonard

This firm markets pole saws, pruner poles and pruning saws, timber carriers, peaveys, cant hooks and other logging tools.

A. M. Leonard & Son, Inc.
Piqua, OH 45356

Anchor Tools

William Day at Anchor makes and sells some of the more primitive woodworking tools like adzes, broadaxes, and drawknives.

Anchor Tools & Woodstoves
618 N.W. Davis
Portland, OR 97209

Dixie

A complete line of logging equipment, replacement parts, specialty forgings, and wood turnings is available here.

Dixie Industries, Inc.
1210 Greenwood Ave.
Chattanooga, TN 37404

Meadows

The Meadows catalog contains 500 pages of forestry and engineering equipment of every description. They carry many specialty items found nowhere else.

Ben Meadows Co.
3589 Broad St.
Atlanta, GA 30366

Forestry Suppliers

They are among the world's largest forestry supply houses. If you can't find it in the FSI catalog, you might be in trouble. A sampling: skidding grapples, bowsaws, crosscut saws, pruning saws, timber carriers, pike poles, tree climbing gear, horticultural knives, and much more.

Forestry Suppliers, Inc.
205 W. Rankin St., Box 8397
Jackson, MS 39204

A German Supplier

Wolf and Bankert produce high-quality cutlery, including machetes and land-clearing knives for every purpose.

Wolf & Bankert
Werkzeug Fabrik
563 Remschied, W. Germany

Fiskars

Manufacturers of a wide range of quality equipment for professional foresters in Europe and North America. A few highlights in the Fiskars catalog are their log hooks, timber stacking claw, skidding grapple, and forest hoe for planting bare-rooted and rolled plants.

Fiskars
Mannerheimintie 14A
Helsinki, Finland

Belknap

This distributor carries a good variety of wood-handling tools, as well as pruners, shears, and machetes.

Belknap, Inc.
P.O. Box 28
Louisville, KY 40201

WHAT TO LOOK FOR IN A CHAIN SAW

The first important rule in chain saw shopping is: look for a nationally known brand and don't spend too much money. You can buy a good saw for under $150 for work around the homestead or farm woodlot. It should last for years if cared for properly.

You'll find models where the chain runs when the motor does, and models that have a centrifugal clutch so you can run the motor without running the cutting chain. The latter kind provides a measure of safety.

Some models have self-oiling features, which keep the chain oiled automatically. They don't seem to offer much advantage over the hand operated oilers that squirt the chain when you push the plunger.

Some manufacturers make a saw with a rotating tip set in the end of the blade. These are supposed to reduce wear on the chain, and this feature is a plus, although not necessary to good operation. You'll also find models with self-sharpeners, but these tend to wear the chain down too fast and require an unusual chain design that may not be as efficient as the standard chain.

Try starting the saw you intend to buy. If it is hard to start in the showroom, it'll probably be hard to start in the woodlot.

An 18-inch blade should be fully adequate for use on the homestead or farm, so don't pay extra for blade length you can't use.

Chain saws have to be sharpened precisely. If you do it yourself, invest a couple of dollars for a saw-sharpening guide. Otherwise, entrust the job to a professional or a friend who does craftsmanlike sharpening. The chain must also be kept at the right tension, and you'll need a wrench and screwdriver for this.

Remember to keep the gas-oil mixture balanced. Too lean on the oil means a burned-out engine. Too heavy on the oil means a fouled motor and a hard start.

Be very careful of secondhand saws. You're more than likely to be buying someone's problem. Since a properly kept new saw lasts for many years, the initial investment is very often worth it.

And finally, use some discretion with the saw. A chain saw is noisy and dirty and doesn't offer the rhythmic harmony of hand sawing or felling trees with an axe. However, it can increase your sawing power ten times over what you can do by hand, and the little bit of gasoline involved can be put to hard, practical use freeing you from what could be a back-breaking chore.

HANDLING YOUR CHAIN SAW

by Walter Hall

If, like me, you are a lover of solitude, chances are you'll pass much of your time in the woods alone. That is why it's important to carry a whistle, a good loud one. If you ever get pinned by a tree or cut yourself, you can give it a good blast. Along with the whistle, when you're preparing to go out for a load of logs, take along all the tools you're likely to need. Take extra fuel and all the extra maintenance parts, such as air filters, spark plugs, and an extra chain and sprocket. Start with a sharp chain and a clean saw. After every hour of work, stop and service your saw. This means you fill the fuel and oil tanks, clean or change the air filter, touch up the chain, and wipe off the saw. If you discover or suspect any problem with your chain saw, stop working until the problem is diagnosed and corrected.

Take frequent breaks. Listen to the living trees around you and don't cut them off for firewood. They are sentient creatures—the tongues of the wind and the earth.

FELLING SMALL TREES

There are two basic cutting operations involved with felling any tree. These operations may be altered or complicated by the size of the tree, the lay of the land, and the required direction of fall. These two operations, the notch, or directional cut, and the felling out, or back cut, are done somewhat differently with a chain saw than with an axe. The notch determines

Notching a small tree.
Allis-Chalmers

and controls the direction of the tree's fall. The notch and the back cut must always be made so as to form a hinge of uncut wood. As the tree falls, it pivots on this hinge, breaking it.

First, you make a notch. The basic notch for a small tree is made with two cuts. Make the upper of the two cuts first, to avoid pinching the bar. It's a lot of work to dig a saw out of a tree with the tree's full weight pressing down on it.

Move to one side of the tree, facing the planned direction of the fall. Aim across the top of your saw, along your front handle or falling sights, at exactly the place where you want the tree to fall. This will correctly line up your guide bar with the trunk of the tree.

Now make the upper cut of your notch, cutting down at an angle. Cut at least a third of the way into the tree, but not as much as halfway. Then make the lower cut. With a small, straight tree on level ground, make this second cut straight in to meet the first. Make the cut horizontal, and cut clear back to remove the whole notch. The hinge will be formed by uncut wood at least two inches thick between the back of the notch end and the felling cut.

Now go behind the tree and make another horizontal cut, two inches or more above the lower, or horizontal cut of the notch. It is extremely important not to make this second cut so it will meet the horizontal notch cut. It must be an inch or two higher. It is also important not to cut through the hinge wood.

When enough of your felling cut is complete, stop your saw and leave it in the cut. Insert a wedge in the cut to prevent it from closing on your saw and to help control the direction of the fall toward the notch. Then start your saw again and continue until the cut is complete, leaving only the hinge. At this time the tree should fall. If not, give it a little push, or use a felling lever. As the tree starts to move, leave your saw on the ground and retreat quickly along your planned escape route (see page 443). Remember that the butt end of the tree may kick backwards as the tree falls and that unseen dead branches may fall straight down, or in any direction, as the tree topples. Take no chances. Retreat quickly and without hesitation along your escape route.

That's how you cut down a tree when its

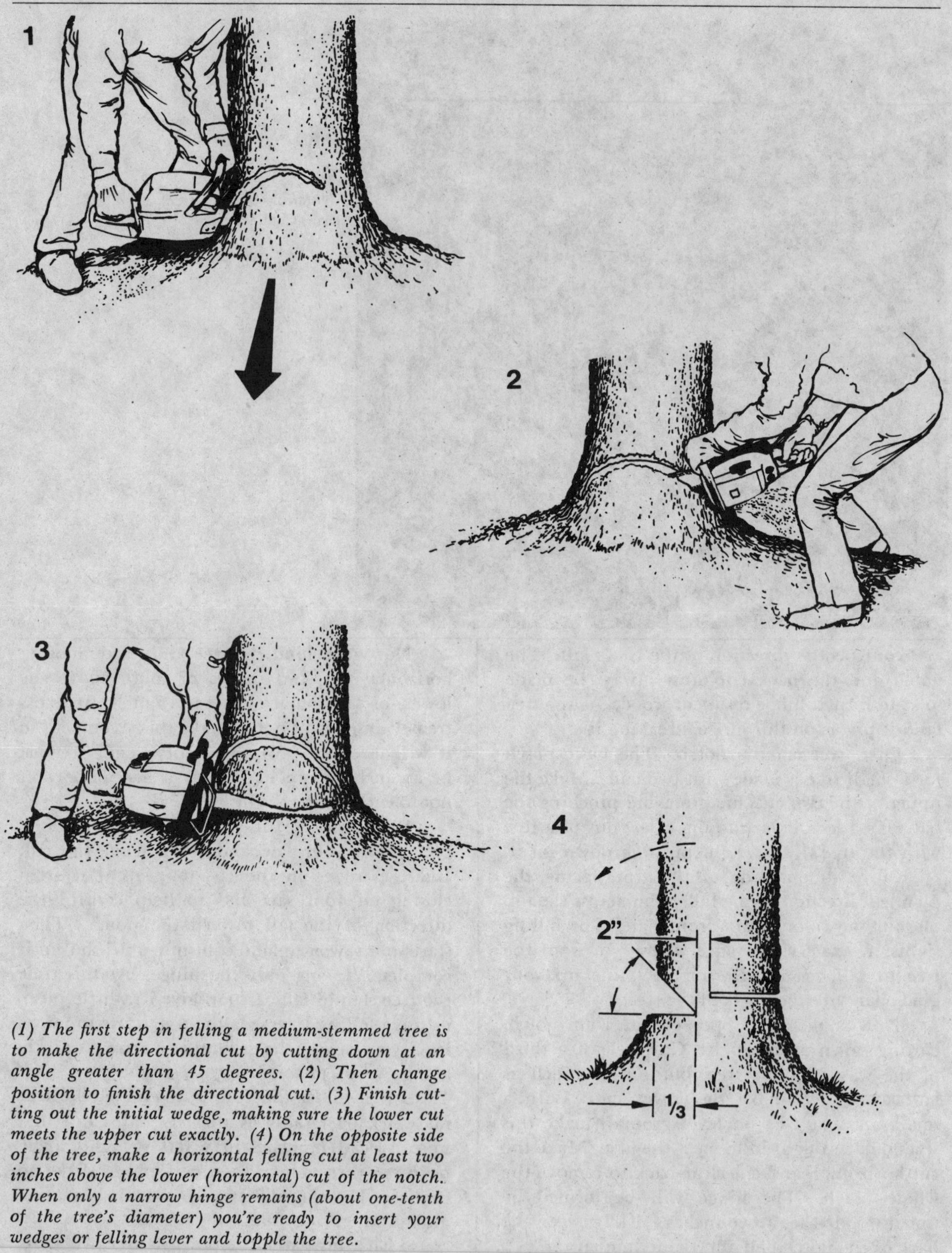

(1) The first step in felling a medium-stemmed tree is to make the directional cut by cutting down at an angle greater than 45 degrees. (2) Then change position to finish the directional cut. (3) Finish cutting out the initial wedge, making sure the lower cut meets the upper cut exactly. (4) On the opposite side of the tree, make a horizontal felling cut at least two inches above the lower (horizontal) cut of the notch. When only a narrow hinge remains (about one-tenth of the tree's diameter) you're ready to insert your wedges or felling lever and topple the tree.

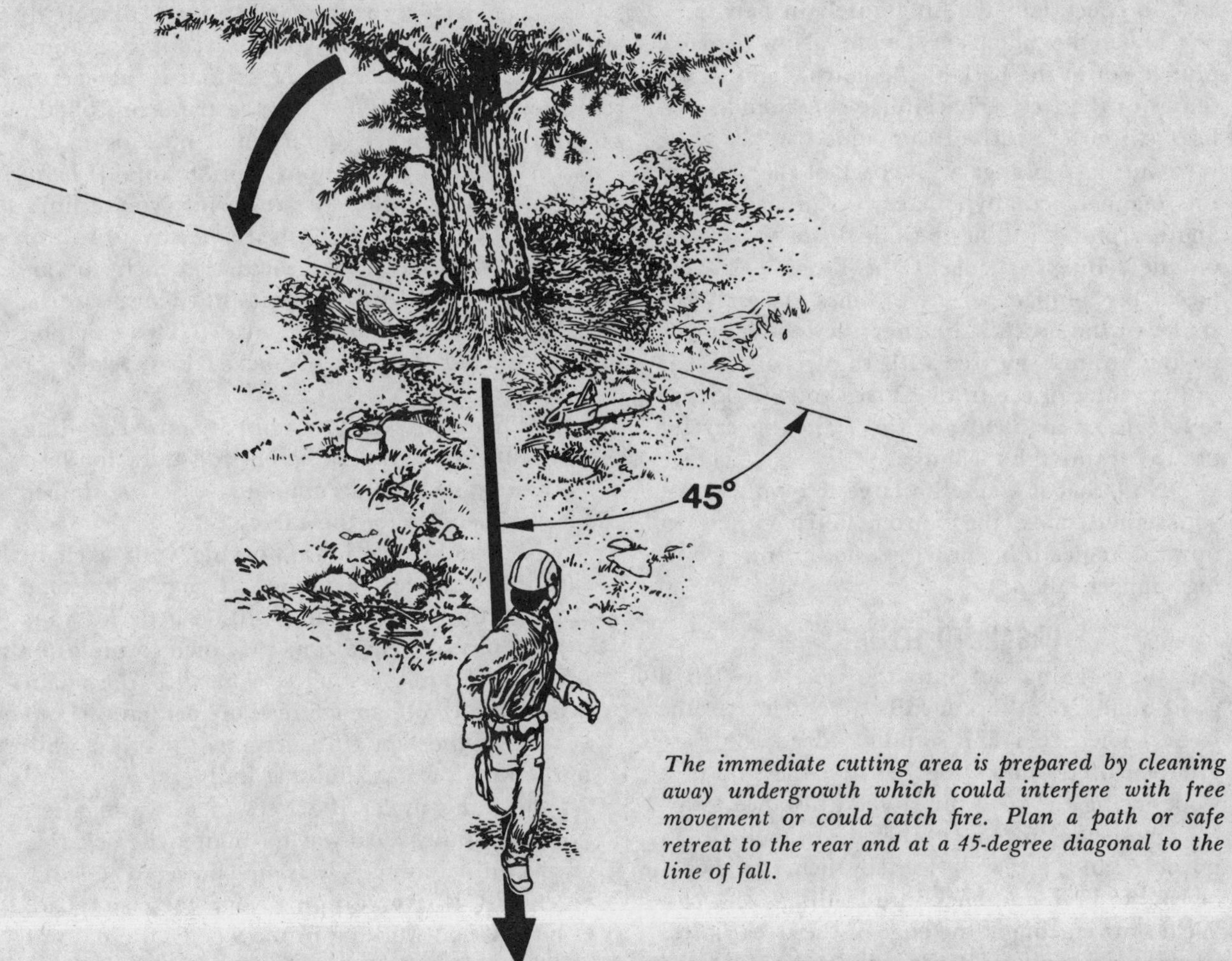

The immediate cutting area is prepared by cleaning away undergrowth which could interfere with free movement or could catch fire. Plan a path or safe retreat to the rear and at a 45-degree diagonal to the line of fall.

diameter is less than the length of your guide bar. But we're also going to be cutting down trees equal to or larger than the length of our guide bars. These situations require a specific sequence of cuts.

FELLING LARGER TREES

To cut a tree with a diameter larger than the length of your guide bar but not twice its size, proceed as follows: Make a notch, as before. Each cut of the notch may require as many as two cuts to complete. You can do this by making one half of the upper notch cut on one side and then moving to the other side of the tree to complete the upper notch cut. Do the same with the horizontal notch cut.

After the notch is formed, make a plunge cut about an inch or two above the notch and on the opposite side of the wood that will form the hinge. Start the plunge cut with the underside of the tip. When the bar has cut a few inches into the tree, straighten the saw to begin sawing straight inward from the tip of the bar.

When your plunge cut is about halfway into the tree and about twice the width of your guide bar, proceed to make the felling cut by sawing around the tree. Make a pivot with the tip of the guide bar in the center of the tree. Be careful not to cut into the hinge wood, and be sure to insert your wedge or felling lever in plenty of time to force the tree in the right direction. If you use a felling lever, be careful not to hit it with your saw. If you use wedges, be sure to use plastic ones, or make your own from wood.

To fell a tree with a diameter equal to or greater than twice the length of your guide bar, only one additional cut is necessary. This time the additional cut is in the notching operation and, in effect, cuts the hinge itself in half.

Make the notch, as before. Now make a plunge cut at the back of the notch, right in the center of the tree. The plunge cut should be at least twice the width of the guide bar.

Cutting a plunge at the back of the notch in this manner actually creates two hinges. Make another plunge cut at one side of the trunk and on the felling-cut side of the hinge. The cut meets the plunge cut that comes through the center of the notch. Continue the felling cut by sawing around the tree with the tip of the bar in the center of the trunk. Place your wedges or felling lever in plenty of time, and be careful not to cut through the hinge.

Note that if you fell a large tree on a slope, you should make the bottom notch cut at an upward angle. This provides more control during a longer fall.

ORGANIZED FELLING

We're going out into the woods to fell a good number of beetle-killed Ponderosa pine trees. The trees are standing dead and are grouped pretty much together, on the side of a slope facing the road but a good distance away.

We want to move the trees as little as possible, and we want to fell them so they'll be easy to limb and buck into loading-sized logs. We'll start cutting at the edge of the trees closest to the road, and we'll use one or more of the trees as a workbench for limbing all the trees that come later.

For a workbench, fell a tree diagonally across the center of your start of operation. Then fell tree number one so that it falls across the workbench. This lifts the trunk up off the ground and makes limbing and bucking easier. Limb the whole tree, from trunk to top. It helps to mark the tree for bucking while you're limbing it. With the tree limbed, it's easy to roll or see-saw the tree across the workbench to one side. Then you can buck it into lengths to be rolled downhill to the road. This method quickly leads to piles of bucked logs, ready for loading.

When you follow an organized felling procedure like this, save the side trees for last. You can use your accumulated piles of timber for workbenches for these trees.

Demanding as it is, working with a chain saw is incomplete exercise. It may add some strength to your arms, but will do little for your overall physical condition. My own formula for unwinding after a long session with the chain saw is to devote some time to meditation and yoga. It's the best cure, for me, though a walk in the woods works almost as well.

Sleeping under the trees on a warm afternoon is another ideal way to counter the negative effects of running a gasoline-powered engine. Sitting by a river dipping your toes isn't bad, either. When working in the woods, the natural woodsperson takes long and frequent breaks. It's the only way to remember who you are, where you fit, and why you're there. For safety's

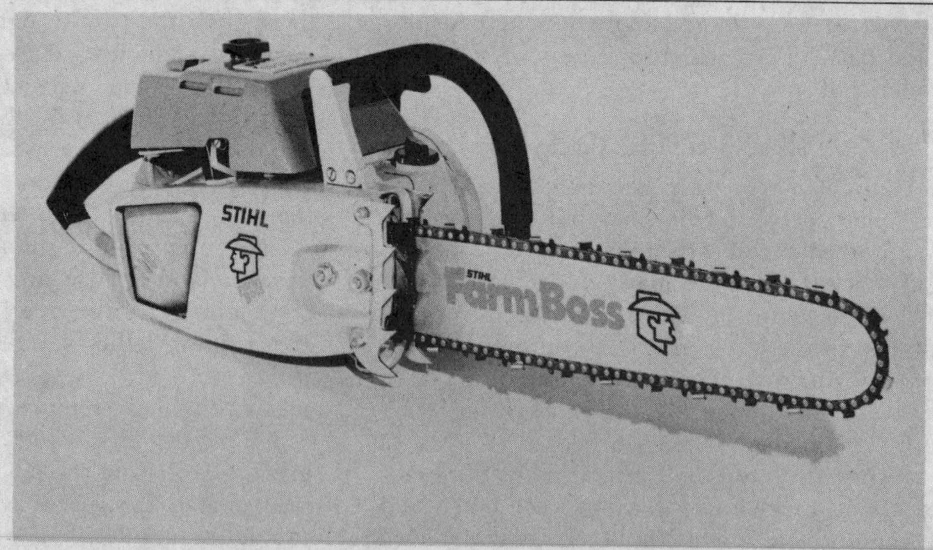

Manufacturers recognize the many uses a chain saw can have on a farm or homestead.
Stihl, Inc.

sake, you should work with a partner whenever you can. For nature's sake, you should each take your breaks in solitude.

ATTACHMENTS FOR A CHAIN SAW

Individuals who haven't had a great deal of experience with chain saws may feel that tree felling and trimming may be the limit of a saw's usefulness. However, with the number of attachments becoming available, the power unit on a chain saw can be a very valuable addition to a tool collection.

The Stihl 08's, a 14-pound unit driven by a single cylinder, two-cycle gasoline engine, is capable of running a cut-off saw, a brush cutter, and one- and two-man earth augers. On many models, power heads can drive hedge trimmers, lumber-making attachments, mills, and drills.

Not all chain saws will drive all the possible attachments, so carefully check into accessories before buying a chain saw. A single power unit running several tools can be much less expensive than buying each tool separately for your woodlot.

CHAIN SAW MANUFACTURERS

Advanced Engine Products
(Savage & Forester Chain Saws)
3340 Emery St.
Los Angeles, CA 90023

Allis-Chalmers
Box 512
Milwaukee, WI 53201

Alpina S.P.A.
31015 Conegliano
S. Vendemiano (TV) Italy

Alpina S.P.A.
Mr. H. J. Hutchinson
Box 313
Trail, British Columbia, Canada

Danarm Chain Saws
Yankee Clipper Trading Post
2405 Boston Post Rd.
Guilford, CT 06437

John Deere & Co.
Moline, IL 61265

Dolmar North American
947 W. Foothill Blvd.
Monrovia, CA 91016

Echo Chain Saws
3240 Commercial Ave.
Northbrook, IL 60062

Frontier Chain Saws
P.O. Box 491, Waneta Road
Trail, British Columbia, Canada

Homelite Division of Textron, Inc.
P.O. Box 7047
Charlotte, NC 28217

Husqvarna
151 New World Way
South Plainfield, NJ 07080

Jobu Chain Saws
Elkem-Spigerverket a/s
1441 Drobak Norway

Jonsereds Chain Saws
Tilton Equipment Co.
4612 N. Chatsworth
St. Paul, MN 55112

McCulloch Corp.
5400 Alla Rd.
Los Angeles, CA 90066

Massey Ferguson
1901 Bell Ave.
Des Moines, IA 50315

Oleo-Mac (Olympic) Chain Saws
Scotsco, Inc.
9180 SE 74th Ave.
Portland, OR 97206

Partner Industries of America, Inc.
255 E. Industry Ave.
Frankfort, IL 69423

AB Partner
S-431 20 Molndal 1,
Sweden

Pioneer Chain Saws
7605 Cushman Dr., P.O. Box 82409
Lincoln, NB 68501

Poulan Chain Saws
Beaird-Poulan Div., Emerson Electric Co.
5020 Flournoy/Lucas Rd.
Shreveport, LA 71109

Remington Chain Saws, Desa Industries
25000 S. Western Ave.
Park Forest, IL 60466

Skil Corp.
5033 Elston Ave.
Chicago, IL 60630

Solo Motors, Inc.
5100 Chestnut Ave.
Newport News, VA 23605

Stanley Hydraulic Tools
13770 S.E. Ambler Rd.
Clackamas, OR 97015

Stihl, Inc.
P.O. Box 5514
Virginia Beach, VA 23455

Stihl Motorsagen
D-7050 Waiblingen
West Germany

SOURCES OF CHAIN SAW ACCESSORIES

Atom

They are manufacturers of chain saw drill attachments.

Atom Industries
15 Reynolds St.
Balmain, N.S.W., Australia 2041

Bailey

Mail-order suppliers of chain saws, tools, and accessories, they also have a logger's job service.

Bailey's
P.O. Box 550
Laytonville, CA 95454

Bell

Formerly known as Nielson, they are manufacturers of home and shop electric saw chain grinders, carb-cutter attachments, and chain saw related machines.

Bell Industries, Saw and Machine Div.
3390 W. 11th Ave., P.O. Box 2510
Eugene, OR 97402

Brookstone

This company markets a chain saw sharpening jig.

Brookstone's Hard-to-Find Tools
125 Vose Rd.
Petersborough, NH 03458

Carlton

They are manufacturers of a saw chain.

Carlton Co., Saw Chain Division
3901 S.E. Naef Rd.
Portland, OR 97222

Defiance

They are manufacturers of the Little Logger chain saw accessory.

The Defiance Co.
Hancock, MI 48830

Davis

They are manufacturers of chain saw testing equipment for mechanics.

Perry Davis Equipment
21353 Endsley Ave.
Rocky River, OH 44116

Granberg

They manufacture chain saw tools, and assorted accessories; ripping chain, Alaskan Mill, Break-N-Mend, and File-N-Joint.

Granberg Industries, Inc.
200 S. Garrard Blvd.
Richmond, CA 94804

Haddon

They are manufacturers of chain saw accessories; the Lumber/Maker attachment.

Haddon Tool
4719 W. Route 120
McHenry, IL 60050

Heli-Coil

They manufacture thread repair kits.

Heli-Coil Products
Shelter Rock Lane
Danbury, CT 06810

Kwik-Way

They manufacture machines and tools for small-engine mechanics.

Kwik-Way Mfg. Co.
500 Fifty-seventh St.
Marion, IA 52302

Lewis

This firm makes chain saw winch attachments.

Fred A. Lewis Co.
40 Belknap Rd.
Medford, OR 97501

Loctite

They are manufacturers of thread-locking compounds.

Loctite Corp.
705 N. Mountain Rd.
Newington, CT 06111

Merc-O-Tronic

They manufacture chain saw ignition-testing equipment.

Merc-O-Tronic Instruments
215 Branch St.
Almont, MI 48003

Omark

This company markets saw chain, tools, and accessories.

Oregon Saw Chain Div., Omark Industries
9701 S.E. McLoughlin Blvd.
Portland, OR 97222

Permatex

They manufacture gasket sealers.

Permatex Co., Inc.
P.O. Box 1350
West Palm Beach, FL 33402

Phelon

They manufacture ignition parts for chain saws.

R.E. Phelon Co.
East Longmeadow, MA 01028

Sandvik

They are manufacturers of forestry tools, guide bars, chain saw tools and accessories. "Swedish Forestry Method."

Sandvik, Inc.
1702 Nevins Rd.
Fair Lawn, NJ 07410

Sears

You'll find accessories, a lumber maker attachment, and sharpeners in the catalog.

Sears, Roebuck & Co.
Farm and Ranch Catalog

Skil Corp.

This company manufactures professional air and electric impact wrenches, and shop tools for chain saw mechanics.

Skil Corp.
5033 Elston Ave.
Chicago, IL 60630

Spencer

They manufacture logger's tape, felling and bucking wedges, and chain saw and logger accessories.

Spencer Production Co.
P.O. Box 224
Pullman, WA 99163

U.S. General Supply

This is a large mail-order tool supply company, with various chain saw accessories for sale.

U.S. General Supply
100 General Place
Jericho, NY 11753

V.I.P.

They manufacture portable, electric, saw chain grinders.

V.I.P. Industries
300 S. Richardson Rd.
Ashland, VA 23005

Walbro

This firm manufactures chain saw carburetors.

Walbro Corp.
Cass City, MI 48726

Whitney

This is another large, well-known, mail-order tool supply company.

J.C. Whitney Co.
1917-19 Archer Ave., P.O. Box 8410
Chicago, IL 60680

Windsor

They manufacture saw chain, guide bars (Timber King), tools, and accessories.

Windsor Machine Co.
3147 Thunderbird Crescent
Burnaby, British Columbia, Canada

Zip Penn

They are mail-order suppliers of saw chain, tools, and accessories.

Zip Penn, Inc.
2008 E. 33rd St., P.O. Box 179
Erie, PA 16512

WHEN AN AXE IS NOT ENOUGH

by Steve Smyser

Log splitters have been on the market for years, but until recently they've been a rather specialized tool used exclusively by professionals. When the energy crunch pushed oil prices up and wood stove sales spiraled, many homeowners started looking seriously at commercial splitters. Certainly nobody is about to predict the demise of the axe, sledge, and wedge. Many folks still cut their entire year's supply of fuel wood by hand, enjoy it immensely, and have no interest whatsoever in mechanical alternatives. The commercial splitter has yet to be invented that can simulate the pure joy of chopping wood on a crisp October afternoon and stacking it away in warm anticipation of winter's worst.

On the other hand, sales figures and a proliferation of new manufacturers in the field bear witness to the steadily increasing number of people who heat with wood and prefer to cut it themselves, but who lack the time or inclination to do it all by hand. For this group, which often includes neighbors making a joint purchase, or individuals interested in starting a part-time cordwood business, the mechanical splitters have been a real boon. It takes most of us the better part of a day to cut, split, and stack a cord of poplar or apple with a chain saw and wedge. With a power splitter, the job takes about half that time.

Wood-splitting devices being sold today are principally of either the hydraulic wedge type or the screw type. The latter variety comes as either a self-powered unit or a bolt-on type that attaches to a tractor PTO shaft or to the rear wheels of a car or truck.

The larger hydraulic units like this go through a cord of wood an hour with ease. Their heavy-duty rams (10 tons of splitting force) make them the choice for frequent splitting of exceptionally dense, stringy wood.

The hydraulic wedge-type splitter used by most professionals is basically a hydraulic cylinder forcing a log through a splitting wedge. The better models generate about ten tons of splitting force from heavy-duty cylinders and gas engines ranging from four to eight horsepower. Most manufacturers offer two sizes of bed (the I-beam or square tubing on which the log rests), one for logs up to 19 inches and another for logs to 26 inches. Cycle times (the time required for the ram to travel to the wedge and return) for various models range from 12 to 30 seconds, a difference that would be important if you are in the cordwood business. Most hydraulic splitters can get through a cord of wood in an hour with no trouble.

As logs are split, they will shift around a bit to follow the grain of the wood. For this reason, the forward speed of the hydraulic ram should be slow enough to give the operator time to avoid a mishap. Some makers offer two-stage hydraulic pumps with this in mind: the two-stage pump provides fast speed with low force for normal operation, then shifts automatically to low speed/high force when additional pressure is needed to split tough or gnarled logs.

The cost of these hydraulic units ranges from $600 for most of the popular four and five horse-power models up to $1,200 and more for some of the more sophisticated professional versions.

A real breakthrough in the design of commercial wood splitters occurred three years ago with the debut of the auger screw-type splitter. Designed largely in response to the burgeoning farm and home market, the screw-type splitters are made to penetrate logs up to 28 inches in diameter and literally screw them apart. In addition to portable, self-powered units, the screw-type splitters come in models that bolt onto auto and truck wheels and tractor PTO shafts. The bolt-on models cost less than the self-powered splitters ($200 as contrasted wih $400 and up), but require an adapter if you switch to a vehicle with different size lug holes on the wheels.

While quite rugged and satisfactory for almost all home-scale splitting requirements, these eight- and nine-horsepower units must take a back seat to the more powerful hydraulic models when it comes to continual cutting of dense, stringy woods like locust, elm, and willow.

To use the bolt-on type of screw splitter, you press the log into the turning screw, making sure each log is offset so that its lower end butts against the ground and prevents the log from spinning. The threads simply pull the log onto the widening screw and split it open, usually in about 10 to

The screw-type log splitter: as a separate unit (left), and as a truck-mounted model (below). Each has advantages and disadvantages.

12 seconds. A safety switch is attached to the engine, allowing the splitter to be turned off from the work area.

Along with the advantage of operating independently of problem-prone small engines and hydraulic systems, the bolt-on screw permits the operator to split large, heavy logs without lifting them off the ground. The self-powered screw units, on the other hand, do not require jacking up your car or truck every time you need to do some splitting.

How do you determine which type is right for you? It depends largely on what kind of wood you work with most often. If you're splitting nonstringy wood like ash, beech, maple, birch, apple, or any wood that splits cleanly with a wedge or an axe, you should probably lean toward the screw-type splitters, which are generally faster and less expensive than the hydraulic units. If you're splitting heavy, dense, and stringy wood like black gum, elm, locust, yellow birch, hackberry, oak or any wood that does not split cleanly with a wedge—any wood that requires an axe to cleave off stubborn strings or strands that prevent a clean spit—then you need a hydraulic unit. If you try to split dense, stringy wood on a screw-type splitter, you will spend as much time trying to pull the wood on the screw as you spend on splitting.

What size machine should you buy? Again, it depends on your objective. If you're splitting logs 12 inches wide by 16 inches long, there's no reason to buy a ten-ton hydraulic ram with a 24-inch bed.

Conversely, don't count on a small screw-type unit to routinely split oak logs three feet long by 30 inches across.

In general, if you're splitting logs under 19 inches in length or 20 inches in width, you can buy what most manufacturers call their homeowner models and be fully confident that the machine will do your work. You can, on occasion, split larger logs if you follow the instructions that come with the machine; but if you're going to split larger logs on a regular basis, you should look at professional models. Buying a homeowner model to split logs 30 inches long by 30 inches wide is like buying a half-ton pickup to deliver ten tons of coal every day—you're going to destroy the machine by forcing it to do more than it was designed for.

Mounted on a three-point hitch, this hydraulic attachment for the Power King Tractor splits logs up to 26 inches in a 15-second cycle.
Engineering Products Co.

An increasing interest in woodlot harvesting has encouraged manufacturers to develop tractor-run equipment. The Wheel Horse D-Series demonstrates both log splitter and saw.

How much should you pay for a splitter? Don't be fooled by price—the least expensive machine you can buy is the unit that fits the requirements of your work. Buy a machine that's smaller than you need, and you're going to spend your savings in repairs. Buying a unit that's larger than you need is wasteful in that you're spending more than you have to in order to get the job done.

When shopping, beware the dealer who stocks one or two models and tells you that his machines will do anything. How does he know? Has he ever split wood? If you're going to buy a splitter, find a dealer who has paid his dues, someone who has split and burned a lot of wood, and who knows the difference between a sledgehammer and a splitting maul.

There is no one machine that will do everything. The inexperienced dealer or manufacturer may try to persuade you that his equipment will handle whatever you're splitting. A good dealer will demonstrate his product thoroughly, and perhaps even let you use it for a week. Who knows, you may discover you prefer swinging that axe after all!

SOURCES OF COMMERCIAL WOOD SPLITTERS

Hydraulic Wedge Types

Mighty Mac

This unit comes in 5 and 7 h.p. models.

Amerind-MacKissic, Inc.
Box 111
Parkerford, PA 19547

Hydra-Splitter

Available in a 4 h.p. unit, the Model 26 TM hooks to tractor hydraulics.

Didier Mfg. Co.
Box 163, 8630 Industrial Dr.
Franksville, WI 53126

Lickity Splitter

This model is available from:
Piqua Engineering, Inc.
Box 605
Piqua, OH 45356

Futura Enterprises
West Bend, WI 53095

Huss Sales & Service
Toledo, OH 43601

Lindig Splitters

These splitters come in a 3 h.p. compact size, and 5 h.p. two-stage model; both have a tractor-mount option.

Lindig Splitters
1875 W. County Rd.
St. Paul, MN 55112

Power King Tractors

This firm markets tractor-mounted hydraulic splitters.

Engineering Products Co.
1525 E. Ellis St.
Waukesha, WI 53186

Farnum Log Splitter
Farnum Companies, Inc.
Box 12068
Omaha, NE 68112

Futura
Futura Master Corp.
5069 Highway 45 South
West Bend, WI 53095

Woodsman
G.S.I. Corp.
Box 39
Jackson, WI 53037

Household Wood-Splitter
Box 143
Jeffersonville, VT 05464

Screw Types

Stickler

This splitter can be wheel-mounted or run from a tractor PTO.

Taos Equipment Manufacturers
Box 1565
Taos, NM 87571

Bark Buster

This is a self-powered screw-type splitter.

FW and Associates, Inc.
1855 Airport Rd.
Mansfield, OH 44903

Quick Split

This self-powered splitter comes in 5 and 8 h.p. models.

Trans America Power Equipment, Inc.
8308 Washington St.
Chagrin Falls, OH 44022

Derby Splitter

This self-powered portable splitter is available as an 8 h.p. model or a tractor PTO-driven unit.

Derby Splitter
Box 21
Rumson, NJ 07760

The Unicorn

This is a wheel-mounted or bolt-on splitter.

Thackery Co.
Columbus, OH 43216

Nortech Splitter

This company offers a self-powered 8 h.p. splitter.

Nortech Corp.
Midland Park, NJ 07432

Knotty Wood Splitter

This unit is driven by a tractor PTO.

Knotty Wood Splitter Co.
Route 66
Hebron, CT 06248

Other Splitters

Pokrandt Splitter

This is a tractor-mounted combination cordwood saw and wood splitter.

Pokrandt's tractor-mounted cordwood saw and wood splitter. Units may be purchased and mounted separately, like the hydraulic wedge splitter.
Richard Pokrandt Manufacturing

MATCHING THE SPLITTER WITH THE WOOD

Clean and Easy-to-Split Woods	Stringy, Hard-to-Split Woods
Hemlock, ash, beech, poplar, hickory, hornbeam, maple, cherry, apple, aspen, white birch, spruce, basswood, oak.	Elm, black gum, hackberry, eucalyptus, pinyon, locust, willow, yellow birch.
For logs up to 19 inches long by 20 inches wide, use a homeowner screw type splitter.	On logs up to 19 inches long by 18 inches wide, use a homeowner hydraulic splitter. (Screw-type units are often inadequate for these woods).
On logs 19 to 36 inches long by 20 to 30 inches wide, use professional hydraulic or professional screw-type unit with a minimum of 8 h.p.	On logs 19 to 36 inches long by 18 to 30 inches wide, use a professional hydraulic splitter. (Screw-type units not recommended for these woods).

Richard Pokrandt Manufacturing
RD. 3, Box 182
Tamaqua, PA 18252

Jiffy Woodsplitter

This is an upright, guided-wedge-type splitter.

C & D Distributors, Inc.
Dept. O, Box 766
Old Saybrook, CT 06475

Thrust Log Splitter

This is a nonhydraulic horizontal wedge.

Thrust Mfg., Inc.
6901 S. Yosemite
Englewood, CO 80110

Knotty Wood

They offer a tractor-driven cordwood saw.

Knotty Wood Splitter Co.
Route 66
Hebron, CT 06248

Woodland Splitters
P.O. Box 976
Oak Brook, IL 60521

Hand-Operated Hydraulic Splitter

Woodland Splitters
P.O. Box 976
Oak Brook, IL 60521

Tractor-Mounted Log Splitter

SI Mac Design
9 Vista Verde
Portola Valley, CA 94025

SAWMILL EQUIPMENT

Gaubert Saws

Gaubert makes a series of electric circular saws with 500 or 600 millimeter blades for both sawing logs and rough-cutting lumber. Tractor PTO and three-point-hitch adaptations are also available.

A. Gaubert 16700
16700 Ruffec
Bordeaux, France

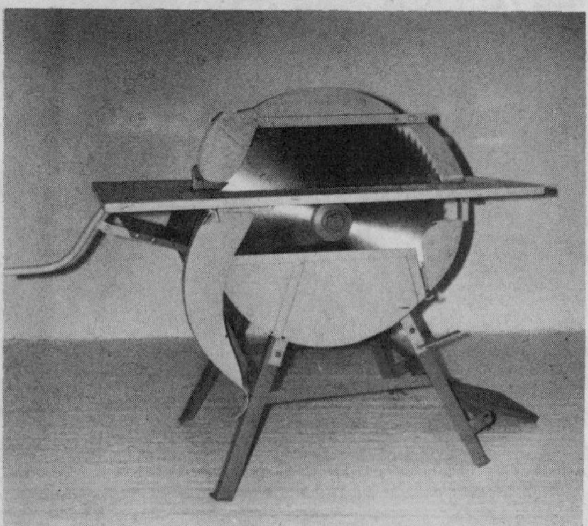

Gaubert Circular Saw Gaubert

Speedy Cord Saw

This saw will cut hardwood slabs or logs to 8 inches in diameter at the rate of 120 cubic feet (about a pickup load full) in 30 minutes time. Three models are available; one trailer, one three-point-hitch mount, and one on skids.

Speedy Cord Saw
Winona Attrition Mill Co.
1009 W. 5th St.
Winona, MN 55987

Mini-Mite

The Mini-Mite can handle logs up to 18 feet in length. Equipped with hydrostatic carriage drive, the unit can produce true dimension lumber with a maximum cut of 4½ inches by 12½ inches. The saw is designed to be towed with a pickup and can be set up on the site in 45 minutes.

Mini-Mite Transportable Sawmill
International Enterprises of America, Inc.
3931 N.E. Columbia Blvd., P.O. Box 20427
Portland, OR 97220

Meadows Portable Mill

Easily moved and set up, the Meadows No. 1 mill features a 15 foot carriage on four sets of roller bearing travelers, 6 inch wheels, and a 48 inch blade.

Meadows Portable Sawmill
North Wilkesboro, NC 28659

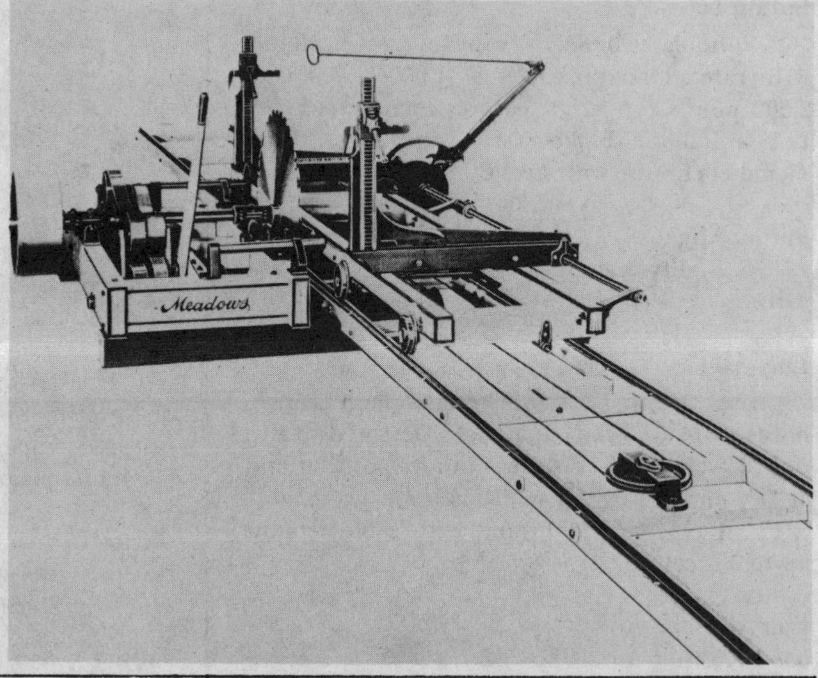

Meadows No. 1 Standard Saw Mill
Meadows Mills Co.

Pokrandt

Pokrandt manufactures a tractor-mounted combination cordwood saw and wood splitter. The saw is driven off a tractor PTO; the woodsplitter is powered by the tractor's hydraulic system. Units may be purchased separately.

Richard Pokrandt Mfg.
RD 3, Box 182
Tamaqua, PA 18252

Belsaw

Belsaw offers a variety of power sawmill equipment, including two sizes of sawmills, a self-feed rip saw, and a chain saw grinder. The smaller mill handles logs up to 18 inches in diameter, 14 feet in length, while the large mill will take a 36 inch diameter, 24 foot log.

Belsaw Power Tools
4103 Field Bldg.
Kansas City, MO 64111

Glen-Bel's Country Store
Rt. 5
Crossville, TN 38555

Laredo

The Saw and Emery Laredo Model SEL-005 requires 3 to 5 h.p., and is available in two models: with stationary engine or three-point tractor PTO. The saw (14 inches in diameter) and the emery (12 inches diameter) will reach a maximum 2,200 rpm.

Laredo, S.A. Industria e Comercio
Rua 1 de Agosto, 11-67
17.100 Bauru (SP), Brazil

WINCHES

Fulton 900

Fulton's 900 Series winches are available with rated load capacities of 1,000, 1,500, and 2,500 pounds. Special features include a Load-Lok automatic brake system and large drum diameters for use with steel cable.

Fulton Mfg. Co.
1912 S. Eighty-second St.
Milwaukee, WI 53219

Lug All

Lug All makes cable ratchet lever winch-hoists in ½ to 3 ton capacities. Designed to lift, pull, lower, bend, or stretch in any position and at any angle, Lug All winch-hoists are available with all types of hooks and with cable lengths up to 50 feet.

Lug All
538 Lancaster Ave.
Haverford, PA 19041

Forestry Suppliers, Inc.
Box 8397
Jackson, MS 39204

Superwinch

These 12-volt electric winches come in 12 different models. The winches bolt on to a vehicle's bumper and draw power from the battery.

Superwinch, Inc.
Connecticut Route 2
Putnam, CT 06260

Trewhella Monkey Winch

Designed for pulling up trees and hedges, and for land clearing, the Monkey Winch is strong and light and has two speeds and a reverse gear. A lightweight model, the Spacemaker, is recommended for pulling, lifting, and clearing small trees. The Monkey Wire Strainer for mending broken fences or stretching new wire is also available.

Trewhella Monkey Winch
Trewhella Bros., Ltd.
Rolfe Street, Smethwick
Warley, West Midlands, B66 2BA, U.K.

Sasgen

Sasgen makes all-purpose winches in 2, 5, and 15 ton capacities. An automatic safety brake handle holds the load in any position.

Sasgen Derrick Co.
3101 W. Grand Ave.
Chicago, IL 60622

Tirfor

The Tirfor is a fully portable pulling-lifting or lowering machine that can be used for many purposes, including tree felling. It can increase the human effort by up to 85 times.

Tirfor Lifting & Pulling Machines
Tirfor, Ltd.
Halfway, Sheffield S19 5GZ, U.K.

Fulton General Purpose Winches

Fulton winches come in load capacities ranging from 900 to 1,500 pounds; all feature a one-piece reinforced frame, two-way ratchets, and gears of high carbon steel. Also listed in these catalogs are free-spooling winches, come-alongs, a variety of hoists, and screw and mine-type jacks.

Cumberland General Store
Box 479, Rt. 3
Crossville, TN 38555

Tirfor Lifting Machine

Glen-Bel's Country Store
Rt. 5
Crossville, TN 38555

Belknap, Inc.
P.O. Box 28
Louisville, KY 40201

Airborne

Airborne, a government surplus store, offers a wide variety of hand and electric winches. Maximum capacities of the hand winches range from 1,200 to 2,000 pounds; the larger electric winches, designed for more rugged use, have 4,000 to 8,000 pound pull ratings.

Also available are hand-operated rope pulls, which combine hoist, winch, and puller for smaller jobs around the home or farm.

Airborne Sales Co.
8501 Steller Dr., P.O. Box 2727
Culver City, CA 90230

More-Power Puller

The More-Power Puller is a portable, two-ton block and tackle unit with $\frac{5}{16}$ inch wire cable in 20, 30, or 40 foot lengths.

Wyeth-Scott Co.
85 Dayton Rd., Rt. 16 East
Newark, OH 43055

Forestry Suppliers
P.O. Box 8397
Jackson, MS 39204

VITA Overhead Hoist

VITA is an international service agency that functions as a clearinghouse for information on village-scale technology and low-energy agricultural methods. Among the voluminous plans they have developed for international distribution (primarily to developing countries) is this easily constructed tripod-type hoist that can be either electrically powered or hand operated. VITA also has a plan for a jack-type post puller made of angle iron and a clevis and chain.

Volunteers in Technical Assistance
3706 Rhode Island Ave.
Mt. Rainier, MD 20822

Levalift

Levalift 117 Pull Hoist, a general-purpose pulling machine, can be used for large jobs, such as extracting trees. It is available in $\frac{3}{4}$, $1\frac{1}{2}$, 3, and $4\frac{1}{2}$ ton sizes.

Herbert Morris, Ltd.
P.O. Box 7
Loughborough LE11 1RL, U.K.

Wire Strainers

Wire Strainers/Stretchers, useful for mending broken fences or stretching new wire around posts, vary in their pulling and holding capabilities. Certain models are for smaller tasks and utilize conventional chain; others require heavy-duty chain and can be used on many types of wire.

G.V. Donald Africa (Pty), Ltd.
P.O. Box 1439
Port Elizabeth 600 S. Africa

Berry-Hill, Ltd.
75 Burwell Rd.
St. Thomas, Ontario, Canada

Trewhella Bros., Ltd.
Rolfe St., Smethwick
Warley, West Midlands B66 2BA, U.K.

Drival, Ltd.
Churchbridge, Wks
Cannock, Staffs WS1 3JP, U.K.

Hans Nicolaisen
Box 18
Plainfield, NH 03781

Banana Conveyor

A winch-powered conveyor has been developed by the Overseas Department of NIAE to meet the needs of banana producers for a simple, mechanical carrying system to transport bananas from the field to the boxing plant. The conveyor, the department feels, may possibly be used in other field transport situations.

Powered either by hand or electric winch, it includes branch lines, ravine crossings, transfer rails, and switch points. A booklet describing the whole system and its components is available from the Overseas Department of the NIAE.

Tropical Agricultural Engineering Information
Overseas Department
National Institute of Agricultural Engineering
Silsoe, Bedfordshire, U.K.

Heavy-Duty Shrub Puller

Anchoring this tool to the ground by foot, the operator grasps the shrub, cotton stalk, thistle, sorghum or maize roots, or young tree in the jaws of this tool, and removes the stem by pulling back on the tall handle. No bending is involved. The maximum jaw opening is two inches.

Project Equipment, Ltd.
Rednal Ind. Estate
Oswestry, Salop, UK

Hans Nicolaisen
Box 18
Plainfield, NH 03781

POWER SCYTHES

Echo SRM

This is a shoulder-type brush cutter with a two-cycle engine integrated into the operating rod. It features a safety guard, muffler, and vibration-damping cushions, with a total weight of 6.8 kilograms.

Echo SRM, Echo Chain Saw Div.
Kiorita Corp. of America
350 Wainwright
Northbrook, IL 60062

CeCoCo Power Scythe

Shoulder- or knapsack-mounted scythe features a 1.2 h.p., two-cycle engine that is independently suspended for minimum vibration and heat. Circular blade automatically stops rotating when it comes in contact with a stone or other obstacle. Weight: 11 kilograms.

CeCoCo Power Scythe
P.O. Box 8, Ibaraki City
Osaka Pref 567 Japan

Stihl Brush Cutters

Stihl produces a complete line of power brush cutters ranging from the very light FS150 to the professional FS202. Larger models are available with either two-cycle or electric engines. The variety of available cutting tools includes brush knives, grass trimmers, chipper tooth blades, and scratcher tooth blades.

Stihl Inc.
Box 5514
Virginia Beach, VA 23455

Andreas Stihl Maschinenfabrik
Postfach 64
705 Waiblingen, West Germany

Kyoritsu Power Scythe
Kyoritsu Noki Co., Ltd.
Seiwa Lbd., 1-6-8
Nishishinjuku, Shinjuku-ku
Tokyo 160, Japan

Hoffco Power Scythe

Comet Industries
25 Washington Ave.
Richmond, IN 47374

Rowco Brushking

Rowco Mfg. Co., Inc.
48 Emerald
Keene, NH 03431

Alpina Brush Cutters

There are three models, ranging from 1.5 to 2.5 h.p., and they can be used by the homeowner or the professional.

Alpina S.P.A.
31015 Conegliano
S. Vendemiano (TV), Italy

Alpina North America
Mr. H.J. Hutchinson
Box 313
Trail, British Columbia V1R 4L6, Canada

Husqvarna Clearing Saw

Accessories for this power saw include a harness for the operator, and two sizes of blade guard. The engine is a two-stroke, single-cylinder, air-cooled model, and weight without harness or transport blade guard is 10.6 kilograms.

Husqvarna Vapenfabriks AB
Husqvarna, Sweden

Husqvarna
151 New World Way
South Plainfield, NJ 07080

ORCHARD HARVESTING EQUIPMENT

Friend Orchard Equipment

Their canvas bags and buckets are durable harvesting bags for all kinds of fruit, including special designs for peaches and easily bruised apples. Picking straps and picking harness are also available separately.

Orchardkraft wood ladders are designed especially for fruit harvesting; they have a wide flare bottom and are well balanced. Available in open top style, pointed top style and three-point step ladders. Also have extra-strong aluminum ladders. Other harvesting equipment is also available.

Friend Mfg. Corp.
Gasport, NY 14067

Maktefot Picker

This is a lightweight pole-and-sleeve-type picker designed to cut stems at exactly the proper length, and thus minimize spoilage. The aluminum rod telescopes to 12 millimeters, with the woven linen chute having internal baffles to cushion the fruit fall.

Maktefot, Ltd.
12 Hadekalim St.
Hod Hasharon, Israel

Pflucki Fruit Gatherer

The Pflucki Fruit Gatherer, a small pole-mounted unit appropriate for cherries and plums, snags the fruit stem in a set of metal tines and drops the fruit into a small plastic box.

Metallwarenfabrik Naegeli AG
P.O. Box CH-8594
Guettingen, Switzerland

Pole Picker

This pole-mounted avocado picker, equipped with a nylon bag to catch fruit, can be mounted on any size pole. A collapsible aluminum pole that extends for several meters for tall trees, as well as grape shears and pruners, are also available.

Tachsir Ltd. Metal Works
25 Hamlacha St.
Holojn Industrial Center, Israel

Pinza Cogliolive (Olive Pluckers)

These pliers have a patented rolling device which allows them to slide along branches to harvest olives without damage to the branches or fruit.

Felli Deidone
Villafranca Verone
Via A. Messedaglia, 20, Italy

Cumberland Fruit Picker

Made from galvanized wire, this fruit picker attaches to any round-ended pole.

NORTH AMERICAN SOURCES OF WOODLOT HAND TOOLS

	PEAVIES	AXES	MAULS	KNIVES, BILLHOOKS	ASS'T. TOOLS FOR WOODLOT	HAND AUGERS, POST HOLE DIGGERS
AMES		X	X	X	X	X
ANCHOR		X		X		
BULLDOG		X				
COUNTRYSIDE			X			X
CUMBERLAND	X	X	X	X	X	X
GLEN-BEL		X	X			X
A.M. LEONARD	X	X	X	X	X	X
STANLEY HYDRAULIC TOOLS				X	X	
TRUE TEMPER		X	X			X
UNION FORK			X			X
MOTHER'S GENERAL STORE		X		X	X	
NASCO		X	X	X		
FORESTRY SUPPLIERS	X	X	X	X	X	X
SEYMOUR SMITH & SON, INC.					X	
SOTZ CORP.			X			
OLEY TOOLING, INC.				X		
TRADEWINDS, INC.						X
SEYMOUR MFG. CO.						X
BELKNAP, INC.	X	X		X	X	X
CENTRAL TRACTOR					X	

Cumberland General Store
Rt. 3, Box 479
Crossville, TN 38555

Cumberland Fruit Picker
Cumberland General Store

Tree Stand

For hunters, photographers, bird and animal watchers, tree trimmers, and fruit pickers, this stand can be locked in a tree with its poly rope and eccentric locking handle without damage to the tree. The tree stand will remain securely fastened in the tree, even with movement of the stand user.

Wamco
1009 W. Fifth St.
Winona, MN 55987

INTERNATIONAL SOURCES OF WOODLOT HAND TOOLS

	PEAVIES	AXES	MAULS	KNIVES, BILLHOOKS	ASS'T. TOOLS FOR WOODLOT
CEAF S.N.C.F. LLISILETTI		X		X	
ENGLISH TOOLS, LTD.		X		X	X
FERFOR		X	X		
FISKARS, AB	X	X		X	
HINDUSTAN ENGINEERING CO.				X	
KUMAON AGRI-HORTICULTURE STORES	X			X	
KUMAON NURSERY		X		X	
KUMAR INDUSTRIES		X			X
GEO. PIKE, LTD.		X			
SOCIETE DES FORGES TROPICALES		X			
FRANZ SONNLEITHNER K.G.				X	
SPEAR & JACKSON TOOLS, LTD.		X		X	X
STANLEY GARDEN TOOLS, LTD.				X	
SYNDICATE DE L'OUTILLAGE		X		X	X
W. TYZACK SONS & TURNER, LTD.				X	
UBUNGO FARM IMPLEMENTS		X		X	X
UNITED REPUBLIC OF TANZANIA				X	
WOLF AND BANGERT WERKEUG FABRIK				X	

-11- Livestock Equipment

Depending on the type of livestock and the actual number of animals or birds a farmer raises, equipment may be a large expenditure or a relatively small one. A handy farmer can build his own pens, coops, fences, feeders, and small buildings.

The following sources carry most of the equipment in which you might be interested for raising poultry, rabbits, pigs, cows, or horses. Other local raisers, the cooperative extension agent, and magazines devoted to a specific animal or breed can also be helpful in locating information on equipment.

GENERAL SOURCES OF LIVESTOCK EQUIPMENT

Brower Mfg. Co.
640 S. Fifth St.
Quincy, IL 62301

Her work is never done! In an old advertisement, we see the family cow separating her own cream with treadle power—illustrating the true meaning of self-sufficiency.
The Farm Implement News, 1894

Nasco Agricultural Sciences
901 Janesville Ave.
Fort Atkinson, WI 53538

A variety of feeders, waterers, hog equipment, nursing equipment, and poultry equipment is offered.

The Pearson Bros. Co.
P.O. Box 192
Galva, IL 61434

They offer a wide variety of specific equipment for most farm animals, a large assortment of veterinary supplies, feeders, waterers, transporting equipment, and related agricultural supplies. Feeders, waterers, stalls, and farrowing crates are available.

Quinn Machinery Division of Zeidlers, Inc.
Box 130
Boone, IA 50036

This company manufactures Daisy gravity and pressure waterers.

Shenandoah Mfg. Co.
Box 839
Harrisonburg, VA 22801

A variety of feeders and waterers, brooders, and metal nests can be found.

Southeast Mfg. Co., Inc.
Route 2 Box 275
Joplin, MO 64801

They carry stock racks for transporting small animals in pickup trucks and large portable hay feeders.

Tomsicek Mfg. Co.
1419 Adams Blvd.
Ithaca, NE 68033

They manufacture portable hay feeders.

Wadler Mfg. Co., Inc.
Route 2 Box 76
Galena, KS 66739

They carry oilers, livestock scales, hay feeders, assorted chutes, and crates.

WLC Co., Inc.
Sedlia, IN 56067

They have a wide variety of feeders, farrowing crates, stock tanks, and gates.

INTERNATIONAL SOURCES OF GENERAL LIVESTOCK EQUIPMENT

Ets Louis Tellier
Athies-Sous-Laon
02000 Laon, France

Large transport equipment for livestock and feeders are available.

SKA s.a.s.
36066 Sandrigo (VI)
Italy

This company offers equipment for small- to large-scale livestock raising, including poultry, rabbits, cattle, and swine.

NORTH AMERICAN SOURCES OF RABBIT SUPPLIES

Bass Equipment Co.
Box 352
Monett, MO 65708

They handle a full line of rabbit-raising equipment.

Maple Grove Rabbit Farm
Chadsey Rd.
Pownal, ME 04069

A wide range of rabbit-raising equipment, rabbits, and books are offered.

Mother's General Store
Box 506
Flat Rock, NC 28730

They stock metal hutches and drinking tubes.

Nasco Agricultural Sciences
901 Janesville Ave.
Fort Atkinson, WI 53538

Feeders are available.

WLC Co., Inc.
Sedalia, IN 46067

Nest boxes, feeders, waterers, and hutches are available.

INTERNATIONAL SOURCES OF RABBIT SUPPLIES

Self-Sufficiency and Small-Holding Supplies
The Old Palace, Priory Road
Wells, Somerset BA 5 1SY, U.K.

Waterers; cage-size hay racks.

NORTH AMERICAN SOURCES OF SUPPLIES FOR COWS, CALVES, AND DAIRYING

American Village Institute
440 Meyers St.
Kettle Falls, WA 99141

They offer a butter churn, butter molds, and a butter paddle.

Belknap, Inc.
Box 28
Louisville, KY 40201

This company manufactures halters, leaders, feeders, weaners, kickers, dehorners, and bells.

Chore-Boy Division
Gloay and Co. Inc.
Cambridge City, IN 47327

They carry milking systems.

Countryside Catalog
Route 1, Box 239
Waterloo, WI 53594

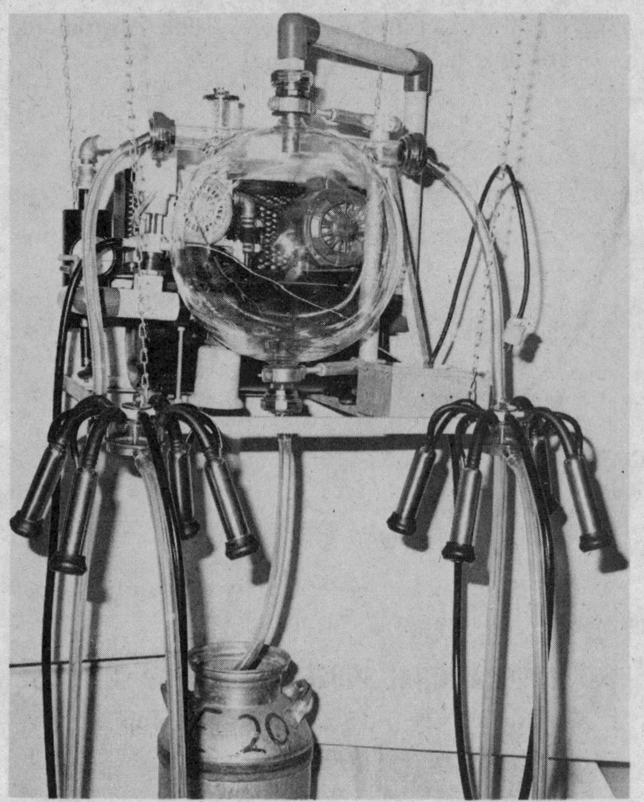

The Chore-Boy Milking System: a two-unit pipeline system that can be installed and in use in an hour. Gloay and Co.

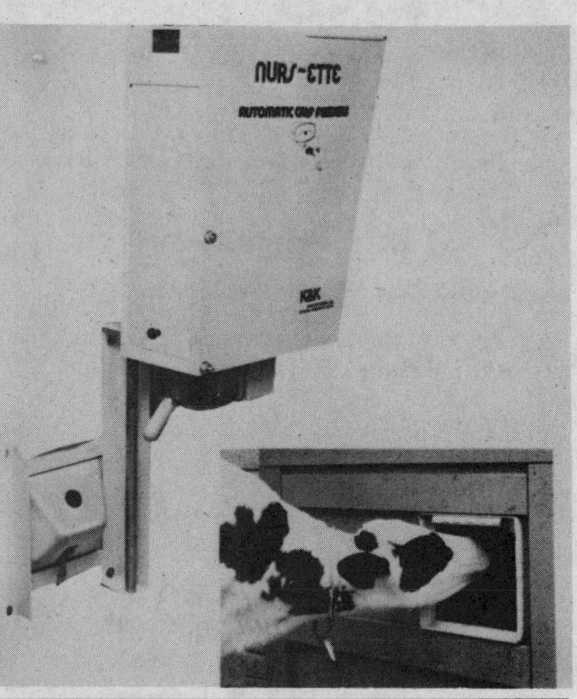

K & K Nurs-Ette Automatic Calf Feeder K & K Mfg.

Milking pails are available.

Cumberland General Store
Rt. 3, Box 479
Crossville, TN 38555

They have nursery items including nipples, calf weaner, cow kicker, bull rings, horn weights, dehorner, bells, halters, and health care accessories.

Glen-Bel Country Store
Rt. 5
Crossville, TN 38555

They offer cattle leaders, dairy halters, bull rings, bells, calf weaners, cow kickers, and grooming aids.

K & K Mfg., Inc.
Rogers, MN 55374

They have Nursette feeders for calves, bottle feeders, and dry automatic feeders.

K-W Mfg. Co., Inc.
800 Marion Rd.
Sioux Falls, SD 57106

They have pole syringes and calfers.

Marting Mfg.
Washington Court House, OH 43160

Feeders, waterers, scales, chutes, shelters, and oilers are available.

Montgomery Ward (catalog)
1000 S. Monroe St.
Baltimore, MD 21232

There are stock tanks, feeders, waterers, tagging guns, home pasteurizers, and milk filters.

Mother's General Store
Box 506
Flat Rock, NC 28731

Halters and bells are available.

Parts are available for making your own feeder.

Nasco Agricultural Sciences
901 Janesville Ave.
Fort Atkinson, WI 53538

There is a wide variety of halters and leads, grooming accessories, hoof and horn equipment, blankets, home pasteurizers, and a wide assortment of dairying equipment including testing supplies.

Sears, Roebuck & Co.
Farm and Ranch Catalog

They have feeders, milk pasteurizers and butter churns.

Schoessow, Inc.
Rt. 2
Pulaski, WI 54162

They have large wagon feeders and gates.

NORTH AMERICAN SOURCES OF GOAT SUPPLIES

Countryside Catalog
Rt. 1, Box 239
Waterloo, WI 53594

They have harnesses and dairying supplies.

Hoegger Supply Co.
Box 490099
College Park, GA 30349

This peculiar-looking device is an aid to keeping those pesky, sometimes dangerous, flies and other insects off your cows. It is a canvas roll which is filled with any absorbent material like cotton rags. The roll is then saturated with rotenone and lubricating oil and suspended between two poles slightly lower than the back height of an average cow. The animals, after an introduction by walking them under the roll once or twice, will return to it on their own, says Gayle Treadwell of Beeville, Texas; it keeps insects under control.

Milking machines and dairying accessories, grooming accessories, dehorners, carts and harnesses, feeders, and cream separators are available.

INTERNATIONAL SOURCES OF GOAT SUPPLIES

Self-Sufficiency and Small-Holding Supplies
The Old Palace, Priory Road
Wells, Somerset BA 5 1SY, U.K.

They offer halters, tethering accessories, milking buckets, and one-cow milking machines with goat adapters.

SOURCES OF HORSE SUPPLIES

Belknap, Inc.
P.O. Box 28
Louisville, KY 40201

They have saddles and girths, halters, bridles (team and work), collars, and grooming equipment.

Cumberland General Store
Rt. 3, Box 479
Crossville, TN 38555

They offer grooming equipment, shears, a wide variety of farrier tools, harnesses, a wide selection of straps, bridles, halters, collars, bits, and hardware.

Glen-Bel Enterprises
Rt. 5
Crossville, TN 38555

There is grooming equipment, straps, shears, and hoof parers.

Mother's General Store
Box 506
Flat Rock, NC 28731

They carry farrier tools.

Nasco Agricultural Sciences
901 Janesville Ave.
Fort Atkinson, WI 53538

Carts, halters, bridles, saddles, girths, straps, blankets, hay racks, feeders, waterers, farrier tools, anvils, horseshoes and nails are available.

NORTH AMERICAN SOURCES OF POULTRY SUPPLIES

Berry Hill Ltd.
75 Burwell Rd.
St. Thomas, Ontario, Canada

There is a wide selection of incubators, brooders, accessories, feeders, waterers, vent equipment, metal nests and pens, egg candlers, handling equipment, scalders, pickers, and processing equipment.

Brower Mfg.
640 S. Fifth St.
Quincy, IL 62301

Egg washers, graders, incubators, and nests can be ordered.

Cumberland General Store
Rt. 3, Box 479
Crossville, TN 38555

Incubators, feeders, brooders, assorted equipment, and books are available.

Marsh Farms
14240 Brookhurst St.
Garden Grove, CA 92643

There are incubators, feeders, and game bird equipment.

Montgomery Ward (catalog)
1000 S. Monroe St.
Baltimore, MD 21232

Feeders, waterers, brooders, incubators and accessories, steel poultry nests, egg washers, cartons, and other kinds of equipment are available.

Mother's General Store
Box 506
Flat Rock, NC 28731

Feeders, waterers, incubators, brooders, and assortments of poultry equipment are available.

Nasco Agricultural Sciences
901 Janesville Ave.
Fort Atkinson, WI 53538

Incubators, feeders, and game bird accessories are available.

New Delphos Mfg. Co.
Delphos, OH 45833

They have a variety of feeders, waterers, metal nests, and vent accessories.

Ronson Farms
P.O. Box 12565
Columbus, OH 43212

They offer feeders, incubators, brooders, cages, poultry pickers, chicks, pigeons, pheasants, waterfowl, quail, doves, books, and aviary accessories.

Sears, Roebuck & Co.
Farm and Ranch Catalog

They list feeders, waterers, steel poultry nests, cartons, chickens, ducklings, goslings, and mallards.

Stromberg's Pets Unlimited
50 Lakes Route
Pine River, MN 56474

They carry feeders, waterers, incubators, chicken pluckers, chicks, bantams, ducklings, goslings, and books.

Productions Master S.A.
Apartado Postal 74-057
Calzada de Tlalpan 1606
Mexico 13, D.F.

Feeders, waterers, and brooders are available.

INTERNATIONAL SOURCES OF POULTRY SUPPLIES

CeCoCo
P.O. Box 8, Ibaraki City
Osaka Pref. 567, Japan

They have egg washers and sorters.

Dalton Supplies, Ltd.
Nettlebed, Henley on Thames
Oxon, U.K.

They carry marking equipment.

PAL, Ets. P. Lecieux & Cie
rue du Riez
59112 Annoeullin, France

Feeders and brooders can be ordered.

Self-Sufficiency and Small-Holding Supplies
The Old Palace, Priory Road
Wells, Somerset BA 5 1SY, U.K.

Feeders, poultry houses, and identification equipment can be found here.

NORTH AMERICAN SOURCES OF SHEEP SUPPLIES

Belknap, Inc.
P.O. Box 28
Louisville, KY 40201

They carry shears.

Columbia Cutlery Co.
P.O. Box 123
Reading, PA 19603

They have a variety of sheep shears.

Countryside Catalog
Rt. L, Box 239
Waterloo, WI 53594

They have shears and wool cards.

K & K Mfg., Inc.
Rogers, MN 55374

They carry Nursette lamb feeders, nipples, and tube assembly parts.

Nasco Agricultural Sciences
901 Janesville Ave.
Fort Atkinson, WI 53538

They offer marking equipment, cards, halters, blankets, nursing supplies, castrators, lambing instruments, and a variety of shears.

INTERNATIONAL SOURCES OF SHEEP SUPPLIES

Dalton Supplies, Ltd.
Nettlebed, Henley on Thames
Oxon, U.K.

They have lamb-bar feeders, lambing instruments, ram harnesses, ewe-bearing retainers, and castration rings.

Kumaon Nursery
Ramnagar
Nainital, U.P. India

Many companies offer the parts for fabricating a feeder at home. . .
K & K Mfg.

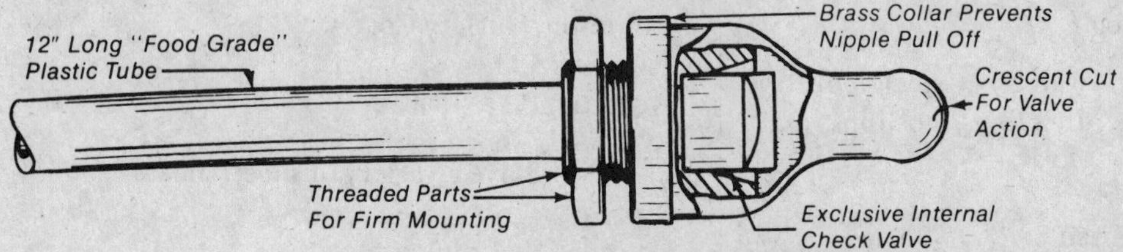

. . . or as a preassembled unit.
K & K Mfg.

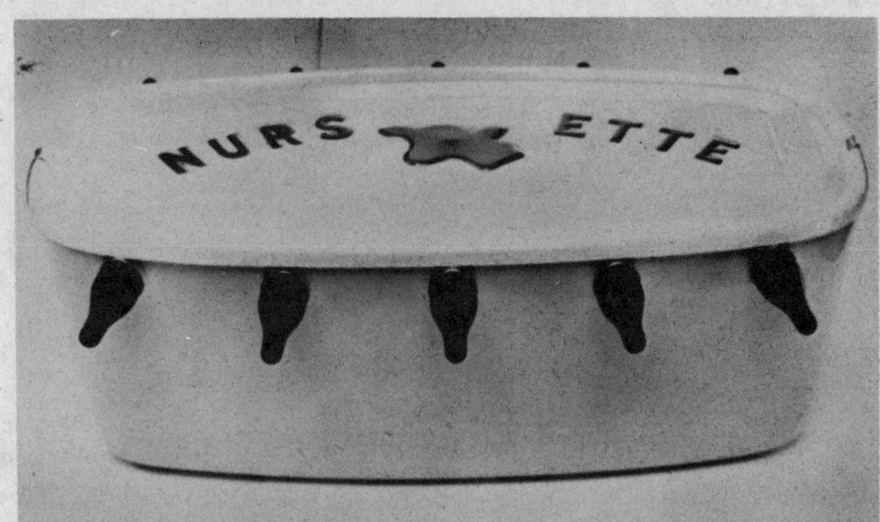

They carry shears.

R.A. Lister Agricultural, Ltd.
Dursley
Gloucestershire GL 11 4HS, U.K.

Electric- or engine-powered sheep shears are available.

Self-Sufficiency and Small-Holding Supplies
The Old Palace, Priory Road
Wells, Somerset BA5 1SY, U.K.

Shears and shepherd's crooks are available.

Ubungo Farm Implements Mfg. Co.
P.O. Box 2669
Dar-Es-Salaam, Tanzania

They carry shears.

NORTH AMERICAN SOURCES OF HOG SUPPLIES

Belknap, Inc.
P.O. Box 28
Louisville, KY 40201

They have feeders, holders, and marking equipment.

Brower Mfg. Co.
640 S. Fifth St.
Quincy, IL 62301

Hog-holding crates, farrowing pens, and pig brooders are available.

Countryside Catalog
Rt. 1, Box 239
Waterloo, WI 53594

They handle harnesses.

Cumberland General Store
Rt. 3, Box 479
Crossville, TN 38555

They offer holders, feeders, waterers, and marking equipment.

Glen-Bel Enterprises
Rt. 5
Crossville, TN 38555

They carry feeders.

K & K Mfg., Inc.
Rogers, MN 55374

They have a nurse-ette piglet feeder.

Marting Mfg.
Washington Court House, OH 43160

They carry a large variety of feeders, waterers, hog houses, holders, oilers, and scales.

Montgomery Ward
1000 S. Monroe St.
Baltimore, MD 21232

They handle feeders, waterers, holding crates, and farrowing stalls.

Nasco Agricultural Science
901 Janesville Ave.
Fort Atkinson, WI 53538

Marking equipment, castrators, holders, feeders, waterers, and scales are available.

New Delphos Mfg. Co.
Delphos, OH 45833

Feeders are available.

Winona Attrition Mill Co.
1009 W. Fifth St.
Winona, MN 55987

They have creep feeders.

INTERNATIONAL SOURCES OF HOG SUPPLIES

Agromet Motoimport
00-950 Warszawa, ul.
Przemyslowa 26, Poland

Waterers and farrowing cages are available.

Dalton Supplies, Ltd.
Nettlebed, Henley on Thames
Oxon, U.K.

They have weighbands.

PAL, Ets. P. Lecieux & Cie
rue du Riez
59112 Annoeullin, France

They offer feeding equipment, waterers, and farrowing pens.

Productions Master S.A.
Apartado Postal 74- 057
Calzada de Tlalpan 1606
Mexico 13, D.F.

They have feeders and waterers.

Self-Sufficiency and Small-Holding Supplies
The Old Palace, Priory Rd.
Wells, Somerset BA5 1SY, U.K.

They carry tethering equipment and harnesses.

SOURCES OF BEEKEEPING EQUIPMENT

Dadant and Sons, Inc.
Hamilton, IL 62341

They have beekeeping equipment and supplies for honey production.

Glen-Bel's Country Store
Rt. 5
Crossville, TN 38555

They also have beekeeping equipment and supplies for honey production.

The Walter Kelly Co.
Clarkson, KY 42726

They have a variety of equipment, supplies for honey production, and books.

Parowan Honey & Mfg. Co.
P.O. Box 305
Parowan, UT 84761

They offer extracting equipment for large or small beekeeping.

The A.I. Root Co.
623 W. Liberty St.
Medina, OH 44256

There are a variety of equipment and supplies for honey production, books, and a magazine called *Gleanings in Bee Culture*.

Sears, Roebuck & Co.
Farm & Ranch Catalog

Beekeeping equipment and supplies for honey production can be ordered.

Sunstream Bee Supply Center
P.O. Box 225
Eighty Four, PA 15330

A variety of beekeeping equipment, honey production supplies, and books are available.

Bee Flat Scale

An interesting production connected with beekeeping is the Bee Flat Scale Kit. This small kit contains all the hardware necessary to construct a permanent scale under the beehive, allowing the beekeeper to easily check on honey production in all seasons with a minimum amount of work.

Bee Flat Scale Company
Route 4 Box 65-F
Reedsport, OR 97467

The Bee Flat Scale
Bee Flat Scale Co.

–12– Tools for Fish Farming

edited by Nancy J. Moore

The uses of a farm pond are as varied as its owners. For some, ponds perform the vital function of providing water for home and livestock. To many people, the pond is a great source of recreation and relaxation—swimming, boating, and fishing in summer, and skating in winter. The pond serves as a catch basin for pasture runoff during rainstorms and is often the only water source for a range area in the event of fire. Insurance companies have been known to lower premium costs for owners of farm ponds.

Pond water is particularly rich in organic material when it contains fish and algae. Resourceful farmers can use this nutrient-rich water for crop irrigation, and benefit from the fertilizer boost as well. The extra bit of work and planning necessary for a successful farm pond is easily offset by these benefits.

AN INTRODUCTION TO AQUACULTURE

by William O. McLarney, Ph.D.

The best argument for aquaculture is based on the ever-increasing need for protein foods. Fish and aquatic invertebrates are efficient food converters, capable of producing more protein per unit area from the same amount of food than their warm-blooded counterparts. The quality of protein is the highest available from animals and is the lowest in fat content.

The farm pond is usually stocked with largemouth bass and bluegills, and is designed to provide sport fishing with food as a fringe benefit. Even when managed with recreation in mind, the farm pond has been shown to produce a substantial amount of edible fish and, it is my belief that, properly managed, it could become a really significant factor in the nourishment of many families.

More than a few American farmers have made the logical transition from eating pond fish to fish culture for the express purpose of food production, often on a commercial scale. They are usually encouraged to go into farming rainbow trout or channel catfish. The former species has produced fantastic yields but requires a large and dependable supply of water at a constant temperature—a condition which can be met by only a few landowners. Catfish farming is more amenable to most farmers as it can profitably be carried out in warm, still water.

Almost all trout farmers use antibiotics, not only in disease treatment, but as a prophylactic measure in their stock's diet. Use of antibiotic feeds is increasing in catfish culture, and many farmers also apply chlorinated hydrocarbon herbicides as a matter of course. Researchers at the New Alchemy Institute in Falmouth, Massachusetts, and at Rodale Resources Incorporated in Emmaus, Pennsylvania, are seeking alternatives, however.

Trout and catfish farming in the United States is further characterized by monoculture and heavy feeding. The latter will almost always increase production and may be necessary in large-scale commercial fish culture, but it certainly is not necessary to produce yields appropriate for personal, family, or community use. Asian fish culturists produce thousands of pounds of food fish which derive their nutrients essentially through organic pond fertilization or enrichment from surrounding farmland, through cut grass, vegetable tops, or other such inexpensive feeds. Similar systems are beginning to evolve in Africa, where considerable success has been achieved with community fish ponds stocked chiefly with herbivorous tilapia.

The direct or indirect utilization of organic wastes by fishes is by no means the only way in which fish ponds can contribute to the recycling capacity of a farm's ecosystem. Excess fish or fish too small for human consumption may be composted or fed to other livestock such as hogs or chickens. Under certain conditions, metabolic wastes from fish and shellfish may be applied beneficially to vegetable crops without harvesting the fish.

Polyculture is a widely applicable technique, with high yields being its most obvious benefit. The Chinese employ a highly refined polyculture technique which supplies them with a substantial supply of fish as it recycles their waste products and fertilizes their gardens. They build their latrines and animal shelters with slatted floors over the pond for organic wastes to fall through and supply the pond with a nutrient source. The pond becomes rich with algae feeding on the manure and provides a foundation for a complicated food chain to build upon. Algae- and manure-rich water is syphoned off to irrigate the garden and fertilize it at the same time.

A further benefit of polyculture includes providing the farmer with greater economic stability. (If one crop fails; there's always something else.) It also reduces the likelihood of a disease or pest destroying the entire crop, with the consequent temptation to use chemical poisons.

It would seem, then, that American food growers at all levels of the economy should not only consider taking up aquaculture, but should also be busy developing modern American analogs of the traditional Oriental pond polyculture systems. When integrated with similar practices on the land, such systems have the potential to revolutionize American agriculture—organically.

WATER QUALITY

When employing intensive fish culture techniques, it is advisable to monitor the water quality. A thermometer is a must for all pond owners, but the intensive aquaculturist must also worry about dissolved oxygen and ammonia content in water. Too much ammonia or too little

Frequent testing of water quality for excesses of ammonia or any oxygen deficiency will warn the fish farmer of problems before they become critical.

oxygen quite often will result in fish kills. And with intensive fish culture, small deficiencies or excesses can rapidly reach dangerous proportions.

There are several companies which manufacture chemical testing kits for under $50, and one company manufactures a meter for measuring dissolved oxygen for a bit over $100.

Several companies manufacture water test equipment, but it is generally designed for precise research work, so prices tend to be high. For example, laboratory-quality oxygen meters, accurate to tenths of a part per million, start at $500. However, the Garcia is designed for fishermen, is less accurate but accurate enough, and costs a little over $100 (1977 price).

The other option for farm pond water testing is to use chemical kits. They require more time, to mix solutions and add chemicals to water samples, but they are much less expensive. The chemicals are premeasured in little packets called pillows to make the procedure as expedient and simple as possible. Chemical test kits are available to measure dissolved oxygen, pH, nitrogen ammonia, hardness, CO_2, and many other factors.

Garcia D.O. Meter

The Dissolved Oxygen meter is available from:
Garcia Dissolved Oxygen Meter
329 Alfred Ave.
Teaneck, NJ 07666

Test Kits

Chemical test kits are available from:
La Motte Chemical Products Co.
P.O. Box 329
Chestertown, MD 21620

Hach Chemical Co.
P.O. Box 389
Loveland, CO 80537

AERATION

Most fish deaths occur because of an oxygen deficiency. Excessive algae and weed growth may rob ponds of oxygen, and the ammonia produced by fish waste products seriously affects water quality. Decomposing plant and animal materials may also contribute to oxygen loss and ammonia buildup. Aeration equipment offers relief from oxygen deficiency and excess ammonia problems.

Aerators can be divided into two main categories, mechanical aerators and agitators which transfer atmospheric oxygen into water, and diffusers, which are tubes that introduce oxygen bubbles into the water under its surface. Anyone who has seen an aquarium filter in operation knows how this type of aerator works.

Floating mechanical aerators use a pump to spray sheets of water above the pond's surface. This spraying action causes the water to absorb oxygen, aids in the removal of carbon dioxide and ammonia, and also may slightly lower water temperatures. Agitators are usually equipped with paddles which stir the water, causing it to oxygenate at the surface.

These positive features are clouded by a few disadvantages as well. Floating aerators and agitators should not be in operation while anyone is boating or fishing because they present an electrical hazard. They also obstruct the natural look of the pond. Some companies have manufactured aerators with decorative spray patterns in an effort to turn this negative feature into an attribute.

Diffusers, on the other hand, oxygenate the water while submerged, so they don't interrupt the aesthetics of the landscape or prohibit swimming or boating. Because of the equipment necessary for installation, such as air compressors and air pumps, diffusers are generally a more-expensive enterprise. Operation costs are generally higher because of a higher power requirement.

SOURCES OF AERATORS

Air-o-Lator

A floating mechanical aerator, the Model AF-14 has a totally submersible 1/3 h.p. (115 volts, 7 amps under full load), stainless steel, electric motor which moves 350 gallons of water per minute, and comes with a 50-foot cord. Shipping weight: 35 pounds.

Air-o-Lator (Div. of Roycraft Industries)
8100 Paseo St.
Kansas City, MO 64131

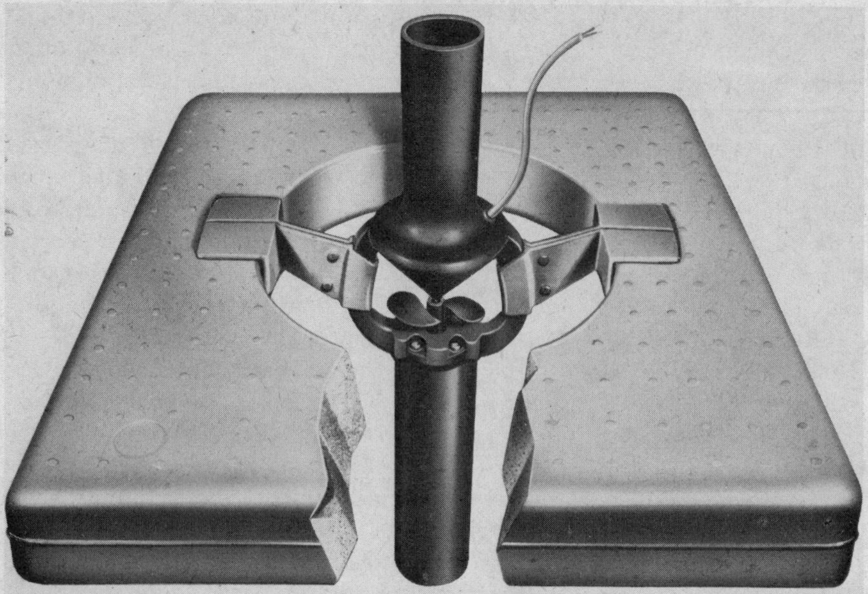

A cross section of the Air-o-Lator illustrates the position of the pump and impeller within the supportive float of a mechanical aerator.
Air-o-Lator

Aquacharger

This unit is a ceramic diffuser-aerator. The manufacturer states that a single unit is sufficient to aerate a 1- to 2-acre lake 10 to 25 feet deep. The diffusing cylinder is 2.25 inches in diameter and 9.5 inches long. It will circulate water to a radius of 20 to 30 feet at the pond surface. Additional equipment needed for operation are a buried electric line with an outlet socket, a waterproof pump house on a concrete slab, an air pump, and copper tubing. Overall life of the unit is estimated at 10 years.

Environmental Management & Design, Inc.
P.O. Box 493
Ann Arbor, MI 48107

Aquacharger Ceramic Diffuser-Aerator
Environmental Management & Design, Inc.

Aqua Puss

The Aqua Puss is an air diffuser-aerator. Air is released from the diffuser in sufficient volume to maintain turbulent uplift at a rate at which oxygen transfer can take place. The water jet propels water enough to carry it above the water surface, making a rise in the pond. The water then flows back upon itself and is converted to a horizontal flow 360 degrees around the rising column.

Schramm, Inc.
901 E. Virginia
West Chester, PA 19380

Boatcycle Company

They are agitation equipment manufacturers. The Big Bull agitator has a 110-volt, 1/3 h.p. motor with a one-year warranty against defective materials and workmanship, provided all repairs have been done by the manufacturer.

Boatcycle Co.
P.O. Box 494
Henderson, TX 75652

Crescent Agitators

Crescent manufactures agitators in a variety of sizes for everything from small hauling and holding tanks to outdoor ponds. Both indoor and outdoor models are available.

Crescent Mfg. Co.
P.O. Box 3303
Fort Worth, TX 76105

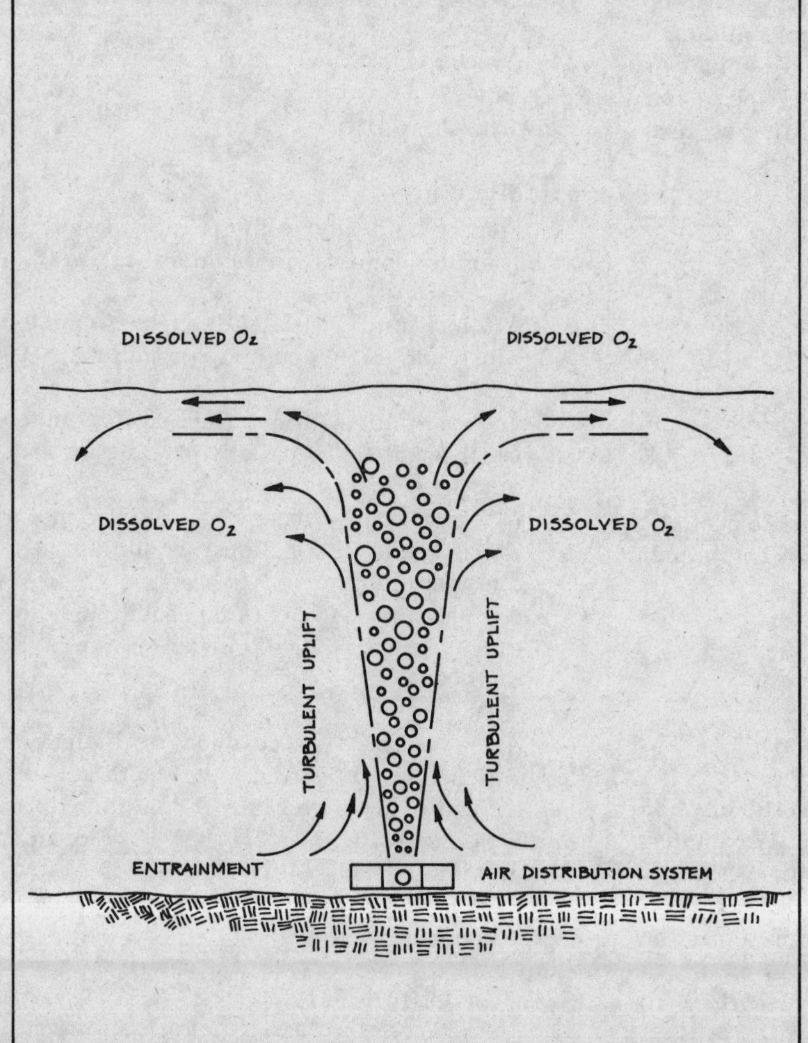

Air distribution system of a diffusing aerator.

Air Jet Aerator

The makers of the Air Jet manufacture various kinds of agitation equipment. In this aerator, air is drawn down through a tube to a propeller and broken up into tiny bubbles. The water level will not alter the effectiveness of the unit. Models for both transport and pond aeration are powered by 110-volt, 1/3 h.p., fan-cooled, continuous-duty ball bearing motors.

Commerce Welding & Mfg. Co., Inc.
2200 Evanston St.
Dallas, TX 75208

Fresh-Flo

In this centrifugal action aerator, a propeller-impeller draws water into the unit and initiates a tremendous force. Water is passed through slots above the water line, and sheets of water are sandwiched with open air. This aerator is mounted on pipes, floats, or overhead installations and provides a continuous circulation process.

Fresh-Flo Corp.
Rt. 1
Adell, WI 53001

GenAIRator

This diffuser-aerator will aerate and circulate 6,000 gallons of water per hour (100 gallons per minute), and add 50 pounds of oxygen to the water per day. The 1/4 h.p. motor has a thermo protector which shuts the motor off temporarily during periods of low voltage or current shortages. There is no float, standpipe, or overhead support; it needs no adjustment to different lake levels. This model poses no hazard to boaters or swimmers, and it has a one-year guarantee.

Kembro, Inc.
P.O. Box 205
Meguon, WI 53092

McDonald Oxidator

Unlike many hanging aerators, water level is not critical with this agitating oxidator. It operates effectively when immersed in 3 to 12 inches of water. Aeration occurs at the surface by an agitating blade and at the bottom of the oxidator by an air rotor. The unit is engineered to aerate more with less agitation.

McDonald Bait Co.
Rt. 2, Box 300
Erin, TN 37061

Micro-por

This air diffuser-aerator consists of ABS thermoplastic tubing containing approximately 1,000 microscopic holes per linear foot. As air is introduced through the tubing at low pressure, it seeps out through these tiny pores along the entire length of the Micro-por pipe. Available in 100-foot coils or in 5-foot straight lengths with ½ inch male thread adapters.

Micro-por, Inc.
P.O. Box 278
Colwich, KS 67030

P.J. Minneau

Floating and submersible aerators are available from this company in the following sizes:

1. A 5 inch unit with a ⅓ h.p. electric motor which aerates 100 gallons per minute at ½ cent per hour;
2. A 5 inch unit with a ½ h.p. electric motor which aerates 200 gallons per minute at 1 cent per hour;
3. A 5 inch unit with a 1 h.p. electric motor which aerates 400 gallons per minute at 2 cents per hour; and
4. A 5 inch unit with a 2½ h.p. gasoline motor which aerates 500 gallons per minute at 10 cents per hour.

A 1½ inch pipe is needed for installation, its length depending upon the water depth and the depth it must be driven into the bottom to be firmly situated (submersible type). (Electrical costs were calculated in 1977).

P.J. Minneau Machine Co.
Lime Kiln Rd., Rt. 6
Green Bay, WI 54301

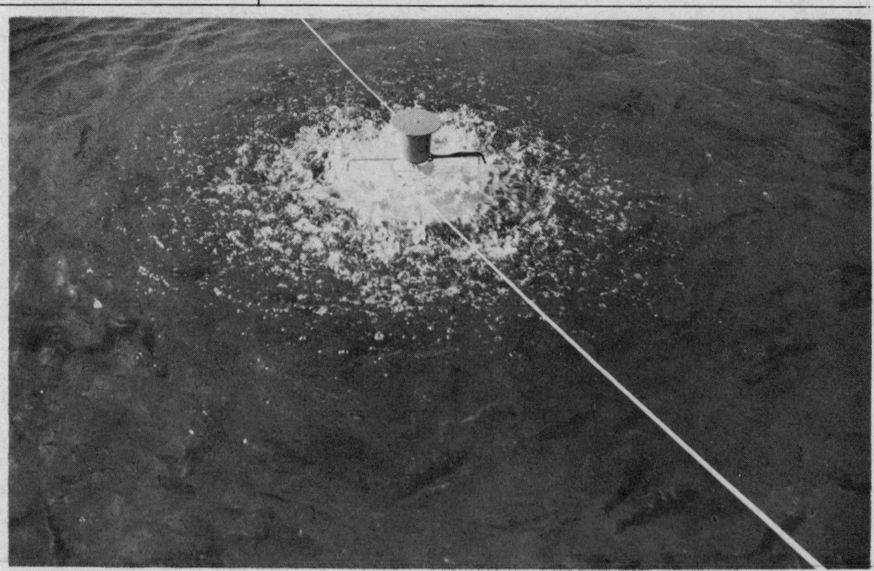

Floating mechanical aerators, like this Otterbine Mechanical Aerator, may need to be held in place by mooring cables.

Otterbine® Aeration Systems

These compact 1, 2, 3 and 5 horsepower floating mechanical aerators are designed to improve water quality in fish ponds by increasing the supply of dissolved oxygen available to the fish and by mixing the water to distribute dissolved oxygen to various depths.

With aeration, fish can be stocked more heavily, reach eating size faster, and are less vulnerable to diseases and parasites.

Otterbine aerators are installed by floating them into position in the pond, and mooring or anchoring them in place. An underwater power cable leads to on-shore electrical service. The 1 and 2 horsepower models require either 115 or 230 volt single-phase power; the 3 and 5 horsepower models require 230 or 460 volt three-phase power.

All Otterbine aerators are warranted conditionally against defects in materials and labor for one full year from date of delivery.

Rodale Resources Inc.
576 North St.
Emmaus, PA 18049

Vulcan Aerator Company

Vulcan's model No. 12 has a 12-volt, ball bearing, totally enclosed motor, with continuous-duty, replaceable brushes. Domes are available for splash-free operation, and it requires 3½ amps at half-paddle. Model No. 10 has a 1.5-amp, alternating current motor which operates at a slower speed.

Vulcan Aerator Co.
N. 113, W. 18830 Carnegie Dr.
Germantown, WI 53022

Xodar Corporation

Xodar's Model 360 is a submersed aeration diffuser. The air flow volume is very low in order to achieve sufficient discharge pressure to produce an effective bubble swarm for the desired maximum oxygen-to-water transfer.

Xodar Corp.
Powder Hill Dr.
Lincoln, RI 02865

FEEDING

Two conditions encourage the use of supplemental feeding of farm pond fish: when the stocking density is higher than what would occur naturally and thus exceeds the natural food supply, and when an increased growth rate is desired. High-protein, pelleted commercial feeds satisfy both conditions and are available at most local feed stores.

Feed pellets are in either floating or sinking form. Floating pellets permit the farmer to watch his fish feeding. He can check growth as well as gauge what amount to feed. The activity with which fish feed is indicative of their health; healthy fish feed actively.

Sinking pellets insure that smaller, more timid fish are fed also. Every fish will eat, not only the big, aggressive fish cruising the water surface. Often pond owners use a combination of floating and sinking feed to reap the benefits of both. Feeding habits are species-specific. Thus, fish farmers should select feed according to recommendations for the variety they are raising.

Fish feeds come with different protein ratios; selection depends upon how extensive the feeding program is. If commercial feed is used only to supplement the fishes' natural diet, a lower protein ratio (25 to 30 percent) is used. If it is the major portion of the diet, then a higher protein ratio (30 to 40 percent) is recommended.

Many pond owners feed their fish by hand. This method is economical, but requires that the owner always be present at feeding time. Purchasing an automatic commercial feeder can easily involve an investment of $100 or more. The simplest feeder is a floating ring which merely confines food to one spot rather than having it float all over the pond. A design carrying the floating ring idea one step further is described in the following build-it-yourself plan. If you have decided to feed by hand, this feeder can make the venture easier while utilizing feed more effectively.

BUILD-IT-YOURSELF FEEDER

This feeder can be used with both sinking and floating feeds. While sinking pellets drop into a sloped screen tray, floating feed remains

A simple feeder will cut down on waste by preventing scattering.

FISH FEEDER

Materials Required

QTY	SIZE & DESCRIPTION	PURPOSE
2	¾″ x 24″ x 2¼″ Pine	Frame
2	¾″ x 38″ x 2¼″ Pine	Frame
2	¾″ x 21″ x 2¼″ Pine	Floating
2	¾″ x 37″ x 2¼″ Pine	Frame
1	44″ x 28″ Aluminum or Plastic Screening	Tray Bottom
1	8″ Strap Hinge	
14	2″–#8 Wood Screws	
	Staples or Tacks	
	Marine Varnish	

confined within a floating wooden square. Surface-feeding fish 'boil' the water as they scramble for food; fish occupying different feeding niches are satisfied with food distributed at different depths on the screen. It is necessary to weight the screened frame with a brick to keep it submerged.

Marine varnish or paint on the frame prevents the wood from rotting, and placing chicken wire over the floating frame keeps birds and other animals from stealing feed. Training fish to feed at one spot will allow you to watch them as they feed. Also, with fish congregated in one spot, harvesting procedures may be simplified.

Pretreat wooden frames with marine varnish before using wood screws in assembling the two frames. One frame will be 21 by 37 inches, the other 24 by 40 inches. The larger frame has screening stretched beneath it, stapled or tacked in place. Use the strap hinge to join the two frames so that the smaller of the two is inside the larger.

For turbulent water, you may wish to make the floating bracket smaller so water currents don't carry feed outside the screen.

Build-It-Yourself Feeder

SOURCES OF COMMERCIAL FEEDERS

A number of commercial feeders are available which automatically dispense feed at timed intervals, while others feed by demand.

E-Z Feed

The E-Z Feed is an automatic feeder with a time-controlled dispensing apparatus. Any type of dry food can be used, and the hopper will hold 40 to 50 pounds. This amount should be sufficient for 6 to 8 weeks for a 1- to 2-acre pond. Suggested installation is over the deepest water up to but not exceeding a depth of 10 feet. Larger or smaller hoppers are available upon request. If no electricity is available at the pond

E-Z Feed Feeder
E-Z Feed Co.

site, E-Z Feed offers a direct current model equipped with a 12-volt battery.

E-Z Feed Co.
P.O. Box 97
Morrisville, NC 27560

Nielsen Model 5-0101

This is an automatic feeder with a 100-pound capacity hopper which has an adjustable gate to control food flow. It is electrically powered by a 115-volt, 60-cycle, alternating current motor which normally draws 3.6 amps. Adjustable mounting brackets are available for installation. Feed dispersion patterns can easily be adjusted manually.

Nielsen Metal Industries
3501 Portland Rd. NE
Salem, OR 97303

Poirot Farm Industries

This company markets an automatic, floating, gravity-operated fish feeder which does not require electricity to operate. It is available with or without a float, and in 100- and 200-pound hopper sizes. The unit is lightweight and can easily be moved to any section of the pond, as it does not require an electrical outlet.

Poirot Farm Industries
Golden City, MO 64748

Sweeney Enterprises, Inc.

Automatic feeding systems are offered here with either 100- or 200-pound hopper capacities and adjustable feed dispersion patterns and flow rates. One model is a front-drop feeder (HF 1). All feeders are battery powered and equipped with a rechargeable dry battery and a DFT-1 Timer. Possible methods of installation include: standing the feeder on its short legs or purchasing extension legs, hanging it from cables and cross arms, or mounting it on a float.

Sweeney Enterprises, Inc.
Rt. 2, Box 145G
Boerne, TX 78006

Sweeney Feeder
Sweeney Enterprises, Inc.

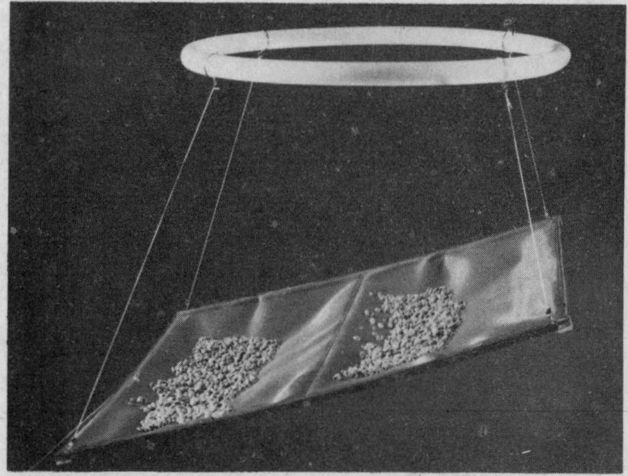

Farm Pond Harvest Feeder
Farm Pond Harvest

Farm Pond Harvest Bluegill Feeder

This feeder utilizes both floating and sinking fish feeds. A floating ring contains floating feed, and a plastic feeding tray suspended under this floating ring holds the sinking feed. This tray prevents the sinking feed from falling to the bottom of the pond. Bluegill may teach bass to eat from the feeder, helping with the harvest of bass. This feeder and feed are available from your local Purina dealer. If they do not have feeders contact:

Farm Pond Harvest
P.O. Box AA
Momence, IL 60954

BUG LIGHTS

Another type of feeder is the bug light, a device which attracts insects by fluorescent lighting. A fan pulls bugs into the water, or a blade cripples their wings, causing them to fall into the water. But depending upon your location, bug lights are often effective only during summer months when insects are prevalent.

SOURCES OF BUG LIGHTS

Will-o'-the-Wisp

This model is an adaptation of the yard bug light; it's an ultraviolet light which attracts insects and is equipped with a fan to blow them down into the water. The shell is made of fiberglass, and the black light is a 32-watt circular fluorescent tube connected to a small electric motor with a fan blade. The only maintenance needed is occasional cleaning and, possibly, replacement of the light bulb. Operating costs (in 1977) are less than 10 cents per day.

Will-o'-the-Wisp Bug Light
Hedlunds of Medford, Inc.

Hedlunds of Medford, Inc.
P.O. Box 305
Medford, WI 54451

Bug-Eater and Security Light

This model is controlled by a photo cell which turns it on at dusk and off at dawn. It is easily plugged into any standard 110-volt outlet, and a direct current operating unit will permit operation where alternating current is not available. A specially designed wire blade rotates rapidly and cripples insects attracted to the light, scattering them into the water below. The unit causes no insect buildup or odor, and operating costs are less than 1 cent per day (in 1977).

Southeast Equipment Co.
P.O. Box 6
Enigma, GA 31749

INSECTS . . . AN UNTAPPED RESOURCE

by Andy Merkowsky

Insects are a natural resource man has yet to utilize to full potential. For most people, bugs are bothersome pests, but viewed differently, they are an excellent source of protein. The protein content of insects is high; some contain more than 60-percent protein. They live almost everywhere and have tremendous reproductive ability.

The squeamishness of most Western societies prohibits human consumption of insects. A more easily accepted method of utilizing insects is to recycle them through other animals. They can be incorporated into pelleted fish feeds or dropped directly into the pond with the aid of a bug light suspended over the pond. Fish congregate under these traps to feed. The high protein content of the

Suspending an easily constructed insect trap over a pond transforms insect pests into fish food.

insects makes for better growth rates in the fish, and as an added benefit, the fish will be easier to catch because they are congregated in one area.

Several types of insect traps have been developed, and companies are now marketing them. Although commercial traps work well, they are very expensive. Homemade traps are cheaper to build and work about as well as commercial models.

DICK'S BUG MACHINE*

Originally designed by Dick Geddes of Winsted, Connecticut, this insect trap was used to supplement his chickens' diet. With only minor alterations, this insect trap can be suspended over a pond to effectively feed fish.

Dick's Bug Machine

* Reprinted from *Build It Better Yourself*. Emmaus, Pa.: Rodale Press, 1977.

MATERIALS

Wood

1–2′ x 4′ sheet, 3⁄4″ exterior plywood or

Sides: 4 pcs. 12″ sq.
End: 1 pc. 12″ x 13½″
Sides: 4 pcs. 8″ sq.

1 pc. 1″ x 1″ x 2″ or

Brace: 1 pc. 1″ x 1″ x 8″
Mounting block: 1 pc. 1″ x 1″ x 4″

Hardware

6d nails

3–½″ #6 screws

1 light bulb clamp and waterproof socket

1–40-watt light bulb

4–1″ #6 screws

Miscellaneous

1 electric fan, approx. 4½″ intake

1 tin can

1 nylon stocking

1 heavy rubber band *OR* 1 elbow tube

CONSTRUCTION

1. From 3⁄4 inch plywood, cut four 12 inch square pieces and a piece 12 inches by 13½ inches. Nail the square pieces together, forming an open-ended box, using 6d nails.
2. Measure the diameter of the fan intake and cut a hole that size in the center of one side of the box. Mount the fan in the box, the intake against the hole cut for it, the exhaust directed out one of the open ends of the box.
3. Place the remaining piece of plywood against the open end through which the fan exhausts. Mark the location and size of the exhaust on the plywood, then remove the plywood and cut out the exhaust hole. Next, cut a similar-sized hole in the bottom of the tin can and secure it over the exhaust hole with three ½ inch #6 screws. Finally, nail the plywood to the box, using 6d nails.
4. Cut four 8 inch square pieces of 3⁄4 inch plywood. Nail them together forming another open-ended box. Cut an 8 inch length of 1 by 1. Nail it across one open end of this box, so the light socket can be clamped to it, with the bulb inside the box.
5. Secure the light box to the fan box, using small corner irons or a homemade mounting, as shown in the photo.

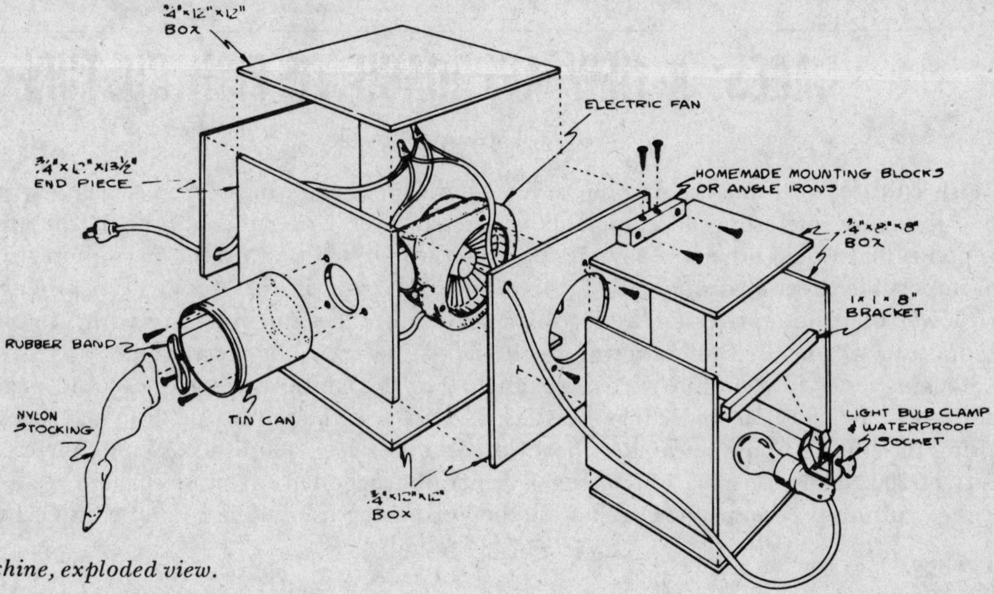

Dick's Bug Machine, exploded view.

6. To trap and collect insects, slip a nylon stocking over the exhaust pipe and secure it with a stout rubber band.
7. For an automatic feed of insects into your pond, replace the stocking trap with an elbow tube directed toward the water.
8. Plug in the light and fan. A 40-watt bulb will provide adequate light.

CAGE CULTURE

There are many advantages to raising fish in cages. Cage confinement means fish can be grown in streams and rapidly moving water without any fear of losing them to the natural environment. Feed waste is greatly reduced since the feeding is concentrated in a very small area. Because the movement of the fish is restricted, they do not need much feed to survive. They just eat and grow! Monitoring fish growth and health is greatly simplified, and the threat of predators is reduced. For a 100-percent harvest, the cages are simply lifted from the water—no fishing, draining, or seining (harvesting with a drag net) is necessary.

Cage culture makes use of bodies of water that are otherwise unsuitable.

CAGES: A NEW APPROACH TO FISH CULTURE

by Andy Merkowsky

Fish culture is an ancient art, but several new approaches have been developed in recent years. One of the more interesting developments is cage culture. Using this approach, the great numbers of farm ponds that would otherwise lay idle because they are without drains or contain stumps that make them impossible to seine, can now be utilized. Floating cages in these ponds can produce fish at a cost much lower than store prices for fresh fish. Cage culture does not interfere with the other pond uses; the pond can still be used for watering cattle, irrigating crops, or recreation.

Stocking rates in cages are amazingly high. For a cage measuring one cubic meter it is recommended that at least 150 fingerlings be stocked. Any less than this and fish may become territorial, resulting in fighting. Some researchers have successfully raised 500 fish per cubic meter, but a stocking density of 200 to 250 fish per cubic meter is generally suggested for most efficient use of cage space.

Cage culture is perhaps the cheapest method of raising fish because pond construction costs can be avoided by using a farm pond already in existence. The movement of fish in cages is restricted so fish do not use as much energy, making feed costs much lower. Fish obviously are much easier to harvest, too.

An easily constructed, durable fish cage.

NORTH AMERICAN SOURCES OF FISH CAGES

Double-Q Cages
Inqua Corp.
P.O. Box 1325
Homestead, FL 33036

Duracraft
Duracraft
Dept. SDEB
Monticello, AR 71655

Aqua-Fab
L & M Aqua-Fab
1853 W. Commonwealth
Fullerton, CA 92633

This small company custom-builds cages to the buyer's specifications.

The Double-Q cage is available from a number of distributors.

Marinovich

Marinovich Trawl Co., Inc.
P.O. Box 294
Biloxi, MS 39533

Distributors of Fish Cages

Act One Supplies
1530 MacArthur Blvd.
Oakland, CA 94602

Aquatic Control, Inc.
P.O. Box 100
Seymour, IN 47274

Astra Chemicals, Ltd.
1004 Middlegate Rd.
Mississauga, Ontario L4Y 1M4, Canada

John B. Fitzpatrick
214 E. North St.
Dwight, IL 60420

Suppliers of Netting for Homemade Cages

Con Wed Corp.
770 29th Ave. SE
Minneapolis, MN 55414

E.I. DuPont De Nemours & Co., Inc.
Specialty Markets Div., Film Dept.
Wilmington, DE 19898

McCrary's Farm Supply
114 Park St.
Lonoke, AR 72086

C.E. Shepard Co.
P.O. Box 9445
Houston, TX 77011

HARVESTING

Any farm pond venture is only as successful as its harvesting methods. Getting the fish from the pond to the table can be approached in a variety of ways. For the sports-minded harvester, there is always the angler's approach. If the fish don't bite or if you want faster results, there are a variety of techniques which employ nets. Seining the pond and using gill nets are two efficient methods of harvesting fish all at once. Dip nets are effective for small harvests and will not injure fish.

SOURCES OF HARVESTING MATERIALS

Commerce Welding and Manufacturing Company

This company manufactures 3/16 inch, nylon mesh, double-frame dip nets with two handle sizes. The nets have 15 inch widths. Handles are available in either 12 or 24 inch lengths.

Commerce Welding & Mfg. Co., Inc.
2200 Evanston St.
Dallas, TX 75208

Crescent Manufacturing Company

Crescent manufactures small dip nets for fingerlings and minnows. The nets have 6 to 9 inch bags of 3/16 inch nylon netting or 3/8 inch net. Nets are available in widths of 10, 12, 14, 18, 20, and 24 inches with handles 10 to 20 inches long. Small-mesh nylon seines are manufactured in depths of 4 to 12 feet and mesh sizes of 1/8, 3/16 and 1/4 inch. Larger mesh seines are offered in sizes of 1/2, 3/4, 1, 1 1/2, and 2 inches and in depths of 6 to 12 feet. Seines are tarred with black net bond for added strength.

Crescent Mfg. Co.
P.O. Box 3303
Fort Worth, TX 76105

Duraframe Dipnet

Dip nets come in three shapes, lengths of 3 1/2, 5, and 6 feet, and mesh sizes of 1/16, 1/4, 3/4, and 1 inch. Seines are made to the purchaser's specifications. Nets and seines are guaranteed for a period of one year: frames are handmade, and those used in cement runways have a second metal rim to keep the net lacing from rubbing and wearing against cement walls.

Duraframe Dipnet
Rt. 2, Box 166
Viola, WI 54664

Nylon Net Company

This firm manufactures a wide variety of nets, seines, and lead sinkers.

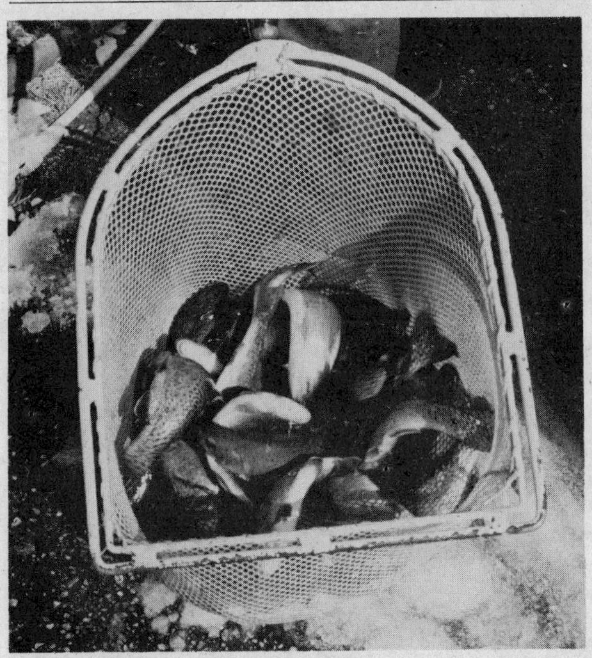

The protective outer rim of the Duraframe Dipnet prevents the net from being damaged if rubbed against the pond wall.
DuraFrame Dipnet

Nylon Net Co.
P.O. Box 592
Memphis, TN 38103

Poirot Farm Industries

The PFI Automatic Fish Harvester models 1-A and 1-B are made of ¾ inch nylon netting tied to three 6-foot pieces of aluminum tubing. When combined with a feeding apparatus, the net will be released when almost all of the feed has been eaten. A 12-volt battery is all that is needed to power the device. Model 2-B is available for minnows and small fish. If a customer is dissatisfied with the units after three weeks, a full refund is given if the system is returned washed. The automatic lift and sensor are guaranteed for 1 year against failure.

Poirot Farm Industries
Golden City, MO 64748

Gill Nets

Gill nets are very large, lightweight nets with mesh averaging about 3 inches. They have little application in fish farming because they catch only very large fish and the fish die shortly after being caught. Particularly useful for commercial fisherman and game and fish associations, they can be manipulated by one person and set up in about an hour. The nets are dropped into a lake or river and left for perhaps 24 hours. Fish are not able to see the fine strands of netting; so they swim right into the net. By the time they realize their peril, they have gone too far and their gills are caught in the net—like a fly in a spider web. Fish are often scarred or marked, and on the threshhold of death when finally pulled from the water. With an immediate market outlet for their catch, commercial fishermen find this technique quite satisfactory, but most people involved in aquaculture prefer to seine.

Seine Nets

Seine nets are used for harvesting all the fish from a pond at one time. Their mesh is much finer and made of a heavier fiber than gill nets in order to hold a whole catch without breaking. Lead weights attached to the bottom ropes prevent any fish from escaping the net as it is pulled across the pond. Floats attached to the top ropes complete the enclosure. To make the catch, the net is drawn across the pond and hauled out of the water at the other end. This is one task which requires a number of helpers.

Catfish Nets

Spines on the dorsal fins of catfish have a

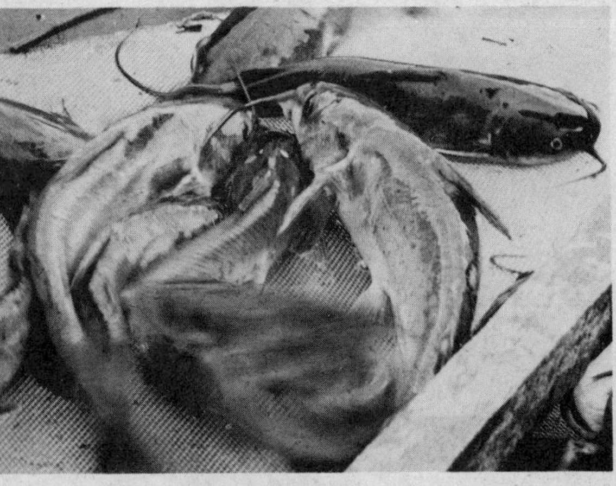

Special netting material must be used for harvesting catfish to prevent snagging and injuring their spines.

tendency to get caught in nylon mesh netting. This can be harmful to the fish and to you if you attempt to free them without gloves, and can create a potential bottleneck in your harvesting project. Special nets coated with tar are available to help you avoid this problem.

AQUATIC PLANTS

The control of aquatic weeds is a problem which plagues everyone involved with fish farming. If allowed to grow unchecked, water weeds will overrun ponds and lakes, reducing their water storage capacity, restricting water flow, and possibly harboring disease-carrying insects.

There is no permanent solution to this problem, but the longer weeds are left to flourish, the greater will be the expense of their eradication. Several methods are employed to remove weeds: mechanical devices, biological controls, chemical treatments, and cultural methods. For ecological reasons, we do not recommend chemicals, especially since sound alternatives are available.

Cultural and biological controls are still in the experimental stages. Certain species of fish, like the white amur and tilapia, feed on aquatic plants. They are illegal in most states because the effects of their introduction into a new environment are unknown. Researchers experimenting with biological control are stocking weed-laden ponds with only male fish to control the population of the species.

Such uncertainties bring us to mechanical devices as the most practical and ecologically

Algae blooms can rob fish of needed oxygen and cause massive fish kills.

sound means of aquatic weed control. Various cutting and dislodging tools are commercially available or can easily be made. Floating and submerged weeds can be controlled by manually picking or cutting them. A number of cutting devices can be used to harvest weeds from the bottom of a pond. It is important to remove cut aquatic vegetation from the water, as many of these plants reproduce through fragmentation (simple cell division) and would soon fill the pond again. Harvesting them for their contribution to the compost pile alone would be worth the effort.

Another effective weed control technique is lining the pond bottom with plastic to prevent plants from rooting. This method is quite expensive, and in larger ponds, is generally used only in the swimming area.

SOURCES OF WEED CUTTERS

Kee Underwater Weed Cutter

This weed cutter is designed to control underwater plant growth. It is comprised of two serrated blades which pivot forward and backward whenever the direction of movement is changed. The cutter comes with a 5-foot handle; an extra extension is also available. The cutter has a 3-month guarantee.

Kee Mfg. Co., Inc.
P.O. Box 2195
Bradenton, FL 33505

Joe Morreale and Son's Pond Sweeper

Plans for building your own pond sweeper are available by sending $3.00 to Joe Morreale. The unit is inexpensive to make, lightweight (12 pounds), and parts should be easy to find. It is operated by two people and is designed to gather weeds as they are cut, considerably simplifying disposal.

Joe Morreale
6805 Pioneer
Richmond, IL 60071

SOURCES OF FISH

Hatchery Listings

A list of all federal, state, and private hatcheries is available from:

National Marine Fisheries Service–National Oceanic and Atmospheric Administration
One Union Plaza, Suite 1160
Little Rock, AR 72201

When purchasing fish it is best to contact the closest hatchery. Transportation costs are high and stress to fish in transport may cause death.

Commercial Fish Farmers Buyers' Guide

The *Buyers' Guide* is published annually and contains a list of distributors and manufacturers of everything the fish farmer may need. The list is comprised of the magazine's advertisers' and subscribers' products.

Commercial Fish Farmer Subscription Service
P.O. Box 4992
Manchester, NH 03105

GOVERNMENT AGENCIES

There are a number of government agencies which provide literature and services for the pond owner. These services vary regionally, as some parts of the country are far more involved with fish farming than others. The best procedure is to contact a local office and ask specifically what information and services are available.

United States Fish and Wildlife Service–Division of Fisheries

The assistance offered by this agency varies in different parts of the country based upon the availability of fish in the area. In the southeastern United States, pond owners can apply to have their ponds inspected and stocked by the Service and receive the assistance of a staff fisheries biologist.

For those fortunate enough to have one of these offices nearby, there is a very important service offered. Each office has a disease control center where pond owners can send samples of dead fish to be analyzed. A staff member will identify the problem and advise what action should be taken. This resource is a comfort when fish appear floating belly up and the cause of death remains a mystery.

Soil Conservation Service

Again, the services offered vary regionally, but in all states the Soil Conservation Service will provide information about the suitability of soil for pond construction, design criteria, and stocking advice. Some states require a formal written request for assistance and will send agents prior to construction, while in other states, agents may stay during the entire construction and may stock the pond for free.

State Fish and Game Commission

In states where this agency is funded by revenue from fishing permits, this commission is forbidden by law to service private ponds. In the South, where fish farming is widespread, services may include free stocking, removal of trash fish, and assistance in restocking ponds. The Fish and Game Commission may also test to see what fish are already in your pond, and advise what should be done with them.

State Cooperative Extension Service

This service generally provides a wealth of information about pond design and management, balance of fish population, and methods of plant control. They can also advise of applicable United States Department of Agriculture publications.

Most extension services have agricultural engineers and/or wildlife experts on staff to advise about fish culture, and in some states, agents will run water-quality tests and assist with pond and stocking management.

United States Department of Agriculture Publications

The following publications are available free of charge (as long as the supply lasts) by writing to:

Publications Division
Office of Communication
U.S. Department of Agriculture
Washington, DC 20250

Write your name and address plainly on your order, and be sure to include your zip code. In general, not more than one copy each of 10 publications is allowed.

+F 2250	Warm Water Fish Ponds
+L 552	Trout Farming: Could Trout Farming Be Profitable for You?
+F 2249	Trout Ponds for Recreation
+MMR 993	Demand for Farm-Raised Channel Catfish in Super-Markets: Analysis of a Selected Market
+F 2256	Building a Pond

INTERNATIONAL DEVELOPMENT OF FISH FARMING

Most countries have government offices specifically geared towards international aquaculture development which are responsible for all project coordination. Often these agencies will contact other countries more actively involved with aquaculture for technical assistance. The United States Agency for International Development (USAID) and the Food and Agriculture Organization (FAO) are the two largest organizations involved with international aquaculture development. Both agencies have staff personnel trained to give technical assistance. Countries can apply to the World Bank for loans to finance their aquaculture projects. Generally, the World Bank will contact aquaculture experts for feasibility studies for a given country.

Addresses of International Offices

World Bank, International Bank for Reconstruction & Development
1818 H Street NW
Washington, DC 20433

USAID
Main State Building
Washington, DC 20523

FAO
Via Delle Terme Di Caracalla
00100 Rome, Italy

RECOMMENDED PUBLICATIONS

Magazines

Farm Pond Harvest

Published quarterly, this magazine includes such features as Aquaculture News, Questions and Answers, Let's Go Farmpond Fishing, various articles about pond species and problems, tips for fish farmers, and advertising for many different types of small-scale equipment. The magazine is geared toward the small farm pond situation.

Farm Pond Harvest
Department M76
P.O. Box AA
Momence, IL 60954

Commercial Fish Farmer and Aquaculture News

Published bimonthly, this magazine features aquaculture news, columns, and sections about all species of cultured aquatic animals, organization news and meetings schedules, new developments both national and international, regular columns by various aquaculture experts, and a new products section. Advertisers are national distributors and manufacturers of aquaculture products and species.

Commercial Fish Farmer
Subscription Department
P.O. Box 631
Penacook, NH 03301

Fish Culture Section/American Fisheries Society Newsletter

You must be a member of the American Fisheries Society to receive this newsletter. Summaries of aquaculture events, conferences, legislation, new publications, workshops and symposiums, lists and directories, and pertinent aquaculture information are presented in this publication.

American Fisheries Society
5410 Grosvenor Lane
Bethesda, MD 20014

Books

The following books will provide fundamental understanding of pond ownership and management. Some are more technical and scientific than others, but all will provide valuable background information.

Hickling, C.F. *The Farming of Fish.* Elmsford, New York: Pergamon Press, Ltd., 1968.

This book provides the reader with an introduction to fish culture and offers an international perspective. It presents information which is basic to understanding pond ecology and productivity—water supply and quality, energy production and consumption within the pond, how the food chain applies to pond life, and the biology of and life cycles within the pond. It also compares aquaculture techniques of various countries.

Bardach, John E.; Ryther, John H.; and McLarney, William O. *Aquaculture: The Farming and Husbandry of Freshwater and Marine Organisms.* New York: John Wiley & Son, Inc., 1972.

The introductory chapter of this book discusses the general principles and economics of aquaculture. The following chapters deal with individual species, describing both commercial and small-scale culture, environmental and biological requirements, breeding information and population controls, and what a particular species has to offer for the fish farmer. It is a must for anyone involved in aquaculture because it provides specific requirements and information about all fish and shellfish commonly cultured.

Bennett, George W. *Management of Lakes and Ponds.* 2nd ed. New York: Van Nostrand Reinhold Co., 1971.

Bennett's book is geared to the professional fisheries biologist or the recreation expert designated to develop a body of water for sports fishing. It provides considerable general information about fish culture and discusses the history and theory of fish management. Other topics covered include water quality, carrying capacity and productivity of a given body of water, behavioral patterns of fish, production and growth potentials, and detailed information about angling.

Chakroff, Marilyn. *Freshwater Fish Pond Culture and Management.* VITA: Manual Series Number 36E, 1976.

This manual is a complete how-to for the aspiring pond owner. It is designed to provide basic information for the Peace Corps worker in Third World countries; so it is not technical or highly scientific. It details pond siting and construction, management and harvesting techniques, and control of diseases, parasites, and predators. The manual is also full of plans, recipes, and homemade treatments.

Scott, W.B., and Crossman, E.J. *Freshwater Fishes of Canada*. Ottawa: Fisheries Research Board of Canada, 1973. Bulletin 184.

Many of the species of freshwater fish found in Canada can also be found in the United States. This book provides detailed information on many species of fish including anatomical sketches, descriptions, distribution, biological requirements, nomenclature, and relation to man. It also has an extensive glossary, many suggested readings, and a lengthy reference section. It is a valuable tool in providing the reader with the means of finding a wealth of material about many species of fish.

Podems, Marc, and Ruttle, Jack. *A Guide to Small-Scale Fish Culture*. Emmaus, Pennsylvania: Rodale Press, 1978.

This primer is a must for any would-be fish farmer. It describes how to raise fish in a pond or a pool or even in your basement in simple, easy-to-understand language. Its chapters include discussions on selecting the right species for given circumstances, caring for the fish, managing the water, estimating costs, and water ecology. In addition, sources for supplies, fish, and references to expert advice are listed in the appendix. It is illustrated with drawings of fish and is available without charge from *Organic Gardening* Readers' Service, Rodale Press, 33 E. Minor Street, Emmaus, PA 18049.

Logsdon, Gene. *Getting Food from Water: A Guide to Backyard Aquaculture*. Emmaus, Pennsylvania: Rodale Press, 1978.

This book, published in fall of 1978, is geared for the hobbyist interested in raising his own food and possibly making a small profit. It covers a wide range of topics from edible water plants to raising ducks to ice and ice houses. This book is not limited to procuring food from a farm pond only, but also tells how to get food from the wild. The first section of the book deals with naturally occurring bodies of water, and the second section deals with constructed ponds, tanks, and raceways.

Hale, P.R., and Williams, B.D., eds. *Liklik Buk*. Lae, Papua, New Guinea: Liklik Buk Information Center, 1977.

This handbook of intermediate technology in Papua, New Guinea has a brief section devoted to the local fish culture project. Dealing with tilapia, its chapters describe the economics, processing, and marketing of the fish.

Liklik Buk Information Center
P.O. Box 1920
Lae, Papua, New Guinea

BIBLIOGRAPHIES

Bibliographies of available publications on aquaculture can be ordered from:

Publications Clerk, 249 Ag Center
School of Forestry & Wildlife Management
Louisiana State University
Baton Rouge, LA 70803

Ask for the aquaculture bibliography:
OG Readers' Service
Rodale Press, Inc.
33 E. Minor St.
Emmaus, PA 18049

Ask for *The Progressive Fish-Culturist:*
Superintendent of Documents
United States Government Printing Office
Washington, DC 20402

Appendix A: NORTH AMERICAN MANUFACTURERS AND DISTRIBUTORS APPEARING ON CHARTS IN THIS BOOK

Agway, Inc.
P.O. Box 1333
Syracuse, NY 13201

Allied Farm Equipment
3721 Mahoning Ave.
Youngstown, OH 44509
or
101 Eastern Ave.
Syracuse, NY 13211
or
124 Labrosse Ave.
Pointe Claire, Quebec, Canada

Allis-Chalmers
Box 512
Milwaukee, WI 53201

Amerind-MacKissic, Inc.
P.O. Box 111
Parker Ford, PA 19457

Ames
Box 1774
Parkersburg, WV 26101

Anchor Tools & Woodstoves
618 NW Davis
Portland, OR 97209

Ariens Co.
655 W. Ryan St.
Brillion, WI 54110

Atlas Tool & Mfg. Co.
5151 Natural Bridge Ave.
St. Louis, MO 63115

Auto-Hoe, Inc.
P.O. Box W121
Lost Dauphin Dr.
DePere, WI 54115

Belknap, Inc.
P.O. Box 28
Louisville, KY 40201

Black & Decker
Towson, MD 21204

Brantly Mfg. Co., Inc.
516 W. Grand
Frederick, OK 73542

Brinly-Hardy Co., Inc.
P.O. Box 1116
Louisville, KY 40201

Brown Mfg. Corp.
Ozark, AL 36360

W. Atlee Burpee Co.
300 Park Ave.
Warminster, PA 18974

J. I. Case Co.
Outdoor Power Equipment Div.
Winneconne, WI 54986

Central Tractor distributed by:

Weaver's Hardware Co.
RD 2, Lyons Rd.
Fleetwood, PA 19522

Chromalloy Farm & Industrial Equipment Co.
Crescent Div., Pear & Tinkham Sts.
Box 549
Havana, IL 62644

Cole Mfg. Co.
1318 Central Ave.
Charlotte, NC 28299

Columbia Cutlery Co.
P.O. Box 123
Reading, PA 19603

Continental Belton Co.
P.O. Box 660
Belton, TX 76513

Corsicana Grader & Machine Co.
P.O. Box 1699
Corsicana, TX 75110

Countryside Catalog
Rt. 1, Box 239
Waterloo, WI 53594

Cumberland General Store
Rt. 3, Box 479
Crossville, TN 38555

John Deere
Moline, IL 61265

DeGiorgi Co., Inc.
Council Bluffs, IA 51501

The Derby Tiller Co.
P.O. Box 21
Rumson, NJ 07760

Detroit Tool & Engineering
The Garden Maid Div.
P.O. Box 232
Lebanon, MO 65536

Edko Mfg. Co.
P.O. Box 111
Rocky Ford, CO 81067

Edko Mfg., Inc.
2725 Second Ave.
Des Moines, IA 50313

Edwards Equipment Co.
4312 Main St.
Yakima, WA 98903

Empire Plow Co.
3140 E. Sixty-fifth St.
Cleveland, OH 44127

Farm & Fleet
1600 E. Lincoln Hwy.
DeKalb, IL 60115

Farnam Equipment Co.
P.O. Box 12068
Omaha, NE 68112

FMC-Bolens
Outdoor Power Equip. Div.
215 S. Park St.
Port Washington, WI 53074

Ford Motor Co.
Troy, MI 48084

Forestry Suppliers, Inc.
205 W. Rankin St., Box 8397
Jackson, MS 39204

Dean Foster Nurseries
Hartford, MI 49057

Fuerst Brothers, Inc.
Rhinebeck, NY 12572

Gantt Mfg. Co.
Box 49
Macon, GA 31202

Gilmore-Tatge Mfg. Co., Inc.
Clay Center, KS 67432

Gilson Brothers Co.
Box 152
Plymouth, WI 53073

Gilson Brothers Co., Ltd.
3325 Orlando Dr.
Mississaugua, Ontario, Canada

Glen-Bel's Country Store
Rt. 5, Box 390
Crossville, TN 38555

Hahn, Inc.
Outdoor Products Div.
1625 N. Garvin
Evansville, IN 47717

Heald, Inc.
Dept. DTB, P.O. Box 148
Benton Harbor, MI 49022

IMCO-Independent Mfg. Co., Inc.
Industrial Park
Neodesha, KS 66757

International Harvester Co.
The Good Earth Catalog
P.O. Box 1008
Tinley Park, IL 60477

International Modern Machinery, Inc.
P.O. Box 790
Beaumont, TX 77704

Jeoffrey Mfg., Inc.
P.O. Box 9114
Amarillo, TX 79105

KMC (Kelly Mfg. Co.)
South Industrial Park
P.O. Box 1467
Tifton, GA 31794

Koehn Mfg. & Dist., Inc.
Watertown, SD 57201

John R. Kovar Mfg. Co., Inc.
6043 Hwy. 10 NW
Anoka, MN 55303

K-W Mfg. Co., Inc.
800 S. Marion Rd.
Sioux Falls, SD 57106

Lehman Hardware & Appliance, Inc.
Box 41
Kidron, OH 44636

A. M. Leonard & Son, Inc.
P.O. Box 816
Piqua, OH 45356

Magna American Corp.
Box 90
Raymond, MS 39154

McDonough Power Equipment
McDonough, GA 30253

The Ben Meadows Co.
3589 Broad St.
Atlanta, GA 30366

Merry Mfg. Co.
Box 168
Marysville, WA 98270

Montgomery Ward
1000 S. Monroe St.
Baltimore, MD 21232

Mother's General Store
Box 506
Flat Rock, NC 28731

MTD Products, Inc.
5389 W. 130th St., P.O. Box 2741
Cleveland, OH 44111

Nasco Agricultural Sciences
901 Janesville Ave.
Fort Atkinson, WI 53538

Noble Mfg. Co.
see Royal Industries

Northeast Carry Trading Co.
110 Water St., P.O. Box 187
Hallowell, ME 04347

Oley Tooling, Inc.
Oley, PA 19547

Pengo Corp.
Sunnyvale, CA 94086

Planet Plows, Inc.
P.O. Box 3779
Amarillo, TX 79106

Roper Sales
1905 W. Court St.
Kankakee, IL 60901

The Roto-Hoe Co.
100 Auburn Rd.
Newbury, OH 44065

Royal Industries
Noble Div., Dept. FI-6
Sac City, IA 50583

G.E. Ruhmann Mfg. Co., Inc.
801 S. Main St.
Schulenburg, TX 78956

Scovil Hoe Co.
P.O. Box 328
Locust Valley, NY 11560

Sears, Roebuck & Co.
Farm and Ranch Catalog
Available at any Sears store.

Sensation Corp.
7577 Burlington St.
Ralston, NE 68127

Seymour Mfg. Co.
3300 N. Broadway
Seymour, IN 47274

Simplicity Mfg. Co., Inc.
Port Washington, WI 53074

Southeast Mfg. Co., Inc.
Rt. 2, Box 275
Joplin, MO 64801

SpeeCo (Special Products)
15000 W. 44th Ave., P.O. Box 592
Golden, CO 80401

Also available from TSC & Central Tractor.

Stanley Garden Tools, U.S. Distributor
Woodcraft Supply Corp.
313 Montvale Ave.
Woburn, MA 01801

Stanley Hydraulic Tools
13770 S.E. Ambler Rd.
Clackamas, OR 97015

Taylor Implement Mfg. Co.
Athens, TN 37303

Tractor Supply Co.
7910 L St.
Omaha, NE 68127

Tradewinds, Inc.
P.O. Box 1191
Tacoma, WA 98401

True Temper Corp., Hardware Div.
1623 Euclid Ave.
Cleveland, OH 44115

True Value Hardware
2740 Clayburn Ave.
Chicago, IL 60614

The Union Fork & Hoe Co.
500 Dublin Ave.
Columbus, OH 43216

United Farm Tools, Inc.
P.O. Box 9175-32
South Charleston, WV 25309

Utility Tool & Body Co., Inc.
Clintonville, WI 54929

The Vassar Co.
Perkins, OK 74059

Wikomi Mfg. Co.
P.O. Box 100
Litchfield, IL 62056

Appendix B: INTERNATIONAL MANUFACTURERS AND DISTRIBUTORS APPEARING ON CHARTS IN THIS BOOK

ACM Equipments
Bienvillers 62111 Foncquevillers
Boite Postale 5, France

African Hoe (Pty.), Ltd.
477 Watt Rd., New Era Industrial Sites
Springs Transvaal, Rep. of S. Africa 1560

Agrator Industrial, S.L.
Ctra. Bilbao por Murguia km. 5,5
P.O. Box 316
Vitoria, Spain

Agria-Werke Gmbh
7108 Moeckmuehl
P.O. Box 47/48
West Germany

Agromet Motoimport
Entreprise Du Commerce Exterieur
Warszawa, Przemyslowa 26, Poland

Bomford & Evershed, Ltd.
Salford Priors, Evesham
Worcestershire WR11 5SW, England

Bulldog Tools U.S. Distributor
Jim Everett, Dobson Park Industries, Ltd.
Suite 400, 4041 N. High St.
Columbus, OH 43214

Caralel Enterprise Co., Ltd.
P.O. Box 59442
Taipei, Taiwan

CEAF
S.N.C. Filli Siletti
24034 Cisano
Bergamasco, Italy

CeCoCo Agricultural & Small Industrial Center
P.O. Box 8, Ibaraki City
Osaka Pref. 567, Japan

Cepelia
236 Fifth Ave.
New York, NY 10017

The Chillington Tool Co., Ltd.
P.O. Box 45, Hickman Ave.
Wolverhampton WV1 2BU, England

Coopexim-Cepelia
Zurawia 4, 00-950 Warsazawa
Poland

Cossul and Co. Pvt., Ltd.
Industrial Area, Fazalgunj
Kanpur, India

E.B.R.A. (Ets Beauvais & Robin)
28 rue du Maine, B.P. 84
49009 Angers, France

English Tools, Ltd. (Bulldog Tools)
Clarington Forge
Wigan, Lancashire, England

Ets Delaplace
02590 Etreillers (Aisne)
R.C. Saint–Quentin 63 A 113, France

Fabriche Riunite Falci
Dronero, Via Cuneo 3/5/7
Cuneo, Italy

Ferfor
Rua Da Amieira, P.O. Box 16
S. Mamede De Infesta, Portugal

Ferunion
Hungarian Trading Co. for Technical Goods
1829 Budapest
P.O.B. 612, Hungary

OY Fiskars AB
P.O. Box 235, Mannerheimintie 14
Helsinki, Finland

Frank'sche Eisenwerke
Aktiengesellschaft Adolfshutte
Postfach 260, D 6340 Dillenburg
Federal Republic of Germany

CG Funcke Sohn
58 Hagen
Postfach 1109, West Germany

Gherardi
Office Machine Agricole Industriali
Jesi (Ancona) Via Gallodoro 68, Italy

Hako-Werke
2060 Bad Oldesloe 1
P.O. Box 1444, West Germany

Herragro
Apartado Aereo 1003
Manizales, Colombia

W. Hertecant
9200 Kwatrecht
Wetteren, Belgium

Hilton Enterprise Co., Ltd.
P.O. Box 36-370
Taipei, Taiwan R.O.C.

Hindustan Engineering Co.
Aban House, 25/31 Ropewalk St.
Rampart Row, Fort Bombay 400 023, India

T & J Hutton Co., Ltd.
Phoenix Works, Ridgeway 11
Sheffield S12 3XW, U.K.

Industrias Metalurgicas Apolo S.A.
Carrera 50-2 Sur-189 Autopista Sur
Medellin, Antioqui, Colombia

ISEKI Agricultural Machinery Mfg. Co., Ltd.
1-3, Nihonbashi 2-chome, Chuo-ku
Tokyo 103, Japan

Jenks & Catell, Ltd.
Phoenix Works, Wednesfield
Wolverhampton, WV11 3PV, England

Jumil
Justino de Morais, Irmaos S.A.
Rua Ana Luiza, 568
Batatais S.P., Brazil

Kuhn S.A.
67700 Saverne
France

Kuhn, U.S.
Box 224
Vernon, NY 13476

Kumaon Agri-Horticulture Stores
P.O. Kashipur
District Nainital U.P., India

Kumaon Nursery
Ramnagar
Nainital U.P., India

Kumar Industries
Edathara Post, Palphat District
Kerala State, South India

Kvernelands Fabrikk A/S
N-4344 Kverneland
Norway

Lasher Tools (Pty.), Ltd.
P.O. Box 254
Germiston 1400 Transvaal, S. Africa

Ralph Martindale & Co., Ltd.
Crocodile Works, Alma St.
Birmingham B19 2RR, England

Mechanized Gardening
Great Gransden, Sandy
Bedfordshire SG19 3AY, U.K.

Mohinder & Co. Allied Industries
Kurali, Dist. Ropar
Punjab, India

Nardi Macchine Agricole
06017 Selci Lama
Perugia, Italy

Nikko Co., Ltd.
1, 5-chome, Shinmachi
Minami-dori, Nishi-ku
Osaka, Japan

Oy Rettig-Strengberg Ab
Metal Industry Purmo
P.O. Box 16
SF 68601 Jakobstad, Finland

Peugeot, Division Outillage
66 a 78, Avenue Francois Arago
92 002, Nanterre, France

Pierce of Wexford—member of:
Britain Group Sales, Ltd.
Agricultural Division
P.O. Box 143, Naas Rd.
Dublin 12, Ireland

George Pike, Ltd.
Equipment Works
Alma St., Aston
Birmingham B19 2RS, England

Polar-Werke, Engels & Sieper
Postfach 14 02 24/25
5630 Remschied 14, West Germany

Purmo Produkt AB
Jakobstad, Sweden

Schanzlin Maschinenfabrik Gmbh
7831 Weistweil
Baden, West Germany

SHW Schwabische Huttenwerke Gmbh
Postfach 1329
7292 Baiersbronn-Friedrichstal
West Germany

Self-Sufficiency and Small-Holding Supplies
The Old Palace, Priory Rd.
Wells, Somerset BA5 1SY, England

Societe des Forges Tropicales
B.P. 706
Douala, Cameroun

Solo Kleinmotoren Gmbh
7032 Sindelfingen 6
Postfach 20, West Germany

Franz Sonnleithner K.G.
4460 Losenstein/Laussa 25
Austria

Spear & Jackson Tools, Ltd.
St. Paul's Rd., Wednesbury
Staffordshire WS10 9RA, England

Stanley Garden Tools, Ltd.
Woodhouse Mill
Sheffield S13 9WJ, England

Staub–Societe des Tracteurs & Motoculteurs
25, BD DeVerdun
Courbevoie Cedex, France

Syndicat de L'Outillage
Agricole et Horticole
15 rue Beaujon
75008 Paris, France

Tanzania Agricultural Machinery Testing Unit
P.O. Box 1389
Arusha, Tanzania

The Tata Iron & Steel Co., Ltd.
43 Chowringhee Rd.
Calcutta 16, India

Tonutti, S.P.A.
Remanzacco
33047 UD 063, Italy

W. Tyzack Sons & Turner, Ltd.
Little London Works
Sheffield S8 OUE, England

Ubungo Farm Implements
P.O. Box 2669
Dar Es Salaam, Tanzania

Vilhard & Co.
Postfach 7
6126 Brombachtal (Odenwald), West Germany

Wolf & Bankert
Werkzeug Fabrik
563 Remschied, West Germany

Wolf Tools for Garden & Lawn, Ltd.
Ross-on-Rye
Herefordshire HR9 5NE, England

Wolseley Webb, Ltd.
Electric Ave., Witton
Birmingham B6 7JA, U.K.

Yanmar Diesel Engine Co.
1-11-1, Marunouchi, Chiyoda-ku
Tokyo, Japan

Appendix C: CONVERSION FACTORS: U.S. AND METRIC UNITS

These conversion tables will come in handy if you're interested in any pieces of foreign equipment. They were supplied by Seedburo Equipment Co.

METRIC TO U.S.

LENGTH

1 millimeter	=	0.04	inch
1 meter	=	3.3	feet
1 meter	=	1.1	yards
1 kilometer	=	0.6	mile

AREA

1 sq. centimeter	=	0.16	sq. inch
1 sq. meter	=	11.0	sq. feet
1 sq. meter	=	1.2	sq. yards
1 hectare	=	2.5	acres
1 sq. kilometer	=	0.39	sq. mile

VOLUME

1 cubic centimeter	=	0.06	cubic inch
1 cubic meter	=	35.0	cubic feet
1 cubic meter	=	1.3	cubic yards
1 milliliter	=	0.2	teaspoon
1 milliliter	=	0.07	tablespoon
1 milliliter	=	0.03	ounce
1 liter	=	4.2	cups
1 liter	=	2.1	pints (liq)
1 liter	=	1.1	quarts (liq)
1 cubic meter	=	264.0	gallons (liq)
1 cubic meter	=	113.0	pecks
1 cubic meter	=	28.0	bushels

MASS

1 milligram	=	0.015	grain
1 gram	=	0.035	ounce (dry)
1 kilogram	=	2.2	pounds
1 metric ton	=	1.102	tons (short)

Temperature °C Celsius x 9/5 and add 32° = °F.

U.S. TO METRIC

LENGTH

1 inch	=	25.4	millimeters
1 foot	=	0.3	meter
1 yard	=	0.9	meter
1 mile	=	1.6	kilometers

AREA

1 sq. inch	=	6.5	sq. centimeters
1 sq. foot	=	0.09	sq. meter
1 sq. yard	=	0.8	sq. meter
1 acre	=	0.4	hectare
1 sq. mile	=	2.6	sq. kilometers

VOLUME

1 cubic inch	=	16.4	cubic centimeters
1 cubic foot	=	0.03	cubic meters
1 cubic yard	=	0.76	cubic meters
1 teaspoon	=	5.0	milliliters
1 tablespoon	=	15.0	milliliters
1 fl. ounce	=	29.6	milliliters
1 cup	=	0.24	liter
1 pint (liq)	=	0.47	liter
1 quart (liq)	=	0.95	liter
1 gallon (liq)	=	0.004	cubic meter
1 peck	=	0.009	cubic meter
1 bushel	=	0.04	cubic meter

MASS

1 grain	=	64.8	milligrams
1 ounce (dry)	=	28.3	grams
1 pound	=	0.45	kilogram
1 short ton	=	9.072	kilograms

Temperature of Fahrenheit x 5/9 after Subtracting 32° = °C.

TONS TO BUSHELS CONVERSION

Conversion factors by grain:

Grain	Short	Metric	Long
Wheat	33.333	36.743	37.333
Corn	35.714	39.368	40.000
Soybeans	33.333	36.743	37.333
Barley	41.667	45.929	46.667
Oats	62.500	68.894	70.000

Wheat	60 lbs. per bu.
Soybeans	60 lbs. per bu.
Corn	56 lbs. per bu.
Barley	48 lbs. per bu.
Oats	32 lbs. per bu.

A Short Ton is 2,000 pounds.
A Metric Ton is 2,204.6 lbs.
A Long Ton is 2,240 pounds.

Index